EXCEPTIONAL

American Exceptionalism
Takes Its Toll

To Katelyn
May There be a future
William Boardman

William Boardman

YORKLAND PUBLISHING
Y͟P

Published by
Yorkland Publishing
12 Tepee Court
Toronto, Ontario M2J 3A9
Canada
www.yorklandpublishing.com

ISBN: 978-0-9697127-8-7

Book Design by SpicaBookDesign
Printed in Canada by Island Blue Book Printing, Victoria, B.C.

For Michael, Benjamin, Diantha,
Samantha, Nicholas, Walker, & Carter,
and any of their progeny –
may the future turn out to be much better
than it's looking right now
5.8.19

The Nuremberg Principles

Principles of International Law Recognized in the Charter of the Nürnberg Tribunal and in the Judgment of the Tribunal (1950)

Principle I. Any person who commits an act which constitutes a crime under international law is responsible therefor and liable to punishment.

Principle II. The fact that internal law does not impose a penalty for an act which constitutes a crime under international law does not relieve the person who committed the act from responsibility under international law.

Principle III. The fact that a person who committed an act which constitutes a crime under international law, acted as Head of State or responsible government official, does not relieve him from responsibility under international law.

Principle IV. The fact that a person acted pursuant to order of his Government or of a superior does not relieve him from responsibility under international law, provided a moral choice was in fact possible to him.

Principle V. Any person charged with a crime under international law has the right to a fair trial on the facts and law.

Principle VI. The crimes hereinafter set out are punishable as crimes under international law:

(a) **Crimes against peace**:

  (i) Planning, preparation, initiation or waging of a war of aggression or a war in violation of international treaties, agreements or assurances;

  (ii) Participation in a common plan or conspiracy for the accomplishment of any of the acts mentioned under (i).

(b) **War crimes**:

Violations of the laws or customs of war which include, but are not limited to, murder, ill-treatment or deportation to slave labor or for any other purpose of civilian population of or in occupied territory; murder or ill-treatment of prisoners of war or persons on the Seas, killing of hostages, plunder of public or private property, wanton destruction of cities, towns, or villages, or devastation not justified by military necessity.

(c) **Crimes against humanity**:

Murder, extermination, enslavement, deportation and other inhumane acts done against any civilian population, or persecutions on political, racial, or religious grounds, when such acts are done or such persecutions are carried on in execution of or in connection with any crime against peace or any war crime.

Principle VII. Complicity in the commission of a crime against peace, a war crime, or a crime against humanity as set forth in Principle VI is a crime under international law.

It is one of the abiding principles of American Exceptionalism that Americans, no matter what they do, are exempt from the Nuremberg Principles or most any other aspect of international laws against war crimes or crimes against humanity. Or as the US recently made clear: as far as any allegations of US crimes are concerned, the International Criminal Court can go pound sand.

Exhibits for the Prosecution

MURRAY NGOIMA

Exceptional Contents

Part Four. Black in America

Part Five. America Saves the World

Part Six. Radiation & Fossil Fools

Part Seven. Impeaching Is Easy, Removal Is Hard

Epilogue/Epitaph

Acknowledgements

First and foremost, thanks to Ed Shiller, my friend for more than 60 years, who saw a book lurking somewhere in my several hundred pieces of recent years and decided to publish this selection of them at Yorkland Publishing.

Essential thanks to Marc Ash and Reader Supported News (RSN) for providing a haven where I could write freely and truthfully to the best of my ability.

Special thanks to my longtime RSN editor, Roberta Hill, for her endlessly friendly, supportive, and acute interactions. She was the first editor for most of the pieces in this book. And I've come to value her kindness and friendship even though we've never met in person.

Thanks to Rosemary Shiller at Yorkland Publishing for her seemingly endless attention to detail in editing the text as the manuscript came together.

Thanks to Nancy Serrell for several sessions on substance that helped develop the book's structure.

Thanks to Murray Ngoima, working under absolutely unfair time pressure, for creating the startling pen&ink drawings, "Exhibits for the Prosecution" and "Thanksgiving for a Grateful Empire."

Thanks to Iryna Spica for creating an attractive design for this complex book.

And thanks of a sort to the rabble of criminals and incompetents, in and out of government, who make a book like this seem not only necessary, but Exceptional.

Tilting at Reality & its Perpetraitors

If I were you, I'd just start reading this book, start anywhere, all of it inter-relates in time. You've already lived through all the events I've written about, whether you were aware of them or not, so you've already been introduced to the subjects, or you can let the subjects introduce themselves. I've tried to make everything accessible whether you know about it in advance or not. But for those still looking for some introductory comments, here goes.

Exceptional – American Exceptionalism Takes Its Toll is an anthology of topical pieces I wrote over an eight-year period for Reader Supported News, where they all first appeared except for a couple that were first in CounterPunch. The pieces are presented here pretty much as they first appeared, with some light editing, but no substantive change from the original. They are sometimes amplified by context or update notes.

American Exceptionalism permeates our culture. Most Americans were taught to believe in American superiority long before we were able to think for ourselves. "America is the greatest country in the world." It's an article of faith. It can't be proved. Other countries didn't vote us #1 in a free and fair election. What is the measure of "greatness" for a country? Do genocide, slavery, racism, imperialism and endemic poverty count? If the United States is really the greatest country in the world, what does that say about the world?

If there's a theme or message or somesuch to this book, it's imposed after the fact, probably by the reader. Each piece is a snapshot in time, when I'm reacting to the moment, whether it's an act of voter suppression, the start of an aggressive war, the police killing of another unarmed black person, or the failed humanity of so many of our "leaders." Whatever the moment, it's something I object to. I try to describe the ways it's wrong and bad for people and bad for the country. Since 2012, I've written over 400 such pieces, about a quarter of which are included here in seven somewhat arbitrary sections intended to make a kind of sense of an inchoate world. These are not the only threads of

American unraveling, but they are surely among the important ones. Within each section the pieces appear chronologically, helping the reader to get a sense of how much – or how little – things change.

I. **Voting vs. Elections.** This is fundamental to everything else. There is an innate tension in our electoral system. There are those who believe in letting everyone vote. And there are those who prefer to game the system to get the "right" election results. My first piece looks at the way Republicans openly boast about fixing the Pennsylvania presidential vote for 2012. The last piece in the section tries to be hopeful about the mixed results of the 2018 election, when Florida voted overwhelmingly to amend the state constitution to allow freed felons to vote. As this is written, Republican state legislators are trying to put up barriers to thwart the clear will of the people as expressed through the ballot box.

II. **America Loses Altitude.** America has been losing altitude for a long, long time. People feel it in different ways, but the feeling seems close to universal. Explanations for the feeling tend to be more varied, ideological and bias-based. I see the American decline as bi-partisan, but driven by the long march of right-wing ideologues since Goldwater/Nixon. This section starts with a mindless 2013 police effort to criminalize free speech that illuminates a continuing trend to shut down rational discussion. The section also covers developments in the American police state and how we've come to have a Supreme Court that defends the interests of the rich and powerful with less and less integrity or shame.

III. **Coming to America.** This illustrates some of the ways a "nation of immigrants" has come to act as if it hates itself. It begins with maltreatment of Dreamers and children at the border in 2013-14. It covers the police-state terrorism of ICE. The section ends with Rep. Ilhan Omar of Minnesota, an articulate Democrat who should be celebrated as one of the first Muslim women in Congress, but is instead subjected to bi-partisan calumny and death threats to which her party responds timorously.

IV.   **Black in America.** It's not easy. Some examples.

V.   **America Saves The World.** From Afghanistan around the world to Afghanistan still, American salvation comes at a steep price to the saved. The examples are Orwellian, "like a boot stomping on a human face – forever." Yemen is the worst, perhaps.

VI.   **Radiation and Fossil Fools.** The nuclear world is inherently dangerous, expensive and profitable (for a few). So is the carbon world. Will enough leaders figure out how to exploit the future in time to preserve it in livable form?

VII. **Impeachment is Easy, Removal is Hard.** This is the Trump-centric section.

The House Democrats could impeach Trump – validly – on a range of offenses. And then what? It's beyond all belief that the Senate would put Trump on trial, never mind convict him. But even if the unbelievable came to pass, that would only result in President Pence, hardly a panacea. The way to the egress is through the 2020 election. Unless there's no way to the egress.

Here's to January 21, 2021 – with hope, but not much optimism. We're in the midst of a presidential election in a country that has been at war all over the world since 2001, and there's no authentic peace candidate (Elizabeth Warren may be the closest, Tulsi Gabbard is a wannabe). There's no strong anti-militarism candidate in a country where the military budget eats our future. Perhaps worse, America seems more responsive to "honoring" the dead than ending the wars that kill them. There's little integrity in our public discourse and less coherence. Truth is optional. Our society is out of rational control, apparently unable and unwilling to prioritize what matters.

Here are a few of the things left out of this book:

- **US meddling in Ukraine.** I wrote a lot about this in the wake of the US-backed overthrow of Ukraine's elected president in 2014. At the moment, Ukraine is on simmer and I talk about it briefly in the NATO piece at the end of the "America Saves the World" section. Ukraine made more news when it elected Volodymyr Zelensky president in the April 21, 2019 runoff election. His preparation for the presidency consists principally of playing the President of Ukraine in the popular TV series *Servant of the People*, after which his Servant of the People Party is named.

- **Keystone XL Pipeline.** I wrote about the pipeline several times as it overrode opposition with law and violence on its march through Texas to the Gulf Coast. A piece published November 30, 2012, was captioned: "Keystone XL: Crime Against Humanity?" The headline was: "Bi-Partisan Senators Urge President to Ignore Science." The piece began: "Based on the same publicly available scientific information, the World Bank issues a report calling for prompt action to ward off global warming, the United Nations reports that greenhouse gas levels reached a new record, and 18 United States Senators (nine from each party) write a letter to President Obama calling on him to approve expanded fossil fuel exploitation without regard for global warming." Even though re-elected by a healthy margin, Obama largely accommodated the fossil fool gang.

- **Vermont's disgraceful embrace of the military-industrial complex.** That embrace expresses itself most obnoxiously by Democrats insisting on basing the nuclear-capable, hugely expensive F-35 fighter bomber at a Vermont airport in a low-income residential area. I have written many times about this. There is nothing redeeming about the F-35 boondoggle, but Democratic Senator Patrick Leahy has been pushing for it shamelessly (and dishonestly, along with the Pentagon) for more than a decade. Democratic Rep. Peter Welch wags dutifully behind, as has the rest of the Vermont power structure. That includes Independent Senator Bernie Sanders. The F-35 is toxic in mission as well as in noise level and materials. The F-35 has yet to prove reliable. An F-35 crashed off Japan on April 9; the pilot is still missing. The F-35 is a weapon of mass destruction, a potential first-strike nuclear weapon, and Vermonters have voted time and again to base it elsewhere. It's a measure of American corruption that Vermont's leaders care so little about the will of the people or making Burlington a target when it comes to caressing the military-industrial complex.

- **The Mueller [REDACTED] Report.** I haven't written about Mueller, Russiagate or any of the other shadowplay that has so preoccupied so much of the media since 2016. As far as I could ever tell, there were never enough serious facts to add up to a critical mass of criminality. The indictments and convictions so far strike me as evidence of common sleaze, but not much more. I assume the Trump campaign at some level colluded with Russia to influence the 2016 election (why wouldn't they?), and I assume the Trump administration is hip-deep in obstruction of justice (why wouldn't it be?). Apparently they're good enough criminals that there's not enough proof to nail them (or maybe they're not guilty?). But here's the more important point: as of now there's no showing by anyone that any Russian (or other) interference in the 2016 election had any significant effect on the outcome. Do you really believe Russian trolls on Facebook mattered more than Hillary blowing off Wisconsin? The 2016 election suffered from enough disabilities as to be a dark bad-news/good-news joke:

  The bad news is that Trump won –
  the good news is that Hillary lost.

As far as I can tell (not that far), the most likely source of meaningful skullduggery in the 2016 election (and others going back a decade or two) would be the deliberate Republican attack on almost all elements of the American voting system. In 2000, Florida Gov. Jeb Bush's administration ran voter suppression and voter caging programs that created an unverifiable vote count that opened the way for the Supreme Court to rule that votes don't really matter when it comes to deciding elections. Republican election fraud, that's more or less where the book begins.

PART ONE

Voting vs. Elections

1.

Partisan Voter Suppression Outsmarts the Law, For Now

Republicans Execute Election Fraud by Legislation

Across the media, the headlines got it wrong.

They claimed, "Judge Upholds Voter ID Law in Pennsylvania," or some variation of that assertion. The reality was more complicated – and better.

Even though it took Commonwealth Court Judge Robert Simpson some 70 pages to explain his decision, the decision did not "uphold" the law. The decision only denied the plaintiffs' application for a preliminary injunction. The grounds were as simple as they were legalistic: Judge Simpson found no basis for suspending the law at once because the plaintiffs could not show it would be unconstitutional in every conceivable circumstance.

The legal issue is "facial constitutionality," or whether the voter ID law is unconstitutional on its face, which is a hard standard to meet. All other questions of substance remain untouched by this decision and remain to be litigated in further court actions, especially any that consider the law "as applied," or as it works in practice.

That's what the judge meant in the summary of his decision, referring to opponents of the Voter ID law:

> Petitioners' counsel did an excellent job of 'putting a face' to those burdened by the voter ID requirement. At the end of the day, however, I do not have the luxury of deciding this issue based on my sympathy for the witnesses or my esteem for counsel. Rather, I must analyze the law, and apply it to the evidence of facial unconstitutionality brought forth in the courtroom, tested by our adversarial system. For the foregoing reasons, I am constrained to deny the application for preliminary injunction, without prejudice to future 'as applied' claims.

In other words, Judge Simpson's decision on the injunction has no weight whatsoever in any future challenge to the law or to any claims of actual harm it may cause.

Judge Simpson is an elected judge, and so has a clear, apparent interest in how his decision might affect the electorate that put him in office. He did not discuss this possible conflict in his decision. He is serving a 10-year term that ends in December 2021.

The judge's ruling is a grand example of where the law takes leave of reality. Majestically, logically, correctly perhaps – but insanely – the law here protects the deliberate, planned perpetration of injustice – Republican suppression of voting groups more likely to vote for Democrats.

This is not a matter of dispute. The voter ID bill was partisan and passed on a partisan vote. The Pennsylvania House Majority Leader Mike Turzai, a Republican from Allegheny, made the political strong-arming crystal clear last June:

> **Voter ID, which is gonna allow Governor Romney to win the state of Pennsylvania – done!**

This isn't subtle. This isn't politics as usual. Both sides don't do it. The Democrats used to suppress the black vote back when the "solid South" voted Democratic. But for at least the past 50 years, Democrats have worked to expand the vote. Perhaps because it has something to do with democracy.

Ever since 1964, the South has been increasingly safe for Republicans and there's an ugly racial element to that. Richard Nixon made that explicit with his so-called southern strategy and Ronald Reagan affirmed it when he started his 1980 campaign in Philadelphia, Mississippi, while that community was still protecting the murderers of Civil Rights workers there in 1964.

Since January 2011, Republican majorities in 11 state legislatures have passed voter ID laws designed to skew the vote toward Republican candidates in those 11 states. The Brennan Center for Justice tracks these laws through its Democracy Program that "seeks to change the ways in which citizens participate in their government by fixing the systems that discourage voting, hinder competition and promote the interests of the few over the rights of the many."

In Texas and South Carolina, with their long histories of suppressing minority voting, the US Justice Dept. has intervened to block both states from implementing their voter ID laws. In Wisconsin, Dane County Circuit Judge Richard Niess ruled in July that the Republican-passed voter ID law was unconstitutional on its face, writing in part: "A government that undermines the very foundation of its existence – the people's inherent, pre-constitutional right to vote – imperils its legitimacy as a government by the people, for the people, and especially of the people.... It sows the seeds for its own demise as a democratic institution. This is precisely what 2011 Wisconsin Act 23 does with its photo ID mandates." So saying, he issued a permanent injunction against the State of Wisconsin, preventing it from further implementing the law. The state has appealed the decision.

Republicans promoting these voter ID laws – and lately it's only Republicans who promote them –argue that the purpose is to prevent voter fraud. Preventing voter fraud is a laudable goal. In reality there is virtually no voter fraud in the United States, especially voter fraud that would be cured by voter ID. In the rare instances where voter fraud occurs, it's much more likely the Indiana Secretary of State, the state's top election official, Charlie White, convicted on six felony counts in January, who commits voter fraud, not some 95-year-old black woman with no birth certificate who had been voting for 50 years after half a lifetime of exclusion. White, while he was still in office, had been an ardent defender of voter ID laws to prevent voter fraud.

Voter fraud is rare in the United States, at least voter fraud by individual voters. Even in the Pennsylvania case, the state admitted before trial that it has no cases of voter fraud to offer as evidence of the need for a voter ID law. Voter fraud is only slightly more common than tsunamis in Arizona – the easiest cure for both non-existent problems is to do nothing. Unless, of course, you have some other purpose in mind, as Pennsylvania House majority leader Turzai made plain.

Disputes over voter ID laws are no small matter, no distraction from more important issues. Voter ID laws are a Republican effort to keep a minority party in office by keeping blocs of ethnic minority voters from voting. It is an effort to rig the system itself, and has worked all too well.

> **Update 2019:** The 2012 Pennsylvania Voter ID Law was one of the most restrictive in the country. It was not enforced in the 2012 elections . In 2014, Judge Bernard L. McGinley ruled the law unconstitutional because a judge ruled on October 2, 2012 that the authorities had not done enough to ensure that voters had access to the required documents.. His decision was not appealed. Nevertheless some Pennsylvania voting districts continued to enforce it.

2.

Is Anti-Semitic Hit on Bernie Sanders a Harbinger of Mud to Come?

Whether incompetent or intentional, NPR produces stunning WTF?! moment

Presidential elections usually bring out the worst in campaign tactics, such as the George Bush/Karl Rove whisper campaign in South Carolina in 2000 that played to the bigot vote by calumniating John McCain with false rumors of his "black child." The pattern is an American chestnut of the worst sort, since any effort to correct the record also spreads the defamation.

A perhaps apocryphal story about Lyndon Johnson vividly illustrates the way it works. "We'll put out the rumor that my opponent fornicates with pigs," Johnson supposedly said in saltier language. When an aide said that his opponent didn't actually fornicate with pigs, Johnson replied, "No, but it will be entertaining to watch him deny fornicating with pigs."

National Public Radio (NPR) recently took part in what looks like a "fornicate with pigs" ploy, only instead of "fornicating with pigs," the proposed slur was having dual American-Israeli citizenship. This WTF moment caused some chatter on the internet, but little or no mainstream news coverage. At this point almost nothing is clear about how public radio came to be part of a "fornicates with pigs" dirty trick, but it deserves as much scrutiny as it can get. The moment happened during a radio interview, with the parties in separate studios miles apart. In the 24th minute of the 50-minute interview, the program host made this statement:

Diane Rehm: Senator, you have dual citizenship with Israel.

7

This is a false statement for which, as Diane Rehm later admitted, she had no factual basis. She had only an unconfirmed listener comment on Facebook alleging the claim (more about that in a moment). Nevertheless, on the June 10 Diane Rehm Show on National Public Radio, Rehm asserted that easily-checked falsehood as fact in her interview with presidential candidate and Independent senator from Vermont Bernie Sanders. Sanders responded unhesitatingly, directly, and unambiguously:

> **Bernie Sanders:** Well, no, I do not have dual citizenship with Israel. I'm an American.... I'm an American citizen, period.

By any credible reckoning, Senator Bernie Sanders is *not* an Israeli citizen, he is only an American citizen. He was born in Brooklyn, New York, to Polish immigrant parents. He is Jewish. All this has been easy to confirm for more than 30 years. But Rehm, having asserted the falsehood once, chose to double down without a pause:

> **Diane Rehm:** I understand from a list we have gotten that you were on that list. Forgive me if that is — [Sanders interrupts]

Rehm made no effort to offer any detail about the "list," nothing about its authorship or its provenance or its reliability or how NPR researchers had confirmed and re-confirmed the accuracy of its substance, nothing like that. Rehm did not even mention who else was supposedly on the "list." Sanders interrupted to say:

> **Bernie Sanders:** Now that's some of the nonsense that goes on in the Internet, but that is absolutely not true.

Rehm did not defend her "list," she did not say it was not "nonsense," she did not claim it was "true," but she reacted as if she believed it was true. She tripled down on the falsehood. Her next response first implied suspicion of Sanders' answer, then expanded the uninvestigated falsehood to the whole Congress:

> **Diane Rehm:** Interesting. Are there members of Congress who do have dual citizenship, or is that part of the fable?

8

At that point Sanders figuratively threw up his hands and said of Congressional dual citizenship, "I honestly don't know." Then he returned to the original question about his own alleged dual citizenship, concluding:

> **Bernie Sanders:** ... I get offended a little bit by that comment, and I know it's been on the Internet. I am an American – obviously an American citizen, and I do not have any dual citizenship.

At that point, Rehm says, "All right," and drops the citizenship question. Rehm, who is of Arabic Christian heritage, switched immediately to a question about Palestinian statehood, which Sanders supports. Rehm, having asked Sanders about the Middle East before launching the "dual citizenship" provocation, seemed to be at least tacitly accusing Sanders of having an improper loyalty to Israel. Earlier, Rehm had asked Sanders questions about Iraq, ISIS, and Syria. Sanders had called ISIS a "barbaric organization" that must be defeated and had called the war in Iraq "a disaster." Sanders had gone on to outline his own approach to the Middle East generally:

> I do not believe the United States can or should lead the effort in that part of the world. What is taking place now is a war for the soul of Islam.
>
> Saudi Arabia, it turns out, has the third-largest military budget in the world. You got Turkey there, you got Jordan there, you got the UAE there. You have – countries are going to have to step up to the plate and lead the effort with the support of the United States and other Western countries.
>
> But here is my nightmare, and I see it moving forward every day. You've got a lot of Republicans there who apparently did not learn anything from the never-ending war in Afghanistan, learned nothing from what happened in Iraq, and want us in a perpetual warfare in the Middle East.
>
> I am strongly opposed to that.
>
> I don't have a magic solution. I'm not sure anybody does. But what has to happen is the Muslim countries in that area, there has got to be a strong coalition. They're going to have to get their hands dirty.

9

> They can't sit aside and wait for the United States of America, our soldiers, our taxpayers, to carry the ball for them. They're going to have to lead the effort.

In her next breath, in a complete *non sequitur*, Rehm unleashed the canard that Sanders has "dual citizenship with Israel." Coming after a call for Muslims to resolve their differences, Rehm's slam played like an accusation, although exactly what the accusation really meant she failed to make clear.

The anti-Semitic source of the "list" is easy to discover

When Diane Rehm claimed to have a "list" of dual Israeli-American citizens, she reminded people of the red-baiting fearmonger of the 1950s, Wisconsin Republican senator Joseph McCarthy, who all too often claimed to have lists of "Communists" but never produced the lists or any other evidence. Despite this, in his heyday, McCarthy's smears were taken seriously by some, and innocent people suffered from the national witch hunts inspired by McCarthyism.

Diane Rehm's response to Sanders – "*I understand from a list we have gotten that you were on that list.*" – is pure McCarthyism. She does not provide the list, she does not offer any credible reason to take the list seriously, and most slippery of all, she says she only "understands" that Sanders is on the list. In other words, she is challenging him with baseless hearsay, which is about as far from professional journalism as it gets.

With little effort, as politifact.com demonstrated in a June 14 post, the reality is much uglier than a mere failure of professionalism. The supposed "list" is actually many lists in various forms going back to 2007, none of which appear to have any reliable basis in fact nor any checkable sources for their claims.

One of the earlier versions of "List of Politicians with Israeli Dual Citizenship," which reappears frequently, apparently dates from around 2007. Authorship is credited to "Dan Eden," who may or may not be a staff writer/editor for a website called viewzone.com, self-described in part this way: "The topics on Viewzone vary widely. The most popular deal with science, mysteries, conspiracies, spirituality and interesting or unusual phenomena." The site has no easily-used search function. The Israeli Dual Citizenship story is not immediately apparent, but it's there, accessible by a Google search for "Dan Eden dual Israeli citizenship." Another, more prominently listed story by Viewzone editor "Gary Vey" (aka "Dan Eden") is titled "Why Yemen is the Next Warfront," and explains:

> In 2001 I was the guest of the Yemeni government because I had accidentally made a discovery that I had no right to make. I discovered strong evidence that the Ark of the Covenant is buried in an archaeological site in a desert outpost called Marib. I know how it sounds … but keep reading.

That's what Dan Eden claimed in his story, which also referred to events in 2009, when the Bush team was out of office. Never mind that. Eden's long list of Israeli-American dual citizens includes Paul Wolfowitz, I. Lewis "Scooter" Libby, Richard Perle, John Bolton, Elliott Abrams, Michael Chertoff, Michael Mukasey, Douglas Feith and some 30 others.

Had Diane Rehm or anyone on her staff done the most basic fact-checking, they might have thought to ask something like: how credible is it to assume that Bernie Sanders runs with *this* crowd? Then, if they'd looked, they would have found a partial answer near the top of the story, where Dan Eden explains his take on Israeli dual citizenship:

> Before I begin I'd like to say something important. There is a new law – the so-called "Hate Speech" law, that just passed the House and is expected to pass the Senate and become law very soon. It was originally designed to guard against discrimination of oppressed minorities but was soon recognized as a way for Israel to forever end any criticism of the state of Israel and Zionism. When it is law, this page, and many like it will be deleted from the internet as yet another mile marker of the infringement of truth and free speech by certain dual-nationals at the expense of true and patriotic Americans. Enough said.

But "this page," as Eden called it, is still there, casting doubt on his imagined power of the vast Zionist conspiracy. On Facebook there's another version of Dan Eden's story, dated 2011, which includes the same cast of Bush characters, but conveniently omits Eden's Zionist conspiracy language.

That language is back with intensity on the website Educate Yourself, which carries the Dan Eden dual citizenship story and a June 11, 2015, piece by Ken Adachi titled "Bernie Sanders and Israel's Law of Return," which speculates that by *telling* Bernie Sanders he was a dual citizen, rather than *asking* him if he was, Diane Rehm may have been *conspiring* with Sanders or others to minimize the story:

> If she had asked him, he would have answered "no" and the moment would not have carried that much weight or interest, but telling him that he's an Israeli dual citizen gave him the perfect opportunity to get on his high horse soapbox and create an instant front page story that reduces the dual Israeli citizen allegation to the stuff of Wing Nuts & Tin Foil Hat cadets. It's only a speculation, granted, but I think it should be mentioned.

Israel's Law of Return does not confer citizenship automatically

After offering an analysis of Israel's Law of Return, arguing that the law provides an easy, simple, and automatic way for Jews around the world to obtain Israeli citizenship, Adachi writes:

> And do you think that ardent, pro-Israel fifth columnists like Bernie Sanders, or Charles Shummer [sic], or Dianne Feinstein, or Jane Harman, or Barbara Boxer, or Al Franken, or Joseph Lieberman, or Benjamin Cardin, or Michael Chertoff, or Richard Pearle, or Paul Wolfowitz, or any of the other former or current American government officials alleged to hold dual Israeli citizenship, are going to tell the government of Israel that they will not accept automatic citizenship status after their 90 day Oleh visa waiting period has run its course? What d'ya think?

Well, politifact.com thinks these people have misread the Law of Return and that it does *not* provide an easy, simple, automatic path to citizenship. According to PolitiFact:

> Applying for citizenship under the Law of Return "is a formal procedure which you could expect normally to take a number of months except under emergency conditions," said Yoram Hazony, president of the Herzl Institute, a Jerusalem think tank. "There is no such thing as receiving Israeli citizenship without submitting a formal request to the Israeli government."

Indeed, guidance from the Jewish Agency – a non-profit group that coordinates immigration into Israel – lists several required steps, including an online application, the filing of documentation, and an interview. (The Israeli Embassy in Washington did not return emails for this article.)

Legitimate question is obscured by its anti-Zionist packaging

Unlikely as it is that Bernie Sanders has dual Israeli-American citizenship, the larger question is legitimate, at least in theory. In the abstract, it's obvious that no coherent government should be populated by people with divided national loyalties. That division clearly constitutes at least the appearance of a conflict of interest, and more likely an actual conflict of interest. That makes it legitimate for any government to require that its decision-makers have citizenship only in the country they are expected to govern. That also makes it a legitimate inquiry, when there is evidence of dual citizenship, to ask if a given office holder has dual citizenship. But dual citizenship is not illegal or unconstitutional. The US Constitution in Article II lays out very limited qualifications to be president:

> **No person except a natural born citizen, or a citizen of the United States, at the time of the adoption of this Constitution, shall be eligible to the office of President; neither shall any person be eligible to that office who shall not have attained to the age of thirty-five years, and been fourteen Years a resident within the United States.**

A dual citizen is still "a citizen of the United States," and a natural born citizen is still a citizen – that's all that is required. In the past there were laws barring dual citizenship, but in 1967, the Supreme Court struck down most of them as unconstitutional in *Afroyim v. Rusk* (387 US 253). In that case the question was not just holding dual citizenship but exercising it by voting in another country's election.

While dual citizenship remains a limited legal issue, it's clearly a relevant political question, as Republican senator Ted Cruz of Texas vividly illustrated recently, when he relinquished his relatively uncontroversial Canadian citizenship. But for dual citizenship to rise to legitimacy as an inquiry, there needs to be some jot of evidence that it

13

might be true; Ted Cruz was born in Canada; his dual citizenship was a fact. Lacking evidence, the inquiry becomes a smear. In Sanders' case, Diane Rehm's only "evidence" was an anonymous "list" of unproven veracity.

Worse, as Diane Rehm could and should have known, her list was most popular with anti-Zionists, who show no apparent interest in substantiation. Sanders was not on earlier lists, but apparently started appearing on Congress lists of senators and representatives around 2012. The basic criterion for getting on such lists seems only to be that the official is Jewish. The Jewish Journal found Sanders in the Congressional list posted May 2 on a Facebook page replete with traditional anti-Semitic tropes.

Diane Rehm's two-paragraph apology to Sanders was a non-apology apology. It centered on her having *stated* that Sanders had dual citizenship rather than having framed it as a question. She blamed the issue itself on a listener who posted on her show's Facebook page. Regarding Sanders, she noted: "He does *NOT* have dual citizenship.... I should have explained to him and to you why I felt this was a relevant question and something he might like to address."

Indeed, Diane Rehm should have explained why she thought the dual citizenship question was relevant, but she didn't. She didn't explain anything. She treated her audience with disrespect. She did not explain how much or how little examination she gave dual citizenship before making it an accusation (which her "apology" seems to justify as "an issue that has come up over the years"). She offered no evidence that the issue was relevant to Sanders. And she said nothing to acknowledge or disown the baggage of bigotry that burdens any honest consideration of dual citizenship with Israel.

NPR ombudsman Elizabeth Jensen probed some of these issues. In response to Rehm claiming to have been a part of putting the rumor to rest, Jensen wrote: "Far from putting anything to rest, Rehm has now taken a falsehood from the fringes of the Internet and moved it into the mainstream conversation." But mostly Jensen wrote sympathetically of Rehm and seemed most interested in keeping NPR's skirts clean: NPR only distributes the Diane Rehm Show, Washington radio station WAMU produces the show and employs Rehm, Jensen emphasized at the start. Jensen seemed as oblivious as Rehm claimed to be to the political reality that anything to do with Israel is a hot-button issue.

Given the Israeli context of the issue, it's even more important that Diane Rehm (and Elizabeth Jensen) failed to mention, much less confront the possibility, that this was an orchestrated political dirty trick in which she could be seen as an all-too-willing participant. The Bernie Sanders campaign is emerging as a real and serious threat to established powers of all sorts, most obviously the Clintons. What could be better for Sanders' opponents than to see him ensnared in a diversionary spat in which his Jewishness can be turned against him?

Diane Rehm had a chance to come clean and chose not to. She continues to have that chance. But so far, her behavior has been slippery, incomplete, and only minimally honest. All in all, her performance is enough to make one think that perhaps "Diane Rehm has indelicate relations with pigs."

3.

Democratic Party's 'Values' Omit Democratic Process

Rigging nominations may or not win elections, but it's despicable

The Democratic Party is showing some ugly faces these days, as entrenched party leaders find both their president and much of their constituency headed in directions that the "party" disapproves. From Sen. Chuck Schumer choosing to risk war to Rep. Debbie Wasserman Schultz stifling supporters of her party's president and the peace deal with Iran, to the insurgent candidacies of Bernie Sanders and Martin O'Malley, party leaders find themselves leading toward goals widely rejected by others.

This is a hopeful sign – that there's resistance. But the struggle to define Democratic values as more than just another oxymoron is still in its early stages. It's also something of a shadowy war in which the party "leaders" seek to deny insurgents oxygen by limiting the number of debates, thereby helping Hillary Clinton ascend to her predicted coronation as the party's nominee. Another way of looking at that is that the party "leadership" is engaged in a delicate game of attempted vote-rigging by public ignorance. What about that can be good for the party, never mind the country?

Leading up to the recent Democratic National Committee (DNC) summer meeting August 26-29, the National Journal (NJ) offered an unintentionally hilarious "insider" assessment of the state of the Democratic Party. "Looming" over the meeting, NJ pontificated, was: A Bernie breakthrough? A Hillary resurgence? O'Malley coming up on the outside? No, none of those. What "loomed" over the meeting was "Joe Biden's phantom candidacy." Seriously, according to NJ,

Biden was getting "much of the buzz" from the party delegates even though he wasn't even attending the meeting. NJ quotes two of the DNC's 450 members as wanting an "interesting race" and not wanting an "anointed candidate" (the unnamed Hillary Clinton). NJ had no trouble mentioning Clinton over and over in its story, treating her as the only looming alternative to Biden (who had a conference call with DNC members on August 26). NJ doesn't even mention Bernie till the last paragraph, and then only to say he will be speaking.

Democratic "leaders" are apparently indulging their dislike of Bernie Sanders so much that their pique threatens to align them with a minority of American voters, committed to nominating a damaged candidate with a 55% *disapproval* rating, and 43% favorable (Sanders is 29% disapproval, 36% favorable, with 33% still unsure). As the certified frontrunner, Clinton remains well ahead of Sanders in national polling, but recently there have been media pieces like the September 1 Huff Post story headlined:

> **Polling Trajectory Shows Bernie Sanders Winning the Democratic Nomination. It's Time for America to Notice.**

Four of the five declared Democratic candidates spoke to the DNC in alphabetical order, which turned out to be in increasing order of intensity, substance, and specificity (Jim Webb did not attend). They were all in agreement in a general way about basic domestic issues and "re-building the American Dream." They all avoided direct criticism of each other, and they all had sharp lines about Republican failures. It was all on C-Span, where differences, both subtle and glaring, emerged, including these:

Lincoln Chaffee spoke only eight minutes, mostly in genial generalizations (everyone else would go over 20). But he pointedly expressed pride in voting against Sam Alito for the Supreme Court. Of Democrats generally, he said, "We're right on income inequality," as well as healthcare, and immigration, and the environment – without getting specific about any of them.

17

Chaffee said he supported the Iran deal, not just on its merits – keeping Iran from building a nuclear weapon – but also because the deal was the result of important international cooperation among the US, China, Russia, Great Britain, France and Germany in negotiations that began in 2003 (joined by the US in 2006). He was alone in saying that that kind of cooperation was needed to solve the world's most serious problems.

And only Chaffee called for ending all American conflicts overseas, calling them "Republican wars." He did not offer specifics.

Hillary Clinton also spoke mostly in familiar generalities – in support of women, children, the middle class, and working-class families. She also took a series of shots at Republican Donald Trump. Clinton said she's worked her "whole life" to even the odds for the poor and middle class. She mostly spoke in a flat, polished manner, carefully waiting at the expected applause lines. She made clear that she was still running as Bill Clinton's wife. (The New York Times inaccurately reported that she delivered "a fiery speech" and "a red-meat speech.") Clinton hit most of the party's major domestic policy clichés without any strong show of passion, punctuating her points with lots of deadpan head nodding.

At the end, Clinton promised to help "re-build" the Democratic Party, a thinly-veiled criticism of the party's present leadership, including the president. She promised to help candidates up and down the ticket nationwide.

Martin O'Malley didn't veil his criticism of the party's leadership, lashing out at policy (but not naming names). He called the party's decision to have only four debates before the primaries a "rigged process" that left the Democratic Party largely silent and unresponsive to unacceptable Republican racism and trickle-down economics. He particularly mocked the party's scheduling of the one New Hampshire debate in the middle of the holiday shopping season when almost no one would watch. "This is no time for silence," O'Malley said, "we need debate."

O'Malley lamented the party's abandonment of a 50-state strategy, a reference to former party chair Howard Dean's effort to turn the Democrats into a truly national party. He proclaimed that "we are the Democratic Party, not the undemocratic party."

But he also touted a fake populism, saying people could make change on their own, claiming that it was "not about big banks, big money taking over elections – it's about us." But O'Malley offered no justification for leaving banks too big to fail or allowing big money to buy politicians. This seems to position him as the "populist" alternative to Sanders, but the one who won't do anything serious to disturb the status quo.

Bernie Sanders was attending his first DNC meeting. After thanking his audience of Democrats "for what you do" for the good of the country, he noted that his campaign "calling for a political revolution" was striking a chord in grassroots America. He compared the current enthusiasm for his message to the Democrats' "abysmal" showing in 2014, when low turnout contributed to Republicans taking control of both houses of Congress:

> In my view, Democrats will not retain the White House, will not regain the Senate or the US House, will not be successful in dozens of governor races across the country, unless we generate excitement and momentum and produce a huge voter turnout. With all due respect – and I do not mean to insult anyone here – that turnout, that enthusiasm, will not happen with politics as usual. The same old same old will not work.
>
> The people of our country understand that given the collapse of the American middle class, and given the grotesque level of income and wealth inequality we are experiencing, we do not need more establishment politics or establishment economics – what we need is a government willing to take on the billionaire class...

Sanders spoke with his usual energy and intensity, enumerating many specific positions unmentioned by others. These included defeating the TPP (Trans-Pacific Partnership), rebuilding US infrastructure, ending "cowardly voting suppression by cowardly Republican governors," leading the world away from fossil fuels, defeating the Keystone

XL pipeline, providing free college tuition to all Americans by taxing Wall Street speculation, providing quality childcare, and expanding Social Security.

Sanders, like Chaffee, affirmed that he stands with the president on the Iran deal.

How divisive is the Iran accord for the Democratic Party?

In the 12 years since negotiations began with Iran over nuclear weapons, Iran has started no wars. Compare that record with the United States. Or Israel. Or even Saudi Arabia. Then ask yourself why you believe Iran is part of an "axis of evil" (if you do believe that). The reality is that Iran has been successfully demonized beyond all rational reality. Iran is even helping the US and others fight ISIS.

All the same, US senators like Schumer and others are willing to turn on their party's president, ready to reject a pact negotiated not just by the US but an international coalition with a wide spectrum of interests, none of which is a nuclear-armed Iran. Hillary Clinton endorsed the deal almost as soon as it was announced. Sanders endorsed the deal. But when an apparent majority of members of the DNC proposed a resolution endorsing the Iran deal, DNC chair Wasserman Schultz barred the DNC from voting on it.

The Iranian nuclear bomb program has never been much more real than President Obama's Kenyan citizenship, yet there are those who fervently believe in each imaginary horror and who will not be swayed by any evidence of an actual reality. With potentially game-changing opportunities of such vitality at home and abroad, it bodes ill for democratic values for the Democratic Party to be so heavily influenced by people so deeply in denial.

4.

Anderson Cooper Offers No Apology for Slandering Bernie Sanders

Who was the richest person in CNN's Democratic presidential debate?

The richest person in the Democratic presidential candidate debate on October 10 was not a candidate. The richest person on that Las Vegas stage was CNN moderator and Vanderbilt heir Anderson Cooper, whose $100 million net worth is greater than all the candidates' net worth combined (about $84 million). In a very real, if unspoken sense, this "debate" was more like an exclusive club interview, with Cooper vetting the applicants for their class credentials.

These class aspects of the debate went unmentioned. In American politics, class issues have traditionally gone unmentioned. The tacit understanding is that if you have the bad taste to ask, then you have no class. If you have class, you will have the right opinions. This year is different because of Bernie Sanders, part of whose popular appeal is that he is so clearly the scion of no great wealth and even less pretension. Sanders is calling for a social revolution against the ruling class of millionaires and billionaires, yet even he did not publicly object to having multi-millionaire Anderson Cooper of the One Per Cent running the show. Sanders likely understands that his best chance to win is not to confront the rich, but to encircle them with the rest of us whose net worth is more like his ($700,000) or less.

Net worth is notoriously hard to pin down with any accuracy, but ballpark figures are good enough at the highest levels, even if the numbers usually come from the candidates themselves. In a candidates' net worth listing published October 13, the Democrats

21

were evaluated as follows (with an alternative set of estimates in parenthesis):

- Hillary Clinton: $45 million ($31.2 herself, with Bill $111 million)

- Lincoln Chaffee: $32 million ($31.9 million, mostly his wife's trust)

- Jim Webb: $6 million ($4.6 million)

- Bernie Sanders: $700,000 ($528,014)

- Martin O'Malley: $-0- ($256,000)

By one recent measure, it takes a net worth of $1.2 million, minimum, to make it into the top One Per Cent of richest Americans (usually accompanied by pre-tax income of more than $300,000 annually). A US senator's salary is $192,600, which is amplified significantly by perks and benefits.

Like most debate moderators, Anderson Cooper seemed most interested in promoting a food fight among the candidates. While he had snark for everyone, his most provocative and least conscionable jibes were saved for Sanders, served up with class-based relish. What does yellow journalism red-baiting sound like? Cooper started with the lurking horror of every unjustifiably rich person:

> Senator Sanders. A Gallup poll says half the country would not put a socialist in the White House. You call yourself a democratic socialist. How can any kind of socialist win a general election in the United States?

How could such a horror happen in America? That's the question he seems to be asking. But to ask it that way, Cooper had to be deceitful and spin the Gallup poll to fit his meaning (Cooper's spin reflects the conventional coverage of the poll at the time). The real news from the June 2015 poll was that 47% of Americans were OK with electing a "socialist" (not further defined by pollsters). That 47% is more than past polls, and those opposed to a "socialist" make up only 50%, a difference close to the margin of error. In other words, more than a year from the presidential election, Gallup finds America more or less neutral on the question of whether a candidate is "any kind of socialist."

Cooper's approach uses "socialism" as something that is by definition pejorative and comes out of a deep, common bias in the US. The American ruling class has cultivated fear of "socialism" for close to two centuries, not because it's a threat to people's freedom, but because it's a threat to the wealth and power of people like the 158 families funding most of the 2016 race for the presidency.

Cooper's life of wealth illuminates his gift as a glib carnival barker

Anderson Cooper was not only born into wealth and power, he has lived the life of that class, as even his official CNN bio affirms. After attending New York's Dalton School, Cooper graduated from Yale College in 1989 with a BA in political science and two summer internships at the Central Intelligence Agency (CIA). He also studied Vietnamese at the University of Hanoi.

Cooper kept his CIA experience in the closet until September 2006, when an unnamed web site reported that Cooper had worked for the CIA. Cooper responded on his CNN blog, in minimizing, dismissive fashion. He said the website didn't have its facts straight but cited no errors. His own facts are well fudged – "for a couple of months over two summers I worked at the CIA headquarters in Langley, Virginia…. It was pretty bureaucratic and mundane." Cooper doesn't say what he did (of course) or even what years he was there (1987 and 1988, in the aftermath of William J. Casey's directorship). Whatever Cooper did at the CIA, he was there when the CIA was running an illegal war in Nicaragua (and another in El Salvador) and the agency's activities were subject to serious congressional efforts to curb them (the Boland Amendment).

When Sanders offered no direct answer to the question of how a "socialist" could win a general election, Cooper followed up more vituperatively and dishonestly:

> The question is really about electability here, and that's what I'm trying to get at.... [T]he Republican attack ad against you in a general election — it writes itself. You supported the Sandinistas in Nicaragua. You honeymooned in the Soviet Union. And just this weekend, you said you're not a capitalist. Doesn't — doesn't that ad write itself?

Cooper's first dishonesty here is asking the "electability" question here only of Sanders. Yes, everyone assumes Hillary Clinton is "electable," but O'Malley, Chaffee, or Webb? They're not even as close to getting nominated as Sanders. Why would anyone assume they're electable in anything but a flip-of-the-coin sense? Cooper's addressing the electability question only to Sanders may be a measure of how strong Cooper believes Sanders is or may be.

Then Cooper stated: "You supported the Sandinistas in Nicaragua." He said it as if there were no question that supporting the Sandinistas was a really bad thing. That's the talking point on Breitbart, National Review, and other right-wing sites for whom Cooper was carrying water. On Just Foreign Policy, Robert Naiman posted a prompt denunciation of Cooper for playing the knee-jerk, pro-war media honcho.

Cooper on record in support of illegal war supported by drug traffic

Supporting the Sandinistas in the 1980s was, and is, a principled position. The Sandinistas had overthrown the Somoza government, one of the most vicious of the US-backed dictatorships in Central America. President Reagan decided to wage an illegal covert war against the Sandinistas, using the CIA to recruit the Contra army to fight in Nicaragua, paid for by CIA-supported drug traffic to the US. Cooper refers to none of this, which was all taking place while he was doing summer internships at the CIA. Is Cooper a CIA asset? Hard to know, but he plays one pretty well on TV. A Cooper-CIA tie is perfectly credible – there's means, motive and opportunity all round. And in 1988, Bob Woodward wasn't getting any younger.

Supporting the illegal Contra war, run on drug money, is an unprincipled position, but Cooper clearly implies that it's still his position. Like the US government, Cooper showed no respect for the International Court of Justice, which issued a 1986 ruling strongly supporting Nicaragua's claims against the US, including the US mining of Nicaraguan harbors. The ruling awarded reparations to Nicaragua that the US never paid. The lone dissent in the decision came from Judge Stephen Schwebel, an American judge. The US defended its position in the UN Security Council in soviet-style, blocking any action with numerous vetoes. The UN General Assembly voted overwhelmingly in support of Nicaragua, with only the US, El Salvador, and Israel opposed.

For Cooper to say that Sanders supported the Sandinistas in Nicaragua would be high praise in most of the world. Only in the boxed-in, unilluminated world of American media can it pass for a criticism without bringing the house down in laughter. That's another of the US government successes brought on by secret agencies like the CIA and fellow-travelers like multi-millionaire Anderson Cooper.

Bernie Sanders challenged the yellow journalist on the issue of Hillary Clinton's emails. His was an act of generosity and presidential stature. None of his fellow candidates had the courage or character to repudiate Cooper's shameless red-baiting, not on Nicaragua, and not on his next slander, "You honeymooned in the Soviet Union."

Integrity is not a quality Cooper showed much interest in

Almost surely, Cooper knew that statement was a dishonest low blow, a neat way to brutalize the truth without actually lying. Again, Cooper was irresponsibly peddling another right-wing trope, used with similar hypocrisy by George Will and others.

As a Daily Kos blog details, the Sanders honeymoon was also part of a 1956 sister-cities program initiated by the Eisenhower administration. In 1988, Sanders and his wife Jane were married, marched in a Memorial Day parade in Vermont, then headed off to the Russian city of Yaroslavl on their "honeymoon." Somehow that doesn't have the same impact as when Anderson Cooper lies about it.

Cooper's last dishonesty was: "And just this weekend you said you're not a capitalist." Once again Cooper acted as if that was an undeniable evil, case closed. But the instance he referred to on NBC was not so simple, and Cooper provided no context. On NBC, Sanders bristled when his interviewer asked if Sanders was a "socialist," since Sanders has referred to himself as a "democratic socialist" for decades. Sanders asked the NBC toady parrot if he ever asked others if they were "capitalists" and the guy cowered out. He asked Sanders if he was a capitalist. And Sanders said, yet again, that he's a democratic socialist.

Returning to his distorted framing bias, a "Republican attack ad," Cooper asked, "Doesn't that ad write itself?" Well, so what if it does? That just means Republican ad writers have as little integrity as Cooper, and maybe that's what they're all paid for.

As Sanders put it on CNN at the end of his opening statement: "What this campaign is about is whether we can mobilize our people to take back our government from a handful of billionaires and create the vibrant democracy we know we can and should have."

We are at the beginning of what might be a long learning curve as we find out what our country is truly about. Bernie Sanders offers an opportunity to look at realities in broad daylight and make up our minds about them. Anderson Cooper is but one of a legion of self-serving, self-preserving One Per Cent propagandists who will do all they can to keep the Sanders message in the dark.

5.

National Mindlessness,
Threats in Cleveland, Yale, & War

"We are in serious times, and this is a really serious job. This is not entertainment; this is not a reality show. This is a contest for the presidency of the United States."

PRESIDENT OBAMA, MAY 6, 2016

Donald Trump is the greatest threat to America today, or so the conventional wisdom, left and right, would have you believe. More realistically, the greatest threat to America today is actually believing that Trump is the greatest threat to America today.

To believe that Donald Trump is the greatest threat to America today, one needs to be a little hysterical or dishonest (or both). Believing in the mortal Trump threat requires believing that the Congress, the Supreme Court, the military, the security state, and all the other agencies of government, as well as all the states and most of the populace will suddenly become helpless to oppose the White House. That is an imaginary helplessness with no basis in reality, as viciously demonstrated by the Republican Congress of the past six years. For better or worse, the Constitution is designed to enable gridlock.

Advanced Trump-phobia is mostly political posturing, as in the president's quote above. The country is drowning in bad faith like this and worse, because the country isn't ready to look itself honestly in the mirror. When your political system produces bad results, it's all too easy, cynical, and dishonest to blame the results. That's just politics. Intellectual integrity is quite a different orientation, one that is in short supply in a country in the near death-grip of decades of national mindlessness. Examples are plentiful.

27

Cleveland: "We'll pay $6 million, but we don't admit doing anything wrong"

On November 22, 2014, Cleveland police officers drove into a playground and executed a 12-year-old boy less than one second after they arrived. The cop who did the killing had had violence problems when he was with another police department. The prosecutor, who failed to get an indictment from a grand jury, later lost a bid for re-election. The family of the boy, Tamir Rice, sued the city in federal court under a civil rights statute. In April 2016, Cleveland agreed to pay Tamir Rice's estate $6 million, perhaps the largest Cleveland settlement in a police-shooting case. Under the settlement, the Rice family will drop its complaint against officers Frank Garmback and Timothy Loehmann, the shooter, who are both still city employees. While paying $6 million, the city admits no wrongdoing, even though the event was rife with wrongdoing.

Failure to admit wrongdoing despite committing wrongdoing has long been an acceptable corrupt practice in the American legal system. Instead of accountability for killing or maiming people, the perpetrators are allowed to lie legally as one means of limiting their damages in a fair trial. Corporations that create Love Canal or Gulf Coast oil spills are the most common beneficiaries of this class-based double jeopardy against the victims. So common is this blatant injustice that it is rarely challenged politically, or denounced, or more than mentioned. But it is a soul-destroying practice embedded in American culture that enriches the rich and protects the guilty. Voters know this viscerally, so when Trump says the system is rigged, they know he's right, and they know almost no one else is telling them that truth.

Yale: "Honoring slavers is our way of showing that slavery was wrong"

On April 28, 2016, Yale University president Peter Salovey tried to explain the Yale Corporation's decision to retain the name of the residential hall Calhoun College, named for South Carolinian John C. Calhoun, Yale 1804. A lawyer, Calhoun owned dozens of slaves and defended slavery as "a positive good." He fought for the expansion of slavery into new territories. He argued that the federal government should defend minority rights, meaning the minority comprising southern slave owners. He defended states' rights in general and in particular the right of the South to secede, either peacefully or by force:

> If you who represent the stronger portion [the North], cannot agree to settle them on the broad principle of justice and duty, say so; and let the States we both represent agree to separate and part in peace. If you are unwilling we should part in peace, tell us so; and we shall know what to do, when you reduce the question to submission or resistance.

In other words, Calhoun was a significant historical figure who was also a slave-owning bigot and traitor, lacking only the opportunity to betray his country because he died in 1850. Yale named Calhoun College after him in 1931, largely based on his achievements – serving as vice president, congressman and senator (as almost no other Yalies had) – not based on his character. After months of public dialogue within the Yale community and private consideration within the Yale Corporation, Salovey explained the decision to continue honoring Calhoun this way:

> We are a university whose motto is "light and truth." Our core mission is to educate and discover. These ideals guided our decisions. Through teaching and learning about the most troubling aspects of our past, our community will be better prepared to challenge their legacies. More than a decision about a name, we must focus on understanding the past and present, and preparing our students for the future.

This explains nothing, and students were unhappy. What in this somewhat lofty rhetoric makes it an educational necessity to honor a slave-owning secessionist? Nothing. These are experiences that are not illuminated by having students live in a place named for a horrible exemplar of a horrific past. Calhoun and the legacy he represents will not be hidden if the place is called by any other, benign name, Salovey's rationalizing notwithstanding:

Ours is a nation that often refuses to face its own history of slavery and racism. Yale is part of that history. We cannot erase American history but we can confront it, teach it, and learn from it. The decision to retain Calhoun College's name reflects the importance of this vital educational imperative.

The decision to retain Calhoun College's name demonstrates a muddy-mindedness that can't or won't distinguish between changing a name and erasing history. By Yale's form of reasoning, Calhoun may as well fly the Confederate flag. Surely people as smart as those at Yale can figure out how to confront the history of slavery and racism without honoring slavers and racists.

Making the Calhoun decision even more indefensible, Yale has also announced the names of two new colleges it plans to build. One will be Benjamin Franklin College, in honor of the recipient of a Yale honorary degree in 1753. While the choice is ambiguous (and was greeted by laughter from students at a town hall meeting), Franklin's brilliance and contributions to learning are undeniable. And the fact that he was a slave owner has real, potential educational value in tracing how Franklin came to be an abolitionist. Calhoun died unreconstructed and apparently unreflective.

Yale's other new college will be named for Anna Pauline (Pauli) Murray, a 1965 Yale Law School graduate and 1979 recipient of an honorary Doctor of Divinity. Born into a poor black family in 1910, Pauli Murray grew up to spend most of her 75 years fighting for positive social change that should make Calhoun roll over in his grave. As Salovey put it, without subterfuge this time:

> **Pauli Murray represents the best of Yale: a pre-eminent intellectual inspired to lead and prepared to serve her community and her country. She was at the intellectual forefront of the battles that defined 20th-century America and continue to be part of our discourse today: civil rights, women's rights, and the role of spirituality in modern society.**

Yale, like most of America, is having trouble dealing fairly with minority students and faculty. Yale, like most of America, is still part of the national mindlessness about race and ethnicity. Of that, at least, Calhoun would be proud. Trump, on the other hand, might note that at Yale's going rate, $250 million could create a Trump College at Yale.

US: "Hey, be grateful, drones kill fewer civilians than carpet bombing!"

For almost pure psychic numbing, let's turn to the White House, where it's needed most (except possibly at the Pentagon). What the Germans did to London and Coventry in World War II constituted war crimes, unlike what our side did to Dresden and Hiroshima. Killing civilians (at least deliberately) violates the law of war, or at least it used to. Having done a lot of saturation bombing in Afghanistan and Iraq, to little military or political avail, the US decided to use the cheaper, more "precise" drone attack tactic, also to little military or political avail. The more meaningful accomplishment of drone warfare has been to turn the president (first Bush, and now Obama, more so) from the chief executive into the chief executioner.

There was a time when having the president of the United States start his day by picking the names of people to kill from a list would have been repugnant. Drone killing is, on the face of it, a war crime. And drone warfare is waged largely in secret (except from the victims). No wonder it goes unchallenged by Congress and presidential candidates alike.

Even Bernie Sanders as president would continue to send drones to kill people on a list, people with no due process rights, no rights of appeal, nothing but the right to be imperial sacrifices in the name of imperial security. In March, Sanders defended his non-pacifist cred, citing the wars he's supported and defending the party line on drone warfare:

> Drones are a big issue, and drones have done some good things. They've been selective; they've taken out people who should be taken out.... [Drones have also done] some terrible things, which have been counterproductive to the United States. But would I rule them out completely? No, I would not. But I am aware that they have in some cases, you know, you use a drone and you end up killing 40 people in a wedding in Afghanistan; that is not a terribly humane thing to do or productive thing to do.

In the past, Sanders said he would continue to wage drone warfare, but would use drones "very, very selectively and effectively." This

31

is American politics today. The good guys want to do as little evil as possible, the bad guys are ok with as much evil as seems necessary. In April, Obama put the lesser-evil argument this way:

> There's no doubt that some innocent people have been killed by drone strikes. It is not true that it has been this sort of willy-nilly, you know, "Let's bomb a village." That is not how it's—folks have operated. And what I can say with great certainty is that the rate of civilian casualties in any drone operation are far lower than the rate of civilian casualties that occur in conventional war.

Never mind that the rate of civilian casualties in conventional war was driven to new highs with the atomic bombings of Hiroshima and Nagasaki. The president is using an obscene level of carnage to make his personal assassination program seem reasonable. Presidential assassination by autocratic fiat was new in American life when President Bush first crossed that line. Presidential assassination, aka executive action, used to be against even American law. A decade after the first drone strike, the country in its muddled mindlessness pretends we're not all proxy assassins. That's too hard to swallow, to admit, to address, to stop, to prosecute. That's reality. It's much easier, and less dangerous, to pit illusion against illusion, to pretend that Donald Trump is a freak-out lethal threat to an America that hasn't existed for a long time. That's a reality show for real. The president and the people collude in the same unconscionable charade: he doesn't want to tell the truth and the people don't want to hear it.

The possibility of healing America continues to recede in the rearview mirror. A nation that creates a torture concentration camp like Guantanamo is not a healthy nation. A nation that maintains a torture concentration camp like Guantanamo is not a healthy nation. A nation that cannot come to terms with a torture concentration camp like Guantanamo and close it down and hold those responsible to account is not a healthy nation. Guantanamo has nothing to do with Donald Trump beyond being another visible symptom of the same metastasizing spiritual cancer.

6.

Clinton to California: 'Drop Dead'

Democratic Party infighting creates false narrative in Nevada

By now, anyone paying the least attention knows that the dishonest Democratic establishment and dishonest mainstream media have created a false narrative of bad behavior by Bernie Sanders supporters at the Nevada State Democratic State Convention on May 14. The evidence-free claims about "thrown chairs" (none) and "death threats" (tasteless insults) have been widely rebutted, but they have served their purpose all the same: taking attention away from the arrogant, autocratic management of the Nevada convention by establishment Democrats working on behalf of Hillary Clinton.

It's a measure of Democratic Party panic that party leaders feel the need to run a despotic state convention, autocratically ramming their preferred results through when there were only two national delegates at stake. Their fear of Bernie Sanders must run deep for them to follow this authoritarian performance with a smear campaign based on lies about the Sanders campaign. Establishment Democrats should be afraid. Almost half the voters allowed to vote in Democratic primaries reject establishment Democrats' "values." But their shamelessness, pusillanimity, and obtuse arrogance march on toward a possibly disastrous November that is wholly self-engineered.

First, let's stipulate that the possibility of Bernie Sanders becoming the Democratic nominee for President is small. But it's also real. Sanders still could pull a rabbit out of the hat for a "miracle ending". Should he be able to get 85% of the California vote, he'd get ALL the California delegates. No wonder establishment Democrats want to pretend the game is already over. It's close to over, to be sure. Let's wait and see what the score is when the game is really over. (In 2008, Clinton

33

played out the game, losing 15 of the last 23 contests; this year, Sanders is winning down the stretch.)

Revolution is hard, non-violent revolution is much harder

Bernie Sanders is fighting for a political revolution. He is doing it with nonviolence, working within the two-party system. The Democratic Party is not a revolutionary party and hasn't even been close since the Johnson years in the sixties. Establishment Democrats like the Clintons are fundamentally counter-revolutionary, which is a problem for a party with ten million voters favoring the political revolution candidate. The Republican party is so intellectually corrupt that it fell apart facing the Trump challenge and is now falling in line with it. Democrats still have enough party discipline (or top-down undemocratic hierarchy) that they can muster the ugly pushback that featured a rigged Nevada convention with no meaningful delegate participation followed by a vicious attack on the victims who have had the temerity to challenge authority.

All this has about it some of the stench of 1968, although the parallel is inexact. But then, as now, a large part of the electorate was incensed at the party hierarchy – then over the party's obdurate support of the Viet-Nam war, now over the party's adamant resistance to social change desired by most of the country. Then as now, the Democratic Party was unresponsive to its anti-establishment dissenters, then preferring a police riot to silence dissent over any rational effort at accommodation, now choosing a rigged convention (with the hint of worse to come). Then as now, the party hierarchy was rigid and intellectually corrupt. Then the Democratic hierarchy managed to get Richard Nixon elected. Now ... well, we'll see.

Top Democrats reacted without bothering to fact check

Nevada senator Harry Reid, the Democratic minority leader, had already taken Sanders to task on May 17, based on the false reports of the Nevada convention – "The violence and all the other bad things that has happened there," Reid falsely told reporters. The New York Times reported that Reid said that Sanders faced "a test of leadership" over the behavior of his supporters, and that Reid said he urged Sanders to "do the right thing." Neither the Times nor Reid, apparently, explained what "the right thing" was, nor did they mention the draconian nature of the convention itself.

The "test of leadership" meme was picked up with equal parrot-like vacuity by Politico, the Washington Post, The Hill, the LA Times, Daily Kos, the Chicago Tribune, and the Drudge Report. The media nadir was reached by the Times with such baldly biased front page headlines as "Sanders Is Urged to Quell Threats by His Backers – Chairs Fly in Nevada" (May 18) and "Bernie Sanders, Eyeing Convention, Willing to Harm Hillary Clinton in Homestretch" (May 19). The unreported reality: it was actually Clinton's Nevada supporters who were harming Clinton with their thuggish takeover of the convention.

What does Harry Reid know about tests of leadership? He can't even lead his 43 fellow Democrats in an effective effort to make the full Senate vote on the current Supreme Court nominee. Harry Reid has called the Chairman of the Joint Chiefs of Staff "incompetent," but during the Viet-Nam war, which he did not oppose, Harry Reid led from behind as a capitol cop guarding the House and Senate. Under Harry Reid's leadership, the Democrats' Senate majority became a minority. Harry Reid called the Iraq War "the worst foreign policy mistake in the history of this country," but he voted for it. Bernie Sanders has characterized Iraq the same way, but he voted against it. The only significant test of leadership that comes to mind with Harry Reid is that he managed to keep nuclear waste from being buried in his Nevada backyard at Yucca Mountain. But he's done nothing to keep anyone else safe from nuclear waste and nothing to stem the production of nuclear waste. Harry Reid is the Democratic establishment personified, and you can count on him for pretty much nothing.

Senate Democratic whip Dick Durbin of Illinois chimed in based on the false narrative, as did Senator Chris Coons of Delaware. Coons shot his foot into his mouth, lecturing Sanders on "the importance of respecting the process," numb to the notion that in Nevada the process was the problem. Senator Barbara Boxer of California was at the convention to give a keynote speech for Hillary Clinton, but when she lit into the Sanders disrupters she was booed. She attacked the crowd, making the booing worse. Boxer claimed she feared for her safety. By contrast, Democrat Nina Turner, an Ohio State Senator who was supposed to speak before Boxer but was bumped to later, used her speaking time to calm the audience: "we got to be calm but committed." Turner, who was at the convention for almost eight hours, attests that there was no violence ("nobody tried to do anything violent whatso-ever") and that reports that she was booed were false, even when she said Bernie Sanders was going all the way to the convention "to make the impossible possible."

Rather tepidly, Democratic House Minority Leader Nancy Pelosi of California semi-praised Sanders as "a positive force in the Democratic Party." She said she was glad to see the energy of Sand-ers supporters but warned that "there are rules that exist." She didn't mention the way Nevada Democrats had treated rules as a variable, but she did reject comparisons between 2016 and 1968 as "ridiculous."

By Friday, May 21, there were reports that Sanders was calling his fellow senators and assuring them of what he'd said all along: that he would support the nominee of the party, once there was a nominee as determined by the convention. There's no report that anyone in the Democratic establishment is assuring him of similar support in the event, however remote, that he is the nominee. That would be a real test of leadership for Harry Reid and his ilk in the face of a popular political revolution to change this country in ways establishment Democrats fear because it threatens their cozy nests of inert but lucrative legalized corruption. Embracing real change for the rest of the country is a test of leadership Clinton Democrats act like they're determined to fail by any means necessary, the consequences be damned.

7.

Platform for Mystification – Democrats at Work

"Our job is to pass the most progressive platform in the history of the Democratic Party"

BERNIE SANDERS CAMPAIGN STATEMENT

"[This is] the most ambitious and progressive platform our party has ever seen"

MAYA HARRIS, CLINTON POLICY ADVISER

The Sanders campaign has more than enough principled reasons to resist conventional political wisdom and carry on its campaign at least into convention floor fights and street demonstrations, not least because Democrats are acting as if they want only to co-opt Sanders supporters and send the Sanders political revolution down the memory hole.

Taken together, the two comments above frame the Democrats' attempt at a "Mission Accomplished" moment for the party's platform draft for 2016. Anyone who wants to read the full text and judge it independently is asking for too much participatory democracy. The Democratic National Committee online offers only two platforms, both from 2015. The Democratic National Convention online offers a press release summarizing the 30-page platform draft, but not the document itself. The apparent purpose of this approach is to persuade people that the party has taken Bernie Sanders into the fold and his followers should now fall in love and fall in line with the Democratic Party. And that's the spin the party got in early coverage from the Washington

37

Post, Associated Press, N.Y. Daily News, CNN ("Clinton campaign hails progressive Democratic platform"), The Hill, and others.

Conventional wisdom has it that party platforms are not to be taken all that seriously, since politicians are notorious for breaking promises, and platforms aren't binding on candidates anyway. But what about the circumstance where the party platform is made up not only of promises, but of many real and veiled threats? How seriously should we take that? Robert Reich suggests that Hillary Clinton's lack of a progressive vision for the country enhances the chances of a Donald Trump presidency.

No wonder, then, that the Democratic Party is working to create the image of a progressive party where there is none. DNC Chairwoman Rep. Debbie Wasserman Schultz thanked the platform committee for "a platform draft that advances our party's progressive ideals and is worthy of our great country." Platform Drafting Committee Chair Rep. Elijah Cummings said, "The draft platform we have produced in an open and transparent manner reflects our priorities as Democrats and demonstrates our vision for this nation." To support these claims, the DNC press release highlights "key progressive policies" in the platform draft, some of which are perennial promises of pie-in-the-sky coming closer to earth. It also leaves out some things that progressives might find important. The following checklist, based on limited available information, is necessarily incomplete in the absence of the 30-page platform draft itself. And in any event, the meaningfulness of any of these platform planks (or omissions) is dependent on the will of a party that has been becoming less and less progressive for 30 years.

Jobs. It's "the most ambitious jobs plan on record," and the sky is full of pie. Focus on restoring infrastructure and revitalizing decaying communities seems encouraging, but that's about as specific as it gets.

Minimum Wage. The committee said a minimum wage of $15 an hour is a nice idea but rejected the Sanders proposal to actually raise the federal minimum wage to $15 an hour. The Clinton members of the committee also rejected indexing any minimum wage to inflation.

Education. For public schools, the platform "reaffirmed Democrats' commitment to supporting teachers, schools and communities." Re-thinking federal mandates, not so much. College education for all who qualify, even less. Eliminating (or just mitigating) student debt, not at all.

Death Penalty. "This is the first time in the Democratic Party's history" that it has called for abolishing the death penalty. A little late, but all the same progress from 1992, when Bill Clinton found it politically expedient to rush back to Arkansas to make sure his state killed a retarded man.

Trade. "Existing deals must be continuously re-examined, and enforcement of those existing agreements must be tougher." Not tough enough now, with TransCanada suing the US under NAFTA for delaying their Keystone XL pipeline? Not a word about that. And not a word about the pending TPP (Trans-Pacific Partnership), opposed by Sanders, sort of opposed by Clinton, but supported by President Obama, so the committee felt politically hog-tied and punted (if you can imagine such contortions). The platform says, "A higher standard [undefined] must be applied to any future trade agreements." Really?

Earned Income Tax Credit. The DNC calls this "looking out for working people," and it helps, but not in day-to-day living, only once a year. Expanding it is a feel-good idea with minimal real impact.

Wall Street Reform. The platform promises expanded regulatory controls, like the ones the party refused to adopt when it could in 2009-2010. The platform hints at adopting a "modernized" Glass-Steagall Act, the one the party abolished to make the crash of 2007 possible, if not inevitable. And the party dangles the bait of breaking up too-big-to-fail institutions that threaten economic stability, a break-up the Obama administration made sure didn't happen. The platform appears to ignore "private equity" threats entirely.

Multi-Millionaire Surtax. The platform is long on rhetoric ("ensuring millionaires can no longer pay a lower [tax] rate than their secretaries"), but short on specifics. Wealth disparity, in any form, is not addressed.

Expanding Social Security. The platform first promises to "fight every effort to cut, privatize, or weaken Social Security," but neglects to mention restoring cost-of-living increases. The committee adopted an amendment promising to expand Social Security, paying for the expansion by taxing annual incomes above $250,000 (roughly five times the American median household income)

Immigration. The platform draft specifically supports "keeping families together, ending family detention, closing private detention centers, and guaranteeing legal counsel for all unaccompanied minors in immigration proceedings," as well as "comprehensive immigration reform" without other specifics. The platform is silent on deportation, which has been higher under President Obama than any previous president.

Universal Healthcare. Reiterating its decades-old assertion that "health care is a right," the platform promotes the Affordable Care Act as a success to build on. The committee, like the president in 2009, explicitly rejected single-payer, Medicare-for-all, despite its manifest popularity and superiority over any other available plan. The Clinton people would have none of it. Universal healthcare is not even serious pie-in-the-sky.

Honoring Tribal Nations. The committee "unanimously adopted the most comprehensive language ever in the party's platform recognizing our moral and legal responsibility to honor the sovereignty of and relationship to Indigenous tribes – and acknowledge previous failures to live up to that responsibility." That's it, no specifics. No promise to clean up uranium contamination on Navajo land, for example.

Climate Change and Clean Energy. In an apparent rebuke to the president's "all of the above" energy non-strategy, the committee adopted a joint Sanders-Clinton proposal "to commit to making America run entirely on clean energy by mid-century." This would be a radical proposal, if the party actually meant it. But the committee also flatly rejected any carbon tax to reduce greenhouse gasses, and it flatly rejected any freeze on natural gas fracking, leaving the air, underground water, and earthquake-prone areas as vulnerable as ever to the largely unregulated, destructive process. The committee also rejected a ban on fossil fuel drilling on federal land or in federal waters.

Reproductive Rights. According to the DNC, the "platform goes further than previous Democratic platforms on women's reproductive rights," which is a measure of how weak previous platforms were. This platform defends Planned Parenthood, opposes the 1973 Helms Amendment (limited US spending abroad on abortion), and opposes the 1976 Hyde Amendment (limiting domestic federal expenditures on abortion).

Criminal Justice Reform. The platform draft "calls for ending the era of mass incarceration, shutting down private prisons, ending racial profiling, reforming the grand jury process, investing in re-entry programs, banning the box to help give people a second chance and prioritizing treatment over incarceration for individuals suffering addiction." This is tantamount to rejection of Clinton-era "reform," as well as an implied rebuke to the sitting president, who has done little to end these horrors.

Marijuana. The platform does not come close to supporting legalization but is for "supporting states that choose to decriminalize marijuana," without specifying how such support would be expressed (no mention, for example, of removing the stupid federal classification of cannabis as a Schedule I Controlled Substance). The committee adopted an amendment recognizing the racial disparity of the impact of marijuana laws on African Americans (and other minorities), but stopped short of saying what, if anything, to do about that injustice.

That is the last item in the full list of issues the DNC chose to highlight from the platform draft adopted (with Cornel West abstaining) on June 25. Unsurprisingly, the DNC did not offer a comprehensive list of all the platform issues, ignoring Israel, for example, although it was reported elsewhere:

Israel. Israel was very much on the platform committee's mind, and the committee rejected a proposal that the US should oppose Israel's ongoing illegal occupation and colonization of the West Bank. The draft platform reflects Clinton's support for the mirage of a "two-state solution" of some sort (not specified). The platform does stake out two new positions for the party: first, that Palestinians "should be free to govern themselves in their own viable state, in peace and in dignity" and second, that Democrats "oppose any effort to delegitimize Israel, including at the United Nations or through the Boycott, Divestment, and Sanctions [BDS] Movement." It's not clear how Democrats will justify both supporting Israel's illegal occupation and opposing the entirely legal BDS Movement.

Iraq And Syria. Although untouted by the DNC, the platform also calls for "more inclusive governance" in Iraq and Syria. What, you thought there was a war there or something? Seriously.

And then there's the highly uncertain, open-ended list of issues possibly important to the American people, but that go apparently unmentioned by the DNC and media coverage. Or maybe they're there and being ignored.

Assault Weapons. Contrary to what you thought you saw on TV, Democrats have no apparent platform plank dealing with assault weapons, 100-shot clips, background checks, or any other aspect of gun regulation. Not a mumbling word.

Military Budget. $600 billion a year for what? Not worth asking.

Intelligence Budgets. Billions more, much in black budgets, and for what? You'd better not ask.

Terrorism. In the unlikely event that terrorism were actually omitted, that would be a sign of maturity and intellectual integrity, moving away from fear-mongering. It *could* happen, right?

Terror War in Yemen. Yes, the Saudis are the international war criminals fronting for the US, but our hands are bloody. And the profits are good, so why bring it up in a party platform? Have you forgotten how divisive Vietnam was?

Afghanistan. Not a word about America's longest war. Long may it wave.

Iran. Saudi Arabia. Turkey. Libya. Etc. Nothing revealed.

Poverty. There are 47 million poor people in America, as Sanders repeatedly points out. They are as invisible in the Democratic platform as they are in everyday life. Why have we become a country where it's considered a tolerable response to round up homeless people and ship them off to somewhere else, anywhere else but here? The platform is as oblivious to America's poor as to the world's poor.

The omissions go on and on – what is the Democratic Party's policy toward any of the unaddressed issues out there? In favor of war in Ukraine? Itching for Naval confrontation in South China Sea? Wanting to accept England as our 51st state? Who knows? If this is the most progressive party platform the Democrats have ever seen, then the Democrats have never seen a truly progressive platform. Not that that is any reason to stop the shuck and jive.

> **Note:** A reader commented at the time that, "We have a national emergency called Trumpism to deal with. Bernie Who is just getting in the way."
>
> My response on June 29, 2016, was:
>
> Yes, there's a national emergency, a longstanding one actually, of which Trumpism is merely the most glaring excrescence. Clintonism is a deeper, more metastasized cultural cancer. Trumpism vs Clintonism neatly frames the existential choice the moral blackmail forced upon us.

8.

Trump's Hillary Email Baiting Sets Off Stupidity Storm

"... Russia, if you're listening, I hope you're able to find the 30,000 emails that are missing. I think you will probably be rewarded mightily by our press. Let's see if that happens. That'll be next."

DONALD TRUMP AT A NEWS CONFERENCE JULY 27, 2016

That's the money quote that was widely reported as what Republican Presidential nominee Donald Trump said that day about Russia and Hillary Clinton's emails. It is hard to read those sentences as anything but cynical joking. But most of the media, the empty-headed commentariat, and Democratic shills all made a fundamentally bad-faith effort to inflate the joke into something sinister to serve their various agendas.

Trump's offhand comment was almost universally misreported in a provocative, interpretive, and stupid manner – even Democracy NOW! headlined the story: "Trump Asks Russia to Hack Hillary Clinton's Email." That is just wrong.

There is nothing in Trump's snide remarks inviting anyone to hack anything. Trump expresses "hope" that Russia can "find" 30,000 emails that are missing because Clinton had them deleted from her private server after unilaterally deciding they were not government property. It would be more accurate to say that Clinton hacked herself to eliminate the emails, except she didn't need to hack, she just needed reassurance from other pliable lawyers that destroying potential evidence was no problem.

As for any invitation to the Russians to hack Clinton's emails now, that's so stupid that it's more than likely *deliberately* stupid. Clinton's

44

private server was disconnected many months ago (or years?) and is literally hack-proof. It's also in FBI custody. And there's no reason to believe it would be worth hacking by anyone, since Clinton has already deleted, disabled, or destroyed pretty much everything on it.

Saying that "Donald Trump invites Russia to hack into Clinton's emails," as the Los Angeles Times did July 27, is at best dishonest mindless sensationalism, but most likely a deliberate political lie. A more accurate interpretation of what Trump actually said would be along the lines of: maybe Russia can find Clinton's deleted emails somewhere, in the cloud or Wikileaks or something, since the US government has failed to figure out what's been concealed from the American public (or has kept it concealed). If Trump was baiting the Democrats, they took the bait – hook, line, and sinker.

Trump called for selective transparency

Trump implied that if the Russians could find Clinton's missing emails, they should share them with the media and "probably be rewarded mightily." There is nothing wrong in asking for this particular transparency, which is clearly in the public interest. But Trump is no more honest than the rest. If reciprocity is a measure of fairness, then he should also be calling for the Russians, or some 15-year-old geek in a basement somewhere, to hack the IRS and release Trump's tax returns. That, compared to hacking Clinton's out of service servers, is at least a theoretical possibility.

Compounding its duplicity, the L.A. Times went on to reiterate the lie that has become a widespread media meme: "Donald Trump dared a foreign government to commit espionage on the US to hurt his rival...." Not only are Clinton's emails beyond the reach of any hacker, it would be impossible to commit espionage even if it were possible to hack them. Clinton had a private server precisely to keep her emails outside US government control and any prying eyes, official or not. Even when the Clinton server was up and running, hacking it would have been legally and morally ambiguous. That hack would have been essentially a crime against another criminal set-up.

45

The larger context for this circling of the media wagons around the Clinton candidacy was the actual hack of the Democratic National Committee (DNC) email system that went undetected for about a year. When Wikileaks started releasing DNC emails, attachments, and voice mails on July 22, the Democratic Party's professional staff was revealed to be small-minded, biased, and dishonest. That was actually a public service. It was also no great surprise, especially to Sanders supporters, but it was a bit startling to see it all revealed so nakedly and shamelessly.

Corrupt DNC exposed just as convention about to begin

Damage control suddenly became a Democratic Party necessity lest the party's venality and corruption become the issue. Within days of the exposure of the campaign, the government rushed to the rescue. Led by the Democrat-in-chief (who kept his hands clean), the partisan executive branch countered with anonymous leaked stories, attributing the DNC hack to one of its favorite scapegoats, Russia. Right on cue, Clinton allies were accusing Trump of treason. Welcome to Cold War II (which has been on for awhile now, actually). The basic framing meme, as it appeared in a New York Times lede July 26, was straight forwardly disingenuous:

> American intelligence agencies have told the White House they now have "high confidence" that the Russian government was behind the theft of emails and documents from the Democratic National Committee, according to federal officials who have been briefed on the evidence.

This is old school Red-baiting (applied to a no longer Red Russia) with even less intellectual integrity than McCarthy-era smearing. No wonder that no evidence was produced by these unnamed spooks, all they had to do was impugn Putin, Putin, Putin, and people's minds started shutting down with pre-programmed fear. A few days later head spook (and the first to go on record) James Clapper, Director of National Intelligence, kept the story alive by pretending to downplay it (sort of) in good spook fashion, while also slyly influencing the presidential election. Some of what Clapper said about the DNC hacks:

46

Was this to just stir up trouble or was this ultimately to try to influence an election? Of course, that's a serious – a serious – proposition… We don't know enough [yet] to … ascribe a motivation, regardless of who it may have been. [emphasis added]

Having said the intelligence community doesn't know who did it or why, intelligence chief Clapper went on to identify and ascribe motive to – you guessed it – Russia:

> **They believe we're trying to influence political developments in Russia, we're trying to affect change, and so their natural response is to retaliate and do unto us as they think we've done to them.**

Is there any reason to think the US doesn't do this stuff to Russia when the US does it to Germany and other allies? Clapper knows better, that's why he made an apparent allusion to the movie "Casablanca," winking to the insiders while hoping most people don't get it:

> **I'm somewhat taken aback by the hyperventilation on this…. I'm shocked someone did some hacking – that's never happened before.**

In "Casablanca," Captain Renault, a cynical state official, bowing to the Gestapo, decides to shut down Rick's café because of illegal gambling:

> *Captain Renault:* I'm shocked, shocked to find that gambling is going on in here! [a croupier hands Renault a pile of money]
>
> *Croupier:* Your winnings, sir.
>
> *Captain Renault:* [sotto voce] Oh, thank you very much.

DNI Clapper seems so shocked to find that hacking is going on in the world that he waxes incoherent:

> I think we're going to be in a state of suppression of extremism in whatever manifestation or form it takes, whether it's al Qaeda or ISIS or some other group that's spawned. This is going to be a long-haul proposition, and I think the same is true in the whole realm of cybersecurity…. I think we just need to accept that, and not be quite so excitable at yet another instance of it.

Wait, say what? Weren't we talking about Russia, or did al Qaeda or ISIS hack the DNC? Or did they all? Is there anyone who didn't hack the DNC?

Political hacking is so much worse than, say, torture, or assassination

In what plays like a comic version of good cop/bad cop, former CIA Director Leon Panetta, an avowed Clinton partisan who spoke at the Democratic Convention, used his speech to add to the hyperventilation over the DNC emails release. Panetta, long a defender of Bush-era torture, raised the stakes of the false political charge that Trump asked Russia to hack Clinton. Panetta, without a scintilla of evidence on display, claimed that Trump was asking Russia to involve itself in the US presidential election on Trump's behalf, all but calling it treason (which others have done):

> He asked the Russians to interfere in American politics.... Think about that for a moment. Donald Trump wants to be president of the United States [and] Donald Trump is asking one of our adversaries to engage in hacking or intelligence efforts against the United States to affect our election.

It would be at least as true to argue that Trump asked the Russians to contribute to American justice, which has failed to hold Clinton meaningfully accountable for her missing emails, or any other aspect of her unilateral effort to personally privatize a corner of government.

Panetta also repeated the lie that Trump asked Russia to hack the currently unhackable Clinton computers. Then he expanded that deceit to include the entire Clinton campaign, which he dishonestly equated with the United States. It's worth remembering that Trump's remarks were directed at the emails that have gone missing from Clinton's private server when she was Secretary of State (2009-2013). The inspector general of the State Department has found that Clinton's server was vulnerable to outside intruders during all or most of the time Clinton was responsible for managing its security. In that respect, it's possible or even likely that Russia (and others) could have copied and kept *all* of Clinton's emails, both the ones she turned over and the ones she deleted. That state of affairs is in itself another kind of joke. It's also an unresolved Clinton scandal. For Trump to make fun of it as he did is to mock a perverse reality. It's a reality that Panetta, like other Clinton loyalists, would like to deny into non-existence. Panetta's demagoguery would have you conclude that Putin is actually Trump's metaphorical running mate:

> No presidential candidate who's running to be president of the United States ought to be asking a foreign country, particularly Russia, to engage in hacking or intelligence efforts to try to determine what the Democratic candidate may or may not be doing.... This just is beyond my own understanding of the responsibilities that candidates have to be loyal to their country and to their country alone, not to reach out to somebody like Putin and Russia, and try to engage them in an effort to try to, in effect, conduct a conspiracy against another party....

Keeping the public's eye off the ball is no laughing matter

Panetta is a smart, experienced guy, so he must be aware of what a colossal joke this is, even though CNN chose to swallow it whole. The DNC hack had little to do with the current presidential campaign and almost everything to do with the Democrats' covert campaign against Bernie Sanders. Any honorable Democrat would denounce that. DNC chair Debbie Wasserman Schultz resigned under pressure, without noticeable contrition, and Hillary Clinton promptly rewarded her with an honorary chairmanship of the Clinton campaign. The last thing Clinton wants is to run against the specter of a martyred Sanders. She would much, much prefer to run against Vladimir Putin and his imaginary alliance with Donald Trump. This is consistent with her decades-long demonization of Russia and support for American/NATO soft aggression against Russia initiated by President Clinton more than 20 years ago.

By omission, Panetta endorses this Clinton policy of needlessly risking war, making endangerment equivalent to patriotic loyalty and, in time-dishonored fashion, equating the reduction of the threat of war between Russia and the US somehow with disloyalty. It's neo-liberal logic, so it doesn't have to make sense. Especially not when it's part of the framing of a false campaign trope.

49

"The Russians are hacking, the Russians are hacking" cry is already losing steam. New reports that someone hacked the Democratic Congressional Campaign Committee (DCCC) or the Clinton campaign itself were downplayed or later minimized in quasi-denial. Early in the week, even before Trump's provocation, Robert Mackey of The Intercept had assessed the sketchiness of evidence that the Russians were to blame.

Principled pushback against Panetta would not be difficult. For all his disdain for Putin's Russia, Panetta has long been a champion of American authoritarianism that is unmatched in the world: the "right" of the president of the US to assassinate by drone, in any foreign country, any person the president determines, in secret, with no due process, to be a legitimate target, even a US citizen. There's a difference between hacking and beheading. Is there any other chief executive in the world with such freedom to kill people with no accountability?

It is a reality of American life these days that there is little public objection to having a president exercise arbitrary, life-or-death power over any one of 7.4 billion people in the world. More common than objection to this plain crime against humanity is widespread acceptance, and sometimes even gratitude for the president's "restraint" in assassinating only a few hundred people, maybe only half of them innocent civilians.

Hillary Clinton has not opposed the US having an executioner-in-chief. Neither has Donald Trump objected. Even Bernie Sanders hasn't objected, although he said the power should be used carefully and sparingly. Trump's sarcastic joke about 30,000 missing emails may not have been all that funny, but the self-serving windbaggery and open deceit the joke provoked are actually hilarious, or would be if the stakes were not so high. Unless something unexpected happens, come January 2017, either Trump or Clinton will have the power to kill at will.

9.

The Presidential Dementia Meme Is Out There – Who Best Fits?

Reliable, verifiable medical records from presidential candidates – what's so hard about that?

In May 2008, presidential candidate Barack Obama released a summary letter of his general health signed by Dr. David Scheiner, who had been Obama's primary care physician for 21 years. Providing limited detail, the doctor found Obama to be in "excellent health" and "in overall good physical and mental health needed to maintain the resiliency required in the Office of the President." The Obama campaign indicated at the time that it was not planning to release any further medical records, and it didn't.

As president, Obama has periodically released health summaries publicly. The most recent report available on the White House website appears to be from June 12, 2014, in which Dr. Ronny Jackson, physician to the president, provides two pages of detail and concludes: "The President's overall health is excellent. All clinical data indicates that the President is currently healthy and that he will remain so for the duration of his Presidency."

This is not a high standard of disclosure for a candidate or a president to meet, assuming that a candidate or a president is in good health. This relatively low standard is also hard, if not impossible, to enforce. John McCain, a cancer survivor in 2008, chose to give selected reporters just a three-hour opportunity to look at some of his health records, but his health did not become a significant issue in the campaign. On his campaign website, McCain posted a health summary more detailed than Obama's. Hillary Clinton in 2008 apparently did not make any health records public (she has released tax returns for the years 2007-2014, with 2015 promised to be forthcoming).

2016 Candidates vary in providing detailed medical records

Green Party candidate Jill Stein is a doctor married to a doctor, and they have two sons who are doctors. She has not released her medical records this year, nor did she when she ran for president in 2012. She has publicly posted the first two pages of her 2015 tax return filed jointly with her husband, Dr. Richard Rohrer.

Libertarian candidate Gary Johnson, president and CEO of a medical marijuana company, appears not to have released any medical records. Of all the presidential candidates, Johnson has had perhaps the most serious physical mishap: On October 12, 2005, Johnson was involved in a near-fatal paragliding accident when his wing caught in a tree and he fell approximately 50 feet to the ground. Johnson suffered multiple bone fractures, including a burst fracture to his twelfth thoracic vertebra, a broken rib, and a broken knee; this accident left him 1.5 inches (3.8 cm) shorter. He used medicinal marijuana for pain control from 2005 to 2008.

Former Democratic candidate Bernie Sanders released a letter from his doctor in January 2016 summarizing his "general health history and current medical evaluation." The letter said that the Senator takes daily levothyroxine to maintain thyroid function and intermittent indomethacin, a non-steroidal anti-inflammatory medication to relieve pain. Dr. Brian P. Monahan, the Attending Physician for the Congress of the United States, concluded: "You are in overall very good health and active in your professional work, and recreational lifestyle without limitation."

Before Republican candidate Donald Trump released any medical report, he promised that "it will be perfection." He also wrote on twitter: "I consider my health, stamina and strength one of my greatest assets. The world has watched me for many years and can so testify – great genes!" On December 4, 2015, Trump's doctor of 36 years issued a brief, four-paragraph letter, the highlight of which was that Trump had lost 15 pounds in the past year. Dr. Harold N. Bornstein of Lenox Hill Hospital,

New York, concluded: "If elected, Mr. Trump, I can state unequivocally, will be the healthiest individual ever elected to the presidency."

The Democratic candidate, Hillary Clinton, released her own medical records letter months ahead of the others. A two-page letter dated July 28, 2015, noted that Clinton had "a deep vein thrombosis in 1998 and in 2009, an elbow fracture in 2009 and a concussion in 2012." (Deep vein thrombosis involves the formation of blood clots, usually in the legs, and is not life-threatening with timely treatment.) Dr. Lisa Bardack of the Mount Kisco Medical Group (near Chappaqua, New York) has been Clinton's personal physician since 2001. She described Clinton's recovery from the noted conditions, adding that as a precaution against further blood clots, Clinton takes an anticoagulant daily. Dr. Bardack concluded: "In summary, Mrs. Clinton is a healthy female with hypothyroidism and seasonal allergies, on long-term anticoagulation.... She is in excellent physical condition and fit to serve as President of the United States."

Drudge dredges old news and Fox News gets sweaty

A year after Clinton's doctor specifically addressed Clinton's already well-publicized falls, the Drudge Report reprised the incidents as if there were something new to them. Drudge was pushing the same Hillary health narrative back in February when it failed to get traction. That was after he pushed the same theory in October, based on Clinton's coughing during the Benghazi hearings. All the same, The Hill of August 8 passed on the re-recycled Drudge story, while noting that a "new" picture of Clinton, apparently needing help up the stairs, was taken in February. Elements of the Drudge story reprise have gone viral, and are still going viral, despite detailed debunking by sites like Mediaite.com and wonderfully extreme rants from Wonkette.com.

There's another internet meme that, if true, would be more troubling. In this case there's a purported leak of medical reports written by the same Dr. Bardack who wrote Clinton's July 2015 health letter. These reports first appeared on a twitter account that was apparently taken down by its owner soon after the post. The documents have a superficial credibility, but may be fake – Snopes.com analyzes the question and calls it "unproven." And that is a problem, because the questions are serious and need to be answered despite the political lynch mob rushing to judgment.

The diagnoses listed in these reports are "Complex Partial Seizures, Subcortical Vascular Dementia." "Dementia" is a scary word. Clinton's opponents are running with it. The Clinton campaign has yet to respond more effectively than to call the attacks "shameful," without further elaboration.

Curiously, the Dr. Bardack "dementia" documents are both dated well before her July 2015 letter affirming Clinton's "excellent physical condition." The authenticity of the July letter is undisputed. The earliest Dr. Bardack "report" dated February 5, 2015, discusses complications continuing from Clinton's December 2012 concussion – blacking out, twitching, memory loss "have become worse over the last few months." The letter refers to a diagnosis of early-onset Subcortical Dementia in mid-2013. The plan included increasing anti-seizure medication and ordering another MRI (brain scan).

The second Dr. Bardack "report" dated March 20, 2015, repeats much of the first, noting that: "Patient is being treated with both an anticoagulant and anti-seizure medications.... Patient is starting to become more depressed about her medical condition and the way it's affecting her life.... We elected to raise the dosage on her antidepressants and anxiety medications. She advised me of her future plans, and I advised her to travel with a medical team." Strikingly omitted from the second report was any mention of an MRI or its results.

Three weeks later, on April 12, 2015, Hillary Clinton announced that she was running for President.

Does the "dementia" meme have legs? And whose legs might it have?

Sean Hannity and other Fox News folks are running one-sidedly with the Hillary Health meme. One of the frequent Fox "experts" is Dr. Marc Siegel, who was chasing the Hillary health question back in April before it was a meme in the twittersphere (@ HilsMedRecords). Fox News seems prepared to pursue this as long as it can, with Hannity hammering away and Martin Shkreli making an on-air diagnosis of Clinton's "Parkinson's Disease."

But there's another question lying in wait for the honest inquisitor, and it goes something like this: so, if Clinton has dementia and sounds cogent all the time, what's up with Donald Trump who always sounds demented?

Salon was making that case back in April, quoting Trumperies like this Q&A sample from a meeting with the Washington Post editorial board:

> *Question:* This is about ISIS. You would not use a tactical nuclear weapon against ISIS?
>
> *Trump:* I'll tell you one thing, this is a very good-looking group of people here. Could I just go around so I know who the hell I'm talking to?

The writer, Sophia McClennen, went on to wonder:

> As we scratch our heads and wonder how someone who says and does such things can still be a frontrunner, I want to throw out a concern. What if Trump isn't "crazy" but is actually not well instead? To put it differently: what if his campaign isn't a sign of a savvy politician channeling Tea Party political rhetoric and reality TV sound bites? What if it's an example of someone who doesn't have full command of his faculties?... At times it can be very hard to distinguish between extreme right-wing politics and symptoms of dementia.

McClennen goes on to analyze Trump's behavior as potentially early Alzheimer's, which his father had for six years before he died. She suggests that Trump should take appropriate tests to demonstrate his mental fitness. Talking about all the ways comics have made fun of the way Trump speaks, she says: "It's not funny if he really has lost the ability to speak like a healthy adult."

Salon on August 10 had another McClennen piece again shredding the idea of Trump's mental competence. One of her points is that when Trump announced his health letter, he got the name of his doctor wrong (naming the doctor's father). The son is a gastroenterologist, whose website has since been taken down.

The Constitution (Article II, Section 1) requires only that a president be a natural born citizen, at least 35 years old, and a resident for at least 14 years. There is no challenge to Clinton or Trump on a constitutional basis. The Constitution is silent on a presidential candidate's mental or physical health. Once in office, a president's failing health is not an impeachable offense. The 25th Amendment (Section 3) allows the president to step aside upon "written declaration that he [sic] is unable to discharge the powers and duties" of the presidency. The vice president then becomes the acting president until the president self-declares in writing the ability to resume the office. The 25th Amendment (Section 4) also provides for the removal of a president who is unaware of an inability to perform, whenever "the Vice President and a majority of either the principal officers of the executive departments or such other body as Congress may by law provide" declare in writing the president's inability and submit it to Congress. In the event that the president disputes the inability, Congress decides.

Everything about Section 4 looks like an opportunity for serious, perhaps long-lasting chaos. We need to know now how healthy Clinton and Trump actually are. Dr. Bardack could help by saying whether the reports with her name on them are genuine. Both candidates could help by taking such medical tests and making such disclosures as are needed to answer fundamental questions about their competence now and in the future (insofar as that's knowable). That's what a rational electorate would expect, that's what responsible political parties would insist on, and that's what honorable candidates would provide.

Update 2019: That was 2016, when the emergence of a rational electorate, responsible parties and honorable candidates turned out pretty much as expected. Dr. Robert Jay Lifton has characterized our continuing condition as *malignant reality*. Optimistically, he quotes the poet Theodore Roethke: "In a dark time, the eye begins to see."

That very much remains to be seen.

Lifton's comments come from the forward to the first edition of *The Dangerous Case of Donald Trump* (St Martin's Press, 2017). The book grew out of an early response by a few psychiatrists to the apparent dangers of a Trump presidency. The April 2017 Yale conference designed to address the threat from a psychiatric perspective was titled: "Does Professional Responsibility Include a Duty to Warn?" The conference was timidly attended by a few, but it's ripple effect continues. The book is a bestseller, in its second edition, but public manifestations of its concern remain hard to perceive.

It's still an open question what to do about Trump. The conference organizer, Dr. Bandy X. Lee, concluded her prologue to the first edition with a psychological conclusion that carries an implicit political demand:

"Collectively with our authors, we warn that anyone as unstable as Mr. Trump simply should not be entrusted with the life-and-death powers of the presidency."

Meanwhile our reality remains malignant as we wait for eyes to begin to see.

10.

Russians Hit Democracy Already Damaged by Republicans

"The F.B.I., as part of our counterintelligence effort, is investigating the Russian government's efforts to interfere in the 2016 president [sic] election...."

FBI DIRECTOR JAMES COMEY, CONGRESSIONAL TESTIMONY,
MARCH 20, 2017

FBI Director Comey let loose the mechanical rabbit of Russian interference, and now all the political greyhounds are chasing it around a circular track as if it were a real quarry worth catching. That gives them all deniability for ignoring the bigger, fatter elephants in the room that actually need to be addressed.

The dominant narrative for the March 20 open hearing of the US House Permanent Select Committee on Intelligence was set in the committee's naming of "its investigation into Russian active measures during the 2016 election campaign." Committee chairman Devin Nunes, a California Republican who has resisted any investigation into Russian ties with the Trump campaign or administration, set a sharp anti-Russian tone with his opening statement that blames the Obama administration for ignoring the committee's warnings. Nunes framed the hearing with his limited exoneration of the Trump operation: "Former Director of National Intelligence James Clapper said publicly he's seen no evidence of collusion between the Russians and the Trump campaign, and I can say that the Committee, too, has seen no evidence to date that officials from any campaign conspired with Russian agents."

Ohio Republican Mike Turner had a darker view, saying, "There is now a cloud over our [election] system.... The goal of the Russians is to put a cloud on our system." Mike Rogers, Director of the National Security Agency, agreed that 2016 campaign activities were "calling into question our democratic process." And Comey said Russian efforts "introduced chaos and discord and sowed doubt" and have worked to undermine and threaten our "wonderful free and fair election system."

These sentiments, echoed over and over like a conventional wisdom mantra, are really ridiculous. Yes, the Russians interfered with the 2016 election, and maybe even influenced it. Yes, Trump operatives had contact with Russian operatives, and they may even have colluded. Yes, these are real problems, but it's a groupthink deception, and self-deception, to treat them as if they comprise the entire problem with the American election system.

American elections went off the rails more than two decades ago and they're been getting worse ever since. Everyone knows this, the government knows this, Congress knows this – and they do nothing to make it better, they work only to make it seem better. The history is in plain sight for anyone who wants to see it, starting well before the 2000 election.

Money in Politics. Corrupt fundraising from corporations and individuals was one of the major elements in Nixon's 1972 Watergate scandal, in spite of reform attempted through the Federal Election Campaign Act of 1971. Post-Watergate reforms that passed Congress were inadequate, leading to the Bipartisan Campaign Reform Act of 2002 (informally known as the McCain-Feingold Act), which also failed to control campaign spending in a rational, democratic way.

Voter Caging. Florida's efforts to take Democratic voters off the rolls and to intimidate them at the polls were state policy under Governor Jeb Bush, carried out by his secretary of state, Katherine Harris, both beneficiaries of great inherited wealth. Without that corrupt preparation of the state, George Bush likely would have lost it outright. The closeness of the vote led to the chaotic recount, also abetted by Bush and Harris, setting up the opportunity to win the presidency in the courts.

Bush v. Gore. The 2000 Supreme Court's 5-4 partisan decision awarded the presidency to the loser of the popular vote. Al Gore, another beneficiary of great inherited wealth, and the wealthy leadership of the Democratic Party chose not to contest this all-American effort to undermine the American electoral system. The Supreme Court ruled, in effect, that elections could be fairly decided without counting all the votes. That continues to be a cloud over the election system.

Citizens United. In January 2010, another partisan 5-4 decision by the Supreme Court upheld the notion that somehow money is speech, and those who have the most money are entitled to the most speech, allowing an already corrupted system to spin out of control. Despite their control of both houses of Congress, Democrats responded impotently and went on to lose the House in the fall.

Voter Suppression. What Jeb Bush oversaw in Florida in 2000 looks almost benign when compared to more recent Republican voter-suppression efforts, and they continue to expand almost unchecked. Even when courts rule them illegal, Republican state legislatures bring them back in modified form. Republican election success depends on reducing the number of voters.

Gerrymandering. Already out of control in places like Texas, where Rep. Tom DeLay stage-managed the Texas legislature's efforts to re-draw districts that increased Republican election winners. As early as 1998, DeLay was the beneficiary of contributions from Russian oil oligarchs. In 2011, DeLay was convicted (and acquitted on appeal) of conspiracy to violate election law in 2002. Gerrymandering has historically been a bipartisan corrupt activity, but the ruthlessness of recent gerrymandering across the country is a largely Republican phenomenon to which Democrats have responded limply if at all.

Voting Machines. Partisan-controlled, privately-owned voting machines is a blatantly corrupt concept that we have lived with for a generation with little response. Why ANY government, from local to federal, ever tolerated election machines controlled by third parties is one of the abiding mysteries of American life. The impact of these machines cannot be good, although how bad they've been is disputed. They seem to be on the decline. At first Diebold and other voting machines were seen as right-wing conspiracies. In 2016, George Soros was accused of owning voting machines in 16 states. Not that it mattered: Trump won eight of them, including Florida, Michigan, Pennsylvania, and Wisconsin.

Voter Registration Rolls. Voter registration is another constant target of Republican voter suppression efforts, which aim at keeping minorities, poor people, and others off the rolls and ineligible to vote. Ruthless voter-roll purging is a common recent Republican technique. The vulnerability of voter rolls to cyber-attacks (by the Russians, for example) is uncertain and came up only briefly at the Intelligence Committee hearing.

Voting Rights Act. The Voting Rights Act of 1965 was a landmark of democratic expansion of the franchise to previously suppressed voting groups, especially black voters. According to legend, when President Johnson signed the act into law, he said that would lose the south for Democrats for a generation. That was optimistic. In 2013, the Supreme Court, in another 5-4 partisan vote, effectively declared that racism was over and gutted the Voting Rights Act. As Chief Justice John Roberts myopically stated: "Our country has changed. While any racial discrimination in voting is too much, Congress must ensure that the legislation it passes to remedy that problem speaks to current conditions."

Roberts is not known to have commented publicly as to the current conditions of American bigotry as expressed by the Trump campaign and its followers, although his opinions in recent criminal cases are more sensitive to race than those of Justice Clarence Thomas. Once again, Democrats have taken the issue of voting rights and done little with it.

Given this history of the self-inflicted collapse of American democratic process, the Russians seem to be relatively minor players of recent vintage. The greater threats to American democracy by far have been the Republican Party and the Supreme Court, with little resistance from Democrats. Together our three branches of government have collaborated to create the corrupt conditions that spawned the Trump candidacy, an all-American target of opportunity the Russians were only too happy to work with.

The Supreme Court and the President seem unlikely to deal with any of this any time soon. That leaves Congress, a Republican-majority Congress, to figure out whether the country is worth saving at this point. The starting point should probably be keeping Americans from interfering with the American democratic process.

11.

Voting Threats Haven't Mattered to National Leadership for Decades

From ghoulies and ghosties
And long-leggedy beasties
And things that go bump in the night,
Good Lord, deliver us!

TRADITIONAL SCOTTISH PRAYER

"Two years after Russia interfered in the American presidential campaign, the nation has done little to protect itself against a renewed effort to influence voters in the coming congressional midterm elections, according to lawmakers and independent analysts."

WASHINGTON POST, AUGUST 1, 2018

Does anyone here have confidence that the American voting system is secure, stable, and designed to protect the voting rights of every eligible American voter?

There's no good reason to believe that after more than two decades of Democratic spinelessness in the face of a consistent Republican assault on voting integrity. The Russians may be long-leggedy beasties, but it's Republicans who have been going bump in the night for all these years, disenfranchising American voters unlikely to vote Republican.

How's this for a proposition: the Democrats elected Donald Trump in 2016 when they decided not to contest the election of 2000 and allowed a partisan Supreme Court to pick the president without allowing a full count of the votes.

63

That election foundered as a result of Florida governor Jeb Bush presiding over a state effort to purge and cage voters, especially non-white voters. The purge-and-cage effort made the election closer than it would otherwise have been and produced a fundamentally invalid vote result from a state-distorted electorate.

The Democrats rolled over then, fighting tactically rather than on principle, and here we are as a country, deep in denial about the integrity of our election system. Instead of addressing real and persistent Republican attacks on voting rights, we imagine nearly omnipotent Russian hacker ghoulies and ghosties somehow subverting a popular will that hasn't been able to express itself fully in a long time. The reality of Russian efforts is at best uncertain, based on available evidence. But "Russian interference" remains an article of bipartisan faith, which serves as a convenient excuse for ignoring the real and present dangers American officials inflict on American voters year after year in state after state.

Possibly the Russians hacked the Democratic National Committee and released damning emails to the public. And that's bad because? The emails showed the DNC to be a corrupt enterprise. Whoever is responsible for the leak, its revelations should be seen as a public service. And it might have been seen as a public service had it led to actual change in the Democratic Party leadership, had it opened the party to the non-corporate voices it has suppressed at least since the Clinton presidency. The DNC emails made no cultural difference; the party is still at war with its progressive members, and that war puts the midterms at greater risk than they should be.

The mindlessness of "leadership" response to the Russian "threat" was neatly expressed, probably inadvertently, by Democratic senator Mark Warner of Virginia, co-chair of the Senate Intelligence Committee on August 1:

> Twenty-one months after the 2016 election, and only three months before the 2018 elections, Russian-backed operatives continue to infiltrate and manipulate social media to hijack the national conversation and set Americans against each other. They were doing it in 2016; they are still doing it today.

Even if Warner is precisely correct, so what? Free speech in a globalized world gets tricky. Does that mean we want to clamp down on free speech the way more authoritarian countries do? One hopes not. But of course, there are those who fervently hope to control free speech to the point of extinction.

How many Russian operatives does it take to hijack a national conversation?

Let's assume, despite evidence to the contrary, that a national conversation is actually happening on social media, where there are millions and millions of voices clamoring to be heard and a much smaller number actually listening. And even with those who listen, there's no way to determine what they actually hear. Does Mark Warner really believe in the alternative reality where Russian-backed operatives have more influence than right-wing operatives at Fox News and elsewhere have had for a generation across all media?

Why doesn't Mark Warner address a real threat to democratic process and demand that his own party have free and fair primary elections? Oh right, that might be a threat to him and his fellow legislators. Or he might address voting in Virginia, where Republicans continue to poison the well by claiming imaginary voter fraud, as they have for years across the country with almost no evidence.

As for substance, the Russian-backed operatives seem mostly to work with political judo, leveraging common American memes to inflame one side or another, even if those sides are already inflamed. American politics have been inflamed for a long time, and the Russians didn't do it. Republicans did most of it, with climate denial and racism and religious bigotry and voter suppression of all sorts and attacking the environment and enriching the rich and impoverishing the poor – where does the list of destructive attacks on decent values end?

The deep irony of our present moment was palpably expressed, most likely by accident, by Republican senator Richard Burr of North Carolina, the other co-chairman of the Senate Intelligence Committee.

Known as a "moderate" Republican, Burr said on August 1, referring to the Russian ghoulies and ghosties:

> This issue goes far beyond elections…. We're fighting for the integrity of our society. And we need to enlist every single person.

Well, the current Republican control of government would not have happened in a society with any real integrity. It's taken a lengthy, bipartisan effort to get us into the morass of today. The Russians are surely grateful for the gift of chaos that they could never have achieved on their own but can now take some advantage of. And the beautiful part of it is that the Russian nibbling gives those responsible for devouring American integrity a great excuse to ignore their own very real responsibility for knocking down an already fragile system.

"The integrity of our society" has never been a reality, only an aspiration at best. The degradation of American society since 1980 has been deliberate and ruthless, to the point that "Make America Great Again" resonates rationally despite its masking of duplicitous purposes. Reagan said it too, word for word.

Richard Burr claiming to be "fighting for the integrity of our society" is hilarious, given the record of North Carolina Republicans enacting racist voter suppression laws that even the US Supreme Court rejected. This was after the Supreme Court enabled racist voting legislation with its 2013 decision gutting the 1965 Voting Rights Act. That element of the integrity of our society was not yet 50 years old when Chief Justice John Roberts wrote the majority opinion based on a masterpiece of doublethink and denial:

> Our country has changed. While any racial discrimination in voting is too much, Congress must ensure that the legislation it passes to remedy that problem speaks to current conditions.

As it turned out, "current conditions" included a North Carolina legislature that promptly passed racist voting legislation that even the Supreme Court couldn't stomach. When the Supreme Court struck down that racist law, the North Carolina legislature went back to work trying to achieve the same racist end by different racist means. Those are the current conditions of the integrity of our society. The Russians have little or nothing to do with any of it. Demonizing the Russians is a bipartisan diversion.

The real existential threat to the integrity of our society has long held office.

12.

Rampant, Racist Voter Suppression in Georgia Goes to Federal Court

"... almost a quarter of a million previously registered voters who may want to vote in this election who will find their registrations cancelled based on an assumption that they had moved when they had not."

"This is a travesty for the people of Georgia whose fundamental right to vote has been taken without any formal notice that their registrations have been cancelled."

FEDERAL COURT COMPLAINT AGAINST GEORGIA SECRETARY OF
STATE BRIAN KEMP

If Brian Kemp wins the 2018 election for governor of Georgia, it will be one more triumph for the massive corruption Republicans have brought to American voting for the past 20 years or more. Brian Kemp is currently Georgia's secretary of state. Part of the secretary's job, as chair of the State Elections Board, is to make decisions that determine who can vote, where they can vote, when they can vote, and whether their votes will be counted accurately – in other words, the whole voting process.

As a secretary of state running for governor, Kemp has a clear conflict of interest, since any of his decisions about voting rights could help his campaign. Many of them already have. Previous secretaries of state who ran for governor have taken themselves out of the voting rights conflict. Kemp has refused to do so. His corruption is so blatantly transparent, his spokesman dishonestly proclaims that "Kemp is fighting to protect the integrity of our elections and ensure that only legal citizens cast a ballot."

68

The claim of illegal voting by non-citizens has been a Republican Big Lie for a long time now. It works, it scares people who don't know any better, but it's not true and has never been true. In 2016, the Brennan Center for Justice analyzed 23.5 million votes for taint. Out of these, only a handful of ballots were flagged for investigation or prosecution. OK, it was a big handful – out of 23,500,000 ballots they found 30 – thirty! – that were suspect. Presumably their intimidation tactics work, or Republicans wouldn't work so hard to suppress the vote, even with recent (October 20), baseless presidential tweets.

Middle-aged white male Brian Kemp's opponent for governor is a progressive Democrat, Stacey Abrams, a middle-aged black woman and Yale Law School graduate who would be the first-ever African-American governor of Georgia. She founded the New Georgia Project, registering some 200,000 voters of color since 2014. Kemp has been disqualifying voters of color even faster. With Kemp recently holding a two-point lead (48-46), their race is considered a toss-up.

The lawsuit cited above grew out of a records request to the secretary of state on March 2, 2018. The request was made under both the Georgia Open Records Act and the 1993 federal National Voter Registration Act (52 U.S.C. 20501 et seq.), the primary purpose of which is "to establish procedures that will *increase the number of eligible citizens who register to vote* in elections for Federal office." [emphasis added] Republicans like Kemp have spent a quarter century in more or less open defiance of this federal law, which was based on Congressional findings that would be unimaginable today:

(1) the right of citizens of the United States to vote is a fundamental right;

(2) it is the duty of the Federal, State, and local governments to promote the exercise of that right; and

(3) discriminatory and unfair registration laws and procedures can have a direct and damaging effect on voter participation in elections for Federal office and disproportionately harm voter participation by various groups, including racial minorities.

69

The plaintiffs in the federal case against Kemp are reporter Greg Palast of Los Angeles and civil rights activist Helen Butler of Atlanta. Palast has built an international reputation with his investigative reporting, especially his reporting on voting rights issues that others in the media (and the Democratic Party) tend to ignore. Butler is the executive director of the Georgia Coalition for the Peoples' Agenda, which has organized state coalitions in more than half a dozen other southern states.

The initial request for legally public records included a request for information about how Georgia uses the Interstate Voter Crosscheck System in managing Georgia's voter rolls. Crosscheck, which has a built-in racial bias against non-white voters, has been used since 2005, especially by Republican secretaries of state seeking to purge voter rolls into a more Republican-friendly form (led by Kansas Secretary of State Kris Kobach). Crosscheck purports to identify "duplicate" voters in different states using only two data points: name and birthdate (different middle names, for example, are considered irrelevant). In 2017, Crosscheck claimed to find 7.2 *million* duplicate voter registrations out of 98 million analyzed in 28 states. Despite Crosscheck's claim of the potential for over seven million voters to vote twice, only 4 – four! – double-voters were identified. Crosscheck is now dormant. The damage is lasting.

Kemp's office did not respond to the plaintiffs' request forthrightly. Instead, Kemp's office demanded exorbitant payment in advance before providing redacted records. Other states acted similarly to stonewall legal "open records" requests.

On June 12, 2018, plaintiffs Palast and Butler filed a new request using only the National Voter Rights Act. The request allowed Kemp 90 days to reply. Kemp did not reply promptly to detailed questions about Crosscheck's lists provided to Georgia in 2016 and 2017, as well as the "list of names and addresses of all those purged or changed to inactive in 2016 and 2017 and the basis for each individual being removed from the voter rolls...."

Kemp's office did not respond in June. Kemp's office did not respond in July. On August 14, plaintiffs sent Kemp a letter reminding him that his 90-day deadline for lawful compliance would expire on September 10. On September 4, Kemp provided a partial response, omitting any information about Crosscheck. In their October filing to compel a complete response to their questions, they wrote:

> Plaintiffs were shocked when they saw that over a half a million Georgians had their registrations automatically cancelled through the inactivity process utilized by the Georgia Secretary of State.

Claiming that Georgians had not voted during a three-year period, Kemp's office in 2017 cancelled the voter registrations of 534,517 Georgians for that reason alone. That is roughly one in 12 Georgians disenfranchised for not voting. That reason is illegal. That reason violates federal law – the National Voting Rights Act – which requires that state voting procedures "shall not result in the removal of the name of any person from the official list of voters registered to vote" *solely* because the person did not vote. Further reasons for removal include moving out of state, being convicted of a felony, or death.

Further analysis of the data showed that of the half-million-plus voters whose registrations were cancelled because they had supposedly moved, at least 340,134 of them – 61% of the total – still lived at the same address. These 340,134 persons did not know their registrations had been cancelled by the state. Palast posted all their names on his website in hopes that some might re-register before the October 9 deadline.

The cancellation of 340,134 registrations of people who have not moved is another violation of the National Voting Rights Act, which requires the state to keep voter rolls that are accurate and current.

This case is now before federal district judge Eleanor Louise Ross, an Obama appointee confirmed in 2014. In an interview with the Atlanta Tribune, Judge Ross said:

> I believe this century has seen enormous strides by women and minorities in general. My having made history as the first African-American female on the US Federal District Court in Atlanta, and one of the first two in the entire state, just continues to blow my mind. There are so many well-rounded, qualified candidates who are ready to also jump in, if provided with the right opportunity. I think

it is crucial that those of us already appointed and elected continue to work together to keep making history until it is not history anymore. It just is!

From that, one might infer that the judge is ready to rule for plaintiffs and deal a blow to Georgia's corrupt voter management system. Restoring the voting rights of 340,134 purged voters would surely be the right thing to do. But even the plaintiffs have not asked for that kind of legal relief. The plaintiffs have asked only that Kemp be found in violation of the National Voter Rights Act and be compelled to provide all the information plaintiffs have requested.

That outcome would reward corruption. That outcome would reward a state official for defying the law until the last possible minute. That outcome would leave purged voters with little useful recourse. That outcome might enable a corrupt secretary of state to become a corrupt governor. That outcome would allow Republicans to crow over protecting the integrity of the vote, when the truth is that they just went on corrupting it.

> **Update 2019:** Brian Kemp maintained his conflict of interest position as Secretary of State overseeing his own election until two days after he was elected.
>
> On December 25, 2018, Greg Palast announced that, with Brian Kemp no longer Georgia's Secretary of State, that office was "throwing in the towel" in the *Palast and Butler v. Kemp* case. Palast wrote: "This opens up the remainder of Kemp's infamous, racially-poisonous voter purge files. Specifically, Georgia will produce the hidden Crosscheck purge files given to Kemp by Kansas Secretary of State Kris Kobach — files Kemp's flunkies told us had been 'lost'.... But there are miles to go before we sleep: Georgia is just one state down, 24 left to go."
>
> As of March 25, 2019, the Brennan Center for Justice reported on seven current federal lawsuits challenging Georgia's voting practices. In one, *Common Cause Georgia v. Raffensperger,* the federal district court has issued an injunction requiring the state to add protections for voters forced to cast provisional ballots.

13.

Shouting Fire in Crowded Theatre, President Courts Votes with Lies

"The fact that this president has been so obsessed with immigrants and immigration as a key component of his message, from the day he announced his desire to become president of the US in 2015, should not make any one of us surprised that he's using the caravan, essentially, to further advance his well-established line against immigrants by demonizing them, by dehumanizing them."

"... we should not be surprised—if I regret one thing, it's that there is no strong counter-narrative from the Democratic Party about an event like this caravan or migration altogether. And I believe that that's a flaw that we need to deal with and find a way of fixing in the US."

OSCAR CHACON OF ALIANZA AMERICAS ON DEMOCRACY NOW, OCTOBER 23

The madness of the day is this: thousands of peaceful migrants are headed toward the US to seek humanitarian asylum and the US president reacts by inciting panic, rage, and hate. The president warns hysterically of a "national emergency" as his deceitful ranting works like a self-fulfilling prophecy, stoking a real emergency from the fevered imaginings of his soul-deep bigotry.

The migrant caravan has been demonstrably peaceful. Mexicans along the caravan route provide food, water, and support. The caravan is estimated at 7,000 people of all ages, mostly whole families. No one has even tried to make an accurate count, but it's reasonable to believe most of the migrants are fleeing from Honduras.

Honduras presents another face of the present madness, but a much older, bipartisan, imperial face. The US has been kicking Honduras around since before the US government in Honduras was just an extension of the foreign policy of the United Fruit Company. The current state of Honduras as a country that terrorizes its own population dates from the Reagan presidency, when ambassador John Negroponte was running Salvadoran death squads out of Tegucigalpa. There followed a brief and uneasy Honduran flirtation with democratic government and an excess of national independence that ended abruptly in a military coup. Satisfied with that outcome, Barack Obama and Hilary Clinton officially certified that no coup had taken place (wink wink), and that the US would continue helping the Honduran government to militarize itself, a policy that continues today. The US is happy with the state of affairs, but Hondurans by the thousands can't find a safe and decent way to live there, so they head north, much to the annoyance of our el Presidente, who, in a remarkably obtuse response, threatens to cut off US military aid to Honduras.

However demagogic politicians may misrepresent this caravan, it has literally nothing to do with illegal immigration. The president falsely claims the people in the caravan are trying to come into the US illegally. They are not. These are asylum seekers. They have standing under international law to seek asylum in another country. The irony is that they're seeking asylum in the country most responsible for creating the conditions that drove them from their homes.

A sensible leader with a human concern for other human beings might have seen something like this coming, since it's been happening more or less twice a year for decades. To be fair, the current caravan is one of the larger ones, but still not the largest ever. But the US doesn't act in good faith when it comes to immigration. The US has a legal obligation to process claims for asylum fairly and promptly. Instead, the US uses force to keep migrants in Mexico, leaves them exposed at border crossings for days, understaffs asylum courts whose backlogs are out of control, and kidnaps children from their parents in a thuggish attempt at deterrence. Now the US president is threatening to meet peaceful asylum seekers at the border with military force. And he's lying about the migrants, providing no evidence to support his lies:

> Go into the middle of the caravan, take your cameras and search.
> OK? ... You're going to find MS-13. You're going to find Middle Eastern.
> You're going to find everything. And guess what. We're not allowing
> them in our country. We want safety. We want safety.

With more demagoguery, unsupported by fact, our Trump refers
to a caravan that is more than 1,000 miles from the US border, where
it might arrive in late November or much later:

> That is an assault on our country and in that caravan you have some
> very bad people and we can't let that happen to our country.... I think
> the Democrats had something to do with it.

The president's rhetoric is of a piece with official Republican bigotry in defense of white people. Using a standard anti-Semitic trope,
his surrogates accuse George Soros of funding the caravan, of course.
Examples of hate speech abound at the state and local level, wherever
there are Republicans running scared. The two Republicans indicted
for corruption, Chris Collins of New York and Duncan Hunter of California, have made especially racist appeals to get re-elected. And when
they're not overtly bigoted, Republicans are busy lying about policies
no Democrat supports (open borders, more crime). When called out
for their dishonest tactics, they whine about civility.

Legitimate coverage of the caravan reveals no gang members,
no Islamic terrorists, no violent people at all. Oh yeah, what about
the internet coverage of those "Mexican Police Officers Brutalized
by Members of a Migrant Caravan"? It's a lie peddled by people on
Facebook and Twitter without reliable sourcing. Turns out the police
were brutalized several years ago (2011, 2012, 2014), but by Mexican
students and teachers, not by any immigrants in any caravan (as documented by Snopes). The false meme purveyors are presumably the
Republican equivalent of Russian bots. One of those spreading this
garbage online was Virginia Thomas, wife of Supreme Court Justice
Clarence Thomas.

In Mexico, official treatment of the caravan is civil and helpful.
Popular response has been mixed, but mostly sympathetic along the
caravan route. One Mexican along the route, Ana Gamboa, offered a

more sensitive, textured response than anything we've heard from
the US president:

> The only thing I can say to people is that they should be more human,
> that we should look into our hearts and imagine ourselves in the
> migrants' shoes, because it isn't easy, what the migrants are doing.
> We Mexicans like to criticize Donald Trump for the way he treats
> Mexicans in the United States, and now we're acting just like him.
> We don't have any walls on our border, but sometimes we ourselves
> are the wall.

Americans are all too often swayed by fear of imaginary threats.
The migrant caravan is an imaginary threat. It's easy enough to find
the facts about this caravan at this time. It's probably easier to find
the falsehoods and the lies, given the media megaphone attached to
the presidential tweeter. Once more we're at the perennial crisis of
American democracy: whether enough voters will both learn the truth
and vote on it.

14.

The Fire This Time – It Will Keep Burning Long After November 6

The election will be a moment of truth for the country, and then what?

Perhaps enough Americans in enough numbers in enough places have woken up to the wildfires consuming our country. Perhaps these woke Americans will throw some water on the fires in the November 6 election. Perhaps an emerging American majority will slow the Republican burn of American idealism, decency, and justice. Perhaps an emerging American majority will elect enough new Democrats to prod old Democrats out of their lazy collusion with burning the country down. Perhaps.

Whatever happens November 6, the fires of political fascism and capitalist authoritarianism will continue to rage out of control. The conniving right has been feeding these flames for decades, and it's likely to take more decades to extinguish them, if that's even possible. The Long March of the right from the debacle of Goldwater in 1964 to the triumph of Trump in 2016 has been astonishingly Maoist in its determination, orthodoxy, and political correctness. One has to acknowledge them for their sheer ruthlessness and determination. Minority rule is no mean trick.

The Republican right had help from supine Democrats with no coherent alternative. They had more help from media quislings and collaborators (yes, that's Fox) whose idea of analysis involved telling "both sides" regardless of what might be true. They had more help from an educational system producing increasingly compliant, ignorant voters who could no longer reliably assess what was real

77

or important or even in their self-interest. And they had still more help from elitist leaders who, rather than engaging the country as a potential unity, dismissed millions of people as deplorables in love with their guns and their religion (as if either of those were unquestionably evil).

Whatever happens November 6, we'll still have a president who aspires to dictatorship, as illustrated by his assertion that he has the power to rewrite the Constitution all by himself. We'll still have a ruling party that relies on racism to maintain power, that enables its bigots to spread hate by graffiti and murder. We'll still have concentration camps full of migrants and migrant children separated from their parents, rounded up and held with no due process of law.

We'll still live in a country where Twitter enables the president to release a shamelessly dishonest racist ad scapegoating immigrants and libeling Democrats. We'll still live in a country where Facebook profits by selling lists of likely customers to white nationalist marketers promoting myths of "white genocide." We'll still live in a country where the dominant culture makes it unsafe and sometimes lethal to be different, where the president invites the military to kill innocent, unarmed people with impunity. This is not politically correct, but it is true: even as we mourn the synagogue murders in Pittsburgh, we remain silent about Israeli executions of innocents in Gaza or Saudi genocide in Yemen.

We'll still live in a country where the government no longer makes grants to organizations fighting US terrorism. We'll still live in a country where the government deliberately pursues policies that threaten the global climate. We'll still live in a country that abrogates nuclear weapons treaties and pursues new, "usable" nuclear warheads and the domination of space.

In a sense, November 6 is a moment of truth for the country. In a deeper sense, that's fundamentally facile and false. Nothing magically changes on November 6, no matter the outcome. The election of a Democratic House looks like the most likely best outcome. But that Democratic majority wouldn't be seated till January, leaving

78

Republicans two months to feed the flames consuming us. The reality is that every moment is a moment of truth. Radical Republican reactionaries internalized that decades ago. Perhaps the realization that the moment of truth is now, always now, has finally generated a humane, tolerant, democratic majority in America – and maybe even an enlightened majority that can sustain itself. It's worth dreaming.

PART TWO

America Loses Altitude

15.

Criminalizing Free Speech

You think the Wall Street Journal has no sense of humor? Think again.

On the Fourth of July – Independence Day – the Wall Street Journal ran a freedom-oriented story with a headline that began: "Teen Jailed for Facebook Posting ..."

In Texas last winter, a working 18-year-old was jailed and is still being held on $500,000 bail, because a Canadian woman reported a single, frivolous Facebook post that he had marked "LOL" (laughing out loud) and "jk" (just kidding). The post was part of a lengthy exchange with the Canadian woman's son. Ignoring those cues, local police went ahead and charged the teen with "terroristic threatening." Really? That is darkly humorous even in post-terrified America.

The Journal didn't frame the story as a First Amendment travesty however, even though by any rational measure a Facebook posting is speech, and the Journal, like most of the rest of us, has a thing about free speech sometimes.

In all too typical mass media fashion, the Journal framed the story with an irrelevant, sensationalist, semi-hysterical reference to the real shooting of real kids half a continent away, two months earlier, in a school in Newtown, Connecticut. The Journal omitted the possibility that Justin Carter was hardly aware of Newtown, but maybe that's more dark humor.

Maybe he was unaware of the news, or maybe he was referring to Syria

"Justin was the kind of kid who didn't read the newspaper. He didn't watch television. He wasn't aware of current events. These kids, they don't realize what they're doing. They don't understand the implications. They don't understand public space," his father, Jack Carter, told KVUE-TV in Austin on June 24. This was the first significant news coverage of the case, which has now gone national.

To be fair to the Journal in its unfair framing and lazy journalism, the Austin Police bought into the "Newtown Massacre" framing from the start, not bothering, apparently, to investigate whether that panic-reaction had any basis in Justin Carter's reality. Or maybe the Austin police were being darkly humorous, too, since they didn't bother to interview their "terrorist" suspect for a month. The New Braunfels police waited about the same length of time to search his apartment, where they reportedly found no weapons or any other incriminating evidence.

This sorry story of law enforcement overreaction and incompetence began innocently enough in February 2013, when Carter and a friend, as they often did, were playing an online video game called "League of Legends." The game involves other online players interacting in real time. It is in the nature of the game, apparently, to talk trash to anyone involved, including strangers.

One Person's Trash Talk Turns Out to Be Terrorist Threatening in Texas

This time the trash talk spilled over onto Facebook, where someone apparently called Carter crazy or said he was "messed up in the head." Carter's mother, Jennifer Carter, talked about the event on freetoplay. tv on June 29:

> February 13th was when he was playing League of Legends and I'm not sure, and no one seems to be sure, why it spilled over into Facebook, but it did. There were a few people involved in this argument and there was some post made on the site while they were playing and so when he was on Facebook the person whose Facebook page it was, said "Well you're f****d in the head and crazy." And Justin, if you knew my son, is incredibly sarcastic.

> He has a very sarcastic, dark sense of humor and he unfortunately said the equivalent of "Oh yeah I'm so messed in the head I'm going

84

to go kill a kindergarten and eat their hearts." Immediately after his statement he posted "lol" and "j/k" and the argument continued from there, but the only evidence we have from the DA's office is a screen capture of his statement and the previous statement. Just Justin's and the previous statement.

Lynching is easier with limited evidence and no context

The nature of that online exchange is all there is to this case. Facebook removed the full exchange from public view. The police and prosecutor chose to cherry-pick the exchange in their court filings, omitting any context and perhaps part of the post itself.

As CNN reported another version: "According to court documents, Justin wrote 'I'm f---ed in the head alright. I think I'ma [sic] shoot up a kindergarten and watch the blood of the innocent rain down and eat the beating heart of one of them.' "

None of this would have mattered any more than the billions of other Facebook posts except that a Canadian woman, self-described as a "concerned citizen," launched into vigilante mode and discovered that there was apparently an elementary school close to an address in Austin where Carter once lived. So, she called the Austin police and made her accusation.

At the time, Carter was 18, working in San Antonio and living with a roommate in New Braunfels.

The authorities arrested him at work, then acted as if it were all over

"The next day, February 14th, he (Justin) went to work," his mother explained. "The Sheriffs came to his job and arrested him. Then he was transported from San Antonio to Austin because the woman in Canada found his father's address where he used to live which is 100 yards from an elementary school. At that point, he sat in jail and bond set at $250,000. His father and I don't have that kind of money. We thought honestly that yeah that was a pretty bad thing that he said, and we can see why they would be concerned after the shooting in Newtown happened a couple months before. So ya, everyone was on edge."

85

Not unreasonably, Carter's parents expected the police to question him, investigate, and figure out that their son had a smart mouth, but wasn't a threat to anyone.

"We thought that once the police talked to him, which we thought would be that day, they would understand it was a stupid comment that he made, a dumb joke, and once they searched his home, they would see there were no weapons and he wasn't a threat."

Why would anyone expect police to be conscientious or thoughtful?

Instead, the police did nothing. The prosecutor did nothing. No one in the government did anything, except let an 18-year-old kid sit in jail, where he was frequently attacked by other prisoners.

There was only one exception to the state doing nothing according to Jennifer Carter: "They went to his father's house [in Austin] a week after he was arrested and asked did Justin live here which his father said no, and they asked if he had any guns or permits for guns which Justin's father said no and that was it."

No one questioned Justin Carter at all for almost a month. He remained in jail, essentially ignored, and no one explained why. His parents advised him not to talk to the police without an attorney present, but he ignored that advice. Eventually, according to Jennifer Carter:

> On March 13th he was questioned by the detectives and he thought best thing for him to do would be to tell the truth. He told them that yes he made the statement and it was a joke and I feel terrible. It was taken badly and I'm sorry for scaring people I didn't mean to. I didn't think people would see it or that anyone would be afraid of it. He told them that he did not live in Austin that he lived in New Braunfels and that was it.

Waiting a month for a search warrant – standard police practice?

Also on March 13, the police in New Braunfels applied for a search warrant to enter Carter's apartment. Police found no weapons, explosives, manifestos of violence, or anything else to support the idea that the

Facebook post was a real threat. The only evidence the police took from the apartment was Carter's computer. A week later, the Comal County Court in New Braunfels issued an arrest warrant for Carter, who was still in jail.

The state transferred Carter from jail in Austin to jail in New Braunfels, because that's where he lived on the day when he made the critical post. The state also asked the court to raise Carter's bail to $500,000, and the court granted the increase, even though Carter's parents were unable to raise enough to meet bail at half that level.

At some point, the court appointed an attorney to represent Carter because he couldn't afford one. On April 10, a grand jury indicted Carter for making a "terroristic threat," a third-degree felony under Texas state statute 22.07(a)(4-6), even though there's no credible evidence that he meets any of the law's six criteria for intent. Without intent, as defined by law, there is no crime. The charge carries a potential penalty of 2-10 years in prison and/or a fine of $10,000.

Some indictments, as is well known, are works of fiction

The indictment claims that Carter intended with a trash talk Facebook post to a stranger to "cause impairment or interruption of public communications, public transportation, public water, gas, or power supply or other public service; place the public or a substantial group of the public in fear of serious bodily injury; or influence the conduct or activities of a branch or agency of the federal government, the state, or a political subdivision of the state."

In May, Carter's court-appointed lawyer waived formal arraignment and a few weeks later Carter turned nineteen.

The prosecutor in the case, the Comal County Criminal District Attorney, is Jennifer Tharp, the first female prosecutor in the county. She was elected with about 81% of the vote in an uncontested race in 2011. The second oldest of 11 children, she described herself this way in campaign literature:

> I was born and raised in Comal County, my husband Dan was raised here, and almost all our immediate family live in this county. My husband and I will raise our two sons here and I am personally vested

in making sure that our county remains as safe as it was when my husband and I grew up here. We have wonderful memories of growing up enjoying the freedoms that come from living in a safe community. My mission as Criminal District Attorney will be to fight to preserve those freedoms.

County prosecutor Jennifer Tharp seemed to want to look tough

She has taken a hard line on the Carter case, avoiding public comment and showing little sympathy for any of the case's anomalies. At some point she offered Carter a plea bargain: a sentence of only eight years. Carter turned it down.

Carter tuned it down even though he continued to be assaulted and battered in jail. His father Jack Carter told NPR on July 3:

> Without getting into the really nasty details, he's had concussions, black eyes, moved four times from base for his own protection. He's been put in solitary confinement, nude, for days on end because he's depressed. All of this is extremely traumatic to this kid. This is a horrible experience.

> Justin Carter is currently being held in solitary confinement, on suicide watch.

And then County Prosecutor Tharp seemed to soften a little

On July 3, Yahoo News reported what might be a softening in the prosecutor's office: "District Attorney Jennifer Tharp would not comment on the details of a pending case but said in a press release that the charge carries a potential penalty of two to 10 years in prison and a fine of up to $10,000. A defendant never previously convicted of a felony may be eligible for 'deferred adjudication community supervision,' which, if served successfully, would not result in a criminal record."

That's better than eight years, but it's not the same as dropping charges that should never have been brought.

One apparent result of Carter's parents' efforts to publicize the case is that Justin Carter now has a new attorney, Donald H. Flanary III, who has taken on the case at no charge. On his San Antonio firm's web site (Goldstein, Goldstein & Hilley) Flanary's statement begins: "I believe that when a citizen is accused of a crime, the best defense is a relentless offense."

Flanary filed his notice of appearance and promptly filed six motions in the case. Two days later he made another flurry of filings, including an application for writ of *habeas corpus*. A hearing on that writ is scheduled for July 16, and one of Flanary's goals is to get Justin Carter released.

Flanary might hold the state accountable for excessive charges and bail

"I have been practicing law for 10 years, I've represented murderers, terrorists, rapists. Anything you can think of," Flanary told NPR on July 3. "I have never seen a bond at $500,000."

New Braunfels police Lt. John Wells tried to sound sympathetic, calling the situation "unfortunate," but then went on to proclaim Carter guilty of the terrorist threat. "We take those very seriously," he said, although the interviewer didn't ask why he hadn't taken it seriously enough to investigate it carefully.

Instead, NPR's Elise Hu concluded with a comment that serves as a paradigm of the soft-headed unctuousness of most mainstream media coverage, tagging the story like this: "A painful reminder of how online comments can have real-life consequences."

At least the National Review showed a bit of moral muscle

Getting it right was an Englishman, Charles C.W. Cooke, writing for the National Review Online. He opened by noting that Justin Carter was "ruthlessly stripped of his freedom for making an offensive joke."

He closed with: "Carter must be set free and this insidious precedent smashed to pieces. Our liberty depends on it."

In between, he noted that "it is not the place of authority to judge what is and what is not acceptable [speech], and it is certainly not the place of the state to designate casual discussion as 'terrorism.'"

He also pointed out that the universal application of sentimentalized pathos, referencing real tragedies like the Newtown killings, is as specious as it is irrelevant, and "does not come close to excusing the Texas police."

Cooke's critique applies equally to the Texas prosecutor, Texas jailers, Texas lawmakers – and all their ilk in other states – as well as most of the media, who can't seem to perceive injustice except, sometimes, when it happens to them.

> **Update 2019:** Carter spent five months in jail on $500,000 bail, until an anonymous benefactor posted bond. Two constitutional challenges to the charging statute failed. On March 28, 2018, in a plea deal, Carter pleaded guilty to a misdemeanour charge of making a false report. He was sentenced to time served and no fine. District Attorney Jennifer Tharp remained sanctimoniously self-righteous, hoping Carter had "learned his lesson." She did not say whether that lesson might relate to prosecutorial abuse and stupidity. Carter moved to Colorado and started a GoFundMe page to try to recoup lost earnings during the five years his bail conditions prevented him from holding a job. In 11 months he raised $2,216.

16.

Talk About Police States

With much of the country aware of the extent of government spying on and lying to American citizens, there is now a limited public discussion of what kind of country we want ours to be. The limits of that discussion are illustrated by recent public utterances of two Democratic senators, Diane Feinstein of California and Ron Wyden of Oregon.

For more than two years, Senator Wyden has been warning that the National Security Agency (NSA) has been operating outside the law for more than seven years. His warnings have been limited and cryptic because he was bound by secrecy law not to tell the truth he knew. That ended when Edward Snowden started sharing truthful information that confirmed everything Senator Wyden had implied and more.

On July 24, a near-majority of members of the House of Representatives supported an amendment to a military spending bill that was intended to put some limits on the NSA's ability to spy on all Americans all the time. President Obama opposed any such limitation and, working with House Speaker John Boehner and Minority Leader Nancy Pelosi, managed to defeat the amendment by a vote of 217-205. Each party split fairly evenly, with 111 Democrats and 94 Republicans voting for greater limits on NSA spying on Americans.

On one side, Senator Wyden calls for more transparency and control

On July 30 on the floor of the Senate, Senator Wyden continued to campaign for more open and effective control of American intelligence agencies and to hold them accountable for violations of law that are still unknown to the public:

> ... the violations that I touched on tonight were more serious, a lot more serious, than the public has been told. I believe the American

people deserve to know more details about these violations that were described last Friday by Director [of National Intelligence James] Clapper. Mr. President [of the Senate], I'm going to keep pressing to make more of those details public. And, Mr. President, it's my view that the information about the details, the violations of the court orders with respect to the bulk phone record collection program, the admission that the court orders had been violated has not been, I think, fully fleshed out by the intelligence community, and I think considerable amount of additional information can be offered without in any way compromising our national security.

And there's the rub – "without in any way compromising our national security" – for in those words, Senator Wyden conceded the conventional framing of the question: the assumption that what the secret agencies do actually does protect national security, even though there's little or no evidence to support that assumption. In a rational world, the burden of proof would be on the intelligence agencies to show that they need to take away freedom to keep us safe, and to prove that any serious, credible threat exists.

Americans have lived for decades in fear of threats identified by the US government without credible supporting evidence. Our government routinely inflated the Soviet threat, as well as that of obviously non-threatening enemies like Libya or Nicaragua or Cuba (still).

On the other side, Senator Feinstein dismisses transparency and control

Rather than fading with the passing of the cold war, American suscep-tibility to threat-mongering was re-invigorated in 2001 by the attacks of 9/11, which demagogic politicians in and out of government routinely invoke to cow those who resist the increasing militarization of domestic society. That's just what Senator Feinstein did during a Senate Judiciary Committee hearing on July 31, referring to two of the hijack-ers who trained in San Diego with the support of a Saudi government contractor during 2000-20001:

> I was on the Intelligence Committee before 9/11, and I remember how little information we had and the great criticism of the government because of these stovepipes, the inability to share intelligence, the

inability to collect intelligence. We had no program that could have possibly caught two people in San Diego before the event took place. I support this [NSA] program. I think, based on what I know, they will come after us. And I think we need to prevent an attack, wherever we can, from happening.

Senator Feinstein ends on a familiar note of fear-mongering, the same fear-mongering that has proved effective for more than a decade now, despite its very thin basis in reality. But this is standard demagoguery, and the senator has plenty of company in using it, even among her peers in the Senate.

Why use fear-mongering and falsehood to defend a "good" program?

More troubling, although perhaps not more uncommon, Senator Feinstein uses falsehood to reinforce her fear-mongering. When she says, "We had no program that could have possibly caught two people in San Diego before the event took place," she is dishonest. While it's perhaps technically correct in a lawyerly style to assert that there was no "program," that is a misleading technicality because the CIA knew about those people in San Diego and decided, for whatever reason, not to tell the FBI.

If the purpose of oversight committees is to take a neutral, skeptical view of government programs, then it's a serious problem that Senator Feinstein has the attitude she has while also serving as the chair of the Senate Intelligence Oversight Committee.

For those on the Feinstein side of the argument, apparently the most important objective is to maintain and expand the American security state. That requires maintaining the appearance of a threat to national security, and if the threat should be minimal or even illusory, that's no reason to change direction, it's just a reason to be grateful that the expansion of the burgeoning police state may proceed with little real danger, unless the American people get wise to the con.

Intelligence expert makes short shrift of Feinstein's assertions

Appearing on Democracy NOW on August 1, intelligence expert James Bamford responded to Senator Feinstein's statement with specificity:

93

... she brings up 9/11. You know, the US government had all the information it needed to prevent 9/11. It didn't need all these bulk data collections and everything else. All it needed to do was have the CIA tell the FBI or the State Department that these two people were coming to the United States – Khalid al-Mihdhar and Nawaf al-Hazmi – because they knew it. They knew it because copies of their visas that had been sent to them. And they knew that they were coming to the United States. The problem here wasn't collecting information; the problem was distributing information. So, justifying all this based on 9/11 is just total nonsense.

At the same committee hearing where Senator Feinstein spoke on July 31, the committee chairman, Senator Patrick Leahy, Democrat of Vermont, questioned John Inglis, deputy director of the NSA, as to just how many terrorist plots the NSA had foiled. Inglis started by saying vaguely, "I would say that the administration has disclosed that there were 54 plots that were disrupted...."

NSA claims 54 successes, one of which might even be real

Under questioning by Senator Leahy, the number of foiled plots quickly dropped to 13, and finally fell to one, one plot that had, maybe, been foiled by the NSA carrying out surveillance that included all Americans. In other words, the NSA is unable to document a single, unambiguous, successful effort at foiling a terrorist plot. But in the best case, the maximum total of successes would be one.

Later the same day, but not before Congress, General Keith Alexander, director of the NSA, repeated the assertion that the NSA had thwarted 54 terrorist events.

Again, on Democracy NOW, James Bamford put the NSA's record in context, noting that despite years of metadata and email collection,

... we had the underwear bomber, the person that was flying to Detroit that was going to blow up a plane Christmas Day, the Times Square bomber, the two people in Boston that just committed the bombing on the marathon day, and so forth. Now, all those people were communicating internationally, basically. They were all communicating either to Chechnya, or the Times Square bomber was communicating to Pakistan, and the underwear bomber was in Yemen, and communicating with other countries in the Middle East, and also to Nigeria, for

94

example. So, if the NSA had been taking all this attention and paying attention to foreign communications and international communications instead of domestic communications, it might have discovered those.

Why are we talking about having any kind of police state?

Apparently, there is general public approbation of the "national conversation" we may be having about Americans spying on Americans. Many in media seem to take a certain smug, self-satisfaction of our "openness" and willingness to confront "hard issues," all of which is bogus in the extreme.

The NSA is only one of 16 secret intelligence agencies under the general control of the Director of National Intelligence. We aren't talking about the others. Even though they have a history of operating outside the law or against it, we aren't talking about them.

We aren't talking about any state intelligence agencies or fusion centers or local intelligence agencies (for example, in New York City or Chicago). Together these number in the thousands.

Fundamentally, we aren't talking about the basic infrastructure of a potential American police state, even though much of that infrastructure is already in place.

For now, the "conversation" is limited to the question of whether the NSA should be spying on US more, or spying on US less. Whether the NSA should be spying on us at all is hardly heard above a whisper.

Our current "conversation" is about the size, shape, and authority of our police state apparatus, not whether we should have one.

17.

Rahm Emanuel, the Face of Democratic Fascism, Deserves to Lose

Chicago's mayoral election may look like a local event, and the media mostly cover it as a local event, but the presence of a large, diverse, and energized opposition demanding change on basic issues of fairness and justice gives the city's local result a potentially important, totemic meaning for the country. The outcome of the April 7 runoff election, which includes 40% of the city council as well, may signify whether peaceful change is possible, or whether the suffocating status quo will grow more stifling.

There is another way of gauging the April vote: is Chicago yet ready to reject the police state practices of its local government? Is Chicago ready to reject a mayor who seems content to allow police state behavior to go unexamined and unpunished? Will Chicago be where a majority of Americans finally confront the nationwide plague of police hate and violence that makes the term "American justice" an oxymoron?

The current mayor since 2011, the arrogant and ineffective Rahm Emanuel, has catered to his rich-folks base (that one observer called "the actions of a mad king"). And he has treated the majority of Chicagoans with destructive disdain, whether he's closing their schools, attacking teachers and other public employees, or ignoring police brutality and killing. (As a congressman in 2002, Emanuel supported the Iraq War right out of the box.) He is endorsed by major Chicago media that laud his "significant accomplishments," but they can't seem to name any. His record is mixed.

Given the preening self-satisfaction of the incumbent pugnacious bully, given the elitist priorities and anti-populist destructiveness

96

of this Clinton-Obama Democrat, the best result for the national Democratic Party – and for the country – would be the clear rejection of regressive, right-wing Democrat Rahm Emanuel for a second term as mayor. Emanuel's defeat could mean the end of almost 30 years of corporate Democrats (including Richard M. Daley, 1989-2011) running Chicago for the 1% and driving the city into heavy debt that the 99% will be expected to pay.

Chicagestapo story breaks, police lie, everyone else starts stonewalling

Chicago is already paying tens of millions of dollars in restitution to people who have been victimized by the Chicago Police Department (CPD) over the past four decades (over $50 million paid in 2014 alone). On election day, February 24, Chicago police-state tactics became a clear and present issue in the current election, when the Guardian newspaper published a report about one of the city's darker open secrets, the Homan Square holding facility that has functioned as a municipal black site for torture and interrogation for years.

In its essence, the story is simple and predictable: the Chicago police have a secure facility where they can take prisoners and hold them more or less indefinitely, keeping no official record of their whereabouts, while treating them with torture techniques made familiar by their application to prisoners at Guantánamo. The Guardian story by Spencer Ackerman, a reliable reporter who used to work for Wired, is based on public records and the personal accounts of both victims and attorneys, none of whom hide behind anonymity. The report provides ample detail that can be independently verified by any responsible public official or investigator or other news organization.

Despite the long Chicago police history of chronic brutality, the department promptly went into denial mode, issuing an unsigned, so-called "fact sheet" that is free of much relevant fact. Beyond that dishonest document, police officials refused to comment. Much of the police "defense" depends on the characterization by witnesses (not by Guardian reporters) of "what lawyers say is the domestic equivalent of a CIA black site."

Homan Square is a large, well-guarded warehouse, secure from scrutiny

Homan Square used to be a Sears, Roebuck warehouse complex built in 1904, on a 40-plus acre site, providing 3.3 million square feet of floor space. In 1978, after Sears moved out, 16 acres of the site became a National Historic Landmark and the rest was re-developed in a variety of ways. In 1999, the police took over part of the Sears complex, one four-story warehouse covering most of a city block. In other words, even this smaller piece of the Sears complex is a big building, as the police acknowledge, without saying just how big the Homan Square Facility is:

> It serves a number of functions, some of which are sensitive and some of which are not, however it is not a secret facility. In fact, Homan Square is home to CPD's Evidence and Recovered Property Section, which is open to the public.... Portions of the facility are sensitive. Homan Square is the base of operations for officers working undercover assignments.... Other sensitive units housed at the facility include the Bureau of Organized Crime (including the narcotics unit), the SWAT Unit, Evidence Technicians, and the CPD ballistics lab.... Homan Square contains several standard interview rooms. Most individuals interviewed at Homan Square are lower-level arrests from the Narcotics unit....

This is an exercise in non-denial denial. The police acknowledge some of what Homan Square contains, but there is no claim that this is all it contains. Most of the facility is "sensitive" and inaccessible to the public. Lawyers and reporters have been barred in recent weeks from entering the grounds. Homan Square also reportedly houses a large number of military vehicles and has plenty of space for a secret section in which to hold and interrogate persons of interest.

The police "fact sheet" claims that there are "always records of anyone who is arrested." That's a non-denial denial. What about people who are NOT arrested. Their allegations of being held and tortured at Homan Square without ever being formally arrested remain completely credible. The assertion that "it is not a secret facility" can be true in a sense, since it does not deny that this "sensitive" facility may hide one or more secret sections. Even in defending themselves against brutality claims, police admit that a prisoner in custody died of a heroin overdose. How does that happen with competent policing?

The second and third pages of the "fact sheet" are even less relevant or persuasive. The second page consists of mostly unattributed opinion from friendly local news media (Tribune, Sun-Times, WBEZ). At least one of the police quotes reinforces the possibility that an actual, unconstitutional detention facility exists: "it's an exaggeration to call it a 'black site,'" according to one law professor. Only an exaggeration?

It's so much easier to disappear someone you haven't arrested

The Guardian report makes consistent allegations supported by testimony that can be independently verified:

- that police take people into custody without arresting them;

- that police hold prisoners incommunicado, sometimes for days;

- that police deny prisoners their right to make a phone call;

- that police deny prisoners any contact with their lawyers;

- that police lie to lawyers about the whereabouts of their clients;

- that police keep prisoners shackled hand and foot.

Mayor Emanuel, police officials, and others choose not to address the specifics of the Guardian report. They have been hiding behind this "fact sheet" charade of a defense, referring questioners to it as if it actually meant something. The Chicago Sun-Times and MSNBC (perhaps others) ran portions of the police "fact sheet" verbatim, as if the anonymous police assertions were an independent news story. As the Columbia Journalism Review noted a week after the Homan Square story broke, it "was huge on the internet – but not in Chicago media." The Review did not go on to note that the Homan Square story was all but invisible in national mainstream media (Democracy NOW covered the story early and in depth). The Review also made a rookie mistake, attributing the "CIA black site" characterization to reporter Ackerman, even though he was careful to attribute it to others.

Police lawlessness in Chicago is an old story – therefore it doesn't matter?

Remember the Chicago police riot of 1968: it was sanctioned by then-mayor Richard J. Daley, who shouted anti-Semitic insults at the Connecticut senator who spoke out against the violent rampage of city cops against unarmed anti-war protestors. Chicago policing was not good before that, and it hasn't improved appreciably since. Government in Chicago, as in so many other places, remains tolerant of illegal, racist, brutal, and sometimes lethal police behavior. That's why it matters.

Rahm Emanuel has responded to the present "black site" report with denial and silence, mostly silence. His only on-the-record comment on The Guardian report is: "That's not true. We follow all the rules.... Everything's done by the books."

It's not credible that he believes that. Emanuel must know that the Chicago police have sheltered their share of serial monsters and may be sheltering others with their code of silence (which he has affirmed).

Emanuel is still dealing with the case of Chicago police detective Jon Burge, who tortured suspects into false confessions for 20 years (1973-1993). Burge was dismissed in 1993. He was never charged criminally. Burge's settlement with the city protected the mayor at the time from having to testify, perhaps embarrassingly, under oath. That mayor was Richard M. Daley (in office 1989-2011), the son of Richard J. Daley (in office 1955-1976). In 2010, Burge was convicted of perjury in civil suits and sentenced to four-plus years in prison. He is now a free man, collecting his $3,000-a-month pension, thanks to a decision (apparently barred by statute) by Chicago's Police Pension Board. Every other taxpayer gets to pay for his crimes through multimillion-dollar settlements to his victims ($67 million to 18 victims and counting) and legal fees. Emanuel has opposed establishing a fund to provide health care and job training to Chicago torture victims.

In 2013, when the city council approved $12.3 million in settlements to two victims, Mayor Emanuel's comments were cold:

> **This is a dark chapter on the history of the city of Chicago.... a stain on the city's reputation.... I am sorry this happened.... Now let us now all move on.**

Or not. Emanuel is also dealing with the more recent case of Chicago police detective Richard Zuley, whose possibly torture-induced convictions are also threatening to come back to haunt the city. Zuley was such a good Chicago torturer (1977-2007) that he went on loan as a Navy reserve lieutenant to Guantánamo, where his torture techniques set the bar high for brutality. Zuley, his attorney, and the Chicago police have refused to answer questions from The Guardian.

Police brutality, torture, black sites still not election factor

Emanuel has never shown any inclination to take on the corrupt history of Chicago policing, even as its costs mount for a city in declining financial health. Other public figures, and the media, are also leaving the issue alone. There have been a few well-deserved calls for an investigation, especially one by the US Justice Department (which so far has refused any comment).

In 2012, Mayor Emanuel attempted to expunge a jury verdict that concluded that the Chicago police "code of silence" was a reality. The mayor backed a court motion to vacate the jury verdict and won the support of a woman who had been beaten by a cop, promising to pay her the $850,000 jury award even after the verdict was vacated. Emanuel effectively reached for a code of silence about the "code of silence," hoping to protect future cops against the consequences of their own brutality. A federal judge rejected the ploy.

The police torture issue is as universal as it is local. The issue cuts deeply. Emanuel is already on the wrong side of it. Even as mild a position as a call for an investigation by the Justice Department would be difficult for traditional Democrats like Emanuel, Obama, Hilary Clinton, and all the rest of the don't-prosecute-torturers crowd that has become the dominant, anti-democratic wing of the Democratic Party.

The defeat of Rahm Emanuel would be at least a momentary check on the smart and soulless drift of the Democratic Party.

Update 2019: Rahm Emmanuel was re-elected Mayor in the 2015 run-off election. Later that year his approval rating dropped to the low 20s in the wake of his stonewalling response to police scandals, including withholding a videotape of police shooting the unarmed 17-year-old Laquan McDonald and opposing a federal investigation of the Chicago PD. In October 2017, he announced that he planned to run for a third term, then dropped out on September 4, 2018, reportedly for family reasons and a reluctance to suffer through another bruising campaign.

As he was preparing to leave office in April 2019, Emanuel was warmly praised by his city council. The Chicago Sun-Times wrote: "Mayor Rahm Emanuel inherited a city on the financial brink. He pushed through an avalanche of tax increases that his predecessor [Richard M. Daley, 1989-2011] wouldn't to lessen the burden on his successor. For that and more, he is not leaving office as a beloved figure in Chicago politics. If he had run for re-election, he would likely have lost. Emanuel has run for office six times and won six times." His mayoral term ended May 20.

According to Emanuel: "A lot of hard things got done that you don't have to worry about. The city is in a better position." His final budget had a $98 million deficit, the lowest of his time in office.

Asked about regret, Chicago's first Jewish mayor said: "How can you regret? I'm blessed. I'm the luckiest guy in the world. I've got three great kids, a wonderful wife. I've had a very fulfilling part of this chapter of my life. Are you kidding?"

Emanuel's successor is Democrat Lori Lightfoot, a former federal prosecutor who is the first black woman (second woman) and the first openly gay person elected as Chicago's mayor. She won her run-off election on April 2, 2019 with 73% of the vote.

18.

USA Police State Celebrated as Defense of Freedom

USA Freedom Act replaces USA Patriot Act, sort of, and so?

One needs a wicked sense of humor these days to fully appreciate the present moment in American history, as a supposedly free country debates which police state practices to adopt, while ignoring any thought that maybe the United States should not be a police state at all.

For a brief shining moment early on June 1, 2015 parts of the USA Patriot Act expired and, miraculously, the republic remained standing. Now the lapsed portions of the USA Patriot Act have been replaced by the USA Freedom Act, and officials from President Obama on down are saying things like "this will strengthen civil liberty safeguards," when the real accomplishment has been an effective defense of the USA Police State. Orwell would be proud.

Quickly signing the USA Freedom Act into law on June 2, the President's first reaction was to complain euphemistically about the brief interruption of some police state powers:

> After a needless delay and inexcusable lapse in important national security authorities, my administration will work expeditiously to ensure our national security professionals again have the full set of vital tools they need to continue protecting the country.

Having the full set of vital police state tools revitalized, the President then felt free to lie about the achievement and give the people propaganda guidance as to how they should react: "Just as important, enactment of this legislation will strengthen civil liberty safeguards and provide greater public confidence in these programs."

The danger is exactly that. The danger is that the American people, fear-mongered into accepting the USA Patriot Act in 2001, will now accept the USA Freedom Act as some sort of reform even though it comes nowhere close to defending civil liberties as the Constitution requires. More honored in the breach than in the observance in recent decades, the Constitution remains "the law of the land," however unenforced it may be:

> The right of the people to be secure in their persons, houses, papers, and effects, against unreasonable searches and seizures, shall not be violated, and no warrants shall issue, but upon probable cause, supported by oath or affirmation, and particularly describing the place to be searched, and the persons or things to be seized.

– Amendment IV, US Constitution, effective 1791

Do we no longer have the courage of our constitutional convictions?

The recent argument between proponents of the USA Patriot Act and self-styled "reformers" calling for the USA Freedom Act had nothing to do with patriotism or freedom. It had nothing to do with the Constitution as written. It was an extra-constitutional argument about raw power, about which set of police state methods the government should be able to use to spy on and, when necessary, to control the American people. Adoption of the USA Freedom Act largely perpetuates the powers of the USA Patriot Act, but with a kinder, gentler image. The argument over them was as meaningless as debating whether prisoners would be happier exchanging their orange jumpsuits for lavender ones.

The mindless rush to reinstate government police powers undreamed of in the Constitution was a bitterly comic charade of American democracy. Some now celebrate the USA Freedom Act as "a cultural turning point for the nation." Others condemn the USA Freedom Act as "a significant weakening of the tools" to protect the country. People on all sides claim to "welcome the debate" on national security.

What are these people talking about? Pontificating and

posturing, the American leadership class pretends it's meaningful to debate the merits of competing legislative efforts to corral personal liberty. Covering their totalitarian impulse in the rhetoric of liberty and security, what they are really talking about is how to decide which authoritarian governmental powers to adopt or expand next.

The USA Freedom Act makes no one any safer from the US government than they were under the USA Patriot Act. That law partially lapsed mainly because of the efforts of a lone US senator, Republican Rand Paul of Kentucky. His filibuster in May and stalling tactics on May 31, 2015 briefly prevented the Senate from voting overwhelmingly to maintain the "security" authorizations later re-dressed in the USA Freedom Act. In effect, Rand Paul was pointing out that the empire has no clothes, that it's a naked police state. But unlike the citizenry in the Hans Christian Andersen fairy tale, most Americans continue to see only what they are expected to see.

Security agencies need more competence, not more power

The drift toward an American police-state long pre-dated the 9/11 attacks that could easily have been prevented by competent national security agencies using the powers they had at the time. They had more than enough information to figure out the threat and prevent the attacks, but they were incompetent to do so. President Bush was even briefed by the CIA on the growing likelihood of an attack, but President Bush summarily dismissed the CIA briefer, telling him: "All right, you've covered your ass now." And then Bush did nothing.

Instead of calm resolve in the wake of 9/11, the Bush administration peddled panic and fear to achieve unrelated political goals, like the Iraq war, based on another, deliberate intelligence failure (a CIA-authored book, *The Great War of Our Time*, quotes Bush saying in a briefing: "F—k diplomacy. We are going to war."). Another post-9/11 failure was the USA Patriot Act, "USA Patriot" being a 10-letter backronym that stands with unintended irony for the "Uniting and Strengthening America by Providing Appropriate Tools Required to Intercept and Obstruct Terrorism" Act of 2001. There is no credible evidence that the law has deterred any terrorism.

Elements of police state legislation had already been written before 9/11, after which they were cobbled together and pushed through a fearful Congress by large majorities in both houses. There were 66 NO votes in the House (including Independent Bernie Sanders of Vermont), but the only senator in opposition was Democrat Russ Feingold of Wisconsin. There was enough constitutional concern in 2001, that sunset clauses were included for constitutionally dubious sections of the USA Patriot Act, but none had any difficulty being renewed until 2015.

A co-sponsor of the "reformist" USA Freedom Act was Vermont Democratic senator Patrick Leahy, the Senate's longest-serving member and former chair of the Senate Judiciary Committee. He voted for the USA Patriot Act in 2001 and has since supported its extensions, while attempting to tinker at the periphery. With all too unfortunate precision, Leahy calls the USA Freedom Act "the most significant surveillance reform in decades." That's a far cry from rolling back police state powers that the lawless NSA continues to exercise without restraint on internet users, as revealed June 4 in documents from Edward Snowden.

Fear still governs reason in considering the USA Police State

Opponents of extreme anti-terrorism laws still don't talk in terms of a police state. They speak quietly of reform, like Leahy. More forcefully, referring to "this sort of Orwellian surveillance," Bernie Sanders wrote in Time recently:

> I voted against the Patriot Act every time, and it still needs major reform....

> Let me be clear: We must do everything we can to protect our country from the serious potential of another terrorist attack. We can and must do so, however, in a way that also protects the constitutional rights of the American people and maintains our free society.

By contrast, former Florida Governor Jeb Bush said May 31, "There is no evidence, not a shred of evidence, that the metadata program has violated anybody's civil liberties." That seems to demonstrate that Bush has no understanding at all of what civil liberties are.

Polls reportedly show that the American people are less afraid of terrorism now than at any time since 9/11. Perhaps that means the American people are appropriately less fearful of angry Islamists. Perhaps it also means that they remain inappropriately unconcerned about assassin police officers, abortion clinic bombers, campus killers, or armed and angry militias. The fearmongers continue to dominate the lack of conversation in the country, as Glenn Greenwald documents in The Intercept, and it's bi-partisan:

> **Sen. Lindsey Graham, R-SC:** We have never seen more threats against our nation and its citizens than we do today.

> **Sen. Diane Feinstein, D-CA:** I have never seen a time of greater potential danger than right now and I've never said that before. [Except she sort of has, in 2013]: I think terror is up worldwide, the statistics indicate that. The fatalities are way up. The numbers are way up. There are new bombs, very big bombs. Trucks being reinforced for those bombs. There are bombs that go through magnetometers. The bomb maker is still alive. There are more groups than ever. And there is huge malevolence out there....

There was a time when the US was a country that took its cues from a president who told us that "We have nothing to fear but fear itself." What happened to that country?

Now we have a CIA chief who lies to Congress and the American people but keeps his job. That's John Brennan, who was peddling fear on CBS recently:

> I think terrorist elements have watched very carefully what has happened here in the United States. Whether it's disclosures of classified information or whether it's changes in the law and policies, they're looking for the seams to operate within. And this is something that we can't afford to do right now, because if you look at the horrific terrorist attacks and violence that's being perpetrated around the globe, we need to keep our country safe.

An FBI official warns ominously of "dark space" where terrorists lurk on the internet. In Boston, a cop-killed suspect has his character assassinated by police reports that he had some connection to ISIS. Fox News promotes the idea that ISIS has recruits in all 50 states. Does anyone mention the sad reality that the best way to reduce terrorist threats in the US is to make the FBI stop organizing plots to entrap people?

Breaking News: Fear is a big winner for the permanent USA Police State.

19.

Police Unions Sustain Police Violence Epidemic

Since when did we decide that police officers should be above the law?

Two of the biggest police unions in the country are now on record in opposition to free speech. They are on record against constitutionally protected free speech that opposes the epidemic of police violence across America (more than 900 killed by police so far in 2015).

The current round of police union intimidation tactics started October 24 in New York, after filmmaker Quentin Tarantino spoke briefly to the "Rise Up October" protest, a "Call for a Major National Manifestation Against Police Terror." The crowd of thousands marched peacefully up Sixth Avenue for two miles and included some 100 families impacted by police violence and killing. Police unions have reacted with violent rhetoric to Tarantino's brief "speech," which offered a non-specific truism (here in its entirety):

> Hey, everybody. I got something to say, but actually I would like to give my time to the families that want to talk. I want to give my time to the families. However, I just do also want to say: What am I doing here? *I'm doing here because I am a human being with a conscience. And when I see murder, I cannot stand by, and I have to call the murdered the murdered, and I have to call the murderers the murderers.* Now I'm going to give my time to the families. [emphasis added]

The event centered on victims of police violence. There is no doubt that police have killed unarmed, innocent people. There is no doubt that few cops have been convicted of murder. The reality of police violence is beyond dispute and longstanding. It goes with the territory, and responsible police leaders everywhere know perfectly well that part of their job is not only to keep their officers safe, but also, and arguably more important, to keep the public safe from their officers. The question is why they do so little about police violence.

In the aftermath of the Rise Up October rally, there were a reported 11 arrests, two of which on video show gangs of police roughing up single, unresisting men. Even though the demonstration was peaceful and had a lawful parade permit, police turned out in force. No police officers were reported hurt, except for their feelings.

Police union goes ad hominem with attack on First Amendment

The day after the rally, Patrick Lynch, president of the New York police union (Patrolmen's Benevolent Association) went on the offensive, as he often does. He ignored the vast substance of the Rise Up October group and chose instead to make an ad hominem personal attack on Hollywood director Tarantino and his right to free speech. Lynch's press release in its entirety:

> It's no surprise that someone who makes a living glorifying crime and violence is a cop-hater, too. The police officers that Quentin Tarantino calls "murderers" aren't living in one of his depraved big screen fantasies — they're risking and sometimes sacrificing their lives to protect communities from real crime and mayhem. New Yorkers need to send a message to this purveyor of degeneracy that he has no business coming to our city to peddle his slanderous "Cop Fiction." It's time for a boycott of Quentin Tarantino's films.

Actually, the police officers that Tarantino calls "murderers" are in fact murderers, which is why Tarantino called them murderers – although they are but a small percentage of the total police cohort, they have murdered people, mostly without significant consequence to themselves. On October 30, Lynch sent another press release featuring Tarantino's father saying, "Cops are not murderers, they are heroes," which is the police union party line. In reality, it should go without saying, most cops are neither murderers nor heroes. Like the first press release, this one also ignored the complaints of police brutality, but it omitted the proposed boycott, too.

Los Angeles police claim victimhood too, and back boycott

Craig Lally, president of the LA police union, the Los Angeles Police Protective League, jumped on the boycott Tarantino bandwagon on October 27 in a somewhat more nuanced press release [in its entirety]:

> We fully support constructive dialogue about how police interact with citizens. But there is no place for inflammatory rhetoric that makes police officers even bigger targets than we already are. Film director Quentin Tarantino took irresponsibility to a new and completely unacceptable level this past weekend by referring to police as murderers during an anti-police march in New York. He made this statement just four days after a New York police officer was gunned down in the line of duty. New York police and union leaders immediately called out Tarantino for his unconscionable comments, with union head Patrick Lynch advocating a boycott of his films. We fully support this boycott of Quentin Tarantino films. Hateful rhetoric dehumanizes police and encourages attacks on us. And questioning everything we do threatens public safety by discouraging officers from putting themselves in positions where their legitimate actions could be falsely portrayed as thuggery.

While this statement begins with support for "constructive dialogue about how police interact with citizens," that very formulation betrays an imagined dichotomy between "police" and "citizens." Police need to think of themselves as our fellow citizens. Worse, Lally immediately moves into his own unconstructive dialogue, mischaracterizing what Tarantino said, launching another ad hominem attack on Tarantino and completely evading the substance of the Rise Up October protest.

Worst of all, Lally reinforces the police-as-victim trope, which is a form of psychological denial. It's not "inflammatory rhetoric that makes police officers even bigger targets," its *inflammatory behavior by police officers*. Given the spate of police horrors since 1999, when NY police shot unarmed Amadou Diallo 41 times, it's fair to wonder why police departments everywhere aren't showing a whole lot more humility. Instead, the NY chief of police has given one of the four killers his gun back (after all four were found not guilty by a jury).

Amadou Diallo's mother, Katiatoo Diallo, was a speaker in the Rise Up October protest. What she said was in stark and humane contrast to the whining victimhood of the police unions:

> We are not bitter. I told the world then, the day when they stood up and told me that the four cops who shot my son had done nothing wrong, that it was the fault of my son, I said to you, I say to you now, I said it then: We need change. Amadou has died. It's too late for him. But we have to prevent this from happening again. When you have tragedies like that, you need to learn what went wrong and correct it....

> Law enforcement community should know that we are not against them. We even feel for those who were shot just recently in Harlem. We are not against them. We are anti-police brutality. We are not anti-cop, because we know some of them are doing a good job. But we need to root out those who are brutalizing our children for no reason.

What should a police union be doing, anyway?

The core issue with police unions, teacher unions and all other public employee unions is how to manage the inherent tension between the good of union members and the good of the public that pays their salaries. Police unions, because their members are empowered to use lethal force, should be especially sensitive to the public perception of what is in the public good. That is almost never going to include killing innocent, unarmed civilians.

In December 2014, NY police union head Lynch actually blamed innocent, unarmed civilians for the ambush assassination of two police officers by a lone gunman. It was a breath-taking manipulation of reality and defiance of both logic and authority:

> There is blood on many hands tonight — those that incited violence on the streets under the guise of protest, that tried to tear down what New York police officers did every day. That blood on the hands starts on the steps of City Hall, in the office of the mayor....

These comments set the stage for a symbolic police mutiny, as officers turned their backs on New York City Mayor Bill de Blasio at a press conference dealing with the assassination ambush. This is a direct challenge to civil order, open defiance of the mayor's lawful authority over the police. And it is a gesture of arrogance, not only against non-violent protests against police killing, but in support of an above-the-law right to continue to execute civilians more or less randomly.

Who is more deserving of protection, police or public?

The same day as the Rise Up October protest, The New York Times ran a front-page story about FBI Director James B. Comey telling a Chicago Law School audience that increased scrutiny of police violence has led to an increase in violent crime, a theory for which he admitted he has no data. The data available does not support the claim. But Comey's perception of "a chill wind that has blown through American law enforcement over the last year" is just a more sophisticated whine than the police unions use. For the head of the FBI to defend police officers from scrutiny for their actions, especially their violent or lethal actions, is little more than a defense of police criminality. As the Times reported:

> **Mr. Comey said that he had been told by many police leaders that officers who would normally stop to question suspicious people are opting to stay in their patrol cars for fear of having their encounters become worldwide video sensations. That hesitancy has led to missed opportunities to apprehend suspects, he said, and has decreased the police presence on the streets of the country's most violent cities.**

Wait a minute, that's pure sophistry. If you have police officers afraid of becoming viral video villains, then you have police officers who are tacitly admitting that they are likely to behave illegally if not lethally. Police officers who act properly make boring videos that don't go viral.

The Times did not cover any of the Rise Up October activities. But it did re-publish the FBI chief story on October 30, with the additional comment: "It's not clear why Mr. Comey decided to wade into this issue now."

On October 18, the Times ran a story in the business section based on FBI statistics of police killings. The story notes that the available data strongly shows pervasive racial bias in many areas of American life. Police behavior is no exception:

The data is unequivocal. Police killings *are* a race problem: African-Americans *are* being killed disproportionately and by a wide margin.

The same persistent pattern of racial bias in police traffic stops was found in North Carolina statistics, as reported by a long analysis in the Times October 25: "The Disproportionate Risk of Driving While Black."

The evidence of racial bias in American life remains powerful and its effects are cruel and unusual. Perhaps the nation is less bigoted than it was in the past, but it remains a long way from being a place where all people are treated equally. And one of the grosser reasons for perpetual racial oppression is the willingness of powerful police unions to deny reality and blame the victims. Police unions need to reflect on the healing words of Kadiatou Diallo and put aside *their* bitterness. Police unions need to protect and serve the public, not the perpetrators of violence and death.

How about: if you're not careful enough to identify a toy gun in the hands of a child before you shoot to kill, then you're not careful enough to be an armed police officer. That seems like a pretty low bar.

20.

Thanksgiving for a
Grateful Empire

"Rooted in a story of generosity and partnership, Thanksgiving offers an opportunity for us to express our gratitude for the gifts we have and to show our appreciation for all we hold dear...."

So begins the official Presidential Proclamation of Thanksgiving Day, 2015, signed and issued by Barack Obama. While it hearkens back to earlier Thanksgivings in St. Augustine in 1565 and Plymouth in 1621, this is an essentially imperial document that gives only vague lip service to giving "thanks for the many blessings bestowed upon us."

When his proclamation gets specific in the third sentence, the President gives the highest place of grateful honor to the source of global American imperial dominance:

> We also honor the men and women in uniform who fight to safeguard our country and our freedoms so we can share occasions like this with loved ones, and we thank our selfless military families who stand beside and support them each and every day.

This is, of course, fatuous pandering and a patent lie that is widely and unthinkingly shared by much of a preoccupied populace. Our country and our freedoms have needed no serious military defense for decades. Even amidst the popular revival of terrorism hysteria these days, our country and our freedoms need no military protection, because they face no credible military threat.

The sad reality seems to be that, as a nation, we no longer know what we hold dear, or even what we once believed we held dear.

Our country and our freedoms are unthreatened by others around the world despite our well-cultivated baseless fear. At home, our country and our freedoms are daily attacked by the cold dead hand of the unelected corporate state. Our country and our freedoms are daily attacked by the shrill, vicious demagoguery of divisive factions that are as dedicated to the dominance of minority views as any Taliban or ISIS or other monomaniacal evangelist. Our country and our freedoms go daily undefended by a feckless, reckless government that would rather control a cowed population than seek conciliation and general well-being for all.

As things now stand in a nation more exceptional for its fragmentation than its collective sense of confidence and purpose, a more honest sampling of appreciation for what some Americans hold dear might include:

- Almost all American people can be thankful that their nation is not involved in any serious wars, just turkey-shoots in Afghanistan, Iraq, Syria, Yemen, much of Africa and other places that produce few American casualties while maintaining the constant expense of ordnance to no useful purpose except steady profit to the international arms industry.

- President Obama and his administration can be thankful that almost none of their totalitarian surveillance and permanent-war-making powers face serious challenges, not even the President's assassination-by-drone terrorism.

- American Muslims can be thankful that they have not been rounded up and confined to internment camps (yet), for the duration of endless hostilities.

- All minority-Americans can be thankful if no one in their family was hurt or killed by police this year. Black families in that category can be super grateful. Even white families can be a bit grateful, since cop brutality isn't as completely bigoted as it sometimes seems.

- Americans in media can be thankful that they will never be held accountable as journalists for their culturally destructive and dishonest hucksterism.

- American police can be thankful for their special above-justice status, since even the most violent among them typically goes unpunished.

- The American prison complex can be thankful for another year of high profits at the expense of decent people jailed for non-violent crimes by a judiciary that has lost its sense of justice (with the significant assistance and insistence of Congress claiming to act for an infantilized and fearful American majority).

- American women can be thankful that it is still mostly lawful to be a woman.

- American terrorists can be thankful that they can go on assassinating doctors, torching clinics, executing church congregations, or shooting up mosques without fear that anyone will call them "terrorists."

- The American public in general can be thankful that it remains generally undisturbed by these or other American realities, and that it lacks a widespread feeling that it has any personal responsibility to fix anything.

- Ben Carson and the rest of the Republican field can be thankful that they have yet to be deemed a danger to themselves or others and have not been forcibly hospitalized.

- Any Americans still nurturing the hope of living in an advanced, civilized nation can be thankful that we have two presidential candidates, a man and a woman, who have credible records of espousing humane values regarding at least some of the critical problems we face. One of them is Bernie Sanders. The other, better one is Jill Stein.

- Upper-income Americans can be thankful for the country that cares for them and neglects others, making sure, year after year, that people who could learn are not educated, that people who could work are not hired, that people who could eat are not fed, that people who could be free are not.

- Any Americans who feel no shame for the state of their country can be grateful for their psychic numbness and failed humanity.

Blessings on all, regardless of just desserts.

21.

Are Most Americans Still Afraid to Be Unafraid?

"Priority number one is protecting the American people and going after terrorist networks. Both al Qaeda and now ISIL pose a direct threat to our people, because in today's world, even a handful of terrorists who place no value on human life, including their own, can do a lot of damage. They use the Internet to poison the minds of individuals inside our country; they undermine our allies. But as we focus on destroying ISIL, over-the-top claims that this is World War III just play into their hands.... they do not threaten our national existence. That's the story ISIL wants to tell; that's the kind of propaganda they use to recruit."

PRESIDENT OBAMA, STATE OF THE UNION, JANUARY 12, 2016

"Even worse, we are facing the most dangerous terrorist threat our nation has seen since September 11th, and this president appears either unwilling or unable to deal with it."

SC GOV. NIKKI HALEY, REPUBLICAN RESPONSE TO STATE OF THE UNION

The Republican consensus these days comes down to this: Be afraid. Don't give peace a chance. Ever.

Pretty much all Republicans and too many Democrats buy into the notion that ISIS is a serious threat to the United States. Of course it's not, as the president reminded us, before pretty much contradicting himself and arguing the need for the US to wipe out ISIS. Why? If ISIS is not a mortal threat, then there's no need to wipe it out. A sane and logical person can't have it both ways. But then we live in a time where sane and logical people are not highly valued in the leadership class, or by much of the population at large.

119

The Republican pitch is a con game with a simple cycle: (1) exaggerate a limited threat, like bin Laden or ISIS, into a monster of terrifying proportions, then (2) promise to protect the homeland from this huge, imaginary threat, and finally (3) take credit for defending America when the threat-that-is-not-so-real fails to materialize. This is an ancient paradigm, most recently played out in America's "victory" in the Cold War, a victory that has left the US politically and culturally gutted and adrift. Seizing on the opportunity of 9/11, the US re-started the same con with "terrorism" in the place of "communism," and the con continues.

The reality, on September 12, 2001, was that two places in the US had been attacked with an effectiveness expected by almost no one. A series of intelligence failures, inattention by law enforcement, sloppy security and unlikely engineering produced the collapse of the World Trade Center and limited damage to the Pentagon, with almost 3,000 dead. 9/11 was sudden and shocking, with powerful optics, but it was a discreet event with virtually zero possibility of repetition.

Statistically, terrorism is an inconsequential threat to Americans

Even counting all 38 American deaths from "terrorism" since 9/11, the 15-year total of American civilians dead from terrorism is still fewer than 3,000. The total of Americans dead from terror doesn't begin to match other killing factors taking out Americans on a near-daily basis. Since 2001, out of some 40 million American deaths, over 400,000 were Americans dead from guns, over 500,000 were Americans dead from cars and over 9 million were Americans dead from heart disease. So why has the US spent $1.7 trillion or more fighting terrorism over the same 15 years? Statistically, terrorism is an inconsequential killer of Americans – so that proves the war on terror works, as a successful con, stopping an almost non-existent threat and saving Americans lives (that weren't in danger).

Americans, on the other hand, are very consequential killers of other nation's people. But these are inconsequential people, apparently, because no one has an accurate civilian body-count of estimated 2,500 dead Pakistanis, 10,000 dead Yemenis, maybe 400,000 dead Afghans, 1,000,000 dead Iraqis, most of them killed by the US and its allies with a reckless disregard for the rules of war. Then there's another 500,000 dead Syrians killed by all sides, including the US and its allies.

Avenging 3,000 dead Americans, the US is responsible, directly and indirectly, for more than 2 million dead civilians in countries attacked in the "war on terror," and yet Gov. Nikki Haley says (above), with a straight face and no serious public challenge, that "we are facing the most dangerous terrorist threat our nation has seen since September 11th."

This is pure fearmongering. There has been no credible threat to the US since 9/11. There is none now. There would perhaps have been no threat before 9/11 if President Bush had taken warnings from the intelligence community seriously. Fear has always been one of the dirtier tools of governing, but after 9/11 the Bush administration drove the country to mindless war using fear on steroids. The administration's cries of wolf were amplified by panic at the top of almost every American institution that had some responsibility to counter such popular delusions.

Institutionally, the US has improved little since 9/11. President Obama does say (above) of the Islamic State (aka ISIL or ISIS or Daesh) that "they do not threaten our national existence." This is abundantly clear and true. Trying to have it both ways, he also articulates the false, dishonest, fearmongering context of reinforcing irrational fear:

> **Priority number one is protecting the American people and going after terrorist networks. Both al Qaeda and now ISIL pose a direct threat to our people....**

This is a continuation of the establishment con, promising to protect the American people from a threat that is hardly real. There's almost no way to fail once people buy into the con. But now, perhaps, a majority of the people is ahead of the leadership's endless, bipartisan deceptions. Popular understanding of the con is strong enough now to keep politicians from being too eager to send in American troops to war in large numbers, but popular opinion is not yet expressing itself strongly enough to change the direction of the present pointless, bloody war in which the most measurable accomplishment is creating more jihadis, more fighters for radical Islam (false Islam), more would-be terrorists on a quest for martyrdom. Wouldn't it be a good idea to shift to tactics that did not perpetuate and enlarge the chaos and devastation that have flowed without surcease from the US's criminal invasion of Iraq?

Is that an ISIS hiding under your bed?

Current estimates of ISIS military strength vary wildly, by orders of magnitude, but even at the most (200,000) ISIS is not a danger to the US, it's not much of a danger to the Syrian government's control of part of Syria. It's something of a danger to the Kurds of Syria and Iraq. The Pentagon and CIA generally estimate that ISIS has about 30,000 fighters in Syria and Iraq combined. This is a force smaller than the New York Police Department's 34,000 officers, who are responsible for 305 square miles with over 8 million inhabitants. ISIS forces cover an area estimated to be more than 12,000 square miles (as much as 35,000) with a population of 2.8 to 8 million.

According to the Pentagon last fall, ISIS is "tactically stalemated." The Pentagon estimates that ISIS gets about 1,000 recruits a month and that airstrikes kill about 1,000 ISIS fighters a month. But the Pentagon also says it doesn't do body counts, and in any event has no one on the ground to count the bodies.

ISIS is committed to holding as much of its territory as it can. Territory is necessary to validate its claim of being a caliphate. ISIS is intent on expanding its territory, if possible. That makes it less of a threat to the US than to the countries that border ISIS (Iraq, Turkey, Syria and Saudi Arabia), two of which (Turkey and Saudi Arabia) support ISIS more than they fight it. Those four countries have one other thing in common: they all want the US to do more of the fighting than they are willing to do. And ISIS, for more perverse reasons, wants the US drawn deeper into the Middle East quagmire. And to achieve that, ISIS issues freakish videos and will (if it can) mount terrorist attacks to provoke another mindless US escalation.

In a communiqué to "All Jihadi Brothers" dated November 18, 2015, ISIS caliph Abu Bakr al-Baghdadi described the success of 9/11 from his perspective:

> Every attack we launch upon the infidel West shows its tenuous hold on its precious civil liberties, their freedoms that we supposedly covet. One attack on the Great Satan was enough to make it torture, spy upon its citizens, kill many Muslim brothers, and entrap yet others through perverse law-enforcement schemes. A few more artfully placed and timed attacks and we will bring the residents of these dens of fornication and perversity to their knees.... In this task, we will be aided, as we already are, by those who continue to disenfranchise their own citizens and commit to oblivion their own esteemed moral, legal, and political principles. They continue to kill our innocent brothers and sisters and their children from the sky; they continue to imprison Muslim brothers without trial, scorning their own precious legal parchments from which the words "due process" have so easily been scrubbed.

A terrorist act is designed to instill fear in the target population, as it did so lastingly on 9/11. A terrorist act is defeated by being brave. A terrorist act is primarily political, designed to make the target population act irrationally, out of fear, against its own interests. At least since 2001, provoked by terrorist-inspired fear, the frightened US government, abetted by American media and other institutions, has acted not only as a global terrorist itself, but also as an effective terrorist enabler and terrorist breeder. This has kept the con and the carnage going, to the benefit of a few office holders and profiteers.

Whether the public has caught on enough to reject the next terrorist provocation as the sucker-bait it is remains to be seen. How afraid will you be?

22.

Wall Street Worldview: Why Are People Upset?

Multi-billionaire Stephen A. Schwarzman says he's puzzled by the amount of discontent apparently felt by other Americans these days

Steve Schwarzman is a bland-looking, somewhat paunchy, not unattractive, balding man of benign demeanor who will be 69 on Valentine's Day 2016. He's worth $12 billion, give or take a few hundred million. He is a poster boy for Wall Street success and self-esteem and cluelessness. He's the co-founder, chairman, and CEO of the Blackstone Group, one of the world's largest financial firms, specializing in private equity, hedge funds and mergers. He's a Republican, and life has been going well for him lately, as it has for decades.

But he freely admits (or pretends to admit) that he doesn't understand why the rest of America isn't just as content as he is. On January 21, at the World Economic Forum in Davos, Switzerland, Schwarzman spoke to a gathering of his peers who run the world about his perception of the US presidential election campaign:

"I find the whole thing astonishing and what's remarkable is the amount of anger whether it's on the Republican side or the Democratic side.... Bernie Sanders, to me, is almost more stunning than some of what's going on in the Republican side. How is that happening, why is that happening?"

One clue to "why is that happening," a clue Schwarzman presumably noticed last October, was the $39 million fine Schwarzman's Blackstone Group advisors had to pay for bilking customers. Blackstone entered into a "consent agreement" with the US Securities and

Exchange Commission (SEC) finding that "it breached its fiduciary duty" to its customers. The consent agreement, admitting no guilt, is a tactic often used by corporate shysters to cut their losses when caught with their hands in other people's pockets. Blackstone's "cooperation" with the SEC was cited as a reason the SEC fined the company only $10 million. Or, as the SEC press release put it:

> Blackstone consented to the entry of the SEC's order.... Without admitting or denying the findings, Blackstone agreed to cease and desist from further violations, to disgorge $26.2 million of ill-gotten gains plus prejudgment interest of $2.6 million, and to pay a $10 million civil penalty.... The settlement reflects Blackstone's remedial acts and its voluntary and prompt cooperation with the Division of Enforcement's investigation.

With revenue of $7.484 billion, Blackstone's $10 million fine represents $10/7484^{ths}$ – or .1336% – of its income.

Blackstone steals millions, pays fine, no one goes to jail

Steve Schwarzman is a smart guy. He went to Yale with George Bush, and like Bush he was in the Yale senior society Skull and Bones. Also like Bush, Schwarzman went to Harvard for his MBA. And then he made billions in an industry that has become a largely deregulated financial racket that brought the country to its economic knees in 2008, under President Bush. So, Steve Schwarzman is no dummy. But he wants you to believe he's not smart enough to figure out the system that made him a billionaire while directly and indirectly impoverishing millions. People resent that system, lots of people resent it deeply for the way it's treated them. Steve Schwarzman is "astonished" by their anger. And he acts as if he expects people to believe in his pose of naiveté, telling a Bloomberg interviewer:

"What is the vein that is being tapped into across parties, that has made people so unhappy?... That is something you should spend some time on."

Schwarzman might have gotten a clue when his president at Blackstone Group (Tony James) hosted a multi-million-dollar fund-raiser for Democrat Hillary Clinton at which she denounced corporate crime (wink-wink, nod-nod). Clinton omitted denunciation of Black-stone for its then-recent fine by the SEC, even though the Blackstone victims included public pension systems in California, Florida and New Jersey (for teachers, firefighters, police and other government workers). And if that didn't seem like enough of a source for anger, Schwarzman might have listened to fellow Blackstone billionaire Byron Wien, who was kicking those public sector workers back in 2010:

> The retirement benefits for state workers, really not only in New York, California and New Jersey, but throughout the country, are very generous. *Too generous.* And it is very hard to change that.... But I think we have to be more realistic. We literally can't afford the benefits we have given our retirees in state and local governments. And *we have to change that.* [emphasis added]

So, Blackstone tried stealing from those pension funds, which may not have been Wien's intent. Either way, when you set about to reduce the retirement income of people who have earned it by contract, why wouldn't you expect them to get angry? And especially why wouldn't you expect them to get angry when their pension "problems" stem from the fiscal deceit of politicians you support? Billionaires attack the life savings of $19,000-a-year workers and expect to be loved? Yes, they do.

Billionaires don't live in the same world most of us live in

Five years later in 2015, Wien was as tone deaf to the situation of most Americans as his baffled Blackstone buddy Schwarzman wondering where all the anger comes from. With no trace of empathy, or irony, Wien wrote in early 2015 about the depleted savings of "many" households:

> Among those who had savings prior to 2008, 57% said they'd used up some or all of their savings in the Great Recession and its aftermath. What's more, only 39% of respondents reported having a "rainy day" fund adequate to cover three months of expenses and only 48% of respondents said that they could not completely cover a hypothetical emergency expense costing $400 without selling something or borrowing money.

Of course, for those in the top-10% of wage earners – "it's all good."

One of the things you don't hear the Blackstone boys or others like them fretting much about is wealth inequality. At the Davos conference, where Schwarzman was expressing his bewilderment, Oxfam had just released a report that 62 *people* own half of the wealth in the world: 62 people own as much as 3.6 billion people own. The scales of wealth are balanced, 62 and 3.6 billion. But Schwarzman would like you to believe that he doesn't see that as a possible source of *irritation*, never mind anger, even though the trend is startling: in 2010 it took 388 people to own half the world's wealth. Schwarzman took no note of this reality in his interview at Davos. How bad can the world look to a guy who spends $5 million on his own 60th birthday party in February 2007 at the New York Armory on Park Avenue, featuring rock star Rod Stewart (for $1 million) and a gaggle of guests from the Let Them Eat Cake crowd? At the time, in all apparent insincerity, when his net worth was maybe only $7 billion, Schwarzman told the New Yorker, "*I don't feel like a wealthy person.*"

Wealthy people pay the highest tax rates, except when they don't

One reason Schwarzman may not feel like a wealthy person is because he and others like him are not taxed like wealthy people. Schwarzman, like Mitt Romney before him, has his income taxed at 15%, the second lowest rate in the tax code (poor people pay a 10% tax rate). The 15% rate is mostly for people earning less than $38,000 a year (or $76,000 for a couple). Schwarzman's income runs into the tens or hundreds of millions of dollars a year, but it is taxed as if it's less than $38,000. It's not magic, and it's not a crime, it's a dishonest tax code that Congress consistently refuses to make fair. Surprise!

The tax gimmick here is called "carried interest" and allows Schwarzman, Romney and the rest of the private equity gang to have their income taxed as if it's "capital gains," for which the (also corruptly low) tax rate is 15%. Because the equity fundsters get this tax break, that means in effect that *every other tax paying household* has to pay another $400 or more a year to subsidize billionaires. Schwarzman is surely smart enough to understand how nurses or truckers or teachers or even most doctors and lawyers might be annoyed at having to pay taxes at a higher rate than a billionaire. But he doesn't seem to get it.

In 2010, when there was some talk of closing the carried interest loophole, Steve Schwarzman strongly objected, as if Wall Street was actually being invaded: "It's a war.... It's like when Hitler invaded Poland in 1939."

In his other public remarks, Schwarzman doesn't seem to have much interest in war, metaphorical or real. On the record, it seems to be war only when it's against him more or less personally. He's smart enough to understand that war can make people angry, but he remains publicly oblivious to politicians who support illegal wars and call for more, to Americans who fight and die in illegal wars that also promote terrorist responses, or to the way America treats its veterans, whether wounded, homeless, or damaged in invisible ways (like the country).

Three big dangers: economic crisis, international crisis and Bernie

In a bizarre four-minute video for the Wall Street Journal on January 21, Schwarzman calmly and smoothly explained what he sees as the three broad reasons for the unsteady state of the world, and especially for shaky market conditions:

- First, the economic slowdown in the US and China, although he called reactions to China "overdone."

- Second, the geo-political situation, which is "concerning ... there are too many unusual things happening in the world now." In a rather random, imprecise blur he mentioned immigration, ISIS, Pakistan, Iran, Korea's hydrogen bomb, "and there are lots of other issues going on in the world.... It's happening with such a frequency, it's actually de-stabilizing and gives the appearance that the world is out of control."

- Third, unsettled markets, "because Bernie Sanders has become a viable candidate, at least in Iowa and New

Hampshire…. He's really on the far left." He added that the Republicans don't seem to have anyone who inspires confidence to handle the job of president. "And really a key to this market collapse is Bernie rising as a viable candidate…."

There you have it, the three pillars of the Schwarzman world view: the world's largest economies, geo-political conflict and Bernie Sanders. Democracy is an unspoken enemy of the established order. Schwarzman doesn't say here which he would tackle first – economic, international, or Bernie issues – but it's hard to believe he cares most about war or peace or inequality of any sort. With nothing to say at Davos about war or torture or drone executions or the predatory American military presence in more than 100 countries around the world, Schwarzman suggested that the country is in "some kind of odd protest moment." He offered, simplistically, that the US needs a president who can bring people together:

> The question is, what is everyone protesting about? There are a lot of things that I guess you could, but what's needed actually is a cohesive, healing presidency, not one that's lurching either to the right or to the left….

Having said that, Schwarzman expressed support for Donald Trump.

23.

The World Stands Aghast at the Moral Vacuum of American Leadership

"I speak as a child of God and brother to the suffering poor.... I speak for those whose land is being laid waste, whose homes are being destroyed, whose culture is being subverted. I speak for the poor of America, who are paying the double price of smashed hopes at home and death and corruption... I speak as a citizen of the world, for the world as it stands aghast at the path we have taken...."

REV. MARTIN LUTHER KING, RIVERSIDE CHURCH,
NEW YORK CITY, APRIL 4, 1967

Fifty years later, with direct references to America's genocidal war in Vietnam removed from the speech, Dr. King's words have more relevance than ever: the world is even more aghast now at the path the US has taken, but the US itself has less resilience, less coherence, less national vitality than ever. In the years leading up to 1967, even as the US escalated war in Vietnam, the country also passed culture-defining legislation supporting civil rights and voting rights and addressing poverty. Now the energy and vision the country needs for resistance remains diffuse, unfocused, ineffective, while ridiculed or ignored by those in power. The country seems subsumed in a moral numbness where only the powerless majority of humane people shares the global horror at the path down which the powerful in our government and corporate society are taking us without our consent.

The Supreme Court seat hijacking is but one vivid example among hundreds now, if not thousands. Republicans shredded the

Constitution by refusing even to consider President Obama's choice for the court. It did not matter to Republicans that Merrick Garland was a relatively bland political choice, a compromise candidate by all appearances (Republican Sen. Orrin Hatch called Garland "a consensus candidate" in 2010). Republicans don't work toward consensus, Republicans don't compromise, Republicans shoot the wounded. Such Republican behavior is as thoroughly corrupt and reprehensible as it is now all too predictable. Given the unacceptability of Republican actions, what is one to make of Democrats responding to these political high crimes with little more than token whimpers? Why did President Obama leave Merrick Garland to twist slowly, slowly in the wind for almost a year (while he, himself, went golfing how many times)? Where was the public outrage of a Democratic president, of the Democratic Party, of that party's presidential candidates, or even a single courageous senator or congressman willing to hold Republicans' feet to the fire in preference to letting them burn the Constitution?

On March 16, 2016, President Obama nominated Merrick Garland to the Supreme Court. On January 20, 2017, that nomination lapsed with the swearing-in of the new president. In the interim, the White House and Democrats in general mostly maintained radio silence on the nomination. (Google searches for "Obama defends Garland" and "Democrats defend Garland" produce nothing more recent than May 2016 until after the 2016 election.) Nowhere in his presidency, despite some real and worthwhile achievements, did President Obama come close to rising to the moral profundity of Dr. King. Early on in the Garland farce, the president was remarkably callow:

> The way I've thought about diversity is not to think about any single seat as 'I've got to fill this slot with this demographic.' ... at no point did I say oh you know what — I need a black lesbian from Skokie in that slot. Can you find me one?... Yeah [Garland is] a white guy, but he's a really outstanding jurist. Sorry. I think that's important.

Certainly it's important to have an outstanding jurist on the Supreme Court, but it wasn't important enough to the president to go to the mat for his nominee, it wasn't enough for the president to defend presidential prerogative in appointing Supreme Court justices, it wasn't important enough to put a centrist justice on the court for President Obama to make it a daily issue on which the Republicans had no principled defense. Neither the president nor his surrogates lobbied the Senate on a daily basis, as they could have. Nor did they maintain a daily media campaign, as they could have. Nor did they go to court to compel the Senate to perform its constitutional duty, as they could have. Collectively, they rolled over and died. Even the American Bar Association was more vocal later in support of Merrick Garland than Democrats. Even Neil Gorsuch has had nicer things to say about Merrick Garland than Bernie Sanders has.

Garland's year of hanging quietly as an ignored piñata is mystifying when viewed through a lens of principle. It's less mystifying as reflected in the distorting mirror of politics, especially the remarkably corrupt Democratic presidential politics of 2016. (A Google search of "Hillary defends Garland" finds her backing him in March and denigrating him in September.) A year ago, remember, pretty much everyone thought the Democrats were going to win the presidency and likely the Senate, too. On March 15, 2016, Clinton won every contested state (OH, NC, FL, IL, MO) and Trump did almost as well, losing only Ohio to Kasich. Here's a whiff of the March magic thinking those primaries produced:

> Crafty of O [Obama] to wait until the morning after Trump's back-breaking wins last night [March 15] to stick McConnell with this [Garland nomination]. Now Senate Republicans will face maximum pressure from both sides.

> If they cave and decide to give Garland a hearing after all, Republican voters who are still cool to Trump might decide to vote for him in a burst of "burn it all down" rage. A betrayal here hands Trump the nomination — assuming there's any doubt that he's already on track to win it.

> If, on the other hand, McConnell stands firm, he's blowing an opportunity to confirm a nominee who's likely to be more "moderate" than what President Hillary will offer next year.

> The conventional wisdom on Trump right now is that he's a dead duck in the general election barring some sort of national crisis. I don't agree with it, but it's not out of left field: His favorable rating,

for instance, is toxic and it's an open question whether he could organize a national campaign capable of matching Hillary's.

If McConnell agrees with that CW, that Hillary's a prohibitive favorite to win *and* that the backlash to Trump will hand Democrats the Senate, then refusing to confirm Garland now clears the path for Democrats to nominate and confirm a young hyper-liberal justice next year. Garland is already in his 60s and is no far-lefty; if Hillary wins big, liberals will insist that she exploit her mandate by engineering a new Warren Court. (Garland, ironically, clerked for the most liberal member of the Warren Court but he hasn't followed the same trajectory as a judge.)

So what do you do if you're Mitch the Knife? Accept a quarter-loaf here by confirming a guy whose centrist credentials will be used to show just how unreasonable and obstructionist the GOP is in blocking him? Or risk having no loaf at all when Democrats win this fall and ram through whoever they want?

This commentator (identified as ALLAHPUNDIT) goes on to consider the possibility of a Trump presidency with a Democratic Senate. And he predicts that Merrick Garland will be confirmed sooner or later. He does not even imagine what we have come to know as reality. In this new reality we have Neil Gorsuch nominated to the Supreme Court, where his stone-cold inhumanity will work to shape the quality of our lives for a generation. Sure, Senate Democrats, most of them, eventually, are putting up a last-minute fight, and maybe they can win it. But even the Republican trashing of the Constitution over Garland wasn't enough to bother Democrats like Joe Manchin or Heidi Heitkamp or Joe Donnelly to reward that daylight robbery (to which none objected at the time), behavior for which The Washington Post, without apparent irony, dubs them "three moderate Democrats."

As this is written late on April 3, the outcome is undecided. But whether the country gets Justice Gorsuch or some other Trump nominee, the credit goes to Democrats. They chose politics over principle for most of 2016 and this is what they achieved. And even now, having lost and lost and lost, the party shows little sign of being able to see itself clearly in a mirror, much less identifying all the ways it needs to change to become anything like a democratic party ever again.

24.

What Would an American Police State Look Like? Are Your Eyes Closed?

The police state impulse is as American as cherry pie

A country doesn't need a monolithic totalitarian government to have an effectively working police state. The United States has had a partial police state in place since before it existed as a "free country." Slavery required a police state structure to maintain "order." Segregation required a police state structure. Ethnic cleansing of native peoples required police state management that still exists, most obviously in North Dakota, but also across the country. Fear of immigrants has fostered police state responses, especially under the Trump administration. Fear of Communists has produced police state responses since 1917, most notoriously during the 1950s McCarthy era. Fear of nuclear weapons and nuclear power and their very real dangers, has produced a permanent police state security network. Fear of terrorism, spiked by 9/11, has produced a host of police state responses such as the 2001 Patriot Act (ready and waiting before the attack); such as expanded citizen surveillance by the NSA and some 16 other, more secret agencies; such as unprecedented punishment of whistleblowers for their truth-telling; and such as a unified police state structure euphemistically called Homeland Security, that encourages citizens to spy on each other.

The American police state has evolved relentlessly for decades, with surges of state control when the opportunity presented itself. It's not perfected yet, but it's working reasonably effectively and flexibly as a hybrid governmental/private sector control mechanism. The American police state has always been more cultural than political, with incremental controls added by whatever elected party happened to be in office at the time. So far, the tension between centralized absolute authority and constitutional checks and balances has preserved something like a democratic republic. Now we're in a zeitgeist where a huge minority of Americans want autocratic government and the party in control of all three branches of the federal government is inclined to deliver. Among the signs (far from an exhaustive list):

Leader worship. Cult of personality is familiar to Russia, China, North Korea and other countries, but not so much the US – until the Trump cabinet meeting of June 12. Flattery and fawning are not a new thing in history, but such over-the-top boot-licking as the president got from his mostly white, male assembly of courtiers may be unique to American government, where "supreme leader" does not usually apply. Figuratively on their knees like a cult group, the assembled Trump flunkies each said things like: "We thank you for the opportunity and blessing to serve your agenda and the American people." What *was* this? What's the opposite of Lincoln's team of rivals? Even conservative stalwart Bill Kristol was appalled, tweeting this obituary: "The American experiment in honorable and dignified self-government. July 4, 1776 – June 12, 2017."

Secret legislation. Republicans won't hold hearings on their so-called healthcare bill, the main features of which are to strip healthcare from millions of the neediest Americans while delivering billions of dollars in tax breaks to the wealthiest (while stripping veterans of tax credits). Under-the-radar regulatory rollback proceeds both by decree (executive order) and through the Congressional Review Act (used only once before Trump). Now, thanks to Republicans, mentally impaired Social Security recipients can buy guns and coal companies can more freely dump mining waste into streams and rivers (four Democratic senators supported more water pollution: Manchin, Heitkamp, Donnelly and McCaskill). In an autocracy (like the Michigan emergency manager system) everyone has the right to be Flint.

Death threats to determine elections. Death threats – direct, anonymous, personal death threats have long been a staple of right-wing politics, although not exclusively, from college campuses to New Orleans to Congress, usually delivered through social media (easier than cross burnings). The right complains about threats, too, but mostly these are symbolic. Recently real death threats drove an Iowa Democrat out of a Congressional race and a New York Democrat (who was also assaulted) out of the Binghamton Mayoral race.

Normalizing injustice. Randomly killing unarmed black, brown and white people with impunity, randomly rounding up and deporting immigrants, randomly and illegally arresting and overcharging protestors – these are all police state tactics. Arrest journalists. (Hasn't the bully in the pulpit told US the media are "the enemy of the people"?) Criminalizing harmless behavior. Charging even nonviolent protesters with the most serious offense possible. Over-charging unpopular (or despised) minorities helps make official lawlessness acceptable. Sometimes intimidation works.

Privatizing government. "Government contractor" is a benign sounding phrase that often means "the right to loot the US Treasury." Defense contractors are notorious examples and have been for years. The Pentagon has never been audited, even though it can't account for somewhere around $125 billion to more than $6.5 trillion (according to its own Inspector General). Outsourcing government responsibilities like justice doesn't seem like a responsible idea, but it's a lucrative one when it comes to private prisons. Private prisons don't save the government money, but they enrich selected politicians and their friends at the expense of inmates. This violent corruption is not new news, but private prisons have paid handsomely for political protection from the Trump administration. Private security forces (mercenaries) have been profitable and problematic at least since Blackwater Worldwide was slaughtering civilians in Iraq. Blackwater's founder helped to set up the Trump-Putin back channel. Mercenaries do government (and corporate) dirty work in the shadows. Their methods are ruthless and corrupt, as shown by TigerSwan International memos treating the peaceful, unarmed Standing Rock protesters opposing the Dakota Access Pipeline as a "jihadist insurgency model." The peaceful protest was crushed by force even though the government acted illegally. In a police state, the government can't be held to account. And a police state needs to protect its police from accountability as well. The Washington Post reports that's just what US Senate Republicans propose to do with their Back the Blue Act of 2017 – "If this bill passes, it would become nearly impossible to sue the police in all but the most egregious instances of abuse, and even then, only in cases where the victim is basically beyond reproach."

No doubt readers can think of other active elements of the American police state – two decades of rampant voter suppression comes to mind. The pieces are in place to make America safe for police state governance. Whether the Trump forces will be satisfied with just a qualified dictatorship remains to be seen. And it also remains to be seen, should the Trump forces try to take full dictatorial powers, whether there is enough of America left to prevent their succeeding.

> **Note:** A reader at the time objected to the emphasis on a US cult of personality, to which I responded: "Certainly cult of personality applies broadly to US Presidents in general (cultural veneration of man/office unsorted out), especially Kennedy, Obama, Reagan. My focus was on the amazing Trump cabinet meeting [June 12, 2017] so chokingly full of political fellatio of the Pres. Perhaps I'm wrong, but that event seems to me unique and without significant precedent in American politics."

25.

Nine Vermont Cops Execute Non-Threatening Addict Holding BB Gun

How many people did it take to waste this life, starting with himself?

Green Mountain homeboy Nathan Giffin was 32, white, and holding a BB pistol at his side when multiple police shot him multiple times outside the Montpelier High School he had once attended. Reportedly, Giffin had admitted addictions to cocaine and heroin, and maybe he even had an intent to die from suicide by cop. If so, he succeeded. Nine Vermont police officers pumped him full of bullets, dropping him on the spot as he stood passively at the far end of a football field after almost an hour standoff.

How is this not an extrajudicial execution that never should have happened?

The video of the shooting is clear. Giffin appears distracted, uncertain, he takes three slow steps forward, one backwards, then four to his left. Then he drops. This is a full-on shooting of a wandering young man by a disorderly firing squad that continues shooting for about three seconds after Giffin is down, mortally wounded.

Police handcuff him on the ground, but the video does not show anyone administering medical attention. Giffin died in an ambulance on the way to the hospital, where he was declared dead.

Before releasing the victim's name, police released information about his criminal record dating back to 2002, when Giffin was 17. It is unclear whether he was known to any of the cops who killed him.

138

This was Tuesday morning, January 16. According to reports, at about 9:30 Giffin used his realistic-looking BB pistol to hold up a State Employees Credit Union. He fired no shots, and no one was hurt. He fled the bank on foot, crossing the street onto the grounds of the high school, which was in session. Somehow (it's not clear how) police cornered Giffin on the bleachers of the fenced-in athletic field at the school. The school went on lockdown. Details of the standoff with the police are few. The "crisis negotiation team" was there, but there are no reports of any negotiation or other meaningful communication with Giffin. Police say that he made both threatening and suicidal statements, and that he ignored orders to surrender his gun. A witness quoted police taunting Giffin: "You going to run away now?" Somehow police were unable to avoid killing a defenseless drug addict who posed no serious threat, all of which they could have known in time. Students in the school reportedly took pictures of the killing as it unfolded.

Giffin's BB pistol, a Umarex 40XP, looked quite real, apparently. Maj. Glenn Hall of the Vermont State Police rationalized the killing of a non-threatening man who hadn't fired a shot this way:

> I certainly can't rationalize why someone would do this, I don't know if there is an explanation, but certainly if you want people to believe that you have a real gun, this is as close as you can get... They look real. It would be literally impossible for anyone to tell it's not real, from a distance certainly, and even sometimes up close.

Hall added that he didn't even know whether the BB pistol was loaded. Asked why the nine officers chose to shoot Giffin, Hall said he had no clue, although he put it this way: "The reason that those officers choose to use deadly force are all part of the investigation. Investigators will want to hear from them, what led them to use deadly force."

Nine police officers with a single reflexive thought? Are they trained that way?

A nurse who knew Giffin when he was younger and hung out with her daughters recalled him as "a sweet kid with a rough life." She said that Giffin as a high schooler was a regular at her house and his nickname was "Milhouse," after a character in the Simpsons.

He was very kind and respectful to me, and grateful to be able to spend time at our house with our family.... The kids group was kind of like an extended family for themselves as well. It's a challenging time in a person's life to be in your teens, so it kind of reminded me of 'The Breakfast Club' a little bit.... We're all heartbroken. Obviously, a lot happened between high school and now, but the person that we knew was a lovely guy.... He was kind of like adorably goofy, and he had glasses, and in little ways he did look like Milhouse....

I know that whatever was going on, he was struggling and suffering, and I will wait to see what the police investigation uncovers about him being shot by nine police officers.

Although she hadn't seen him for more than ten years, the nurse said her daughter also remembered Giffin as "a very sweet soul who was very caring."

A former 2003 classmate remembered Giffin similarly: "He was a great kid all the way through school. He was very friendly, very upbeat, very funny – funny to be around."

As reported by police, Giffin's criminal record includes convictions for cocaine possession, theft, burglary and armed bank robbery (state and federal), but no violent crimes. He was sentenced to two years for the federal bank hold-up. He was most recently arrested for Christmas day burglaries. In a police affidavit after his arrest, Giffin said he was "sick of living like this." He was to appear in court on those charges two days after he died. That court appearance had been delayed allowing Giffin to get drug treatment.

The nine police officers who shot or shot at Giffin are on paid administrative leave while the investigation continues.

Two of the nine officers have been through this before. Sgt. Lyle Decker and Trooper Christopher Brown were among five officers who shot and killed another 32-year-old man with a realistic-looking BB pistol in Poultney, Vermont, last summer. The crisis negotiation team was also there. Even though the perceived threat turned out not to be actual, the officers were cleared of wrongdoing in the case where the man, an accused wife-beater, was pointing the BB pistol down at them from a second story window. After an investigation, the state's attorney ruled that the killing was justifiable homicide under the law and the officers' decision to use deadly force was reasonable.

Giffin's life and death appears to be a years-long personal and social failure. The challenge to society is to figure out how to care for a damaged child before he drops out of high school, becomes a drug addict, a criminal, a convict, with less and less chance of recovery until he is publicly executed.

It's small consolation that no police officers or others were physically hurt in this cultural crime.

UPDATE 2019: Three months after the shooting, Vermont prosecutors decided not to prosecute any of the officers involved. On April 17, 2018, according to the Burlington Free Press: "Attorney General T.J. Donovan and Washington County State's Attorney Rory Thibault both said Tuesday it was reasonable for the nine officers to fire more than a dozen shots at 32-year-old Nathan Giffin after he had robbed a credit union on Jan. 16." Seven of the shots had hit Giffin. Vermont State Police Col. Matthew Birmingham said the shooting led the agency to revise its use-of-force policies. One change was to have officers involved in a shooting take more time off afterwards. Additionally, state police training will include de-escalation techniques and use of non-lethal means of resolving a standoff, such as plastic bullets or beanbags. Body cameras are planned for all state troopers.

One of the officers who shot Giffin was involved in two other fatal shootings in a six-month period.

26.

Dark Foreboding: Is the American Democratic Experiment Over?

> Things fall apart; the centre cannot hold;
> Mere anarchy is loosed upon the world
> The blood-dimmed tide is loosed, and everywhere
> The ceremony of innocence is drowned;
> The best lack all conviction, while the worst
> Are full of passionate intensity.

WILLIAM BUTLER YEATS, THE SECOND COMING, 1919

Apocalyptic thinking has been with us for a long time, and it sometimes foreshadows actual apocalypses, albeit at human scale, without biblical finality. For a century now, the Yeats poem quoted above has served as an increasingly common reference point for those who fear apocalyptic events approaching. Today such fears are varied, the threats are real, and reactions range from crisis-mongering to self-serving denial, making any rational, coherent societal response almost impossible.

We've been heading this way for decades. We finally got here in 2016. It's taken awhile, but the forces of chaos and greed seem to be cohering, tightening their grip on power, on government and culture, facing little or no effective opposition. An election is coming. It will matter. But how?

Things fall apart; the centre cannot hold;
Mere anarchy is loosed upon the world

Worse, things are under attack, the center is the enemy. The US president veers toward dictatorial powers and seeks out new targets to disrupt or destroy. The US wages war around the world in at least 7 countries (with combat forces in 146 according to Seymour Hersh). The US Environmental Protection Agency wages war on the environment along with public health and safety. The US Education Department wages war on public education. The US Justice Department wages war on Justice, turning law enforcement into a profit-making, human-trafficking criminal enterprise. The US Department of Housing and Urban Development wages war on the poor, as do other agencies. The US Labor Department wages war on labor. The US Supreme Court wages war on most of the population. And so it goes: almost everywhere one looks, there is almost no center left to hold. Resistance is scattered, ineffective, inconsistent, fragmented – mere anarchy is loosed upon the world.

The blood-dimmed tide is loosed, and everywhere
The ceremony of innocence is drowned

This is our country that has loosed a blood-dimmed tide across the globe for decades, this is American exceptionalism that has flooded countries from Iran to Guatemala with its citizens' blood for American ends. This endless flow of American violence and death has drowned our innocence, and still so many of us pretend there is no blood on our hands, no blood up to our eyeballs, no blood vengeance haunting our future.

That's not the way we see the border, but that's the way the border is. American-sponsored dictatorships and genocides are sending the children of their victims to our borders where we victimize them again and again and again. And finally, at least more than just a few people notice who and what we are, and who and what we have been for so long, and there is horror, at least for some. No border guards are yet showing signs of conscience as they carry out unlawful orders, but at least one immigration judge has expressed embarrassment at asking a one-year-old if he understood the court proceedings the US was putting him through.

The best lack all conviction, while the worst
Are full of passionate intensity.

And so, we head for another election on November 6, bitterly divided as a country. It's a so-called off-year election (no presidential race), but it may be darkly viewed as the last stand for the American democratic republic. Some say that 242-year-old experiment has already failed, and there's logic to that opinion. The decline has been long, slow, relentless and the end will not likely be apocalyptic.

When did we lose the possibility of a country of freedom, tolerance and honesty? OK, the Constitution allowed slavery. More recently, was it our willingness to incinerate Japanese civilians with atomic weapons? Was it our willingness to accept Reagan as president despite his dealing with Iran to rig the election? Was it our willingness to let the Supreme Court choose Bush for president? Was it our willingness to let Bush lie us into wars that haven't ended yet? Was it our willingness to accept yet another bloody dictatorship in Honduras (after all the others over so many years)? Was it our willingness to accept a Supreme Court decision (Citizens United) that turned democratic elections into plutocratic power auctions? Was it our acceptance of Republicans stealing a Supreme Court seat? Was it our election of minority-president Trump? Any of these points (and no doubt others) were turning points where the best lacked all conviction, while the worst rode their passionate intensity to the verge of total control of the US government. From there, it could be but a short distance to totalitarian control.

We're heading into the 2018 election with polling that shows only a slight majority of Americans – around 53% – opposed to the direction of the country, opposed to Republicans, opposed to Trump. Republicans currently control the presidency, both houses of Congress and the Supreme Court (with another justice online). The election can't change the presidency. The election can't change the Supreme Court directly (especially if Kavanaugh is approved beforehand). The election can change either house of Congress, neither of which is anything like a sure thing. If the House gets a Democratic majority, that puts all legislation on the negotiating table and raises the possibility of articles of impeachment for which this president has qualified since day one of his presidency. If the Senate gets a Democratic majority, that also makes all legislation negotiable and makes it harder for Republicans to pack the courts. If both houses of Congress get Democratic majorities, that gives the American experiment a chance to continue, dependent on Democratic courage, long in short supply.

**And what rough beast, its hour come round at last,
Slouches towards Bethlehem to be born?**

So ends The Second Coming by Yeats, inconclusively, suggestively. There's no knowing what may happen to head off our own rough beast slouching toward November. Perhaps Mueller will go public on Trump crimes. Perhaps the trade war will implode the US economy. Perhaps Trump will sack Mueller (or some other critical figure). Perhaps enough people will recognize – and reject – the already functional police state created by ICE jurisdiction. Perhaps Republican Senator Richard Burr, already on record as chair of the Senate Intelligence Committee that Russian collusion in 2016 happened, will seize the moment to hold hearings to learn "What did the President know and when did he know it?"

Or perhaps the fascist coup, the totalitarian American state, is already upon us and we're only waiting for massive popular passivity to confirm it. There are those, after all, millions who seem to believe that Donald Trump really is the Second Coming.

27.

The Shame of Dianne Feinstein, the Courage of Christine Blasey Ford

"Any talk of a hearing on Monday, frankly, is premature, because she just came forward with these allegations 48 hours ago. And since that time, she has been dealing with hate mail, harassment, death threats. So she has been spending her time trying to figure out how to put her life back together, how to protect herself and her family. And there hasn't been an investigation. And these are serious allegations."

ATTORNEY LISA BANKS, REPRESENTING DR. CHRISTINE BLASEY FORD,
SEPTEMBER 18

Attorney Banks doesn't quite get her facts straight. You have to suspect that your story is going badly when you've taken care to do it right in coming forward with a dark accusation against a powerful man and even your lawyer manages to misrepresent your reality in a way that favors the powerful man. What does it take to confront reality with care, accuracy and integrity?

Let's concede that at this point, nothing is proved. On balance, however, it's fair to say that Dr. Christine Blasey Ford's bona fides are significantly more credible than Brett Kavanaugh's honesty, integrity, or fundamental decency.

When Attorney Banks says of Dr. Christine Blasey Ford, "she just came forward with these allegations 48 hours ago," attorney Banks is flat out wrong (Wikipedia makes the same distortion). She is also framing the case in a manner favorable to the accused, Supreme Court nominee Brett Kavanaugh. Why would Banks do that? The truth is that Dr. Christine Blasey Ford came forward, albeit somewhat tentatively, even before Kavanaugh was nominated on July 9. From then till

146

now she has been consistently betrayed, by public officials unwilling to defend the rule of law.

Everyone deserves to be taken seriously, but that's hardly the governing standard in American public life. Despite the prevailing bias, one might expect a serious response to a well-credentialed credible professional woman coming forward with an allegation that, as she acknowledges, may well destroy her life and leave her attacker unscathed. We've seen this story before. Unless he's impeached for his wife's gross political conflict of interest activities (or other misbehavior), Clarence Thomas will spend the rest of his life polluting American culture with his corrupt jurisprudence. And Thomas owes his seat to the cowardice of Joe Biden and the rest of the Democrats who refused to call three witnesses, three credible women, who would have testified in support of Anita Hill with their own stories of Thomas's disgustingness. That was 1991, when Anita Hill was 35 and Dr. Ford was 24.

Dr. Christine Blasey Ford knew the Anita Hill story; she knew the very real risks she would run by coming forward. Dr. Ford is a psychologist, with two master's degrees and a doctorate from the University of California. She is a professor in clinical psychology at Palo Alto University. One can only imagine what it takes for a successful professional woman whose life would remain secure in silence to break that silence and face huge, unknown risks for speaking truth to power. She began cautiously, as the Washington Post reported on September 17:

> She contacted The Post through a tip line in early July, when it had become clear that Kavanaugh was on the shortlist of possible nominees to replace retiring justice Anthony M. Kennedy but before Trump announced his name publicly. A registered Democrat who has made small contributions to political organizations, she contacted her congresswoman, Democrat Anna G. Eshoo, around the same time. In late July, she sent a letter via Eshoo's office to Sen. Dianne Feinstein of California, the ranking Democrat on the Judiciary Committee.

In the letter, which was read to The Post, Ford described the incident and said she expected her story to be kept confidential. She signed the letter as Christine Blasey [Ford], the name she uses professionally.

Christine Blasey Ford was never anonymous in telling her story, but she didn't want to go on the record. That's why the Washington Post, with little more to go on, didn't pursue the story at first.

It's not clear why Rep. Anna G. Eshoo, a Democratic member of Congress since 1993, did little more than forward a letter to Dianne Feinstein. Eshoo met with Blasey Ford for more than an hour on July 20 and recently said: "At the end of the meeting, I told her I believed her." On Eshoo's advice, Christine Blasey Ford wrote a letter to Dianne Feinstein that Eshoo's staff hand-delivered on July 30.

Using Christine Blasey's request for confidentiality as an excuse, Feinstein kept the letter secret for six weeks – secret from the public, secret from the Judiciary Committee, secret from her fellow Democrats, secret from the FBI, secret. Feinstein appointed herself judge, jury and executioner of a cover-up of a credible claim by an established professional woman, vouched-for by her own congresswoman, asserting that a Supreme Court nominee attempted to rape her when she was fifteen.

For six weeks, as Kavanaugh's steamroller nomination proceeded, flattening all propriety and procedure, Feinstein did nothing to determine whether or not he was an attempted-rapist of women. So why did Feinstein do nothing? Why did Eshoo apparently do nothing? Why did these women not support Christine Blasey Ford? Why did they not explore the allegation, test it, and develop a strategy to keep a would-be rapist off the Supreme Court? Why did they waste time, contributing to the likelihood of a circus atmosphere when the story broke? Did they really think they could enforce an effective cover-up? And if so, why did they think that was any sort of a good idea? Who ARE these people supposedly serving our country?

Christine Blasey Ford consulted a lawyer who advised her to take a polygraph test. In early August she took the lie detector test administered by a former FBI agent. The result, according to the Post, "concluded that [Christine Blasey Ford] was being truthful when she said a statement summarizing her allegations was accurate." By late August, still getting little support from her representatives, Christine

Blasey Ford had decided not to come forward, her confidentiality still intact.

On September 12, the Intercept reported on the letter in Feinstein's possession and on Feinstein's refusal to share the letter with colleagues. The author remained unnamed. Feinstein refused to answer questions about the letter. During Kavanaugh's hearings, Feinstein had questioned him without even veiled reference to the rape accusation. On September 13, the FBI confirmed that it had received the letter and, with the author's name redacted, included it in the Kavanaugh background file available to all members of the Judiciary Committee. On September 14, Feinstein's office issued a self-serving statement that explained nothing:

> The senator took these allegations seriously and believed they should be public. However, the woman in question made it clear she did not want this information to be public. It is critical in matters of sexual misconduct to protect the identity of the victim when they wish to remain anonymous, and the senator did so in this case.

Feinstein has set the stage for the predictable, dishonest posturing that promptly emerged to discredit whatever it was without trying to find out what it was. Texas senator John Cornyn, second ranking Republican on the Judiciary Committee, delivered a tweet very much in the spirit of the Watergate cover-up conspirator who told an underling, "I don't want to know, and you don't want to know." Cornyn chose sarcasm for his evasion tweet:

> Let me get this straight: this is statement about secret letter regarding a secret matter and an unidentified person. Right.

The circus had begun. How it will end, nobody knows, but if the past is any guide, pessimism is in order. Dr. Christine Blasey Ford, in a fruitless effort to tell her own story in her own way, has come forward. Republican senator Chuck Grassley, chairman of the Judiciary Committee, continues to recklessly railroad one of the most dishonest, incomplete, reckless Supreme Court nominations with continuing disregard for any effort to see the nominee in full dimension. Dr. Christine Blasey Ford has said she's willing to testify, but that should come after

EXCEPTIONAL

an FBI investigation. The president has lied and said the FBI doesn't do such investigations. Grassley, true to his own emptiness, says there's no reason for more delay of this hurried process, no investigation is needed, better to have a one-on-one, reality show shouting match with Kavanaugh and Christine Blasey Ford together before the committee that has no track record of delivering the truth about anything. The potential for a category 5 Capitol Hill storm is building.

Psychologist Blasey Ford's position is calm and rational, as outlined in a letter from lawyer Banks to Grassley, promising full cooperation with the committee and law enforcement and arguing that investigation should precede judgment (although many Republicans have already expressed judgment):

> ... a full investigation by law enforcement officials will ensure that the crucial facts and witnesses in this matter are assessed in a non-partisan manner, and that the Committee is fully informed before conducting any hearing or making any decisions....
>
> We would welcome the opportunity to talk with you and Ranking Member Feinstein to discuss reasonable steps as to how Dr. Ford can cooperate while also taking care of her own health and security... She is not prepared to talk with them at a hearing on Monday [September 24].

Rather than investigate, Republicans have chosen to threaten. Grassley has rejected calls even to delay the hearing on Monday, saying that if Christine Blasey Ford doesn't testify, the committee might just go ahead and vote on Kavanaugh and be done with it. There's nothing in the Constitution that prevents the Supreme Court from having two sexual predators.

Anita Hill has weighed in with a cogent and sensitive op-ed in The New York Times, reviewing the mistakes the Senate made with its 1991 Clarence Thomas hearings and suggesting ways for the Senate to do better this time, and maybe even get it right:

> Do not rush these hearings. Doing so would not only signal that sexual assault accusations are not important — hastily appraising this situation would very likely lead to facts being overlooked that are necessary for the Senate and the public to evaluate. That the committee plans to hold a hearing this coming Monday is discouraging.

Simply put, a week's preparation is not enough time for meaningful inquiry into very serious charges.

Finally, refer to Christine Blasey Ford by her name. She was once anonymous, but no longer is. Dr. Blasey is not simply "Judge Kavanaugh's accuser." Dr. Blasey is a human being with a life of her own. She deserves the respect of being addressed and treated as a whole person.

The evidence of Christine Blasey Ford's being not just a whole person, but a kind and competent person with a powerful social conscience, is so far overwhelming (even in the Wall Street Journal). There is, to date, no reason not to believe her story. As others have noted, she has nothing to gain by coming forward, and much to lose. She has already lost some of it, and the worst is still ahead. Sympathy for her is widespread, as evidenced by an online support site that raised more than its $100,000 goal in less than 24 hours.

Kavanaugh is already credibility-challenged on numerous fronts. He has no record of protecting women, minorities, civil rights, workers, or anyone else in a vulnerable position. His written opinions have excoriated humane principles. He wants a lifetime appointment. The burden is on him to show that he deserves it. He has already denied any sexual assault; he has even denied being at a party that, as yet, has no precise time, date, or place.

Isn't it Kavanaugh's turn for a polygraph?

28.

Fox News Reveals: Brett Kavanaugh Does Not Tell the Truth

"I've always treated women with dignity and respect."

JUDGE BRETT KAVANAUGH ON FOX NEWS, SEPTEMBER 24, 2018

This is not true. Brett Kavanaugh has not always treated women with dignity and respect, unless you mean that abusing his judicial authority to prevent a woman from having the legal abortion she wants somehow constitutes "dignity and respect."

This is clear in the 2017 case of Garza v. Hargan. This is the one abortion case Brett Kavanaugh has ruled on as a federal judge. In it he treated a pregnant 17-year-old with no dignity and no respect, and he went out of his way to do it. The woman was a Jane Doe fleeing from family violence in Central America, where her parents had beaten her pregnant sister so badly she miscarried. Jane Doe was in US custody, she wanted an abortion, and the US refused. She sued and won the right to an abortion. The US appealed and the case reached the US District Court where Kavanaugh sat. The court ruled to allow Jane Doe (J.D. in the court's opinion), then at least 15 weeks pregnant, to have her abortion. In an opinion concurring with the majority decision, Judge Patricia Ann Millett wrote:

> Fortunately, today's decision rights a grave constitutional wrong by the government. Remember, we are talking about a child here. A child who is alone in a foreign land. A child who, after her arrival here in a search for safety and after the government took her into custody, learned that she is pregnant. J.D. then made a considered decision, presumably in light of her dire circumstances, to terminate that pregnancy. Her capacity to make the decision about what is in her

best interests by herself was approved by a Texas court consistent with state law. She did everything that Texas law requires to obtain an abortion. That has been undisputed in this case.

What has also been expressly and deliberately uncontested by the government throughout this litigation is that the Due Process Clause of the Fifth Amendment fully protects J.D.'s right to decide whether to continue or terminate her pregnancy. The government—to its credit—has never argued or even suggested that J.D.'s status as an unaccompanied minor who entered the United States without documentation reduces or eliminates her constitutional right to an abortion in compliance with state law requirements.

Where the government bulldozed over constitutional lines was its position that—accepting J.D.'s constitutional right and accepting her full compliance with Texas law—J.D., an unaccompanied child, has the burden of extracting herself from custody if she wants to exercise the right to an abortion that the government does not dispute she has. The government has insisted that it may categorically blockade exercise of her constitutional right unless this child (like some kind of legal Houdini) figures her own way out of detention by either (i) surrendering any legal right she has to stay in the United States and returning to the abuse from which she fled, or (ii) finding a sponsor—effectively, a foster parent—willing to take custody of her and to not interfere in any practical way with her abortion decision....

The irreparable injury to J.D. of postponing termination of her pregnancy—the weekly magnification of the risks to her health and the ever-increasing practical barriers to obtaining an abortion in Texas—have never been factually contested by the government.

Ignoring the health risk question, Kavanaugh's nine-page dissent argued for waiting for Jane Doe to find a sponsor with little consideration of her as a person with a complicated problem. His summary of Jane Doe's situation lacks Millett's humane concern, as he wrote with dry starkness:

Jane Doe is 17 years old. She is a foreign citizen. Last month, she was detained shortly after she illegally crossed the border into Texas. She is now in a US government detention facility in Texas for unlawful immigrant minors. She is 15-weeks pregnant and wants to have an abortion. Her home country does not allow elective abortions.

He might as well say she is just a pawn in the game, she doesn't matter. Kavanaugh later treats the majority opinion reductively, as if it was only about abortion ideology, not the time-constrained needs of a 17-year-old girl. And in doing so, he uses the loaded language of an anti-abortion ideologue:

> The majority apparently thinks that the government must allow unlawful immigrant minors to have an immediate *abortion on demand.* [emphasis added]

And later Kavanaugh writes similarly:

> The *en banc* majority, by contrast, reflects a philosophy that unlawful immigrant minors have a right to immediate *abortion on demand*, not to be interfered with even by government efforts to help minors navigate what is undeniably a difficult situation by expeditiously transferring them to their sponsors. [emphasis added]

This is not honest, truthful argument. This is tendentious and false. Kavanaugh makes clear that he would choose a legalistic rigidity requiring Jane Doe to find a sponsor, regardless of how long that might take or whether it was even possible. Clearly, delay might make her abortion medically more difficult, or impossible. That, although he is not forthright enough to say so, seems to be Kavanaugh's preferred outcome. That inference is reinforced by Millett's response to Kavanaugh:

> Judge Kavanaugh's dissenting opinion (at 4) suggests that it would be good to put J.D. "in a better place when deciding whether to have an abortion." That, however, is not any argument the government ever advanced. The only value of sponsorship identified by the government was that sponsorship, like voluntary departure from the United States, would get J.D. and her pregnancy out of the government's hands.

Judicial courtesy presumably restrains Millett from saying outright what she clearly describes: that Kavanaugh is arguing speciously and dishonestly. Jane Doe had already decided to have an abortion. Kavanaugh is not telling the truth to suggest otherwise. Kavanaugh's argument serves only a callous, ideological purpose, lacking any of the human decency Millett expresses in her conclusion:

The government's mere hope that an unaccompanied, abused child would make the problem go away for it by either (i) surrendering all of her legal rights and leaving the United States, or (ii) finding a sponsor the government itself could never find is not a remotely constitutionally sufficient reason for depriving J.D. of any control over this most intimate and life-altering decision. The court today correctly recognizes that J.D.'s unchallenged right under the Due Process Clause affords this 17-year-old a modicum of the dignity, sense of self-worth, and control over her own destiny that life seems to have so far denied her.

Kavanaugh told Fox News: "I've always treated women with dignity and respect." That's simply not true. He did not treat Jane Doe with dignity and respect. Not even close. As a pridefully professing Christian, Kavanaugh seems not to have accepted the lesson of Matthew 25:45: "Truly I tell you, whatever you did not do for one of the least of these, you did not do for me."

"I'm a good person," Brett Kavanaugh keeps telling us. But Brett Kavanaugh doesn't tell the truth.

Would a good person conceal his involvement with government torture and other human rights abuses? Would a good person conceal his involvement with mass surveillance of American citizens? Would a good person conceal the rest of his record in the executive branch? Would a good person have so much to hide as Brett Kavanaugh has relentlessly kept hidden? Brett Kavanaugh refuses to tell the truth.

Does that mean he's a liar? Does that mean he's delusional? Does that mean he's in deep denial approaching pathological dimensions? Does that mean he's an unscrupulous political operative for whom facts are what he says they are at any given moment? Does any of this matter? Why should we care why he doesn't tell the truth? It doesn't matter.

The Supreme Court Justice we deserve would be a reliable truth-teller.

Update 2019: Despite Kavanaugh's efforts, Jane Doe managed to have an abortion at fifteen weeks, thanks to the Appeals Court ruling. The Supreme Court later vacated the ruling, too late to affect Jane Doe. Attorney Rochelle Garza, the named plaintiff representing Jane Doe, testified against Kavanaugh before the Senate Judiciary Committee on September 7. Garza testified to the mistreatment of Jane Doe by the federal detention authorities, pro-life counsellors and the courts:

"The pain that this caused Jane is something I can't even describe – knowing that her life's path, whether she would be forced to carry a pregnancy to term, was completely in the hands of people she would never know made her feel desperate, hopeless and alone."

Referring to Kavanaugh's icy reasoning in the case, Garza said in an interview:

"There was no consideration for the fact that Jane ... already had a ruling from a state court judge, who is more apt to determine her best interest. He didn't consider that she was being followed one-on-one, that she was completely under the thumb of the federal government. These are all things that should have been taken into account and weren't."

29.

Will Federal Judges Cover Kavanaugh's Butt – or Whup It?

Context 2019: Judge Kavanaugh was rushed through the confirmation votes without anything like due diligence in examining his record. As I wrote at the time, Republicans "destroyed due diligence the moment they decided to keep most of Kavanaugh's government service records secret. Think about that. It doesn't seem the Democrats thought about it much. They made some token complaints before rolling over and saying, in effect, that's OK, this guy worked for the executive branch on polarizing, partisan issues for years, but we don't really need to know what he did even though taxpayers were paying him to do it. Seriously, according to Democrats on the Judiciary committee, whatever his involvement with politicizing Vince Foster's suicide or the Starr investigation into Monica Lewinsky or shutting down the vote count in the 2000 election or building a bogus case for an illegal war in Iraq or developing justifications for torture and other war crimes, we don't need to know any more about any of that now do we?

A bipartisan conspiracy of silence was accepted as a reasonable approach to vetting a chronic liar whose known views would take this country in the opposite direction from where a majority of the people want it to go. With that corrupt two-party bargain in place, the risk of an actual, factual record for the candidate was too great a risk to take. And then Dr. Christine Blasey Ford finally emerged with a credible tale of Kavanaugh and Mark Judge, both drunk and laughing hysterically, trying to rape her in an eerie enactment of a "devil's triangle" (which Kavanaugh, with presumably unintended irony, would later testify falsely was a "drinking game" – a game for the drinkers, perhaps, but not so much the victim).

Kavanaugh lied when he testified: "Dr. Ford's allegation is not merely uncorroborated, it is refuted by the very people she says were there, including by a long-time friend of hers. Refuted."

This is false. None of Dr. Ford's allegations was refuted by anyone. Dr. Ford's allegations have not been effectively rebutted by anyone. Kavanaugh has denied them. His supporters have said, in effect, I can't imagine he'd do such a thing. The FBI performed a sham investigation. But there is NO evidence that counters Dr. Ford's allegations. And Kavanaugh must know that.

Kavanaugh's televised performance before the nation on September 27 caused a number of serious lawyers and legal scholars to file judicial conduct complaints challenging Kavanaugh's honesty, partisanship, and other factors making him unfit to be judge or justice.

Judge Kavanaugh was long past his sell-by date as a credible human. Nevertheless, the Senate confirmed him October 6 on a 50-48 vote, the closest ever for a justice. He was sworn in the same day. Judicial conduct complaints continued to pour in till they numbered 83 and the chief judge of the DC District was forced to deal with them.

"This whole two-week effort has been a calculated and orchestrated political hit, fueled with apparent pent-up anger about President Trump and the 2016 election, fear that has been unfairly stoked about my judicial record, revenge on behalf of the Clintons and millions of dollars in money from outside left-wing opposition groups.

– JUDGE BRETT KAVANAUGH'S SENATE TESTIMONY, SEPTEMBER 27, 2018

The integrity of the US judicial system is actively, albeit quietly, in play. A sitting federal judge, or more likely a panel of sitting federal judges, will be required in the near future to render an assessment of the honesty, integrity and fitness of a Supreme Court justice to retain his lifetime appointment. The process and the result of the federal judges' decision will, together, render a judgment as to the integrity of not just one Supreme Court justice but the federal courts as a national institution.

The stakes are as high as they are simple: Will our court system choose to defend the position one of its own members or will it choose to defend the integrity of the US judicial system? There is no possibility it can do both with any credibility.

This is a morality play that began at a time uncertain, reaching back decades. The curtain opened as the president named Brett Kavanaugh to fill a seat on the Supreme Court despite – or because of – his long history of playing Republican hardball against the Clintons over Whitewater, against the Clintons over Monica Lewinsky, for George Bush over the Florida vote count in the 2000 election, for fake intelligence in the lead-up to the Iraq War, and for the White House in its efforts to spy on or torture anyone they chose. On occasion even as a federal judge, Kavanaugh has proved the perfect partisan.

Kavanaugh's history was a concern when he was first nominated for the federal bench in 2004, but he managed then to get confirmed with only limited doubt about his ability to tell the truth under oath. This year, when his Senate confirmation hearings began on September 4, the concerns about his integrity were still there, but Kavanaugh was protected from his own record because the White House kept most of it secret. Kavanaugh's refusal to give full and complete answers to questions about his career as a political operative prompted the first formal ethics complaints (even before the Dr. Christine Blasey Ford story broke). One of those complaints, filed by attorney J. Whitfield Larrabee on behalf of two clients – all "under penalty of perjury" – summed up the case against Kavanaugh this way:

> Kavanaugh received stolen information taken from Democratic members of the Senate Judiciary Committee while he worked in the White House and he perjured himself while testifying about the matter in Congress in 2004, 2006 and 2018. Kavanaugh violated Canons 1 and 2 of Code of Judicial Conduct by committing crimes of dishonesty while he was a federal judge, by obtaining confirmation of his appointment as a federal judge by false and perjurious testimony, by concealing and covering up his criminal actions and by obstructing justice. He is unfit to serve as a judge by reason of his corrupt, unscrupulous, dishonest and criminal conduct.

This indictment is followed by five pages of factual allegations citing chapter and verse of some of Kavanaugh's perjurious representations. The complaint concluded with a call for an investigation leading to a recommendation to Congress:

... that Kavanaugh be impeached in accordance with Rules 20 and 23 of the Rules for Judicial-conduct and Judicial-Disability Proceedings.

This is only one of a reported 15 or more formal ethics complaints made about Kavanaugh before the Dr. Blasey Ford farce or his confirmation to the Supreme Court. All the complaints made their way to the chief judge of the Court of Appeals, DC Circuit, on which Kavanaugh then sat. That chief judge is Merrick Garland, whose own appointment to the Supreme Court in 2016 was stonewalled by Mitch McConnell and Senate Republicans (illegitimately making the seat available to usurper Neil Gorsuch). Garland, faced with the complaints against Kavanaugh, did the non-partisan thing and recused himself, leaving the first assessment of the complaints to someone else.

According to an October 6 press release from DC Circuit judge Karen LeCraft Henderson (a Bush appointee and Kavanaugh's colleague on the bench):

> After the start of Judge Brett Kavanaugh's confirmation hearings, members of the general public began filing complaints in the D.C. Circuit about statements made during those hearings. The complaints do not pertain to any conduct in which Judge Kavanaugh engaged as a judge. The complaints seek investigations only of the public statements he has made as a nominee to the Supreme Court of the United States.

This characterization is misleading if not just false. The complaints *may* only refer to false public statements (most of the complaints have not been made public), but those false public statements were in fact made by a sitting judge (just not while he was in court, apparently). Judge Henderson is implicitly arguing for a judicial standard that allows judges to lie whenever they want when they're off the bench. This is not the standard of judicial temperament most of us thought we signed up for.

According to a letter from Chief Justice Roberts on October 10, he first heard officially about the Kavanaugh complaints starting on September 20. By October 6 he had received 15 complaints that were deemed worthy of review (it's uncertain how many, if any, were dismissed as frivolous). In conveying the complaints to the chief justice, Judge Henderson, concerned "that local disposition may weaken public confidence in the process," requested that the complaints be transferred to another circuit (as provided by Rule 26). In his October 10 letter, the chief justice did exactly that:

> I have selected the Judicial Council of the United States Court of Appeals for the Tenth Circuit to accept the transfer and to exercise the powers of a judicial council with respect to the identified complaints and any pending or new complaints relating to the same subject matter.

The chief judge of the 10th circuit, based in Denver, is Timothy M. Tymkovich (a Bush appointee). He was also on the White House short list with Kavanaugh. And now he is, at least for the moment, in charge of 15 or more Kavanaugh complaints. As of October 15, he had not yet announced how the complaints would be handled. Nor has he publicly addressed his own political bias or his clear conflict of interest in the matter. Early reporting on the Kavanaugh complaints has been somewhat sketchy and sometimes dismissive.

On October 4, the House Progressive Caucus sent a letter to the president in a last-ditch effort to have the Kavanagh nomination withdrawn. The letter, signed by 39 members of Congress, outlined Kavanaugh's partisan political past and his efforts to minimize or hide it. The letter demanded a full investigation of Kavanaugh's record and promised impeachment proceedings if the Senate's accusations of lying under oath were borne out. The letter concluded: "The credibility and reputation of the country's highest judicial body is at stake."

Even if the Kavanaugh complaints continue to get scant media coverage, the issue seems unlikely to go away. The Supreme Court is on trial and the chief justice knows it. He also knows that Rules for Judicial Conduct say unambiguously: "As long as the subject of the complaint performs judicial duties, a complaint alleging judicial misconduct *must* be addressed." [emphasis added] The chief justice also knows that

Kavanaugh's partisan outburst (quoted above) seems to clearly violate the judicial conduct rule against "making inappropriately partisan statements." The Supreme Court, led by a man with a reputation for defending institutional integrity, is faced with finding a way to justify its own probity – or join the rest of the wreckage of the Trump era.

30.

Supreme Court Sustains Compassion and Law by 5-4 Vote, for Now

"Any alien who is physically present in the United States or who arrives in the United States (whether or not at a designated port of arrival and including an alien who is brought to the United States after having been interdicted in international or United States waters), irrespective of such alien's status, may apply for asylum in accordance with this section or, where applicable, section 1225(b) of this title."

U.S. ASYLUM LAW, STATEMENT OF SCOPE (8 US CODE 1158 (A)(1))

United States asylum law, duly enacted by Congress and the president of the United States, has remained unchanged and largely unchallenged since 2008. The clearly stated intent of the law is to allow *any* alien physically present in the US to apply for asylum, in a legal process consistent with both international and federal law. The unstated subtext of the law is that the US should be a compassionate country where people fleeing oppression, persecution and violence may find a safe haven.

This one of America's founding myths, that we are a country of immigrants, in the best sense of the word. Despite glaring violations, the myth has served as the basis of consensus national policy until very recently. And it has been the settled law of the land.

On November 1, 2018, in a provocative and less than honest speech on immigration, President Trump set out on a campaign to change all that, as he challenged the law of the land and the constitutional process by which law is created. Masking the constitutional challenge, Trump distracted attention with threats that US military would kill asylum seekers if they threw stones. Despite his deliberate demagoguery, Trump's extreme language failed to have a discernible effect on the fall election.

On November 9, in the latest strike in his unrelenting war on immigrants, Trump issued a proclamation asserting that he, as president, had the unilateral authority to change any law passed by Congress – in this case, the asylum law. The proclamation implemented a 78-page "interim final rule" issued the previous day by the US Departments of Justice and Homeland Security. The Washington Post, adopting Trump's false framing, disingenuously and falsely headlined this move as "Trump administration tightens immigration asylum rules as caravans continue to push for US border." NBC News had a somewhat different take on the interim final rule:

> The Trump administration expects to be sued over the draconian new immigration plan it unveiled Thursday afternoon, say two senior administration officials with knowledge of the discussions — but with Justice Brett Kavanaugh now on the Supreme Court, it expects to win.

Lawsuits followed, as expected. In San Francisco, the ACLU (American Civil Liberties Union) promptly filed suit on behalf of four organizations involved with immigrant rights.

On November 20, US District Judge Jon Tigar issued a temporary restraining order that barred the administration from implementing the interim final rule until it had been fully litigated. In his ruling, Judge Tigar wrote:

> The rule barring asylum for immigrants who enter the country outside a port of entry irreconcilably conflicts with the INA [Immigration and Nationality Act of 1965] and the expressed intent of Congress. Whatever the scope of the President's authority, he may not rewrite the immigration laws to impose a condition that Congress has expressly forbidden.

The White House responded by attacking the judge for being appointed by President Obama. The White House also issued a statement falsely describing reality on the border and falsely representing the president's authority. The White House appealed to the full 9th US Circuit Court of Appeals to stay Judge Tigar's ruling. If granted, the stay would allow the White House to move forward with the interim final rule.

On December 8, a three-judge panel of the 9th Circuit upheld Judge Tigar and rejected the White House request. Writing for the unanimous court in a 65-page decision, Judge Jay Bybee (previously well known in the Bush administration for writing memos justifying torture) began by reiterating the legal and historical baseline for considering applications for asylum in the US:

> For more than 60 years, our country has agreed, by treaty, to accept refugees. In 1980, Congress codified our obligation to receive persons who are "unable or unwilling to return to" their home countries "because of persecution or a well-founded fear of persecution on account of race, religion, nationality, membership in a particular social group or political opinion. Congress prescribed a mechanism for these refugees to apply for asylum and said that we would accept applications from any alien "physically present in the United States or who arrives in the United States *whether or not at a designated port of arrival* ... irrespective of such alien's status. [Emphasis in original]

Judge Tigar's temporary restraining order lasted only until December 19, when he held a hearing on the White House appeal. After hearing argument from both sides, Judge Tigar concluded that "Plaintiffs [ACLU] have established an overwhelming likelihood that the new rule barring asylum is invalid." The judge then granted a preliminary injunction barring the White House from implementing unlawful restrictions on asylum seekers.

The White House had already applied to the Supreme Court to stay Judge Tigar's restraining order and allow the new rules to go forward. The Supreme Court rejected the request without comment on a 5-4 vote. The entire Supreme Court order reads:

> The application for stay presented to Justice Kagan and by her referred to the Court is denied. Justice Thomas, Justice Alito, Justice Gorsuch, and Justice Kavanaugh would grant the application for stay.

It's not really news that Justices Thomas, Alito, Gorsuch and Kavanaugh have no objection to the president rewriting Congressional legislation on his own, without review even by the judiciary. These men are all well known for their shaky adherence to constitutional law when the opportunity to support authoritarianism presents itself.

Nor is it really news that Justices Kagan, Ginsberg, Sotomayor and Breyer come down in support of the rule of law.

The news – and it really looks like good news – is that Chief Justice John G. Roberts is the swing vote here in opposition to legislation by presidential diktat. As NBC News reported, the White House expected to win this in the Supreme Court. We should be grateful that their expectation was wrong, at least for now. The asylum case is far from over. The White House is almost surely going to go on trying to create a presidential dictatorship. But for now, we're still one justice shy of the end of constitutional government.

31.

Court Uses Law's Absurdity to Allow Unfit Kavanaugh to Remain as Justice

"The allegations contained in the complaints [against Judge Kavanaugh] are serious, but the Judicial Council is obligated to adhere to the Act. Lacking statutory authority to do anything more, the complaints must be dismissed because an intervening event – Justice Kavanaugh's confirmation to the Supreme Court – has made the complaints no longer appropriate for consideration under the Act.... Because it lacks jurisdiction to do so, the Council makes no findings on the merits of the complaints."

ORDER OF THE JUDICIAL COUNCIL OF THE US TENTH CIRCUIT,
DECEMBER 18, 2018

That is the sound that eight federal judges make when they know full-well they're doing something rotten but can't bring themselves to defend the integrity of their own judicial system.

This order deals with complaints against federal judge Brett Kavanaugh, whose reputation for perjurious testimony is documented at least as far back as 2004. Last summer, the US Senate gave only cursory attention to whether Kavanaugh had repeatedly lied under oath on a variety of occasions, including the Senate judiciary committee hearings of 2018. Kavanaugh was a federal district judge from May 30, 2006, until October 6, 2018, when he was sworn in as a Supreme Court justice. At that time, the majority of 83 ethical conduct complaints addressing his behavior as a district judge had already been filed. In an unusual procedure, the Tenth Circuit Judicial Council has made these 83 complaints public on its website, while concealing the identities of the complainants.

The first batch of Kavanaugh complaints went to the DC Circuit, which passed them to Supreme Court Chief Justice John Roberts, who passed them on to the Tenth Circuit on October 10. At that time, I wrote in Reader Supported News that the credibility of the US judicial system was the core issue in the Kavanaugh case:

> The stakes are as high as they are simple: Will our court system choose to defend the position one of its own members or will it choose to defend the integrity of the US judicial system? There is no possibility it can do both with any credibility.

This is still true, as the Kavanaugh complaints appear headed back to the Chief Justice's lap for further action, or inaction.

It took the eight judges of the Tenth Circuit Judicial Council just over two months to decide to do nothing about any of the 83 misconduct complaints against Judge Kavanaugh. Worse, the court's order asserted in a strained legal argument that there was nothing that *could* be done legally about the 83 misconduct complaints against Judge Kavanaugh for one reason, and one reason only – because he had become Justice Kavanaugh. That's the whole argument: that Kavanaugh gets to escape judicial accountability, and his getaway car is his seat on the Supreme Court. This is cultural madness and legal absurdity. What were those Tenth Circuit judges thinking?

What they actually do is create a legal fiction, starting with a false assertion in the first sentence: "Complaints of judicial misconduct have been filed against Supreme Court Justice Brett M. Kavanaugh...." In fact, most of the complaints were filed against Kavanaugh when he was a district judge. All the complaints cite judicial misconduct by Kavanaugh as a district judge. The false statement of reality is necessary to support the wonderland the judges need to escape dealing with what the court saw as the substance of the charges:

> ... that Justice [sic] Kavanaugh made false statements during his nomination proceedings to the D.C. Circuit in 2004 and 2006 and to the Supreme Court in 2018; made inappropriate partisan statements that demonstrate bias and a lack of judicial temperament; and treated members of the Senate Judiciary Committee with disrespect.

Much of this is beyond reasonable dispute. Both professional and lay witnesses abound. More than 2,400 law professors are on record opposing Kavanaugh as unfit to serve on the Supreme Court. Even Kavanaugh has acknowledged and quasi-apologized for some of the behavior in the 83 complaints. The Tenth Circuit judges acknowledge that the complaints are "serious" but then choose to make "no findings on the merits of the complaints." How is this not deliberate judicial malpractice?

The answer to that is a legal quibble. According to the Tenth Circuit judges, the applicable statute for federal district judges is not applicable to Supreme Court justices. This is certainly true in the sense that if the complaints made against Kavanaugh referred to his behavior as a justice, the statute would not apply. The statute is the Judicial Conduct and Disability Act, 28 USC 351 *et seq.*, which applies specifically to federal circuit judges, district judges, bankruptcy judges and magistrate judges. It is one of the abiding scandals of American government that the Supreme Court is subject to no rules of ethics of its own and that Congress has done little to remedy the ridiculous result: that those with the most authority, are held the least accountable. Or as the Tenth Circuit judges put it:

> ... the complaints must be dismissed because, *due to his elevation to the Supreme Court,* Justice Kavanaugh is no longer a judge covered by the Act. See 28 USC 352(b)(1)(A)(i). [emphasis added]

The court thereby creates a reality in which:

(1) Over a period of 13 years as a judge, Kavanaugh committed objectionable acts;

(2) Complaints were lawfully filed in response to his objectionable acts;

(3) Some complaints were based on objectionable acts Kavanaugh committed before he was a circuit judge and subject to the Act, but these complaints were not dismissed;

(4) Despite unambiguous jurisdiction at the time of the acts and unambiguous jurisdiction at the time of the filing of the complaints, the Tenth Circuit claims it's helpless to act.

The Tenth Circuit does not explain, or even address, this absurdity. The court's order argues that "The Act thus applies only to complaints that allege that one of those covered judges [which Kavanaugh was] 'has engaged in conduct prejudicial to the effective and expeditious administration of the courts'" [which Kavanaugh patently did as a circuit judge]. The court holds that whatever Kavanaugh did as a judge that was complained about while he was still a judge can all be ignored because of an "intervening event," such as a judge's death. Kavanaugh did not die, although he kind of went to heaven. The court cites Rule 11(e) to justify its abdication of anything like the rule of law. Rule 11(e) in its entirety says:

> Intervening Events. The chief judge may conclude the complaint proceeding in whole or in part upon determining that intervening events render some or all of the allegations moot or make remedial action impossible.

Kavanaugh's elevation to the high court did not make any of the complaints moot. If anything, his elevation made them more pertinent than ever. Kavanaugh's elevation to the high court hardly made remedial action impossible, although it probably makes remedial action more difficult. The court's order cites four precedents for its action, three of which are irrelevant (involving judges who were transferred, retired, or whose objectionable behavior was before becoming a judge). The one relevant citation involves several judges for whom the dismissed complaint is ruled "frivolous" as well as Supreme Court Justice Clarence Thomas, who is dismissed "for want of jurisdiction" as a sitting justice. The relevance here is about as slim as it gets, comparing one "frivolous" complaint to Justice Kavanaugh's 83 complaints acknowledged by the court to be "serious."

As described by the court's order, the judicial council held no hearings, examined no evidence for its probative value, or otherwise investigated any of the 83 complaints against Kavanaugh. The court dismissed those complaints solely on the tenuous jurisdictional basis that they were out of the court's reach. The court chose not to discuss any other possibly more judicious responses to the prickly Kavanaugh case, leaving the country still saddled with a justice palpably unfit for his office.

The court defended its conclusion by noting that Congress, in other instances, had indeed included justices under its statutes and offered as an example 28 US Code 455 – "Disqualification of justice, judge, or magistrate judge." This statute is likely to become increasingly important as long as Kavanaugh remains on the bench, since it mandates that a justice "shall disqualify himself in any proceeding in which his impartiality might reasonably be questioned." Kavanaugh's televised performance of personal bias against Democrats and his stated conspiracy beliefs should be enough to disqualify him from a wide range of political cases. With 83 serious conduct complaints to be examined, it might take less time to assess what cases there are where Kavanaugh could reasonably *avoid* disqualification.

Nor is the impeachment of Justice Kavanaugh off the table. That's a distant outcome under present circumstances, but as the court's order notes in its penultimate paragraph:

> The importance of ensuring *that governing bodies with clear jurisdictions are aware of the complaints* should also be acknowledged. See Nat'l Comm'n on Judicial Discipline and Removal, "Report of the Nat'l Comm'n on Judicial Discipline & Removal," 152 F.R.D. 265, 342-43 (1994). Accordingly, we request that the Committee on Judicial Conduct and Disability of the Judicial Conference of the United States *forward a copy of this Order to any relevant Congressional committees* for their information. [emphasis added]

For now, the Republican judicial atrocity represented by Justice Kavanaugh sits undisturbed. The Tenth Circuit's order is subject to appeal until January 29, 2019. As of January 9, a Tenth Circuit court spokesperson declined to say if any appeal had yet been filed, citing appellant confidentiality. One of the self-identified complainants, retired attorney Larry Behrendt, filed his five-page complaint October 2, concluding:

> Judge Kavanaugh made repeated, inappropriate partisan statements to the Senate Judiciary Committee during his testimony on September 28, and is thus guilty of misconduct under the Act [28 USC 351ff]

and the Rules. This misconduct is particularly egregious, as it took place in front of millions of people, at a time when scrutiny of the law and the judiciary is at its highest, and where Kavanaugh had a clear duty to display judicial temperament and deportment.

After the Tenth Circuit Judicial Council skirted any serious consideration of Behrendt's complaint or the 82 others, the attorney published an op-ed explaining why he thought the court was wrong. He noted that the law is silent on how to handle a nexus of offenses under transitional circumstances like Kavanaugh's. That hardly makes it likely that the intent of Congress was to give a lying partisan a free pass to the Supreme Court. Behrendt says he hasn't decided whether to appeal the Tenth Circuit order. Maybe the Tenth Circuit will find some backbone. Maybe the chief justice will care more about his court's integrity than the slippery hack who is its newest member.

Until *someone* finds the courage to confront the truth of this legal fiasco the rest of us are stuck with a lifetime travesty of justice.

Update 2019: The handling of Kavanaugh's 83 judicial conduct complaints has turned into a spectacle judicial due process as farce, with no happy ending in sight.

In March 2019, a 6-1 majority of the Tenth Circuit Judicial Council reviewed its own initial decision and declared it to be just fine. One Judge entered a dissent, arguing that it was improper for the council to consider an appeal of its own decision. Another judge recused himself, on the basis that reviewing his own decision would be a conflict of interest.

In April 2019, several petitions challenging the Tenth Circuit's decisions were filed with the federal Committee on Judicial Conduct and Disability. That committee, citing "confidentiality," refuses to reveal the number, nature, or authors of any petitions.

A fundamental issue going unaddressed is the probity of a system that allows a judge to avoid the consequences of misconduct by retiring, resigning, or most absurdly, being elevated to the Supreme Court.

In December 2018, Judge Alex Kozinski retired to avoid being investigated for allegations of sexual misconduct.

In April 2019, Judge Maryanne Trump Barry – the president's older sister – retired to avoid being investigated for committing tax fraud.

The judicial follies of the Tenth Circuit have allowed Judge Kavanaugh to avoid accountability for 83 judicial conduct complaints (some filed while he was still a judge) solely because he was elevated to the Supreme Court. It is ritual judicial rhetoric that the court should avoid absurd results. Never mind.

Despite secrecy of the Committee on Judicial Conduct, two petitioners have revealed themselves and their petitions. New York lawyer Jeremy Bates, a member of the New York City Bar Association committee on professional ethics, argues that the Tenth Circuit "entirely failed to analyze the real issue," whether judicial misconduct should be judged as of the time a complaint is filed. Non-lawyer Paul Horvitz, a financial news editor, argues that the Tenth Circuit committed ignored its clear responsibility (under Rule 18) to analyze the propriety of Kavanaugh's conduct regardless of any ability to sanction it.

Presumably Chief Justice John Roberts and much of the rest of the federal judiciary hope the issue of Kavanaugh's judicial misconduct will somehow disappear into the swamp of federal procedure, never to be seen again. That hope would be a violation of a judge's oath of office and that would a direct rejection of the best interests of the nation.

32.

Swing Vote for Bigotry, Chief Justice Roberts Strikes Again

"Openly transgender persons have been serving in the military for two and a half years and leaders from each branch have testified that their service has not harmed the military. Although the government cries that the sky is falling, it has offered no evidence to support its dire claims."

WASHINGTON ATTORNEY GENERAL BOB FERGUSON

Here's another level of madness: The Supreme Court ruled on January 22 that the Trump administration could force the Pentagon to adopt bigoted transgender policies, even though a lower court had already held the policies likely to be unconstitutional. The swing vote putting the court on record supporting baseless discrimination was Chief Justice John Roberts. Roberts could as easily have voted on the side of tolerance and the rule of law. His decision looks cowardly. It is unexplained. The court offers no argument – none – to support its decision. The court offers no supporting evidence to justify its arbitrary and capricious reinstatement of gender bias as a lawful policy under the Constitution. And the body politic, never mind the general public, hardly responds at all to an action that replaces due process of law with government by decree to which there is no avenue of appeal. Governance by tweet has brought us to a place of judicial anarchy.

In the ordinary course of events, a plaintiff – here, several transgender soldiers affected by the Trump administration's ban – will file a case seeking to block (or overturn) an action in federal district court. Typically, cases will be decided first at the district court level, then appealed to a higher court where it is affirmed or reversed (or some of both). Only after this careful process builds a solid record of evidence and argument will the Supreme Court even consider hearing a further appeal. Out of some 7,000 appeals to the Supreme Court each year, it decides maybe 130 (holding hearings on about 80). It is extremely rare for the court to deviate from this orderly process. The Supreme Court's rules allow such deviation "only upon a showing that the case is of such imperative public importance as to justify deviation from normal appellate practice and to require immediate determination in this court." [Rule 11] The court identified no such "imperative public importance," but for some reason allowed these transgender bias cases to jump the line.

On January 22, the Supreme Court threw out regular procedure, without explanation. The court issued orders in two cases – *Trump v. Karnoski, et al.* (18A625) and *Trump v. Stockman, et al.* (18A627). The cases are similar but come from different jurisdictions in California and Washington. The initial plaintiffs (Karnoski, Stockman, et al.) won their case at the district level, where the court not only ruled in their favor voiding the transgender ban, but also issued an injunction preventing the government from implementing the ban before the litigation was completed. The government appealed the decision but did not appeal the injunction issued December 11 (or the one issued December 22). That is an indication that there was no arguable emergency in December 2018.

In issuing the injunctions, the district courts also found, on the record, that the government's forcing the military to adopt a transgender ban was likely to be found unconstitutional by higher courts.

As defendants in a companion case, *Trump v. Jane Doe 2* (December 2018), argued:

> The district court correctly concluded that the government's ban on military service by transgender individuals is likely to be found unconstitutional and that a preliminary injunction is necessary to prevent irreparable harm to respondents while the parties work toward final resolution of respondents' claims on the merits.

The merits are what should matter in any legal proceeding that purports to be a search for truth. The district court issued its injunction after concluding the government's transgender ban was likely unconstitutional, a substantive judgment on the merits. The Supreme Court, without considering the merits, lifted the injunction without explanation. How does this not corrupt the process below? How is this not a signal that five justices are ready to find transgender prejudice constitutional? How is this not a rather genteel but blatant obstruction of justice?

How did we get to this place of radical cruelty by an unaccountable, authoritarian court without raising a ruckus among those who still pretend the Constitution means something? The court has a solid bloc of reactionary justices in the quartet of Thomas, Alito, Kavanaugh and Gorsuch, all of whom voted for the transgender ban. Roberts chose to join them, just as he chose to join the reactionaries in 2013 in gutting the Voting Rights Act when he preposterously argued that racial bias was a thing of the American past. Since that case, *Shelby County v. Holder*, almost 1000 polling places have been closed, mostly in minority districts, one of the more obvious tools of racist voter suppression enabled by the Supreme Court.

The justices voting to defend voting rights included Ruth Bader Ginsburg, who wrote a dissent joined by Justices Breyer, Sotomayor and Kagan. These same four justices voted this year to maintain the injunction against the military transgender ban.

What is it with Roberts that, faced with a clear opportunity to vote for democratic process, for inclusion, for tolerance, he opts for repression and bigotry? In gutting the Voting Rights Act, Roberts voted against allowing despised minorities to participate as political equals in a society he pretends is colorblind. He voted in denial of reality and in disregard of Congressional findings. With the transgender cases, he again chooses bigotry over decency and he again votes to undermine constitutional processes, this time of the US judicial system. What kind of legacy is he building?

There are maybe 15,000 transgender military personnel on active or reserve duty now, no one knows for sure. There are maybe 134,000 transgender military veterans. The Supreme Court has unsettled their futures, with no guideline for how anyone should proceed. All the court did was lift injunctions, and that may not take effect before the end of February. After that, no one is required to do anything. The Defense Department, facing no immediate crisis it can see, does not have to reinstate the transgender ban in its previous or any other form. There is concern that any significant change from the status quo would create a crisis of its own. A Pentagon spokesman said with careful fuzziness:

> It is critical [that the Defense Department] be permitted to implement personnel policies that it determines are necessary to ensure the most lethal and combat effective fighting force in the world.

Transgender personnel have served in the military since the American Revolution. For most of that time, the military treated the issue with a blind eye. More recently, as more and more minority groups struggled for rights and self-respect, openly bigoted resistance came out of other closets. At the urging of evangelical Christians, Trump placated them with his July 26, 2017, tweet: "that the United States Government will not accept or allow Transgender individuals to serve in any capacity in the US Military..." This caught the Pentagon by surprise, setting off the policy chaos the Supreme Court just added to.

The transgender community has reacted with predictable fierceness, since the administration seems bent on their metaphorical if not literal extinction. In a powerful New York Times op-ed, 1997 Annapolis graduate and transgender Navy Air Force pilot Brynn Tannehill describes the recent evolution of humane policy, a process in which she participated. She also describes her effort to return to active duty, apparently sabotaged by the Supreme Court, and adds:

> All of this makes the administration's dogged attempt to undo everything achieved over the last few years even more baffling. The ban was developed in secret, without the sort of careful study that went into the policy it reversed. It does not reflect any current medical understanding of transgender people, and it has been denounced by the American Medical Association, the American Psychological Association and the American Psychiatric Association.
>
> No one, including the lawyers for the Trump administration, has been able to show that inclusion of transgender service members or

providing care to them has had any measurable negative impact on morale, readiness or unit cohesion.

The bigotry of the Trump administration and now the Supreme Court is so palpable as to seem perhaps a distraction from something else, but what? US Solicitor General Noel Francisco offers a possible higher stake in his filing on the transgender cases. In a single passing sentence without further amplification, the solicitor general complains:

> The accelerating trend of lower courts' enjoining enforcement of federal policies nationwide, including as to nonparties, reflects an abandonment of settled principles and underscores the need for this Court's review.

This is not your average throwaway line. It is a sweeping attack on the court system in general for its efforts to protect the American people – those annoying "nonparties" – from unconstitutional power grabs by this administration. The shibboleth of "activist" judges has long been a staple of right-wing propaganda, but now it's shape-shifted into an attack on courts who defend the nation against "enforcement of federal policies" when those federal policies fail to meet constitutional or legislative standards. (As one judge wrote: "Whatever the scope of the President's authority, he may not rewrite the immigration laws to impose a condition that Congress has expressly forbidden.") Who better to rid the president of these troublesome judges than a Supreme Court well-stocked with ideologues who believe in the expansion of executive power? With this ugly decision in favor of transgender bigotry, the court also sends a message to lower courts: if you go too far checking the president's power then we'll have to disempower you – human decency, justice, those are a chump's game.

33.

NO Biden – Some of the reasons why NOT Biden

"We are in the battle for the soul of this nation.... But if we give Donald Trump eight years in the White House, he will forever and fundamentally alter the character of this nation, who we are, and I cannot stand by and watch that happen."

– JOE BIDEN'S CAMPAIGN ANNOUNCEMENT VIDEO (3:30), APRIL 25, 2019

Biden's candidacy announcement video is an elaborate exercise in false consciousness, opening with a misleading invocation of the Declaration of Independence. He never mentions the Constitution. The video segues into a shameless bit of soulless exploitation, manipulation, and misrepresentation of the racial events in Charlottesville in 2017. The portentous music together with Biden's funereal tone work hard to create the sense that there was meaning and substance where there was neither. Biden can only fake gravitas. He goes on and on about "American values" and "who we are" without naming a specific value or saying who he thinks we are. This is political pandering in the form of a Rorschach blot. This is crude demagoguery that boils down to an appeal to elect a familiar under-achiever just because he's NOT Trump.

Last time anyone looked, ALL the candidates were NOT Trump. And a good many of them actually stand for both articulated values and thought-out policies to put them into practice.

Most of Biden's career has been spent standing by and letting things happen, things that attest to the historic character of "who we are," but are anywhere from not admirable to despicable. Biden's announcement video suggests that Biden would promote racial healing. He never has before, why would anyone believe he could now?

179

Trump calls Biden "Sleepy Joe." That's actually a compliment in the context of his record. "Sloppy Joe" would be more apt. Trump grabs women by the pussy, Biden grabs women by the shoulders. There's a difference, but they're both grabbers. Maybe the most realistic thing to call him is "Creepy Joe."

In reality, Biden has been horrendously awake and active on the wrong side of too many issues. Here are some of them, unranked.

Biden actively supported the Iraq War, helping President Bush lie the country into war.

Biden actively supports the Afghanistan War and always has. He supports drone strikes and CIA-trained death squads without any apparent concern for civilians maimed and killed.

Biden is silent on Saudi Arabia's criminal war on Yemen, green-lighted by President Obama.

Biden has advocated a non-specific "military solution" for Syria, but not recently.

Biden's son Hunter had lucrative interests in Ukraine that were under investigation by Ukraine's top prosecutor. Biden has boasted of leaning on Ukraine President Poroshenko, who fired the prosecutor.

Biden backed the aggressive and deceitful eastern expansion of NATO, knowing it would likely lead to unnecessary confrontation with Russia.

Biden has long supported tax cuts for the rich.

Biden supports cutting Medicare and Social Security.

Biden voted for the banking "reforms" that loosened banking regulation and opened the way to the 2008 crash.

Biden actively supported credit card companies and other lenders in their efforts to gouge the public with usurious interest rates and other debt enforcement mechanisms.

Biden has supported the War on Drugs through all its failed permutations. He opposes any legalization of marijuana.

Biden opposed bussing to integrate schools, without offering any alternative to promote integration. He joined with racist Senators Jesse Helms and Strom Thurmond to craft regressive "bipartisan" legislation. He falsely claimed to have once been a civil rights activist.

Biden has been a relentless demagogue on crime issues. He has been comfortable with their underlying racist bias, contributing to the massive, unjust incarceration that enriches private corporations. Biden pushed for harsh minimum sentencing, not justice. He supported civil asset forfeiture. He voted for racist sentencing for possession of crack cocaine (harsh for blacks) and powder cocaine (light for whites).

Biden has backed numerous new death penalty laws.

Biden has claimed, falsely, that he has the most progressive record of any candidate.

Biden is not a firm supporter of a woman's right to choose.

Biden has yet to offer anything positive and humane with regard to immigration. Biden has backed draconian deportation law and police state tactics of border enforcement.

Biden has backed US policies that have made Central America unlivable, including support for the military coup in Honduras.

Biden voted for NAFTA.

Biden was the chair of the Senate Judiciary Committee during Supreme Court nominee Clarence Thomas's hearings. Biden treated Anita Hill abysmally. Worse, Biden refused to call corroborating witness who would have supported Hill's account of Thomas's awfulness. Biden is singularly responsible for one of the least qualified justices in our history. And recently, creepy Biden called Hill to say he regretted what she went through. But he didn't apologize and has yet to accept personal responsibility for his own actions. He has yet to attempt anything to atone for them.

Biden is a corporate money candidate. His first campaign fundraiser was a lobbyist-rich event at the home of a Comcast executive, signaling Biden's opposition to net neutrality.

If Biden has any new – never mind progressive – views on health care, criminal justice, education, climate change, war, or any other important issue, he has yet to articulate any of them.

Does Biden stand for anything concrete that you care about?

Biden is like Trump-Lite. Biden may be no more than Trump polite. Biden is a substantively empty vessel with a shiny self-reflecting surface.

Biden pitches himself as a "return to normalcy." A close reading of his record would define "normalcy" as endless war, endless racial divide, endless injustice, endless enriching the rich, endless grabbing heads and pressing noses as if that were some token of sincerity and authenticity.

Running as the NOT-Trump is a reasonable approach for most candidates, but for Biden, it's ridiculous. Biden has no identifiable attribute that will move the country forward toward a better, more honest, more civilized condition.

Biden was once, perhaps, "who we are" in a negative sense of the phrase. Now he's who we were, and that's how it should remain, for the sake of the soul of the nation.

PART THREE

Coming to America

ILLEGAL IMMIGRATION BEGAN IN 1492

34.

US Detains Dreamers in Solitary Confinement

Solitary confinement is a form of torture, all torturers agree

The United States officially opposes the humanitarian parole of nine young people who grew up in this country, but came here as children without proper documentation. Now matured, they are acting like citizens and committing civil disobedience against the laws that stigmatize them as un-people.

For these Americans-in-all-but-papers-please, the US government's Department of Homeland Security has decided, without due process apparently, that the Constitution's 8th Amendment prohibition against excessive bail or cruel and unusual punishment may be disregarded with impunity.

While this is just another routine constitutional crisis obscured from most Americans, it's a vivid illustration of the moral brutality with which the American government acts almost reflexively in response to immigration issues – issues it has spent decades making little effort to fix, for fear of depriving politically generous agribusiness and other corporate employers of cheap, semi-slave labor.

As of July 29, the Dream 9 had been jailed for a week in Arizona, at the Eloy Detention Center. Six of the Dream 9 are in solitary confinement as punishment for the hunger-strike they undertook in protest against Corrections Corporation of America's denial of telephone access to their lawyers and family. The Corrections Corporation of America is a publicly traded, for-profit company contracted by the US government, which apparently sanctions torture by this contractor. Solitary confinement is internationally recognized as an element of torture.

185

Government Decides How to Enforce the Law, Doesn't Explain

Homeland Security, Immigration and other officials refuse to discuss these cases. Eloy Detention Center's officials did not respond to a request for information. Reportedly officials will meet with detainees early in the week.

The Homeland Security website as of July 29 offered a policy statement that says, in part, regarding Deferred Action for Childhood Arrivals (DACA):

> As the Department of Homeland Security (DHS) continues to focus its enforcement resources on the removal of individuals who pose a danger to national security or a risk to public safety, including individuals convicted of crimes with particular emphasis on violent criminals, felons, and repeat offenders, *DHS will exercise prosecutorial discretion as appropriate to ensure that enforcement resources are not expended on low priority cases, such as individuals who came to the United States as children....*" [emphasis added]

All nine members of the Dream 9 being held in Eloy prison first came to the United States as children under 16, one as young as four months old.

The Dream 9 Protest Started with the Dreamers in Graduation Garb

On July 22, they were all wearing graduation caps and gowns, signifying their high school and college diplomas and degrees, as they walked from the Mexican side of the border in Nogales to the US immigration offices, where they sought to re-enter the US legally.

Six of them had come to this country as children and had lived most of their lives here, becoming American in almost every way but legally, eventually getting caught up in the byzantine application of immigration law enforcement that effectively exiled them from their own country. The other three members of the Dream 9 voluntarily left the US in order to take part in this action, to highlight the injustice of US immigration law and to test the government's ability to exercise prosecutorial discretion and to act justly.

At the US immigration office in Nogales, the Americans promptly took the Dream 9 into custody, even though each of them presented officials with documents that supported their individual stories, along with formal requests for admission to the US.

Tucson attorney Margo Cowan represented the Dream 9 and formally asked the federal officials to grant each of the nine a humanitarian parole, which would allow them to return home in the US to await formal proceedings. She argued that her clients were not a flight risk and wanted only to go home and continue their lives. Each of the Dream 9 also requested asylum in the US, a request the US has ignored, unlawfully.

The Private Prison Contractor Has an Ugly Public Reputation

The government promptly and arbitrarily denied every request, without holding any hearing. The government sent the nine to prison, first in Florence and then to the private prison run by the for-profit Corrections Corporation in Eloy. The nine remained there as of July 29, six of them in solitary confinement, with no action scheduled on their cases.

The Eloy prison has a horrific reputation as a savage place going back at least as far as 2007, when detainee deaths in Homeland Security custody drew attention even from the New York Times. Already this year there have been two more detainee deaths, apparent hanging suicides by two men aged 24 and 40. At least one other prisoner, a US military veteran, is currently being force-fed because he was on a hunger strike.

The website DREAM ACTIVIST: The Undocumented Students Action & Resource Network offers brief biographies of some of the Dream 9, whom some now consider prisoners of conscience or political prisoners:

- Claudia Amaro, 37, from Monterrey, Mexico, moved to Colorado when she was thirteen years old. Her mother fled Mexico after her father was murdered and the family was threatened. In 2006, while living in Wichita, Kansas, Claudia's husband was detained while driving to work. ICE detained Claudia while she was interpreting for her husband. Living in Mexico has been hard for Claudia and her thirteen-year-old US citizen son. Finally, her mother gained legal status last year and was able to visit her grandson for the first time in seven years. Claudia is coming home to put the family that deportation tore apart back together.

- Adriana Diaz, 22, from Mexico City, first came to Phoenix, Arizona, when she was just four months old. Adriana graduated from Crestview Preparatory High School in 2010 with many accolades, including the Citizenship Award. To this day, two of her murals decorate the school's walls. Adriana left Phoenix three months before DACA was announced. She left because she was tired of living in fear under County Sheriff Arpaio, not knowing each night if her mom was going to come home. Once in Nogales, Adriana tried to go to school. Because she had lived so long in the US, Mexico recognized her as a foreign student and would not accept her US degree. Instead of going to school, Adriana has been working with migrants at the Juan Bosco shelter in Sonora. Adriana is coming home because she has no memories in Mexico. Her entire life was in Phoenix. She has memories of school, birthdays, going to prom ... even her partner of four years lives in Phoenix. Everyone deserves to come home.

- Luis Gustavo, 20, from Michoacán, Mexico, has lived in North Carolina since he was five years old. He graduated from McDowell High School. Luis left Marion, North Carolina, in August 2011 with the hopes of being able to finally go to school in Mexico. Luis, unable to stand being away from his family, tried to come home in June 2012 when the Deferred Action for Childhood Arrivals (DACA) program was announced. Luis never made it; he was caught by border patrol. The responding agent sympathized with him, and filed for DACA on his behalf, but saw it rejected. Luis was subsequently deported.

Desperate to come home, Luis attempted to re-enter three more times, and failed on each attempt. Luis is coming home to be with his mother, sister and four brothers.

- Maria Peniche, 22, from Mexico City, first came to Boston when she was just ten years old. She graduated from Revere High School in 2010 and went on to attend Pine Manor College. By 2012, paying the high price of tuition became too difficult, and she dropped out. Three days before DACA was announced, Maria left for Mexico to continue her schooling. "Here in Mexico you can only do one thing, either work or go to school," she said. Maria has had to put off her studies and work in order to provide for her family. Maria is coming home to provide for herself and her family and to pursue her education.

- Ceferino Santiago, 21, came to Lexington, Kentucky, at the age of thirteen in order to be with his older brother, Pedro. Ceferino is a permanent part of the Lexington community; he helped paint a mural at one of the local middle schools. During high school, Ceferino ran for the school cross-country team and was honored as one of the program's top student athletes in 2010. After graduating from high school, Ceferino was forced to return to Oaxaca, Mexico, because of an ear infection which required surgery that cost $21,000. Ceferino is coming home so he can be with his brother, his community and to continue with his studies.

- A sixth member is Mario Felix, who joined this action at the last minute. He is currently being held in solitary confinement, along with Claudia Amaro and Ceferino Santiago. All three are currently in solitary confinement.

- The other three members of the Dream 9 all voluntarily left the US in order to take part in this demonstration of immigration injustice.

- Lizbeth Mateo came to the US before she was 16 and grew up in Los Angeles. Before returning for the Dream 9 action, she had not seen her family in 15 years.

- Lulu Martinez, who came to the US at the age of three, has spent years as an activist for justice in immigration rights and LGBT rights.

- Marco Saavedra is a poet and painter who graduated from Kenyon College in Ohio. Before joining the Dream 9, he worked at his family's restaurant in New York City. He came to the US before he was 16.

Dream 9 attorney says government policy amounts to "A War on the Poor"

The attorney representing the Dream 9 is a long-time activist for immigrants' rights and is a staff attorney at the Pima County Public Defender's office, where her biography is posted:

> Margo Cowan – Graduate of the Antioch School of Law, Washington D.C., 1985; admitted to the State Bar of Pennsylvania in 1986; admitted to the State Bar of Arizona in 1995; substantial experience as an attorney in general immigration practice since 1986; General Counsel, Tohono O'odham Nation 1993-2003; Of Counsel, Congressman Raul Grijalva, 2004; extensive pro bono work, mainly in the areas of border/immigration policy development and representation of undocumented persons and refugees; Defense Attorney in the Law Offices of the Pima County Public Defender since 2004. In March 2007, the National Association for Social Workers – AZ Branch II awarded Margo with the Cesar Chavez Humanitarian Award for her dedication in advancing human rights for over thirty-five years. An example of this dedication is her co-founding of the group No More Deaths. This group provides assistance to migrants returning from the US to the border towns of Mexico, and their sole purpose is to reduce the amount [sic] of deaths in the Arizona Desert.

In a book published in 2010 by Beacon Press, "The Death of Josseline: Immigration Stories from the Arizona Borderlands," author Margaret Regan refers to Cowan as "the indefatigable pro bono attorney for No More Deaths." Regan quotes Cowan as describing US immigration policy as "a war on the poor."

About her own work, Cowan said: "Everything we do is transparent. We're just a group of people who think migrants shouldn't die in the desert on their way to clean toilets."

> **Note:** At the time of this artile, an unsympathetic reader wrote uncomprehendingly that: "They are only in detention since they refused to return to their real home which is Mexico." I responded that he was wrong, adding:
>
> They did not choose to break the law.
>
> They were brought here as children.
>
> They are being punished by a government that is too feckless to get its own act together.
>
> Are we really such a cold country with so little empathy?
>
> **Update 2019:** On August 7, 2013, the Dream 9 were released from Eloy. In 2015 they were the subject of an NPR Latino USA documentary. Details of their lives since 2013 are scarce.
>
> Claudia Amaro was granted temporary asylum in 2013. Her husband, Hector Yaujar, was held for two and a half years before being released and granted temporary asylum in 2015. He had been deported for driving without a license. While in Mexico he was kidnapped for ransom. As of 2018, Amaro was living with her family in Wichita, Kansas, where she continues her DACA activism, has a weekly radio show, and goes to college part time
>
> While she was held at Eloy, Maria Peniche agitated for free legal counsel for the DREAM 9. Eloy responded by putting her in solitary confinement, where she ended up on suicide watch. As of 2014 she was living with her family in Boston and going to college on a scholarship.
>
> In March 2018, attorney Lizbeth Mateo, a Santa Clara University graduate, became the first undocumented immigrant appointed to a statewide position in California, as a member of the California Student Opportunity and Access Program Project Grant Advisory Committee (Cal-SOAP). Its mission is to help underserved communities send their children to college. Mateo is in private practice, having earned her law degree from Santa Clara in 2016.

On April 26, 2018, a Chicago immigration court judge granted Lulu Martinez permanent asylum in the US after she argued that as an outspoken lesbian and LGBT activist, she would not be safe in Mexico. Judge Eva Saltzman rejected the Homeland Security lawyer's argument that Mexico was safe because Mexico City had legalized same-sex marriage in 2010 and has "a vibrant gay community." Martinez graduated from University of Illinois at Chicago in 2017 with a degree in gender and women's studies.

Marco Saavedra graduated from Kenyon College in 2014. As of November 2016 he was working in his family's restaurant and living in the Bronx, New York.

35.

Children at the Border,
Another US Foreign Policy Debacle

This isn't theatre. This is a problem.
I'm not interested in photo ops.
I'm interested in solving the problem.

PRESIDENT OBAMA IN TEXAS, JULY 9, 2014

If he's saying he's too busy to go down to the border but you have time to
drink a beer, play pool, the appearance means that he's not paying attention
to this humanitarian crisis.

CONG. HENRY CUELLAR, TEXAS DEMOCRAT, JULY 9, 2014

Seeing through the tear-jerking to the guilty U.S. government

The pictures of thousands of children huddled in shelters are upsetting, and the tales some tell are horrifying, and that is all a real but
sentimental distraction from the entrenched American power that
created these conditions. American power uses these children and
their families and their countries for its own ends. American power
is not likely to make any meaningful changes to solve what is essentially a permanent crisis. Whatever official alleviation there is will
be just enough to get those heart-rending images off the front pages,
so that the profitable stream of human exploitation can be managed
more "effectively." American power insists that these are "illegal immigrants," rather than face the reality that they are refugees from the
exercise of American power.

So, it's no wonder President Obama doesn't want to have his picture taken amid the terrible results of American policy at work. It's

a policy to which he has been as much a guilty party as every other president at least since Polk. By his actions over the years, the president appears committed to the U.S. imperial role in the world, especially in "our backyard." There is little serious debate among the governing classes, who seem to feel their mandate is expressed by racist rioting against brown children.

This humanitarian crisis is not new. Nobody has been paying meaningful attention to it for decades. It's getting attention now only because the flood of refugees has topped the figurative levees and threatens to inundate higher-priced real estate. Almost everyone talking about it is fundamentally cynical, focusing only on symptoms, offering nothing approaching a cure for the underlying pathology.

President Obama is referred to as the deporter-in-chief, since his administration has deported record numbers of people. This administration has also detained record numbers of people crossing the border. This administration has record numbers of officers patrolling the border, and even shooting people across the border.

On June 20, the White House announced what was reported as "a slew of aid programs to El Salvador, Guatemala, and Honduras. They include $US9.6 million in aid for the countries to 'receive and reintegrate' their citizens who have been denied entry into the U.S., as well as multi-million-dollar crime and violence protection programs in each of the three Central American nations."

Calling $9.6 million "a slew" of aid to three impoverished countries is something of a joke when you compare it to the $300 million per year the US spends to support the Honduran military alone. Who even thinks the non-military aid will reach the neediest people, much less reintegrate them? That comparison shows a roughly 30-to-1 disparity of spending on the rich over the spending meant for the poor. That's already a structural problem in Central America and it's a growing one in the United States. Most of the US spending in all four countries is for military and para-military means of protecting plutocracy.

President Obama is referred to as the deporter-in-chief, since his administration has deported record numbers of people. This administration has also detained record numbers of people crossing the border. And this administration has record numbers of officers patrolling the border, and even shooting people across the border.

Or, as the White House puts it, this program "involves our partners in Central America who have acknowledged that we all share a responsibility to make sure we stop this situation before it starts." It's too late for that.

What do El Salvador, Guatemala, and Honduras have in common?

El Salvador, Guatemala, and Honduras are not "our partners" in any meaningful sense, any more than they are free and independent democracies. They are out client states. Each of them shares borders with the other two. More than anything, they share more than a century of exploitation by American power, both governmental and corporate. Since the 1950s, they have all suffered brutal, anti-democratic coups d'état orchestrated or approved by the United States. They have all suffered especially cruel dictatorships supported by the United States for the benefit of a tiny elite that controls most of the wealth in each country. The United States has brutalized these countries for decades, the US has helped make them unlivable, and now the US pretends to wonder why people don't want to live there.

El Salvador, Guatemala, and Honduras account for almost 75% of all the refugee children coming out of Central America.

Almost no children are fleeing Nicaragua, a former American enemy (full of phantom threat and against whom the U.S. committed war crimes). On the contrary, Nicaragua is a host country for asylum seekers, as the United Nations High Commissioner for Refugees (UNHCR) found in a study ("Children on the Run") released in March 2014:

> While the United States is receiving the majority of the new asylum claims, UNHCR has documented a 712% increase in the number of asylum applications from citizens of these three [El Salvador, Guatemala, Honduras] countries in Mexico, Panama, Nicaragua, Costa Rica and Belize, combined, from 2008 to 2013.

When the White House says there's "a responsibility to make sure we stop this situation before it starts," it's time to start some

White House soul-searching, not just about American military and corporate predation over decades, not just about trade agreements (NAFTA and CAFTA) that have hurt the poorest people in these poor countries, but especially about the Obama administration's own deeply bloody role in what has happened in Honduras since 2009.

When it came to Honduras, America offered no hope and no change

Five years ago, Honduras had a democratically-elected government that was beginning to make reforms. Five years ago, most of the Honduran population of 8 million were safely staying home.

On June 28, 2009, Honduras suffered a military coup. Almost immediately, the Obama administration blessed the new dictatorship and soon set about lying to the American people in order to avoid enforcing American law that's supposed to apply to any coup (later the administration did the same dishonest dance around the Egyptian coup).

The United Nations, the Organization of American States (OAS), and the European Union all condemned the Honduran coup. On July 5, 2009, the OAS voted unanimously to suspend Honduras from membership (the suspension was lifted two years later). None of this affected unwavering U.S. support for the coup (which some people officially argued was not a coup).

Less than a month later, the U.S. embassy cabled a report to Washington titled, "Open and Shut: The Case of the Honduran Coup," asserting that there was no doubt that the military coup was unconstitutional, and the removal of the Honduran president was a "kidnapping" with no legal authority. The cable went to the White House and to the Secretary of State. No one in the Obama administration – not Barack Obama, not Hillary Clinton, no one – told the truth about Honduras. They kept this cable secret and they lied about it.

The embassy cable remained secret till November 28, 2010, when Wikileaks released it (as part of the release of 251,287 confidential State Department documents). Reported then by Just Foreign Policy, the cable had little impact.

The coup – and the continued degradation of Honduran governance – had the quiet, bi-partisan support of American power. The United States has dirty hands throughout the hemisphere, dirty hands that are equally at home in strangling democratic governments or children's futures.

History professor Dana Frank on Huffington Post blog describes some of the deep corruption among Honduran politicians, police, prosecutors, and judges, which even the U.S. State Department acknowledges:

> Among the most serious human rights problems were corruption, intimidation, and institutional weakness of the justice system leading to widespread impunity; unlawful and arbitrary killings by security forces, organized criminal elements, and others; and harsh and at times life-threatening prison conditions.

In response to his country's police corruption, Honduran president Juan Orlando Hernández has increased the country's militarization, as Frank reports:

> Not only does the regular military now patrol residential neighborhoods, airports, and prisons, but Hernández's new 5,000-strong military police force is fanning out across the country.

> On May 13, the new military police surrounded, tear gassed, brutally beat up, and forcibly ejected from the main hall of congress all 36 congress members of the center-left opposition party LIBRE.

Ultimately the surge of child refugees into other countries has less to do with gangs and extortion, or with rape and murder, or even with poverty and political repression, than it has to do with the American role in the world – the American power that promotes and profits from all these horrors and expects gratitude in return.

This is what the United States government has become, and it is despicable.

36.

Unregistered Immigrant Votes Republican, Republicans Punish Her

Scapegoating minorities is useful in building a police state

Rosa Maria Ortega, 37, came to the United States as an infant. She has a sixth-grade education. When she was about eleven, her mother was arrested and deported. Her two younger brothers, born in the US, became citizens. She became a permanent resident, with a green card. She is a mother of four children, ages 12-16, who are all citizens. She is engaged to marry Oscar Sherman, a citizen.

When she lived in Dallas County, she registered to vote on forms that had no box to check for "permanent resident," only "citizen." She registered in 2012, as a Republican. She voted for Mitt Romney. She voted again in May 2014. When she moved to Tarrant County, she again registered to vote in October, on a different form, with a box for "non-citizen," which she checked. That registration was rejected. She explained to election officials that she had voted in Dallas County without difficulty, they said she had to be a citizen. In March 2015 she filed another form claiming to be a citizen. Apparently, no one thought to sort the situation out humanely, with someone who didn't know the difference legally between permanent residency and citizenship.

Instead, in October 2015, she was arrested and charged with "Illegal Voting," a second-degree felony under a Texas law that took effect January 1, 2012. She was indicted in November 2015. According to Rosa Maria Ortega's attorney, Clark Birdsall, the Texas Attorney

General's office agreed to dismiss all charges if she would agree to testify on voting procedures before the Texas Legislature. But Tarrant County district attorney Sharen Wilson vetoed any deal and demanded a trial to showcase how tough she was on "voter fraud." State and county officials refused to comment on this to The New York Times, but a spokesman for Wilson offered a non-denial denial saying any negotiations had been only "discussions."

On February 8, 2017, after about two hours of deliberation, a jury found Rosa Maria Ortega guilty on two counts, thereby rejecting her testimony that she was confused by and didn't understand the law. The statute requires that the court determine that a person had cast an illegal ballot "knowingly." Each count carried a possible sentence of 20 years in prison. The following day, the Texas county judge sentenced Rosa Maria Ortega to an eight-year sentence on each count (to run concurrently) and fined her $5,000.

Attorney General Ken Paxton was elected in 2014 after years of crusading against "voter fraud." (He has his own legal issues these days, Texas criminal securities fraud charges and a federal lawsuit, but he denies any wrongdoing, with a trial coming up May 1.) After Rosa Maria Ortega's sentencing, Ken Paxton was all over the news boasting in an email:

> This case shows how serious Texas is about keeping its elections secure, and the outcome sends a message that violators of the state's election law will be prosecuted to the fullest. Safeguarding the integrity of our elections is essential to preserving our democracy.

Republican governor Greg Abbott, a long-time promoter of fantasy voter fraud, pushed his way into the Rosa Maria Ortega spotlight with a tweet of absurd intensity for a fellow party member:

> In Texas you will pay a price for Voter Fraud: Noncitizen Sentenced to 8 Years in prison for Illegal Voting. #txlegetillage

The judge who sentenced Rosa Maria Ortega is a Republican. So is the Attorney General. In 2014, Rosa Maria Ortega voted for him.

Rosa Maria Ortega's ordeal is a Republican zeitgeist story

Since 2002, a total of 72 million Texas votes have produced to voter fraud prosecution in – wait for it – fewer than 100 cases (in which convictions led to light sentences or probation). But politicians pursuing an imaginary monster tend to inflate any evidence they can find of their particular Big Foot. That's just Rosa Maria Ortega's bad luck, that and Republicans' savage indifference to inflicting needless pain and cruelty.

Texas voter laws have for years rewarded Republican cruelty in pursuit of hobgoblins. Last year the US Court of Appeals for the Fifth Circuit, by a 9-6 vote, struck down part of the Texas Voter ID law. Considered the country's most conservative appeals court, it held that the Texas law discriminates against black and Latino citizens. For now, the US Supreme Court has rejected a Texas appeal of the lower court's ruling. The law would have eliminated 16,400 legal voters from the election. Texas governor Greg Abbott issued a statement at the time:

> The 5th Circuit rightly reversed the lower court's finding of discriminatory purpose, but wrongly concluded the law had a discriminatory effect. Voter fraud is real, and it undermines the integrity of the election process. As Attorney General I prosecuted cases against voter fraud across the State, and Texas will continue to make sure there is no illegal voting at the ballot box.

At about the same time, Abbott also FALSELY claimed: "The fact is voter fraud is rampant—and in Texas, unlike some other states and unlike some other leaders, we are committed to cracking down on voter fraud." Politifact called Abbott's claim a "Pants on Fire" lie. In Texas it's a crackdown on rampant voter fraud when a court judicially lynches an under-educated woman who voted Republican. (In Iowa, a woman charged with voting twice for Trump is, according to her attorney, mentally incompetent to stand trial.)

Rosa Maria Ortega's attorney Clark Birdsall is outspoken about the injustice of this Texas prosecution and the fatuous Republican self-grandiosity that goes with it:

These people are beating their chests and wrapping themselves up in the flag and trying to impress our current occupier of the White House, and they're like a big-game hunter, one foot on the carcass, with their gun in their hand and with a big smile on their face.

This is such a miscarriage.

And the taxpayers are going to pay a minimum of $300,000 or $400,000 to house this woman, just so a local politician can curry favor with Trump, or with Abbott, who is just as out of control.

With mindless immigrant persecution continuing across the country in the current ICE rampage, Rosa Maria Ortega's story is emblematic of the inhumanity Republicans bring to governing. Whether it's cruelty to the sick, or cruelty to immigrants, or cruelty to disabled people, or cruelty to the LGBTQ community, it's always cruelty at the heart of the approach.

> **Update 2019:** On November 28, 2018, the Texas 2nd Court of Appeals upheld Rosa Maria Ortega's conviction. She has chosen not to appeal further and serve her sentence. She returned to Tarrant County Jail on January 31, 2019. She has lost custody of her children. She is potentially eligible for parole within a year. Then she will be subject to deportation. And Texas justice will have been served.
>
> Attorney General Paxton was re-elected in 2018. The Texas and federal cases against him for alleged securities fraud remain unresolved as of May 2019.
>
> In November 2018, Paxton's wife, Angela Paxton, was elected as a new Texas State Senator. In February 2019, she introduced legislation (Senate Bill 860) that would empower the Attorney General – her husband – to decide on his own which entrepreneurs could be exempted from certain state regulations that regulated "innovative financial products or services."
>
> As the Texas Tribune reported at the time: "One of those exemptions would be working as an 'investment adviser' without registering with the state board. Currently, doing so is a felony in Texas — one for which Ken Paxton was issued a civil penalty in 2014 and criminally charged in 2015."
>
> Senate Bill 860 was referred to the Senate Business & Commerce Committee.

37.

Why Expect Justice for Children from a Category 5 Presidency?

Why isn't innocence enough to protect any child from the law?

Historically, bigotry has served as the basis for US policy and law often enough that no one should be surprised that we're at it again, targeting people who had no meaningful choice when they were brought to this country as children. To mask our bigotry, we call these innocent young people "childhood arrivals." We pretend they broke the law as minors by accompanying their parents who brought them to our country in violation of our constitutionally squalid immigration statutes. But we also pretend we are big-hearted because we will hold off on "deferred action" against these criminals in our midst. Yes, that's DACA, Deferred Action for Childhood Arrivals, the 2012 executive program that is fundamentally a moral hoax and a legal joke, neither of which is among the reasons President Trump has given for throwing the program into deferred chaos.

In fact, President Trump has offered no rational explanation for his decision to punt the problem to Congress for six months while promising to revisit it later if Congress doesn't act to his liking (whatever that turns out to be). That re-visitation is a reasonable likelihood, since Congress hasn't acted since August 2001 when the Development, Relief, and Education for Alien Minors Act, known acronymically as the DREAM Act, was introduced as a bipartisan proposal from Senators Dick Durbin of Illinois and Orrin Hatch of Utah and 16 co-sponsors of both parties. The legislative history of the DREAM Act's multiple failures to treat innocent children with something like fairness and decency is a story of dysfunctional government now in its third presidency. The standards in the DREAM Act are truly double standards, expecting these forced immigrant children to be paragons of virtue that some native-born citizen children couldn't match.

Well, never mind, that's what America does to its masses of immigrants — it treats them harshly to see if they're tough enough to become real Americans. There are two obvious exceptions to that rule. The rich or talented immigrant has a much softer ride. Those brought here as slaves are never forgiven.

Hurricane Trump spins in circles with random chaos

The president's moral vacuity regarding "childhood arrivals" was underlined by his chickening out on announcing it himself. These DACA children arrived in the US when they were an average age of six (now they're 26 on average, but their children are citizens). So, for the president to pass the announcement of this bigoted decision to serial hater Attorney General Jeff Sessions was a neat Trumpian ploy to distance himself from his own inhumanity. At a press conference last February, the president rambled semi-coherently, as if he were trying to persuade himself of his own decency:

> We're going to show great heart. DACA is a very, very difficult subject for me. I will tell you. To me, it's one of the most difficult subjects I have.... But you have some absolutely incredible kids — I would say mostly. They were brought here in such a way. It's a very — it's a very very tough subject. We are going to deal with DACA with heart. I have to deal with a lot of politicians, don't forget. And I have to convince them that what I'm saying is, is right. And I appreciate your understanding on that.... But the DACA situation is a very very, it's a very difficult thing for me because you know, I love these kids. I love kids. *I have kids and grandkids and I find it very, very hard doing what the law says exactly to do* [emphasis added].

Announcing that DACA would end in six months or so, the US attorney general both lied about the program and misrepresented it in a ritual Republican manner. Most egregiously, he called them "adult illegal aliens" and said they could participate in the Social Security program. Responding to the predictable outcry against his decision, President Trump tweeted, without substance: "Congress now has 6 months to legalize DACA.... If they can't, I will revisit the issue!" The next day the president was widely reported as saying he had no second thoughts about cancelling DACA.

Even before Donald trump announced his candidacy for the presidency, anyone who was paying attention knew he was unfit for the office. He wasn't taken seriously. With major media playing the Trump Campaign for comedy ratings, Trump ran roughshod over Republican candidates made to look like pallid clowns, whether more qualified than Trump or not. And still he was not taken all that seriously by a Democratic Party and candidate that stood for little more than being not-Trump. Now we are where we are, wherever that really is, and the leaders of the country in both parties, in business and the arts, in media and academia, in whatever field, mostly resemble chickens in the barnyard with the fox, having no better plan than to be the last one eaten.

There are some exceptions to our widespread panic

Fifteen states and the District of Columbia filed suit September 6 to block Trump's DACA plan the day after it was announced. New York attorney general Eric Schneiderman, who is part of the suit against the Trump administration, told an anti-Trump rally:

> We understand what's going on in Washington. And we know that when bullies step up, you have to step to them and step to them quickly. And that's what we're here to do today.... By definition, Dreamers play by the rules. Dreamers work hard. Dreamers pay taxes. For most, America is the only home they've ever known. They deserve to stay here.

This is the essence of what makes DACA a moral hoax and a legal joke. Just to qualify for deferred action as a childhood arrival, Dreamers are required to provide evidence that they are better than average people. Roughly 800,000 of them have done just that. These are children who are being punished for being good children. They did not break the law, yet the law holds them accountable for the sins of their parents. Innocence should be enough to protect a child from the government.

And there is a Gordian Knot solution to this largely imaginary problem. It's a mystery why President Obama didn't do this instead of crafting another Rube Goldberg structure destined to be a problem as long as it lasted (the immigration equivalent of Obamacare). That Gordian Knot solution is simple and constitutional. These Dreamers, for reasons that defy human decency, are charged with violating immigration law, an offense against the United States. The Constitution (Article II, Section 2) gives the president the "Power to grant Reprieves and Pardons for Offenses against the United States." President Obama could have pardoned these innocent "criminals," but big gestures have not been his style and, as a lawyer, he presumably could list a bunch of complications flowing from such pardons. But so what? They would have been fair and just and decent. They would have served the intent of the Constitution's preamble to establish justice, insure domestic tranquility and promote the general welfare. The possibility of pardons transforms the debate, removing it from some unclear, mean-spirited, bigoted challenge to alleged "illegal aliens." Instead, considering pardons for inadvertent lawbreakers forces one to explain why we should lynch innocent children.

The pardon option remains on the table. If Joe Arpaio is pardonable for committing crimes against humanity, why not pardon Dreamers for doing nothing more wrong than making a bad choice of parents? President Trump could do it tomorrow. Or the tomorrow after that. Or the tomorrow after that…. What are the odds?

> **Update 2019:** The DACA lawsuit of 2017 first produced a temporary injunction from a federal court preventing Trump from changing the DACA program. A federal appeals court affirmed the lower court's injunction. The Trump administration has appealed the injunction to the Supreme Court, where it sits and waits. If the court takes it up, oral argument can't be scheduled until October 2019 at the earliest.

38.

ICE Is a State-Sponsored Terrorist Organization – Abolish ICE

"ICE has strayed so far from its mission. It's supposed to be here to keep Americans safe, but what it's turned into is, frankly, a terrorist organization of its own, that is terrorizing people who are coming to this country."

CYNTHIA NIXON, DEMOCRAT FOR GOVERNOR OF NEW YORK, JUNE 21, 2018

ICE (US Immigration and Customs Enforcement) is the country's largest police agency: some 20,000 employees, offices in 50 states and 48 foreign countries, all part of in the Department of Homeland Security. Created with little serious thought in the post-9/11 government panic, ICE was supposed to be a bulwark against the inflated threat of international terrorism. Over the past fifteen years, lacking enough serious criminals to justify its $6 billion budget, ICE has reduced itself (with poisonous political pandering in support) to the horrifying monster we're finally seeing more clearly. Thanks to ICE, American life is littered with caged parents and children, broken families, incarcerated innocents, unemployed working taxpayers, and disrupted American businesses. This is a full range of social mayhem chosen by the past several presidents in preference to any humane, decent policy rooted in justice. In 2002, Congress voted to make ICE a national police force with Gestapo-like powers. Corrupt law and corrupt politics have produced corrupt results. What a surprise.

How best to respond to this paramilitary police state operation that mostly produces human carnage (including widespread sexual abuse of detainees since 2010)? How best to end the chronic violation of human rights law by this brutal regime that denies asylum to the persecuted and sends them back to suffer or die? The current movement to abolish ICE began last winter with a piece in The Nation magazine, in which Sean McElwee concluded: "It's time to rein in the greatest threat we face: an unaccountable strike force executing a campaign of ethnic cleansing." Abolishing ICE is no panacea, but it is a necessary step to creating immigration policy based on law, compassion, and our own better history. The political will to reinvent American idealism may or may not emerge in the face of vicious, bipartisan opposition.

On June 21, Cynthia Nixon apparently became the first high-profile politician to call ICE by its rightful terrorist name and to call for its abolition. She's running for Governor of New York against Democratic establishment hope-crusher Andrew Cuomo, who supports ICE. But two days before Nixon spoke out, Cuomo announced his plan for New York to file a multi-agency lawsuit against the Trump administration for "violating the Constitutional rights of thousands of immigrant children and their parents who have been separated at the border." The treatment of families at the border is only one part of ICE's assault on human rights, as Cuomo surely knows, indicated by his apparently ironic comment: "I think ICE *should be* a *bona fide* law enforcement organization that prudently and diligently enforces the law." [emphasis added]

Nixon first spoke out against ICE at the St. Paul and St. Andrew United Methodist Church in New York City. The church has given sanctuary to a 32-year-old Guatemalan mother, Debora Berenice Vasquez, and her two children (both US citizens), after ICE threatened them with deportation. How do these facts square with ICE's promise: "We vow to continue our mission to protect the United States by promoting homeland security and public safety through the criminal and civil enforcement of federal laws ..."? What "homeland security" or "public" is served by taking 13 years to bring a case that robs a mother of her job and freedom while traumatizing her two American children? At the church's press conference announcing the sanctuary, Nixon said:

> Thank you, from the bottom of our hearts, for offering sanctuary to Debora and her children. And thank you for giving us all a place to gather today to stand up with one voice as New Yorkers and say, 'No,' and say, 'No, not in our name. Not in our name.'

This event didn't happen in a vacuum. On June 26, New Yorkers voted in their Democratic primary. In one race, voters rejected a member of the House leadership, who carefully supports ICE (he voted to create it) and who doesn't live in his district, in favor of a 28-year-old Latina whose campaign targeted ICE and the party's aging, out-of-touch leadership. Alexandria Ocasio-Cortez grew up in the district that covers much of the Bronx and Queens. She graduated from Boston University and came home and organized. She was the first to challenge the incumbent in more than a decade. She said of her campaign:

> It's time we acknowledge that not all Democrats are the same. That a Democrat who takes corporate money, profits off of foreclosure, doesn't live here, doesn't send his kids to our schools, doesn't drink our water or breathe our air cannot possibly represent us.

She was describing the media-cliché "powerful Democrat," ten-term congressman Joseph Crowley, crony to Nancy Pelosi and Steny Hoyer and presumed easy winner of the seat to which he was surely entitled, along with his predicted rise to Speaker of the House. The race got little attention until the media and professional politicians woke up "surprised" to find that a former organizer for Bernie Sanders had won the nomination with more than 57% of the vote. Trump and the rest of the right-wing dishonest noise machine are already lying about what Ocasio-Cortez and other Democrats stand for, as Trump called Democrats "now officially the party of impeachment, open borders, abolishing ICE, banning the 2nd Amendment and unbridled socialism." What Ocasio-Cortez actually said about ICE has had nothing to do with open borders:

> Abolishing ICE doesn't mean get rid of our immigration policy, but what it does mean is to get rid of the draconian enforcement that has happened since 2003 that routinely violates our civil rights, because, frankly, it was designed with that structure in mind.

The day before the primary, June 25, a Democratic candidate for New York Attorney General published an editorial in the Guardian titled: "ICE is a tool of illegality. It must be abolished." Fordham law professor Zephyr Teachout is challenging at least three other candidates in the September 13 primary for the open office, but the filing deadline doesn't close the race till July 12. The temporary attorney general, Barbara Underwood, is not running. She replaced AG Eric Schneiderman (also a Democrat) who resigned in May amidst sexual misconduct allegations. Teachout appears to be the only candidate calling for the abolition of ICE, writing in The Guardian:

> Let's be clear: ICE is a fairly recent development. When the George W Bush administration successfully pushed to place immigration enforcement within the Department of Homeland Security (DHS), it transformed decades of past practice where internal immigration policy was conducted by the justice department. The new policy sent a clear and chilling signal: immigrants should be treated as criminals and a national security threat.

The same day as Teachout's editorial, four current Congress members – Mark Pocan (D-Wis.), Earl Blumenauer (D-Ore.), Jim McGovern (D-Mass.) and Pramila Jayapal (D-Wash.) – said they would support legislation to abolish ICE. Representative Pocan explained his motivation in a press release:

> During my trip to the southern border, it was clear that ICE, and its actions of hunting down and tearing apart families, has wreaked havoc on far too many people. From conducting raids at garden centers and meatpacking plants, to breaking up families at churches and schools, ICE is tearing apart families and ripping at the moral fabric of our nation. Unfortunately, President Trump and his team of white nationalists, including Stephen Miller, have so misused ICE that the agency can no longer accomplish its goals effectively....
>
> I'm introducing legislation that would abolish ICE and crack down on the agency's blanket directive to target and round up individuals and families. The heartless actions of this abused agency do not represent the values of our nation and the U.S. must develop a more humane immigration system, one that treats every person with dignity and respect.

A weeklong barricade of ICE offices in Southwest Portland, Oregon, has been broken up by police. Representative Blumenauer spoke in favor of the protestors at a rally at City Hall. He voted against the creation of ICE in 2002. In support of Pocan's legislation, Blumenauer wrote:

We should abolish ICE and start over, focusing on our priorities to protect our families and our borders in a humane and thoughtful fashion. Now is the time for immigration reform that ensures people are treated with compassion and respect. Not only because it is the moral thing to do, but it's better policy and will cost less.

Rational, moral, and humane as these voices are, they still represent only a small minority of Democrats, most of whom have run for cover on the issue. Media coverage tends to treat "abolish ICE" as a trivial issue or, at Fox, an offense against the state. Democrats of note appear intimidated by the issue. Bernie Sanders voted against ICE, now doesn't want to abolish it. Nancy Pelosi voted against ICE, now supports it. In all, 120 Democrats in Congress opposed ICE in 2002, but today only four are on record to abolish it. In 2002, Democratic senators overwhelmingly supported creating ICE in a 90-9 Senate vote. None of the 9 Democrats opposing ICE in 2002 remain in office.

Maybe this is changing, maybe Ocasio-Cortez's strong victory will be a shock to the all but dead party of Democrats. On June 28 on CNN, New York Democratic senator Kirsten Gillibrand was caught in a high-pitched defense of her failure to respect Ocasio-Cortez as a candidate. The interviewer read a tweet from Ocasio-Cortez, calling out Gillibrand's lockstep party orthodoxy. Then, on the defensive, Gillibrand suddenly expressed support for abolishing ICE, almost as if she meant it. Now how hard was that? November is coming and Democrats continue to cling to old notions detached from current reality (the Crowley Democrats). Under pressure, Gillibrand took the right position for the moment. For November to be worth celebrating, the party will have to do much better than that. It will have to find a heart and a soul and a brain and apply them all to the criminal atrocities our government commits daily at home and abroad.

39.

ICE Agents Are Kidnappers and Sociopaths, Trump Honors Them

"In June of 2014, the ACLU and the International Human Rights Clinic at the University of Chicago Law School filed complaints with the Department of Homeland Security. And the complaints documented the cases of 116 unaccompanied children, ranging in age from 5 years old to 17. According to these organizations, a quarter of the children said they were physically or sexually abused. They said they'd been placed in so-called stress positions and were at times subjected to beatings by Customs officials. More than half of the kids reported receiving death threats from US government agents."

REPORTER JEREMY SCAHILL, THE INTERCEPT PODCAST,
"INTERCEPTED", MAY 30, 2018

"You are the patriots and you are the heroes. You keep us safe and you keep us free. I'm honored every single day to serve as your Commander-in-Chief. I will never leave your side, I will never leave the fight."

PRESIDENT TRUMP HONORING ICE AGENTS, AUGUST 20, 2018

US immigration agencies have been committing crimes against humanity for decades. The Obama administration raised immigration ruthlessness to a new level, earning the president the derogatory title of deporter-in-chief, balanced by no redeeming effort to resolve an issue more rooted in hate than harm. Now the Trump administration has taken official viciousness and stupidity to a whole new level, prompting Human Rights Watch to object strenuously to US immigration policy and practice:

> Misdemeanor illegal entry (for entering the US without authorization) and felony illegal re-entry (for re-entering the US after deportation) have been crimes since the early 20th century. But prosecutions were

limited to immigrants with serious prior criminal histories or repeat offenders. In 2005, Operation Streamline was introduced in Del Rio, Texas, permitting rapid-fire mass prosecutions of migrants.

The Trump administration's policy is the first to target parents traveling with children for prosecution and to couple criminal prosecution of asylum seekers with policy changes intended to restrict eligibility for asylum to those who enter the US illegally. Penalizing asylum seekers for entering without authorization is a *violation of international refugee law*. [emphasis added]

How inhumane can the US government get before a majority of the American people begin to care? Why should Americans tolerate law-breaking that should be an impeachable offense? How long before a majority of us have zero tolerance for official cruelty, abuse and lawlessness?

Abusive treatment of a woman about to give birth should shock anyone's conscience, but it hasn't, apparently. For now, ICE (the US Immigration and Customs Enforcement) can get away with almost any atrocity.

On the morning of August 15, in San Bernardino, California, Joel Arrona-Lara, 36, was driving his nine-months-pregnant wife to the hospital to give birth by C-section. Two ICE SUVs surrounded their car at a convenience store, for no apparent reason except racial profiling. The ICE agents did not know who they were stopping and first asked the wife, Maria del Carmen Venegas, for her ID, which she had. She and her husband have lived in the US for 12 years and have four other children, three of whom are citizens.

When the ICE agents turned to the husband, the driver, for identification, he didn't have it with him, having left hurriedly for the hospital. He had his ID at home, a few blocks away. His wife pleaded with the ICE agents to let him get his ID. The ICE agents didn't care enough to check it out. Instead they handcuffed Joel Arrona-Lara and took him into custody. They searched the car, finding nothing amiss. With two vehicles available, the ICE agents could easily have escorted the wife to the hospital. They didn't. They left her alone to drive herself, which she managed to do. The baby was later born safely.

The ICE agents still have no reason for arresting Joel Arrona-Lara other than his not having proper ID on his person. The surveillance camera video of this arrest went viral online and was picked up by media. On Friday, ICE officials claimed Joel Arrona-Lara had been arrested for "illegally residing in the United States," an assertion patently false, since he was arrested before ICE knew who he was. According to ICE's Friday statement, ICE considered Joel Arrona-Lara someone "who poses a threat to national security, public safety and border security."

On Saturday, under media scrutiny, ICE officials issued another probably false claim, that Joel Arrona-Lara was arrested for an outstanding homicide warrant in Mexico. This not only fails to persuade for its belated timing, as well as ICE not knowing who he was when they arrested him, but there's no evidence yet that such a warrant even exists. Joel Arrona-Lara said he knows of no warrant; his attorney has seen no warrant. The Mexican consulate has said it has no warrant. Maria del Carmen Venegas, 32, says her husband has never had trouble with the law, not even a traffic ticket. She said his brother had done jail time in Mexico, maybe that was the source of confusion.

(Elsewhere, in fake news, Tucker Carlson of Fox News lied on Monday about the homicide warrant, claiming other media coverage omitted it. They did omit it for a while, because ICE hadn't made it public. He is right about the story being propaganda, but it's ICE propaganda. Over on Fox & Friends, the headline was "Media Slams ICE Over Illegal Immigrant Arrest" – nice ambiguity – while they misrepresented facts and tried to justify this arrest because some other unrelated person was killed in a head-on car crash with some other illegal immigrant. This message was delivered by a well-programmed "angel mom" who said that "there's an American victim for every illegal alien criminal who's in our country." Really? Twelve million victims? Almost all going unreported? Now, THAT's propaganda.)

The fact remains that ICE arrested someone before they knew who he was, they didn't explain why they were arresting him, and then they changed their story about why he was arrested. That is fundamentally corrupt. ICE has been an invitation to corruption since it was created, since it is not accountable to the US Justice Department but to the Department of Homeland Security which was created to run both sides of the law to protect us from "terrorists."

The legally dubious arrest is bad enough, and common enough for ICE, but leaving a nine-months-pregnant woman to fend for herself by the side of the road is a new cruelty for ICE. "ICE acted in total disregard for the health and wellbeing of the mother," said attorney Emilio Amaya Garcia.

To ICE's credit, perhaps, the ICE agents did not take the mother and unborn child into custody, even though the mother is also undocumented. ICE can always go after the mother later and do untold damage to this harmless, self-supporting family. Meanwhile, ICE can take pride in having created a situation in which an American-born child may never get to meet his father.

That seems unlikely, according to Russell Jauregui, staff attorney for the San Bernardino Community Service Center, who represents Joel Arrona-Lara, currently being held in the Theo Lacy detention center:

> He does have a right to a bond hearing before an immigration judge in immigration court. He does have the right to counsel. We're going to represent him *pro bono*. He does have the right to pursue a bond hearing to see, determine if he can be released. We're hoping that he can, given his length of time here in the United States and the fact that he does have three US citizen children. And then, if he is, hopefully, released on bond, then his case will continue with the immigration courts, where he'll be pursuing his, hopefully, relief during a removal hearing before an immigration judge, where he'll have to prove that, you know, his US citizen kids will suffer exceptional and extreme and unusual hardships without him if he's removed.... And this process could take one or two years.

Politicians of both major parties have demagogued the immigration issue for decades, numbing the public to the unlawful and inhumane treatment of a vast, undefined victim class that includes citizens and non-citizens alike. Even more horrific abuses of immigrant children under the Trump administration have finally sparked some outrage, but nowhere near enough to change the police-state practices of ICE. Sadistic, perverted, police-state abuses of children by American border police flourished during the Obama administration, whose foreign policy drove millions of people to seek asylum from their American-sponsored Central American police states. Under Trump, it's all the same only worse. Now the US policy is to take children hostage – and then abuse them and lose track of them. As far as immigrants go, President Trump ("They're not people – these are animals") is betting there's no limit to what atrocities Americans will tolerate as long as his demonized victims are non-white.

So far, he's winning that bet.

40.

US Prosecutes Religious Workers for Attempted Life-Saving

"No More Deaths is a humanitarian organization based in southern Arizona. We began in 2004 in the form of a coalition of community and faith groups, dedicated to stepping up efforts to stop the deaths of migrants in the desert and to achieving the enactment of a set of Faith-Based Principles for Immigration Reform. We later developed into an autonomous project. Since 2008 we have been an official ministry of the Unitarian Universalist Church of Tucson."

NO MORE DEATHS WEB PAGE

It is a measure of American corruption that the Trump administration has officially criminalized selected acts of Christian mercy. It is a further measure of American corruption that the official criminalization of actions taken to save lives goes little reported and is less discussed. Those conclusions are aptly illustrated by the selective prosecution of four women volunteers with No More Deaths for leaving water and food in a desert where thousands of migrants have died in recent years.

Federal Magistrate Judge Bernardo Velasco convicted the women of all the nine misdemeanor charges against them. Each charge carries the potential penalty of a $500 fine and six months in federal prison. He delivered his verdict on January 18, the day after a trial that lasted three days. There was no jury. The court will schedule a sentencing hearing sometime in February. The judge found that the women's placing of water and food in a lethal environment violated statutes against trespass and littering. There is no dispute that the women did these things in August 2017. The women's defense rested in part on their assertion that their acts of conscience were protected

216

by the Religious Freedom Restoration Act passed by Congress in 1993 (42 USC 2000bb-1).

Judge Velasco, in his three-page (650-word) verdict, begins by mischaracterizing the complex 803.48-acre region of the Cabeza Prieta Refuge and Wilderness Area, which has a variety of names and sub-names, and parts of which are subject to the jurisdiction of various federal agencies (including the Departments of Defense and Interior, the US Border Patrol and the Fish and Wildlife Service, as well as the Department of Justice as needed) and the Tohono O'odham Indian Nation. The northern section of the wilderness, to which the Department of Defense allows no public access, is the Barry Goldwater Bombing Range, which is irrelevant to the case against No More Deaths. Twice in his order, Judge Velasco emphasizes the "pristine nature" of the area. Nevertheless, the judge also falsely characterizes the wilderness in an apparent effort to impugn the defendants' good judgment:

> ... the preserve is littered with unexploded military ordinance, the detritus of illegal entry into the United States, and the on-road and off-road vehicular traffic of the US Border Patrol efforts to apprehend illegal entrants/undocumented immigrants.

The judge refers to the federal law requiring "people who access Cabeza Prieta to obtain a permit authorizing entry," although he does not cite the law. He asserts *ex cathedra* and inaccurately that:

> Violators of the access regulations may be verbally admonished to comply with the rules of the Refuge, cited for a violation of the pertinent regulations, banned from the area, or summoned into Court for criminal prosecution. The choice of action to be taken is at the sole discretion of the Refuge's law enforcement officer, except the latter, which requires the US Attorney's exercise of its discretion to authorize the criminal prosecution.

There's much to unpack in this paragraph, which amounts to an invisible masking of federal actions during the Trump administration that bear directly on the case at hand. During the trial, Judge Velasco commented: "This trial is not about the government's obligations."

This case is the first federal prosecution of its kind since the Bush administration. The prosecution of No More Deaths volunteer

Dan Millis for littering in a different wildlife refuge ended in conviction in 2009. That was overturned the following year by the US Court of Appeals ninth circuit (with a dissent by Judge Jay Bybee, better known for his pro-torture memos). The majority based its ruling in part on the government's obligation to be clear and precise in its rules and regulations:

> We begin by noting that the rule of lenity "requires courts to limit the reach of criminal statutes to the clear import of their text and construe any ambiguity against the government." ... The rule of lenity applies "only where 'after seizing every thing from which aid can be derived, the Court is left with an ambiguous statute.'" ... In such a case, fundamental principles of due process mandate that "no individual be forced to speculate, at peril of indictment, whether his conduct is prohibited."

Or in layman's language, the court required that Millis be able to tell, from the language of the statute, what he was and was not allowed to do. After a painstaking analysis of the statutory language, the court concluded that the arresting officer (and the dissenting judge) was trying to punish Millis for doing something that was not precisely prohibited in the law. This is a standard of legal clarity that is not only reasonable but a clear protection against abuse of authority.

Judge Velasco does not mention this precedent, the only previously adjudicated case similar to the one before him. Nor does he examine the particular language of the rule under which the No More Deaths women were charged. From the judge's analysis, there is no way to assess whether the rule, as it was written in 2017, was legitimate. We know, from extensive reporting in The Intercept, that early 2017 was a time when the Trump administration was ratcheting up pressure on migrant-rights groups, in particular No More Deaths. Attorney General Jeff Sessions visited Tucson in April 2017 to demand tougher immigration control.

During the Obama administration, Border Patrol and No More Deaths had reached an agreement that the Border Patrol would not interfere with a humanitarian aid facility run by No More Deaths, but would treat it as a medical facility. In mid-June 2017, the Border Patrol broke the agreement and raided the camp with 30 agents, 15 trucks, 2 ATVs and a helicopter. A No More Deaths volunteer published an op-ed predicting the Border Patrol raid would lead directly to more migrant deaths in the Sonoran Desert: The raid "sends the message that people crossing the desert are unworthy of medical care, food and water: unworthy of life. Tougher border policy is not just political rhetoric — it is death by dehydration, without a funeral." The written agreement had protected migrant lives for thirteen years. No More Deaths responded to the raid with a statement that said in part:

> Obstruction of humanitarian aid is an egregious abuse by the law enforcement agency, a clear violation of international humanitarian law and a violation of the organization's written agreement with the Tucson Sector Border Patrol.

During the same period, Fish and Wildlife manager for the Cabeza Prieta Refuge, Sidney Slone, set about tightening rules, including seeking voluntary compliance from No More Deaths. No mutual understanding was reached, and a new rule went into effect July 1, 2017, requiring visitors getting permits to enter the refuge to sign a pledge not to leave any food or water behind. At a July meeting, an assistant US attorney was heard to say the US had no interest in prosecuting volunteers for dropping off water and food. Without mentioning the rule of lenity, Slone later said the new rule was intended to "make it really clear so there's no question in someone's mind what the rules are."

On August 13, when the four women from No More Deaths entered the refuge, they did not seek a permit. There is no certainty as to what they knew or didn't know. They knew they were committing something of an act of civil disobedience, but their action was not designed as a direct challenge to the law. They may have known – and No More Deaths almost surely knew – that in recent years, none of the citations issued in the refuge had been referred to the Justice Department for prosecution. Judge Velasco's 2019 recitation of the risk of prosecution is at best disinguous as applied to 2017 when it simply was not happening as he explains it. The No More Deaths women were cited in August 2017, and then nothing happened.

Months passed. Border Patrol pressure increased. Border Patrol agents sabotaged or destroyed caches of water and food. Border Patrol agents raided a No More Deaths aid station. On January 17, 2018, No More Deaths released a lengthy report documenting arguably criminal behavior by Border Patrol agents. The report described agents destroying humanitarian aid and included videos of agents pouring water on the ground. Within days after the report came out, the four women were charged for their action five months earlier. Five other No More Deaths volunteers were also charged in that period. All these prosecutions, as Judge Velasco points out, had to be approved by the Justice Department under Jeff Sessions.

The only such prosecutions approved by the Justice Department have all been against No More Deaths volunteers. No More Deaths has asserted that it is being selectively prosecuted. The four defendants presented evidence including Fish and Wildlife records that they said showed they were being singled out for prosecution. The government denied that. Judge Velasco does not address the question in his verdict.

Update 2019: At a hearing on March 1, 2019, the four No More Deaths volunteers convicted of federal misdemeanors were each sentenced to pay fines of $250 and serve 15 months of unsupervised probation.

Earlier, at a hearing on February 21, federal prosecutors had dropped all federal criminal charges against four other No More Deaths volunteers who had been arrested after searching fruitlessly for three missing migrants. Border Patrol picked up two of them the next day. The third has not been found. The four volunteers were issued civil citations with a fine of $250 each.

The ninth No More Deaths volunteer facing federal prosecution is Scott Warren. He faces federal felony charges in a case that looks very much like entrapment. His trial was scheduled for some time in May 2019. Warren is accused of providing two migrants with food and shelter for three days. The feds, who had the migrants under surveillance well before they arrived at Warren's desert cabin, say he committed the crime of "harboring," even though they could have prevented it and chose not to.

41.

Moment of Truth for Democrats: Censure Trump for Inciting Violence?

"... we're the party of love, we're the party of compassion, we're the party of inclusiveness. What we are fighting for is not for the few, but for the many. Every single one, just this week, when we've had the attack in California on a synagogue, it's the same person who's accused of attempting to bomb a mosque. So I can't ever speak of Islamophobia and fight for Muslims, if I am not willing to fight against anti-Semitism. We collectively must make sure that we are dismantling all systems of oppression."

REP. ILHAN OMAR, MINNESOTA DEMOCRAT, APRIL 30, 2019

Of the 435 members of Congress elected in 2018, Ilhan Omar won her race with more votes than 428 of her colleagues of both parties won theirs. She is a black woman born in Somalia, an immigrant, a Muslim, intelligent and outspoken. From her first moment in Congress, right-wing bigots have targeted her with whatever smear seemed useful. The most effective has been the bogus claim that she's anti-Semitic, rooted in imaginary evidence. Democrats failed to understand the fraud and still haven't rallied around a party member whose life has been endangered by the occupant of the White House. Media reports routine include comments referring to the accusations of anti-Semitism, as if they were real, giving continuing credence to political lies. All in all it is a massive cluster-fiasco of incompetence and bad faith from a huge portion of the supposed "leadership" class in the US.

On April 30, Black Lives Matter organized a rally on Capitol Hill calling for "Hands Off Ilhan Omar." More than a hundred African American women leaders in and out of Congress gathered in Omar's support, issuing a call to Congress to censure President Trump for endangering the life of a sitting member of Congress. There is no doubt that a Trump tweet on April 12 constituted reckless endangerment with an incendiary but false incitement against Ilhan Omar. The Tweet sparked a sharp increase in death threats against the congresswoman by tying her to the collapse of the twin towers on 9/11, with no basis in fact.

> WE WILL NEVER FORGET!
> – **Tweet from Pres. Trump**, 6:35 PM, April 12, 2019, accompanying a 43-second fraudulent attack video dishonestly suggesting that Rep. Ilhan Omar was somehow accountable for the attacks of 9/11, a fascistic meme of Islamophobic demagoguery of the first order

The 43-second video is a polished production, with the same manipulative slickness as the Nazi propaganda films of Leni Riefenstahl. This was more than just another apparently casual Tweet from the White House. This Tweet required production and planning. It was apparently inspired by an April 9 Tweet from Rep. Dan Crenshaw, a Texas Republican who once called for toning down political rhetoric. Crenshaw supports Trump's border wall, denies climate change, opposes any ban on assault weapons, and voted against the election reform act of 2019. His tweet about Rep. Omar used an out-of-context quote to create a political lie based on a racist trope:

> First Member of Congress to ever describe terrorists who killed thousands of Americans on 9/11 as "some people who did something". Unbelievable.
> – **Tweet by Rep. Dan Crenshaw**, April 9, 2019

The Omar's choice of words is similar to what President Bush's language in the immediate aftermath of 9/11, and both require context to determine meaning. Crenshaw's policing of right-wing political correctness had its own problems, since he forwarded, without qualification, a tweet that called CAIR, the Council on American-Islamic Relations, "a terrorist organization" – another lie.

Piling on in the endless demonization of Ilhan Omar, GOP chairwoman Ronna McDaniel called on Democrats to enforce dishonest Republican perceptions. Well, Democrats had done it before, right?

Ilhan Omar isn't just anti-Semitic – she's anti-American. Nearly 3,000 Americans lost their lives to Islamic terrorists on 9/11, yet Omar diminishes it as: "Some people did something." Democrat leaders need to condemn her brazen display of disrespect.

– **Tweet from Ronna McDaniel**, April 9, 2019

The next day, Omar responded to Crenshaw:

This is dangerous incitement, given the death threats I face. I hope leaders of both parties will join me in condemning it. My love and commitment to our country and that of my colleagues should never be in question. We are ALL Americans!

– **Tweet from Rep. Ilhan Omar**, April 10, 2019

Two days later, the president raised the ante with his unconscionable 9/11 Big Lie. For the Democrats, whether they liked it or not, this was a moment of truth.

Establishment Democrats have failed dismally to react responsibly to the dishonest attacks on Ilhan Omar, mustering neither courage nor coherence in the face the latest form of McCarthyite bullying over the past four months. The president's over-the-top Tweet using 9/11 as a bludgeon gave Democrats another chance to behave honorably. Some of the presidential candidates did, but the first response appears to have come from New York Democrat Rep. Alexandria Ocasio-Cortez. [The Twitter date stamps are mysterious, there are two sets, an hour apart; I have followed the same sequence for all the Tweets so, while the exact time may be wrong, the interval seems correct.]

Members of Congress have a duty to respond to the President's explicit attack today. @IlhanMN's life is in danger. For our colleagues to be silent is to be complicit in the outright, dangerous targeting of a member of Congress. We must speak out. "First they came…"

– **Tweet from Rep. Ocasio-Cortez**, 8:39 PM, April 12, 2019

The first Democratic presidential candidate to respond was Bernie Sanders, with prompt and unambiguous support:

Ilhan Omar is a leader with strength and courage. She won't back down to Trump's racism and hate, and neither will we. The disgusting and dangerous attacks against her must end.

– **Tweet from Sen. Bernie Sanders**, 9:07 PM, April 12, 2019

A few minutes later, Elizabeth Warren issued an even stronger condemnation, with a direct rebuke to the president and a direct challenge to her fellow elected officials:

> The President is inciting violence against a sitting Congresswoman—and an entire group of Americans based on their religion. It's disgusting. It's shameful. And any elected leader who refuses to condemn it shares responsibility for it.
>
> – **Tweet from Sen. Elizabeth Warren**, 9:23 PM, April 12, 2019

As the evening wore on, Gov. Jay Inslee tweeted that Trump was jeopardizing Omar and all Muslims. Former Rep. Beto O'Rourke tweeted that Trump's action was "incitement to violence" without mentioning Omar. Mayor Pete Buttigieg's Tweet accused Trump of using 9/11 "to incite his base against a member of Congress, as if for sport," without mentioning Omar. Senator Amy Klobuchar's tweet tried to have it both ways, referring to an arrest for a threat on Omar's life but noting that she had disagreed with Omar before. And that was reportedly all the significant Democratic response to a president deliberately putting a congresswoman in the crosshairs. The next day's responses were generally weaker or absent. There was no word of note from Speaker Nancy Pelosi or the rest of the House "leadership."

Since April 13, there has been no effort to censure the president for reckless endangerment of a Congress member's life. The president committed this crime in plain sight and House Democrats do nothing. By doing nothing, House Democrats signal that as far as they're concerned, Ilhan Omar is fair game. Most of the presidential candidates are no better. This is shameful. My guess is that most Trump supporters look at Democrats with greater scorn than ever for their unwillingness to defend one of their own. As far as Ilhan Omar is concerned, most Democrats have acted and continue to act without principle, without courage, without integrity. This doesn't seem like a really great way to win an election in 2020. Standing up to bigots should be one of the easier things to do politically. If Democrats can't do that, what can they do?

It looks like the Democratic establishment has been doing things the Washington way for so long they can't see themselves clearly in the mirror anymore. No matter who Ilhan Omar truly is, no one has a right to lynch her and those who stand by and watch the lynching happen are just despicable. Here's the way Ilhan Omar described herself to her supporters on April 30:

> Here's the thing that really offends a lot of people and the reason that we are here. I was born—I was born as a very liberated human being, to a country that was colonized, that recognized that they can colonize the land but they can't colonize your mind, to people who recognized that all of us deserve dignity and that no human being was ever, ever going to tell you that you are less than them. Thirteen people organized for our independence in Somalia. So I was born in that breath of recognizing that they might be more powerful than you are, that they might have more technology than you have, they might think that they are wiser than you, they might control all of the institutions, but you control your mind, and that is what sets you free.

> ... the thing that upsets the occupant of the White House, his goons in the Republican Party, many of our colleagues in the Democratic Party, is that—is that they can't stand—they cannot stand that a refugee, a black woman, an immigrant, a Muslim, shows up in Congress thinking she's equal to them. But I say to them, "How else did you expect me to show up?"

> ... So, I know my place in this society. All of you know your place in this society. And it's one that is equal to every single person that walks in it.

Protecting Ilhan Omar should he a reflexive no brainer. Protecting Ilhan Omar is so obviously the right thing to do, it should come easily to anyone of conscience. This is not rocket science. This is not morally ambiguous. To protect Ilhan Omar is to protect us all. The Democratic Party doesn't seem to have a clue that it is in the midst of an existential litmus test. Does the Democratic Party actually stand for anything anymore? There's still time to figure it out, if they start soon. A good starting place would be to stop going for the bait of trolling Republican bigots. Is it some perverse political calculation that brings on timidity, silence, cowardice, a betrayal of the best American values to appease the values of the worst Americans? If the Democratic Party lacks the strength to defend and protect Ilhan Omar just because she's human, then all the talk of American values and freedoms and principles and "the soul of the nation" is just more political garbage.

PART FOUR

Black in America

Every time you see me you want to mess with me.

I'm tired of it. It stops today...

I'm minding my business, officer, I'm minding my business

Please just leave me alone.

I told you the last time, please just leave me alone.

Please.

Please don't touch me.

Do not touch me.

I can't breathe.

I can't breathe.

I can't breathe.

I can't breathe.

I can't breathe.

I can't breathe.

I can't breathe.

I can't breathe.

42.

Assata Shakur, FBI's White Whale?

FBI Terror List: Bombers of US Embassies, Pan Am Flights, Khobar, & USS Cole

> **Author's note:** As you read this article, keep in mind an undisputed, convicted terrorist who bombed hotels and nightclubs in Havana and blew up a Cuban Airliner, killing 73. Luis Posada Carriles has denied the airliner, admitted the rest. The US has refused to deport him to either Cuba or Venezuela or to prosecute him for terrorism because, after all, he was our terrorist, an anti-communist and a CIA asset.

Why does the FBI consider a 65-year-old woman a "Most Wanted Terrorist?"

The World's Number One Terrorist on the FBI web site, at the top of the FBI's official list of "Most Wanted Terrorists," is Joanne Deborah Chesimard, whose birth name is Byron and whose current name is Assata Shakur.

Shakur, 65, is the aunt and godmother of the late hip-hop icon Tupac Shakur. A fugitive since 1979, she has lived in Cuba under political asylum since 1984. In her twenties, she was a leading black liberation activist in New York, relentlessly pursued by authorities until she was jailed in 1973. Dubiously convicted of murder in 1977, she escaped from prison while her appeal was pending. In 2005, the FBI, without alleging any terrorist acts, retroactively labeled her a "domestic terrorist." And on May 2, 2013, the FBI named her the Terrorist List's first woman, first black woman, first mother, first godmother and perhaps even first grandmother.

"She's a danger to the American government," said FBI agent, Aaron T. Ford, with a straight face, at a news conference called to

229

make the Most Wanted Terrorist announcement. Ford is the agent in charge of the FBI's Newark, New Jersey, division. The FBI scheduled the media event on the 40th anniversary of the crime for which Shakur was convicted in 1977, and about which she has always maintained her innocence.

"She continues to flaunt her freedom in the face of this horrific crime," State Police superintendent Col. Rick Fuentes said at the same news conference, where he called the case "an open wound" for troopers in New Jersey and around the country.

As it turns out, she's not widely perceived as a threat by much of anyone. She continues to advocate revolutionary change, she writes books and shorter pieces, she has a YouTube channel, "Assata Shakur Speaks Out." Her life and work are included in black studies courses at colleges like Bucknell and Rutgers. The Cuban government pays her something like $13 a day to help keep her alive.

Officially, the FBI says she "should be considered armed and dangerous"

Outside the law enforcement community, those who know about Assata Shakur perceive an entirely different person. The newly-elected mayor of Jackson, Mississippi, considers her "wrongfully convicted." A sociology professor at Columbia University says there's "just no material evidence" to support the lone conviction that resulted from seven different trials. A New York City councilman has called for the bounty on Shakur to be rescinded.

For both sides, for all Americans, this case represents some of the unfinished business of the "Sixties."

The critical event that is perceived so differently by different people took place on May 2, 1973, when two white New Jersey State Troopers, in separate cruisers, stopped a Pontiac LeMans with Vermont plates on the New Jersey Turnpike for a "broken taillight." The car held two black men and Shakur, all members of the revolutionary Black Liberation Army. In the shootout that followed, a trooper and one of the black men died. Shakur and the other trooper were wounded. The other black man, Sundiata Acoli, drove away in the Pontiac with

Shakur seriously wounded, and they were arrested separately not long after.

FBI Says, "Her standard of living is higher than most Cubans"

The FBI's current version of the event has no ambiguity: "On May 2, 1973, Chesimard [Shakur], who was part of a revolutionary extremist organization known as the Black Liberation Army, and two accomplices were stopped for a motor vehicle violation on the New Jersey Turnpike by two troopers with the New Jersey State Police.... Chesimard and her accomplices opened fire on the troopers. One trooper was wounded and the other was shot and killed execution-style at point-blank range. Chesimard fled the scene but was subsequently apprehended. One of her accomplices was killed in the shoot-out and the other was also apprehended and remains in jail."

In fact, Shakur was shot twice, apparently with her hands up, while turning away. The bullets wounded her upper arms, armpit and chest, all of which is undisputed. Expert medical testimony at trial held that her wounds rendered her incapable of firing any weapon. There was no forensic evidence to show that she had fired a weapon, no gunpowder residue, no fingerprint on any weapon. The surviving trooper admitted on the stand that he had lied to the Grand Jury and testified at trial that he had never seen Shakur with a gun. After a New Jersey legislator reportedly lobbied the jury for conviction while they were sequestered, the all-white jury delivered a guilty verdict.

FBI COINTELPRO crimes give context to Assata Shakur's actions

One of her attorneys, Lennox Hinds, now a law professor at Rutgers University, put this event in the context of the time, when the FBI was regularly violating the law with its COINTELPRO program that targeted people the FBI deemed too radical, especially anti-war protestors and black power advocates. The FBI says all COINTELPRO operations ended in 1971, adding somewhat delicately: "COINTELPRO was later rightfully criticized by Congress and the American people for abridging first amendment rights and for other reasons."

Those other reasons might include law breaking, since COINTEL-PRO activities included burglaries, wiretaps, physical threats, vandalism and other illegal actions, even alleged assassinations. There have been no prosecutions of COINTELPRO crimes.

As Lennox Hines told Democracy NOW! the day after the FBI's Terrorist List press conference:

> In the FBI's own words, they wanted to discredit, to stop the rise of a black messiah – that was the fear of the FBI – so that there would not be a Mau Mau, in their words, uprising in the United States. And they were, of course, referring to the liberation movement that occurred in Kenya, Africa.

> Now, the FBI carried out a campaign targeting not only the Black Panther Party. They targeted SCLC [Southern Christian Leadership Council]. They targeted Martin Luther King. They targeted Harry Belafonte. They targeted Eartha Kitt. They targeted anyone who supported the struggle for civil rights, that they considered to be dangerous.

William Kunstler, one of Shakur's several defense attorneys, had successfully introduced COINTELPRO evidence at a trial of members of the American Indian Movement (AIM). His motion to do so in Shakur's trial was denied.

Perjury to indict, jury tampering to convict – the New Jersey way?

Referring to the FBI's sometimes criminal political repression, attorney Hines said:

> It is in that context we need to look at what happened on the New Jersey Turnpike in 1973. What they call Joanne Chesimard, what we know as Assata Shakur, she was targeted by the FBI, stopped. And the allegation that she was a cold-blooded killer is not supported by any of the forensic evidence.

> If we look at the trial, we'll find that she was victimized, she was shot. She was shot in the back. The bullet exited and broke the clavicle in her shoulder. She could not raise a gun. She could not raise her hand to shoot. And she was shot while her hands were in the air.

Now, that is the forensic evidence. There is not one scintilla of evidence placing a gun in her hand. No arsenic residue was found on her clothing or on her hands. So, the allegation by the state police that she took an officer's gun and shot him, executed him in cold blood, is not only false, but it is designed to inflame.

An example of such inflammatory rhetoric came from Special Agent Ford at the May 2 press conference: "Openly and freely in Cuba, she continues to maintain and promote her terrorist ideology. She provides anti-US government speeches espousing the Black Liberation Army message of revolution and terrorism. No person, no matter what his or her political or moral convictions are, is above the law. Joanne Chesimard is a domestic terrorist who murdered a law enforcement officer, execution-style." And even worse, according to the FBI, "Her standard of living is higher than most Cubans".

Presumably Agent Ford is aware that Sundiata Acoli remains in prison for killing the "law enforcement officer execution style," that the label "domestic terrorist" was arbitrarily applied in 2005, and that Assata Shakur considers "Joanne Chesimard" her slave name. Agent Ford may also know that acknowledging any of those facts would run the risk of possibly humanizing this sexagenarian "danger to the American government." And Agent Ford is likely trained to understand that the FBI's inflammatory rhetoric can help distract people from facts

The FBI press release of May 2 dishonestly fudges the case, saying, "Chesimard [Shakur] and Squire [Acoli] were charged, convicted, and sentenced for the murder," as if there hadn't been two separate trials, four years apart; and as if the second trial of Shakur hadn't taken place while the convicted murderer of the trooper was already serving his sentence.

The first person convicted of the trooper's murder has been in prison since 1973, a point that goes unmentioned in most media coverage of the Shakur case. In an egregious example of slanted reporting, The New York Times on May 2 not only fails to mention Acoli, but frames the story with the trooper's "execution," thus leaving the reader little room to infer anything but Shakur's sole guilt, even though that's false even if she's partly guilty as an accomplice according to law.

Special Agent Ford sounds a bit obsessed as he hurls verbal harpoons

According to NBC News, Agent Ford said there was no specific new threat that led the bureau to add Shakur to the list. He said she "remains an inspiration to the radical, left-wing, anti-government, black separatist movement.... Some of those people, and the people that espouse those ideas, are still in this country. So, we'd be naïve not to think that there's some communication between her and the people she used to run around with."

While over-the-top comments at a press conference might be hyperbole in the heat of the moment, Agent Ford's comments three weeks later were much the same in an interview with Christine Amanpour as reported by Yahoo! News on May 23:

> It's unfortunate that someone involved in the murder of an officer, kidnappings, hostage takings and robberies in a 14-year span is revered by a segment of society.... For us, justice never sleeps, justice never rests. We're looking to bring her to justice because she committed a heinous act. She is a member of an organization [Black Liberation Army] which espoused hate against the US government....

Agent Ford was apparently not asked how one should feel about the US government when it executes such illegal programs as COINTELPRO. And he didn't say what the government knows of Shakur's communications through the PRISM program of the NSA [National Security Agency] or other electronic surveillance.

Talking about a 65-year-old woman effectively confined to Cuba, Agent Ford called her "a supreme terror against the government" and said without apparent irony: "We absolutely still consider her a threat. She is a menace to society still. She has connections and associations from members of that party she belonged to years ago. They are still espousing anti-government views...." The FBI seems to have a problem distinguishing between political thought crime and actual terrorism.

Shakur's letter to the Pope has biography, polemic, analysis, confession

In 1997, when Pope John Paul II was planning to visit Cuba, the New Jersey superintendent of state police wrote asking him to intervene on the state's side in the Shakur case by persuading Cuba to extradite her. Superintendent Carl Williams did not make his letter to the Pope public, but he made sure his request was well publicized.

Learning of this, Shakur wrote the Pope her own open letter, which she also broadcast. Aired on Democracy NOW! in 1998 and again on May 2, the letter details her story of her life and resistance, with an early reference to the secret New Jersey letter:

> Why, I wonder, do I warrant such attention? What do I represent that is such a threat? Please let me take a moment to tell you about myself. My name is Assata Shakur and I was born and raised in the United States. I am a descendant of Africans who were kidnapped and brought to the Americas as slaves. I spent my early childhood in the racist segregated South. I later moved to the northern part of the country, where I realized that Black people were equally victimized by racism and oppression....

Later she admits to harboring the very thoughts the FBI still considers criminal: "I think that it is important to make one thing very clear. I have advocated and I still advocate revolutionary changes in the structure and in the principles that govern the United States. I advocate self-determination for my people and for all oppressed inside the United States. I advocate an end to capitalist exploitation, the abolition of racist policies, the eradication of sexism, and the elimination of political repression. If that is a crime, then I am totally guilty."

At the end of her fundamentally political, 1800-word-plus statement, written on Martin Luther King's birthday, she concluded with her request to the Pope:

> I am not writing to ask you to intercede on my behalf. I ask nothing for myself. I only ask you to examine the social reality of the United States and to speak out against the human rights violations that are taking place.

To judge by the public record, the Pope chose not to get involved.

Pursuing Assata Shakur has taken on a ritual aspect

The FBI and other agencies first became interested in Assata Shakur (then still Chesimard: she changed it around 1970) in the mid-1960s, perhaps at the time of her first arrest in 1967, when she and about 100 other students demonstrated at the Borough of Manhattan Community College. Many charges and sometimes arrests followed, but she wasn't held or tried, not even in 1971, after she was shot in the stomach. Later she reportedly said she was glad she was shot, so she wouldn't be afraid to be shot again. That case was dismissed.

In the early 1970s, Shakur had been accused of enough crimes that she was the subject of a nationwide manhunt as the "revolutionary mother hen" of a Black Liberation Army cell accused of a "series of cold-blooded murders of New York City Police officers." Police pursuit of Assata Shakur became an increasingly ritualistic hunt.

Deputy Commissioner Robert Daley of the New York City Police called Assata Shakur "the final wanted fugitive, the soul of the gang, the mother hen who kept them together, kept them moving, kept them shooting."

By early 1973, the FBI was issuing nearly daily reports on her status, activities and allegations. She was even the apparent namesake of the FBI operation CHESROB, though it was not limited to her in focus. For all the attention and earlier allegations, when Assata Shakur was captured on May 2, 1973, she was not charged with any of these earlier alleged crimes. Starting in December 1973, once Shakur had recovered sufficiently from her gunshot wounds, various jurisdictions brought her to trial for various charges, with mostly dismal results:

- Dec. 1973 – bank robbery – hung jury, dismissed.
- Dec. 1973 – re-trial, bank robbery – acquitted.
- Jan. 1974 – murder of NJ trooper – mistrial due to her pregnancy.
- May 1974 – two separate murder indictments – lack of evidence, dismissed.

- Sept. 1975 – kidnapping – acquitted.

- Jan. 1976 – bank robbery – acquitted.

- Feb. 1977 – murder of NJ trooper – convicted.

Shakur would spend more than six years in various prisons, often under deplorable conditions, with brutal treatment. In 1979, the United Nations Commission on Human Rights found that her treatment was "totally unbefitting to any prisoner."

The UN investigation of alleged human rights abuses of political prisoners cited Shakur as "one of the worst cases" – in "a class of victims of FBI misconduct through the COINTELPRO strategy and other forms of illegal government conduct who as political activists have been selectively targeted for provocation, false arrests, entrapment, fabrication of evidence and spurious criminal prosecutions."

On November 2, 1979, Shakur's brother Mutulu Shakur brought two other men and a woman to see her in the prison visitors' room. Prison officials did not search them. Prison officials did not run checks on their false identification papers. They had guns. They took two guards as hostages and left with Shakur. No one was hurt, the guards were left in the parking lot.

The hunt for Assata Shakur goes on in fourth decade

For the next five years, Shakur was a fugitive with the FBI searching for her, and her community protecting her. Three days after her escape, more than 5,000 demonstrators rallied in her support. The FBI circulated wanted posters; her supporters circulated "Assata Shakur Is Welcome Here" posters. In 1980, the head of the FBI complained that residents weren't cooperating. Residents were alienated by heavy-handed police tactics including a crude, door-smashing raid that turned up nothing and by surveillance of Shakur's daughter going to grade school.

Although the intensity of the search has waned – the FBI knows where she is, after all – both the FBI and the New Jersey State Police reportedly have an agent assigned to the case fulltime.

237

In recent years, the pursuit has taken on an anniversary pattern. On May 2, 2005, the FBI named Shakur a domestic terrorist and posted a $1 million reward for her capture. On May 2 this year, the FBI promoted her to the Most Wanted Terrorist list and New Jersey added another $1 million to the reward pool.

How and why these decisions are made is unclear. In response to an inquiry, the FBI Office of Public Affairs stated: "The inner workings of how people get selected to the List are not something the FBI shares with the general public." According to the same office:

People are added to the List when they meet the following criteria:

- They have threatened the security of US nationals or the national security of the USA.

- They are considered a dangerous menace to society.

- They are the subject of a pending FBI investigation and have an active federal arrest warrant.

- The worldwide publicity must be thought to be able to assist in the apprehension of the terrorist.

The FBI did not respond to a request for a definition of "terror" or "terrorist." Nor did the FBI respond to specific questions about Chesimard/Shakur "due to the ongoing investigation into her whereabouts."

Joanne Deborah Byron, then Chesimard for three years ending in 1970, took her new name then for its specific meaning: Assata ("she who struggles") Olugbala ("for the people") Shakur ("the thankful one").

At her trial in 1977, Shakur gave an opening statement to that all-white jury that concluded:

Although the court considers us peers, many of you have had different backgrounds and different learning and life experiences. It is important to me that you understand some of those differences. I only ask of you that you listen carefully. I only ask that you listen not only to what these witnesses say but to how they say it. Our lives are no more precious or no less precious than yours. We ask only that you be as open and as fair as you would want us to be, were we sitting in the jury box determining your guilt or innocence. Our lives and the lives that surround us depend on your fairness.

Ten years after her trial, Shakur was living in Cuba, re-united with her daughter there, but still an engaged activist. In 1987, she published "Assata: An Autobiography," which remains available as an e-book. That same year, in Public Enemy's hip-hop hit "Rebel Without a Pause," Chuck D shouted "supporter of Chesimard" and brought her to the attention of a new generation.

Assata Shakur became a hip-hop meme. The hip-hop artist Common was unapologetically supportive in "A Song for Assata." This allowed others to raise a stink when Common played the White House on 2011.

Writing in The Grio, Chuck "Jigsaw" Creekmur sees Assata Shakur's appeal this way: "In a quintessentially American way, some folks in hip-hop just appreciate the raw 'gangsta' of a woman who didn't back down, stood firm in her convictions, completely bucked the system, and lived to tell the Pope about it."

The Question for History May Be: Which Side Needs Rehabilitation More?

An attorney who once represented Shakur, himself a long-time black nationalist, Chokwe Lumumba was recently elected mayor of Jackson, Mississippi, by a wide margin. He told Democracy NOW!:

> I've always felt that Assata Shakur was wrongfully convicted, so she shouldn't be on a wanted list at all. She never should have been in prison. She was actually shot herself and wounded and paralyzed at the time that the person who she was convicted of killing was shot. So she obviously couldn't have shot him. And she also was arrested, which caused the incident, for about eight different charges which she later was found not guilty of or were dismissed. So I think it's unfortunate. Assata Shakur, I believe, will historically be proven to be a hero of our times....

That's just what the Ahabs of the FBI seem to fear most.

Update 1: In 2017, President Trump demanded that Cuba return "the cop-killer Joanne Chesimard" to the US and announced the US was reversing President Obama's opening to Cuba. Cuba ignored the demand. In February 2019, to honor Black History Month, the airline JetBlue put up an exhibit of posters at the JFK airport in New York. The posters (ready-made by a third party vendor) included Assata Shakur, calling her a "Civil Rights activist and a member of the Black Panther Party." The poster bullet points also said: "Became the first woman to be placed on the FBI's Most Wanted list after escaping to Cuba from prison where she was serving a life sentence for the 1973 murder of a police officer" and that "Many people believe Shakur to be a political champion who is innocent of the criminal accusation against her."

The NY Post reported on the poster, saying that it "had been circulating on pro-cop websites." Three weeks after the exhibit went up, on February 23, a tweet from @Jennymz76Jenny went to @JetBlue saying: "Rumor has it that you are celebrating Black History Month at LGA by celebrating Assata Shakur? She is a convicted cop killer. Please tell me this is not true." There were no other complaints, according to the airline.

Jet Blue responded by removing the poster and apologizing "for any offense the poster may have caused." The New Jersey Patrolmen's Benevolent Association expressed appreciation. Assata Shakur, now in her seventies, remains on the FBI's Most Wanted List. The FBI is offering $1 million as a reward "for information directly leading to the apprehension of Joanne Chesimard." Another $1 million reward is offered by the New Jersey State Police.

Update 2: Cuban exile Luis Posada Carriles died on May 23, 2018, at the age of 90 in Florida. In 2005, Posada was arrested and charged with being in the country illegally, a judge blocked his deportation to Venezuela and granted him asylum on the basis that he might be tortured. The US Justice Department sought to keep him in jail because he was "an admitted mastermind of terrorist plots and attacks." He was released in 2007.

43.

Trayvon Martin in the United States of Zimmerman

Context 2019: On February 26, 2012, in Sanford, Florida, Afro-Peruvian George Zimmerman, 28, shot and killed African-American Trayvon Martin, 17, who was unarmed. On April 11, a special prosecutor charged Zimmerman with second-degree murder. On July 13, 2013, the jury of six women (5 white) found Zimmerman not guilty. The verdict was widely seen as unjust. A Facebook post included the phrase "back lives matter," leading to the Black Lives Matter movement. In 2018, Zimmerman demonstrated to a court that he was $2.5 million in debt, was assigned a public defender, and ended up pleading no contest to a charge of stalking a private investigator for a documentary film company. In 2019 he was banned from the dating app Bumble.

A jury verdict is not the same as moral judgment

The most important thing about the Zimmerman verdict is that it's a clear demonstration of how the American legal system is only about law. It is not about justice. It is not even about the consequences of killing another person.

The verdict demonstrates that, despite the protestations of the law that it is about justice, that's only a pretense to cover the reality: that when the law produces justice, it's a coincidence, an accident, a surprise. The law is only about the law.

And it's no wonder, when you stop to think about who makes laws and why. Justice is one of the last things on the legislative mind, if it ever gets there at all.

And so, the Zimmerman verdict can be seen as a metaphor for the American way of life and death these days, a psychic Rorschach

241

blot of our culture, a measure of the zeitgeist in the United States of Zimmerman, the US of Z.

In the distorting mirror of the Zimmerman verdict we glimpse all too much of who we are today as a nation – not what each of us is, nor what all of us are, but an inescapable collage of how exceptional we are in so many ways of which we should be ashamed. Some of those reflections are collected here:

A Rough Guide to Life in the US of Z – United States of Zimmerman

In the US of Z the law allows people to hunt each other.

In the US of Z you can be a self-appointed volunteer vigilante, and you have permission to decide that a person is up to no good based solely on the color of his skin, and maybe the time of day and your own bigotry.

In the US of Z you may racial profile to your heart's content and the judge won't let it be used against you in court.

In the US of Z, you don't have to feel remorse if you kill someone, even if that person did nothing wrong, even if you went out of your way to get to kill him. You can just believe it was God's plan.

In the US of Z, there is confusion about whether Trayvon Martin is another Medgar Evers or Emmett Till. He might have grown up to be a Medgar Evers. He died an Emmett Till.

In the US of Z, the acquittal of someone who stalked and killed a young black man comes as no surprise. But it's still surprising that Zimmerman's defense attorney asserted, in all apparent seriousness, that in the same circumstances, Zimmerman would not even have been charged if he was black.

In the US of Z, it is no surprise for a black man to go uncharged when he does not survive his arrest. That's not what the defense attorney meant, because in the US of Z, it's the killer Zimmerman who is somehow the victim.

In the US of Z, there are white people who believe that black people don't care about dead black boys except when whites kill them.

Is it ever fair to arrest a judge's son?

In the US of Z, some people still think it's unfair that Zimmerman was ever arrested, even 44 days after the killing. They don't believe that George Zimmerman's father, Robert Zimmerman, a retired Virginia Supreme Court magistrate, reportedly talked the police out of arresting George the night he killed Trayvon. Is it even fair to arrest a judge's son?

In the US of Z, the Zimmerman verdict no doubt gives some hope to Michael David Dunn, 45, a Florida white man who killed an unarmed black teenager in the back seat of a car for having the music too loud, shooting him at least eight times. Dunn has pleaded not guilty, saying he felt threatened and acted in self-defense, and besides the law gives him the right to stand his ground.

In the US of Z, having rap music too loud for the guy who drives up beside you in the parking lot is an even worse offense than walking home in the rain with Skittles and iced tea while black.

In the US of Z, WWB – Walking While Black – is risky behavior that sensible people avoid. So is SITBSWB – Sitting in the Back Seat While Black.

In the US of Z, your older brother can go on TV (CNN) and trash talk your victim and pretend he's starting a healing dialogue and the news people will just nod. "Healing dialogue" for the Zimmermans starts with "blacks are bad".

In the US of Z your brother's behavior doesn't seem so odd because your father, the retired Virginia magistrate decides to publish an e-book right before your trial started, with the title: "Florida v. Zimmerman – Uncovering the Malicious Prosecution of My Son George."

In the US of Z, Judge Zimmerman makes clear, among other things, that in his view the "True Racists" in the US of Z are all African-American. And the judge names among others, the Congressional Black Caucus, the NAACP, the Black Chamber of Commerce, the United Negro College Fund and Trayvon Martin's undertaker.

In the US of Z, someone puts up a "Kill Zimmerman" page on Facebook that gets more than 7,000 "likes" in just a few hours, gets reported by an unknown number of people, and doesn't get taken down right away.

In the US of Z, perhaps counterintuitively till you think about it, the Zimmerman verdict, like the O.J. verdict, went to the money side.

In the US of Z there is little appreciation of the dark irony that the Zimmerman verdict was delivered in Seminole County.

44.

Democrats Join Republicans in High-Tech Lynching of Black Nominee

Context 2019: On November 18, 2013, President Obama nominated Debo Adegbile, then senior counsel on the Senate Judiciary Committee, to serve as Assistant Attorney General for the Civil Rights Commission. His qualifications for the job went unchallenged, but there was considerable objection (much of it in seeming bad faith) to Adegbile's participation as a defense attorney in an appeal to the Supreme Court on behalf of convicted (in 1982) cop-killer Mumia Abu-Jamal, who may well be innocent. Abu-Jamal's case is riddled with pieces that don't fit. As a result the case has a long and torturous history. Adegbile's involvement was short term and limited. He took part in a brief challenging jury selection tainted by race. Abu-Jamal's jury, 10 whites and 2 blacks (after the judge removed a third black) reached a unanimous verdict at the end of a chaotic trial in which Abu-Jamal was denied his right to counsel of his choice. When Adegbile was nominated, Senators from both parties who should have known better objected to his nomination on the basis of his participating in the appeal for Mumia Abu-Jamal. When his nomination came to the floor in March 2014, Republicans mounted a filibuster. The vote to end the filibuster failed 47-52 (45 Republicans and 7 Democrats). In September 2014, Adegbile withdrew his nomination and went into private practice at the firm of Wilmer Cutler Pickering Hale and Dorr.

Seven Democratic dwarves prefer police state veto to due process of law

When the United States Senate voted against the United States Constitution on March 5, 2014, the anti-constitutional majority included, as expected, all the Republican senators voting, plus seven principle-free Democrats.

The majority vote represents an affirmation of imaginary guilt by association, with deep racial overtones, in what amounted to a Senatorial lynching of an attorney who dared participate in the constitutionally-mandated legal defense of a pre-judged black man long since found guilty and still in prison after thirty years. These senators were less persuaded by the Supreme Court's finding of a flawed trial than by the orchestrated baying by white vigilantes whose police state mentality allows no nuance when they want someone dead no matter what.

The Senate vote in question on March 5 was whether to end a Republican filibuster against President Obama's nominee to serve as the United States Assistant Attorney General in charge of the Civil Rights Division of the US Department of Justice – attorney Debo Adegbile, 48, who is currently senior counsel for the Senate Judiciary Committee. A native New Yorker, he was born Adebowale Patrick Akande Adegbile (his father Nigerian, his mother Irish) and raised by his single mother. As a child he was an actor on Sesame Street for nine years. He earned his law degree from New York University law school in 1994.

After seven years in private practice at the N.Y. law firm of Paul, Weiss, Rifkind, & Garrison, Adegbile joined the NAACP Legal Defense and Education Fund, where he was a respected litigator from 2001 to 2013. He argued his first Supreme Court case in 2009, defending the Voting Rights Act. His career path, without the major cases, is similar to that of the late Supreme Court justice Thurgood Marshall, but only up to this point.

Republicans opposing Adegbile are vehement, adamant and dishonest in their opposition, which is rooted in passion and prejudice. Their critique does not challenge Adegbile's competence or qualifications to be in charge of the Civil Rights Division, which currently has an acting head. Arguing Adegbile's nomination on its merits is not something Republicans even tried to do. Their "case" against Adegbile was an ugly, demagogic stew of partisanship, race baiting and irrelevance worthy of the late Senator Joe McCarthy at his worst. Republican Senator Ted Cruz of Texas expressed this well on the Senate floor, March 4, 2014:

I stand with the Fraternal Order of Police in opposition to Debo Adegbile.... We all should agree that those who go out of their way to celebrate, to lionize, convicted cop killers are not suitable for major leadership roles at the Department of Justice. Under Adegbile's supervision, LDF lawyers fanned the flames of racial tension through rallies and protests and a media campaign all to portray Mumia Abu-Jamal, an unrepentant cop killer, as a political prisoner.

In this brief statement, Cruz manages to:

- Defend what amounts to a police lobby veto over presidential appointments to the Justice Department;

- Lie about Adegbile's activities (no evidence to support Cruz's smear);

- Invent "lionization" of the man at the center of a case that is genuinely about due process and the death penalty, a case that has been found wanting by the Supreme Court;

- Pretend that racial tensions have not been present in this case since the moment it started (the trial judge promised "I'm going to help them fry the nigger," and a higher judge found the comment not prejudicial);

- Lie about Adegbile's "supervision," offering no evidence, using only a kind of "guilt" by association that also attacks free speech;

- Reach final judgment on a case in which he has played no role, and in which both sides have arguable positions for which neither side has managed to provide ultimately definitive evidence;

- Illustrate one of the ways Abu-Jamal is used as – and is, in fact – a political prisoner, whatever else he may be.

Cruz and other senators opposing Adegbile got many of their distorted talking points from the National Fraternal Order of Police

(FOP), a Washington-based labor union and lobbying organization that claims membership of more than 330,000 police employees and whose motto is "Building on a Proud Tradition." (According to FBI statistics, there are more than a million full-time law enforcement employees in the US.) In a letter to the president dated January 6, 2014, FOP president Chuck Canterbury expressed his organization's opposition to Adegbile with a rambling argument in which FOP's apparently real issue doesn't appear until the fourth paragraph, which complains: "The Administration did not consult the FOP during the decision-making process for this nomination.... This nomination can be interpreted in only one way: it is a thumb in the eye of our nation's law enforcement officers."

More raw emotionalism came earlier in Canterbury's fundamentally racist letter:

> As word of this nomination spreads through the law enforcement community, reactions range from anger to incredulity. Under this nominee's leadership, the Legal Defense Fund (LDF) of the National Association for the Advancement of Colored People volunteered their services to represent Wesley Cook, better known to the world as Mumia Abu-Jamal – our country's most notorious cop-killer. There is no disputing that Philadelphia Police Officer Daniel Faulkner was murdered by this thug. His just sentence – death – was undone by your nominee and others like him who turned the justice system on its head with unfounded and unproven allegations of racism.

As Canterbury is presumably well aware, Abu-Jamal remains in prison under a life sentence, and his death sentence was undone by the Supreme Court under John Roberts (who has also done pro bono work for a man who killed eight people). But logic requires the FOP to falsify the facts in order justify their untenable and seemingly race-based argument: "We are aware of the tried and true shield behind which activists of Adegbile's ilk are wont to hide – that everyone is entitled to a defense; but surely you would agree that a defense should not be based on falsely disparaging and savaging the good name and reputation of a lifeless police officer."

This claim, unsupported by evidence and rooted in irrelevance (even if true in any respect), is essentially an attack on the US

Constitution's Sixth Amendment – not an effort to eliminate completely the right of a defendant to have legal representation, but an effort to give others the power to decide which defendants shall have constitutional protection, and which shall not.

The Sixth Amendment does not allow for such intervention by hostile parties like an enraged and frustrated police union. The amendment says, in pertinent part: "In all criminal prosecutions, the accused shall enjoy the right ... to have the Assistance of Counsel for his defense." In its own brief statement of Goals, the FOP states: "We believe that Law is the safeguard to freedom, and it is our duty to defend it." The effect of the FOP's letter to the president is to carve out arbitrary exceptions to its stated "belief" and "duty" whenever constitutional law serves a defendant that the FOP just wants to kill. The FOP stands ready to defend the law only to the extent that the law does its bidding.

The FOP's attack wasn't intended to have integrity, logic, or supporting evidence. Its primary purpose was political, to block a non-white defender of civil rights whose record suggested he would be effective in the civil rights job at Justice. The shortest, quickest route to blocking Adegbile would be to panic enough Democrats to prevent the Senate from even voting on his nomination. Democrats, with a 54-46 vote advantage in a party line vote, could lose four members and still shut down the Republican filibuster against Adegbile (with Vice President Biden present to break a tie). The challenge for Republicans was to terrorize more than four Democrats into cutting and running. What better way to panic politicians than to scream, irrelevantly, "cop-killer" and imply that a vote for a qualified attorney was the same as supporting a hated black man? To Democrats' shame, the deceitful race-baiting worked.

Quick to pick up on the FOP's "thumb-in-the-eye" letter was the FOP in Philadelphia, where the killing took place in 1981. Philadelphia in 1981 had been close to open race war for years, with Police Chief/Mayor Frank Rizzo often making matters worse with pre-emptive raids, a vicious cycle that culminated in the Police bombing of the MOVE house, home of a black collective in a black neighborhood. MOVE was a black liberation movement started in 1972 and a continual target of police confrontation until the 1985 bombing that killed 11 MOVE members, five of them children. The bombing set off a massive fire that destroyed 65 homes. Survivors sued the city and the police, winning a $1.5 million jury award in 1996.

That's lethal context of mass killing suppressed by the FOP's tunnel vision: "It's [Adegbile's nomination] an absolute slap in the face to every police officer, especially those who gave their lives in the line of duty. There's outrage, there's resentment there's disapproval – you name it and our cops are feeling it," said the Philadelphia FOP president, adding that he'd be lobbying his senators on the nomination, meaning Democrat Bob Casey, since Republican Pat Toomey was already in the bag (and among the vigilantes).

A few weeks later, Senator Bob Casey abjectly caved to the pressure in a sadly craven political statement, issued on a Friday (February 28):

> I believe that every person nominated by the President of the United States for a high-level position such as Assistant Attorney General for Civil Rights should be given fair and thoughtful consideration as senators discharge their responsibility of 'advise and consent.' I respect that our system of law ensures the right of all citizens to legal representation no matter how heinous the crime. At the same time, it is important that we ensure that Pennsylvanians and citizens across the country have full confidence in their public representatives – both elected and appointed. The vicious murder of Officer Faulkner in the line of duty and the events that followed in the 30 years since his death have left open wounds for Maureen Faulkner and her family as well as the City of Philadelphia. After carefully considering this nomination and having met with both Mr. Adegbile as well as the Fraternal Order of Police, I will not vote to confirm the nominee.

Instead of "fair and thoughtful consideration," Casey voted for a filibuster. Instead of respect for our system, this lawyer and Democrat voted for random application of the law, sometimes dictated by dishonest hate-brokers.

Casey was the first Democrat to collapse completely in the face of the emotional illogic of anti-constitutionalists. Casey, 54, a child of white privilege and a career politician, was first elected to the Senate in 2006. Even though he's not up for re-election this year (not till 2018), he could not find the strength to stand for principle against a baying mob.

Public reaction was even harsher on philly.com, where "Attytood" was able to distinguish between his own feeling about Abu-Jamal ("the guy murdered a cop in cold blood") and the value of the Constitution:

> Faced with the choice of voting for a good man or responding to the bullying tactics of the Fraternal Order of Police, Casey wilted. I don't know why that's a surprise. Spinelessness has been a trademark of Casey's career.... What does Bob Casey stand for? Cowards tend to congregate, and so Casey's chickenry encouraged six other feckless wonders – [Senators] Pryor, Walsh, Manchin, Heitkamp, Donnelly, and Coons (say it ain't so, Chris) – to join in....

Senator Mark Pryor of Arkansas, 51, another son of white privilege and career politician, is running for a third term in the Senate. After two easy races in 2002 and 2008, he's now considered one of the most vulnerable Democrats in 2014. His record has no well-known highlights. He has voted to keep prisoners in Guantanamo, to set up extra-constitutional military commissions, and to block background checks for gun purchases. Pryor issued no statement explaining his vote against his party's president's nominee, and if he made any public comment, it remains obscure.

Senator John Walsh of Montana, 54, was appointed to the Senate on March 9, 2014, having already announced his plan to run for the seat in the 2014 election. He's not a career politician, but as a retired National Guard general, he's presumably drawing both a pension and a salary from the government. Walsh's campaign website slogan is "Montana courage," but the site has no information about his vote against Adegbile, or much of anything else requiring courage. A Montana newspaper reported that: "Walsh said through a spokeswoman that he voted against Adegbile because the controversy over his appointment would 'follow him to the Justice Department and distract from the important work of defending civil and voting rights.' " A few days later, Walsh was criticizing his opponent in the Montana Senate race of having "a cruel ideology, a cowardly ideology."

Senator Joe Manchin III of West Virginia, 67 and a former governor, was first elected in 2010 (a special election) and won a full term in 2012 with 60% of the vote. He is devoted to the coal interests of his state, supports the Keystone XL pipeline, and was named second most bi-partisan senator in 2011 by Congressional Quarterly. After voting against Adegbile, according to the Washington Post, the usually chatty Manchin was tight-lipped with reporters, saying only, "I made a conscientious decision after talking to the wife of the victim, I made a conscientious decision, I made a conscientious decision" repeatedly. Manchin's campaign website offers an "editorial" written by the campaign claiming Manchin was "Right to Follow Conscience." The "editorial" does not mention the Constitution.

Senator Heidi Heitkamp of North Dakota, 59, an attorney and former state attorney general, was first elected to the Senate in 2012. A search for "Adegbile" on her official webpage turns up nothing. In an email statement, Heitkamp explained her anti-constitutional vote with suitably craven illogic in support of the demagoguery that intimidated her, affirming the right of police state tactics to trump due process:

> Mr. Adegbile has had an impressive career advocating for civil rights. But, as a former Attorney General, I was very concerned about a nominee who would face such staunch opposition from law enforcement officers from day one, as that will only make it more difficult for the Civil Rights division at DOJ – a very important and needed group – to do its job. I agree with North Dakota law enforcement officers that the President would be better served by nominating another individual who is not so controversial.

The speciousness of this argument prompted Ari Melber of MSNBC to write Heitkamp an open letter calling her on the hypocrisy of claiming to defend voting rights in a fundraising letter sent out after she has just undermined a strong defender of voting rights. His letter concludes, "President Obama called the vote a 'travesty.' And if this is the precedent you want to set – that no one who's defended 'controversial' clients can serve the public – then it's a travesty for all of us."

Senator Joe Donnelly of Indiana, 59, an attorney, former Congressman and child of white privilege, was elected to the Senate in

2012. His official website has no mention of "Adegbile," but touts a ranking that rates him slightly more conservative than liberal, neither of which explains a vote against constitutional principle by a lawyer. Appearing briefly on an Indiana TV station, Donnelly followed the Heitkamp script to explain his vote against Adegbile: "In Sen. Donnelly's interview with Amos, Donnelly stressed that while he respected Adegbile's qualifications for the job, Donnelly was convinced that the controversy would 'undermine' Adegbile's 'ability to work with law enforcement officials,' given the fierce opposition by police organizations, including the Fraternal Order of Police, to Adegbile's involvement in the Abu-Jamal case." Or in other words, why defend a qualified non-white man from being hounded by police bigots who don't even tell the truth?

Senator Chris Coons of Delaware, 51, a child of white privilege, has Yale graduate degrees in both divinity and law. A former county council president, Coons won the 2010 Senate special election against Christine O'Donnell. He is running for a full term in 2014. Coons initially came out in support of Adegbile, only to cave under pressure and make this statement after flip-flopping on his vote in favor of Adegbile in the Judiciary Committee: "At a time when the Civil Rights Division urgently needs better relations with the law enforcement community, I was troubled by the idea of voting for an Assistant Attorney General for Civil Rights who would face such visceral opposition from law enforcement on his first day on the job. The vote I cast today was one of the most difficult I have taken since joining the Senate, but I believe it to be right for the people I represent."

If, as Coons says, the "Civil Rights Division urgently needs better relations with the law enforcement community," why is that not a sign that the law enforcement community is having trouble enforcing the law? Coons's full statement, on his official website, only makes his weakness look more pathetic:

> Last month, I voted in the Judiciary Committee to move his nomination to the Senate floor because I believed his nomination should be debated and considered by the full Senate. As a lawyer, I understand the importance of having legal advocates willing to fight for even the

most despicable clients, and I embrace the proposition that an attorney is not responsible for the actions of their client.

The decades-long public campaign by others, however, to elevate a heinous, cold-blooded killer to the status of a political prisoner and folk hero has caused tremendous pain to the widow of Philadelphia police officer Daniel Faulkner and shown great disrespect for law enforcement officers and families throughout our region. These factors have led me to cast a vote today that is more about listening to and respecting their concerns than about the innate qualifications of this nominee.

These seven Democratic dwarves agree on one thing: when a thuggish police-based minority dishonestly attacks democratic due process, it's the Constitution that should suffer. These people, like the rest of Congress, have sworn an oath to defend the Constitution, even against a mob of cops outraged by the courts' denying them their own lynching of Abu-Jamal. They have enabled a cowardly tactic, but one that works: that the best way to avoid losing an argument is to prevent it from happening.

"Cop-killer" is a powerful epithet, rooted in an understandable outrage, but it is also a conversation-stopper, a verbal barrier to any disinterested understanding of the underlying case, the 1981 murder of officer Daniel Faulkner, which is an undisputed fact. Also a fact, Mumia Abu-Jamal (born Wesley Cook) was convicted in 1982 of the murder. Another fact, usually omitted from summaries of the event, is that Abu-Jamal was also shot, in the lower abdomen, a wound that prevented him from fleeing the scene. This matters because none of the eyewitness statements describe the officer or anyone else firing any weapons, and no one says Abu-Jamal shot himself. That's only the beginning of the evidentiary strangeness of this case. It appears, from a brief review, that the jury verdict was supported by at least a preponderance of not very strong evidence, but perhaps not enough to meet the standard of beyond reasonable doubt. Unlike some cases of wrongful conviction, this one lacks any credible alternative to the central conclusion reached by the jury, but there are enough contradictions, omissions and procedural failures to make anyone wonder, with some humility, just what really happened.

With Abu-Jamal in prison for life, the appearance of justice has been met – except for those who will settle for nothing but the death penalty. But that is an emotional demand, not a legal or rational one. It is the reflexive but unreflective emotional cry of pain from Faulkner's widow and his fellow officers that overwhelmed good sense. Here is widow Maureen Faulkner's online petition on change.org, with extreme bitterness:

> In the three decades that followed [the murder], Abu-Jamal filed appeal after appeal – each rooted in lies, distortions and allegations of civil rights violations. Today, as Officer Faulkner lies in his grave, Abu-Jamal has become a wealthy celebrity and continues to spew his vitriol from prison.

This isn't an argument, it's a baseless, *ad hominem* attack. Here the consequences do not include thousands of dead Iraqis and Americans, but this hysterical manipulation is every bit as unconscionable as the scare-mongering of "a smoking gun in the form of a mushroom cloud." And yes, it is also a protected form of free speech. But it is not a reasonable basis for governing, especially when it stampedes a majority in the Senate. That majority has done a lynch mob's job metaphorically and the White House called them on it with startlingly mild language:

> The Senate's failure to confirm Debo Adegbile to lead the Civil Rights Division at the Department of Justice is a travesty based on wildly unfair character attacks against a good and qualified public servant. Mr. Adegbile's qualifications are impeccable. He represents the best of the legal profession, with wide-ranging experience, and the deep respect of those with whom he has worked. His unwavering dedication to protecting every American's civil and Constitutional rights under the law – including voting rights – could not be more important right now. And Mr. Adegbile's personal story – rising from adversity to become someone who President Bush's Solicitor General referred to as one of the nation's most capable litigators – is a story that proves what America has been and can be…. The fact that his nomination was defeated solely based on his legal representation of a defendant runs contrary to a fundamental principle of our system of justice….

That Senate majority – but especially those seven Democratic Senators – who voted against Adegbile's nomination did much worse than merely deny advancement to a capable and principled lawyer without any cogent reason for doing so. Adegbile may well be hurt, but he seems likely to survive this assault, which he has apparently suffered with a silent grace.

The seven timorous Democrats, in their collaboration with a nihilistic Republican strategy, have added to the damage from which American democracy will be a long time recovering, if it ever can.

These seven democrats represent profiles in no courage, running scared on a vote that should not have required any courage. These seven Democrats have colluded in a vote that reeks of racial bigotry:

- A vote that attacks due process of law;

- A vote that undermines vigorous enforcement of the Voting Rights Act by politicizing the Justice Department's Civil Rights Division appointments;

- A vote that ignores relevance, logic and facts;

- A vote that promotes filibuster as an acceptable evasion of public responsibility;

- A vote that punishes civility and allows the screeching of a hate mob to overwhelm reasoned debate;

- A vote that punishes an innocent man for serving the Constitution;

- A vote that punishes the Constitution for giving rights to all.

After these seven Democratic quislings had collaborated in stopping Adegbile's nomination in its tracks, another Democrat switched his vote to join them. The eighth Democratic vote to sustain the filibuster was majority leader Harry Reid of Nevada who changed his vote for tactical reasons. Under Senate rules, only a senator who has voted against the nomination is entitled to bring it the floor again, which Reid was prepared to do. That's just one of many good deeds the other seven Democrats can't be trusted to do.

45.

'It's Not Polite to Say Nigger in Public....'

Author's note: This piece will end with a brief personal experience I had recently, an experience that illuminates what the President is saying and raises the question of whether it's polite to say "nigger" in private. My experience underscores that what the President is saying is obviously and profoundly true and has been since long before he was born. And my recent experience illustrates the abiding armor of denial and determined ignorance that allows people to enjoy the advantages of a racist society without having to acknowledge that it exists.

"Racism, we are not cured of it. And, and, and it's not just a matter of, uh, it not being polite to say nigger in public. That's not the measure of whether racism still exists or not. It's not just a matter of overt discrimination. Societies don't, overnight, completely erase everything that happened two to three hundred years prior."

PRESIDENT OBAMA, JUNE 22, ON MARC MARON PODCAST

One form of denial is feigned shock that "Obama said the N-word!"

Assorted television babble-heads on CNN, NBC, MSNBC, CBS, Fox and elsewhere got all a-twitter over the President's saying "nigger," which they sanitized to "the N-word" with such characterizations as "extremely direct language" and "shock value" and "jarring comment" and "electric" and "one of the most charged racial slurs in the English language" – all of which are projections of the commentator's subjectivity. They are not at all accurate descriptions of what the President said, which was detached, measured, analytical and precisely accurate.

257

But who wants to hear that on TV? As Wolf Blitzer put it on CNN, "Many people may find this offensive." CNN's black legal analyst said the word should never be used. In sharp disagreement, CNN black anchor Don Lemon articulately defended adult conversation about difficult issues on television (for example, on Democracy NOW).

By paying attention only to the President's use of the word "nigger" and not to his much broader context, television's purveyors of conventional wisdom manage to deny the relevance of the President's larger point: that racism has been endemic to American (and pre-American) culture for some 400 years and that racist thinking remains alive and well in many forms. Focusing on the President's use of "nigger" as an excuse not to talk about racism in America is, arguably, just another form of racism in America.

Larry Wilmore on *The Nightly Show* reduced the TV babble to its ultimate Fox-accusing absurdity, President Obama saying "nigger" in a State of the Union speech. Wilmore also played clips of other presidents saying "nigger," albeit in a less thoughtful way than Obama:

- **Nixon:** "Our niggers are better than their niggers"
- **LBJ:** "there's more niggers voting there than white folks"

Wilmore also indicated that, while there's apparently no record of presidents like Washington or Jefferson saying "nigger," they did own one or more.

Another effect of all the empty blather about the President saying "nigger" is to distract from the empty gestures about various Confederate flags. American devotion to the Confederate flag is, literally, insane or dishonest or hypocritical, or all three, or pick your word. Why? All Confederate flags are symbols of treason against the United States of America, and somehow, it's OK to celebrate them and merchandise them and pretend they're something they never were. The Confederacy committed treason as defined by the Constitution and too many people would do it all over again, for the same racist reasons.

Another form of denial is cultured obtuseness

An unintendedly brilliant example of self-induced moral blindness to racist behavior comes from Pat Boone, the octogenarian multi-millionaire musician whose fortune was built on racist exploitation of black music in a racist music industry devoted to catering to America's white racism. Boone's fundamentalist Christian self-delusions about race appeared on WND (aka WorldNetDaily), self-described as "an independent news company dedicated to uncompromising journalism, seeking truth and justice and revitalizing the role of the free press as a guardian of liberty."

According to Boone, it's President Obama's fault there are racial issues in America. Boone faults Obama for not preaching that "racial divides and prejudice had greatly diminished and that our society was truly becoming colorblind." Having said that, Boone provides a white racist analysis of the killing of two black children, Trayvon Martin and Michael Brown, unarmed and shot by reckless white men. As for Charleston, where an avowed white racist killed nine black people in church in hope of starting a race war, Boone explains it away as having a "racist element," but being "inspired by Satan"! While blaming Obama for "erasing" God from public life, Boone pleads for a return to America as a Christian nation – but he does not mention that American Christianity was a powerful defender of American slavery.

This mode of thinking, or rather this mode of avoiding real thought, is endemic to a large section of the American population and has been, in one form or another, since before there was a United States. How else do you get a Constitution in which slaves don't get to vote, but do get counted as three-fifths of a person in order to inflate Congressional representation of slave owners? Orwell called it Doublethink in "1984," but it's a much older American tradition.

What does one young South Carolinian tell us about America today?

So, here's the personal experience I mentioned. Over the weekend of June 20-21, I was at a family wedding in northern Maryland. The

Sunday before Obama's podcast became public, I was at a post-wedding cookout with maybe 20 people of various ages, many in their twenties. It was a definitely non-political social gathering.

One young man in his mid-twenties was there as the new beau of the bride's sister. He was pleasant, attractive, well-spoken, polite, and had grown up in South Carolina. During our first conversation with several other people in the kitchen, David (not his real name) spoke enthusiastically of his work with horses and Brahma cattle. He described a roping gone wrong when he was forced to jump his horse over a fallen Brahma cow, whose horn scored his horse's underbelly. He seemed comfortable and at ease as the conversation shifted from person to person. He gave no hint of any socially disruptive opinions or behavior. But he was drinking.

Sometime later I wandered into a conversation David was having with the bride's mother on the screen porch. This conversation was already political. David was complaining about Jon Stewart on *The Daily Show* for calling out Charleston for having streets named after Civil War generals and otherwise ridiculing South Carolina's history. Stewart was about to start a race war, David argued, without mentioning Dylann Roof killing nine people. David said he was concerned about a race war because someone had already shot at the Confederate flag at the Capitol. David said we should just let history be history, and besides some people treated their slaves well.

By the time our hostess came into this conversation, David was talking about Obama being Kenyan. Our hostess told him firmly not to talk like that in her house. When he didn't seem to get the point, I leaned in and suggested that maybe we should both be quiet. He admitted he'd been drinking, but throughout this conversation he remained polite, friendly, quiet, apparently sincere in beliefs he didn't seem to think anyone would find unusual. He came across as a basically sweet kid.

The last thing he said to me before others took him swimming, he said with the same earnest pleasantness: "I don't hate niggers."

46.

Black Lives Matter, Just Not to Hillary Clinton

Black voters support a fantasy champion for black lives

Over 50 years ago, in a 1963 Chicago protest against school segregation, one of today's Democratic candidates for president was chained to a black woman and then arrested for resisting arrest. Now that moment appears in an unofficial campaign poster emphasizing the candidate's commitment to civil rights. That protestor for black rights in 1963 was *not* Chicago native Hillary Clinton, then a politically active Republican supporting Barry Goldwater for President, even though he opposed the Civil Rights Act. Now Clinton is politically strongest in the same southern states Goldwater won in 1964. The protestor chained and arrested in 1963 was Bernie Sanders. Ponder that irony.

In 1962, Hillary Clinton's youth minister took her and her class to hear Dr. Martin Luther King preach a sermon titled "Sleeping Through the Revolution," referring to the civil rights activism of the time. She shook Dr. King's hand. Recalling the event in 2014, Clinton said:

> Probably my great privilege as a young woman was going to hear Dr. Martin Luther King speak.... I sat on the edge of my seat as this preacher challenged us to participate in the cause of justice, not to slumber while the world changed around us. And that made such an impression on me.

But it did not make such an impression on her that she couldn't support Goldwater (to be fair, he helped integrate the Arizona Air National Guard). And it didn't make such an impression on her that she actually participated in the Civil Rights Movement. That makes Clinton-supporter Rep. John Lewis's denigration of Sanders's civil rights

261

record look like a pretty hypocritical cheap shot, but that's what happens when the establishment circles the wagons. It's not that Hillary Clinton is terrible on civil rights, she usually manages to end up on the side of the angels, more or less, but she has never shown the willingness or capacity to lead them.

Hillary Clinton: "We have to bring them to heel."

On February 24, 2016, in Charleston, South Carolina, Hillary Clinton held a private fundraiser at a posh private home before a predominantly white crowd of about 100 who paid $500 each to attend. Clinton had just started to speak when a young black woman (who also paid $500 to get in) quietly held up a pillow case with a handwritten message in capital letters – "WE HAVE TO BRING THEM TO HEEL", followed by #WhichHillary. Making nice at first, Clinton started reading the message aloud and the following exchange took place.

Ashley Williams: I'm not a superpredator, Hillary Clinton.

Hillary Clinton: OK, fine. We'll talk about it.

Ashley Williams: Can you apologize to black people for mass incarceration?

Hillary Clinton: Well, can I talk? OK, and then maybe you can listen to what I say.

Ashley Williams: Yes, yes, absolutely.

Hillary Clinton: OK, fine. Thank you very much. There's a lot of issues, a lot of issues in this campaign. [...]

Ashley Williams: I know that you called black youth superpredators in 1994. Please explain your record. Explain it to us. You owe black people an apology.

Hillary Clinton: Well, I'll tell you what, if you will give me a chance to talk, I'll—I'll tell you something. You know what? Nobody's ever asked me before. You're the first person to ask me, and I'm happy to address it, but you are the first person to ask me, dear.

By this time the audience has become hostile, and security is leading Ashley Williams away (filmed by her confederate who appears to be ignored).

Hillary Clinton: Um, OK, back to the issues.

The issue Clinton ducks here is massive black incarceration

In 1994, President Bill Clinton signed a vicious crime bill (to go with his vicious welfare reform bill) that has had a devastating impact on black families and communities across America. In 2010, Michelle Alexander published *The New Jim Crow* (a New York Times bestseller) to address "mass incarceration in the age of colorblindness." In her preface, Alexander wrote that "something is eerily familiar about the way our criminal justice system operates, something that looks and feels a lot like an era we left behind... America's latest caste system." (The scandal of over-imprisonment in America is or should be well known to any sentient reader, along with the scandal of disproportionately locking up people of color, along with the scandal of making imprisoned black people a profit center for largely white-owned private prisons.)

For the February 10, 2016, issue of The Nation, Michelle Alexander wrote a piece titled "Why Hillary Clinton Doesn't Deserve the Black Vote," in which she summarizes the Clinton record on racial justice:

> What have the Clintons done to earn such devotion? Did they take extreme political risks to defend the rights of African Americans? Did they courageously stand up to right-wing demagoguery about black communities? Did they help usher in a new era of hope and prosperity for neighborhoods devastated by deindustrialization, globalization, and the disappearance of work? No. Quite the opposite.

Campaigning for President Clinton's re-election in 1996, Hillary Clinton chose to defend the 1994 crime bill and its increased mass incarceration, with hard-edged, unsympathetic rhetoric, based in part on the scare tactic of invoking imaginary "super predators." (Clinton has since offered a non-apology apology for the rhetoric: "Looking back, I shouldn't have used those words, and I wouldn't use them today.")

To date, Clinton has not addressed the substantive issue of mass incarceration, which seems a pretty clear systemic injustice of long standing. Clinton has taken contributions from the private prison industry and has given a small proportion of the money to a charity that helps women prisoners adjust to society on release. In October 2015, after months of pressure from civil rights and immigrant justice groups, the Clinton campaign had promised not to accept clearly labeled prison industry contributions.

By July 2015, the injustice of the American justice system had become plain enough that even Bill Clinton sort of apologized for the 1994 Violent Crime Act. Speaking before the annual meeting of the National Association for the Advancement of Colored People (NAACP) on July 15, Clinton said: "I signed a bill that made the problem worse.... And I want to admit it." He did not propose to do anything about it. Nor has Hillary Clinton proposed to do anything about the mass incarceration of black Americans or other minorities. She has offered, at best, kinder, gentler rhetoric.

And at the same time, she claimed in Charleston: "You know what? Nobody's ever asked me before. You're the first person to ask me, and I'm happy to address it, but you are the first person to ask me, dear."

Clinton lies – what else is it – and the media can't tell it's a lie?

The reality is that Hillary Clinton has been asked before about mass incarceration, she has been asked before about mass incarceration by Black Lives Matter people, she has been asked before about mass incarceration of black people only to turn pettish and say, "if that is your position, then *I will talk only to white people about how we are going to deal with a very real problem.*" That was on August 11, 2015, in the course of a 15-minute videotaped meeting in which Daunasia Yancey pressed Clinton on her role in oppressing black people:

> ... you and your family have been personally and politically responsible for policies that have caused health and human services disasters in impoverished communities of color through the domestic and international war on drugs that you championed as First Lady, Senator and Secretary of State. And so, I just want to know how you feel

264

about your role in that violence and how you plan to reverse it?... those policies were actually extensions of white supremacist violence against communities of color. And so, I just think I want to hear a little bit about that, about the fact that actually while ... those policies were being enacted, they were ripping apart families ... and actually causing death.

In response, Clinton tried to change the subject. (On August 25, 2015, Reader Supported News published my long report on Clinton's dismal and unresponsive meeting with Black Lives Matter people in Keene, New Hampshire. The event was reported by others as well, but not widely.) Perhaps that limited coverage contributed to Clinton's willingness to claim, absolutely falsely, that nobody had ever asked her before. Perhaps she gambled that no one would remember, or even google, the truth.

And she would have won that bet with one of the best columnists at The New York Times, Charles M. Blow, whose work is consistently probing and thoughtful. Just not this time – in his February 29 piece, "I'm Not A Super Predator," about Ashley Williams, he quotes Hillary Clinton saying, "You're the first person to ask me ..." about mass incarceration of minorities.

"How could this be true? How was this possible?" Blow wrote, with instinctive, accurate skepticism. But he accepted the Clinton claim's veracity at face value, apparently not bothering to do basic fact-checking of a claim that is not even close to being true. This Clinton dishonesty was not widely reported. And Blow, having accepted the truth of Clinton's falsehood, used it in a weird kind of victim-blaming:

> In that moment, I knew that the people of my generation had failed the people of Williams's. Her whole life has borne the bruises of what was done, largely by Democrats, when I was the age she is now.
>
> She said she has grown up knowing families and whole communities devastated by vanishing black people, swept away into a criminal justice system that pathologized their very personage. That night, Williams forced a reckoning.

But that's not true. There has been no reckoning, not so far as Clinton is concerned. There is no Clinton acceptance of responsibility or accountability for inhumane policies, the Democratic Party is still in bed with those who want to privatize government. The establishment candidate and her party have yet to promise any serious change, much less any real improvement. The private prison scam will continue to be just one more way to loot the public treasury, while having the perverse effect of pressuring governments from local to federal to keep arresting people fast enough and jailing them long enough to keep the profits flowing to people who have no vested interest in justice, rehabilitation, or freedom. Black lives don't matter to the bottom line of the prison-industrial complex any more than they matter to Hillary Clinton.

What *does* matter to Hillary Clinton? Or Bernie Sanders?

Clinton gives the game away at the end of her brief encounter with Ashley Williams in Charleston. As the black college graduate student is led away by security for objecting to policies that destroy black lives, Clinton says calmly, revealing her actual priorities, "OK, back to the issues."

In other words, more than two decades of life-destroying criminal policy that she helped implement and support is not an issue for her. She might just as well have said, "I will talk only to white people," which is pretty much what she did for the rest of the evening.

Ashley Williams has also criticized Sanders for voting for the 1994 Violent Crime Act. At the time, April 13, 1994, he also spoke out strongly against the likely – now actual – consequences of the crime bill, concluding:

> Mr. Speaker, it is my firm belief that clearly, there are some people in our society who are horribly violent, who are deeply sick and sociopathic, and clearly these people must be put behind bars in order to protect society from them. But it is also my view that through the neglect of our Government and through a grossly irrational set of priorities, we are dooming tens of millions of young people to a future of bitterness, misery, hopelessness, drugs, crime, and violence. And Mr. Speaker, all the jails in the world, and we already imprison more people per capita than any other country, and all of the executions in the world, will not make that situation right. We can either educate or electrocute. We can create meaningful jobs, rebuilding our society,

or we can build more jails. Mr. Speaker, let us create a society of hope and compassion, not one of hate and vengeance.

This demonstrates that the consequences of the crime bill were knowable in 1994, and that some people knew them. This also illustrates the political pressure politicians were feeling about "crime" issues, leading some like Bernie Sanders to vote for a "solution" that he did not believe to be any solution at all. There is no such contemporary prescience expressed by either of the Clintons, leaving their supporters to defend horrible policies with weak excuses like, well, lots of people supported it. One of them in 1994 was Hillary Clinton, whose hardline defense of more cops and more prisons contains no compensating humane concern even close to what Sanders expressed.

More than fifty years of commitment to civil rights has earned Sanders only a tiny fraction of the black vote in primaries so far, despite articulate and heartfelt support from black rapper Killer Mike talking about Hillary Clinton's cold dismissal of Ashley Williams and Black Lives Matter: "The only person that I have the conscience to vote for is Bernard Sanders, I know that the only person that my logical, beautiful black mind will allow me to vote for is Senator Bernie Sanders!" His argument has yet to gain significant traction with black voters. On February 29, before the black vote crushed him in South Carolina, Sanders told a rally:

> There is no rational reason why a black male baby born today has a one-in-four chance of ending up in jail. That's a disgrace. And together, we are going to bring justice to a broken criminal justice system.

Hillary Clinton could have said something like that to Ashley Williams at that mostly-white fundraiser in Charleston. She didn't say anything like that. She didn't even make the effort. With the removal of the black nuisance, Hillary Clinton said only: "OK, back to the issues." Three days later, at a Hillary Clinton rally in Atlanta, two Georgia State University students were removed for holding "Black Lives Matter" signs.

The Clinton campaign denied any responsibility.

47.

Ali's Biggest Win: As Clay v. United States in Supreme Court

"No Viet Cong never called me nigger."

MUHAMMAD ALI

Much of the coverage of Muhammad Ali's death kind of ducks how polarizing his life was in the 1960s as a brash young black man who loudly touted his own talents and called out the world for what it was. He was loved and he was hated, and he was especially hated by mindless sports writers reflecting the mindless prejudices of their (and our) time (with some courageous exceptions like Robert Lipsyte, Howard Cosell, Dave Anderson and others). Some of the hate still shows in the grudging tone of some postmortems, and perhaps as well in the general downplaying or omission of what was arguably Muhammad Ali's greatest victory, his unanimous Supreme Court decision *in Clay v. United States*. The case emerged naturally enough out of American racism, eventually involving imperial war and government criminality, a nexus that plagues us still.

In early 1960 Louisville, Kentucky, 18-year-old Cassius Marcellus Clay Jr. dutifully went to his local Selective Service Board #47 to register for the draft. Because he performed poorly on the Army's minimum intelligence test, his classification was 1-Y, not 1-A: his government did not consider him eligible for military service. The US was not at war in 1960, despite covert and not so covert military and paramilitary operations around the world, including "advisors" in Vietnam. Cassius Clay was already a well-known amateur boxer, with 100 victories in 108 bouts and a host of Golden Gloves titles. And even though Cassius

Clay won the Olympic heavyweight boxing gold medal that summer in Rome, back in Louisville he was not considered eligible for restaurant service, and people still called him (among other things) "boy."

Clay won his first professional fight on October 29, 1960, and 18 straight more after that, while taunting heavyweight champion Sonny Liston into fighting the undefeated 22-year-old. On February 25, 1964, Liston lost his championship when he refused to come out of his corner for the seventh round. At a press conference the next day, Clay announced that he had accepted the teaching of the Nation of Islam, also known as Black Muslims, and that he had changed his name to Cassius X (later to Muhammad Ali). Reportedly this announcement prompted FBI Director J. Edgar Hoover to inquire into Ali's draft status.

Needing more bodies for Vietnam, the US lowered draft standards

In February 1966, Louisville Draft Board #47 met to reconsider Clay's case in new circumstances. Muhammad Ali had long since become the world heavyweight boxing champion, defending the title twice, but they still called him Clay. Although Ali had failed the Army's intelligence test twice, the Selective Service had lowered the mental standards enough to make him eligible to be reclassified 1-A and eligible to be drafted to fight in Vietnam. While acknowledging that Ali (whom he called Clay) had a right to appeal any reclassification, the draft board chairman said, "This is a routine thing. There just isn't any way out for him as far as I can see."

After Ali was re-classified 1-A on February 17, 1966, the wire service UPI reported it with some editorializing:

> LOUISVILLE, Ky. (UPI) – Cassius Clay, the self-styled "greatest," appeared headed today for the greatest fights of his career, proving he's a good soldier and winning the public approval that eluded him after ring victories. The heavyweight champion received a 1-A classification Thursday from his Louisville draft board, making him extremely vulnerable to the Army draft and placing his March 29 title defense against Ernie Terrell in jeopardy. If Louisville's March draft quota is the same as in recent months. Clay will be in the Army

before the fight, which cannot be moved to an earlier dale. If Clay is drafted, his title will be frozen until his discharge, a minimum of two years. "Why pick me?" was the immediate reaction of Clay, who was contacted at his Miami Beach training headquarters. "Why seek me out and hold a special one-and-a-half-hour meeting on it? I pay the salaries of at least 2.000 men a year. For two fights I pay for two modern bomber jets. *I can't understand why they picked me without testing me* to see if I'm wiser or worser. I'm fighting in a game nine out of 10 soldiers wouldn't want to take part in," Clay added. [emphasis added]

At a press conference soon after, on a TV hookup in Miami, Ali answered questions about his situation. Recalling that event, at which he read a short poem, Ali later said: "Of all the poems I wrote, all the words I spoke, all the slogans I shouted ... none would have the effect on my life or change the climate around me."

> Keep asking me, no matter how long,
> On the war in Vietnam, I sing this song:
> I ain't got no quarrel with the Viet Cong ...

According to the US, some ministers are more religious than others

On February 28, 1966, Ali applied to the Louisville local draft board for draft exemption as a conscientious objector, based on his religious beliefs as a minister in the Nation of Islam that: "to bear arms or kill is against my religion. And I conscientiously object to any combat military service that involves the participation in any war in which the lives of human beings are being taken." The Louisville board denied his claim and he appealed to the Kentucky Selective Service Appeal Board. In May, the Kentucky Appeal Board affirmed the local board, but it also referred Ali's case to the US Department of Justice for an advisory opinion. The Justice Dept. then, in effect, sought its own advisory opinion, requesting an FBI investigation (that interviewed 35 people), followed by a special hearing on Ali's "character and good faith."

On August 23, 1966, Ali petitioned the appeals board directly for draft exemption, asking the board to re-classify him as a conscientious objector as a minister of the Lost Found Nation of Islam.

That same day, a retired federal judge presided at the Justice Department's special hearing on Ali's character. Hearing officer Lawrence Grauman reported his conclusions to the Justice Dept.: that Ali had stated his views "in a convincing manner, answered all questions forthrightly," and was "sincere in his objection on religious grounds to participation in war in any form." Judge Grauman recommended that Ali be granted conscientious objector status.

The Justice Dept. rejected the opinion it had sought and advised the Kentucky Appeal Board to deny Ali conscientious objector status. The Justice Dept. withheld the hearing board record from both Ali and the appeals board. Instead, the Justice Dept., ignoring the hearing record, asserted falsely that Ali's objections to war "rest on grounds which are primarily political and racial. These constitute objections to only certain types of war in certain circumstances, rather than a general scruple against participation in war in any form ... only a general scruple against participation in war in any form can support a claim for conscientious objector [status] ... [Ali] had not consistently manifested his conscientious objector claim and had not shown overt manifestations sufficient to establish his subjective belief where his claim was not asserted until [conscription] became imminent."

The Justice Dept.'s argument is clearly specious, since Ali had no reason to assert it till he was reclassified. But it was good enough for the Kentucky Appeal Board. On January 10, 1967, that board denied Ali's conscientious objector claim without explanation. In February, the National Selective Service Appeal Board denied Ali's appeal of the Kentucky decision.

Racial prejudice doesn't make draft boards unqualified to pick victims

Taking a new tack, Ali requested and received a change of his induction center from Louisville to Houston, Texas, where he then lived. He then challenged induction on the basis that the under-representation of African-Americans on local draft boards violated anti-discrimination laws and removed any constitutional authority from those boards to induct African-Americans into the Army. The US District Court for

Western Kentucky chose to ignore Ali's argument that the law was unconstitutional on its face or the underlying assertion that African-Americans were "systematically excluded" from Kentucky draft boards. Instead the court held that none of that mattered until and unless Ali was personally harmed, and he could then seek redress. Preventing unconstitutional behavior was not a "substantial constitutional question," the court held, "unless and until [Ali] presents himself at an Induction Station and either submits to induction or refuses to submit to induction."

At about the same time, late March 1967, Ali issued a longer statement of principle:

> Why should they ask me to put on a uniform and go ten thousand miles from home and drop bombs and bullets on brown people in Vietnam while so-called Negro people in Louisville are treated like dogs and denied simple human rights?

> No, I am not going ten thousand miles from home to help murder and burn another poor nation simply to continue the domination of white slave masters of the darker people the world over. This is the day when such evils must come to an end. I have been warned that to take such a stand would put my prestige in jeopardy and could cause me to lose millions of dollars which should accrue to me as the champion.

> But I have said it once and I will say it again. The real enemy of my people is right here. I will not disgrace my religion, my people or myself by becoming a tool to enslave those who are fighting for their own justice, freedom and equality...

> If I thought the war was going to bring freedom and equality to 22 million of my people they wouldn't have to draft me, I'd join tomorrow. But I either have to obey the laws of the land or the laws of Allah. I have nothing to lose by standing up for my beliefs. So I'll go to jail. We've been in jail for four hundred years.

On April 28, 1967, Ali appeared as summoned to the Houston induction center, but when called to step forward, he refused. Three times he refused induction. He was arrested and jailed. Ali sought injunctive relief from the US District Court for the Southern District of Texas. The court denied any relief because he could not show any "irreparable harm." He had to be inducted first, then go to court. Again, a federal court was making it clear the court wasn't going to prevent any harm but might or might not consider the damage later. Ali had a radically different perspective:

> I strongly object to the fact that so many newspapers have given the American public and the world the impression that I have only two alternatives in this stand — either I go to jail or go to the Army. There is another alternative, and that alternative is justice. If justice prevails, if my constitutional rights are upheld, I will be forced to go neither to the Army nor jail. In the end, I am confident that justice will come my way, for the truth must eventually prevail.

An all-white jury for Muhammad Ali

On May 8, 1967, a federal grand jury indicted Ali for draft evasion. Ali's petition to the US Fifth Circuit Court of Appeals to restrain the pending trial was denied. On June 20, an all-white jury of six men and six women heard little more than an hour of testimony, mostly by government witnesses. The jury deliberated about 20 minutes before unanimously finding Ali guilty of refusal to submit to induction into the Armed Forces. Judge Joe Ingraham, a World War II vet, gave Ali the full maximum sentence: five years in prison and a $10,000 fine. He also stripped Ali of his passport. Ali was released on $5,000 bond. The Fifth Circuit Court of Appeals later upheld the verdict and Ali appealed his case to the US Supreme Court.

"Clay Guilty in Draft Case; Gets Five Years in Prison" was the headline in The New York Times, with a story that took its time to mention an all-white jury. Deeper in, the Times reported: "After Judge Ingraham had ruled that a study of the huge draft board file of the Clay case had convinced him that the draft boards had not acted 'arbitrarily or capriciously' in refusing the deferment, Clay's conviction became a foregone conclusion." This would turn out to be false, a judicial error that contributed to the Supreme Court overturning the verdict.

In 1969, while the Supreme Court petition was pending, the US government revealed that FBI wiretaps on other people had illegally picked up Ali in five conversations. Based on this information, on March 24 the Supreme Court vacated Ali's almost two-year-old conviction and sent it back to the district court to determine if the illegal surveillance had tainted the verdict. The same trial judge, Joe Ingraham, privately reviewed the wiretaps and ordered four of them revealed to Ali. The fifth wiretap he withheld, stating that it had been lawful. Subsequently, with no public hearing, Judge Ingraham ruled that the government's illegal wiretaps had not tainted its case against Ali and reinstated the full sentence.

Ali returned to the Fifth Circuit Court of Appeals, contesting the withholding of the secret wiretap. The appeals court blinked in the face of the government's "national security" argument. The court held, in effect, that it would be "intolerable" for courts to review and possibly rule against government actions taken in secret, unless the court had "relevant information" that it couldn't get because it was secret. The court claimed it had balanced the rights of the government and the defendant but omitted any discussion of the Constitution's Fourth Amendment prohibition against warrantless searches and seizures. The court upheld Ali's conviction and Ali again appealed to the Supreme Court.

Boxing authorities wrongly stripped Ali of his license, championship

During 1969-1970, Ali fought another prolonged legal battle to get his boxing license reinstated by the New York State Athletic Commission (which had rescinded his license before he was convicted of any crime). The US District Court for the Southern District of New York eventually found that the Commission had exercised its legal authority to regulate boxing, but that in Ali's case the "deliberate and arbitrary discrimination or inequality in the exercise of [the Commission's] regulatory power, not based upon differences that are reasonably related to the lawful purposes of such regulation," violated the Equal Protection Clause of the Fourteenth Amendment. The Commission did not appeal the ruling, and Ali was reinstated.

On October 26, 1970, Ali fought Jerry Quarry in Atlanta, Georgia, over the strenuous objections of Georgia governor Lester Maddox, a notorious racist famous for distributing ax handles to use on African Americans. "We shouldn't let him fight for money if he didn't fight for his country," Maddox argued while urging a boycott, but the fight went on and Ali won commandingly, after more than three years of forced retirement. After another warm-up fight, Ali took on the champion named in his absence, Joe Frazier, on March 8, 1971, and lost a unanimous decision. Both men went to the hospital after the fight, Frazier for three weeks.

On June 21, 1971, the Supreme Court decided *Clay v. United States* in Ali's favor by an 8-0 vote. The ninth justice, Thurgood Marshall, the first African-American justice, recused himself from the case because he had been US Solicitor General when the case began, before his appointment to the court in October 1967.

The unanimous decision wasn't as simple as it seemed. The initial vote of the eight justices in April was 5-3 to uphold Ali's conviction, with Justice John Marshall Harlan II among the majority. With encouragement from his clerks, Justice Harlan did further research into Black Muslim doctrine and came to believe Ali's conscientious objection was sincere. More pointedly, Justice Harlan found fault with the Justice Dept.'s rejection of its own hearing officer's advisory opinion, that Ali was sincere. Further fault was found with the Justice Dept.'s false analysis of Ali's guilt and the Kentucky Appeal Board deciding the matter without explanation. The court's *per curiam* decision states:

> The petitioner's criminal conviction stemmed from the Selective Service System's denial of his appeal seeking conscientious objector status. That denial, for which no reasons were ever given, was, as we have said, based on a recommendation of the Department of Justice, overruling its hearing officer and advising the Appeal Board that it "finds that the registrant's conscientious-objector claim is not sustained and recommends to your Board that he be not [so] classified." This finding was contained in a long letter of explanation, from which it is evident that Selective Service officials were led to believe that the Department had found that the petitioner had failed to satisfy each of the three basic tests for qualification as a conscientious objector.

In fact, the Justice Dept. had misled the board. During Supreme Court proceedings the government admitted it was wrong in its allegations on two of the three tests for conscientious objection but argued there was some basis in fact for the third. The court was not impressed. Sidestepping the trickier issues in the case, the Supreme Court ruled unanimously that Ali's guilty verdict be reversed, based on the appeals board denying him conscientious objector status without giving any reason for the ruling.

Other than four years of unjust punishment, *Clay v. United States* ended fairly well for Muhammad Ali, who reflected on it with real grace (and dubious assumptions of the good faith of others) after the Supreme Court decision was announced. When a reporter asked if he would take legal action to recover his damages, Ali answered: "No. They only did what they thought was right at the time. I did what I thought was right. That was all. I can't condemn them for doing what they think was right." Much later he said:

> Some people thought I was a hero. Some people said that what I did was wrong. But everything I did was according to my conscience. I wasn't trying to be a leader. I just wanted to be free. And I made a stand all people, not just black people, should have thought about making, because it wasn't just black people being drafted. The government had a system where the rich man's son went to college, and the poor man's son went to war. Then, after the rich man's son got out of college, he did other things to keep him out of the Army until he was too old to be drafted."

We haven't come far in fifty-plus years. Real draft dodgers have become presidents and vice presidents. There is little widespread appreciation of the courage of Muhammad Ali's convictions or of the full vindication of his unpopular public stance. On June 7, the chairman of the Congressional Black Caucus in the US House of Representatives introduced a somewhat generic resolution honoring Muhammad Ali for his "extraordinary life, accomplishments and countless contributions." The resolution has only 42 co-sponsors so far, only one of whom is a Republican, Rep. Mia Love of Utah, also the only Republican member of the Black Caucus. Of the 393 other congressional representatives not supporting the Ali resolution, it's unlikely there are any who have taken or will ever take as courageous and personally costly stand as Muhammad Ali took for fundamental American principles.

> **Update 2019:** The resolution honoring Ali, H.Res.766, eventually had 82 co-sponsors, all Democrats except Rep. Love. On June 6, 2016, it was referred to the House Committee on Oversight and Government Reform. That Republican-controlled held no hearing and no votes on the resolution, which never came back to the floor of the House.
>
> In the Senate, Orrin Hatch, R-Utah, and Cory Booker, D-NJ, introduced a similar resolution on June 10 and it was agreed to by unanimous consent.
>
> In January 2007, Resolution H.Res.58 to honor Muhammad Ali on his 65th birthday passed on a vote of 421-0.
>
> On January 16, 2019, Louisville, KY, announced that it would rename its airport in honor of Muhammad Ali.
>
> On January 17, 2019, Rep. John Yarmuth, D-KY, introduced H.R.635, the Muhammad Ali Legacy Act, proposing to establish grants in Ali's name to promote global character and leadership. It was sent to the Foreign Affairs Committee.

48.

Official Stupidity Killed Keith Lamont Scott

Shooting a man slowly backing away is no way to serve or protect

Some reasonable people are weighing the available evidence and waiting for more definitive proof of various allegations before they decide whether or not they think the death of Keith Lamont Scott, 43, in broad daylight in a parking lot in a housing development in Charlotte, North Carolina, on the sunny afternoon of September 20 was a police execution.

Those reasonable people are being unreasonable: the police clearly executed Keith Lamont Scott as he was slowly backing away from them, his hands at his sides, his body slack. The question that needs answering is: why did they execute this non-threatening, possibly unarmed black man?

The most obvious answer, up and down the line, is official stupidity, official lethal stupidity, the same sort of official lethal stupidity that protects the powerful against the powerless everywhere.

As of September 25, the Charlotte-Mecklenburg Police Department (CMPD) had not made full disclosure of evidence in the shooting, but had posted a timeline (below, in bold, annotated) declared to be "Facts from the CMPD Investigation." The most remarkable thing about these "facts" (maybe) is that they do not include *any* reference to the presence of Rakeyia Scott, Scott's wife of 20 years, during the shooting. She was there, that's a fact. She shot video that includes the shooting, that's a fact. In the video she screams at the police not to shoot her husband ("Don't shoot him"), she screams that he has no gun ("He has no weapon"), she screams that he has a book, she screams that he has a brain injury ("He has a TBI [traumatic brain injury], he is not going to

278

do anything to you guys, he just took his medicine"), she screams for her husband to comply ("Keith, don't let them break the windows. Come on out the car"), she screams, "Keith, don't do it. Keith get out the car" (it's not clear what "it" is), and she screams again, "Keith! Keith! Don't you do it. Don't you do it." Interspersed with Mrs. Scott's screams, police in the background are also screaming, mostly "Drop the gun." Fifty seconds into this video a police officer executes Keith Lamont Scott with four quick shots (he will die later, at a hospital). There is no way to make sense of this shooting as anything but an execution without including this video in any honest assessment (even if it can be debunked). The CMPD "Facts" omits Mrs. Scott's video, withheld two police videos for days, and reportedly is still withholding other videos. All this strongly suggests that the CMPD "investigation" is neither thorough nor honest.

But that's not just on CMPD. The state of North Carolina has passed a law that requires dishonesty and cover-up, actually barring public police agencies from releasing police videos to the public. Other states have passed similar laws. Transparency is an enemy of the state. The CMPD stall in releasing video may have something to do with the North Carolina gag law that takes effect October 1, 2016. The CMPD timeline begins:

> On Tuesday, September 20, 2016, at 3:54 p.m., officers from the Metro Division Crime Reduction Unit were searching for a suspect with an outstanding warrant at The Village at College Downs.

Keith Lamont Scott, apparently randomly, arrived soon after and parked his car beside the unmarked police car in a public parking lot. If he saw the police, what he saw was two men in civilian clothes, still sitting in their unmarked vehicle. The CMPD's saying they "were searching for a suspect" is right at the edge of false. That's what they should have been doing. Their job was to serve a warrant on some other person. For unexplained reasons, they stopped doing their job and turned their attention to Keith Lamont Scott, who was still sitting in his car. That seems stupid on its face, but might be justified under extraordinary circumstances (which don't include a man sitting in his car minding his own business).

> Officers observed a subject, Mr. Keith Lamont Scott, inside a vehicle in the apartment complex. The subject exited the vehicle armed with a handgun. Officers observed the subject get back into the vehicle at which time they began to approach the subject.

If, in fact, "subject exited the vehicle armed with a handgun," that might be an extraordinary circumstance – but arguably not, in a state where open carry is legal, and the cops are in plain clothes. There is, as yet, no video showing the cops identifying themselves to Keith Lamont Scott. And how long was the subject outside the vehicle? What did he do while he was outside the vehicle? When he got back inside the vehicle, handgun or not, why wasn't that the end of the episode? Why was there no presumption of innocence? Why did the officers approach the subject only after he was back in the car (if he ever actually got out)?

This is critical. A man in a parked car is not an overt threat to anyone. A man in a parked car with a handgun in his possession (not pointed at himself or anyone else) is not a threat to anyone. So what actually motivated the cops to move in for the kill?

> Officers gave loud and clear verbal commands, corroborated by witnesses, for the subject to drop the weapon.

These commands are, oddly, inaudible in the police body cam video, which is silent for 28 seconds, until after the shooting, which occurs roughly 23 seconds into the 71-second video. In Mrs. Scott's video, the commands *are* audible and clear: "Hands up!" "Drop the gun," [at least nine times] and "Drop the fucking gun." There is also an unidentified voice, not Mrs. Scott, shouting "Don't shoot" once. Otherwise this seems like typical, semi-hysterical police screaming – until one realizes that police were screaming at Keith Lamont Scott to put his hands up *inside his car*. That certainly seems stupid.

A website called "Bearing Arms" claims that the police body cam video clearly shows Keith Lamont Scott was wearing an ankle holster on his right leg. The website also says the video does not clearly show that Scott's right hand is empty. The image is grainy, and both conclusions are uncertain. What the image shows more clearly is a police handgun pointed directly at Scott, who appears to be looking at the police officer holding it.

What the body cam video shows most clearly is the agitated state of the officer wearing it, as he scrambles about like a squirrel, reinforcing the sense of danger and crisis, when a calm, thoughtful demeanor might have saved a life.

> In spite of these verbal commands, Mr. Scott exited the vehicle still armed with the handgun as officers continued to tell him to drop his weapon.

This assertion is problematical, even if it's true as stated. The police dash cam video shows Keith Lamont Scott getting out of his car – backwards – about six seconds into the video. He continues to walk slowly, backwards, in a half circle away from the visible cops, who continue to shout indistinctly. Keith Lamont Scott's gait is slow and unsteady. There is nothing in his right hand. His left hand is obscured. He was right-handed. Roughly nine seconds of non-threatening behavior later, Scott is executed by four quick shots.

> The subject posed an imminent deadly threat to the officers and Officer Brentley Vinson subsequently fired his weapon striking the subject. The officers immediately requested Medic and began performing CPR.

There is nothing – absolutely nothing – in any of the videos to support the claim that "subject posed an imminent deadly threat" to anyone in the universe. Officer Vinson, 26, who is also black (as is CMPD police chief Kerr Putney), has been a police officer for two years. Vinson is also the son of one of the first black detectives in Charlotte. Vinson has not yet spoken publicly, but one of his friends told CNN that Vinson is "distraught", as well he might be for any number of reasons. Even if legally justified, his execution of Keith Lamont Scott looks wholly, unnecessarily stupid.

The remainder of the CMPD timeline deals with events after the shooting.

On September 24, four days after the shooting, according to the Charlotte Observer, the CMPD gave another, enhanced, but hardly more credible account of the event:

Two officers in plain clothes were in an unmarked car waiting to serve a warrant when Scott's white SUV pulled in beside them.

They saw Scott roll what they believed to be "a marijuana 'blunt.'" They returned to watching for their suspect, and then Vinson saw Scott hold up a gun.

They withdrew to a spot nearby and put on duty vests that said "Police" that would identify them as officers.

When they came back, Scott still had the gun. They identified themselves as police officers, the department said, and told him loudly and repeatedly to drop the weapon. Scott did not comply.

Then a uniformed officer in a marked SUV drove up to assist, and an officer started pounding on the front passenger window.

Scott then got out with the gun and backed away from the vehicle, police said, but did not drop the weapon.

This is the narrative pretty much accepted in mainstream media, including a New York Times "What We Know" article September 26. That "responsible" piece is full of responsible "experts" speculating about ways the cops could have been doing the right thing, even though the official narrative is patently flawed and raises questions that go unanswered.

Why does the "blunt" not appear in the initial account? How is it that cops sitting in one car can see what someone is doing in another car, even one relatively close? If they saw Scott "roll" a blunt and later produced a partly smoked blunt in evidence (as they did), why don't they say they saw him smoking it? If Scott was rolling a blunt, why would he be "holding up a gun"? Why would he be holding up a gun at all? What does that even mean, "saw Scott hold up a gun"? When the cops decide to put on vests, what does that show about their state of mind? Here is where the timeline becomes important – how long does all this take? When Mrs. Scott's video begins, the cops are already screaming at Keith Lamont Scott, who is still in his car.

Why do the cops pay no attention to Keith Lamont Scott's wife, who is trying to get them to de-escalate? The man is still in the car and they're threatening to break the windows. If you think a man in a car has a gun, why would you try to break his passenger side front window where you'd be a close target? Forcing such a man out of the car only makes the situation more dangerous. As long as he's in the car, surrounded by police (at least four), there is minimal risk to pausing to talk to the wife, to learn who he is, what injury he has, what medication he's on, and any other de-escalating information.

The cops didn't do that. The cops acted like caricature cops. The cops acted stupidly, unnecessarily stupidly. But they are trained to be stupid. Police training includes a certain amount of reflexive stupidity like this. The police hierarchy that requires this training is stupid. Police stupidity is protected by legislators who protect them from their own lethal stupidity by passing laws that conceal the evidence that reveals that stupidity. Legislators are protected from their stupidity by courts that stupidly accept the legality of withholding evidence of lawful stupidity. It's culturally endless, but on the positive side, at least law enforcement isn't as stupid as the prison system in America. But that's another story.

For now, the Charlotte police are showing pictures of a gun and a holster and a blunt they say belonged to Keith Lamont Scott and asking you to believe that that justifies their executing him. But it's still an open question whether the gun or the holster or the blunt – or all of them – were planted by cops whose behavior was too stupid to preserve his life.

Update: Following standard procedure after the killing, CMPD placed Officer Vinson, a Liberty University graduate, on paid administrative, pending investigation. On November 30, 2016, the Mecklenburg District Attorney announced that Vinson would not be charged. The DA's report said Vinson "acted lawfully" and that "All of the credible and available evidence suggests that he [Scott] was in fact armed." The report confirmed that Scott had not raised his gun, but video did not confirm that he had a gun.

Investigations by the state of North Carolina and the US Justice Department faded quietly into oblivion.

On August 29, 2018, Keith Lamont Scott's family filed a $60,000 wrongful death lawsuit against the City of Charlotte, CMPD, and

Officer Vinson. According to the lawsuit, Vinson was the least experienced officer on the scene. When other officers decided to a technical maneuver called a "vehicle takedown," they ordered Vinson to stay in his vehicle because he had never done such a maneuver. Vinson didn't stay in the vehicle and was the only officer to fire his weapon. For this, the lawsuit calls him "willful, wanton and/or reckless."

As of June 2019 the case had not come to trial.

49.

Charlottesville: Robert E. Lee Was a Traitor to the United States

Unite the Right is about defending treason

Unite the Right is the organizing name for the group that brought a torchlight march (chanting "white lives matter") and violent demonstrations to Charlottesville, Virginia, on August 11-12. Unite the Right organized those demonstrations to honor the memory of a famous traitor, Gen. Robert E. Lee.

That's what their Charlottesville march was about, objecting to the removal of a statue of a traitor to the US. Unite the Right organized these demonstrations in defense of the core value of treason. In a video after the event, Jason Kessler of Unite the Right said he had worked for two months to have a peaceful, free speech rally "in support of white advocacy" working closely with Charlottesville police. In the chaotic aftermath, Kessler accused the Charlottesville police of sabotaging the rally by not providing the pre-arranged security and shutting it down half an hour before it was scheduled to start. He said: "They didn't give a damn about public safety.... The only thing they cared about was stopping the alt-right.... This is an act of war against the American people, in my mind." He also accused the police of failing to show up as promised on Friday night when fights broke out.

In April, the Charlottesville City Council voted (3-2) to remove and sell a bronze statue of General Lee on horseback from Lee Park in downtown Charlottesville. The Council also voted unanimously to rename the park as Emancipation Park. Those votes triggered a series of protests by right-wing groups including the Ku Klux Klan (KKK).

In May, in a lawsuit brought by the Sons of Confederate Veterans and other groups, a federal judge delayed the removal of the 1924 Lee statue for six months. This order remains in force while the lawsuit is pending. The judge allowed the renaming of Lee Park to stand, as well as changing the name of a park named after Gen. Thomas "Stonewall" Jackson to Justice Park.

At its dedication in Lee Park on May 21, 1924, Edwin Alderman, president of the University of Virginia, said of the General Lee statue:

> Here it shall stand during the ages at the center of our lives, teaching, through the medium of beauty, the everlasting lesson of dignity and character, of valor and unselfish service ... And now, in this hour of reunion and reconciliation, we know how ... he symbolized the future for us as it has come to pass, and bade us to live in it, in liberal and lofty fashion, with hearts unspoiled by hate and eyes clear to see the deeds of a new and mightier day.

In 1924, "this hour of reunion and reconciliation" was at the peak of Jim Crow, the peak of segregation, the peak of separate and decidedly unequal, and the peak of racial lynching across the South. 1924 was also a peak time for racist white supremacy, the year the KKK marched in hooded regalia in Montpelier, Barre and Northfield, Vermont.

1924 was not a time when polite society thought of Gen. Robert E. Lee as a traitor to his country, the United States. More likely he was thought of as a heroic leader against "the War of Northern Aggression." But the Civil War was a sectional rebellion, a rebellion every bit as much as the American Revolution, where the rebels ran the risk of being hanged.

The liberal magnanimity of Abraham Lincoln spared Robert E. Lee from the noose he so clearly earned. As a graduate of the United States Military Academy and a military officer, Lee acted consistently with his oath of loyalty to his country. In April 1861, Lee knowingly and deliberately committed treason by joining and fighting for the Confederacy. The Constitution that Lee swore to uphold is clear on the point in Article III, section 3:

Treason against the United States, shall consist only in levying War against them, or in adhering to their Enemies, giving them Aid and Comfort.

Some traitors treated more courteously than others

When Lee surrendered to Gen. Ulysses S. Grant at Appomattox on April 9, 1865, he was taken into custody and promptly released, paroled as a prisoner of war.

On May 29, 1865, President Andrew Johnson issued a Proclamation of Amnesty and Pardon "to persons who had participated in the rebellion against the United States." There were exceptions to this blanket pardon, and Lee was among them. On June 13, 1865, Lee wrote the President seeking his full pardon:

> Being excluded from the provisions of amnesty & pardon contained in the proclamation of the 29th Ulto; I hereby apply for the benefits, & full restoration of all rights & privileges extended to those included in its terms. I graduated at the Mil. Academy at West Point in June 1829. Resigned from the US Army April '61. Was a General in the Confederate Army, & included in the surrender of the Army of N. Va. 9 April '65.

On October 2, 1865, Lee signed the Amnesty Oath required to restore his citizenship. Once again, Lee swore to "faithfully support, protect, the Constitution of the United States, and the Union of the States thereunder...." But Lee's oath was diverted, he was not pardoned, and his citizenship not restored. In 1970, Lee's Amnesty Oath was found among State Department records. In 1975, Congress restored his citizenship, effective June 13, 1865 (more than three months before Lee signed the Amnesty Oath) and President Gerald Ford signed the fiction into law, saying:

> General Lee's character has been an example to succeeding generations, making the restoration of his citizenship an event in which every American can take pride.

Not everyone is mystified by the imaginary image of Robert E. Lee. The staunchly conservative National Review magazine published this clear-eyed assessment of Lee in June:

Lee was no hero; he fought for an unjust cause, and he lost. Unlike the Founding Fathers (even the slaveholders among them), he failed the basic test of history: leaving the world better and freer than he found it.

Whatever saintly qualities or myths are attributed to Robert E. Lee, he was plain and simple a traitor to his country. In 1865 he would likely have received his pardon as a traitor, but by 1975 his hagiography was in place and the South had long since risen again. Gerald Ford was hardly unique in whitewashing a traitor who might well have been justly hanged. And he foreshadowed our present host of alt-right super-patriots so intent on making America great again by defending its greatest traitors.

Update 2019: As of late February 2019, the Lee statue remained in place, fenced off by city construction fencing and No Trespassing signs. A lawsuit filed in March 2017, meant to preserve the statue of Lee and another of Stonewall Jackson, entered settlement talks on January 31, 2019. A possible jury trial was pending. The Lee statue was spray-painted with "Native Land" in July 2017. It was spray-painted again on February 19, 2019, with "FREDOM" (sic) in red letters.

50.

Trump's Racially Obtuse Transcript Highlights, Annotated

Is silence on racism still racism? Does it matter?

White supremacy survives on violence, but the President of the United States can't, or won't, bring himself to condemn either. Most Americans, it seems, don't have that difficulty, judging by the outpouring of disgust with the President and the hail of statues coming down around the country.

That's the encouraging early public response to President Trump's reactionary news conference in Trump Tower in New York on August 15. The news conference was supposed to be about the nation's highways and other physical infrastructure. Even though the actual remedy was limited to an executive order that's supposed to reduce regulatory delays, Trump summarized his accomplishment by saying: "We are literally like a third-world country. Our infrastructure will again be the best. And we will restore the pride in our communities, our nation. And all over the United States will be proud again."

The first question from a reporter was not about bridges and highways, it was about Charlottesville and its aftermath. And the President promptly hijacked his own announced message by inflaming America's psychic infrastructure. What looked at first like yet another Trumpian offense to decency now looks like a possible catalyst for national self-awareness and maturity.

We shall see. Meanwhile, here are excerpts from the news conference that may have unintentionally opened pathways for millions of people to get in touch with their better angels. A reporter asked why the President has waited so long to say something responsible and healing about Charlottesville. The President offered a layered lie:

289

> I didn't wait long. I didn't wait long. I wanted to make sure, unlike most politicians, that what I said was correct, not make a quick statement. The statement I made on Saturday, the first statement, was a fine statement but you don't make statements that direct unless you know the facts....

What he said on Saturday, August 12, in the wake of two days of racist chanting, under-policed conflict, and a terrorist-style killing by car was this, and only this: "We condemn in the strongest possible terms this egregious display of *hatred, bigotry and violence, on many sides. On many sides.* It's been going on for a long time in our country. Not Donald Trump, not Barack Obama. This has been going on for a long, long time." [Emphasis added.] This was not a "correct" statement; it does not express "the facts." It's not a "fine" statement, it is an easy statement worthy of the cheapest politician trying to sound good without accepting any responsibility. It's "been going on for a long, long time," said the man who has spent years feeding and prolonging racist hatred in America. But President Trump spun out his lie for minutes until he figured out how to make the killing of Heather Heyer all about him:

> In fact, the young woman, who I hear is a fantastic young woman, and it was on NBC, her mother wrote me and said through I guess Twitter, social media, the nicest things. And I very much appreciated that. I hear she was a fine, really actually an incredible young woman. Her mother, on Twitter, thanked me for what I said. And honestly, if the press were not fake and if it was honest, the press would have said what I said was very nice.... How about a couple of infrastructure questions?

In reference to nothing that was asked, the President irrelevantly said, "I didn't know David Duke was there," and left it at that. It would be mind-reading to say that reflected a guilty conscience about one of America's most notorious aging racists. It would be a reminder of the record that candidate Trump had a hard time disavowing former KKK Grand Wizard David Duke's support during 2016, though he did so on occasion, making it seem as if the media were persecuting him. David Duke still loves him.

The second statement [on August 14] was made with knowledge, with great knowledge.

> There are still things — [cross talk] excuse me. There are still things that people don't know. I want to make a statement with knowledge. I wanted to know the facts.

That second statement, carefully prepared apparently by White House staff, was careful, hitting the right notes ("We are all made by the same almighty God") but without much sign of genuine feeling. Politically, at least, it seemed to make up for the moral squalor of violence "on many sides" that the President emphasized in his first statement. Possibly the President had done enough damage control to keep Charlottesville from morphing into a larger crisis. He undid that possibility with his Tuesday news conference where, despite terrorist car attacks in France, England, and elsewhere, he had trouble calling the Charlottesville car attack terrorism:

> Well I think the driver of the car is a disgrace to himself, his family and this country. You can call it terrorism. You can call it murder. You can call it whatever you want.

The posture is defensive, protecting the driver's Vanguard America and other alt-right, white supremacy groups like the KKK, neo-Nazis, white nationalists, or neo-Confederates from being officially labeled terrorist organizations. Asked if the "alt-right" was responsible for Charlottesville, the President feigned ignorance:

> Well, I don't know. I can't tell you.... When you say the alt-right. Define alt-right to me. You define it. Go ahead. No, define it for me. Come on. Let's go.

The term "alt-right" was invented by those on the alt-right, such as White House advisor Steve Bannon, as a term to describe their movement. The alt-right is self-named. The alt-right also invented the term "alt-left" as a term with no specific meaning other than to label whoever the alt-right considers an enemy. President Trump so seemingly baffled by "alt-right," had no trouble blaming an undefined "alt-left," that has no specific membership, for causing trouble in Charlottesville. Invited to compare the alt-left to neo-Nazis, the President shifted gears:

> So — excuse me — and you take a look at some of the groups and you see and you would know it if you were honest reporters, which in many cases, you are not. But, many of those people were there to protest the taking down of the statue of Robert E. Lee. So this week, it is Robert E. Lee. I noticed that Stonewall Jackson is coming down. I wonder, is it George Washington next week? And is it Thomas Jefferson the week after? You know, you really do have to ask yourself, where does it stop?

This is nonsense, and a common argument from the alt-right. It has no merit. Washington and Jefferson were instrumental in creating the United States, whatever else they may have done. That they were slave owners and still could argue that all men are created equal only illustrates the human capacity to harbor contradictory beliefs (as a devout Christian, Stonewall Jackson taught Sunday school to his slaves). No matter what, Washington and Jefferson betrayed their king and risked being hanged as traitors, all for the sake of getting our imperfect country going. Lee chose to fight to destroy the country to which he had sworn allegiance. To support Lee is to support treason and to discard the United States as no longer valuable. That's the logic underlying what the President says. If that's what President Trump believes, then he should say so and we should all confront that, for what it's worth.

Unfortunately, this President seems to believe things that are not true, even though he says he's seen the reality with his own eyes. He made this distinction between the torchlight parade of Friday night and the aborted rally of Saturday:

> I looked the night before. If you look, they were people protesting very quietly the taking down the statue of Robert E. Lee. I am sure in that group there were some bad ones. The following day, it looked like they had some rough, bad people, neo-Nazis, white nationalists, whatever you want to call them. But you had a lot of people in that group that were there to innocently protest and very legally protest.

Their innocent protest included chants of "You will not replace us," "Jews will not replace us," and the quintessentially Nazi slogan

"Blood and soil." This is not nonviolent language, but the parade was nonviolent for the most part. The parade came onto the University of Virginia campus and there forced a confrontation with a much smaller number of peaceful, unarmed counter-protestors. The counter-protestors had joined hands in a circle protecting a statue of Thomas Jefferson. The Unite the Right parade pushed and shoved the counter-protestors, who pushed and shoved back, while the police mostly watched and made one arrest. President Trump didn't mention the defense of Thomas Jefferson – or the alt-right's threatened attack on Jefferson.

As the news conference was winding down, the narcissist-in-chief returned to what seemed to be his favorite part of the Charlottesville events:

> I thought that the statement put out, the mother's statement, I thought was a beautiful statement. I tell you, it was something that I really appreciated. I thought it was terrific. Under the kind of stress that she is under and the heartache that she is under, I thought putting out that statement to me was really something I won't forget. Thank you all very much. Thank you.

Then the President went back to lying gratuitously, saying he owns a house in Charlottesville, actually a winery, "one of the largest wineries in the United States." Only it's not. And his son Eric seems to own it. (After hearing this news conference, Heather Heyer's mother, Susan Bro, is refusing to take calls from Trump: "I'm not talking to the president now, I'm sorry. After what he said about my child. You can't wash this one away by shaking my hand and saying, 'I'm sorry.'")

Whether Donald Trump is an actual racist bigot in his heart, what does it matter? He's still defending racist and bigoted words and actions and symbols. That's something White House advisor Steve Bannon is accused of doing as well, although on August 15, when he called the American Prospect, he referred to his erstwhile alt-right colleagues disparagingly: "Ethno-nationalism — it's losers. It's a fringe element. I think the media plays it up too much, and we gotta help crush it, you know, uh, help crush it more.... These guys are a collection of clowns." Contradicting the President when Bannon's own job is rumored to be on the line is an interesting tactic, although at his news conference, the President said of Bannon: "I like Mr. Bannon. He is a friend of mine.... He is a good man. He is not a racist. I can tell you that. He is a good person. He actually gets a very unfair press in that regard."

In that same American Prospect interview, Bannon also talked about North Korea and said something smarter and truer than President Trump has ever said about North Korea:

> There's no military solution [to North Korea's nuclear threats], forget it. Until somebody solves the part of the equation that shows me that ten million people in Seoul don't die in the first 30 minutes from conventional weapons, I don't know what you're talking about, there's no military solution here, they got us.

But not to sound too much saner than his boss, Bannon went on to push instead for greater confrontation with China: "the economic war with China is everything. And we have to be maniacally focused on that. If we continue to lose it, we're five years away, I think, ten years at the most, of hitting an inflection point from which we'll never be able to recover."

Meanwhile we have President Trump's lawyer forwarding an email that supports alt-right arguments and claims that Black Lives Matter "has been totally infiltrated by terrorist groups." The subject line on the email is "The Information that Validates President Trump on Charlottesville." Among the email's assertions: "You cannot be against General Lee and be for General Washington, there literally is no difference between the two men." Literally, that's pure hokum.

So here we are, looking at a President and his lawyer fostering white race rage and a now former presidential advisor looking to man up against China, and war with North Korea just barely off the front pages, any one of which could be an inflection point from which we may never recover.

Comment:

One reader from Massachusetts wrote:

Trump actually said, "Racism is evil. And those who cause violence in its name are criminals and thugs, including the K.K.K., neo-Nazis, white supremacists and other hate groups that are repugnant to everything we hold dear as Americans."

I'd say that, contrary to Boardman's claim that Trump can't or won't end violence, the President managed to issue a clear and unambiguous condemnation.

My response included:

What [the reader] doesn't seem to appreciate is that Trump says one thing one day, another thing another day. [The reader] is correct about the Trump quote he offers, as referenced in my article. This was Trump's SECOND statement, on August 14, clearly prepared to mitigate his FIRST statement, on August 12.... [The reader] sees "clear and unambiguous" where I see changing and uncertain. My conclusion has long been that there is NO way to know what Trump believes by listening to what he says. And ultimately what he believes matters much less than what he does (or what is done in his name). Here are some of the Trump policies likely to warm the cockles of a white supremacist's heart:

- immigration – more white people, fewer non-white people, and a special kick in the teeth for Muslims

- voting rights – search for imaginary voter fraud, suppress voting by minorities

- civil rights – reduce (or reverse) enforcement

- health care – increase vulnerability of poor and minorities

- affirmative action – challenge it as "reverse discrimination despite little or no actual evidence

- policing – calling for rougher treatment of suspects

No doubt more, but running out of space.

51.

NFL Plantation Owners Ban Uppity Quarterback

American Shame: Colin Kaepernick is jobless for thought crime

To watch America's structural racism at work, one need look no further than the National Football League (NFL) and its treatment of nonviolent unorthodoxy as expressed by Colin Kaepernick going to one knee during the national anthem in support of the unacceptable thought that black lives should matter as much as anyone else's. Of course, that's still a relatively new idea in the United States, dating from 1863 in law and still not fully accepted in much of the country.

Colin Rand Kaepernick, who turns 30 in November, is a proven professional football quarterback who chose to become a free agent after the 2016 season. He led San Francisco to the Super Bowl in 2012. He is good enough to play for most any of the NFL's 32 teams, but none have signed him. A year ago, when unarmed black men shot by cops were getting heavy news coverage and while presidential candidates Clinton and Trump disparaged Black Lives Matter, Kaepernick undertook a solo protest, sitting during the national anthem before the first NFL pre-season game. In subsequent games, Kaepernick went down on one knee in silent, respectful protest during the Star-Spangled Banner. Asked by an NFL Network reporter why he was doing that, Kaepernick said:

> I am not going to stand up to show pride in a flag for a country that oppresses black people and people of color. To me, this is bigger than football and it would be selfish on my part to look the other way. There are bodies in the street and people getting paid leave and getting away with murder....

This is not something that I am going to run by anybody. I am not looking for approval. I have to stand up for people that are oppressed.... If they take football away, my endorsements from me, I know that I stood up for what is right.

At the time, official football – the league, his team, his coach – all spoke carefully about respecting Kaepernick's "right as a citizen," without engaging the issue he was raising. Kaepernick is bi-racial. He was adopted by white parents and raised in Wisconsin with white siblings.

Zeitgeist signals: Kaepernick blacklisted, Arpaio pardoned

In November 2016, a Miami Herald reporter asked Kaepernick about a shirt he had worn showing Fidel Castro and Malcolm X with the caption: "Like Minds Think Alike." In discussing the shirt, Kaepernick reportedly said: "One thing that Fidel Castro did do is they have the highest literacy rate because they invest more in their education system than they do in their prison system, which we do not do here, even though we're fully capable of doing that." That sort of truth, spoken out loud, does not endear one to the overlords of the NFL or other American authorities, especially the ones who created and profit from the unaddressed, unending scandal of prisons for profit.

A year after he first spoke out by kneeling in silence, Colin Kaepernick is unemployed. Unarmed black men are killed by cops at a faster rate now than in 2016, but it's not news so much anymore. Kaepernick had his free speech, now he's paying the price. The country has moved on to a more ardent defense of free speech by Nazis, white supremacists, the KKK, anti-Semites and other bigots.

The Trump administration is contributing to social calm and order by setting out to give local police more military weapons, from armored troop carriers to grenade launchers.

The ugliest sign of the country's darkening racial zeitgeist is President Trump's pre-emptive, unprincipled, unconditional pardon of one of America's most notorious police bigots, former sheriff Joe Arpaio of Arizona, a man who spoke proudly of his own brutal and deadly prison system as a "concentration camp." Arpaio was awaiting sentencing when the President interdicted the judicial process with a hasty pardon, granted without any of the usual review and consideration. The brief White House announcement concluded with these lies:

> Throughout his time as Sheriff, Arpaio continued his life's work of protecting the public from the scourges of crime and illegal immigration. Sheriff Joe Arpaio is now eighty-five years old, and after more than fifty years of admirable service to our Nation, he is a worthy candidate for a Presidential pardon.

Arpaio's record is reasonably clear that he did little protecting of the public or the Constitution. His office operated with racist standards that encouraged police brutality and led to prisoner deaths from violence and neglect. Arpaio's service as sheriff was not admirable but self-serving, obsessed with targeting Latinos regardless of guilt, while ignoring real criminal offenses, including domestic abuse and child abuse.

Kaepernick and the irony of the Star-Spangled Banner

Some argue that Kaepernick is the victim of a blacklist. Others deny what seems obviously true. One of the deniers makes much of a few other players who made similar gestures without consequences. But he leaves out critical facts: that these are all players currently under contract and that they have a union to defend them. He makes a point of saying that "NFL rosters are 70 per cent Black," without wondering why NFL rosters are close to 100 per cent without any expressed social conscience. He does not mention that NFL owners would be 100 per cent white but for some limited partners like Reggie Fowler of the Minnesota Vikings.

American racism is structural, institutional, shameless and intractable. Electing Barack Obama in 2008 didn't make the country a post-racial society any more than electing Donald Trump in 2016 makes the country a post-sane society. The abiding ambiguity of American madness can be seen in our "national anthem," which has been our national anthem less than 100 years (adopted 1931).

The Star-Spangled Banner celebrates the defense of Fort McHenry in Baltimore Harbor in 1814 in Maryland, a slave state. The attacking British force included numbers of escaped slaves fighting for the British on the promise of earning their freedom. Francis Scott Key, who wrote the Star-Spangled Banner, was a lifelong slave owner. A lawyer who served as US Attorney, Key used his office to prosecute abolitionists. In an 1837 prosecution of abolitionist Dr. Reuben Crandall for instigating a slave rebellion, Key said in his summation to the jury:

> Are you willing, gentlemen, to abandon your country, to permit it to be taken from you, and occupied by the abolitionist, according to whose taste it is to associate and amalgamate with the negro? Or, gentlemen, on the other hand, are there laws in this community to defend you from the immediate abolitionist, who would open upon you the floodgates of such extensive wickedness and mischief?

Rendered in modern language, these are the same sentiments the racists of Charlottesville expressed in their exercise of free speech. In 1837, the jury acquitted Dr. Crandall. On the Charlottesville hordes, the jury is still out.

Maybe our public consciousness should come to grips with the reality that our national anthem is a slave owner's paean to the defense of a slave state. Maybe, whenever it's played, we might think more seriously about kneeling ourselves. That might be a better way to express our hope to become, truly, the land of the free and the home of the brave.

52.

Flag Idolatry Is a Pathology That Crushes Real American Values

What, if anything, does it mean to respect the American flag?

The flag is a symbol, and there is no agreement as to what it actually symbolizes. By design, the flag's thirteen stripes stand for the original 13 states, none of which would ban slavery. The 14th state, Vermont, was the first state to ban slavery, doing it weakly in its 1777 state constitution (not that the principle was enforced: in 1802 the Town of Windsor sued a State Supreme Court justice to get him to take care of an elderly, infirm slave he had dumped on town welfare; the town lost the case). The original flag had 13 stars for those same original 13 states, and it took over 70 years before all 36 stars in the 1865 flag represented states without slavery (but not states without racist Jim Crow laws and the freedom to lynch without consequence). The colors of the stars and stripes had no meaning in 1777, when it was adopted, as distinct from the colors of the Great Seal that did have meaning.

Then there's the Star-Spangled Banner, written by a slave owner in celebration of the defense of a slave state in a battle against the British. The British force included a contingent of former slaves who were promised freedom if they fought for the British. How many people at the beginning of a sports event understand "the land of the free and the home of the brave" in its deepest historical irony?

All in all, the typical American flag ritual is an exercise in mindless obedience in which any talk of real meaning interferes with the underlying objective of fealty to the state. The ritual is totemic and totalitarian, but not so extreme as the Two Minutes Hate required by the Party in George Orwell's novel "1984." The difference is one of degree, not kind, and the enemy in both instances is rational, individual thought.

Mindless obedience has long been a goal of self-appointed patriots, wrapping themselves in the flag to defend indefensible domestic injustice or criminal wars (both of which we have more than our share these days). There is no meaning in the demand to "respect" any abstract symbol, much less one as drenched in horrifying contradiction as the American flag. In a mature world, respect is what you earn, not what you demand. In a mature world, a person is respected for who and what he or she is and does, not for any office or position of authority. We do not live in a mature world.

More than a year ago, San Francisco quarterback Colin Kaepernick first sat quietly, then kneeled during the national anthem at the beginning of his team's games. The gesture was quiet, respectful and principled. And Kaepernick was articulate in his explanation that he was objecting to bigotry and injustice in America, and especially to police suffering no consequences for shooting and killing unarmed black men. For this objection, he has been blacklisted by the National Football League owners, the same owners who turkey-danced in all directions last weekend in a panic to find the right response to an intensity of protest they mostly neither shared nor understood, beyond the need for public relations management.

No one has a coherent argument for saluting the flag, because there isn't one. The flag ritual is an expression of our secular religion, American Exceptionalism. Coherence and reason are at best irrelevant and require suppression before they spread and become a threat. The result is widespread confusion among a large portion of the population. Historically, all the flag worship in the world has done little to assure justice. Yes, it sort of sounds good, until you try to figure out what it means. Knee-jerk reactions are not about knees but jerks. And when people are standing for the national anthem, what are they really standing for?

Is this a tipping point? Are we watching a fad or a movement?

When Colin Kaepernick was protesting alone in 2016, it's doubtful even he expected to see so many NFL players and owners expressing such solidarity and support in 2017. Granted, the message was muddled, as some players kneeled, some linked arms, some stayed in the locker room, and so on, with no clear message emerging beyond, perhaps, some disgruntlement at being dissed by Trump. The game is on, but it's not clear yet what the game is, and no clear leadership has emerged. But the legitimacy of professional American athletes protesting, even in the mildest way, is a new thing. If the protest expands and endures and coheres, it could be a very good thing for the country. These protestors include an inordinate number of new millionaires who have decided not to forget what they know about being black and brown in this America. And for anyone wondering what that means, there's America's response to storms in Texas and Florida, and America's virtual abandonment of Puerto Rico, as Trump blames the looted colony for being at the mercy of the United States. Puerto Ricans are American citizens who serve in the US military at disproportionately high rates. Tell them about saluting the flag.

And now sports protest has spread from professional football to major league baseball, although just barely. On September 23, Oakland Athletics rookie catcher Bruce Maxwell became first major league baseball player to kneel for the national anthem, hat over his heart and a teammate's hand on his shoulder. Maxwell was born on a US military base in Germany. He is the son of a career soldier. Maxwell's statement after the event had enviable coherence:

> The point of my kneeling is not to disrespect our military. It's not to disrespect our constitution. My hand was over my heart because I love this country. I've had plenty of family members, including my father, that have bled for this country, that continue to serve for this country. At the end of the day, this is the best country on the planet. I am and forever will be an American citizen, and I'm more than forever grateful for being here. But my kneeling is what is getting the attention, because I'm kneeling for the people that don't have a voice. This goes beyond the black community. This goes beyond the Hispanic community. Because right now we're having a racial divide in all types of people. It's being practiced from the highest power that we have in this country, and he's basically saying that it's OK to treat people differently. My kneeling, the way I did it, was to symbolize the fact that I'm kneeling for a cause, but I'm in no way or form disrespecting my country or my flag.

Maxwell is, intentionally or not, echoing Abraham Lincoln's first inaugural address in 1861, when he said, with seven states already seceded from the union for the sake of slavery:

> We are not enemies, but friends. We must not be enemies. Though passion may have strained, it must not break our bonds of affection. The mystic chords of memory will swell when again touched, as surely they will be, by the better angels of our nature.

We have no president today capable of such words, and even less capable of such sentiments. That understanding is part of what drives NFL players to demonstrate, however inchoately. From Kaepernick to Maxwell, professional athletes are in touch with our better angels, and this is something new in American life. It is enough to give one hope, at least for the moment. Maybe they will be bullied back into silence and mindless obedience by the screechers demanding respect – respect for the flag, respect for the military, respect for the police even though they keep killing unarmed black people (and others). The screechers know no boundaries and are unburdened by integrity; they want only consent by any means necessary. But they are screeching for a despicable president who earns disrespect daily, so maybe hundreds, even thousands of over-privileged professional athletes will become America's saving grace. We're a long way from there. But wouldn't that be an amazing example of giving something back?

> **Update 2019:** Blacklist or not, the NFL hasn't signed any contract with Colin Kaepernick as of March 2019. In October 2017, Kaepernick filed a collusion grievance against the NFL (later joined by Eric Reid). On February 15, the NFL settled the grievance with an agreement that remains confidential. Speculation was rife that Kapernick was paid handsomely. He already had a Nike endorsement deal. In the NFL, objections to cultural racism, police violence, and other offenses had been pretty well snuffed out.
>
> Bruce Maxwell, indicted for pointing a gun at a delivery worker, gave up kneeling in protest during 2018 spring training. In July he was sentenced to two years probation. Also in July, Maxwell was sent to the minors during the season and by December 2018 was an unsigned free agent facing a possible Major League Baseball blacklist.

53.

Bigoted and Unprofessional Police Chief Backed by Michigan Governor

"Dear NFL: We will not support millionaire ingrates who hate America and disrespect our Armed Forces and Veterans. Who wins a football game has ZERO impact on our lives. Who fights for and defends our nation has every impact on our lives. We stand with the Heroes, not a bunch of rich, entitled, arrogant, ungrateful, anti-American, degenerates. Signed, We the people."

This is an unsurprisingly nasty internet meme that was publicly shared by the director of the Michigan State Police on her Facebook page on Sunday, September 24. Director Col. Kriste Kibbey Etue apparently gave no thought to her pre-packaged, knee-jerk reaction to NFL players kneeling during the national anthem in protest of police treatment of African Americans in America. Col. Etue was apparently unprepared for the intense reaction to her casual castigation of fellow citizens, predominantly black athletes, acting on principle. A Michigan State Police spokesperson actually asserted that Col. Etue's slanderous social media post was "not about race" — even though the issue wouldn't exist without a racist justice system that allows cops (mostly white) to kill unarmed, innocent black people without suffering significant consequences.

Roughly two days after the posting, Col. Etue issued a brief, substance-free non-apology apology for it, posted on the Michigan State Police website (not on Facebook):

It was a mistake to share the message on Facebook and I sincerely apologize to anyone who was offended. I will continue my focus on unity at the Michigan State Police and in communities across Michigan.

This is the nature of systemic racism. This example happens to be in Michigan, but its general pattern can be found almost anywhere in the US: some official makes a casually racist remark, perhaps even unaware of its racist import, and then when objections come, the official apologizes "to anyone who was offended" — which is a second offence compounding the first.

Col. Etue should not only be apologizing to everyone for embracing a dishonest, insupportable opinion, she should be apologizing for the opinion itself. And if she has the humanity for it, she should be ashamed. She should be ashamed both as an individual and as the head of the Michigan State Police.

As an individual, she is entitled to her opinion, even though this isn't even her own opinion. She is also responsible for the falsehoods and provocation of her opinion: she has owned the false "disrespect" meme, she has ignored the real, racial roots of this protest, and she has adopted the divisive false dichotomy between "heroes" and "players" since there are players who are veterans. She has, in a word, publicly posted her own stupidity, and she could learn from that, but not until she recognizes and understands her actual offense.

As the leader of the Michigan State Police, she has additional responsibility beyond whatever personal bias she harbors. She is an appointed representative of the people charged with enforcing the law even-handedly. Her meme post is incredibly stupid from a professional perspective. A true professional learns to hide her bias, maybe even repair it, not broadcast it to the population that already distrusts her and police in general. In that sense, her mindless post was a form of incompetence and she should apologize for that, too.

It's not as though racial insensitivity is a new issue in Michigan. As of March 2017, the Michigan State Police was essentially a white male institution (88% white, 90% male) that reflects no population anywhere. Of 1875 enlisted officers, there were 182 minority officers (121 African Americans, 47 Hispanics and 14 Asians). 187 of the 1875 were women. Michigan's state population of 9.5 million is 79.7% white and more than 50% female. Two troopers who won a racial discrimination suit against the Michigan State Police in 2013 (a $5.2 million jury verdict) later claimed they were targeted for retribution within the police force. Col. Etue said Michigan State Police would never discriminate or retaliate against one of its own (a second lawsuit based on retaliation is still pending).

Faced with charges of racial profiling, Michigan State Police have changed their record-keeping to be more accurate. A Detroit attorney who has won several lawsuits against the Michigan State Police said he wasn't surprised by Col. Etue's ugly post because, as he said, "I've become familiar with the display of coarse bigotry, narrow-mindedness and racism throughout the ranks of the Michigan State Police department."

In late August, a Michigan state trooper fired a taser from his moving cruiser (a policy violation) causing the death of a 15-year-old black boy driving an ATV (currently under investigation by the Detroit police and subject to the family's $50 million lawsuit over a "drive-by shooting").

Col. Etue's post and apology do not pass any credibility test unless she's so obtuse that she should be removed from office on that basis. Col. Etue has promised she won't resign till 2018. She will continue to draw both her salary of $150,000 a year and a state pension of $80,000 a year until she retires. After her October 5 meeting with leaders of the Michigan Legislative Black Caucus, Col. Etue told reporters:

> Obviously, my comments on a personal Facebook post was very offensive, and I'm truly sorry, that was never my intent. There's a lot of issues in Michigan that I think we should be dealing with, and I'm going to stay focused on working throughout the state to make Michigan a safer place, and I will work with everyone in this legislature. Primarily we have some work to do with our minority populations. If I offended anyone I am truly sorry. I am not resigning. Thank you.

As soon as the story broke, before he had a chance to assess it meaningfully, Michigan governor Rick Snyder made clear he would not seek Col. Etue's resignation. As of October 10, he had not met with the Legislative Black Caucus. Col. Etue is subject to internal discipline since her post apparently violated state police guidelines. For that, she might get a 5-day suspension or just a reprimand. That's the way institutional racism works. Get caught at it, maybe you get a slap on the wrist. On October 5, Gov. Snyder illustrated the institutional racism playbook with his response about Col. Etue's post:

> **I don't agree with those statements.... Again, I said she made a mistake. She did something wrong, but part of being human is people do make mistakes, and the key thing is you apologize and you learn from those.**

What you learn is to lay low. You don't have to make a real apology to anyone specific. You don't have to make an apology for your egregious and offensive remarks. You don't have to retract any racist sentiments, you don't have to acknowledge your racist bullying, you don't have to make even false promises to fix actual problems.

A governor who wanted to fix a racist police force and establish something like even-handed justice in his state would have repudiated the race-baiting and offered some gesture toward equality and decency. Such a governor might have sought Col. Etue's suspension until she made some credible effort to repair the damage she caused, until she actually made some act of atonement for reinforcing the racial divisiveness that keeps white people in power. But Gov. Snyder is in power in part thanks to his own racist dog whistles, the same racist dog whistles that have helped Republicans into high office at least since Nixon's southern strategy and Reagan's campaign kickoff in Philadelphia, Mississippi, the dark heart of racist murder.

This is what the party of Lincoln has become, a vehicle for racism and white supremacy that doesn't mind poisoning a whole city like Flint, Michigan, and then letting it stay poisoned — because how many white voters live there anyway?

> **Update 2019: Col. Etue, reappointed by Gov. Snyder, served through December 2018. On retirement she reportedly received a one-time payment of $500,000 and a pension of $92,000 a year. Governor-elect Gretchen Whitmer appointed Capt. Joe Gaspar to replace Col. Etue. He took office on January 1, 2019.**

54.

Marine General Shreds Integrity Image in Defense of Trump

Context 2019: On October 4, 2017, around 11:30 in the morning, a military patrol comprising 10 US Special Forces and 35 Nigerien soldiers was in a convoy returning to its base. The convoy had left Tongo in Niger, near the Mali border, when it was ambushed from the rear by a force of Islamic State in the Greater Sahara fighters estimated at 50-120 militants. The chaotic firefight lasted several hours before reinforcements arrived. Casualties included four US Special Forces sergeants, 8 Nigerien soldiers, and at least 21 militants killed. Three of the US sergeants, all white, were recovered quickly. The fourth, a black sergeant named La David Johnson, wasn't recovered for two days. Children found him, almost a mile from the location of the convoy, shot 18 times and badly decomposed. His funeral on October 21 in Cooper City, Florida, was attended by some 1,200 people including US Rep. Frederica Wilson, a Democrat and a family friend. The black congresswoman had sponsored "5000 Role Models," a mentoring program that had helped prepare Sgt. Johnson for the military. He was survived by his wife Myeshia and three children (one as yet unborn).

Four days earlier, Myeshia Johnson and her mother, along with Rep. Wilson and several other people were in a car on the way to the airport to meet the Delta flight that was returning Sgt. Johnson's body to Florida. That's when the president called the widow, talking to her for about five minutes while others in the car listened on speaker phone. At the end of the call, Myeshia Johnson was upset and in tears, but said only, "Thank you" to the president.

Shortly after, Rep. Wilson was describing the call to reporters. She quoted Trump as telling the widow, "he knew what he signed up for... but when it happens, it hurts anyway."

"So insensitive," Rep Wilson said, "He should not have said that. He shouldn't have said it."

This touched off a flurry of nasty, dishonest responses from the White House, none even attempting to comfort the widow. The Johnson family confirmed Rep. Wilson's account.

John Kelly backs president with lies, evasions, irrelevancies — not truth

What motivated White House Chief of Staff John Kelly to bring himself to the White House briefing room October 19, only to perform something like a self-immolation?

He began with abrupt fuzziness:

> Well, thanks a lot. And it is a more serious note, so I just wanted to perhaps make more of a statement than an — give more of an explanation in what amounts to be a traditional press interaction.

OK, not clear what that might mean, reporters understood that he was there to defend President Trump's handling of his suddenly infamous phone call to Sgt. La David Johnson's widow and mother of three, comforting her with "your guy ... must have known what he signed up for." Kelly is not in the habit of engaging with reporters, but he had been a witness to the call. So, the next thing he said was:

> Most Americans don't know what happens when we lose one of our soldiers, sailors, airmen, Marines, our Coast Guardsmen in combat. So let me tell you what happens....

Wait, this is not relevant to Trump's tone-deaf effort at empathy. Nobody's asking what happens to the fallen in combat. That's easily found out by the curious. Why is he leading with this red herring? He goes on with his explanation:

> Their buddies wrap them up in whatever passes as a shroud, puts them on a helicopter as a routine, and sends them home. Their first stop along the way is when they're packed in ice, typically at the airhead. And then they're flown to....

Kelly is telling us what's supposed to happen. He is probably telling us what often happens. He is absolutely not telling us what happened to Sgt. Johnson. Kelly had just said, "when we *lose* one of our soldiers." That was a tipoff, consciously or otherwise. During the ambush, Sgt. Johnson and several Nigerien soldiers were literally lost. No one knew where they were for a couple of days. We don't know who found Sgt. Johnson, or how. We don't know if anyone wrapped his body in ice. We do know that his body was so decomposed that an open casket was not appropriate. Kelly's recitation of by-the-book treatment of military casualties was not only irrelevant, it was misleading. And in the midst of this distraction, Kelly tossed in another deceptive aside:

> A very, very good movie to watch, if you haven't ever seen it, is *"Taking Chance,"* where this is done in a movie — HBO setting. Chance Phelps was killed under my command right next to me, and it's worth seeing that if you've never seen it.

All of a sudden, the White House chief of staff is doing a promo for a mediocre, maudlin HBO movie from 2009. What's his point? See, Widow Johnson, maybe there's a movie deal in your future? So, what's wrong with this? For starters, the movie is about the feelings of the colonel (Kevin Bacon) who delivers Private Phelps home to Wyoming in 2004, complete with fawning media coverage at the time. Sgt. Johnson got very different treatment.

But then there's this weird sentence from Kelly: "Chance Phelps was killed under my command right next to me, and it's worth seeing that if you've never seen it." Syntactically, Kelly seems to be saying that it's worth seeing Phelps, 19, getting killed right next to Kelly, in the heat of combat — what Kelly apparently means is that it's worth seeing the movie. But still, what is that "killed under my command right next to me" all about? It's all about a sort of true thing that Kelly distorts into falsehood. Phelps was in a unit guarding a convoy that came under fire. Gen. Kelly was somewhere in the convoy. The official story is that Phelps was wounded while defending the convoy as it got away; somehow, he dies later. Another story came from US Naval Hospital. Corpsman Doc Peabody: "I am the corpsman who was sitting next to PFC Phelps when we got hit on April 9th, 2004. I was sitting right next to Phelps in the vehicle as the enemy initiated the ambush. I am convinced that Chance died instantly but his head was in my lap and cradled in my arms just seconds after he was hit."

There's not much of a story in that, and this was 2004, when the Bush administration desperately needed heroes to keep selling its travesty of a war in Iraq and PBS was happy to help. And so was HBO. "Taking Chance" is a reverent look at idealized treatment of military dead, and generals have been grateful for the sycophancy ever since. Kelly's long-winded recitation of "what happens when we lose" a soldier is an idealized echo of a Hollywood fantasy sponsored by the Pentagon.

In the midst of these layered diversions from what actually happened to Sgt. Johnson in Niger, Kelly adds the irrelevancy of how he felt when his own son was killed, and his son's buddies called him. He abruptly segued into his half-baked non-defense defense of Trump:

> If you elect to call a family like this, it is about the most difficult thing you could imagine. There's no perfect way to make that phone call. When I took this job and talked to President Trump about how to do it, my first recommendation was he not do it, because it's not the phone call that parents, family members are looking forward to. It's nice to do, in my opinion, in any event.

Kelly went on to say that when his own son was killed in Afghanistan, President Obama had not called him, but that "was not a criticism." Then he said, "I don't believe President Obama called." Kelly did not mention that Obama invited him to a dinner at the White House. Finally, Kelly got to the calls to next of kin of the four soldiers killed in Niger on October 4, again drifting into details of military protocol. And when Kelly finally addressed the substance of the calls, he said he advised Trump to use the insensitive formulation that makes emotional sense only to a deeply militarized mindset. Kelly said to tell the dead soldier's survivors that:

> ... he was doing exactly what he wanted when he was killed. He knew what he was getting into by joining that 1 percent. He knew what the possibilities were because we're at war. And when he died, in the four cases we're talking about, Niger, and my son's case in Afghanistan — when he died, he was surrounded by the best men on this Earth: his friends.

So, a mind-numbed former general advised his insensitive president to go with a hard truth laced with a self-deception, most likely a lie. Kelly just lays it out there: the four dead in Niger are just like his son in Afghanistan. How many ways is that just not true? The US has been at war in Afghanistan since 2001; the US war in Niger has come as a surprise to most people. Kelly's son was the child of a general serving his third tour of duty. Sgt. Johnson joined the Army in 2014. He had a wife and family at home, and a congresswoman who had known him as a child.

It is a common delusional fantasy to suggest that "he was doing exactly what he wanted to do when he was killed." No, when he was killed, he was trying to survive. The greater glory is all in someone else's head. In the metaphorical sense, perhaps a career soldier like Kelly's son was doing what he wanted that got him killed, but was that true of any of the sergeants killed in Niger? And how would anyone know? Sgt. Johnson hadn't joined the one percent like Kelly's son, and he had not signed up for a still mysterious mission that got him killed thanks to decisions made higher up the chain of command, which has been engaged in a butt-covering exercise in finger-pointing and stonewalling ever since. Kelly really doesn't want to talk about what happened in Niger, or why the Pentagon won't say what happened, or why the Pentagon and Niger military have different versions of what happened, or who was responsible for four dead Americans and uncounted (by the US) Nigerien soldiers, all travelling in unarmored non-military vehicles.

Contrary to Kelly's kneejerk rainbow patriotism, Sgt. Johnson did not die "surrounded by the best men on this Earth: his friends." Sgt. Johnson died surrounded by Nigeriens he hardly knew. He had no friends nearby when he died. He was left on the battlefield for two days without being reported missing, and when he was found, Nigeriens found him. Kelly may even believe the military mythology he spouts, but that hardly makes it true or relevant or even decent in relation to Sgt. Johnson. But Kelly doubled down on the shibboleths of coercive patriotism as applied to Sgt. Johnson:

> ... he knew what he was getting himself into because he enlisted. There's no reason to enlist; he enlisted. And he was where he wanted

to be, exactly where he wanted to be, with exactly the people he wanted to be with when his life was taken.

That is the language of emotional numbness, that is the lie that lets generals live with themselves, and that is a widespread self-delusion that enables the US to go on and on and on killing people in most of the other countries in the world. "There is no reason to enlist," says Kelly, clearly contradicting his own rhetoric about service and duty. Maybe his sons felt that way, or maybe they had an obdurate general for a father. But even in a volunteer army, most soldiers are there because they have no better choice to bring hope to their lives. That's not a good thing, that's a sad thing — a raw indictment of American culture.

Then Kelly launched into his vituperative and wholly dishonest attack on Rep. Frederica Wilson of Florida. Kelly flatly misrepresented the Congresswoman's appearance at the dedication of an FBI building in 2015. Kelly was there; he was a witness to what happened. Four years later, his version of what happened was wrong. What he remembered, or said he remembered, was not what the videotape of the event showed. Not even close. Does Kelly have memory problems of some sort? Does he not have enough integrity to vet his opinions against reality? Did he just lie and carry out a deliberate political smear? He gave us a clue to his state of mind:

> It stuns me that a member of Congress would have listened in on that conversation. Absolutely stuns me. And I thought at least that was sacred. You know, when I was a kid growing up, a lot of things were sacred in our country. Women were sacred, looked upon with great honor. That's obviously not the case anymore as we see from recent cases. Life — the dignity of life — is sacred. That's gone. Religion, that seems to be gone as well.

A good psychiatrist could unpack that passage for years. Why does Kelly think a widow can't have anyone she wants to be present to comfort her, especially during a cold call from her president? Why does Kelly suggest something sneaky — "listened in" — when the congresswoman was clearly invited to be present and the call was heard on speakerphone by five or six people? Kelly says he is "stunned." He said that frequently in this appearance. Is this a measure of his insulation from the real world, that he expects everyone to live by some unspoken military code?

And then there's the bombshell about being a kid growing up and things being sacred. He grew up in Boston, where one of the demonstrably sacred things was white racism. Kelly doesn't mention that. He starts with the male chauvinist classic: "Women were sacred." Right, especially Catholic women for whom autonomy was all but a venial sin. Kelly turned 10 in 1960 and was apparently stunned to see his sacred cows challenged: women's rights, civil rights, human rights, and peace activism. Ironically, Kelly's life in the sixties was remarkably free-wheeling, including hitchhiking cross-country, riding freight trains back, and joining the Merchant Marine, where his first overseas trip was taking beer to Vietnam. He even chose to avoid the draft — but it was by joining the Marines.

And now here he is saying that women are no longer "looked upon with great honor ... as we see from recent cases." He names no one, but this skates stunningly close to his pussy-grabbing boss. He laments the loss of "the dignity of life," by which he presumably means a woman's right to make her own medical decisions. A broader meaning of "the dignity of life" is hardly possible for a man whose career depends on killing people. Kelly's career is prima facie evidence of his complicity in torture and other war crimes, including the use of depleted uranium weapons, white phosphorous, and the indiscriminate killing of civilians. All those are virtually sacred to the military mentality. Kelly laments the loss of religion, but that's his religion and it's far from gone.

Answering a few questions after his statement, Kelly bobbed and weaved about the Niger mission that got Sgt. Johnson killed. Kelly keeps saying how wonderful our soldiers are doing what they do. He offers not a shred of apparent regret at their deaths. As Kelly sees it, with stunning incoherence and self-contradiction, American soldiers:

> ... put on the uniform, go to where we send them to protect our country. Sometimes they go in large numbers to invade Iraq and invade Afghanistan. Sometimes they're working in small units, working with our partners in Africa, Asia, Latin America, helping them be better.... That's why they're out there, whether it's Niger, Iraq, or

whatever. We don't want to send tens of thousands of American soldiers and Marines, in particular, to go fight.

So why do we send them to fight anyway, to fight and die in wars that never end, wars that never should have begun? Why do we threaten new wars with North Korea or Iran or even Russia? How does that "protect our country" exactly? Kelly's "patriotic" delusions are widely held. They've been driving national policy for decades, and on steroids since 9/11. But like Kelly's appearance in the press room, the expression of these delusions never makes sense; they always come down to a question of faith, preferably blind faith. And with that, as we see in Kelly, goes a sense of priesthood, a sense of superiority masked by disingenuous false humility:

> We don't look down upon those of you who that haven't served. In fact, in a way we're a little bit sorry because you will never have experienced the wonderful joy you get in your heart when you do the kinds of things our service men and women do — not for any other reason than they love this country. So just think of that.

Yes, think of that. Think of what our service men and women do not only in Afghanistan, Iraq, or Syria, but also in less closely observed places like Okinawa, El Salvador, or Yemen. The kinds of things our service men and women do, following orders from men like Kelly, are not particularly appreciated in the countries they destroy. Local elites may appreciate our torturing or assassinating their political enemies, but only the most inhumane among them can really appreciate the war crimes that devastate their home countries. Ex-general Kelly imagines a military full of starry-eyed heroes doing wonderful things, and expects the rest of us to believe that, too. The reality on the ground is that sexual assault within the military has reached record levels, the military serves in part as a training ground for white supremacists and other militants, and the capacity of the American military to promote positive change anywhere in the world is pretty much nil. Hip deep in the Big Muddy, John Kelly says to push on. For love of country.

55.

Just Another Pregnant Black Woman Jailed Unjustly

Siwatu-Salama Ra stood her ground in Michigan. Black people can't do that.

Detroit's attitude toward guns is supposed to be different. In December 2013, Detroit's chief of police publicly encouraged Detroit residents to arm themselves legally. Two years later Chief James Craig observed, "When you look at the city of Detroit, we're kind of leading the way in terms of urban areas with law-abiding citizens carrying guns."

By the summer of 2017, Siwatu-Salama Ra was one of Detroit's lawful gun owners and an active community leader who believed she had a right to stand her ground when threatened with vehicular attack at home. Now she's 26, married, pregnant with her second child, sentenced to two years in prison for a nonviolent gun offense, and facing the prospect of giving birth in jail while shackled. That's the way they do it in Michigan. Sometimes, during hard labor, they take the shackles off for a while.

Siwatu-Salama Ra was sentenced and incarcerated on March 1, but her story has been slow to get much media attention. It is a Kafkaesque nightmare of systemic incompetence, irrationality and injustice. A search of the Detroit Free Press produced no results for "Siwatu-Salama Ra." The Grio ran a piece on March 6 by Patrisse Khan-Cullors, a co-founder of Black Lives Matter, calling out the ugly dishonesty of America's current hate-filled politics:

> We can't expect gun lobbyists to come to this Black woman's defense for standing her ground and we know that anti-choice activists will never lift a finger to prevent an unborn Black child from going to jail.

Siwatu's case only highlights the linked contradictions of these two right wing movements. We must take on her case ourselves and navigate within a criminal justice system that unfortunately continues to be steeped in hypocrisy.

If anything, that characterization is an understatement. Siwatu-Salama Ra has spent the past decade as an activist, working to change the system and improve the lives of the people of Detroit. Now, it seems, the Michigan justice system – police, courts, prisons – is paying her back with an excess of the vicious cruelty it usually lavishes on despised minorities. Fighting some powerful establishment forces, she was outspoken, honest and insistent. As the Detroit Metro Times described her recently:

> Siwatu-Salama Ra is the kind of young Detroiter who inspires hope. Raised between Northwest Detroit and California, the black mom began fighting for environmental justice in the city at just 19 years old, taking on polluters like Southwest Detroit's Marathon Oil Refinery and the Detroit Renewable Power trash incinerator.
>
> Now, seven years later, the 26-year-old is the co-director of the Cass Corridor's East Michigan Environmental Action Council. In recent years she channeled her energy toward educating other young Detroit moms about nutrition and how to avoid harmful chemicals in food. Before that, she developed programs in Detroit schools to engage kids in environmental causes, and some of those students are now graduating college and building their own careers around environmental justice. She represented Detroit in events at the Paris Climate talks, and is organizing a large conference in the city that will bring together environmentalists from around the nation in May.

The freakish sequence of events that put her in prison began late on a Sunday afternoon in July 2017 (described in detail on Democracy NOW! April 18). Siwatu-Salama Ra and her two-year-old daughter were at home in the single-family house where she lives with her mother, sister, brother and nieces. Ra and her mother, Rhonda Anderson, were sitting on the front porch, watching the two-year-old play in Ra's parked car. Ra's 14-year-old niece (Rhondish's grandchild) was inside. Unexpectedly, a 38-year-old acquaintance, Chanell Harvey, drove up unannounced, dropped off her 14-year-old daughter to play with Ra's niece, and left hurriedly. Some weeks earlier the girls had had a falling out because the Harvey girl reportedly "beat up" Ra's niece in a bathroom at school. The girls had apparently made up in the interim, but Ra and her mother knew only about the violent incident. Ra called the sister, who had not given her daughter permission to have this friend visit. Under protest from both 14-year-olds, the friend called Chantell Harvey to come pick her up. When Harvey arrived about ten minutes later, she was "very upset, very angry," according to Ra:

> She started yelling at me, screaming at me, cursing at me. In the midst of this, I'm asking this woman to leave, right? I'm asking her to leave, just go, you know, and she wouldn't. And so the next thing that she did was ram her car into my car. Plus, my baby was in the car. She was in the car playing. That shocked fear in me, and I jumped and got my baby out of the car. So, she's literally going back and forth with this car, putting it in reverse and fixing herself to come at us again and go after my mom. My mother, who was also standing very close to me, wasn't able to run.

Ra's mother confirms this, saying, "She was so close to hitting me that I can feel the car on my clothes." Harvey, with her own daughter in the car, continued to lurch it forward and back, without hitting anyone or anything else, until Ra went to the glove box in her car and pulled out her licensed handgun. Knowing it was not loaded, Ra pointed it at Harvey. Harvey stopped, took three pictures of Ra with her cell phone, then left. The squabble might have ended there, when the only damage was what Harvey had inflicted on the side of Ra's car running into it.

Harvey escalated her response, going directly to the nearest Detroit Police station to file a complaint against Ra. A few hours later, Ra went to the same station to file a complaint of her own against Harvey. At that point, one might think the Detroit police would investigate the case before moving ahead. One would be wrong. For whatever brain-dead reason, the Detroit police have a policy that the first one in the door becomes the complainant, the victim, the unquestioned righteous testifier. The other party is mindlessly labeled the "aggressor" and nothing she can do will change that. Her own affidavit becomes a legal nullity to which the justice system gives no weight. Because Siwatu-Salama Ra filed her report second – and for no other reason, apparently – Ra was permanently considered "aggressor," even though Chanell Harvey had attacked her, her mother and her car. Attorney Victoria Burton-Harris described this strange police policy:

> And it was testified at trial by the investigating officer, the officer in charge, that their practice is, when a report is made and someone is noted as the aggressor, they are not allowed to speak to that person. There is no interview that is had with that aggressor. So, when Siwatu made a police report, she was never considered a victim. Her police report went nowhere, because it was made second. She was already, by the time she made her police report, again, deemed to be the aggressor. So no one followed up with Siwatu. No one did an interview with Siwatu. Siwatu was not called back to the station two weeks after she made her report, like the complaining witness and her daughter were, to give a written statement.

That was July 17, after which, by their own account, the police did no investigation to determine any facts and made no credible assessment of the alleged facts they had. On August 3 the police sought and got a warrant for Ra's arrest, then sent a SWAT team to arrest her. She was arraigned on August 29 on two counts of felonious assault and one firearm felony. On its face this farce has no reasonable justice-based explanation, raising questions as to what was really going on among the participants, known and unknown.

It's reasonable to assume that, even before the complaints were filed, both women were well known to police and others in the justice system.

On April 5, 2015, Chanell Chatell Harvey was charged with two counts of felonious assault with a deadly weapon and two other felony firearm counts, including possession by a felon. On April 22 the police got a warrant for her arrest as a habitual offender. She was arraigned on December 13, pleading not guilty by standing mute. On February 26, 2016, Harvey entered into a plea deal, pleading guilty to one count of felonious assault with the other three charges dismissed. On April 4, 2016, Harvey was sentenced to three months in Wayne County Jail, followed by two years' probation (which would include the July 2017 incident with Siwatu-Salama Ra). By then, Ra had established a very public persona as an environmental activist over the previous decade.

In November 2013, a 54-year-old white male homeowner, living alone, shot and killed a drunken, unarmed 19-year-old black girl who was on his front porch at 4:30 a.m., pounding on his door, looking for help several hours after she'd had a car accident. Wayne County prosecutors were slow making up their minds what if anything to do about it. There were public Black Lives Matter protests and one of the leaders was Siwatu-Salama Ra, then 22. Under a 2006 Michigan law, the homeowner had a right of self-defense, but that depended on whether he credibly believed his life was in danger. Almost a year later, a jury convicted the homeowner of second-degree murder and a judge sentenced him to 17 years in prison, including a mandatory two years required by a Michigan weapons law. He had failed to persuade the jury of his right to a stand your ground defense. On March 9, 2018, the Michigan Supreme Court rejected the homeowner's appeal of the judge's jury instructions on self-defense.

There is perhaps no way to know what impact any knowledge of these two women had on the attitudes or decisions of authorities. But it is more than passing strange that the habitual offender somehow comes off preferentially to the habitual challenger to authority. How do any of these people justify their roles in this process? While Harvey's version of events may have swayed the jury despite internal inconsistencies, she also had three other versions in the course of the case. How do police, prosecutors, judges, jurors, jailers tell themselves it's OK to decide, against the overwhelming preponderance of the evidence, that a victim, a pregnant young black woman, deserves to be jailed in primitive, punishing conditions?

Lurking in the charges against Siwatu-Salama Ra was the possibility of a mandatory sentence, enacted by the Michigan legislature as a delusory "deterrent." As University of Minnesota law professor Michael Tonry wrote in 2009, in an unwitting prediction of the outcome of Ra's case:

> There is no credible evidence that the enactment or implementation of such [mandatory] sentences has significant deterrent effects, but there is massive evidence, which has accumulated for two centuries, that mandatory minimums foster circumvention by judges, juries,

and prosecutors; reduce accountability and transparency; produce injustices in many cases; and result in wide unwarranted disparities in the handling of similar cases.

Siwatu-Salama Ra's trial was its own kind of special farce, starting with an all-white judge and jury. The judge, Thomas John Hathaway (sworn in in 2017), has a respectable resume that includes no experience relevant to a case like this. He told the jury it would be a two-day trial, but it ran five days over two weeks. On the fifth day, jury deliberations were pressured by an approaching snowstorm. The judge told the jury if they didn't decide, they'd have to come back the next day. As it turned out, court was closed the next day because of the storm.

Meanwhile the jury reached an incomprehensible decision. None of them would talk about it afterwards. What they decided was that Siwatu-Salama Ra was guilty of assaulting Chanell Harvey in her car, but *not guilty* of assaulting Harvey's daughter in the same car at the same time. The assault, consisting of pointing an empty handgun at the car, somehow managed to assault only one of the people in the car, according to the jury, hurrying to get home ahead of the storm.

Other indications of jury distraction to the point of irresponsibility were the jury notes to the judge during the trial. The notes concerned irrelevant but charged questions about why Ra's two-year-old daughter was in a car with a gun in the glove box. This had nothing to do with the charges. It's not clear whether the judge gave the jury a clear instruction to stick to the case at hand, as was his duty. Ra's attorney, Victoria Burton-Harris thinks the irresponsible outcome was unrelated to the merits of the case:

> I believe that they couldn't come to an agreement, so they said, "Let's just split the baby."

What the jury didn't know, because the judge didn't tell them, which is legitimate in Michigan, is that any guilty verdict on the felony firearm charge would mean an automatic two-year sentence under Michigan's arbitrary gun law. The judge sentenced Ra to two years of probation on the felonious assault charge. This is similar to what a different judge had sentenced Harvey to on an identical charge. Harvey's felony firearm charge – with its two-year mandatory sentence – was dismissed as part of her plea bargain that included three months in jail.

For reasons that are not apparent, Siwatu-Salama Ra has not been granted release on bail while her lawyers pursue an appeal. Judge Hathaway denied a motion to delay sentencing till after Ra gives birth. Her first pregnancy had complications that are expected to be repeated in her current pregnancy, so compassionate release would seem a no-brainer. But the Detroit justice system has shown no brains from beginning to end in this case. And now the prison system is doing its part by providing the seven-months-pregnant mother with poor health care and treatment. According to attorney Burton-Harris, on a recent trip to the hospital for treatment of an infection that caused contractions, guards shackled her so tightly it was tantamount to torture:

> They put the shackles so tight around her ankles that she couldn't even walk and lost all feeling in her feet. She's six to seven months pregnant, so ankles are already swollen. She doesn't have access to good health care, and it's totally inhumane to shackle a pregnant woman's feet to a bed as she's getting a vaginal exam.

Ra is a practicing Muslim and is subject to religious discrimination, according to court filings. CAIR, the Council on American-Islamic Relations, charges the Michigan Department of Corrections with violating Ra's constitutional right to free expression of religion by serving her food with pork products, denying her a hijab, and denying her access to a Qur'an or religious visitation. A prison spokesman more or less denies the claims. This sort of discrimination is not a new issue with Michigan prisons.

The Wayne County Prosecutor's Office, which is as responsible for this travesty of justice as any of the players, has a reasonable mission statement:

> The mission of the Wayne County Prosecutor's Office is to pursue justice, to safeguard the community by demanding accountability for those who commit crimes and to enhance the quality of life by changing the culture of violence.

By every measure of their own criteria, the prosecutors – and the rest of the justice system – failed to pursue justice, failed to safeguard the community, failed to demand accountability and did nothing to change the culture of violence. They have all participated in an apparently gross miscarriage of justice – "Let's just split the baby" – that threatens to be literally lethal for an unborn child.

> **Update 2019:** Siwatu-Salama Ra spent about eight months in prison, where she gave birth to her son Zakai Siklar Ra Muhammad who is healthy as of 2019. She was released on bond in mid-November 2018 while her case is on appeal. She told Metro-Times: "I will say that giving birth in prison is, for any woman — any woman that gives birth in prison — it's something that she will have to heal from for the rest of her life. That's going to be one of the most traumatic and unnatural things that she will ever experience.... that I was not able to breastfeed my baby. I will never forget being separated from him. I will never forget having to put him down and to have them put chains on me all over again and then escort me out of the hospital and put me in the back of a MDOC car to transport me back to the prison. I will never forget that. I'll never forget leaving him behind.... No woman deserves that. No woman should be separated from their child. Like somebody says, 'There is no such thing as an infant — there's only an infant and his mother. You can't separate the two. But in this country, you see a lot of it. You see a lot of it at the border and you see a lot of it in these women's prisons."
>
> In October 2018, Judge Donald Knapp denied Ra's motion to be released while her appeal was pending. Knapp ruled, without explanation, that Ra was a danger to the community, even though the prosecutor had filed a motion saying she was not a danger.
>
> On appeal, the Michigan Court of Appeals sent the ruling back to Knapp, saying that he needed to "articulate on the record why defendant did not establish by clear and convincing evidence that she does not pose a danger to other persons. Conviction of the crime alone is not a sufficient basis."
>
> Rather than further shame the Michigan justice system, Knapp let her go.

56.

FBI Goes Trumpian, Hypes Imaginary Terrorism Threat as Fake News

"Protecting our citizens and our nation remains the Justice Department's top priority," US Attorney [Justin] Herdman said. "This defendant plotted and scouted locations in downtown Cleveland for an attack on July 4th, when he knew it would be packed with people celebrating our nation's birthday. We will continue to do all we can to identify, arrest and prosecute those threats while working to keep our communities safe and secure."

FBI PRESS RELEASE, JULY 2, 2018

Well, that sounds like pretty good news, doesn't it? The supposed July 4th attack sounds like it could have been horrendous, right? And your Justice Department saved us all yet again, right? That must be why the Justice Department headlined its press release:

> Ohio Man Arrested for Attempting to Assist a Foreign Terrorist Organization with Homeland Attack Plot

Actually, no, that's not quite what happened. This is fundamentally a big government lie. It's a tissue of lies.

The government press release begins with some facts:

> Demetrius Nathaniel Pitts, aka Abdur Raheem Rafeeq, aka Salah ad-Deen Osama Waleed, 48, of Maple Heights, Ohio, was charged with one count of attempting to provide material support to al Qaeda, a designated foreign terrorist organization. Pitts was arrested Sunday [July 1] by members of the FBI's Joint Terrorism Task Force.

This press feed is well-framed to make readers think the worst – "al Qaeda" and "terrorist" and "Terrorism Task Force." And all those aliases – that's scary stuff. But what did Pitts actually do? And why only one count? And who else was involved? The details fail to live up to the hype.

324

Instead of clarifying the arrest, the press release then continues for its next four fat paragraphs with chest-thumping government officials offering bloated, irrelevant and largely false rhetoric – "the dangerous threat posed by radical Islamic terrorism" and "plans to attack innocent civilians" and "working to keep our communities safe and secure." This is all good, solid Orwellian language as it avoids lying without actually telling the truth. And it makes one wonder: Good lord, what on earth was Demetrius Pitts up to all by himself? According to the press release:

> Pitts, a US citizen living in Ohio, pledged his allegiance to al-Qaeda, a foreign terrorist organization, and was planning to conduct an attack in Cleveland on Independence Day, the very day we celebrate the freedoms we have in this country," said Special Agent in Charge [Stephen] Anthony. "The FBI commends the public for reporting individuals that espouse their radical beliefs and/or engage in behavior that threaten the lives of our military personnel and community.

This is the only – mysterious – reference in the press release to thank "the public for reporting individuals." And does the FBI now consider it a crime for people to "espouse their radical beliefs"? Isn't that a radical belief? And does the thanks to informers mean that there was NO independent investigative work? The balance of the press release comprises a summary of a court-filed affidavit that completely supports such a conclusion. Apparently, this heroic defense of public safety consisted of someone giving Pitts's name to the FBI some time ago and the FBI then executing a sting operation bordering on entrapment (or more likely actual entrapment) of a man of less than full competence or significant ability. Not only that, it's taken the FBI almost two and a half years to instigate Pitts to allegedly criminal action, as the FBI admits (indirectly) in its 31-page affidavit filed by Special Agent Andrew Wilson, a 22-year veteran assigned to the Cleveland Joint Terrorism Task Force:

> On December 31, 2015, a Facebook profile for ABDUR RAHEEM RAFEEQ (which was ultimately determined to be PITTS) came to the FBI's attention after RAFEEQ sent a private Facebook message to "The Craig Sewing Show," a California-based political commentary program, stating: "Fuck America and there arm[sic] forces. The USA will be destroy. Allahu Akbar."

First of all, this is all Constitutionally-protected free speech. Secondly, no serious terrorist is going to out himself to the Craig Sewing Show. What Pitts probably unwittingly did was to set himself up as a clay pigeon for the FBI to take pot shots at. There is a long, shameful pattern of FBI agents manipulating marginal people into imaginary threats to build a bogus arrest record that actually undermines freedom by "defending" it. Who knows how many people rot in jail as "terrorists" only because they were entrapped by the FBI in "plots" that never actually existed as real-world threats? The FBI apparently ignored Pitts for a year until he made another post, on Facebook, according to the FBI affidavit:

> On January 25, 2017, PITTS used his Facebook account Abdur Raheem Rafeeq (UID 100010669985661) to comment on pictures believed to be from a jihad training camp. PITTS posted, "We as Muslim need to start. Training like this everyday. We need to know how to shoot guns. Throw hand grenades hand to hand combat. How survey out in the woods. Look at the bed blue eyed devils. They teach their little dogs on how to shoot and Hunt. If you fear death. Then don't say you love Islam. The Rasool saw said. We should always be prepared to fight in the name of Allah Akbar. All cowards stay home. Walsalaam. Abdur Raheem sahl Rafeeq. Allahu Akbar Allahu Akbar Allahu Akbar."

The FBI slouched into action, reviewing Pitts's Facebook account in February 2017 and observing it into June 2018. According to the affidavit, during those 16 months, the FBI believed Pitts was "threatening violence against the United States," "expressed a desire to recruit people to kill Americans," and was "willing to conduct a US based attack." The FBI took no action. Neither did Pitts.

As of early 2018, Demetrius Nathaniel Pitts, 48, an African-American US citizen, had apparently been living a quiet life in Willoughby, Ohio, about 19 miles east of Cleveland on Lake Erie. In May he apparently moved to Maple Heights, about 13 miles south of Cleveland. It's not clear what he did for work, or whether he was employed. He apparently lived alone. After the FBI arrested Pitts, Diane Stoudemire, his aunt near Cincinnati, expressed bewilderment, even though she hadn't heard from him in two years:

He's never been a violent person, so that's what I don't understand.... He had had some problems with drugs and everything. He came up without his father, which is my brother, that was killed before Demetrius was born. His mother passed away while Demetrius was in penitentiary, so he's been having such a hard time....

Diane Stoudemire said Pitts lived "on the fringe" of society, but had no idea he'd been living near Cleveland:

We've been worried about him, because I was his favorite aunt. And he used to would come to me, and I haven't heard from Demetrius in a few years.... He was a good person. I never knew him to get in no trouble, like hurting somebody or fighting or anything. Anything he ever done was to himself.

According to the FBI at a July 2 press conference, Pitts has a criminal history that includes felonious assault and aggravated robbery in 1989, when he was 19. He served less than a year before being released on probation. He was arrested in 2006 but charges were dismissed. He was arrested again in 2007, convicted on a theft charge and placed on probation. He was arrested in 2016 for absconding from probation in 2009.

On June 18, 2018, everything started to change from bad to worse for Pitts. That was the day the FBI sent an undercover agent posing as al Qaeda to meet with Pitts in Willoughby and surreptitiously recorded their conversation (excerpted in the FBI affidavit). The conversation is full of violent fantasy to which the FBI agent contributes, but nothing like a plan or even a credible threat emerges. Pitts makes it clear that he has not joined al Qaeda but would take a test to join. The FBI agent suggests a test: "take out a soldier? A US Army soldier?" Pitts responds: "He dead. He dead. He dead. It's like I said." Then Pitts seems to back off the idea. They go through a similar loop talking about killing a Marine. Nothing is decided, or even promised. Pitts does not ask the FBI agent to prove he's from al Qaeda.

On June 22, the FBI agent met with Pitts in Walton Hills and surreptitiously recorded the conversation (excerpted in the affidavit). The FBI agent starts with a pitch that fits an effort at entrapment:

And so that's part of, part of the question. Part of the in and out is understanding what al Qaeda is about and then wanting to know are you willing to, I mean any brother that's gonna be in al Qaeda has to be willing to do all the things that we've already talked about.... That's why I mean, I mean, I mean I'm excited I went back but of course the brothers, they wanna build trust by steps. And they're willing to send a brother out to meet you but we gotta make, we gotta get to that level too. The other thing too is I mean there is, there is risk with all this and that's why we gotta, we gotta start somewhere. I mean I think we are there but I gotta go back and convince.... I mean I think that can happen pretty soon. But-but this is, but I think this is what this is a big thing that was asked of me cause I told him I told him about hey the value in the knife fighting. The possibility of like what we talked about last time. Finding places where we could get in and set up a bomb. I mean if they provide the bomb maker and we find the path in. Then man, dude we can do, I mean you wanna talk about if doing something like that, that from, from, from within, that will shake them more than 9/11. 9/11 mashallah was amazing.

Pitts doesn't buy into any this. He volunteers that he been thinking about the 4th of July, but nothing specific. Pitts says: "I'm trying to figure out something that would shake them up on the 4th of July.... See I-I that's why I like chess." Pitts mentions "a bomb to blow up at the 4th of July parade," then rejects it because of too many surveillance cameras in the city. The FBI agent abets the "planning" by googling a map of downtown Cleveland. Later the same day, the FBI agent promises to provide Pitts with a bus pass and a cell phone.

On June 25, a second FBI agent posing as "a trusted 'brother'" met with Pitts in Maple Heights, delivering the bus pass and cell phone.

On June 26, Pitts texted the first FBI agent that he had scouted out downtown Cleveland, as discussed. Pitts said he planned to go to Philadelphia (his hometown) for further surveillance. The FBI agent talked to Pitts on the phone and asked if Pitts was going through with the July 4th plan that other "brothers" were building devices for. The conversation was inconclusive.

On June 27, Pitts met with the second agent posing as a "brother" and turned in his cell phone. The second agent gave Pitts a black flag as a terrorist symbol. Later the same day, Pitts met with the first FBI agent for two and a half hours to discuss "the impending July 4th bombing" (according to the FBI affidavit). Pitts says he's going to spend the day July 3 casing the surroundings, "We're just takin' pictures, takin' video." Pitts says he wants to see the explosion on the 4th and the FBI agent says:

> You wanna see it – you wanna see that fireball go flying – you wanna see the body parts flying into the sky?... Alright. Well you know what? Like where we were standing when you can overlook the whole lake, off by that – on top of that parking garage, you can get a pretty good view from way up there.

At this point in the affidavit, neither party has specified just what kind of bomb might be used and they've discussed a few possibilities. They have no specific target. The FBI agent seems confused: "Oh, so you're talking like uh – like uh full car bomb in the whole van." Pitts, who has no way of knowing about and no connection with any bomb, agrees. The FBI agent says: "Alright. I mean this is a – we're going from a remote-control car bomb to a full-size van." Pitts seems to agree but talks about remote-control toy cars with bombs. This seems to fluster the FBI agent, the conversation wanders, "this is gonna take an adjustment and my plan was for the – well what we kinda – they gonna bring in the bomb guy for us...." They seem to reassure each other that they're going through with the plan even though they haven't settled on the plan. Pitts isn't planning to be involved with the bombing directly:

> My part is just to go scope, get the information we need, and bring it back.... See you gotta have Brothers who don't nobody never see. Like I don't wanna meet all the Brothers. No.

> The FBI agent agrees to this. Later in the day, Pitts texted the FBI agent that the plan was impossible, too much security. Pitts talks about pushing on, maybe in Philadelphia:

> Ahki (brother) I want to do this by myself. I have no reason to live. Since I know Philly very well. All I need from the brother. Is some chicken eggs that go [emojis inserted that appear to be explosions]. I will put my life on the line. This will be done in September labor day. Just help me get there. So ahki you must show me. How to drive again. Now can you do that. You don't need to be in this. Ahki you have a family. So keep your hands clean ahki.

On June 28, on the direction of the first FBI agent, Pitts carried out instructions relating to the imaginary bombing, including searching for a vehicle. Pitts said a purchase would be difficult because he'd have to provide a driver's license. The FBI agent suggested a strawman purchase. Pitts found several possible vehicles but bought none.

June 30, the FBI agent "told Pitts that the attack Pitts planned in Cleveland for July 4th was a "go" and that the al Qaeda brothers were happy with Pitts' plan for Cleveland" (according to the FBI affidavit), even though there was still no clear record of any specific plan. The FBI agent egged Pitts on with false promises of a "large explosion ... on behalf of al Qaeda."

On July 1, the FBI agent met with Pitts in Garfield Heights to learn what plan Pitts had for Philadelphia. Pitts explained he was still planning an attack that he wanted to be bloody. The FBI showed Pitts a "remote control car ... [that] contained C-4 explosives and BB's" rigged by the FBI, a toy that could roll under a police vehicle. Pitts freely speculated on uses for remote control cars as well as a larger bomb that he assumed existed. The meeting ended with his arrest.

On July 2, the Justice Department issued its deceitful press release, claiming to have protected the country from a fearsome terrorist attack, even though the FBI knew that attack was never even close to taking place, and even though the FBI knew Pitts had zero capability of carrying it out on his own. The FBI makes no claim to the contrary, but merely asserts the sort-of-true claim that Pitts "did knowingly attempt to provide material support or resources to a foreign terrorist organization." The FBI does not acknowledge that the "foreign terrorist organization" was an FBI fiction and that Pitts's attempt was based on a delusion.

The FBI filings make very clear that no terrorism and no threat of terrorism existed before the FBI decided to pump one up, using a troubled, angry, isolated black man as its pawn to inflate its own institutional ego with fake news. And the news media bought the fake news as presented, uncritically parroting the FBI spin that they stopped an attempted terror attack.

CNN: Man accused of plotting terror attack on July 4th parade in Cleveland

New York Times: Man Arrested in Cleveland Terror Plot After F.B.I. Sting

ABC News: Man accused of planning terrorist attack in Cleveland had San Francisco travel plans

USA Today: FBI: Man who planned attack on Cleveland wanted to give explosive-filled cars to military children

And so, it went across the news media, with a presumption of guilt fostered by FBI lies taken at face value. FBI agent Stephen Anthony set the tone for media coverage:

> Law enforcement cannot sit back and wait for Mr. Pitts to commit a violent attack.... We don't have the luxury of hoping an individual decides not to harm someone or get others to act.

This is disingenuous to the point of deceit. This is a totalitarian mindset. Anthony knows full well that Pitts has never committed a terrorist act, that Pitts has never attempted a terrorist act, that Pitts is known to have "planned" a terrorist act only with FBI incitement. The FBI knows it has no evidence that Pitts is even capable of committing a terrorist act. Based on the available evidence, Pitts has done nothing worse than exercise his First Amendment rights in politically incorrect ways, expressing deep anger and hostility toward the US for its endless slaughter of Muslims. What Pitts was incoherently expressing was rage at his own country's terrorism. For that, his country makes him the terrorist.

That's not a reality that many Americans can perceive from their 9/11-induced fear bubble (that the FBI cleverly invoked). The hysteria of 9/11 has not abated much. We continue to spend endless millions on terrorism task forces, so of course they're going to find terrorists even where there are none – that's their job. And if they can't find terrorists, they'll invent them as they did with Demetrius Pitts, who was essentially helpless once the FBI targeted him. His case should bring shame to anyone serious about law enforcement and justice. Instead it has brought on nothing better than official empty strutting and craven media credulity.

As for Demetrius Pitts, he has been serially lynched – first by life, which could happen to anyone. But then he was lynched by an FBI in search of easy prey, next he was lynched by the Justice Department in search of easy praise, and now he is being lynched by news media in search of easy answers. In due course, he will likely be lynched by the court system and then by the prison system.

This case is what societal failure looks like. Police-state tactics can railroad an innocent man, and no one questions the police state's flimsy official story.

Update 2019: Pitts has been in jail since July 2018. Public defender Charles Fleming represents him and sought a competency evaluation because Pitts has "longstanding mental concerns." A court appointed psychologist found Pitts competent to understand court proceedings and assist in his defense. In mid-November 2018, the court found Pitts competent to stand trial. On January 17, 2019, the US Attorney indicted Pitts "on one count of attempting to provide material support to al Qaeda." The rest of the indictment presents the same weak case, creating the appearance of a government face-saving gesture at Pitts' expense. This is a far cry from justice.

57.

Not Safe to Be Black at Smith College

Dispatch: Campus Police, recorded line.

Reporting Caller: I was just walking through here in the front foyer of [REDACTED] and we have a person sitting there laying down in the living room area over here. I didn't approach her or anything but um he seems to be out of place ... umm ... I don't see anybody in the building at this point and uh I don't know what he's doing in there just laying on the couch.

Dispatch: Can I have your last name please?

Reporting Caller: *[REDACTED]*

Dispatch: I'll send someone over and check it out.

Reporting Caller: Alright. I'll wait over here.

CAMPUS POLICE CALL TRANSCRIPT,
JULY 31, 2018, AS RELEASED BY SMITH COLLEGE ON AUGUST 3

It's very hard to see this call by a white Smith College employee as anything but a racist reaction once you know the person on the couch is a black woman, even though the caller doesn't reference race. The dispatch officer doesn't ask about that. The Smith employee isn't even sure what gender the person is but complains to the police, "I don't know what he's doing in there just laying on the couch." The police dispatcher is remarkably uncurious about why anyone should care about a person lying on a couch, much less why the police should investigate at all. Why are these supposedly security-conscious people so casual about such a non-offense offense? Are the redactions in the transcript more substantive than they appear?

Smith College should provide the full, unredacted transcript.

333

The white employee waits for the campus police to arrive. A second white person of the opposite gender joins the first. The second person has not been identified either.

The "out of place person" turns out to be nothing of the kind, not even close. She turns out to be a black woman with very short black hair. She is Oumou Kanoute, 21, 5'2" tall, an academically gifted Smith College sophomore working for the summer teaching chemistry to high school students in the college's STEM program. She is also a member of Smith's cross-country team. To get into the student common room in the first place she had to use her college-issued keycard. The white Smith employees weren't likely to have known who this person was, but they almost surely knew it took a keycard to get into the room, and they should have considered that along with the absence of any sign of forced entry.

While a uniformed police officer talked briefly to Kanoute, the white employees apparently waited in the foyer, possibly with a second police officer. The record is incomplete.

None of the parties have said what happened next. Presumably the police officer left Kanoute to carry on. But if the white employee was still there, did the officer explain what happened? Why didn't the white employee own the mistake and apologize on the spot? Why didn't the police officer facilitate such an opportunity? All this should be just obvious institutional behavior in an institution actually serious about promoting harmony, never mind racial harmony. Failing to resolve it in the moment is a form of institutional negligence, and it could have been avoided had either the white Smith employee or the white campus cop acted with reasonable human decency.

Oumou Kanoute grew up in New York City and is the first member of her family to go to college. She speaks four languages. She was an outstanding student at Westminster School in Simsbury, Connecticut, class of 2017. She worked hard, against long odds, to get into Smith College (roughly 5% black) in Northampton, Massachusetts (4% black). As the college describes itself: "one of the largest of the prestigious Seven Sisters women's colleges, Smith educates women of promise for lives of distinction." Smith is notoriously difficult to get into.

The casual, mindless cruelty of a still-anonymous Smith employee set off a sequence of events that continues to unfold. That same evening, Oumou Kanoute posted on Facebook:

> I am blown away at the fact that I cannot even sit down and eat lunch peacefully. Today someone felt the need to call the police on me while I was sitting down reading, and eating in a common room at Smith College. This person didn't try to bring their concerns forward to me, but instead decided to call the police. I did nothing wrong, I wasn't making any noise or bothering anyone. All I did was be black. It's outrageous that some people question my being at Smith College, and my existence overall as a women of color. I was very nervous, and had a complete meltdown after this incident. It's just wrong and uncalled for. No students of color should have to explain why they belong at prestigious white institutions. I worked my hardest to get into Smith, and I deserve to feel safe on my campus.

Beneath that, Kanoute posted a video she made of her police interview. The picture quality is weak, and the audio is poor. Over the video she wrote: "So I'm sitting down minding my damn business and someone calls the cops on me while I'm just chilling. This is why being black in America is scary." The police officer's tone in the video is mild. Kanoute adds: "Now he is apologizing on behalf of the racist punk who called the police on me for absolutely nothing." Later that same evening, Kanoute posted again on Facebook, this time asking readers to forward her story to their followers: "I demanded that the administration share the name of the person who made the [campus police] call so that they can confront and acknowledge the harm done to me as a student.... I'd appreciate any message you could send to your followers in order to put pressure on the administration...." Kanoute's Facebook posts went viral.

This incident illustrates just how thin the veneer of "feeling safe" is for a black person in America these days. Only it's not just these days, it's effectively forever, and white society – as Smith College is currently demonstrating – still has a long way to go to achieve any decent version of that "post-racial society" so many callow idiots were crowing about in late 2008.

The next day, August 1, the Smith College "Interim Director of Inclusion, Diversity and Equity," Amy Hunter, posted a sterilized response to the event. She did not say how it came to her attention, and she named no names. In the midst of her flat, bureaucratic text, she included: "I have reached out to the student to offer support and discuss next steps and will conduct an investigation of the incident with the employee, with Human Resources and with Campus Police."

As a personal response, this is worthless, but even as an institutional response it seems rather lame. By then Amy Hunter knew, or should have known, what distress Kanoute had expressed. Personal contact, not mere "reaching out," is what a responsible institution would require. Perhaps that has happened since.

By August 2, Massachusetts media were running the story, as was The New York Times, which quoted the college president's response and put the incident in the context of similar racist cop callers in recent months, targeting black people doing ordinary things. The Washington Post, the Daily Mail, ABC, CBS and CNN also covered the story over a two-day period. As of August 6, the story was still trending on YouTube with 30,972 views.

On August 2, Smith College president Kathleen McCartney made her first public statement in a letter to "Students, Staff and Faculty." She refers to the event, then says:

> I begin by offering the student involved my deepest apology that this incident occurred and to assure her that she belongs in all Smith spaces. This painful incident reminds us of the ongoing legacy of racism and bias in which people of color are targeted while simply going about the business of their daily lives. It is a powerful reminder that building an inclusive, diverse and sustainable community is urgent and ongoing work.

By omission, McCartney implies that she, too, has not felt that any personal contact with the unnamed Oumou Kanoute was necessary or desirable or something. Her letter goes on for another page or two coldly articulating all the right thoughts. She announces that – for the first time: "Beginning this fall, every Smith staff member will be required to participate in mandatory anti-bias training." There will also be workshops. And Amy Hunter's office will work with the campus police not to go off half-cocked, though she put it more delicately: "to strengthen protocols by which they triage, assess and respond to calls for assistance." McCartney's letter also announces engaging an outside law firm as a "third-party investigator" whose investigation will remain secret, at least insofar as protecting the privacy and concealing the identity of the perp who called the cops in the first place.

Personal responsibility, anyone? Smith College says no, racial harassment is protected speech, apparently, or maybe it's a form of academic freedom. The college should be ashamed of putting itself in the position of protecting the instigator while attending minimally to the victim. McCartney shows no sign of shame, or even awareness of her structural culpability. With apparently unintended irony, she ends her letter with an appeal to the community to send her ideas: "we need everyone's input, and we pledge to listen to you."

Late on August 2, Oumou Kanoute posted again on Facebook to address the unexpected "volume of response to come from this situation," promising to respond to everyone. She addressed the media, saying she was the only contact and not to contact anyone else for interviews. She addressed family and friends and allies, thanking them for support. And she addressed Smith College:

> I recognize and appreciate the effort that you all continuously put into inclusion on this campus. However, we must be intentional about addressing this racist incident and systemic racism on campus. Your response has been helpful, but it is incomplete. I will be unable to move forward from this incident without the following personal demands
>
> 1. The name of the employee (confidentially or publicly);
>
> 2. A private conversation between me, that employee, and the administration focused on reconciliation and acknowledgement of this wrongdoing from the employee and the college;
>
> 3. An apology from the school and the employee during that meeting – This process must precede any type of decision for or against punishment for this outrageous and racist act. This process must also be accompanied by beginning a mandatory campus-wide conversation and new school policy

concerning racism, gender, and policing that centers the voices of students and faculty of color when we return from summer vacation in Fall 2018.

On August 3, Inclusion director Amy Hunter announced, "Updates on the Investigation," including releasing the call transcript and naming the Sanghavi Law Office as the college's "external investigator." Hunter also wrote, without revealing the identity, that: "The employee who placed the call to Campus Police has been placed on leave pending the outcome of the external investigation."

Smith has struggled with race issues in the past. President McCartney stakes out an honorable if somewhat bloodless position (smacking of white privilege?). Oumou Kanoute stakes out a heartfelt demand for a humane institutional response that offers an opportunity for meaningful institutional growth, especially in the current presidentially-induced atmosphere of racist pollution.

Update 2019: On September 17, 2018, the Boston Globe reported: "Smith College sophomore Oumou Kanoute no longer runs alone along the hilly Northampton roads. She has skipped out on campus celebrations. And she now prefers to eat in her room, avoiding leisurely meals and potentially uncomfortable run-ins in the dining halls.... she guards her privacy after weeks of public exposure.... she doesn't regret her decision to broadcast her experience on social media."

Earlier in September Smith students staged a mass walkout from convocation, demanding that Smith come to grips with racial bias issues.

On October 30, 2018, Inside Higher Ed reported: "Investigators concluded that the caller provided 'legitimate, non-discriminatory' reason for calling campus police on a black student who was eating her lunch in a residence hall living room.... According to the report, the caller, whose name has not been publicly disclosed, called campus police because 'he thought it was strange that a person was in the un-air-conditioned living room of Tyler House, when the nearby dining area was air conditioned, and the building was 'closed.' ... Kathleen McCartney, Smith College president, emphasized in a letter to students, faculty and staff that the college still had work to do to prevent racial bias on campus."

There is no indication that anyone has yet apologized to Oumou Kanoute.

338

58.

Police State Mindset Sees One-Year-Old and Mother as Threat

"The mission of the New York City Police Department is to enhance the quality of life in New York City by working in partnership with the community to enforce the law, preserve peace, reduce fear, and maintain order. The Department is committed to accomplishing its mission of protecting the lives and property of all citizens of New York City by treating every citizen with compassion, courtesy, professionalism, and respect...."

MISSION AND VALUES OF NYPD, ISSUED APRIL 5, 2016

This mission was spectacularly not accomplished on Friday afternoon, December 7, at a Brooklyn office of the city's HRA – Human Resources Administration (irony presumably unintended). The stunningly abject failure of police to live up to their professed mission featured several police officers violently separating a one-year-old boy from his mother as she lay on the floor crying for help. The end of the event was documented in a video posted on Facebook the same day by a witness who commented:

> So I'm At 275 Bergen Street Handling My Business Or Whatever & There Wasn't Any More Chairs For This Lady To Sit Down So She Sat In The Corner On The Floor. The Security Guard Came Over Said What Ever She Said To Her & She Made The Security Guard Feel Dumb So She Called The Cops On Her & This Was The Outcome SMH Mind You She Had Her Baby In Her Hands The Whole Time. I'm So Fucking Disgusted with The NYPD. EVRYBODY PLEASE SHARE!!! I'm a mother myself & I would've lost my fucking mind if this was me they would've had to kill me.

Here's what apparently happened, starting with the arrival of Jazmine Headley, 23, at the HRA office, carrying her one-year-old son. She was there to get a child care credit so that she could take a cleaning job. One account has her waiting four hours. She had no place to sit but

339

the floor. None of the human resources workers offered her an extra chair. Instead, a security guard told this woman holding an infant that she had to stand. When Jazmine Headley refused to stand, the security guard or someone else called the cops.

That might not have been a bad thing, since New York has recently started training its police officers in de-escalation techniques that presumably help to "preserve peace, reduce fear, and maintain order." How hard would it have been to sort out a situation where a mother and child are waiting patiently to get served? That really depends on the mindset of the enforcement officers. The security guards had already escalated a non-event into a confrontation. The NYPD officers, mostly (or all) women, turned it into a human rights violation, an unjustified assault on both the mother and the infant. When bystanders objected to the way the cops were acting, one of the cops threatened the bystanders with a taser. A police spokesman later refused to identify any of the cops involved or to say they had followed proper protocols.

This really should have been a no-brainer for every authority figure involved. A woman and her baby sitting in a corner pose what kind of threat to whom? Who is responsible for the way the hired security guards impose "order"? Where is the simple humanity of those who run a crowded "human resources" office? What possible rationale does anyone have for demanding that the woman stand with her child while she waits her turn? Why did the police not de-escalate the non-threating situation instead of turning it into a violent arrest of the mother and violent detention of the infant? No wonder the video went viral and sparked widespread outrage.

Official response by higher-ups was little better and came days later. Mayor Bill de Blasio tweeted that the police assault was "a disturbing incident." The NYPD issued a statement calling the assault "troubling." The police statement apparently misrepresented the sequence of events, claiming HRA security "made unsuccessful attempts to remove this individual from the facility due to her disorderly conduct towards others and for obstructing the hallway." The NYPD statement includes this inconsistent passage:

> The woman was then informed by police numerous times to leave the location, and she refused. As NYPD officers were attempting to convince the woman to depart the facility, HRA peace officers brought the woman to the floor. NYPD officers then attempted to place her under arrest. She refused to comply with officers' orders, and was then taken into custody.

She was "informed" to leave? Why? Did she not have every right to be there? What right did any of the authorities have to raise this barrier to her finding work when it was the job of at least some of them to help her? "HRA peace officers brought the woman to the floor." What? She was standing, then tackled? With a child in her arms? Then she was arrested for what, littering? And why does the NYPD statement omit the child's existence, as well as the assault on the child? After all, one of the charges against Headley was "acting in a manner injurious to a child."

The bogus arrest of a young black woman on a Friday in Brooklyn didn't generate much news coverage until the video went viral and public reaction pushed it into the news on December 9. The next day NY Police Commissioner James O'Neill tweeted:

> As we investigate Friday's arrest in Brooklyn, I'll tell you the video is very disturbing to me — as PC, & as a dad. Also, #NYPD cops have a very tough job. We were called to a chaotic situation & we're looking at all available video to determine why certain decisions were made.

The credible accounts available so far all suggest that if there was any chaos, then the private security guards created it, and the NYPD made it worse. Training in de-escalation – bringing a calming effect to an intense situation – began about four years ago, after a NY police officer killed Eric Garner with a stranglehold even though the underlying offense was selling single cigarettes on the street. Eric Garner, 43, was an unarmed black man and father of six when a gang of cops swarmed him. His last words were: "I can't breathe." Garner's killer, Daniel Pantaleo, was not indicted by a grand jury in 2014, but he still faces an internal police disciplinary charge of using excessive force. Pantaleo's hearing started December 7, the same day NY cops used Jazmine Headley to demonstrate that de-escalation techniques have not yet taken hold, although there was no stranglehold and Headley survived.

Pantaleo is defended by his police union, the Patrolmen's Benevolent Association. Union head Patrick Lynch responded to protesters that this trial is a "kangaroo court." He accused the Civilian Complaint Review prosecuting Pantaleo of rushing the 2014 case. Lynch was also quick to absolve the police of any blame in tearing Jazmine Headley's baby from her arms. Lynch said: "These police officers were put in an impossible situation. They didn't create the dispute at the HRA office." Yes, that's true as far as it goes. But it ignores the reality that the police made the impossible situation into a disaster. Kind of reminds one of Chicago mayor Richard Daley's exquisite malapropism during the 1968 police riots: "The police are not here to create disorder, they're here to preserve disorder."

Fifty years after the Chicago police riots, police violence remains an American plague. Police executions of innocent, unarmed, usually non-white victims continue to go unpunished. The same day Jazmine Headley became news, The New York Times published a study of excessive police violence in Phoenix. The piece starts with a cop roughing up and arresting a blind man who "came too close" to him in a men's room. City officials did not dispute the statistics showing Phoenix police were more violent than police in other cities of similar size. Instead, the officials blamed Phoenix citizens, based on no statistics or other evidence. When the Phoenix police chief hired a non-profit research firm to study the violence issue, the Phoenix police union called that "second-guessing police officers who have done nothing wrong."

That's a police state mentality, the presumption that the police have done nothing wrong, without evidence or analysis. Patrick Lynch of the NY police union expressed the same poisonous attitude: "The event would have unfolded much differently if those at the scene had simply complied with the officers' lawful orders." The idea that we should obey the police whatever they say is raw authoritarianism. In a free country, police need to be as accountable as the rest of us. And in the case of Jazmine Headley, accountability seems to have begun.

On December 11, the Brooklyn district attorney dropped all charges against her, saying:

> I was horrified by the violence depicted in the video and immediately opened an investigation into this case.... An HRA officer escalated the situation as Ms. Headley was about to leave the premises, creating an awful scenario of a baby being torn from his mother. The consequences this young and desperate mother has already suffered as a result of this arrest far outweigh any conduct that may have led to it. She and her baby have been traumatized, she was jailed on an unrelated warrant and may face additional collateral consequences.

The same day, Headley was released from Rikers Island prison after five days there. Ordering her release, Judge Craig S. Walker called her arrest a "horrific scene that was broadcast all over the United States." While the viral video and subsequent outcry influenced the judge, Headley had only limited awareness of the media storm until she was released.

Headley was jailed because of a New Jersey warrant relating to credit card fraud charges for which she had missed at least one court appearance. The NY judge released her on her own recognizance, meaning that she did not have to post bail but was expected to appear at a New Jersey hearing next week. Brooklyn Defender Services, which has represented Headley, assured the judge that she would appear as required. The agency has also filed a motion in New Jersey asking for the dismissal of the charges there.

This represents partial justice of a sort for Jazmine Headley, but it's hardly restorative or compensatory. Meanwhile, the police union's Patrick Lynch continues to whine for police supremacy: "The immediate rush to condemn these officers leaves their fellow cops wondering – when confronted with a similar impossible scenario, what do you want us to do? The answer cannot be 'do nothing.'"

What do we want police to do? Have they not been trained in de-escalation? Are they not capable of making sensible, proportionate decisions? How willing are they to live up to their mission of "treating every citizen with compassion, courtesy, professionalism, and respect..."?

Update 2019: On February 4, 2019, Jazmine Headley testified to the New York City Council about her experience. When she finished, she received a standing ovation and numerous apologies from Council members. One of them, Laurie Cumbo, herself a new mother, invited Headley and her son to attend Cumbo's son's birthday party.

One of the guards in the incident has resigned. The city is seeking to fire another.

Several bills mandating civil and humane behaviour by the Human Resources Administration have been introduced by the Council.

PART FIVE

America Saves the World

59.

US 'Secures' War in Afghanistan, Also War Criminals

"This year we will conclude our combat mission in Afghanistan."

PRESIDENT OBAMA, MAY 27, 2014

Actually, in line with US policy of permanent war somewhere, our combat mission in Afghanistan has been extended indefinitely. Amidst the more clamorous public freak-outs over ISIS and Ebola, the moment of the Afghan war extension went largely unnoticed in the media and went without serious discussion by the public or the vacationing Congress. It's just more war, and just more of the same old war at that, what's to discuss?

The more war moment occurred on September 30, when the US and Afghanistan signed a 30-page Bilateral Security Agreement that, among other things, prolongs what is already the longest war in US history well into the indefinite future. The agreement also prolongs the backdoor war on Pakistan. On May 27, President Obama said, "This is the year we will conclude our combat mission in Afghanistan." That statement is now "inoperable." Maybe the next president will end the Afghan war.

Under the security agreement, the US will keep about 9,800 troops in Afghanistan, where their combat missions will include special forces operations in-country and Afghan-based drone strikes in Pakistan as well as Afghanistan. A similar agreement between NATO and the Afghan government will keep another 2,000 or so foreign troops in the country. The US-NATO troop level of 12,000 compares with troop levels in Afghanistan in 2002 – or troop levels in Vietnam

347

in 1963 – in similar efforts to suppress an indigenous insurgency with "advisors" and other euphemisms.

When it was signed in Kabul, the security agreement was variously described as "long-term," which it is; "long awaited," which it was by some; "an important step forward," which it may be from some perspectives; "vital," which has yet to be demonstrated; and "crucial," which can't be known for decades. Or, in the words of US secretary of state John Kerry:

> The signing of the Bilateral Security Agreement sends a long-awaited and unequivocal message that the United States and Afghanistan are determined not just to sustain, but to build on more than a decade of progress. This is a milestone moment... an exclamation point... a bond.... The gains of the past decade have been won with blood and treasure. They must not be lost, and we all have a stake in ensuring they're a foundation upon which to build.

Once the agreement enters into full force on January 1, 2015, it will become virtually permanent. According to Article 26:

> This Agreement shall also supersede any prior agreements and understandings ... contrary to the provisions of this Agreement. The Agreement may be amended by mutual agreement of the parties, but it may not be terminated by either party alone except upon two years written notice to the other Party.

Does anyone actually know what's real in Afghanistan?

Afghanistan remains divided, with the government and the Taliban each controlling about half the country. Without the security agreement, all foreign troops were likely to withdraw by the end of this year, raising the possibility of a Taliban takeover of the whole country. A shipping company working in and through Afghanistan, the Icon Company, estimates heavy Taliban activity in 80% of the country.

The US continues to frame its purpose in Afghanistan as part of a fight against terrorism. US policy pronouncements continue to conflate al Qaeda with the Taliban, even though the Taliban rejects al Qaeda as being as foreign as Americans. Even in 2001, the al Qaeda training bases in Afghanistan were established and run by Saudis.

The Taliban, also known as the Islamic Emirate of Afghanistan, frames its purpose in Afghanistan as a jihad against foreign invaders and a determination to establish "a pure Islamic government" – in other words, repelling a foreign invasion and fighting a civil war against Afghan collaborators.

As soon as the bilateral agreement was signed, the Taliban issued a statement condemning US-Afghan security cooperation, saying in part:

> The American stooges further exposed their true faces to the Afghan nation.... these people are the paid employees of America... whose only mission is to cement American interests.... [They] obediently signed away an official document of enslavement of this nation to America....

> We consider this action by the new officials of Arg (Presidential Palace) as an act of disgrace and regret which is considered an unforgettable treason with their own religion, people, history and nation and with it has paved the way for continuation of the current crisis for their own immediate political interests.... Afghans have now realized their calls of reconciliation and peace are mere deceitful slogans while the infidel transgressors who were on the verge of fleeing the country have been provided with an excuse to stay....

> We once again want to clarify our stance regarding the occupation; the presence of armed infidel forces, their military structures and intelligence agencies on the land of Muslims as well as their unrestricted access to the land and airspace of an Islamic country are in direct conflict with all religious, national and human principles.... therefore we shall never back off from our Jihadi duties in the presence of infidel armies.

> ... we shall continue our sacred Jihad and struggle for freedom against you until we have saved our country from the savage American claws, restored a strong Islamic government and endowed our nation with another historical distinction.

> Our nation ... intends to hand out the same Shariah judgment and punishment to the signatories of the current American pact which was meted out to the previous stooges here, Inshallah.

The day before the security pact signing in Kabul, a Taliban suicide bombing killed six people; the day after the signing, another suicide attack in Kabul against an Afghan army bus killed seven and injured 21 (according to Western reporting; the Taliban claimed over 50 deaths). In recent months, Taliban attacks throughout the country have inflicted high casualty rates on government security forces and exposed logistical shortcomings. As a RAND Corporation analyst put it:

> The fact that the US and other partner nations will be present doesn't suggest that this is going to be an easy fight. This year, the Taliban killed more Afghan soldiers and police than it has in any year since it fell from power, and there are no signs that it is easing up.

> "10,000 US troops to stay in Afghanistan until at least 2024. News greeted with collective beltway shrug." – Rachel Maddow tweet, September 30, 2014

At the end of her MSNBC program on September 29, Maddow concluded by noting that in Congress, out of 100 senators and 435 representatives, a total of 14 (four senators, 10 representatives) "say they're embarrassed by what Congress has done and Congress ought to come back in order to vote on the war in Syria and Iraq." It's even worse when it comes to the US-Afghan security agreement that prolongs the war by executive action. As Maddow said, understating the open-endedness of the US commitment:

> But it is both members of the Congress and us the public who actually have to decide if we make overt decisions as a country about what wars to wage and where our troops should serve and whether these decisions are just going to happen outside the political system and nobody answering for them who debate, without hard wisdom about what we're doing not only going unanswered, but in most cases, going unasked. Amazing.

> But tonight's breaking news, breaking precisely nowhere is 10,000 US troops in Afghanistan for a decade. They are signing that deal tomorrow. Not a peep in Washington.

Nor have there been many peeps since the signing. Afghanistan has faded in the news. The official narrative has taken hold. US security interests in Afghanistan are "vital," "crucial," blah-blah-blah – and in no need of examination. The mainstream media generally reinforce the official narrative, typically by bland acceptance, or silence, occasionally by overt propaganda. Just four days before the signing of the security agreement, Maddow's parent network NBC ran a blatantly fear-mongering, thinly-sourced story with the headline:

ISIS-ALLIED MILITANTS BEHEAD 15 DURING AFGHANISTAN OFFENSIVE: OFFICIAL

According to the US government, the Taliban and al Qaeda are supposed to be indistinguishable. According to NBC News, the Taliban and ISIS, the Islamic State in Syria, are also supposed to be indistinguishable. The propaganda point seems to be that we are facing some kind of global conspiracy of massive proportions and all the propaganda about "Communists" can be re-cycled by replacing "Communists" with "Islamists" or a variant. This is how NBC sold the new fear on September 26:

> Militants aligned with ISIS launched a brutal offensive in Afghanistan alongside Taliban fighters that has left more than 100 people dead, local officials said Friday. Insurgents carrying the black flag of ISIS captured several villages in Ghazni province, according to Deputy Governor Ali Ahmad Ahmadi and Deputy Police Chief Gen. Asadullah Ensafi. Fifteen family members of local police officers were beheaded and at least 60 homes were set ablaze ...

NBC offers no independent confirmation of any of the supposed facts in this story, although NBC fails to say that outright. Dishonestly, NBC presents the story as true, without actually owning it. The Ghazni attacks, part of a week-long offensive, threatened to give the Taliban control of a province roughly midway between Kabul and Kandahar, two of Afghanistan's largest cities. The attacks appear to be real enough, but unlike NBC, others, including Reuters, N.Y. Times and The Guardian, report the possible Islamic State connection only tentatively or not at all.

NBC omits any mention that this is just one more attack in a civil war now in its fourth decade, or that the Taliban insurgency started in 2002. And NBC fails to note that the report is based solely on sources within a government with one of the worst human rights records in the world.

Is Afghanistan now "secure" from spinning out of control?

Despite the US-Afghan security agreement, "Afghan security" remains an oxymoron. No civilians are safe: not from the Taliban, not from the Afghan government, and certainly not from US and NATO night raids and drone strikes. None of the fighting forces are safe. The Second Afghan Civil War that began with the Saur Revolution in 1978 has entered a new phase, but unlikely a better phase. Despite the drawdown, foreign troops may keep the Taliban in check for awhile. But the Afghan military has yet to perform well and is significantly infiltrated by its enemies. The foreign troop drawdown will also allow more space for other outside intervention. Pakistan, India, and international Islamist forces are already in the game, and others could easily join.

So, what does the Bilateral Security Agreement actually secure? Here's an incomplete checklist of what the US-Afghan agreement, together with the NATO-Afghan pact, are designed to secure for now in one of the poorest countries in the world:

Permanent War. The security agreements keep war alive for at least two years and set the framework for a war that can be extended indefinitely into its fifth and sixth decades and beyond. Subsidizing the war will cost about $5.1 billion a year, mostly paid by the US. The direct military subsidy is necessary, according to official Washington, because the Afghan government can't afford to pay its army. But this military subsidy is down from recent years, $11 billion in 2012 and $5.7 billion in 2013. It appears that the agreements provide just enough assistance to keep the Afghan government from losing control of its share of the country, probably, but not enough to defeat the Taliban. No one is talking much about peace negotiations.

US Immunity from Afghan law. That was the potential deal-breaker. American exceptionalism requires the exception that US forces not be subject to the laws of any country in which they may commit war crimes. The US has been immune from Afghan law since 2001. The US has prosecuted some of the most egregious war crimes US forces have committed, but not those policy-based war crimes like bombing civilians and night raids. Former Afghan president Hamid Karzai balked at giving immunity for bombing civilians and entering their homes, among other things. In Iraq in 2008, Nouri al-Maliki also balked at giving the US immunity for the crimes US forces committed there. Failing to get US immunity in Iraq, lame duck President Bush in late 2008 signed the US military withdrawal agreement that some people now blame on President Obama.

US Drone Bases. Even though drone strikes are arguably war crimes and arbitrary presidential execution is arguably an impeachable offense, US drone bases are now secure to continue killing people in at least two countries.

Permanent U.S Bases. The US currently has something like 30 bases in Afghanistan. The White House says that "the US does not seek permanent military bases in Afghanistan." On the ground, US bases will remain effectively permanent until the US decides otherwise. The security agreement also contemplates the US building new bases. There's no need to "seek" what the US already has. Afghan President Ashraf Ghani reportedly "assured Afghanistan's neighbors that the extended presence of US troops would pose no threat to them," as if he had any control over what a rogue state like the US might choose to do to Pakistan, Iran, or China.

Torture, Secret Prisons. Officially denied, these practices reportedly continue with US blessings, outsourced to contractors and the Afghan government. The US may transfer some of its secret prisoners in Afghanistan to the concentration camp in Guantanamo. The security agreement is politely silent on torture, secret prisons and human rights abuses generally. UNAMA, the United Nations Assistant Mission in Afghanistan, reports a bleak picture of human rights there. The US continues to embrace human rights abuses around the world, to the extent that they are seen to serve US policy goals.

Private Contractor Corruption. In June 2013, the Congressional Research Service reported that there were 108,000 private contract workers in Afghanistan, outnumbering US troop strength of 56,700.

That report noted: "the ineffective use of contractors can prevent troops from receiving what they need, when they need it, and can lead to the wasteful spending of billions of dollars. Contractors can also compromise the credibility and effectiveness of the US military and undermine operations, as many analysts believe have occurred in recent operations in Iraq and Afghanistan." Blackwater, for example, gunned down civilians, with little or no response from the Pentagon. A report by the US Government Accountability Office underscored Pentagon management shortcomings. While spending on contractors reached $195 billion in 2010, contractor reporting was inadequate to assess whether contractors actually did the jobs they were paid to do. Contractors, some of whom have been hired for combat work, will not be immune under the security agreement from Afghan laws and courts.

Forced Labor at US Bases. The US, while officially forbidding the use of forced labor on US bases, has tolerated the practice for decades now. The perverse practice is a direct result of US policy outsourcing military jobs to contractors who squeeze their workers to increase corporate profit. Two of the more notorious abusers are Fluor and Dyncorp International. The Pentagon knows all this and chooses to do nothing about it. The exploited workers, mostly third-country migrants, get little protection from the US or the host countries that don't care how the US treats non-locals.

Afghan Poverty. Afghanistan is one of the poorest countries in the world. Estimates of the Afghan population range from roughly 27 million to 35 million. Of these, roughly half live in poverty. Almost half are food-insecure. Half the children under five are malnourished. More than 80% of Afghans are illiterate. Claims of "recent progress" ring hollow in the echo chamber of endless war and exploitation. The security agreement makes it more likely that Afghans will be killed than taught to read, fed, or lifted out of poverty.

Afghan Hunger. In early 2014, as hunger and malnutrition increased across the country, even in the capital, some officials found it "baffling." Others, such as an Afghan doctor in a malnutrition ward, noted that conditions were the worst since 2001, and maybe decades of war and a large uprooted internal population might have something to do with it. Other contributing factors are mines in agricultural fields, a decline in breast-feeding and reduced food shipments because of sanctions on Iran.

Afghan Government Corruption. One of the ideas behind the United States' role in arranging the new Afghan government was to reduce Afghan corruption. A UN report found that in 2012, 50% of Afghans receiving free public services had to pay bribes to get them. Any reduction in corruption would have to be huge to be meaningful. According to generally accepted ballpark figures, the US has spent more than $100 billion ($100,000,000,000) in reconstruction aid to Afghanistan since 2001, of which about $85 billion has apparently been stolen. In a 2012 ranking, only North Korea and Somalia were considered more corrupt than Afghanistan. President Ghani recently announced the re-opening of an investigation into the Kabul Bank scandal, in which $1 billion disappeared and 10% has been recovered. Full recovery would still be a drop in the bucket, suggesting that the investigation's true purpose may be to serve as a check on former President Karzai. In April 2014, even the Pentagon realized that US policy since 2001 has fostered corruption in a corrupt state, through this war on which the US has spent close to $1 trillion. Lacking any useful solution of its own, the Pentagon pretty much blamed then-President Karzai for the mess the US has fostered.

Afghan Judicial Corruption. In a well-functioning judicial system even the guilty – perhaps especially the guilty – are treated with fundamentally fair due process. A recent case against several rapists turned into a kangaroo court and rush to execution, despite calls from some in the international community for a competent, impartial and independent review of the flawed trial. Despite pleas to stay the execution ordered by President Karzai, President Ghani chose not to act, allowing the men to be hanged as the result of an unarguably corrupt judicial travesty based on confessions made under torture. The verdict would almost surely have been the same in a fair trial.

Heroin and Opium Business. The drug trade represents an estimated one quarter of Afghanistan's economy of about $34 billion a year. By 2001, under the Taliban, the Afghan government reduced opium poppy cultivation to less than one-tenth of its previous acreage (roughly from 202,000 acres to 19,000 acres). In the wake of the US invasion, opium poppy cultivation returned quickly to previous levels. Protected by the US military, the drug trade continues to expand and flourish. According to the UN's Afghanistan Opium Survey, poppy cultivation covered more than 400,000 acres for the first time in 2013. The crop is worth an estimated $1 billion a year to farmers and much more to traffickers as the product moves to the global market. Afghan heroin reportedly represents 90% of the world's supply, "managed" by the CIA and "secured" by the US military. Over at the State Department, they've come up with "Myths and Facts about Fighting the Opium Trade" in which the first myth is that opium poppies can be refined into biodiesel fuel.

War Criminals. War crimes have characterized the US presence in Afghanistan since 2001. Hundreds of prisoners of war in US-Afghan custody that December were murdered by suffocation and shooting, then the US participated in a cover-up that continues to the present. Under the auspices of the UN, Physicians for Human Rights compiled compelling evidence of the mass killing, including mass grave sites. The Bush administration consistently stonewalled requests for an official investigation. Democracy NOW first covered the story in 2003. When James Risen broke the story in mainstream media (New York Times of July 10, 2009) the Times editorial board characterized the murders and cover-up as part of the "sordid legacy" of the Bush administration. At the heart of the mass killing of POWs was an Afghan warlord on the payroll of the CIA, Gen. Abdul Rashid Dostum. Afghanistan's current president Ghani has publicly called Dostum a "known killer." A few days after Risen broke the story, President Obama acknowledged that the massacre had not been "properly investigated" and asked his "national security team ... to collect the facts," seeming to imply that he would order an investigation. Instead he has maintained the cover-up. As covered in depth by Democracy NOW on September 30, the "known killer" Dostum is now the vice president of Afghanistan, personally secured by a bilateral agreement with the US.

Those are some of the things the Bilateral Security Agreement is likely to secure. As Secretary of State Kerry said, with no hint of irony, "The gains of the past decade have been won with blood and treasure.... and we all have a stake in ensuring they're a foundation upon which to build."

That helps to explain why the US is planning to deploy 9,800 troops to defend a mass murderer.

60.

Yemen Matters – As a Target, as a Market, as a Culture

US supports Saudis and others in war of aggression on Yemen

Arab aggression, in the form of a blitzkrieg unleashed by Saudi Arabia with the support of the United States among others, currently pits a coalition of five Sunni Arab police state monarchies in the Gulf Cooperation Council against the poorest country in the Middle East, Council non-member Yemen, where the Shia Houthi insurgency has taken control of perhaps one third of the country.

Yemen, insofar as there is a state entity that can be called Yemen, has attacked no other country and has little capability of doing so. For years, over at least two presidential administrations, Yemen has persisted as a disintegrating quasi-democratic kleptocracy. Years of systematic Saudi state bribery have reinforced chronic instability by supporting tribal independence and political disintegration. Yemen is roughly the size of Morocco, Germany, or California. It is also the same size as Iraq, with about three million fewer people and many more political and cultural fault lines.

What did Yemen do to provoke weeks of US-supported terror-bombing carried out primarily by Saudi pilots flying US jets armed with US munitions? Yemen has a population of about 25 million people who are overwhelmingly dependent on food imports for survival. What terrible crime has Yemen committed to be subjected also to an international naval blockade that will cause widespread malnutrition, hunger and in time starvation?

The proximate cause, it would seem, is the interruption of what US Ambassador to the UN Samantha Power called the "peaceful, inclusive, and consensus-driven political transition under the leadership of the legitimate President of Yemen, Abdo Rabbo Mansour Hadi." One problem with this formulation is that Hadi's "legitimacy" derives from his being installed as president by an international diplomatic coup, followed by his election in a race in which he was the sole candidate. Essentially, there is no legitimate government of Yemen and has not been for decades at least. The present war of aggression by outside powers intervening in a multifaceted civil war relies for its justification on fiction.

The US, the Saudis and the rest of the aggressors are committing daily war crimes with their bombing and their blockade in an undeclared war that increasingly kills civilians. Each civilian death is a crime against humanity.

Responding to Arab aggression, UN embargoes those under attack

In the United Nations, where peace and universal human rights are supposed to matter at least a little bit, the Security Council has imposed an arms embargo on the Houthis. The vote on April 14 was 14-0, with Russia abstaining. Among the aggressor nations voting in support of their own actions were the US, UK, France and Jordan. Those with no obvious conflict of interest voting for the embargo included China and that American-designated threat to world peace, Venezuela.

The Universal Declaration of Human Rights states in part in the preamble:

> Whereas it is essential, if man is not to be compelled to have recourse, as a last resort, to rebellion against tyranny and oppression, that human rights should be protected by the rule of law ...

This addresses the fundamental irony of Yemeni reality, that a long mistreated minority, the Houthis, are rebelling against the tyranny and oppression of the Yemen government, only to be opposed by a coalition of even more tyrannous and oppressive states, as well as Al Qaeda and ISIS, not to mention imperial powers who have colonized Yemen one way and another over the past 200 or so years.

The Security Council ignoréd all this. Its vote took place with apparent obliviousness even to the UN report a week earlier warning that the Saudi war was driving Yemen toward a humanitarian catastrophe. Implicitly, the situation on April 7 was somehow not yet a humanitarian catastrophe, even though the UN Office for the Coordination of Humanitarian Affairs reported: that civilians in need could not be reached with aid; that more than 100,000 Yemenis had been displaced since March 26 when the bombing started; that of the 560 reported killed, more than a third were civilians. The report concluded:

> This year, humanitarian partners estimate that about 15.9 million people – 61 per cent of the population – will require humanitarian assistance, a number that is expected to increase if violence continues to escalate.

Given the number and diversity of combatants in and around Yemen, there is almost no chance that violence will abate any time soon. Russian calls for a ceasefire and talks are widely ignored. An Iranian proposal for peace talks was angrily and preposterously rejected by the Saudis as they continued their unopposed daily bombing of Yemen, while at the same time accusing Iran of meddling in Yemen. "Iran is not in charge of Yemen," said Saudi foreign minister Saud al-Faisal, rather contradicting the Saudi justification for bombing Yemen because of too much Iranian influence.

Whatever Iran's role in Yemeni affairs, and no doubt it's real if not extensive, it can't compare to the Saudi interference in a neighboring, supposedly sovereign state. During recent decades, the Saudis have fought the Yemenis over northern Yemeni territory, have bribed and intimidated Yemenis leaders, and played divide and control with Yemeni tribes.

Saudis happy to bomb the helpless, reluctant to invade the combative

Saudi bombing of Yemen has met no significant resistance even though the Yemen air force is said to have about 195 attack aircraft, mostly aging Soviet MIGs and some US F-5s. Neither the Yemen air force nor

360

any ground-to-air defenses appear to have had any deterrent effect on the Saudi ability to hit any targets it chooses, which so far include a number of schools, hospitals, refugee camps, a dairy factory and other civilian facilities. The assault is reminiscent of the Spanish Civil War when the fascist bombing of defenseless Guernica created the atrocity vividly re-created in "Guernica," the painting by Picasso. The US-backed Saudis are on their way to creating a Muslim Guernica.

Yemeni helplessness is no surprise to the Saudis and their allies in the bombing, any more than Guernica's defenselessness was a surprise to Francisco Franco and his Nazi allies in 1937. More than three years ago, the Yemen air force was known to be "barely functional," suffering from low morale, inadequate training and equipment shortages that limited planes to flying only in daylight. Analysts doubted the ability of the Yemen air force to defend its own air space. The Saudis had little trouble bombing Houthi targets in Yemen in 2009. During that same time (2004-2012), the Yemeni air force was also bombing defenseless Houthi targets.

The fiction of a functional Yemen air force had at least one useful application: giving the US deniability for its criminal drone strikes in Yemen. The Yemen government willingly took credit for strikes it had no ability to carry out, much to the satisfaction of Americans seeking deniability, as confirmed in a 2010 cable released by Wikileaks:

> "We'll continue saying the bombs are ours, not yours," [Yemen President] Saleh said, prompting Deputy Prime Minister Alimi to joke that he had just "lied" by telling Parliament that the bombs in Arhab, Abyan, and Shebwa were American-made but deployed by the ROYG (Republic of Yemen Government).

The American drone campaign in Yemen is now widely known as one of the most intensive of US drone programs. Like the US drone strikes in Pakistan, the Yemen strikes have also killed civilians. Drone-killings of civilians have not become as controversial in Yemen, where protest is diffused by government connivance in the killings and the number of opposing sides in the country's civil war. The charade of who-did-the-airstrike continued on April 14, when Al Qaeda announced on Twitter the killing of a leader in a "crusader airstrike," while US and Yemen government officials refused to say if it was a drone strike.

Who is my enemy when the enemy of my enemy is my enemy's enemy?

In May 2014, the Yemen army was fighting on two fronts in Yemen: against the Houthis in the northwest and against Al Qaeda in the southeast. Now the army itself is divided and the number of forces opposing each other has multiplied to the point where speaking of "fronts" is almost nonsensical.

The absurdity of the fighting in Yemen is encapsulated in the presumed drone killing of the Al Qaeda leader at the behest of US and Yemen government interests, even though Al Qaeda is a fierce enemy of the Houthi rebels, who are being bombed by the Saudis, who are another target of Al Qaeda, even though Al Qaeda grew out of private Saudi money and influence, but now Al Qaeda is being targeted by the Islamic State moving into Yemen, the Islamic State having emerged out of the chaos and sectarianism inflicted on Iraq by the US invasion of 2003, and that was the house that George built. As Al-Monitor reports, Iraq is divided in its response to Saudi aggression:

> Operation Decisive Storm has also divided Iraq's religious institutions. The Sunni Association of Muslim Scholars announced its backing of the campaign in a statement issued March 29, referring to it as the "Arab effort aimed at supporting the Yemeni people and confronting the Iranian tide." On the other hand, the cleric Muqtada al-Sadr, leader of the Sadrist movement, categorized the operation in a March 27 interview as "interference in the affairs of the Yemeni people."

In Kuwait, one of the aggressor countries, the daily paper Al-Ray viewed its undeclared war this way: Kuwaiti daily Al-Ray: "The Gulf has been forced to go into war despite its heavy price and painful results. If it had not been for the US administration's policy in the region, the Gulf would not have faced the hard choice."

On April 15, Iraqi Prime Minister Haider al-Abadi, visiting Washington, sharply criticized the American-backed Saudi bombing campaign in its 22nd day, saying: "There is no logic to the operation at all in the first place.... Mainly, the problem of Yemen is within Yemen." Then the prime minister raised a much more sinister implication of the Saudi aggression:

> The dangerous thing is we don't know what the Saudis want to do after this. Is Iraq within their radar? That's very, very dangerous. The idea that you intervene in another state unprovoked just for regional ambition is wrong. Saddam has done it before. See what it has done to the country.

Whatever else may be going on in Yemen, the 25 million Yemeni people are not a coherent body, and pretty much everyone involved is interfering with their affairs. Presently, there are five major factions fighting within Yemen, as well as an unknown number of smaller factions and independent militias. There seem to be no reliable reports of the numbers of these fighting forces. Of these factions, it appears none is strong enough to govern the whole country, leaving Yemen to be governed by a shifting assortment of forces:

The Hadi Forces, or the Yemen Government, such as it is, is headed in name at least by President Abed Rabbu Mansour Hadi, who has spent this year being held in house arrest in his capital, Sana'a, then fleeing to Aden, where he claimed he was still president, and now fleeing to Saudi Arabia with the same claim. His government is fragmented, and its area of control probably changes, probably shrinking, every day. But an estimated half the Yemen military remains under government control and makes up most of the Hadi forces in Aden and southwest Yemen.

The Houthis have populated northwest Yemen for generations, fighting off most of those who would control them. Some 8 million Houthis (about a third of Yemen's population) provide the base for Houthi military strength, which has been growing during the past year. In September 2014, Houthis took control of Yemen's capital and in January 2015 forced President Hadi to resign and held him in house arrest. During February and March, the Houthis took control of more of the south, putting Aden under threat, with heavy urban combat reported in mid-April. Houthis are Zaidi Muslims whose cohort ruled North

Yemen (the Kingdom of Yemen) off and on from the 17th century until 1962.

The Saleh Forces mainly comprise the Yemen military no longer loyal to the Hadi government. In 2012, in the midst of an "Arab spring" uprising, an international diplomatic coup headed by the Gulf Cooperation Council intervened in Yemen to install then-vice president Hadi in place of Yemen's 33-year president Ali Abdullah Saleh, in a peaceful transition of power that included immunity from prosecution for Saleh. Planning to run for president again in 2015, Saleh allied himself with Houthi dissidents, among others. With roughly half the military on his side, Saleh has contributed to Houthi success. Like the Houthis, Saleh is a Zaidi Muslim, but not a member of the historic ruling faction.

Al Qaeda, or Al Qaeda in the Arabian Peninsula (AQAP) is perhaps the second strongest force in Yemen, after the Houthi/Saleh alliance. This Al Qaeda is made up of Yemeni and Saudi factions, as well as foreign recruits, and controls most of the eastern part of Yemen, mostly low-population desert with several hundred miles of largely undefined border with Saudi Arabia. With an effectively autonomous region for now, Al Qaeda opposes both the Houthis and the Hadi forces, but faces a new challenge from the Islamic State. On April 2, Al Qaeda forces captured a prison in the eastern port city of Mukalla, freeing some 300 prisoners, many of whom are Al Qaeda fighters.

The Islamic State (ISIS/ISIL) established a presence in southern Yemen probably during 2014, with declared enmity toward everyone else, especially Al Qaeda, although American intelligence officials have floated the idea that ISIS might join forces with Al Qaeda in an effort to hit the US. On March 20, 2015, ISIS sent suicide bombers into Sana'a to attack Houthis at prayer in two mosques, killing 142 and wounding 345. ISIS also opposes US-supported Saudi attacks, as one supporter wrote:

> We will not allow America to interfere in the Arab world by using an Arab proxy. Arabs will only succeed when they leave the control of the Americans and move outside their circle of influence and control....

> The ongoing war in the area is mostly an internal one, one that is fought between people who follow the rules and justice of Allah in its most basic form, and between the traitorous and corrupted ruler.... The revenge is not only against the evil Shiites, and not only against the tyrants, but against those who provide them with the weapons and the missiles they use to draw our blood.

US is OK with terrorizing civilians, not evacuating them

Four days before the Saudi bombing began, the US evacuated about 100 special forces troops from their Yemen base (the US evacuated embassy personnel in late September). The British by then had already evacuated their own special forces. Saudi bombing, naval bombardment in and around Aden, as well as ground fighting involving, at a minimum, the Houthis, Saleh forces, Hadi forces, Al Qaeda, and assorted independent militia, quickly created a crisis for more than 16,000 foreign nationals trying to flee the fighting, including thousands of Yemeni-Americans – a crisis about which the US felt compelled to do nothing, not even for its own citizens.

India evacuated 4,640 Indian nationals and 960 others by ship and by plane. Pakistan also evacuated Pakistanis, Indians and others. Pakistan has considered a Saudi request to join the attack on Yemen but has rejected it.

China used its navy to evacuate more than 900 people of many nations from Yemen, mostly from Aden, where they sent troops ashore to secure the rescue.

The Russian navy evacuated 308 people from Yemen, including 18 Americans. Another 300 people were evacuated on Russian planes. Even Somalia rescued its citizens and others from Yemen, as did Djibouti. The two countries have given refuge to at least 1,260 people, according to the UN Refugee Agency, which expects another 130,000 people from Yemen to come to Somalia and Djibouti in the next six months.

Oman, the only member of the Gulf Cooperation Council not to cooperate in the attack on Yemen, has also taken in civilians fleeing the fighting. Oman is the only country that shares a border with both Saudi

Arabia to the north and Yemen to the west. Despite its past history as a mediator between Iran and Arab states, Oman's offer to mediate talks between Yemen and its attackers has been ignored so far.

For Yemeni-Americans, their country abandoned them. Roughly 4,000 of them got no help from their government. Some got out on their own. Three civil rights groups in the US have established "Stuck in Yemen," a website that asks, "Are you a Yemeni-American stuck in Yemen?" and collects information to help. The three civil rights groups – the American-Arab Anti-Discrimination Committee (ADC), the Council on American Islamic Relations (CAIR) and Asian Americans Advancing Justice (AAJC) – have also sued the State Department to force the US to rescue its citizens.

Officially, the US doesn't explain or defend its decision to leave American citizens of Yemeni descent hanging in harm's way, twisting slowly in the wind. Asked by reporters why the US isn't evacuating Americans from Yemen the way it has evacuated Americans from so many other places over the years, State Department spokesperson Marie Harf responds coldly to a reporter asking, "There are no plans to evacuate Americans from Yemen?":

> *Marie Harf:* "That is true.... It's not that we can't. There's always a decision. Different factors are weighed, whether it's the security situation, whether it's how we would be able to do this.

In other words, according to Marie Harf, the US could evacuate its citizens from Yemen if it wanted to – it just doesn't want to. And why not? Because based on a politically motivated bigotry, the US treats Yemeni-Americans as second-class citizens.

American policy kills people – now it's become Yemeni-cidal

One view of the past half-century of American and western world predation is that it's all deliberate, as Gulam Asgar Mitha wrote recently in Oriental Review:

> Since the Western powers were kicked out of Indo-China, they along with Israel have managed to create wars, civil wars and wars of terrorism in Muslim countries over the past four decades – in Algeria,

Egypt, Pakistan, Iraq, Afghanistan, Syria, Jordan, Palestine, Mali, Libya, Yemen and Iran. *These wars have killed at least 15 million Muslims in those four decades.*

In sharp contrast, Southeast Asia has seen peace and economic prosperity. If Muslims desire peace and economic prosperity, they'll have to adopt the SE Asian model. In a civil war, it will be Muslims eating the flesh and drinking the blood of each other. Some sense should prevail among Muslims by not falling into the western trap. Will it? Time will tell if the western powers will be able to impose their civil war agenda in the Middle East or will Muslims get their sanity to defeat the western agenda and opt for peace?

In Dissident Voice, Peter Konig, a former World Bank economist, writes in a similar vein:

> The recent brutal attack on Yemen is US-supported and led by Saudi Wahhabis, an aggressive fundamentalist off-shoot of Sunni Islam. Fighting a proxy war against the Shia Muslims in Iran and the Yemeni Houthis, a secular off-spring of Shia Islam, as well as Syria with its ruling Ba'ath party (a socialist faction of Sunnis) – is a win-win, serving the big trans-Atlantic master, as well as Riyadh's key objectives – regime change in Syria and annihilating Iran.

Perhaps inadvertently reinforcing the Iran-obsessions distorting US policy are comments of Republican congressman Ed Royce of California, who is chairman of the House Committee on Foreign Affairs. Now cheerleading aggressive war, Royce wrote in February, getting the basic fact of who controls Yemen absolutely wrong:

> This takeover of Yemen by the Iranian-supported Houthi militia is a very dangerous blow to our national security. Iran is consolidating its grip on the region, our embassy is on lockdown, and al-Qaeda has more room to operate. The Administration must come to grips with the increasingly destructive role Iran is playing in the region.

One thing Iran hasn't done is to arm all sides in the Middle East. The US and its allies have done that, through commerce and through arming countries who can't hang onto their weapons. Yemen, for example. In February, the Guardian reported that the Pentagon had lost track of $400 million worth of weapons in Yemen, weapons that went to the Houthis or Al Qaeda or whoever happened to pick them up.

Of course, it's necessary to have large, coordinated losses like this if you want the arms business to boom. And the arms business is definitely booming, not just with Saudi Arabia, with current arms orders of $46 billion. It's salesmanship like that that not only keeps wars going, especially in the Middle East, but also boosts President Obama's presidency to the most successful arms dealing administration in history, even after adjusting for inflation. As William Hartung, the director of the Arms and Security Project at the Center for International Policy, has written:

> ... the volume of major deals concluded by the Obama administration in its first five years exceeds the amount approved by the Bush administration in its full eight years in office by nearly $30 billion. That also means that the Obama administration has approved more arms sales than any US administration since World War II."

No wonder the US, from a humane perspective, continues to cover itself with blood and stupidity.

61.

Saudis Try Yemen Peace Initiative – For More Than an Hour

US-sponsored war crimes resume as Yemenis fail to give up their country

While the US publicly plays Pontius Pilate washing his hands clean, the Saudi-led coalition of Arab police states continue to enjoy US support for crucifying Yemen in their one-sided war. The same Arab dictatorships that continue to wage aggressive war with impunity against a defenseless Yemen have, at the same time, scaled back on fighting the militant Islamic State despite its hold on large parts of two other Arab countries, Syria and Iraq. Seriously, why fight someone who might do you harm in return?

In a rational world, the unprovoked aerial and naval attacks on an impoverished Yemen by Saudi Arabia and its allied monarchies would seem more likely to draw objection than military support from the US and its somewhat-democratic allies. In a comprehending world, the public explanations for criminal aggression by the Saudis and the US would provoke howls of derisive laughter for their preposterous fabrications. In a principled world, a dedicated peace movement and a motivated left would be filling the streets with protest.

But we don't live in a rational, comprehending, or principled world. In our world, opposition to the criminal bombing of an internationally peaceful, defenseless, collapsing state draws scant objection from the international community except for quiet, *pro forma* critiques by China, Russia and Iran. No nation actually threatens to defend the territorial integrity or independence of Yemen. As is traditional, the Yemenis are left to defend themselves, which they haven't been able

369

to do in the past. Now the Yemenis' greatest offense is achieving some success in their chaotic search for a more representative government than any of their neighbors will allow.

Seldom has such a clear case of criminal war, of naked aggression, drawn such yawns from the world at large. Describing the current mad consensus of power in the American imperium, with a quiet objectivity to which no reaction is expected or forthcoming, The New York Times of April 22 reports in deadpan prose the irreconcilable contradictions of an insane policy – or if there is no policy, just crazed tactics – in the second paragraph of its lead story, under this headline:

Saudis Announce Halt to Yemen Bombing Campaign

... The announcement followed what American officials said was pressure applied by the Obama administration for the Saudis and other Sunni Arab nations to end the airstrikes. The bombing campaign, which has received logistical and intelligence support from the United States, has drawn intense criticism for causing civilian deaths and for appearing to be detached from a broad military strategy.

Written before the world realized that the bombing "halt" was actually only a brief pause in the Saudi terror campaign, the Times' "explanation" was nevertheless ridiculous. With masterful flat affect, the Times assured us that the US applied pressure to get the Saudis to stop doing what we had helped them do from the beginning and were continuing to help them do. Say what?

Has there ever been a better use of the word "detached" in a piece not openly critical of authority? Not only is the Saudi air attack detached from any broad military strategy, it is detached from any military strategy at all, and it is detached from reality. Detachment from reality is one measure of insanity.

Another measure is one's insistence on continuing to do what one has been doing while at the same time claiming that what one has done has accomplished all its objectives. Or, as Adel Al-Jubeir, Saudi Arabia's ambassador to the US, put it in his official statement on April 22 [with imagined honest annotations]:

We destroyed their air force.

Even though Yemen didn't really have an actual air force, due to corruption and neglect, which is why we were able to bomb the planes they had while they were still on the ground. And, technically, that was the Yemen government air force under the command of President Hadi, who happens to be living in Riyadh these days, but never mind about all that.

We destroyed their ballistic missiles, as far as we know.

Because, after all, we don't really know if anyone in Yemen actually has any ballistic missiles. We know or we think we know they had some in 1979 and for awhile after that, but we don't know if they ever used any and by 2010 they had, maybe, 6 launchers and maybe 33 SCUD missiles and maybe 22 other SAMs, which are surface-to-air missiles which could shoot down Saudi F-15s, for example, if they had them, and if they knew how to use them, and we know none of our planes have been shot down, so you figure it out.

We destroyed their command and control.

That sounds impressive, doesn't it, but I don't know what it really means either, in Yemen, where there are so many different factions under so many different commands and no perceptible control, except maybe the Houthis, who've been fighting for their independence for more than a decade without the need for sophisticated command and control bunkers and electronics and stuff.

We destroyed much, if not most, of their heavy equipment.

Also, an impressive accomplishment, until you ask how much heavy equipment they have, besides the handful of tanks we haven't destroyed. But we've destroyed schools and hospitals and food aid depots and other heavy equipment like that, so when you add it all up, it comes to a lot of damage.

And we made it very difficult for them to move, from a strategic perspective.

Never mind that, strategically, they don't really need to move, since they've held the capital city, Sana'a, for months now and they've pretty well got Aden and the eastern part of the country, which is pretty much all they really want. So never mind that part. And never mind the reality that it hasn't been easy to move around Yemen for years, but that hasn't stopped the Houthis. What we've done, destroying roads and bridges where we could find them, is make it harder for people to move around Yemen when it wasn't easy in the first place, and that includes refugees and internally displaced people, and, really who cares, we did what we could with what they had.

> So we've degraded their capabilities substantially, and thereby elim-inated the threat that they pose to the kingdom of Saudi Arabia and, in a process, ensured the safety of our borders, our territory and our citizens.

That is such a good line, absolutely my best line, and Western media lap it up like limp puppies, they talk about how we've ensured the safety of our borders and our territory and our citizens and they never ever even stop to think: Hey, Joe, wait a minute – what was the threat to Saudi Arabia? There was NO threat to Saudi Arabia, and that goes a long way toward making it possible for us to secure our unthreatened safety. And what about their capabilities, you might ask, are they not degraded? And the answer is, of course, they've always been degraded and now they're a little more degraded, which makes them even less of the no threat they posed to Saudi Arabia, and also has the benefit of making the Houthis more vulnerable to Al Qaeda and to the Islamic State, and we're counting on them to go in and finish off the Houthis, because we certainly don't want to send Saudi boys to do the job Yeme-nis boys on one side or another should be doing themselves.

> That was the objective of Operation Decisive Storm, in addition, of course, to the protection of the legitimate government of Yemen. Those objectives have been achieved.

Sounding a little Monty Python here, that was the objective here, protect Saudi Arabia and the Yemen government, those were the two objectives here, but the Yemen government part is tricky because we had to bring it to Riyadh to protect it, those are the three objectives here, even though having the Yemeni government in the Saudi capital rather curtails its ability to run things in Yemen, at least it's protected and, having installed it undemocratically once, we have every hope of installing it undemocratically again because, after all, nobody expects the Saudi Installation. So those are the objectives that have been achieved by our chief weapons, fear, surprise and ruthless efficiency, except the ones that haven't been achieved.

Having accomplished their objectives, the Saudis resume bombing

Having been the poorest country in the Middle East, and one of the poorest in the world when the US-supported Saudi attacks began a month ago, Yemen's humanitarian condition has deteriorated. According to Robert Mardini of the International Committee of the Red Cross, on April 22, after a three-day visit there: "Nowhere is safe in Yemen. People are really facing a lot of challenges – no electricity, no water, no fuel, no public services, no garbage collection...." The next day in Geneva Mardini emphasized the predictable result of US-supported Saudi war crimes: "The humanitarian situation is nothing short of catastrophic."

In a meaningless word game, the Saudis say the short bombing halt marked the end of so-called Operation Decisive Storm, which has decided nothing. The Saudis call their new intensive bombing campaign Operation Renewal of Hope, as if to say that they are continuing to bomb defenseless targets in order to accomplish the same objectives they claim to have already achieved, in hope that achieving them anew will be made easier by already having claimed to have achieved them.

Or, as Saudi ambassador Jubeir said of the Houthis: "The decision to calm matters now rests with them." At the same time, Saudi prince Al-Waleed bin Talal announced that he would give a $200,000 Bentley luxury car to each of 100 Saudi fighter pilots, in apparent appreciation of their crimes against humanity, although he didn't put it that way.

An estimate by the UN's Office for the Coordination of Humanitarian Affairs, based on Yemeni sources, reports the air war and ground fighting together have displaced some 150,000 people. The UN also estimates that of Yemen's population of about 25 million, at least

7.5 million require humanitarian assistance, and the number continues to grow.

Asked to sponsor peace talks, the UN has delivered a limited embargo

For their part, the Houthis again called for UN-sponsored peace talks and political negotiations in which they have an equal role. This is a longstanding Houthi position that has yet to be honored by Saudi Arabia or anyone else. When the international cabal comprising the Saudis, the US, and others deposed Yemen's President Saleh in 2012 and installed President Hadi in an undemocratic process, the Houthis were excluded from the process. Quite reasonably and accurately, the Houthis maintain that there is NO legitimate government of Yemen.

Because the UN did not authorize the Saudi-led war, it is by definition illegal. There is little evidence to suggest that the UN will address the questions of US-supported Saudi-led aggression in violation of the UN Charter any time soon, if ever. The UN Security Council did impose an arms embargo on Yemen, however, by a 14-0 vote, with Russia abstaining. Comparing this international behavior to American frothing over Ukraine illustrates the flexibility of application inherent in international law and the roundly pontificated moral principles supposedly underlying them.

The delusion making all this irrational, criminal and murderous behavior seem plausible to the perpetrators and their camp followers is the claim that the Houthis are a hand puppet of Iran. President Obama says, with a straight face in public, that "We've indicated to the Iranians that they need to be part of the solution, and not part of the problem."

The big problem with that perspective is that it is detached from reality. There is no credible evidence available to suggest that Iran is anything more than a minor, largely insignificant player in Yemen, where most of the fighting on all sides is heavily supported by American weapons that have been flooding the region for decades.

Reporters at the State Department on April 21 asked what kind of evidence the administration has to support its claims against Iran, including the recent claim that Iran has been supplying the Houthis with weapons. In an evasive non-answer answer to the question, State Department flack Marie Harf effectively revealed that there's no cat in the bag:

> Well, we've – this isn't something new, unfortunately. We've long talked about the support when it comes from funding or whether it's weapons supplies that the Iranians are sending to the Houthi. This has been really an ongoing relationship for a very long time. I'm happy to see if there's more evidence to share publicly of that, but this has been something we've expressed concern about for some time.

In other words, Harf is saying: look, this is something we've been saying for a long time, we don't have evidence and we don't need evidence because usually when we make the same claim over and over and over you come to accept it as true, that's the way propaganda works, that's the way propaganda is supposed to work, why are you giving us a hard time now? You can't possibly care about a minority cohort of Yemenis like the Houthis, can you?

For objective reporting of propaganda as news, try PBS or the Times

Frontline has a reputation for being about the best thing going in news reporting on PBS, which says more about PBS news reporting than it does about Frontline, none of it good. Here's Frontline's lead for an April 22 Yemen story, perfectly recapitulating the false Saudi line:

> Late on Tuesday, the Saudi Arabia-led coalition that launched a military campaign – dubbed "Operation Decisive Storm" – against Houthi rebels in Yemen nearly a month ago announced that it was ending the operation. Taking its place would be "Operation Renewal of Hope."

The story quoted a Saudi general and a Saudi ambassador and went on to create the impression that American involvement consisted only of pressure to end the bombing, not an ongoing month of American logistical and intelligence support to the undeclared war on a neutral country.

Following up on its front-page "Saudis Announce Halt to Bombing" story that became so quickly inoperative, the next day's Times had a front-page headline claiming that:

SAUDI DEFIANCE REFLECTS LIMITS OF US STRATEGY

Later online editions of the story changed "defiance" to "resolve," adding nuance to the propaganda. The story began by explaining that this all just goes to show "the difficulty of finding a political solution to the crisis." Actually, it doesn't show that so much as it shows the intransigence of the US and the Saudis and others in their unwillingness to accept the reality that the "political solutions" they have imposed on Yemen in the past have fallen apart because of the corruption and injustice on which they were built. And it shows how unwilling the US and Saudis and others are to enter into – and abide by – a genuine political solution that treats fairly the interests of all relevant parties.

And then there's the Saudi ambassador again, invoking the largely imaginary threat from Iran as a reason Iran should have no part in any peace talks relating to Yemen. Echoing President Obama, or cueing him, Ambassador Jubeir is quoted making the same propaganda point, that Iran is "part of the problem, not part of the solution."

In fact, based on the evidence to date, the US and Saudi Arabia and its allies are the problem, and none of them are interested in what the Yemenis might accept as a solution.

And besides, they're all betting no one will ever hold them accountable for this package of war crimes and crimes against humanity any more than anyone has been held accountable for such crimes relating to Iraq, or torture, or drone strikes.

62.

Saudis Drop US-Made Cluster Bombs in Criminal War on Yemen

Saudi-American rogue state alliance flouts global decency norms

Costa Rica condemns Saudi Arabia's dropping US-made cluster bombs on Yemen, in defiance of international law, including the Convention on Cluster Munitions that specifically outlaws the development, production, distribution, stockpiling and use of cluster munitions, including the cluster bombs the Saudis have used since March 26 in their uncontested air attack on Yemen with an estimated 215 jet fighters from nine countries. (The Saudis are also bombing people in Syria and Iraq.)

Human Rights Watch presented evidence of the Saudi cluster-bombing campaign in a widely under-reported analysis presented May 3. The New York Times had a story datelined Cairo on page A8 of its May 3 print edition covering the Human Rights Watch report, but the paper has had no follow-up. The online version of the Times story noted, near the end, that both the Saudis and Americans have used cluster bombs in Yemen as long ago as 2009, without provoking significant protest.

Amnesty International issued a report May 8 documenting Saudi bombing of densely-populated areas of Yemen where the Saudis mostly killed civilians. An earlier Amnesty report documented the Saudi killing of hundreds of Yemeni civilians in its US-supported bombing campaign. Also on May 8, the Saudis announced that it would begin a unilateral ceasefire beginning at 11 p.m. on May 12, conveniently timed to precede meetings of President Obama and Arab dictatorship representatives, including the five countries leading the attacks on Yemen, starting May 13.

Cluster munitions are a particularly hideous weapon of war, designed primarily to kill people indiscriminately, both immediately and for years after they have been dispersed. Anti-personnel cluster munitions, whether delivered by air or artillery, burst in mid-air, spreading submunitions or bomblets that can remain lethal for years, as they have, for examples, in Vietnam, the Falklands, Chechnya, Croatia, Afghanistan, Iraq, Georgia, Libya, Vietnam, Syria and now Yemen.

By condemning Saudi and others' use of US cluster bombs, Costa Rica is an exception among the "civilized" nations of the world. Costa Rica is one of 116 current signatories to the Convention on Cluster Munitions, which entered into force on August 1, 2010. Most countries in Europe and North America have signed the convention, but the United States and Russia have not. Neither have China or Israel. Nor has the coalition of Arab dictatorships attacking Yemen: Saudi Arabia, Jordan, Kuwait, Bahrain, UAE, Egypt, Sudan and Morocco. (Among Middle East countries, the only ones that have forsworn cluster bombs are Lebanon, Palestine and Iraq.)

Cluster munitions help hold down the cost of global militarism

The United States position, as expressed in 2011 by the Heritage Foundation, is a morally duplicitous defense of American militarism's ability to do whatever it considers its imperial necessity:

> The Convention on Cluster Munitions is a misbegotten treaty that neither advances the laws of war nor enhances security. It is an unverifiable, unenforceable, all-or-nothing exercise in moral suasion, not a serious diplomatic instrument. It creates perverse incentives for insurgents to use civilian populations as human shields, undermines effective arms control efforts, inhibits nation-states' ability to defend themselves, and denigrates the sovereignty of the United States and other democratic states.

> The US should emphatically reject both the convention and the undemocratic Oslo Process that produced it and should instead continue to negotiate a realistic and enforceable protocol on cluster munitions that balances US military requirements with the humanitarian concerns posed by unexploded ordnance.

This thoughtless think tank expression of the establishmentar-ian's view of the need for heavily-muscled US exceptionalism had been expressed considerably more forthrightly in May 2008 by then-Acting Assistant Secretary of State for Political-Military Affairs Stephen Mull:

> Cluster munitions are available for use by every combat aircraft in the US inventory, they are integral to every Army or Marine maneu-ver element and in some cases constitute up to 50 percent of tactical indirect fire support. US forces simply cannot fight by design or by doctrine without holding out at least the possibility of using cluster munitions.

What that really means is that cluster munitions cost a lot less than standard ordnance, so the military can kill lots more people with many fewer airplanes, rockets and artillery. In one test, the alternative to cluster munitions was found to be nine times as expensive and to take 40 times as long to create equivalent destruction.

Current US policy relies on diversion and moral obtuseness

The US State Department spins the issue along the lines of moral rel-ativism, as well as irrelevance, by bringing in landmines (unexploded cluster bombs become, in effect, landmines) – without mentioning that the US is NOT among the 162 signatories to the landmine treaty of 1997 (along with China, Egypt, Iran, Israel, Russia, Saudi Arabia and 26 others). The publicly stated US policy on "Cluster Munitions" is, in its entirety, morally bankrupt:

> The United States shares in the international concern about the humanitarian impact of the indiscriminate use of all munitions, including cluster munitions. That is one of the reasons that it spends more than any other country to eliminate the risk to civilians from landmines and all explosive remnants of war, including unexploded cluster munitions.

> Cluster munitions have demonstrated military utility. Their elimina-tion from US stockpiles would put the lives of its soldiers and those of its coalition partners at risk. Moreover, cluster munitions can often result in much less collateral damage than unitary weapons, such as a larger bomb or larger artillery shell would cause, if used for the same mission.

The essential perversity of US policy is demonstrated by its banning the export of almost all cluster munitions, but allowing export of the CBU-105 that is used in Yemen on the basis of the humanitarian argument that this state-of-the-art cluster munition has a lower failure rate than earlier designs. The CBU-105 is banned under the Convention on Cluster Munitions as posing an unacceptable risk to civilians.

Financing of cluster munitions manufacturing is predominantly American. In 2012, Pax Christi found that of 137 cluster-munition financing institutions, 63 were US-based, followed by South Korea with 22 and China with 16. Together these banks and others invested more than $43 billion in cluster bomb makers during 2009-2012. Among the leading US-based investors in cluster bombs are AIG, Wells Fargo Bank, JP Morgan Chase and Goldman Sachs. Investment in cluster bomb making continues to grow worldwide, according to Pax Christi. Two years ago, companies that make cluster munitions thought they were feeling some heat and thought there was jeopardy to their profits from "a global advocacy campaign that targets manufacturers of military hardware," according to National Defense, NDIA's Business and Technology Magazine. In an April 2012 article, the magazine fretted about the possibility of no more war, according to senior fellow Steven Groves at the Heritage Foundation, attacking Code Pink and others, arguing that they:

> ... don't like drones because they're a projection of American power. But if you ban drones, you'd have to also ban cruise missiles and F-16 fighter aircraft.... You start with the most unpopular weapons and you work your way back. You attack the munitions, the depleted uranium, the drones, all the way to tanks and soldiers. Antiwar activists want to ban war by banning all weapons of war.

That threat still hasn't materialized.

Meanwhile the Saudis lie, bomb and kill with US blessings

Search for "cluster bombs" on the Saudi Embassy website, then wait quite awhile, and eventually it tells you: "This webpage is not available." Chances seem good that a Saudi webpage about cluster bombs has never been available. Search for "Yemen" and you get the same result online. On the ground in Yemen you can find Saudi cluster bombs all too easily, but that is reality, and reality for the Saudi dictatorship is a variable that must be carefully and unscrupulously manipulated.

Even though the Saudi site search finds no "Yemen," the Saudi Embassy Public Affairs page of May 8 featured a Yemen story of May 6, accusing Yemenis of attacking Saudi civilians, under the headline:

FOUR KILLED, ELEVEN INJURED IN SHELLING FROM YEMEN

That story, in its entirety, reads: "A spokesman of the civil defense in Najran Province announced today that four people were killed and eleven injured as a result of shelling originating from Yemen. The spokesman said that shells have hit civilian targets."

The rest of the sanitized Saudi propaganda version of its illegal, aggressive war on Yemen is covered on another page for "Operation Decisive Storm" that begins with one Orwellian headline on March 25 – "Saudi Arabia launches military operations in support of legitimate Yemeni government" – and ends with another on May 4 – "Saudi Arabia to establish unified coordination relief center for Yemen."

The so-called "relief center" doesn't appear to be a "center" at all but refers to promised Saudi efforts to consult with its co-aggressors and with donor nations to coordinate the delivery of international human relief aid already waiting to go to Yemen but delayed by the continuing Saudi bombing campaign. The Saudis already control the unchallenged air war that is devastating a defenseless Yemen, the poorest country in the region. Now, as they make it clear in their May 4 press release, the Saudis are determined to decide which Yemenis get fed and which starve:

> Minister [of Foreign Affairs Adel bin Ahmed] Al-Jubeir said that Saudi Arabia is consulting with coalition members and all countries supporting the coalition's efforts in Yemen in order to determine specific areas in Yemen where humanitarian aid to be delivered. The foreign minister added that all air operations would cease at specific times in these areas to allow the delivery of relief supplies....

> Mr. Al-Jubeir warned that Houthi militias and forces loyal to former Yemen President Ali Abdullah Saleh will try to exploit the ceasefire

and prevent the people of Yemen from receiving aid. He reiterated that Saudi Arabia will respond to any violations of this ceasefire by resuming air attacks targeted at Houthi militia groups.

Waging aggressive war with cluster bombs is a war crime within a crime against humanity, not that there is much international outrage at these US-supported atrocities. The Houthis in Yemen are a designated despised minority, like the Jews of Europe or the Armenians of Anatolia, and if the world ever cares, it will be a belated, contrived contrition too late to matter to the dying and dead now.

63.

Yemeni Genocide Proceeds Apace, Enjoying World's Silence

Note: Shortly after this story was filed, the UN announced a "humanitarian pause in the country's ongoing conflict" starting July 10 and expected to last a week. As framed by the UN, the "pause" was agreed to by "Yemen's President Hadi" as well as the Houthis and "other parties" in Yemen, as if there were no other significant combatants. This deceitful framing omits the most aggressive, undeclared war-making carried out against Yemen by the US, Saudi Arabia, and sundry other UN members. The UN missive makes no mention of the months of Saudi-American bombing, even though the bombers must have agreed to a "pause" to make it happen. In the author's view, the pause is a good thing from a humanitarian perspective, although the previous 5-day pause in May was relatively ineffective. From the perspective of policy and politics, the "pause" is a sham and a delusion that will have the effect of keeping some Yemenis from starving long enough so they can be bombed. In other words, the UN continues to collude in a complex of continuing war crimes and crimes against humanity, as the article that follows argues.

US and ISIS join efforts to kill Yemenis

Turns out the United States and the Islamic State, ISIS, are de facto allies of Saudi Arabia and its alliance of dictator states, all bent on exterminating Yemeni Houthis and pretty much any other Yemeni in the neighborhood. This Yemenicide started in earnest in March 2015. After years of US drone strikes proved too slow and ineffective at wiping out people in the poorest country in the Arab world, it was time to expand the arsenal of war crimes. Rarely, in discussions of Yemen, does one hear much about the violations of international law that have reduced the country to its present war-torn and devastated condition.

Failing to acknowledge a foreign policy disaster in Yemen, the Obama administration has chosen instead to trash international law by supporting the criminal, aggressive war that Saudi Arabia's coalition of police states launched on Yemen on March 26. Now, despite more than three months of Saudi-American terror bombing, the Houthis remain in control of northwest Yemen, their tribal homeland, as well as much of the southeast of Yemen, having overthrown the internationally-installed puppet government, later "elected" without any opponents, of President Abd Rhabbuh Mansur Hadi.

President Obama praised Hadi as his "successful" partner in attacking terrorists, by which Obama meant he was grateful to Hadi for not objecting to the US drone attacks against his own people. Hadi's legitimacy always depended on foreign puppeteers, and it still does. Having resigned as president, fled the capital, and rescinded his resignation, Hadi fled again, to Saudi Arabia the day before the Saudi blitz began. The official story is that Hadi requested the undeclared Saudi attack on his own country. Hadi remains in the Saudi capital of Riyadh, free to go nowhere while he pretends to head a government-in-exile that is the presently desired fiction of his captor-protectors.

On July 8, from Riyadh, Hadi reportedly proposed a ceasefire in Yemen to start before the month of Ramadan ends July 17. On July 1, UN Secretary-General Ban Ki-moon had called for a "humanitarian halt" in combat "until the end of the holy month of Ramadan." So far, Hadi's Saudi controllers have used the Muslim holy month to rain increased terror on populated areas of Yemen, killing hundreds of civilians and Houthi fighters, with no accurate count available. July 7 saw the highest death toll in Yemen since the Saudi bombing campaign began. This bland-seeming coverage of the carnage by Reuters is riddled by propaganda deceits:

> The United Nations has been pushing for a halt to air raids and intensified fighting that began on March 26. More than 3,000 people have been killed since then as the Arab coalition tries stop the Houthis spreading across the country from the north.
>
> The Iran-allied Shi'ite Houthis say they are rebelling against a corrupt

government, while local fighters say they are defending their homes from Houthi incursions. Sunni Saudi Arabia says it is bombing the Houthis to protect the Yemeni state.

The Reuters perspective represents the mainstream consensus, which also typically includes some of the same threads of media deceit as these:

- *"The UN has been pushing ..."* No it hasn't. The UN as a body has done little to protect the Yemenis, but the Security Council has done less for a country in which civil war has spanned generations. Security Council resolutions are determinedly "even-handed" in their equal treatment of aggressors and victims. In June 2015, after two months of Saudi bombing, the Security Council expressed its "full support" for an impossibility: "a peaceful, inclusive, orderly and Yemeni-led political transition process that meets the legitimate demands and aspirations of the Yemeni people."

- *"pushing for a halt to air raids ..."* No it hasn't. The air raids are being carried out by the nine UN member states in the Saudi Coalition, including Security Council member Jordan. The US, a permanent Security Council member, has supported the aerial war crime campaign with logistics, in-flight refueling of bombers, intelligence, air-sea rescue, and naval support for the blockade (which is also an act of war).

- *"intensified fighting that began on March 26 ..."* Intensified fighting began long before March 26. Yemen's civil war has waxed and waned over several decades. What began March 26 was the war crime nexus of bombing civilian targets by the nine-member Saudi Coalition that includes Egypt, Morocco, Jordan, Sudan, UAE, Kuwait, Bahrain and Qatar. The Houthi rebellion is more than a decade old and gained intensity in the fall of 2014. The Houthis drove out the Yemeni government and now control the western half of the country, where most of the population lives and most of the bombing takes place.

- *"the Arab coalition tries to stop the Houthis spreading across the country from the north ..."* Reuters is just wrong on this. The Houthi spread was a fact, and the "Arab coalition" failed in an ill-conceived campaign. Faced with an army advancing on the ground, the "Arab coalition" has not deployed ground troops. Without serious objection from the international community, the "Arab coalition" attacks military forces in another country with which they are not at war, as well as terror-bombing that country's civilians with US-made cluster bombs.

- As for spreading *"from the north,"* that is at best wrong, if not duplicitous. Saudi Arabia has declared the northernmost province of Yemen, Saada, a military zone in which every civilian is a presumed combatant. This is the same bloodthirsty policy that leads the US to count every drone victim as a combatant until proven otherwise. This is the same moral numbness that led the US to establish free fire zones in Vietnam, where every living thing was deemed an enemy. This is total war as waged by the powerful, at a distance, against the weak and almost defenseless. This is as bad as any Nazi onslaught of World War II.

- The absurdity of the Reuters characterization is illustrated by another UN Security Council position in support of a *"political solution to Yemen's crisis in accordance with the Gulf Cooperation Council Initiative."* The Gulf Cooperation Council is an oxymoron, in that it includes six of the seven Arab states (not Iraq) on the Persian Gulf who allied determinedly NOT to cooperate with the other Persian Gulf state, Iran. Further, the Security Council absurdly supports the "Gulf Cooperation Council Initiative" when five of the six Gulf Council members (not Oman) are busily bombing Yemen in violation of international law.

- *"The Iran-allied Shi'ite Houthis ..."* There is no evidence of an alliance between Iran and the Houthis, certainly not in any sense equivalent to the overt alliances waging undeclared war on Yemen. The Houthis are Shi'ite Muslims, and Iran has almost surely supported them to some extent, but most claims of Iranian involvement in the current fighting are patently over-stated and lack supporting evidence. Reuters here is parroting Arab, American and Israeli propaganda about the "threat" from Iran.

- *"say they are rebelling against a corrupt government ..."* Who says? Reuters doesn't say. This is specious journalism. Yemen has a long history of corrupt government, but perhaps the Hadi government allowing US troops to wage war on Yemeni territory, killing Yemenis at will, raised the corruption bar to a new level.

- *"local fighters say they are defending their homes ..."* is worse than specious journalism, it's pretty much a lie since the main opposition to the Houthis comprises forces loyal to Hadi, as well as cohorts of both Al Qaeda and ISIS.

- *"Sunni Saudi Arabia says it is bombing the Houthis to protect the Yemeni state"* would be a laugh line were it not such a dark lie. Saudi bombing is destroying the Yemeni state in order to "save" it. The Saudis may be "protecting" the Hadi government, but only in the sense that the Mafia provides protection in a protection racket. The Saudis have longstanding territorial conflicts with the Houthis along the northwest Saudi-Yemeni border. And the Saudis are acting as if they believe their own demonizing propaganda about Iran. Saudi Arabia is more likely bombing the Houthis because they are defenseless and Saudi Arabia doesn't dare bomb Iran.

Nobody seems to care about Yemen, not even The New Yorker

The widespread, bland disinterest in the unending victimization of Yemenis facing unrelenting, daily crimes against humanity is hardly unique to obtuse observers like Reuters. The New Yorker, which eventually distinguished itself in opposition to the horrors of Vietnam, last published a piece on Yemen on May 1 (according to a site search). That piece conveys the American denial of its own terrorism with a tone of mild distaste suitable to Eustace Tilley, whose monocled default opinion is to blame the victim, as Robin Wright wrote little more than a month after the Saudi-American bombardment began:

> The current Houthi rebellion – the seventh – is only the latest. The Houthi clan are Zaydi Muslims, who make up about a third of Yemen's twenty-six million people. A once powerful people from the rugged northern highlands, they ruled an imamate for a millennium and deeply resented their reduced influence under [former President] Saleh [now a Houthi ally]. Between 2004 and 2010, they fought six other wars against his government....
>
> The quarter-century experiment in uniting Yemen has definitively failed. There is no military solution, and there are unlikely to be any winners out of such a multilayered conflict, whatever the territorial gains....
>
> Last week, the United States dispatched the aircraft carrier USS Teddy Roosevelt to supplement seven American warships off the Yemen coast. Washington strongly supports a political solution to the conflict in Yemen, but without interested players the risks of unintended consequences increase.

Rhetorically the US may support a "political solution" (to its own liking) and gullible reporters may accept that as some sort of reality. The reality on the ground (and on the water) is that the US supports and participates in endless terror bombing and a naval blockade. That is to say, the US supports and participates in the war crimes that are leading toward mass starvation and human devastation, what the discreet Ban Ki-moon refers to as a "humanitarian crisis" or a "catastrophe," as if there were no agency causing it.

An editorial July 7 in The New York Times takes the same concerned-but-oblivious-to-the-genocidal-actors tone that reinforces the general pretense that no one is responsible:

> Yemen has now been added to the United Nations' list of most severe humanitarian emergencies, along with South Sudan, Syria and Iraq.

It is a tragic distinction, highlighting the peril to 80 percent of the country's 25 million citizens. The international community, including the United States, is not doing enough to push for an immediate cease-fire in the war that is ravaging the country to make it possible to deliver aid.

Yemen, a poor country, was deeply unstable even before a coalition, led by Saudi Arabia and backed by the United States, started bombing the Houthi rebel movement in late March. Last week, Ban Ki-moon, the United Nations secretary general, declared the situation a "catastrophe."

Is it possible to commit a long string of war crimes in self-defense?

Having tiptoed up to the edge of US war crimes, the Times retreated. The rest of the editorial comprises little more than helpless hand-wringing, without even hinting at the most effective way to save Yemeni lives: stop the bombing. That means you, "Saudi Arabia ... backed by the United States." Like most of the rest of the world, the Times settled for asking for a reasonable-sounding impossibility, which it then undercut with another wisp of Saudi reality:

> What is needed is a permanent political solution that will ensure the Houthis, who have some legitimate grievances and are unlikely to give up, get a significant role in any new government. Negotiations should be started without preconditions. But Saudi Arabia and its allies have appeared intent on forcing the Houthis to surrender, no matter what the cost to civilians and Yemen's cities and villages.

Well, "Saudi Arabia and its allies" includes the US and others. The Times needs to look in the mirror without flinching. Saudi Arabia and its allies need to stop their bombing.

Ironically, they are not bombing Al Qaeda or ISIS forces in Yemen with anything like the same intensity they're bombing Yemenis. In fact, Al Qaeda and ISIS are supplementing Saudi-American bombing with their own terror-bombing of Yemenis. For whatever reason, if there is one, the Saudi-American aerial genocide against Yeminis is making most of Yemen a much safer haven for terrorists. Yet this lunatic policy continues without serious opposition apparent anywhere. Who decided that Yemen should be treated as if it were the Haiti of the Arab world?

If any of the umpteen candidates for president of the United States has said anything humane, useful, or even dimly relevant about Yemen, it is hard to find (and I have found nothing). And nowhere have I found any call to establish the appropriate International War Crimes Tribunal to judge the illegality of the multiple, heinous predations of the United States, Saudi Arabia and their sundry allies, all members in good standing of the world peacekeeping authority.

64.

Do War Crimes in Yemen Matter to an American President?

The US added Yemen to its 14 years of continuous war somewhere

The American-backed genocidal war on Yemen is in its fifth month, making it one of the hotter issues in the 2016 Presidential campaign, right? Wrong.

If *any* announced candidate has said anything about Yemen, it's hard to find. None of our would-be leaders of the free world are calling for a halt to the war of aggression that violates international law, none are demanding a stop to the war crimes and crimes against humanity that flow from the terror-bombing carried out by Saudi Arabia and its allies, with US tactical and intelligence support. None of our White House aspirants are demanding a halt to this criminal war or demanding justice against its war-criminal perpetrators.

Of course, neither is the present president, whose administration seems to have adopted a policy variant on the way we won the west ("the only good injun is a dead injun"). Now the American mantra amounts to "the only good Houthi is a dead Houthi." The slogan may change, but the genocide remains the same.

The good news here, in its way, is that there's no cheerleading section for multi-state savagery against largely defenseless people. Little reported, even less discussed, the US-Saudi terror bombing of Houthi rebels in Yemen goes relentlessly on, like the fascist intervention in the Spanish Civil War, causing a Yemenicide of displaced, starving and dead civilians, along with a few dead fighters whose enemies include not only the US and Saudi coalition, but also Al Qaeda and the Islamic State (ISIL) in Yemen as well.

In other words, President Obama's policy amounts to a declaration that the enemies of our enemies are also our enemies. Why? Who knows? Because the Saudi Sunnis say so? Because the US thinks killing Shi'ites en masse is a good thing? Is it pure, homicidal cynicism for the sake of Saudi oil? Is it just a continuation of the recent American proclivity to get in on the wrong side of stupid wars, as the president said of Iraq?

Is American foreign policy built on institutional stupidity?

There's plenty of evidence for a prima facie case that American policy on war and peace has been rooted in stupidity at least since Vietnam. The underlying question is whether stupidity is a product or a cause of capitalism or imperialism. And a related question is whether it's really stupidity, since it's the consistent policy of a tiny minority, the bipartisan American elite that continues to benefit from being consistently wrong from a moral or humanitarian perspective. That's another reason a healthy country needs war crimes trials for people above the rank of lieutenant.

One of the major stupidities still raging through American political discourse, such as it is, is that Iran is all bad. This is an article of faith for which the evidence is very thin. Any honest indictment of Iran would be far briefer than an indictment of Saudi Arabia, Israel, or the United States. Clearly, no honest indictments are in the offing.

Caught in this web of Iran inanity as he tries to establish a sane relationship with Iran (a signatory to the nuclear non-proliferation treaty, unlike Israel), President Obama recently undermined the prime Saudi rationale for reducing Yemen to rubble. The Saudis are Iranophobic, blaming Iran for the Houthi rebellion against decades of repression by the Yemeni government. Now President Obama has quietly said that actually Iran tried to restrain the Houthis when they started to take over Yemen:

> When the Houthis started moving, that wasn't on orders from [the head of the Iranian Revolutionary Guard Qasim] Soleimani, that wasn't on an order from the IRGC [Iranian Guard]. That was an expression of the traditional Houthi antagonism towards [the Yemeni

capitol] Sanaa, and some of the machinations of the former president, [Ali Abdullah] Saleh, who was making common cause out of expediency with the Houthis...We watched as this proceeded. There were moments where Iran was actually urging potential restraint. Now, once the Houthis march in and there's no *there* there [the government fled] are they interested in getting arms to the Houthis and causing problems for the Saudis? Yes. But they weren't proceeding on the basis of, come hell or high water, we're moving on a holy war here.

Whatever. That didn't keep the Obama administration from joining the Saudis in committing war crimes if there was a holy war. Obama argues, heretically in the present American belief system, that Iran is a rational state actor. What he doesn't say is that, in recent history, Iran has been a more rational state actor than the US. Having called US anti-terrorist policy in Yemen a success, President Obama has been all but silent about the criminal war that resulted from that "success."

If no one talks about a genocide, it's not really happening, is it?

Like their president, the current candidates' silence on Yemen is just as deafening. That silence is aided and abetted by a passive press corps that chooses not to ask questions about why the US is aiding the Saudi coalition in trashing international law and destroying one of the poorest countries in the world. That's similar to the Turkish Rule about Armenians: if you forbid mention of genocide, then it never happened.

As a former Secretary of State, Hillary Clinton might have some insight into what's happening in and to Yemen. She might even have an opinion. But if she does, she hasn't shared it much. She has a record of voting for and tolerating criminal wars. Her official website, skimpy on foreign policy generally, doesn't seem to mention Yemen at all. Surely her reticence has little to do with gifts to the Clinton Foundation from Saudi Arabia, Morocco and Yemen (the former government, whose president has fled to Saudi Arabia), all of which are among the criminal belligerents in the Saudi coalition.

Bernie Sanders doesn't seem to have anything to say about war crimes in Yemen, either. But then Bernie Sanders doesn't have much to say about war and peace issues, defense spending (more than half the US budget), or militarism generally. He's made a point of supporting

393

wounded American veterans, which is decent and politically easy, but fails to address the pathology that creates wounded veterans in the first place. He's said the US needs to fight terrorism, but so do Saudi Arabia and Turkey ("Those countries are going to have to get their hands dirty, it cannot just be the United States alone"). This implies that Sanders is OK with Turkish attacks on its Kurds and Saudi depredations against Yemen. He doesn't actually say.

Jill Stein of the Green Party apparently hasn't said anything about America's criminal war on Yemen in particular. She has, however, expressed sanity about Iran, called the wars in Iraq and Afghanistan illegal, and in 2012 she noted that:

> It's very clear that there is blowback going on now across the Middle East, not only the unrest directed at the Libyan embassy. 75% of Pakistanis actually identify the US now as their enemy, not as their supporter or their ally. And, you know, in many ways, *we're seeing a very ill-conceived, irresponsible and immoral war policy come back to haunt us,* where US foreign policies have been based, unfortunately, on brute military force and wars for oil. Under my administration, we will have a foreign policy based on international law and human rights and the use of diplomacy. [emphasis added]

As for the 17 Republican candidates running for president, that's a running joke, with a potential punch line that's not too funny. Given their collective performance on the Fox News "debates," none of them has a coherent view of the US place in the world beyond doing whatever it pleases. The Fox News reporters didn't ask any probing questions.

There were some hilarious responses about foreign policy, as Juan Cole noted. Ted Cruz seemed to praise Egyptian President al-Sisi for killing hundreds of opponents and establishing a military police state. Ben Carson seemed to defend torture and other war crimes. A Fox reporter asked Scott Walker, "Which Arab country not already in the US led coalition has potential to be our greatest partner?" Walker's effectively answered "none" when he said:

> ... we need to focus on the ones we have. You look at Egypt, probably the best relationship we've had in Israel, at least in my lifetime, incredibly important. You look at the Saudis — in fact, earlier this year, I met

with Saudi leaders, and leaders from the United Arab Emirates, and I asked them what's the greatest challenge in the world today? Set aside the Iran deal. They said it's the disengagement of America. We are leading from behind under the Obama-Clinton doctrine — America's a great country. We need to stand up and start leading again, and we need to have allies, not just in Israel, but throughout the Persian Gulf.

All of this seems to confirm the observation attributed to Ambrose Bierce more than a century ago, that "War is God's way of teaching Americans geography."

65.

Nobel Peace Prize Winner Bombs Afghan Hospital

Tabloid headline (above) is a crystallization of present reality

No, it's not really fair to blame President Obama *personally* for the waves of aerial bombing that took more than an hour on October 4 to destroy a neutral hospital operated by Doctors Without Borders in Kunduz, Afghanistan, even though it appears on its face to be yet another US war crime.

But it's totally fair to blame President Obama for giving the world another six years (so far) of President Bush's policy of bringing chaos and devastation to whatever part of the Middle East happens to be annoying the folks who have decided these things since 2001. Not that it was all bread and roses before that, given the century-plus of unrelenting Western subjugation of the region by direct force and by establishing vicious proxy dictatorships (exhibit #1 is Iran).

So when Donald Trump and people like him say that the Middle East was more stable under Saddam Hussein or Muammar Gaddafi, therefore the US should be supporting Russia's effort to keep Bashar al-Assad in power in the bits of Syria his government still controls, it makes a kind of superficial sense – unless you actually believe the region is a better place now than it was 15 years ago. And if that's your belief, maybe someone should explain their good fortune to those millions of refugees.

Trump's argument would have been relevant in 2001, when he had nothing useful to say in opposition to the national predation our government proudly unleashed on the world as a war on "terrorism" and then claimed as a "mission accomplished," even though there's

396

still no let-up as innocent people continue to be killed by American weapons in the hands of Americans and others. In 2011, Trump was equally ineffective in opposition to US engagement in Libya. To be fair to Trump, principled opposition to America's permanent war on largely imaginary enemies (until we attack them, creating new ones) is hard to come by, and no principled opponent of the US warfare state is presently running for president or most other offices.

At any meaningful level, Trump's notion of "stability" is absurd except for people who can imagine it being cool to live in an unimaginably brutal police state. That's what they had in Iraq and Libya, and the US accomplishment was making it worse for Iraqis and Libyans. Will Syrians now reap the same benefits?

Slaughtered wedding parties, maimed children – Hey, stuff happens

Just as Jeb Bush is the "stuff happens" candidate now, his brother George (like his father George) were "stuff happens" presidents. Officially, as Defense Secretary Rumsfeld said, "Stuff happens" – describing US forces who protected only themselves as looting and revenge killings went unchecked in "liberated" Iraq. Rumsfeld himself fleshed put the full cynicism of the Stuff Happens Doctrine, explaining an American mentality that continues to shape decisions of state without a trace of its inherent, ugly irony:

> Stuff happens, and it's untidy. Freedom's untidy, and free people are free to make mistakes and commit crimes and do bad things. They're also free to live their lives and do wonderful things. And that's what's going to happen here.

Seriously, the US occupation makes you free. How Orwellian is that? And how's that working out across more than 4,000 miles of aggressive US intervention, military and otherwise, from Tripoli to Kunduz? The ghastliness of American behavior around the world has been plain to anyone with the wit to look at it, as Harold Pinter did in 2005 in his Nobel acceptance speech, which has a humanity long missing from American leadership. Reviewing past American crimes, and anticipating future American crimes, Pinter referred to the pitiless American assault on Nicaragua:

> The United States finally brought down the Sandinista government. It took some years and considerable resistance, but relentless economic persecution and 30,000 dead finally undermined the spirit of the Nicaraguan people. They were exhausted and poverty stricken once again. The casinos moved back into the country. Free health and free education were over. Big business returned with a vengeance. "Democracy" had prevailed.

> But this "policy" was by no means restricted to Central America. It was conducted throughout the world. It was never-ending. And it is as if it never happened.

> The United States supported, and in many cases engendered every right-wing military dictatorship in the world after the end of the Second World War. I refer to Indonesia, Greece, Uruguay, Brazil, Paraguay, Haiti, Turkey, the Philippines, Guatemala, El Salvador, and, of course, Chile. The horror the United States inflicted upon Chile in 1973 can never be purged and can never be forgiven.

In the United States, Chile is hardly remembered and rarely discussed, except perhaps when our leaders confer honors on a fellow war criminal like Henry Kissinger.

"Hope and Change" fooled people in 2008, what will work in 2016?

Peace is not yet at hand, but the world continues to wait, rather fecklessly for the most part, while the US peace prize president pursues the same deluded war polices (sometimes watered down) that produce the same disastrous results. Meanwhile a numbed homeland populace is encouraged to fret about its own security, to accept the cost of stuff happening to other people and to ignore fifteen years of failed leadership's repeated failures.

Still there's some restlessness in the land and Trump speaks to that, however irrelevantly, blaming the past while offering nothing new for the future. In that, he's not alone. No one among Republicans and Democrats takes on the US warfare state of today – that empire has no clothes, and everyone admires its exceptional wardrobe.

US combat role ended in Afghanistan – only it didn't. The end of the US combat role in Afghanistan was never more real than a three-card monte hustle. The US would base more than 10,000 troops in Afghanistan indefinitely, but they wouldn't have a "combat role" on paper. But there was never any question that these troops would be fighting whenever and wherever someone in authority considered it necessary, as authorized by the commander-in-chief. US military activity in Afghanistan in 2015 included regular air strikes against presumed "insurgents."

Despite US and other coalition support for Afghan government forces, the Taliban made significant gains during 2015. By September, in an eerie echo of Vietnam, the Taliban controlled most of the Afghan countryside while the government still controlled the cities. One of those cities, Kunduz, in the northeast of the country, came under Taliban control on September 28 and has had extreme fighting ever since. US bombing of Kunduz began September 29.

Also in Kunduz, in 2011, Doctors Without Borders had established a hospital that treated anyone who was hurt: civilians as well as combatants from any side. The hospital was well marked as a hospital. Doctors Without Borders made sure that authorities on all sides, including Kabul and Washington, knew the hospital's coordinates. It's the only hospital of its kind in the region. It was outside the Taliban-controlled area when the US bombed it. Hospital staff notified the US and Afghan forces that they were bombing a hospital, after which the bombing continued for another half hour.

When the bombing started, there were 80 staff and 105 patients in the hospital. The death toll was 12 staff and 10 patients (three children), some of whom burned to death in their beds in the critical care unit. More than 35 others were injured. Doctors Without Borders calls the attack a war crime. And they have closed the hospital.

The first US lie in response was that they bombed the hospital because there were Taliban inside. That would still be a war crime. But there were no Taliban inside, and no Taliban shooting at Americans nearby, and there were no Americans nearby, as other US lies variously claimed. Now US officials have acknowledged that, after a "rigorous US procedure," the US bombed the hospital intentionally. That is a war crime.

Is an unprosecuted war crime still a war crime?

So far, the American public's reaction to this war crime is of a piece with public reaction to almost all-American atrocities – stuff happens. Harold Pinter described the process a decade ago:

> It never happened. Nothing ever happened. Even while it was happening it wasn't happening. It didn't matter. It was of no interest. The crimes of the United States have been systematic, constant, vicious, remorseless, but very few people have actually talked about them.

> You have to hand it to America. It has exercised a quite clinical manipulation of power worldwide while masquerading as a force for universal good. It's a brilliant, even witty, highly successful act of hypnosis.

Why would the US, even at Afghan request, deliberately commit a war crime? A cynic might speculate that, since they were losing Kunduz to the Taliban, they might as well deny the Taliban the use of the only available hospital.

Like President Obama, Doctors Without Borders has won a Nobel Peace Prize. Unlike the president, Doctors Without Borders has not established policies responsible for killing thousands of civilians in dozens of countries.

What happened in Kunduz is dwarfed by the horrors that happen in the US-supported Saudi coalition total war on Yemen. On September 29, coalition airstrikes there killed more than 130 people in a wedding party. At his press conference three days later, the peace prize president did not have the grace to mention it, much less to call it unimaginable brutality.

66.

Saudi Arabia a Force for Stability? Dream On!

Enabling Saudi militancy is an irrational US policy

The Saudi mass beheadings on January 2 proved nothing new to a world that well knows Saudi Arabia is still a tribal police state with a moral code of medieval barbarity. Saudi Arabia is a Sunni-Muslim country that executes people for witchcraft, adultery, apostasy and homosexuality (among other things). And the Saudi regime is perfectly willing to torture and kill a Shi'a-Muslim cleric for the crime of speaking truth to power, knowing that his judicial murder will inflame his followers and drive the region toward wider war. The Saudi provocation is as transparent as it is despicable, and yet the Saudis are held to no account, as usual.

Yes, the predictable reaction in Iran included street protest and breaching the security of an annex to the Saudi embassy in Tehran. Protestors ransacked the annex and set it on fire. Police responded quickly, put out the fire, and arrested some 40 protestors. No Saudis were hurt or taken hostage. As such things go, the annex attack was pretty much a non-event – but it was enough for diplomats and media to create a false equivalency, as if vandalizing an empty building carried the same moral weight as the ISIS-style execution of Sheikh Nimr al-Nimr for nonviolent protest against a brutal dictatorship.

Hiding behind this false equivalency, governments around the world call for both sides to act with restraint, even though Iran has acted with restraint all along, while Saudi Arabia threw restraint to the winds from the start with the deliberate provocation of a political murder. Of course, there's nothing inherently wrong – ever – with both

401

sides exercising restraint, it's just a meaningless bromide as applied here, with a caution bordering on cowardice. These are, after all, the same people who mostly say nothing in opposition to the Saudi coalition's brutally aggressive war against Yemeni fighters and civilians alike in daily violation of international humanitarian law.

The speed with which Saudi Arabia seized on the embassy attack as a pretext for cutting off diplomatic relations suggests that this was a Saudi goal from the start. The diplomatic break also complicates (or even scuttles) this month's peace talks that contemplated Saudi Arabia coming to the same table with Iran to discuss the wars in Syria and Iraq. The Saudis are fighting in both wars. Iran has fighters with Iraqi and US forces fighting the Islamic state in Iraq, and Iraq has something like "advisors" supporting President Assad in Syria. The Saudis allege that Iran has troops in Yemen on the side of the Houthis there, but there is no persuasive evidence that this is true. Whatever the reality on the ground, any restraint on Iran resulting from the Saudi provocation would likely help the Saudis in their unrestrained wars, neither of which is going all that well. The Saudis unilaterally ended the ceasefire in Yemen, killing more civilians there the same day it beheaded 43 prisoners and shot four others at home.

When does US complicity in Saudi violence come to an end?

The long game for the Saudis – regional dominance – requires relative Iranian weakness. The sanction-enforced weakness forced on Iran in recent years is about to end as a result of the multinational nuclear agreement between Iran and most of the civilized world (China, France, Russia, United Kingdom and the US – the five permanent members of the UN Security Council – plus Germany and the European Union). The return of Iran to the world community can only increase its challenge to Saudi regional hegemony. Whether this is good or bad for the rest of the world is arguable, but the current Western conventional thinking that Saudi Arabia is a force for stability in the region is pure fantasy.

There is not a lot of moral high ground in the Middle East, where the most democratic nation is Israel, which treats its Palestinians worse (perhaps) than the Sunni dictatorship of Bahrain treats its Shi'a majority (with the blessing of the US 5th Fleet based there). When it comes to executing people, Iran and Saudi Arabia are #2 and #3 globally, behind China, and followed closely by Iraq, North Korea and the US.

In the midst of this moral quagmire, President Obama once again has an opportunity to actually earn that Nobel Peace Prize he received in 2009 in anticipation of his someday doing something to deserve it. He can act to contain and calm the nations of the Persian Gulf. Instead of relying on mealy-mouthed bromides from low-level State Department officials, the President of the United States could step up to defend his administration's signal accomplishment to date, the multinational nuclear agreement with Iran, by telling the Saudis to behave like a mature nation and stop beheading clerics just to annoy the neighbors.

The White House website has no searchable comment about recent Saudi actions. On January 4, White House Press Secretary Josh Earnest commented on the mass beheadings with seemingly helpless plaintiveness more reflective of weakness than any kind of leadership: "And, you know, this is a concern that we raised with the Saudis in advance, and unfortunately, the concerns that we expressed to the Saudis have precipitated the kinds of consequences that we were concerned about."

Well, if the White House had been truly concerned about heading off mass executions, or even just heading off the beheading of Sheikh al-Nimr, the White House could have done any number of things to give the Saudis pause, something other than what it did, including approving another $1.2 billion in arms sales.

US has the choice of not abetting Saudi war crimes in Yemen

Instead of weeping for American children already beyond his help, President Obama could act immediately to save still-living Yemeni children by withdrawing US support of the Saudi-led war on Yemen (carried out with weapons from the US and others). President Obama has been complicit in the Saudi criminal war since the US helped launch it in March 2015. The US could end its role in the naval blockade that keeps Yemenis from fleeing the war zone, a blockade that keeps food and other humanitarian aid from Yemeni children and adults alike, a blockade that enforces mass hunger and one of the worst humanitarian crises in the world. For the US merely to abstain from its active role in crimes against humanity in Yemen would allow it to seize something like the moral high ground in a region where almost none exists. Pulling back from mindless support for one of the most depraved governments in the Middle East would seem, by contrast, like reaching a moral mountaintop. Why does the US support the Saudis anymore anyway, when the Saudis are most useful now for heating the world beyond habitation?

The Saudis have demonstrated time and again that the US has no significant influence on Saudi Arabia. In 2001, when Saudis hit the World Trade Center, Saudi Arabia (with the connivance of President Bush) withdrew its people from the US before the FBI could have a word with any of them, even those who had had contact with the dead terrorists. Again and again, the US bows to Saudi pressure on issues large and small (with some magnificent exceptions like the multinational nuclear agreement with Iran). At some point the US should ask itself: if we have so little influence with Saudi Arabia, why should we let the Saudis make us look like their puppet?

Saudi betrayals of trust and good will have a long history

There has been no doubt about Saudi duplicity at least since 1996, when the Khobar Towers bombing killed 19 Americans (wounding some 500) and the Saudis obstructed the FBI and other American investigators every step of the way, even though the Saudis knew from the start the identity of the Saudi terrorist who planned the attack. Even so, the US eventually indicted 14 people (13 Saudis and one Lebanese), but blamed it all on Iran. Iran denied any involvement, and also promised no further attacks. Having obstructed the investigation, after the indictment Saudi Arabia refused to extradite any of the suspects. According to Bruce Reidel, then a deputy assistant secretary of defense, at that time the Saudis were most worried about the US starting another Gulf War by attacking Iran and acted to avoid that escalation:

In my meetings with senior Saudi officials in Dhahran in the days immediately after the attack, they pointed the blame at Saudi Hezbollah. It became clear the Saudis had a great deal of information on the group and had probably foiled an earlier bomb attack without telling Washington. The Saudis were certain it was not the work of Osama bin Laden. They knew Mughassil was the mastermind from the start. [Ahmen Ibrahim Al-Mughassil has been identified as head of the military wing of the pro-Iran Saudi Hizballah.]

Now, in 2016, President Obama asks in vain for the Saudis to join the peace talks on Syria but authorizes billions of dollars of arms sales to Saudi Arabia to pursue its covert support for the Islamic State (ISIS) and its criminally brutal war on Yemen. And Secretary of State Kerry asks in vain for the Saudis to spare the life of a cleric whose crime is speaking truth to power, but Saudi Arabia cuts off his head along with 42 others, just to make a point. Saudi Arabia has long since broken with the US whenever it felt like it. Will the US finally get it *this* time that our Saudi ally is not only unreliable but is not an ally?

The multinational nuclear agreement with Iran is, if it holds, an actual achievement worthy of a Nobel Peace Prize. Yet this President acts as if the Saudi kingdom of corruption and war is somehow worthier of protection and support than a world with a diminished threat of nuclear war.

67.

US/Saudi Aggression in Yemen Celebrated by Co-Aggressor UAE

The National is an English-language publication owned and operated by Abu Dhabi Media, the government-run media organization of Abu Dhabi, the capital of the United Arab Emirates (UAE). There is no press freedom in the UAE. Government media report the government point of view, which rarely includes criticism of the government.

On March 26, the first anniversary of the UAE's unprovoked attack on Yemen as part of the Saudi-led coalition of mostly Arab states, the UAE's official media published a document about the carnage in Yemen illustrative of George Orwell's observation: "If you want to keep a secret, you must also hide it from yourself." The truth about the war in Yemen is a largely unreported secret. The UAE officially hides that truth from itself in an editorial in The National (which follows in its entirety, section by section). It begins with the headline:

AFTER A YEAR IN YEMEN, OUR RESOLVE IS FIRM

After a year in Yemen, the US/Saudi coalition has managed to reduce the region's poorest country to an almost unthinkable condition, where some 20 million Yemenis – about 80% of the population – need humanitarian assistance. In a country both under attack and on the verge of mass famine, what does "our resolve is firm" really mean if not continued crimes against humanity? The UAE editorial's first sentence has no discernible meaning at all:

> The start one year ago of Operation Decisive Storm comes as a reminder of the importance of the war in Yemen.

The anniversary of an aggression – that the Saudis proclaimed would be brief and decisive – is important mostly for its irony. An official Saudi press release of March 25, 2015 quoted the Saudi ambassador to the US saying: "The operation will be limited in nature and designed to protect the people of Yemen and its legitimate government from a takeover by the Houthis. A violent extremist militia." By then the "legitimate" government of Yemen had fled to the Saudi capital of Riyadh. Not only has more than a year of US/Saudi-led war failed to achieve any significant military success, it has produced collateral damage on a massive scale, making the country of 25 million people perhaps the worst humanitarian crisis in the world today. This reality makes a mockery of the UAE editorial's next assertion:

> The UAE joined the Saudi-led coalition campaign driven by its commitment and dedication to maintaining security and establishing peace in the region.

This is, almost literally, Orwellian in its "war is peace" mindset. From the start, the US/Saudi aggression has violated international law and committed war crimes against Yemeni civilians, using cluster bombs made in the USA (and sold to the Saudis with US taxpayer subsidies). The recently-released US State Department annual human rights report on Saudi Arabia for 2015 soft-pedals the allies' slaughter of civilians in Yemen and omits Saudi-dropped US cluster bombs entirely (perhaps because their lingering impact killing children over years and decades is deucedly hard to assess accurately, whereas profits can be tallied almost immediately). The full despicability of the Obama administration's position on these inhumanities is revealed in its official unwillingness to speak on the record about the blatant hypocrisy of its morally indefensible defense of the murder of civilians for profit, as reported in The Intercept:

> A State Department spokesperson, who would only comment on background, pointed out that the US has called on both sides of the conflict to protect civilians. He also claimed that the use of cluster munitions is not a human rights violation because the United States has not signed the ban on cluster munitions.

The State Department spokesperson did not acknowledge that only one side bombs civilians (in schools, hospitals, markets and homes) with US-made planes dropping US-made munitions. This follows a years-long US campaign in Yemen to kill civilians with US-made drones (still in use from outside the country).

Yemen is drawn as a coherent state on maps, but most of the Yemeni-Saudi border has never been officially defined. Yemen has an ancient culture in the western part of the country, but it has never been a coherent state. The Saudis and Yemenis have engaged in sporadic, armed conflict for decades. In particular, the Saudis and the Houthis have fought over northwest Yemen and neighboring southwest Saudi Arabia, which is home to a large Houthi population. Security in the region is not directly threatened by the Yemeni civil war. For any Arab state to talk like the UAE of establishing "peace in the region" is fundamentally hilarious.

The UAE has long been a source of support for the Islamic State (aka ISIS, ISIL, or Daesh), as have Saudi Arabia, Qatar and Kuwait – all part of the coalition waging war on Yemen. Editorially, the UAE cloaks itself in the mantle of state legitimacy:

> The coalition responded to the call by Yemen's president Abd Rabbu Mansour Hadi to restore his internationally recognised government to power.

To call the Hadi government "internationally recognized" is to fudge the reality that the Hadi government has only limited recognition among Yemenis. Hadi came to power through what US Ambassador to the UN Samantha Power called, somewhat falsely, the "peaceful, inclusive, and consensus-driven political transition under the leadership of the legitimate President of Yemen, Abdo Rabbo Mansour Hadi." One problem with this US formulation is that Hadi's "legitimacy" derives from his being installed as president by an international diplomatic coup, followed by his election in a race in which he was the sole candidate. Essentially, there is no legitimate government of Yemen and has not been for decades at least. The present war of aggression by outside powers intervening in a multifaceted civil war relies for its justification on a variety of dishonest fictions. The Houthis are a sub-group of the Shi'ite Zaidis, who number about eight million in Yemen. The Zaidis governed northwest Yemen for 1,000 years, until 1962. The UAE editorial invents a different historical identity:

> Houthi rebels had captured the capital of Sanaa, with the support of Iran and loyalists to former president Ali Abdullah Saleh, and were advancing towards the southern city of Aden. On the way, they had killed civilians and destroyed neighbourhoods, leading to a vast humanitarian crisis.

Iran is widely scapegoated as a nefarious influence in Yemen, but there is little or no evidence of Iranian involvement on a scale that could possibly make a difference on the ground in Yemen. Iran's support of the Houthis, their fellow Shi'ites, has been largely diplomatic, political and presumably financial. Former president Saleh, who has a wide following of non-Houthis, was deposed in the coup that installed Hadi. When Saleh was president of Yemen, he also fought a Houthi insurrection. While there is little doubt that all sides in the Yemen civil war (including al Qaeda and ISIS) have committed war crimes of various degree, only the US/Saudi coalition has bombed defenseless civilian populations. There is a special deceit in the UAE suggestion that the Houthis in 2015 are the cause of the Yemen humanitarian crisis in 2016. A year of largely indiscriminate bombing by the US/Saudi forces is the more proximate and powerful cause, as is the year-long US/Saudi naval blockade that keeps Yemenis caught in the bomb range while at the same time denying them food, medicine and other essentials for survival. Nevertheless, according to the UAE editorial, the Houthis – who have suffered attacks by ISIL – are somehow responsible for ISIL attacking coalition forces in the south:

> The Houthis' disregard for Yemen's security created fertile ground for extremism to thrive, leading to the latest attacks by ISIL that killed 20 people in Aden on Friday.

Whatever "security" Yemen has had in recent years has been largely illusory. The US drone program in Yemen spent years creating insecurity and killing civilians until the US withdrew just ahead of the fall of the Hadi government (president Saleh had also sanctioned the lethal US military presence in Yemen). And why was the US there? Because Yemen was already "fertile ground for extremism," in particular AQAP, al Qaeda in the Arabian Peninsula, which now controls roughly half of Yemen's southern coast, about 370 miles including the port city of Mukalla, with a 500,000 population. The effective allies in the US/Saudi war on the Houthis include not only the UAE and other coalition members, but also al Qaeda and ISIS – not in the sense that these "allies" share the same goals, but in the sense that the US/Saudi genocidal obsession with the Houthis has allowed and helped both ISIS and especially al Qaeda to expand and solidify positions in Yemen.

All the same, the UAE tries to blame the ISIL (ISIS) suicide bomb attacks in Aden on March 14, 2016, on the Houthis, when Aden is more or less under the military control of the Hadi government. Saudi and UAE forces have been deployed to Aden at least since July 2015, in limited numbers, to protect the Hadi government. The UAE has also secretly deployed hundreds of Colombian mercenary soldiers to Yemen, along with other mercenaries from Panama, El Salvador and Chile, frequently commanded by Australians. During this same time period, neither Saudi Arabia nor the UAE deployed any troops to fight ISIS in Syria. UAE troop strength in Yemen reportedly peaked in the fall of 2015 at about 5,000 troops of one nationality or another. Currently the UAE is estimated to have about 2,500 troops in Yemen as well as other deployments in Libya and Afghanistan. The UAE, with a population of about 6 million, has a military of some 65,000 active frontline personnel.

The UAE's editorial summary of its year of war-making in Yemen relies on an imaginary threat of a wider war that would somehow have magically emerged from the possibility that the Houthis might secure their own country, or just part of it:

> The precarious situation last year required swift intervention to guard against a wider conflict in the region. Saudi Arabia and its Gulf Cooperation Council allies, including the UAE, realised that the security of Yemen was critical for the Arabian Peninsula at large and that a military operation would be required. Iran, which has a history

of meddling in regional affairs, has been backing the Shiite Houthi group to fulfil its own nefarious agenda of expanding its footprint in the Middle East. Quite simply, unless we had taken firm action, our security would have been at risk. This has come at a great cost, including the lives of more than 80 UAE martyrs.

More than a year after collaborating in an aggressive war against Yemen, the UAE can cite no credible or rational or legal basis for joining the attack – unless "a nefarious agenda" turns out to be an obscure *casus belli* under international law. Worse, the UAE doesn't even acknowledge, much less try to justify, the criminal brutality of its war.

This criminal brutality has been documented over and over by non-governmental organizations. Most recently, on April 7, Human Rights Watch issued a report centered on the war crime of bombing a civilian market, killing 97 civilians, 25 of them children. This is no isolated incident. The responsibility and guilt for these atrocities extends to those who sell the weapons as well as those who use them. As Human Rights Watch reported in part:

> Since March 26, 2015, the UN and nongovernmental organizations have documented numerous airstrikes by coalition forces that violate the laws of war. The UN Panel of Experts on Yemen, established under UN Security Council Resolution 2140 (2013), in a report made public on January 26, "documented 119 coalition sorties relating to violations" of the laws of war.

> Human Rights Watch has documented 36 unlawful airstrikes – some of which may amount to war crimes – which have killed at least 550 civilians. Human Rights Watch has also documented 15 attacks in which internationally banned cluster munitions were used in or near cities and villages, wounding or killing civilians.... The coalition has used at least six types of cluster munitions, three delivered by air-dropped bombs and three by ground-launched rockets....

None of these war crimes could possibly be committed by the Houthis and their allies, since they have no air force. Whatever the atrocities committed by Houthis, Saleh's forces, or others, the humanitarian suffering in Yemen is overwhelmingly the responsibility of the US/Saudi coalition, however the UAE editorial may spin it:

> The UAE has also contributed greatly to humanitarian efforts in Yemen, especially as Operation Restoring Hope got under way. More than Dh1.6 billion has been spent on infrastructure and aid programmes to provide our brothers and sisters there with electricity, food, health services, water, sanitation, fuel and transport. We will continue to help the civilian population. Of course, the ultimate goal is a political solution that restores the legitimate government.

In late April a year ago, the Saudis announced that Operation Decisive Storm was over and had achieved its goals. Saudis also announced the beginning of Operation Restoring Hope, which included airstrikes and other military actions, as well as some relief missions.

The claim that the UAE has spent more than 1.6 billion Dirham ($436 million) in and on Yemen is misleading. In 2015, the UAE apparently contributed that amount to United Nations humanitarian programs in Yemen, an amount exceeded only by Saudi Arabia. A contribution in the hundreds of millions of dollars appears generous but represents only a couple of days of the cost of the war. Saudi Arabia is reportedly picking up most of the cost of the war: $200 million per day ($6 billion per month).

> Joining a military campaign is never an easy decision to make, but in this case it was a necessary one. As the Minister of State for Foreign Affairs, Dr Anwar Gargash, said on Friday, the UAE is more powerful today with the sacrifice of its martyrs, and history will remember the important role Operation Decisive Storm has played in drawing "a line between acceptance and submission, and determination and will."

So ends the official UAE version of its Yemen adventure, a version that imagines with complete falsity that the Houthi rebellion somehow put the UAE under threat of having to accept and submit. Accept and submit to what? The Houthi rebellion was a thousand miles from the UAE and has yet to go beyond Yemeni borders (except for the sporadic fighting along the Saudi border in the northwest). In reality, the US/Saudi coalition has long demanded that the Houthis accept and submit to domination by their Sunni enemies of a thousand years. Now, in mid-April 2015, an open-ended ceasefire of sorts is settling over Yemen, with the Houthis still in control of much of the country, and the Saudis continuing to bomb at will. Ironically, if anyone has so far shown true determination and will, it is the Houthis, in their resistance to a ruthless and relentless international coalition.

As for "joining a military campaign," which the UAE officially says is "never an easy decision to make," the UAE has apparently managed the difficult choice once again. Now the UAE has reportedly asked the US for significant increases in military support in order to escalate the war in Yemen against AQAP, al Qaeda in the Arabian Peninsula. Officials in the US and the UAE refuse to comment on the report, which would be an expansion of fighting long under way. According to Iranian Press TV, tensions between Saudi Arabia and the UAE emerged after the UAE withdrew large numbers of troops following defeats in late 2015, leading to a recent plan by the Saudis to replace UAE troops with Jordanians.

On April 15, despite the five-day old truce, US drone strikes, and US-made apache helicopters attacked the city of al-Houta, near Aden in south Yemen. Coalition officials said al Qaeda forces had withdrawn, and the government controlled the city, with five soldiers reportedly killed in an operation that took four hours.

The ceasefire that started April 10 has continued to remain in effect around most of the country, despite some violations. In the Yemeni capital of Sanaa, more than 100 miles north of al-Houta and still under Houthi control, tens of thousands of demonstrators turned out on April 15 for peaceful protest against continued airstrikes by the US/Saudi coalition.

The UN special envoy leading the peace talks scheduled to begin in Kuwait says peace has never been as close as it is today. Those talks include only "government" and "rebel" representatives. Most of the belligerents, including the US/Saudi coalition, al Qaeda, and ISIS, will not be taking part.

68.

Saudis Should Kill Civilians More Slowly, two US Senators Say

How broken is American government? Other senators A-OK with current killing patterns, or prefer increase

It sounds a little like a joke (in a sense it is): Two US senators introduce a resolution based on fraudulent representations of reality, seeking to make the president insist that the Saudis bomb fewer civilians in Yemen – and this darkly hilarious hoax is still better than anything the other 98 senators (and the whole House) are doing about the US illegal war in Yemen. Our would-be heroic duo in the Senate doesn't actually oppose the US war on Yemen, even though they acknowledge its savage daily violations of international law (currently suspended during a tenuous ceasefire). Regardless, these two senators are simultaneously misrepresenting US participation in those ruthless crimes (which the rest of the Senate simply ignores, and the State Department trivializes).

Following 15 years of special ops there, the US has been openly at war against Yemen for more than a year, in support of a genocidal Saudi coalition (mostly the Gulf Cooperation Council that President Obama met with privately recently). Once again, the US is in a war undertaken without Constitutional consultation with Congress, and without Congress raising a peep of an objection. This is a criminal war in which the US is at least accomplice to war crimes and crimes against humanity. The US drone war's toll on civilians arguably makes the US guilty of committing both sets of crimes.

Most of this is acknowledged in Senate Joint Resolution 32, which the senators introduced on April 13, after which it was referred to the Senate Foreign Relations Committee for further consideration possibly. Resolution 32 states in part:

> Whereas the Panel of Experts established pursuant to United Nations Security Council Resolution 2140 (2014) reported on January 22, 2016, that the military coalition led by the Government of Saudi Arabia in Yemen "had conducted *air strikes targeting civilians and civilian objects, in violation of International Humanitarian Law,* including camps for internally displaced persons and refugees; civilian gatherings, including weddings; civilian vehicles, residential areas, medical facilities, schools, mosques, markets, factories and food storage warehouses, and other essential civilian infrastructure such as the airport in Sanaa, the port in Hudayadah, and domestic transit routes".... [emphasis added]

The same UN Panel of Experts cited in Resolution 32 also reported attacks on civilians by the Houthi-Saleh forces (usually referred to as the "rebels") in Aden and Taiz, but the panel did not accuse the Houthi-Saleh forces of a systematic, countrywide campaign in violation of international humanitarian law. Yemen has been engulfed by civil war time and again in recent decades, but the current civil war is overwhelmed in brutality and carnage caused by the international aggression of the US/Saudi coalition. Theirs is the only bombing campaign in a largely defenseless country. The US/Saudi allies are responsible for most of the war's 3000-plus civilian deaths and the destruction of at least three Doctors Without Borders hospitals among other atrocities.

Resolution 32 fails to acknowledge that this is a war that could not have begun without US blessing. The resolution obliquely acknowledges that this is a war that could not be fought without US weapons, or certainly not fought as easily and devastatingly. But the resolution does not oppose the war. The resolution seeks to leverage the Yemen war in favor of a preferred war elsewhere, in places where civilians might be more easily disregarded as would-be "enemy combatants."

Senate response to criminally murderous war: use fewer bombs, maybe

There is no peace movement in the US Senate. There is no anti-war movement in the US Senate. There is no anti-criminal-war in Yemen movement in the US Senate. There is no active anti-war-crimes movement in the US Senate. But there are two senators who have co-sponsored Resolution 32, the gist of which is to put pressure on Saudi Arabia to drop fewer bombs on Yemeni civilians unless they start dropping more bombs on ISIS, the Islamic State in Syria and Iraq. Resolution 32 is not a proposal designed to save lives, merely to take different lives in different places, and not necessarily fewer lives. Fortune Magazine reported the resolution with standard, unexamined foreign policy clichés and an appropriate emphasis on the weapons business:

> **A major US ally is in the crosshairs**
>
> The US defense industry has sold at least $33 billion worth of weapons to its Persian Gulf allies over the past year as dual bombing campaigns against the Islamic State in Iraq and Syria and Houthi rebels in Yemen have depleted stores of aerial bombs and other munitions. But as civilian casualties mount in Yemen in particular, a bipartisan duo in the US Senate is working to tighten the free-flow of weapons and cash between the US and one of its most important Gulf allies. Sens. Chris Murphy (D-Conn.) and Rand Paul (R-Ky.) introduced legislation on Wednesday [April 13] that would restrict the sale of US aerial bombs and missiles to Saudi Arabia unless certain conditions are met.

Fortune has a funny way of seeing things: Saudi Arabia, without significant military risk, bombing civilians to the point of running out of bombs, is somehow seen as "in the crosshairs." These so-called crosshairs are merely an empty threat by two senators to sell them fewer bombs. So long as the Saudis get the president to certify that they'll bomb ISIS more, then everyone involved can go on about the business, the very lucrative business, of random killing as usual, even if the Saudis don't bomb ISIS more. There is no purpose here beyond more killing, with little regard for who gets killed. Well, that's pretty much a summary of the post-9/11 American zeitgeist, isn't it?

Is the United States capable of governing honestly about anything?

Senators Murphy and Paul falsely describe the American role in the war on Yemen this way in Resolution 32:

> Whereas the United States Armed Forces provide dedicated personnel and assets to the armed forces of Saudi Arabia to support their military operations in Yemen, including over 700 air-to-air refueling sorties, and to assist with effectiveness and reduction of collateral damage....

This is true as far as it goes, but it minimizes complicity: how much bombing would be possible without air-to-air refueling? The answer to that question would provide a measure of direct US responsibility for bombing at will in a country with no air defenses.

The senators refer in deceitfully benign language to US personnel who "assist with effectiveness and reduction of collateral damage" the US/Saudi bombing raids. In reality US personnel work side by side with Saudi counterparts in Riyadh, planning, authorizing, and assessing the bombing missions that began over a year ago and have produced a world-class humanitarian crisis. That result suggests that any effort to reduce collateral damage has been limited, incompetent, or both.

But the senators also deceive by omission. Resolution 32 omits the moral (if not legal) war crime that the US commits every time it supplies the Saudi coalition with a cluster bomb, a devastating anti-personnel weapon, that leaves explosives littered around each bomb site, where they remain lethally dangerous, especially to children. That's why most of the rest of the world has banned cluster bombs, while the US and other rogue states have not. Senators Murphy and Paul, like their 98 peers, lack the courage even to admit they're on the wrong side of the law of war on this.

And while the senators acknowledge "the systematic and widespread blockade" that has substantially deprived Yemen of food, fuel, medicine, humanitarian aid and commercial goods, they omit any hint of US participation in that blockade by land, air, or sea. The US Navy in the Red Sea and the Indian Ocean reinforces the Saudi-dominated blockade. Yemen, the poorest country in the region, has long depended on food imports to feed its population of some 25 million. The result of the blockade, not unexpected, is that Yemen has been brought to the verge of mass starvation by the US/Saudi coalition. And the blockade further heightens the crisis by preventing Yemenis from leaving this nation-sized prison purgatory.

An elaborate, meaningless charade is better than nothing, right?

The US has been militarily engaged in Yemen since 2000, when suicide bombers attacked the US Navy destroyer Cole while refueling at port in Aden. The attack killed 17 crew members and wounded 39. US counter-terrorism operations in Yemen since then have included Special Forces, an extended drone campaign, and the current US/Saudi war. In that time, the al Qaeda presence in Yemen has increased to control much of the eastern part of the country, including the port of Mukalla, where Saudi battleships control access from the sea. As of April 23, Saudi coalition forces, including a large contingent from the United Arab Emirates, were massing for an attack on Mukalla, according to UAE official media.

In almost identical press releases from Sen. Murphy and from Sen. Paul, they define the intent of Resolution 32 as a means:

> ...to prevent the United States from continuing to support Saudi-led military campaigns in places like Yemen where Saudi Arabia's year-long campaign has led to a devastating humanitarian crisis and a security vacuum that has empowered our terrorist enemies al Qaeda and ISIS. The Murphy-Paul bipartisan legislation will require the President of the United States to formally certify that the Government of Saudi Arabia is demonstrating an ongoing effort to target terrorist groups, minimize harm to civilians and facilitate humanitarian assistance before Congress can consider the sale or transfer of air-to-ground munitions to Saudi Arabia.

In other words, Resolution 32 is a Rube Goldberg contraption designed to give the impression of moral decency while leaving the reality of the US/Saudi war unlikely to be affected even in the unlikely eventuality that this proposal becomes law. (A companion resolution has now been introduced in the House, where it too will be sent to committee to await further action, if any.)

We pay senators $174,000 a year (plus their perks and staff) and this is the best any of the hundred of them can suggest "to prevent the United States from continuing to support Saudi-led military campaigns in places like Yemen"? Seriously?

The conventional beltway banalities, the bipartisan deceits, the continuing failure of business as usual are worthless.

69.

US Okay with Surgical Strikes
on Yemen Hospitals

Nuremberg: "a war of aggression ... is the supreme international crime"

Presumably no agenda for talks among the US, Saudi Arabia, and the Gulf Cooperation Council has ever included an item for discussion of "Waging Genocidal War on a Defenseless Country," even though they are all parties to just such a war on Yemen. Theirs is just such a war of aggression, started by Saudi Arabia.

American participation in this war of aggression was a war declared by press release from the National Security Council on March 25, 2015, another example of the imperial presidency's ability to act by fiat without fear of serious objection from the public, the media, or even Congress:

> President Obama has authorized the provision of logistical and intelligence support to GCC [Gulf Cooperation Council]-led military operations.

The fundamental crime in Yemen is waging a war of aggression, which encompasses all the subsequent war crimes including bombing civilians, using cluster bombs, bombing hospitals, bombing food supplies, and trying to starve a population to submission or death. Yemen, with a population of 26 million people, was the poorest country in the region even before it was attacked. What the US supports and sanctions against Yemen makes any US complaint about Russian actions in Crimea sound like howling hypocrisy.

For all that the Saudis frame their war on Yemen as a defense against a threat from Iran, there has never been any credible evidence of any credible threat to Saudi Arabia from any element of the miniscule Iranian presence in Yemen. Yemen is fighting a civil war, a new version of the same old civil war Yemenis have been fighting for decades, both before and after Yemen was two separate countries. The Iran "threat" is the paranoid delusion supposedly justifying a merciless war on a civilian population already beset by a four-sided civil war.

There is no way that those who decided to wage this war of aggression could not have known the reality in Yemen if they had wanted to know it. Presumably they knew it all full well and chose a war of aggression anyway, recklessly, perhaps even thoughtlessly, but criminally all the same. The Saudi goal was always to get rid of a longstanding threat on its southwestern border, where the tribal land of the Houthis lies both in Yemen and Saudi Arabia. When the long-oppressed Houthis, a Shia minority in a Sunni world, drove out the Sunni government of Yemen in 2015, the Saudis, without saying so in so many words, decided on a course of action that could lead to a final solution. And everyone knew, at the time, and no one objected, according to this account by the highly reliable Andrew Cockburn on Democracy NOW! (whose piece in Harper's Magazine for September 2016, ironically titled "Acceptable Losses," provides an excellent exegesis of the war on Yemen, but with a more elegiac tone):

> I was told, very early on in the war, Deputy Secretary of State Tony Blinken went to Riyadh to ask the—this is two weeks—yeah, it was two weeks into the war [mid-April 2015], when they had already been bombing away, using the US bombs, US-supplied bombs, using US weapons, killing already dozens, if not certainly, you know, hundreds of civilians, destroying factories. And finally, Blinken turns up in Riyadh and asks, "By the way, what are you trying to accomplish here?" And the Saudis effectively said, or at least the Americans understood them to say, "Well, we basically want to wipe out the Houthis." Well, they termed it as "end all Iranian influence in Yemen." So, the Americans—Blinken was a bit shocked by that, so I'm told, and said, "Well, you know, that's going a bit far. But it's—you should certainly stop the Houthis taking over the country." And that, effectively, gave the Saudis carte blanche to continue this kind of mindless carpet bombing....

By 2015, American hands were already bloody with the US drone assassination program that had killed not only innocent civilians, but American citizens, without a trace of due process of law. In effect, already enmeshed in its own nexus of war crimes in Yemen, the US green-lighted the Saudi-led war of aggression that would make American crimes pale by comparison. As American policy over the years would have it, American weapons have been dispersed all over Yemen since 2006.

Kerry to consult on terrorism, but not US or Saudi terrorism

Terror bombing, an example of which is Saudi pilots flying American planes dropping American bombs on defenseless Yemeni civilian targets, is probably not the terrorism Secretary Kerry wants to discuss – ever – with the Saudis and their allies, never mind other weapons suppliers like France and the United Kingdom. As the official State Department notice put it in deadly opaque prose:

> Secretary Kerry will travel to Jeddah, Saudi Arabia, for a series of meetings with senior Saudi leaders, his counterparts from the Gulf Cooperation Council, the United Kingdom, and the United Nations Special Envoy for Yemen. His discussion will focus on the ongoing conflict in Yemen and efforts to restore peace and stability....

Those "efforts to restore peace and stability" notably include the destruction of two schools, another hospital and a potato chip factory, along with the associated men, women and children, especially at the schools. Perhaps the latest great military "victory" achieved by the war criminals known as the Saudi-led coalition is to drive the world's leading medical crisis-zone organization out of Yemen by targeting its hospitals over and over and over and over since March 2015. Of course, America the Exceptional does not stand for this betrayal of human decency, and our presidential candidates of all parties have railed ceaselessly against this indiscriminate murder of patients, their families, their doctors and other medical personnel, forcing the White House to take action to bring to an end 17 months of aggressive war and other war crimes and crimes against humanity – no, wait, that's not happening, is it?

Actually, if *any* presidential candidate of *any* political party has expressed the slightest objection to the Saudi-coalition's genocidal war on Yemen, such evidence is so hard to come by that it may as well not exist. (In August 2015, Jill Stein of the Green Party mentioned in passing that the Saudis "are committing war crimes right now in Yemen," and more recently she called for an end to US funding for Saudi Arabia and Israel because of their violations of human rights laws, but she does not tend to make a point of the US support for a war of aggression. Still she's better than any other candidate on Yemen.) At this point, a year and a half into our shared war of aggression, *every* candidate is complicit in this horrendous, unjustified war promoted and pursued with smug disdain for anything like peace by our peace prize winning President Obama. The blood drips from all their hands, their feet, their tongues and eyelashes, but most of all from every pore of our Nobel Laureate in the White House. (As the book *Double Down* reported in 2012: "*Turns out I'm really good at killing people,*" Obama said quietly, "*Didn't know that was gonna be a strong suit of mine.*")

With the US at war, Congress has nothing to say about any of it

The US is at war with Yemen, in support of the Saudi-led coalition that launched its undeclared war of aggression on March 26, 2015. US war-making includes, but is not limited to: US intelligence services providing intelligence to the aggressor nations; US military personnel participating in daily target planning and attack assessment; US tanker aircraft re-fueling aggressor nation aircraft bombing Yemen (46,500 acknowledged sorties in the first 11 months of war); US drones targeting and attacking under US control; US military contractors servicing the Saudi F-15s that bomb Yemen; US personnel training Saudi military; US military personnel operating in Yemen; and the US Navy reinforcing the Saudi blockade intent on starving Yemen into submission.

The US Congress has never debated, never authorized US participation in a war of aggression against Yemen. The US president has never asked Congress for such authorization of a war of aggression against Yemen. Neither house of Congress has acted on any bill that directly addresses the war of aggression against Yemen. More than a year after the war started, two Democratic members of Congress (joined by two Republicans) introduced identical bills intended to respond to the war. California congressman Ted Lieu (joined by Florida congressman Ted Yoho) and Connecticut senator Christopher Murphy (joined by Kentucky senator Rand Paul) asked their colleagues to address the horrors of the war (briefly enumerated in the bill), not by ending the war, but only by *temporarily limiting US arms sales to Saudi Arabia*. That's it. They did not mention US participation in the war. Both their bills were referred to committee. At the time there was a spotty ceasefire in Yemen while peace talks proceeded in Kuwait (the talks were suspended in early August, leading to the Saudi escalation currently killing more civilians).

Incredibly, this non-response response to war crimes in Yemen has gotten Rep. Lieu some recent positive press coverage, in The Intercept of August 22 and elsewhere, even though his bill is designed to have no immediate impact on the carnage. Rep. Lieu is a colonel in the US Air Force Reserve. When he was on active duty, he taught the law of war to other Air Force officers. His interview rhetoric, like most of his public action, is soft-edged even though he knows perfectly well his country is committing war crimes. He almost said as much in an August 15 statement objecting to the Saudi attack on a school in Haydan, Yemen, that killed 10 children:

> The indiscriminate civilian killings by Saudi Arabia look like war crimes to me. In this case, children as young as 8 were killed by Saudi Arabian air strikes. By assisting Saudi Arabia, the United States is aiding and abetting what appears to be war crimes in Yemen. The Administration must stop enabling this madness now.

Rep. Lieu and others have also objected to the State Department's certification of another arms sale to Saudi Arabia: this one is $1.15 billion for 153 tanks, hundreds of machine guns and other war materiel. This is in addition to the record $100 billion in arms sales to the Saudis already made by the Obama administration. The latest arms deal suggested to Rep. Lieu "that the administration is, at best, callously indifferent to the mass number of civilians dying as a result of the Saudi-led coalition's bombing." He did not openly consider whether 153 Abrams Main Battle Tanks and other weaponry might open the way for the air war of aggression to be matched by an escalation of the ground war of aggression as well. Twenty of those new US tanks are specifically designated as replacements for tanks lost in combat, some of them in Yemen. On the other hand, the official State Department notice of the Abrams Tank sale assures Congress: "The proposed sale of this equipment and support will not alter the basic military balance in the region." That's hardly reassuring in a region where wars of attrition and military quagmires are killing not only thousands of Yemenis, but Palestinians, Israelis, Lebanese, Syrians, Saudis, Turks, Kurds, Iraqis, Afghans and god knows who else, more often than not with Made-in-USA weapons and munitions.

The proposed US tank sale has drawn the attention of several NGOs (non-governmental organizations) looking to wash American hands of the war on Yemen by blocking the sale, or at least having a debate about it in Congress. Human Rights Watch (HRW) wrote a letter to Secretary Kerry August 19, with temperate language of concern about several countries, including Yemen. HRW asked Secretary Kerry "to emphasize the potential consequences if Saudi Arabia fails to improve its conduct." But it did not suggest what those consequences might be in light of the reality that the US has coordinated and condones all Saudi conduct to date. CODEPINK is supporting a petition to support the Congressional letter that urges President Obama to postpone the US tank sale to the Saudis.

Even The New York Times is expressing something shy of anguish over "American complicity" and "carnage" and targets that are not "legitimate" under international law as it supports efforts to block the tank sale in Congress. The Times doesn't mention that this is the same Congress that in June – supporting a White House request – refused to block the sale of cluster bombs to Saudi Arabia for fear of "stigmatizing" cluster bombs. That's a reflection of the American version of reality, since cluster bombs are already stigmatized by most countries of the world and using them on civilians, as US-Saudi forces do in Yemen, is widely understood to be a war crime. The solution, according to the Times:

> Congress should put the arms sales on hold and President Obama should quietly inform Riyadh that the United States will withdraw crucial assistance if the Saudis do not stop targeting civilians and agree to negotiate peace.

That can't happen in the real world, where the president and the Saudis all know they are war criminals and are, like Macbeth, so steeped in blood "that should I wade no more, /Returning were as tedious as go o'er."

There is no reason to expect any good to come to Yemen until a whole lot more Americans face the reality of their country's support for a genocidal war of aggression. When enough Americans recognize that, then they will have to do a lot more about it than stop selling tanks to the aggressors. Until then the US-sponsored atrocity of ethnic cleansing in a poverty-stricken country that threatens no one will continue unabated.

70.

New US Policy: Kill the Kurds

Syria: what do you do when you don't know what to do?

The continuing incoherence, insanity and ultimate inanity of US policy in and around Syria was highlighted brilliantly, albeit perhaps inadvertently, by Vice President Joe Biden on a state visit to Turkey August 24, when he threatened the most effective fighting force against the Islamic State – the Kurdish militias – with American punishment if they didn't play nice with the Turks, who have spent years supporting the Islamic State (aka ISIS or ISIL), attacking "bad" Kurds in Turkey and Iraq, and who are now attacking "good" Kurds in Syria.

This is not quite as complicated as it is stupid, self-defeating and ultimately deceitful. Let's review the bidding:

- The Turks are a NATO ally whose reliability is an on-and-off thing unrelated to Turkey's actual treaty obligations. The only reason Turkey is part of NATO is because somebody during the Cold War thought it would be a good idea to counter the USSR. With the USSR gone, Turkey is more like a dagger pointed at the heart of NATO, hence the delicate psycho-diplo-military dance NATO nations have had to follow for years, unwilling to cut Turkey loose from NATO, even now, as the Turkish government devolves toward authoritarianism and tighter ties with Russia. Putting it in perspective, Turkey's longstanding, abysmal record on political and human rights is a prime reason that the European Union continues to deny Turkey EU membership. Turkey is not a truly modern state: Turks waged a genocidal campaign against its Armenian citizens a century ago, but it's still against the law to

427

mention that genocide in Turkey (by comparison, Americans can talk freely about the greater American genocide against native peoples, but the progress toward anything like justice is about the same in both countries).

- The Kurds are, for the Turks metaphorically, the 21st century Armenians. The Turks exhibit all the signs of wanting to wage genocidal war on the Kurds but they are held off by multiple factors, not least the current taboo on genocide upheld by NATO and the EU, at least publicly, most of the time. The Kurds are also more militarized than the Armenians ever were, and the Kurdish home territory is a mountainous region that has resisted invaders for centuries. Also the Kurdish region is spread over four countries, so any Turkish genocide of the Kurds would work only if it included attacks on Iran, Iraq and Syria. Each of those countries has also gone through periods of Kurdish repression, so there is always the theoretical possibility of an allied genocide of the Kurds. Right now, the Kurds in Turkey, having survived an attempted Kurdish genocide in the 1930s, continue their low level conflict with the Turkish military, punctuated by periods like the current high level conflict. The Kurds long for their own country, a Kurdistan, and no one else wants them to have that for reasons that are obscure and chronically destabilizing. (A similar situation keeps Afghanistan unstable, where the Pashtun are spread across southern Afghanistan and northwestern Pakistan, and no one wants them to have their own Pashtunistan, either.)

- The US has no vital interests in any of these places. To be clear, the country of the United States has no vital interests. The empire of the United States is a different, undemocratic, self-directed global power structure that sees vital interests in faraway yurts in the most distant desert. That part is not up for debate. But the distinction between the US as a country and the US as an empire helps to understand why the country is pushed into doing things that are stupid, self-destructive and planet-threatening on behalf of the empire. Everybody pretty much knows, even if they won't admit it, that with a nod from the US the Turkish genocide of the Kurds could begin tomorrow, if not sooner. That is the context for the creative tension within which the US VP makes his not so veiled threats.

Biden to Kurds: defend yourselves from the Turks and we will hurt you

August 24, the day that VP Biden was talking tough in Ankara, was the same day the US and Turkey went to war against Syria, although it mostly wasn't reported that way. It was advertised as Turkey finally responding to pleas to fight ISIS. Some called it an "escalation" and some called it an "incursion," echoing official lines in Vietnam, but it was an invasion. As invasions go, it was pretty small potatoes, unreported in detail, but involving probably a few hundred troops with heavy artillery support, and maybe dozens of tanks and aircraft. This was not the first Turkish attack on Syria, but it's the first to seize and hold territory, and to do so with US sanction and air support (even though US special forces are on one of the other sides).

The reality is that Syria is still a sovereign country with a legitimate government still in place. No matter what may be true about the Syrian government or the all-but-uncountable forces arrayed against it and within it, the government remains legitimate, which is why the US and others keep calling for its overthrow. The Syrian government is fighting a very complicated, five-year-old civil war against combatants both Syrian and foreign, some of whom control significant areas of Syria, over which they're fighting with the Syrian government and each other. As civil wars go, this one is particularly messy, not only because Syria was made up all along of different ethnic groups. Since Syrian citizens took up arms against their government, they have enjoyed, if that's the right word, outside support of various kinds and quantities of fighters and materiel from the US, Turkey, Iraq, Saudi Arabia, Iran,

Israel, Lebanon and probably Jordan (which, with Turkey, has sheltered millions of Syrian refugees).

Even so, when the Turkish military with US air support crosses the border and captures the town of Jarabulus (population around 26,000), that's a new thing in this war where other countries mostly use proxies to fight for whatever they think they're fighting for, not their own armed forces. Russia is an exception, fighting for the Syrian government at the invitation of the Syrian government. Every other combatant is an uninvited guest. When the US-backed Turkish military crossed the border and captured Syrian territory, that was an act of undeclared war (like the US war with the Saudis on Yemen).

So who is the target, who is the enemy, and are they the same?

Billed as "a significant escalation of Turkey's role in the fight against the Islamic State" (New York Times), the Turkish attack seems more seriously directed at the Kurdish citizens of Syria who have lived there right along. The Syrian Kurds have proved the most effective fighting force in Syria opposing ISIS, other than the Syrian government. And the Syrian Kurds enjoy the support of several hundred US Special Forces, who now find themselves facing the prospect of being attacked by a NATO army supported by their own country.

Jarabalus is on the west bank of the Euphrates River, which separates it from the Kurdish-dominated region of northern Syria. In 2013, ISIS forces took control of Jarabalus and have held it until recently, with little objection from Turkey. ISIS used this Turkish-Syrian border town as one of several crossing points for fighters and supplies with little interference from the Turks. In 2015, Syrian Kurdish forces threatened to attack ISIS in Jarabalus. Turkey's President Erdogan warned the Kurds that such an attack would be met by the Turkish military, securing ISIS control of the town for another year. Now it's the US vice president warning the Syrian Kurds not to interfere in their own country. Referring to the Kurdish desire to control that part of Syria where they live along the Turkish border, Biden said there would be no Kurdish "corridor" (as fragmentarily reported in the Washington Post):

Period. No separate entity on the border. A united Syria.... We have made it absolutely clear to ... the YPG [Kurdish People's Protection Units in Syria] that ... they must move back across the river.... They cannot, will not, and under no circumstances will get American support if they do not keep that commitment. Period.

The "corridor" referred to by Biden is a hypothetical area that, if controlled by the Kurds, would connect western "Kurdistan" near Aleppo with the rest of "Kurdistan" in northeastern Syria. The Turks are dead set against this, as they consider all Kurds "terrorists." The US has gone along with the Turks calling the Kurds in Turkey terrorists, but the US considers the Kurds in Syria non-terrorists, mostly because of their success fighting ISIS. Part of that Kurdish success was working with US Special Forces to take territory south of Jarabulus (Manbij and surrounding towns). According to Biden, that operation was carried out under a Kurdish promise to go back across the Euphrates and leave the area to Syrian rebels (who had been unable to take it on their own).

Turkey has long been shelling Kurdish communities in Syria, killing civilians with indifference, since Turkey's main objective vis à vis the Kurds is ethnic cleansing. Now, with US blessing, Turkey is using its invasion of Jarabulus to attack Kurdish settlements to the south, killing dozens of civilians in attacks on Jub al-Kousa and al-Amarna. These are not Kurds who should have gone back across the Euphrates, these are Kurds who live in those towns.

There are roughly two million Kurds in Syria and about 30 million in the region. The Kurds have been subjugated and marginalized in all the countries where they live at one time or another. They have long been restive in Turkey. Then the chaos Americans brought to Iraq gave Iraqi Kurds some independence. In Syria, the Kurds earned greater independence by fighting ISIS more effectively than anyone else.

Having invaded Syria to fight ISIS, Turkey is now joining with Syrian rebels (of some sort) to attack Kurds. This is American policy at work. In effect, VP Biden has said: Hey, you Kurds, you're subjugated people, you've been subjugated people long enough to be used to it, and you're gonna stay subjugated, OK, so suck it up.

431

So we leave the Kurds to the mercy of their perennial persecutors, and for what? Some dim hope that Turkey will improve its human rights record and stop torturing prisoners? Or perhaps our wishful thinking is that if we abet the Turks in their darkest whims, maybe they won't cozy up to the Russians so much? Whatever the Obama administration is thinking – assuming there is any thinking going on in this secretive government – American policy seems politically incoherent, as if it's enough to say: This is what the American empire requires, don't ask questions. But it is more than politically incoherent. American policy toward a people yearning to be free is morally repugnant.

71.

US Cluster Bombs Kill Children for Decades in Laos, and Now Yemen

Does anyone think America is accountable for its own actions?

The preposterous ironies of President Obama's unapologetic visit to Laos on September 6 have not yet generated the attention they deserve, but they provide an excellent measure of the self-righteousness of the monstrous continuity of American violence inflicted on the world from Vietnam in the 1950s to Yemen more than sixty years later.

The baldest irony of Laos is that the US spent nine years bombing Laos, at a cost of more than $100 million per week in current dollars (on the order of $45 billion in all), powerfully documented in Mother Jones in 2014. Having tried to bomb Laos back into the stone age and then walked away, now, decades later, as the bombs continue to blow up Laotian civilians, the US president is promising $90 million (the equivalent of less than a week of bombing) over the next three years to help clean up the mess the US made. This promise of more bomb-removal aid was one of the few lines in his speech to elicit applause from his 1,000-person audience, who were likely more aware of the brutal context than most Americans. As the US president described the bombing of Laos, then a neutral country:

> At the time, the US government did not acknowledge America's role. It was a secret war, and for years, the American people did not know. Even now, many Americans are not fully aware of this chapter in our history, and it's important that we remember today.

There are minor ironies in that passage. The US government did not acknowledge bombing Laos then, just as it does not acknowledge now that bombing Laos was a war crime of major magnitude.

The president says it was a secret war, which isn't really true, since the Laotians and the Vietnamese certainly knew, and any American who wanted to know could find out, but now the number of Americans in denial is probably larger. And in saying "it's important that we remember today," isn't it ironic that the president says this in the capitol of a country that has never forgotten, but in the US his voice is as silent about these war crimes as it has been about the war crimes of his predecessor, as well as his own, in the Middle East. That allows for some future president to go to Yemen, for example, and echo President Obama by promising to help clean up the deadly debris from years of US cluster bombs and drone strikes on the poorest country in the region (like Laos in Southeast Asia). The US-supported atrocities in Yemen are only a few years old now but, with no end in sight, could eventually compare to the devastation dropped on Laos. In the US president's words:

> Over nine years – from 1964 to 1973 – the United States dropped more than two million tons of bombs here in Laos – more than we dropped on Germany and Japan combined during all of World War II. It made Laos, per person, the most heavily bombed country in history. As one Laotian said, the "bombs fell like rain." Villages and entire valleys were obliterated. The ancient Plain of Jars was devastated. Countless civilians were killed.

In Laos, the US made a whole country into collateral damage

Laos was doubly victimized by a war in which it had no part. The US bombed Laos with unmerciful futility because Laos was unable to defend its eastern border with North Vietnam, which used the mountainous region with impunity along the Ho Chi Minh Trail that was a supply route to guerrillas in the south. So, when the US president says with Orwellian sanctimoniousness that he acknowledges "the suffering and sacrifices on all sides of that conflict," he's speaking to people who were not on any side of the Vietnamese civil war or the US criminal intervention in that civil war, thereby blaming the victims in Laos. Accepting responsibility for its own actions is not something the United States does. But the US president has still another revision of history to offer:

And from the anguish of war, there came an unlikely bond between our two peoples. Today, the United States is home to many proud Laotian Americans.

A large proportion of those Laotian Americans are from the Hmong tribes that lived in the mountains along the Vietnamese border. US Special Forces (Green Berets) recruited Hmong to help attack the Ho Chi Minh Trail. Once the US lost the war and pulled out of Vietnam, the Hmong were left to fend for themselves like so many local US allies in other war zones (as in South Vietnam, Afghanistan, or Iraq for example). Faced with the communist Pathet Lao takeover of Laos, thousands of Hmong fled, mostly to Thailand and beyond. Laos, the Lao People's Democratic Republic, remains a one-party state with close ties to China.

The US is presently waging another criminal war mercilessly attacking civilians in Yemen, but this time the US is on the side of the one-party state that is the lead aggressor, Saudi Arabia. Few if any American media have made the ironic connections between Laos and Yemen, but the Hong Kong based Asia Times nailed it despite running a half-wrong headline:

US APOLOGIZES TO LAOS OVER CLUSTER BOMBS, THEN SELLS THEM TO POUND YEMEN

The story that followed, by Johns Hopkins Fellow Christina Lin, does not mention the apology that never happened. She reports on President Obama's speech in Laos this way:

Obama said, "Given our history here, I believe that the United States has a moral obligation to help Laos heal." This gesture of trying to make amends for the damage US caused in the past is laudable, especially since Obama is the first US president to visit Laos. However, one wonders how sincere this gesture is, when US turns around and sells the same cluster munitions to Saudi Arabia for a similar bombing campaign of another poor country—Yemen—that is maiming children and will likewise keep the population trapped in dire poverty and devastation for the next several decades.

The assertion, despite its relatively cautious academic prose, is as devastating and undeniable as the hypocrisy and war crimes it describes are palpable. But Lin, like others "concerned" about Yemen, keeps her rhetoric modest to the point of obscuring the truth. She describes the inhumanity of using cluster bombs without mentioning their criminality. She points out that the White House has approved another arms sale to Saudi Arabia for $1.15 billion to benefit US arms makers. She does not say that without US support, weapons and ordnance the Saudi-led war on Yemen could not continue. She does manage to hint at outrage when she notes: "As a token gesture, Secretary Kerry announced a $189 million humanitarian aid for Yemen, a Band-Aid compared to the multi-billion-dollar arms packages used to inflict harm on the very same people." She does not connect this payment to the much smaller amount of conscience-salving money promised to the much smaller, but much more damaged Laos.

Reuters offers example of how to do journalism really, really badly

Whatever its shortcomings, this Asia Times piece is better than any of the non-coverage by most American mainstream media. For serious reporting on Yemen one must go to this or other sources like Dissident Voice. International coverage is generally consistent with the official US-Saudi line that usually alleges the necessity to resist Iranian influence, for which there is precious little evidence. At its worst in "respectable" media, Yemen coverage is like this Reuters filing that begins:

> Egypt will host an international conference in March to coordinate humanitarian aid for Yemen, which has been devastated by a civil war, a minister in Yemen's Saudi-backed government said on Tuesday.

It's bad enough that Reuters leads with a press release by one of the combatants. That's sloppy and dishonest, but common enough, and at least the source is named for the careful reader to identify. It's unconscionable to omit the Saudi role in bombing Yemen on a daily basis, and it's unacceptable to hide that role behind the assertion that Yemen "has been devastated by a civil war," when most of the devastation comes from the US-Saudi criminal war. In this case, Reuters is in the tank for war criminals, which it makes clear in its third deceitful paragraph, which claims: "The conflict pits the Iran-allied Houthis and supporters of former President Ali Abdullah Saleh against President Abd-Rabbu Mansour Hadi, who is supported by an alliance of Arab states led by Saudi Arabia." This neat bit of propagandizing ignores the essential US support that makes the war on Yemen possible, and also omits the reality that half the country or more is currently controlled by the forces of al Qaida and the Islamic State that are fighting each other as well as everyone else. As for that humanitarian aid conference in Egypt six months from now, Reuters reports that Egypt has said nothing about it.

J. Michael Springmann is a former US diplomat who served in Saudi Arabia in 1987-1989, until he was fired in a whistleblower incident. To hear him criticize the US participation in "a war of aggression" against Yemen, one has to go to an Iranian PressTV clip on YouTube (which the Yahoo search engine warns against). In that clip he accurately expresses skepticism about the US "withdrawing" military forces from Saudi Arabia. The incident he described in August involved moving the US-Saudi command and control center for the bombing campaign from Saudi Arabia to Bahrain, which Springmann calls "political theatre."

Opposition to US war on Yemen is tepid, laced with "Moral Idiocy"

A recent piece in Consortium News discusses the century-old psychological term "moral idiocy" in the context of American war-making since 1949. Lawrence Davidson's main point is that the rules of war, in particular the Geneva Conventions, are not widely observed and that there's rarely any penalty for committing war crimes, a term he eschews. He blames this on moral idiocy, the inability of our leaders to understand moral behavior and act on that understanding. He does not use the word "sociopath." And his list of moral idiots contains only Republicans like Nixon, Bush, Cheney and Kissinger. But is Barack Obama with his drone strikes not a moral idiot? Is Hillary Clinton with her Qaddafi killing glee not a moral idiot? Is John Kerry not a moral idiot when he says, as he did in June 2016, "I think the Saudis have expressed in the last weeks their desire to make certain that they're acting responsibly and not endangering others." Davidson doesn't mention Yemen or other current wars. He doesn't even wonder why there is virtually no anti-war movement in America today. He doesn't seem to understand that his anodyne detachment is part of the problem, not least when he concludes: "And, who are those who most often take advantage of this loophole? Ironically, it is the very people who lead our societies and those assigned to defend the culture and enforce the law. Lack of accountability makes for very poor public hygiene."

If Americans want to do something decent for Yemen, then Americans need to hold their own country accountable.

72.

What War Are We Buying with Another $58 Billion for the Military?

"We have to start winning wars again. I have to say, when I was young, in high school and college, everybody used to say we never lost a war. We never lost a war, remember?...

America never lost. And now we never win a war. We never win. And don't fight to win. We don't fight to win. We've either got to win or don't fight at all."

PRESIDENT TRUMP TO THE NATIONAL GOVERNORS ASSOCIATION, FEB. 27, 2017

"Don't fight at all" has a pleasant, fresh ring to it, like any good salesman's con. The President was about to announce a proposed military budget increase of $58 billion, making the world's biggest military budget that much bigger. So he probably wasn't thinking, "Don't fight at all." In fact, almost as soon as he said that, he turned to his frustration with the Middle East after 17 years and a cost of $6 trillion. "That's just unacceptable. And we're nowhere," the President said:

> Actually, if you think about it, we're less than nowhere. The Middle East is far worse than it was 16, 17 years ago. There's not even a contest. So we've spent $6 trillion. We have a hornet's nest. It's a mess like you've never seen before. We're nowhere. So we're going to straighten it out.

The Middle East is a big place, so straightening "it" out could be even more complicated than health care. And the President hasn't proposed a strategic plan that we know of, so how he plans to go about straightening it out is a little murky. Still, we're already at war there, so that's a start. We're at war under a 2001 Authorization to Use Military Force (AUMF), passed then by a mindless and panicked Congress, and

439

left in place ever since by a feckless Congress (Rep. Barbara Lee the lone exception). With his AUMF in place, with the world's largest military, and with virtually no American opposition to war in other places, the President pretty much has carte blanche to wreak havoc as he chooses.

Escalation in Syria is well under way, especially bombing raids

As part of Operation Inherent Resolve, more US troops have been deployed in northwestern Syria (how many is unclear, but the total force is about 500). According to US Centcom, their mission is a "reassurance and deterrence [mission] ... designed to be a visible symbol to other parties there that Manbij has already been fully liberated" from the Islamic State (which held it from January 2014 to August 2016). Manbij is a city that once had a population of 100,000, located roughly midway between Aleppo and the Turkish border. Military forces nearby in the region include Syrian, Russian, Turkish and Kurdish troops, as well as elements of the Islamic State and Syrian rebels. The American role, in cooperation with the Russians at least, is to keep others from interfering in Manbij, which was governed for awhile by a mostly local military council. Now the Kurdish Democratic Union Party (PYD), a leading force of Syrian Kurds, is trying to establish Manbij as a democratic autonomous administration that would, in effect, be part of a de facto Kurdistan in northern Syria. The Turks are adamantly opposed to Kurdish autonomy and would have attacked Manbij but for the US and Russian forces in their way.

US Weapons of Mass Destruction might get wider use

The US Central Command (CENTCOM, based in Tampa, Florida) has recently confirmed what it had previously denied: that the US has used depleted uranium weapons in Syria against the Islamic State. For decades now, the US has been using – and denying that it uses – depleted uranium weapons in Iraq, Afghanistan and other countries in the region. Depleted uranium weapons have long been controversial, and their use is arguably a war crime, since the radioactive impact of the weapons does not discriminate between combatants and civilians and leaves radioactively poisoned areas behind for decades.

Under international law as well as 18 US Code sec 2332c, depleted uranium weapons are considered weapons of mass destruction (WMDs). Use of depleted uranium weapons arguably violates numerous international treaties, including the Geneva Conventions and the Universal Declaration of Human Rights. More than 150 countries have worked to control or ban depleted uranium weapons, an effort always opposed by the US despite the connection between depleted uranium and the poisoning of US troops called Gulf War Syndrome.

Yemen: an undefended target of opportunity for any murderous impulse

The pace of drone strikes by the US on *suspected* terrorists has increased more than fourfold since Trump took office. At the same time, Trump has abandoned personal responsibility for ordering drone strikes, leaving it to others down the chain of command to kill unlucky civilians at will. The US carried out more than 30 drone strikes against Yemen in the first days of March alone. According to the US CENTCOM, the ostensible target was "al-Qaida in the Arabian Peninsula" and the drone strikes "were conducted in partnership with the government of Yemen." The "government of Yemen" is essentially a legal fiction that controls a small portion of the country around Aden and is significantly controlled by Saudi Arabia.

The US CENTCOM characterizes al-Qaida in the Arabian Peninsula as "a local and regional threat" with manpower in the "low thousands." US CENTCOM also says this al-Qaida "has more American blood on its hands" than the Islamic State of Iraq and Syria does, and that it is a "deadly terrorist organization that has proven itself to be very effective in targeting and killing Americans, and they have intent and aspirations to continue doing so, ... This is a dangerous group locally, regionally and transnationally, to include against the United States, the West and our allies." US CENTCOM provides no specific details.

Meanwhile Yemen is on the verge of mass starvation and the US continues to support the Saudi-led blockade of the poorest country in the region.

That's one way to "straighten out" the Middle East.

73.

Gas Attack in Syria, Gorsuch Attack in US

"Assad had an air force, and that air force is the cause of most of the civilian deaths, as we have seen over the years and as we saw again in the last few days. And I really believe that we should have and still should take out his airfields and prevent him from being able to use them to bomb innocent people and drop Sarin gas on them."

HILLARY CLINTON AT THE WOMEN IN THE WORLD SUMMIT APRIL 6, 2017

What happened at dawn in the "rebel-held" town of Khan Sheikhoun in northwest Syria on April 4 remains in dispute, with little reliable evidence to support any version of events. Apparently indisputable is that whatever happened killed perhaps as many as 100 people and caused severe suffering to many more in a community of about 48,000, and that carnage was the result of chemical weapons dispersed by an airstrike. From there the versions of events diverge, usually according to the teller's self-interests. Even the meaning of "rebel-held" is uncertain. As Deutsche Welle reported April 4: "Idlib province, where Khan Sheikhoun is located, is mostly controlled by the Tahrir al-Sham alliance, which is dominated by the Fateh al-Sham Front, formerly known as the al-Qaeda affiliated al-Nusra Front."

Let us stipulate, for the sake of maintaining focus, that the official Western version of the event is correct, and that it occurred very soon after the US government had announced that regime change in Syria was no longer a goal. Both the US secretary of state and the UN ambassador publicly said that it was no longer US policy to remove Syrian president Bashar al Assad as a precondition to a cease-fire. By what logic, then, does the Syrian air force launch a startling and deliberately provocative chemical weapons attack that could not go undetected and would surely push human rights buttons around the world? All but inexplicable, but it is the official version and it seems to be widely accepted with little serious skepticism.

Whatever really happened in Syria, the event has sparked a spasm of political response rooted more in emotion than anything resembling reality. On April 5, for example, President Trump responded ungrammatically, semi-coherently, maudlinly and without any apparent need to know what actually happened:

> It crossed a lot of lines for me. When you kill innocent children, innocent babies, babies, little babies, with a chemical gas that is so lethal—people were shocked to hear what gas it was—that crosses many, many lines, beyond a red line. Many, many lines.

President Trump is not known for having great concern for any babies, much less dead babies killed with US participation in Mosul or all across Yemen (where the US helps starve children as well). But it's nice that he can express the sentiment, however insincerely and unconvincingly. He could have used the opportunity to offer humanitarian aid or to allow more Syrian babies into the US. But, like the good con he is, our Trump moved without a beat to the snide "red line" reference that alludes to President Obama struggling with another Syrian attack. In 2013, Trump pleaded by tweet with the President not to bomb Syria: "President Obama, do not attack Syria. There is no upside and tremendous downside. Save our 'powder' for another (and more important) day!"

The 2013 chemical weapons event in the Ghouta district of Damascus is widely misused these days to prove one point or its opposite, so it's useful to remember what's real about it. More than 1,400 people were killed in a rebel-held area. To this day there is no certainty as to who did it. President Obama indicated he favored a military response, but did not act impulsively. Public opposition (including Trump's) to US military escalation in Syria grew, followed by Congressional opposition when the president sought authorization for the use of military force. Before Congress acted, the Russians brokered a deal under which Syria would give up its chemical weapons under international supervision (the deal did not include chlorine). Within a year a substantial amount of Syria's chemical weapons had been destroyed, with no way to know if everything was gone. There was no inspection regime or other means to prevent Syria from redeveloping chemical weapons. According to the United Nations, the Syrian government, rebel groups and ISIS all have used chemical weapons on multiple occasions since 2014, almost always without provoking international notice.

Likewise, the US has been using chemical weapons in the region for decades, also without provoking much notice. The US chemical weapon of preference is depleted uranium (DU), which lacks the ability to create dramatic video of dying and dead babies, but does manage to leave a radioactive residue that promotes childbirth deformities and cancer in all ages for generations. The US continues to use DU weapons in the region, at least in attacks on ISIS. Tomahawk missiles, a Raytheon profit center, have long been suspected of delivering a DU payload. So President Trump's loosing of 59 Tomahawk missiles on Al Shayrat Airfield was answering a chemical weapons attack with a chemical weapons attack. And an act of war against a sovereign nation. And a war crime.

The US missile attack has received mostly bipartisan support in the US, as well as support from national leaders and cheerleading across much of the mainstream media. "America is back," crowed Charles Krauthammer on Fox. On MSNBC, Brian Williams called the missile launches "beautiful" without apparent irony. Senate Democrat Chuck Schumer called it "the right thing to do" and House Democrat Nancy Pelosi called it "a proportional response." But both hedged on approving further military action without Congressional involvement (not that Democrats can have much influence).

"I believe we have a restoration of American moral clarity," claimed Scott Jennings, former aide to President Bush and Sen. Mitch McConnell: "We now have a president who's willing to act when it's in our best interests and when it's in the best interests of the world, to stop a genocidal mad man, which Bashar Al Assad certainly is."

Today, for Jennings, Assad is a "genocidal madman" in charge of Syria. But what was Syria in 1991 when the Syrian Air Force helped the first President Bush bomb Iraq? And what was Syria around 2006, when it helped the second President Bush outsource torture to Syrian facilities that were happy to do things Americans were too squeamish to do?

Within a week, US policy on Syria shifted 180 degrees away from regime change, only to complete the full 360 to an act of war, all in reaction to an event that had no great military, political, or philosophical importance. The killing at Khan Sheikhoun was an atrocity, with accompanying emotional impact magnified by social media, but far from any sort of serious threat to US national security (despite President Trump's claim to the contrary).

Phyllis Bennis on Democracy NOW! explored the oddness of the moment:

> ... now, suddenly, because of Trump's emotional reaction to the deaths of these particular children... —the hypocrisy, the selective outrage, that this group of children somehow sparks the outrage that didn't exist when children were slaughtered under US bombs in Mosul, when children were killed trying to make the crossing with their parents to a United States that would not accept them, that was slamming a door in their face, and drowning on the beach as a result. You know, this is not about a strategy. This is about a lashing out. It may be tied to concerns about all the political ways that the Trump administration is losing support. That's certainly part of it.

The Tomahawk attack is lethal political kabuki. Did anything really happen? There were media shows of rockets flying. The US warned the Russians who warned the Syrians, so the missiles hit an almost abandoned airfield. How does that send a message of anything but wink-wink, non-nod to anyone? It gets a few people in Congress wound up, but the majority hasn't cared since 2002 when they voted to give the president effectively unlimited war power. The four-minute missile attack was good for days if not weeks of empty media coverage, overwhelming the rest of the news.

The Syria strike took attention away from the Senate changing its rules to elect Supreme Court nominee Neil Gorsuch with 54 votes (the fewest since Clarence Thomas, thanks only to three Democrats). And Syria also distracted attention from the Republican achievement of electing perhaps the first confirmed plagiarist to the Supreme Court. Politico reported on Gorsuch's academic plagiarism, where he borrowed heavily from several authors for his 2006 book and an academic article—without citing their work. In one chapter in "The Future of Assisted Suicide and Euthanasia," Gorsuch lifted entire passages from an Indiana Law Journal article, with minor additions and changes to verb tenses. Syracuse University writing professor Rebecca Moore Howard told Politico, "Each of the individual incidents constitutes a violation of academic ethics. I've never seen a college plagiarism code that this would not be in violation of."

That's probably not the worst to be said about Gorsuch, whose judicial record is as heartless and merciless as a chemical weapons attack. It's not a stretch to imagine that, over twenty or more years on the bench, Gorsuch will be responsible for killing more "helpless men, women and children" (in President Trump's phrase) with a pen than Bashar al Assad can gas. And Gorsuch-style judicial killing is less obvious, messy, or public.

Mission accomplished?

74.

In Afghanistan: America's Longest War Will Never Be Won

"I'm very, very proud of the people. Another—really, another successful job. We're very, very proud of our military. Just like we're proud of the folks in this room, we are so proud of our military. And it was another successful event."

PRESIDENT TRUMP'S ANSWER TO THE QUESTION,
"DID YOU AUTHORIZE THAT BOMB?"

The US war in Afghanistan, by proxy and/or direct intervention, is approaching the end of its fourth decade. And now the US is running short on big bombs to use there that are still smaller than thermonuclear weapons. On April 13, for the first time in combat, the US used its GBU-43B, a Massive Ordnance Air Blast (MOAB) explosive that weighs 21,000 pounds and creates an air blast equivalent of 11 tons of TNT. The aerial fireball effectively sets the air on fire within a one-mile radius, above and below ground, incinerating, burning alive, or suffocating anyone within its reach. Official reports, as in The New York Times, were suitably bland and non-specifically threatening:

> US forces in Afghanistan on Thursday [April 13] struck an Islamic State tunnel complex in eastern Afghanistan with "the mother of all bombs," the largest non-nuclear weapon ever used in combat by the US military, *Pentagon officials said.* [emphasis added]

To hear mainstream media and the Pentagon tell it, this is just war business as usual for the current NATO mission, "Operation Resolute Support." The official line is that the mission of 8,400 US troops there is training and support, not combat (except sometimes fighting terrorists). Just before the big bomb drop, on April 8, a US Army

447

Special Forces officer (Staff Sgt. Mark R. De Alencar, 37) was killed in action when his unit was attacked during anti-ISIS combat operations in Nangarhar Province, along the Pakistan border. That's where the MOAB was dropped (in one of more than 460 US airstrikes in Afghanistan this year). Nangarhar Province has been a difficult to conquer military terrain for at least 2,500 years (Alexander the Great held it for a few years after 331 BC). These days, no one really controls Nangarhar, much less the rest of Afghanistan, certainly not the Afghan government, despite NATO and independent US support. Conventional wisdom at the moment has it that the Taliban is winning, though it's not clear what that might mean. Despite US attention to ISIS forces, real or imagined, ISIS is nowhere close to controlling the country and is at war with the Taliban as well. That reality makes White House Press Secretary Sean Spicer's highlighting of an essentially irrelevant explosion in a relatively remote location somewhat surreal:

> The GBU-43 is a large, powerful and accurately delivered weapon. We targeted a system of tunnels and caves that ISIS fighters used to move around freely, making it easier for them to target US military advisers and Afghan forces in the area. ... The United States took all precautions necessary to prevent civilian casualties and collateral damage as a result of the operation. Any further details, *I would refer you to the Department of Defense on that.* [emphasis added]

Other than the novel notion that one might "move around freely" in caves and tunnels, the press secretary's announcement is so opaque that one wonders if the White House knows what actually happened. This sense is reinforced later in the same press session when a reporter asks: "On the GBU-43 bomb – the first time it's ever been used. Why did you choose this particular location? And would you say that this bomb won't be used again in another flashpoint around the world, like Syria? Like North Korea, for instance?" The question assigns a significance to the bomb that has yet to be demonstrated. But the question's policy points regarding Syria and North Korea are nevertheless germane. Spicer does not even try to address that, but again defers to the Pentagon, as if that's where policy is being made these days.

When the White House and the Pentagon promote "a strike on an Islamic State of Iraq and Syria-Khorasan tunnel complex in Achin district, Nangarhar province, Afghanistan, as part of ongoing efforts to defeat ISIS-K in Afghanistan" they are focusing on a currently minor opponent with a long historical shadow. This is the same region in which the US failed to capture bin Laden before he escaped into Pakistan's tribal region. According to the US, over the past six months or so it has reduced ISIS-K's strength in Achin district from as many as 3,000 fighters to some 600 presently (though it's not clear how many may have tactically withdrawn to Pakistan). The air blast took out another 30-90, according to different reports, and "only" another 10-12 civilians, including four children. The commander of US forces in Afghanistan, Gen. John Nicholson, indicated that there were no reports or evidence of civilian casualties, although US and Afghan forces had withdrawn to a safe distance before the bomb blast. As the Times headlined it April 14:

A GIANT US BOMB STRIKES ISIS CAVES IN AFGHANISTAN

But here's the funny thing about the cave and tunnel complexes in Nangarhar Province: the US helped create them. During 1978-1988, the US, through the CIA, supported the mujahideen opposition to Soviet control and invasion of Afghanistan. Although the US has now used the "mother of all bombs" to attack caves and tunnels built with US support, the US couldn't hope to destroy them because they were built deep into mountains to be largely impervious to aerial attack. Referring to "ISIS caves" is both ahistorical and misleading, since ISIS is merely the current tenant. The US did not use its "bunker buster" bomb, the GBU-57A/B Massive Ordnance Penetrator (MOP), which delivers a larger payload than the MOAB. Nor did the US use any of its somewhat smaller, non-nuclear bunker buster bombs on the bunker-like complex of caves and tunnels.

The MOAB is an anti-personnel weapons, it's designed to annihilate soft targets, especially people. One of its predecessors, named the BLU-82B, or "Daisy Cutter," was used in Vietnam to cleanse suspected Viet Cong areas of most living things for a one-mile diameter. The Daisy

Cutter was also used in Iraq and Afghanistan, before the last one was dropped on a Utah test range in 2008. Its primary use has often been psychological more than strictly military.

The US, in the person of Gen. Nicholson, chose to use the weapon with the media-friendly nickname "mother of all bombs," which of course it isn't at all, though it does serve very well as a good, shiny-object distraction for the media. With an explosive power of 11 tons of TNT, the MOAB is not even as big as the "small" Hiroshima atomic bomb, nicknamed "Little Boy," with its 15 kilotons of explosive power. The "mother of all bombs" is a tiny dwarf next to the US arsenal of nuclear weapons rated by the megaton (1,000 kilotons) of destructive power. The most powerful US nuclear bomb (as distinct from a warhead) is the B83, a "nuclear bunker buster" (or 1.2 million tons, more than 100,000 times the size of the "mother of all bombs").

Nuclear weapons have remained unused in war since 1945, subject to an international taboo that President Trump is eroding, perhaps quite deliberately. Using a nuclear weapon in Afghanistan remains, for now, "unthinkable," as they say. But how close to "thinkable" is it becoming for North Korea? And who decides what's thinkable now, who's doing the thinking? Depending on the time of year, prevailing winds would carry radioactive fallout from an attack on North Korea either to Japan or China. President Trump and the White House provide almost no clarity or guidance to their thinking, as this April 13 shouted press exchange illustrates:

> *Shouted Question:* How about that bomb, sir? Did you authorize that bomb?
>
> *President Trump:* I'm very, very proud of the people. Really another successful job. We're very, very proud of our military. Just like we're proud of the folks in this room, we are so proud of our military, and it was another successful event.
>
> *Reporter:* Did you authorize it?
>
> *Trump:* Everyone knows exactly what happened. So, and, *what I do is I authorize my military.* We have the greatest military in the world, and they have done the job, as usual.

We have given them total authorization, and that's what they're doing, and frankly, that's why they've been so successful lately. Take a look at what's happened over the last eight weeks and compare it with the last eight years. There is a tremendous difference. Tremendous difference.

We have incredible leaders in the military, and incredible military, and we are very proud of them.

Reporter: Does this send a message to North Korea?

Trump: I don't know if this sends a message, it doesn't make any difference if it does or not. North Korea is a problem, the problem will be taken care of.... [emphasis added]

The president went on to suggest vaguely that China will resolve the North Korea problem somehow. But what he has just described is unconstitutional government. The supposed commander-in-chief has confirmed the abdication of civilian control of the US military. If there are any exceptions to the "total authorization," the administration has not made clear what they or, or even if they include nuclear weapons. It's small comfort that this abdication by the president is a bookend to the similar abdication by the Congress on September 14, 2001, in a resolution giving "total authorization" to the president to make war at will. That Congressional action, driven by the panic of 9/11, was the Authorization for Use of Military Force Against Terrorists. It passed both houses without any reflective consideration and with only one vote in opposition – Rep. Barbara Lee, a California Democrat (two cowardly Republican Senators, Larry Craig and Jesse Helms, were "present/not voting"). Barbara Lee has been trying in vain ever since to have the authorization rescinded and to return the country to traditional constitutional order, under which the power to declare war belongs to Congress.

Insofar as the 2001 Authorization for Use of Military Force has contributed to making the US an increasingly militarized, emerging police state, the terrorists are winning, mostly with our help.

75.

Trump Honors Saudi Family Police State as His Government Ideal

"Let me now also extend my deep and heartfelt gratitude to each and every one of the distinguished heads of state who made this journey here today. You greatly honor us with your presence, and I send the warmest regards from my country to yours. I know that our time together will bring many blessings to both your people and mine".

PRESIDENT TRUMP, MAY 21, IN RIYADH, SAUDI ARABIA

Addressing the Sunni Summit, a motley host of countries with little freedom, democracy, justice, or other human rights, President Trump might well have wished he could just begin by saying, "Greetings, my fellow dictators...." The circumstance was not so auspicious for America's would-be strongman. Unlike the autocrats of Egypt and Bahrain, Kuwait and Qatar, Jordan and Saudi Arabia, President Trump's authority remains shaky, his control of the emerging American police state insecure, his future somewhat uncertain. No wonder he was "exhausted" just two days into his first foreign trip as president, the same day his former national security advisor decided to plead the Fifth – Gen. Michael Flynn, the same guy Trump apparently tried to protect from an FBI investigation, chose to refuse to testify before the Senate rather than risk incriminating himself in criminal activity. It's enough for a man to send his daughter out to speak for him, which is what the president did, at an event intended to promote the use of social media for counter-terrorism, a police state activity if there ever was one.

The Trump family must envy the Saudi family business, with its own oil-rich, dissent-free nation, where the preposterously rich royal family is above the law, but the justice system sends unlucky gang rape *victims* to prison, but not before giving them 200 lashes. Saudi treatment of women makes Trump's treatment of Melania look almost polite. In an international situation where saying anything honest is out of the question for any but the most courageous speakers, our American president instead symbolically bows obsequiously and begins by thanking "the magnificent Kingdom of Saudi Arabia for hosting today's summit. I am honored to be received by such gracious hosts. I have always heard about the splendor of your country and the kindness of your citizens, but words do not do justice to the grandeur of this remarkable place and the incredible hospitality you have shown us from the moment we arrived."

The Trump Traveling Carnival's big achievement during its two-day performance in Riyadh was a further grand distortion of an already tortured reality in a region where the only country considered free is Tunisia (Freedom House ranks all the Middle East countries as not free, except for "partly free" Israel and Turkey, which gives you some idea of the low standard for freedom at work). Standing out among the non-stop carny acts of the Trump road show was the president's flat-out commitment of the United States to take sides in the centuries old Islamic civil war. This makes little sense for a "Christian" country, but at least is coming in on the side of the Sunnis, who outnumber the Shi'ites roughly nine to one. The president even got some of the Sunni dictatorships to sign a memorandum of agreement to help fight terrorism, which sounds like it might make sense, but makes no sense at all for all kinds of reasons, including: (1) terrorism has been fueled for decades by the Saudis globally promoting Wahhabism, a radically conservative form of Sunni Islam that considers all other Islamic practitioners heretics; (2) most of the 9/11 hijackers were Saudi nationals, and the Saudis spent untold amounts of money lobbying Washington to keep reports of Saudi involvement secret and to prevent victims from suing the Saudi government; and (3) the Saudis and other Gulf states have played both sides of the terrorist/ISIS wars for years now.

But the US taking the Sunni side in the Islam war makes a kind of perverse sense in that it pits the US against Iran, although there's no decent reason to single out Iran in a region of blood-drenched bad actors among whom Iran is far from the worst. Saudi Arabia's human rights record is significantly worse than Iran's. Iran just elected a new, moderate president with 57% of the vote, a result the minority Trump White House yearns for, even though it seems to have benefitted from more electoral interference than the Iran winner. Another level of senselessness is President Trump's blindly unexamined condemnation of the multinational agreement that virtually all careful observers agree is keeping Iran from developing a nuclear weapon.

Instead of a *rational* approach to a real problem, President Trump used religious incantation to call for a witch hunt, a jihad, a holy war of Arab-American zeal:

> **A better future is only possible if your nations drive out the terrorists and extremists. Drive. Them. Out.**
>
> **DRIVE THEM OUT of your places of worship.**
>
> **DRIVE THEM OUT of your communities.**
>
> **DRIVE THEM OUT of your holy land, and**
>
> **DRIVE THEM OUT OF THIS EARTH.** [emphasis in original]

Instead of something resembling reality, the US is now basing its policy on the mad view of Saudi King Salman, "saying the Arab world had no problems with that country [Iran] until its 1979 revolution brought a theocratic government that quickly turned to terrorism and regional ambitions." Translated: as long as the CIA-supported Shah of Iran ran one of the grimmest police states in the world, the Saudis were happy to exchange torturers with the Iranians. President Trump is dragging the US into bed with thugs and dictators from the Philippines to Russia. And the rationale is that it's all good for fighting terrorism and promoting trade.

Well, the administration did trumpet that $110 billion arms sale to Saudi Arabia, claiming in the process that it was even bigger than the $115 billion arms sale to Saudi Arabia last September. Perhaps the math was thrown off by the glitter of the Saudi gift of $100 million to an

Ivanka Trump pet project for the advancement of women, even though the Saudis suppress their women pretty much as well as anyone, without drawing an audible tut-tut from any Trump. That looks like corruption in plain sight.

The arms deal also looks like continued genocide in less plain sight in Yemen. "Above all, America seeks peace — not war," President Trump told his Saudi audience. Surely, they all knew better. More than two years ago, the US encouraged and supported the Saudi coalition of Gulf states to attack Yemen from the air, to bomb defenseless civilian populations, to use cluster bombs and other anti-personnel weapons, to impose a naval blockade, to create conditions of mass hunger and near-starvation, to turn the country into a virtual prison. This action is an ongoing violation of international law, a war of aggression waged with a nexus of US-sponsored and US-supported war crimes that have been impeachable offenses for the American president every day since March 2015, with no end in sight.

Some in Congress have attempted to block previous weapons sales to the Saudis, and maybe some in Congress will do so again. No one is Congress has yet shown any inclination to confront the reality that we are now on our third consecutive president who is a war criminal.

76.

Saudis Try Hostage-Taking as Diplomacy

Assault on Qatar gets Trump tweet support, but US government demurs

The Persian Gulf nation of Qatar has been held in a weird kind of hostage situation since June 5. That's when Saudi Arabia, the United Arab Emirates (UAE), and a few other countries decided to try to isolate and manipulate Qatar by cutting diplomatic relations and imposing an embargo and something of a blockade. A blockade is, by definition, an act of war, but the blockaders didn't declare war, or send troops, or even make a clear statement of *casus belli* at the time. Qatar has long been a scapegoat for hardliners devoted to "regional stability" on their own terms only.

The hostage-taking, terrorist-supporting nations accused Qatar of supporting terrorists, expelled Qatari diplomats and Qatari citizens, called their own nationals home from Qatar, closed Qatar's only border (with Saudi Arabia), and shut down air and sea routes to the tiny emirate, generally regarded as a near-absolute, hereditary monarchy with little freedom to begin with. Qatar is a small country, smaller than the state of Connecticut. Its military of 11,800 is the second-smallest in the region. Qatar has a population of roughly 2.6 million, only 300,000 of whom are citizens. The rest are foreign workers, a quarter of them from India, with other large contingents from Nepal and Bangladesh. Qatari citizens have the highest per capita income in the world.

This surprise hostage move was duly reported as the "biggest diplomatic crisis in years" in the region, as the Saudis acted with Egypt, Bahrain and the UAE to de-stabilize the region in response to what they

456

claimed was Qatar's de-stabilizing of the region. So what kind of crisis is it when a coalition of dictatorships takes a neighboring state virtual hostage, for no coherently stated reason, and then takes more than two weeks to present any hostage demands (never mind how absurd)?

Let's review the bidding here. The region, from Israel to Afghanistan, is not known for its stability in recent years, decades, centuries, or millennia. The current period of extreme de-stabilization was touched off by "I'm a war president" Bush, backed by a supine Congress (except for Rep. Barbara Lee). The Middle East of the past 14 years is a Republican-led, bipartisan master disaster that has destroyed millions of lives for nothing more apparent than the appearance of American "leadership." But the US has had plenty of help in the worst sense of the word from just about every other country in the region, except possibly Oman, some of the time. Also pitching in to spread the carnage have been several NATO allies, as well as Russia. If that leaves out anyone, don't worry, there's more than enough blood to go around for every official hand and a good many feet.

The governments holding Qatar hostage now are mad because Qatar had the effrontery to offer some support to the democratic elements of the Arab Spring of 2010-2011, when there was some hope to rid the region of the brutal police states that stabilized the region. Only Tunisia has survived. Egypt's present military dictatorship is mad at Qatar for supporting the Muslim Brotherhood in Egypt and elsewhere and sees this hostage taking as a chance for revenge.

Qatar is not exactly a stalwart defender of political freedom and human rights, but judged by its enemies, Qatar looks pretty good. And Qatar is also home to the largest US military base in the region, the Al Udeid Air Base. That air base runs the bombing campaigns in Syria, Iraq, Afghanistan and elsewhere, much to the benefit of the Qatari hostage-takers. Better yet, Qatar is a member of the Gulf Cooperation Council, the other members of which are hostage-takers Saudi Arabia, Bahrain, Kuwait and UAE, as well as Oman. The US air base also runs the bombing campaign in Yemen, where Qatar is allied with its hostage-takers in the illegal, genocidal war that has brought Yemen to the verge of mass starvation. Presumably the aggressors believe that mass death in Yemen will help stabilize the region. The government of Yemen, housed in Saudi Arabia, is also a titular Qatari hostage-taker.

> During my recent trip to the Middle East I stated that there can no longer be funding of Radical Ideology. Leaders pointed to Qatar – look!

@realDonaldTrump tweet, June 6, 2017

With mad tweets like that, the president took credit for the hostage-taking, even as his secretaries of State and Defense would try to distance their country from the mess. Trump's business history provides a clear basis for asking whether his decisions with regard to Qatar are shaped by conflict-of-interest. The Saudis have been doing millions of dollars of business with Trump for decades. The UAE has paid Trump millions of dollars for putting his name on golf courses. Qatar has not done business with Trump.

On June 14, the Defense Dept. signed a $12 billion deal to sell Qatar dozens of F-15 fighter jets. On the same day, Secretary of State Rex Tillerson expressed support for the arms deal approved by his department and said the Saudi-led blockade was creating problems for the US military effort against ISIS. Asked about the apparent gap between his comments and what Trump had been tweeting, Tillerson assuaged Congress, "There is no gap between the President and myself or the State Department on policy, ...there is no daylight between he and I."

On June 20, State Dept. spokesperson Heather Nauert rebuked the Saudi-led hostage takers:

> Now that it has been more than two weeks since the embargo started, we are mystified that the Gulf states have not released to the Qataris, nor to the public, the details about the claims they are making toward Qatar.... The more that time goes by, the more doubt is raised about the actions taken by Saudi Arabia and the UAE.... At this point, we are left with one simple question: were the actions really about their concerns regarding Qatar's alleged support for terrorism? Or were they about the long-simmering grievances between and among the GCC [Gulf Cooperation Council] countries?

Noticeably absent from State's official view was any mention of Iran, even though the hostage-takers complained about Qatar's normal engagement with Iran. President Trump has long joined in demonizing Iran, regardless of the weight of evidence that Saudi Arabia (for example) has long been a greater supporter of terrorists than Iran. Iran, like Russia and Turkey, has called for a peaceful resolution to the hostage-taking.

Turkey has directly supported Qatar diplomatically, militarily, and with supplies, in defiance of the embargo and blockade. Qatar, like Yemen, imports most of its food. Turkey has an army base in Qatar, with about 150 troops who train Qataris. Turkey, like Qatar, supported the Muslim Brotherhood during the Arab Spring and has taken in hundreds of political refugees from Egypt, which arrested and killed unknown numbers of people opposed to the military coup. Among the hostage-takers' demands presented June 23 is that Qatar shut down the Turkish military base.

The demands viewed as a totality amount to a demand that Qatar hand over its sovereignty to Saudi Arabia and its fellow hostage-takers. The hostage-takers want Qatar to shut down Al Jazeera, the Qatari news organization that has been far too truthful about the region. The hostage-takers want Qatar to break off diplomatic relations with Iran, a regionally de-stabilizing act that is consistent with the suspected Saudi desire to bring on a full-scale religious war between Sunni and Shiite Muslims. Iran is Shiite. Qatar and its hostage-takers are all Sunni.

Given the nexus of contradictions and conflicts of interests surrounding the Qatar hostage situation, it's no surprise the German foreign minister has referred to it as the "Trumpification" of regional politics: "Such a Trumpification of relations with one another is particularly dangerous in a region that is already rife with crises."

Update 2019: Apparently this hostage taking was even stranger – and more corrupt – than it seemed at the time. On March 21, 2019, Democracy NOW reported he outline of the story, based on Vicky Ward's new book, "Kushner, Inc.: Greed. Ambition. Corruption. The Extraordinary Story of Jared Kushner and Ivanka Trump."

Before getting to the White House, before being identified as a security risk and getting clearance anyway, Jared Kushner's business had bought 666 Fifth Avenue. That white elephant turned out to be a masterstroke of bad business leaving Kushner facing a $1.4 billion debt that would come due in February 2019. No American bank would lend him money and Kushner was getting desperate. His search for foreign financing led to his forming a close relationship with Saudi Arabia's Prince Muhammad bin Salman (MBS). But MBS didn't help with Kushner's 666 Fifth Avenue problem.

In the spring of 2017, Kushner manipulated President Trump into making his first state visit to Saudi Arabia. Subsequently, independent of the US security establishment, Kushner gave MBS the green light to move against Qatar. MBS's goal was to invade and take over Qatar, US air base and all, it seems.

Instead of leading to an invasion, the blockade quietly and mysteriously faded away. The Qataris were the second-largest investor in a Canadian holding company, Brookfield Asset Management. Brookfield and Kushner Cos talked. The blockade of Qatar slowly relaxed. Brookfield reportedly paid Kushner Cos $1,3 billion for a 99-year lease of 666 Fifth Avenue. Brookfield paid the $1.3 billion for the lease up front. The Kushner debt was wiped out. Terms of the deal were not revealed. Congress is investigating.

77.

North Korea Does Not Threaten World Peace, the US Does

Petulant leadership risks war to what end?

President Donald Trump is 71 and Supreme Leader Kim Jong Un is 27, but if they ever met, would there be a grown-up in the room?

One of them knows full well that North Korea is not a threat to world peace and is not even a serious threat to South Korea. The one who knows that is not Donald Trump. Or if he does know it, he's choosing to inflate the North Korean "threat" even more than some of his predecessors.

But wait, didn't North Korea just fire a missile in the general direction of the United States? Yes indeed, and like every other North Korean missile (except the ones that blew up on launch), it hit smack dab in the Sea of Japan, unpleasantly for aquatic life but a danger to no one else. This is, after all, exactly what the US does periodically to the Pacific Ocean from California's Vandenberg Air Force Base, generally causing yawns around the world.

Deputy Defense Secretary Robert Work witnessed just such a US test (the 15th or so in five years) in February 2016, after telling reporters the purpose was to demonstrate an effective US nuclear arsenal to Russia, China and North Korea:

> That's exactly why we do this. We and the Russians and the Chinese routinely do test shots to prove that the operational missiles that we have are reliable. And that is a signal ... that we are prepared to use nuclear weapons in defense of our country if necessary.

Not only is that perspective less than comforting, it includes a major tell. For reasons that may be obvious but unspoken, North Korea

461

is not allowed to do what the US, Russia and China do. That's the price of being a member of the US-determined Axis of Evil. That may be a stupid foreign policy position (Exhibit A: Iraq), but it's American stupidity, not Korean stupidity. The North Koreans are well aware that they do not have "operational missiles that ... are reliable."

Do as US says, not as US does

US-imposed rules forbid other countries like North Korea or Iran from following rational patterns of self-defense, even in the face of overt US threats. And when North Korea ignores US rules and hits the ocean with another rocket, the US ratchets up the hysteria as if the North Korean launch were a hostile act while the Vandenberg launches are only benign peace-keeping splashes. The US framing of the world is clearly nuts, but we're so used to it we hardly notice anymore.

Not only does North Korea pose no serious threat now, its hypothetical future threat is largely imaginary. Whatever military might North Korea has is unlikely to be used outside its own country unless the US or someone else attacks it first. That might well lead to all hell breaking loose, but it's the only thing that will as far as North Korea is concerned. Washington is baffled: What doesn't North Korea understand about its duty to do what the US tells it to do?

Fear-mongering over North Korea hasn't worked — ever

Assessed objectively, North Korea's missile tests demonstrate a missile program proceeding haltingly, with frequent failures as well as "terrifying" successes. What terrified Washington about the July 3 North Korean missile launch is the presently imaginary threat that the Independence Day ICBM prototype could deliver a nuclear warhead to the United States. It can't. That's a pure future threat, if it's a threat at all. Capturing the widely proclaimed fear with merely modest hype, Business Insider led its report on the new North Korean missile with this: "North Korea claims that it has launched its first intercontinental ballistic missile, or ICBM, which experts say could have the ability to reach Alaska." (Reuters upped the ante, reporting that "some experts believe [the missile] has the range to reach Alaska and Hawaii and perhaps the US Pacific Northwest." As with other reports, these experts go unnamed and unchallenged.)

Unpack all that and what do you have? A North Korean claim, inflated by anonymous experts, selling a worst-case scenario. The North Koreans also claimed that the missile could hit any location on the planet. So, nobody's even trying to tell the truth here. The missile actually went about 580 miles, which isn't even close to qualifying as an ICBM. The nearest point in Alaska (not target, just rocks) is about 3,000 miles away. Any point on the planet is 12,000 miles away, give or take a few thousand.

But the North Koreans have nuclear weapons. Yes, they do, maybe even 20 of them, all smaller than the one the US dropped on Hiroshima. At this point there's no evidence North Korea can deliver its nuclear weapons anywhere by any technology much more advanced than donkey cart. By comparison, the US nuclear arsenal, which was once over 31,000 warheads, is now down to 4,000, with about 1,900 methods of delivery to anywhere on the planet, and almost all those warheads are many times more powerful than the Hiroshima bomb. For all that some worry about aging nuclear weapons, the US is not even close to being an inviting target to attack with impunity.

Not to minimize nuclear weapons of any sort, but seriously, some sense of proportion is expected of mature leadership. Chicken Little cluckings of impending doom is not mature leadership.

Isn't 64 years long enough to get a peace treaty?

The Korean War began June 27, 1950, when North Korea invaded the south. The armistice was signed July 27, 1953, ending hostilities, but not the war. There is a cease-fire but no peace treaty. The US entered the war under UN auspices. Congress never declared war but supported the war with appropriations. Currently, some in Congress are seeking legislation to prevent the president from taking any military action against North Korea without explicit permission from Congress. That hardly seems to matter.

The new president of South Korea wants to negotiate with North Korea, but that hardly seems to matter either. South Korea engaged in perennial massive war games with the US that North Korea deems threatening, as would any neighboring country facing the same reality. Worse, the US has introduced anti-missile weapons into South Korea without telling the South Korean president.

And President Trump publicly blames China for not bringing North Korea to heel, as if China had either that responsibility or ability. China has increased trade with North Korea by a reported 40 percent, which should be a stabilizing factor, especially over the long term. But the US is demanding short-term results.

What could the world community do to reverse this growing threat, real or imagined, from North Korea? It would help to allow North Korea to feel safe and unthreatened, maybe even as safe and unthreatened as Vermont. That, as Korea expert Christine Ahn argued on Democracy NOW, would require President Trump to do what he claims to be good at: negotiating, making a deal. Something very like this view was formally articulated to President Trump in a June 28 letter from such policy experts as former secretary of state George Schultz, former defense secretary William Perry and former senator Richard Lugar:

> As experts with decades of military, political, and technical involvement with North Korean issues, we strongly urge your administration to begin discussions with North Korea…. Talking is not a reward or a concession to Pyongyang and should not be construed as signaling acceptance of a nuclear-armed North Korea. *It is a necessary step to establishing communication to avoid a nuclear catastrophe.* The key danger today is not that North Korea would launch a surprise nuclear attack. Kim Jong Un is not irrational and highly values preserving his regime. Instead *the primary danger is a miscalculation or mistake that could lead to war.* [emphasis added]

A more colloquial way of saying much the same thing might be that you don't control a bratty child by burning down the house, unless you're another bratty child yourself, and you don't really care all that much about the house.

78.

Biological Warfare: US & Saudis Use Cholera to Kill Yemenis

"Chemical/biological warfare is the term used to describe the use of chemical or biological agents as weapons to injure or kill humans, livestock, or plants. Chemical weapons are devices that use chemicals to inflict death or injury; biological weapons use pathogens or organisms that cause disease. Pathogens include bacteria, viruses, fungi, and toxins (poisons produced by animals or plants)."

LIBRARY OF CONGRESS, SCIENCE REFERENCE SERVICES

Since March 2015, the US has supported Saudi Arabia and its allies in their criminal war of aggression against Yemen, committing daily war crimes, especially against civilians, who are now suffering a cholera epidemic with more than 400,000 victims. Cholera is caused by the bacteria Vibrio cholera and has been weaponized by the US, Japan (in World War II), South Africa (under apartheid), Iraq (under Saddam) and other states. To be most effective, cholera must be spread through water supplies. That's what's happening in Yemen now. More than two years of bombing has largely destroyed Yemen's infrastructure, water and sewage systems are destroyed, hospitals and clinics are destroyed, and the population of about 25 million has almost no protection against the spread of cholera. The UN says Yemen's cholera epidemic is "the largest ever recorded in any country in a single year since records began."

This may not be literal biological warfare, but it is certainly biological warfare by other means. This is biological warfare in reality, if not in law. This is biological warfare in one of the world's poorest countries, supported across two American administrations, with no

465

sign of letting up. US slaughter of civilians has been ratcheting up in recent months, not only in Afghanistan but in places like Iraq (Mosul) and Syria (Raqqa). This is what empires do, especially as their authority begins to wane.

And in Yemen, the US continues to support and participate in this panoply of criminal acts with little objection from Congress, most news media, or the general public. Few seem to care about the deliberate spread of a toxin that affects mostly children and that "causes a person's intestines to create massive amounts of fluid that then produces thin, grayish brown diarrhea." Where treatment is unavailable or impossible, cholera can be lethal in a matter of days. As a NOVA program on bioterror put it, "because cholera is readily treated with proper medical attention, it is less likely to be used as an agent of terror in the United States." And since rehydration is essential to recovery, cholera is most effectively deployed in a place like Yemen where the water and sewage systems have been bombed into a state of high lethality.

There are laws against all this, not that it matters much...

At present, 124 nations are member states of the International Criminal Court (ICC), established by international treaty (the Rome Statute) to have jurisdiction over the international crimes of aggression, genocide, crimes against humanity and war crimes. The United States is not among the member states, having signed the original treaty and then withdrawn its signature. Sudan, Israel and Russia also signed the original treaty, then withdrew. Yemen voted in 2007 to ratify the treaty, then re-voted to retract ratification. There are 41 other countries, including India, Pakistan, Turkey and China, that have rejected the treaty.

The US did not sign the war crimes treaty until December 31, 2000, when President Clinton was a lame duck who had not asked the Senate to ratify the treaty. On May 6, 2002, John R. Bolton, the Bush administration's Under Secretary of State for Arms Control and International Security, communicated the US position to the UN. Here is the full text of the letter to UN Secretary General Kofi Annan:

This is to inform you, in connection with the Rome Statute of the International Criminal Court adopted on July 17, 1998, that the United States does not intend to become a party to the treaty. Accordingly, the United States has no legal obligations arising from its signature on December 31, 2000. The United States requests that its intention not to become a party, as expressed in this letter, be reflected in the depositary's status lists relating to this treaty.

There was a time when the US, lacking "legal obligations" not to commit war crimes, might still have felt some moral obligation not to do so (as well as the capacity to overcome it, for example, in Hiroshima and Nagasaki). Now our national interests, usually undefined, put us in the company of thuggish police states like Saudi Arabia, Egypt, the United Arab Emirates, Bahrain and Kuwait in their unprovoked, savagely genocidal assault on a defenseless Yemeni population whose Houthi minority had the effrontery to want to be left alone and was willing to fight for that right.

There was a time, before there was a United States, that this country fought for the same right. We've long since become a country that doesn't want to leave anyone else alone. Now we have a president who demands complete personal loyalty, and who's more than happy to molest anyone who even appears to fall short, which happens to include the majority of Americans. This can't end well.

79.

Megadeaths From America – Yemen Is the Worst Case Among Many

"Let me be clear: The use of starvation as a weapon of war is a war crime."

UN SECRETARY GENERAL BAN KI-MOON, JANUARY 15, 2016,
WARNING THE WARRING PARTIES IN SYRIA

"People are dying; children are suffering not as a result of an accident of war, but as the consequence of an intentional tactic – surrender or starve. And that tactic is directly contrary to the law of war."

U.S. SECRETARY OF STATE JOHN KERRY, FEBRUARY 1, 2016,
DENOUNCING ATROCITIES IN SYRIA

As Americans get ready for Thanksgiving 2017 over-eating, their government is on the verge of successfully starving millions of Yemenis to death by siege warfare. The US naval blockade of Yemen has been unrelenting since March 2015. The US Navy is an essential element of this perpetual war crime, this endless assault on a civilian population of about 25 million. This is the kind of collective punishment of innocents that we once put Nazis on trial for at Nuremberg. The US Department of Defense Law of War Manual, however, advises (section 5.20.1, page 315) that: "Starvation is a legitimate method of warfare." So now the US is a blithe mass-murdering state with impunity, qualities hardly ever mentioned in the world's freest media (with one remarkable exception in Democracy NOW, where coverage of Yemen has been excellent at least since 2009).

Well, never mind, at least Taylor Swift's reputation is soaring, and everyone gets to throw figurative rocks at Roy Moore, Harvey Weinstein, Kevin Spacey and other serial predators. Predator is also the name of one of the US drones that the US President sends to assassinate people who may or may not have done anything wrong, but who showed up at the wrong time on the wrong list, and what more due process do un-white foreign people deserve anyway? You don't hear Congress complaining, do you? Or mainstream media? Or the courts? This is beyond bipartisan thrill killing, this is national consensual mass murder.

OK, to be fair, there has been some tepid, insincere, sporadic objection to wiping out millions of innocent people. Why, just as recently as October 10, The New York Times ran an op-ed article – NOT an editorial – that began with a fair summary of the carnage being visited on Yemen by the US and its allies:

> Imagine that the entire population of Washington State — 7.3 million people — were on the brink of starvation, with the port city of Seattle under a naval and aerial blockade, leaving it unable to receive and distribute countless tons of food and aid that sit waiting offshore. This nightmare scenario is akin to the obscene reality occurring in the Middle East's poorest country, Yemen, at the hands of the region's richest, Saudi Arabia, with unyielding United States military support that Congress has not authorized and that therefore violates the Constitution.

The headline on this op-ed piece is "Stop the Unconstitutional War in Yemen," which is something of a deception since the war is truly criminal by any standard of international law and its "unconstitutionality" is but one aspect of its overall criminality. Like the Times, the authors of the op-ed have yet to face the raw criminality of the aggressive war on Yemen. The authors are three members of Congress, two Democrats, Ro Khanna of California and Mark Pocan of Wisconsin, together with a rare Republican of some integrity, Walter Jones of North Carolina. But they do not call out the gross criminality of American siege warfare against Yemen, they come hat in hand arguing that the war is unconstitutional because Congress hasn't approved it formally. Congress has approved it with silence. No party leadership on either side has joined with these three in their gentle effort to "Stop the war." These three Congress members, with Republican Thomas

Massie, were the original sponsors of the House resolution introduced September 27, as a hint "to remove United States Armed Forces from unauthorized hostilities in the Republic of Yemen." The resolution has so far gathered an additional 42 co-sponsors (one more Republican) from the House's 435 members. One measure of where we are as a country is that something as bland and incomplete as this resolution is seen somehow as a radical act that gets little support in Congress or coverage in the media, where the forced starvation of millions of people is not a big issue.

Yemen is a nation under siege from the air with daily bombings. The Saudis and their allies control the air over Yemen, which has almost no air force and almost no air defenses. Nothing flies in or out of Yemen without Saudi permission, which is rarely given, even for food or medical supplies. The Saudi air force could not function without American support. US military forces select targets, provide intelligence, re-fuel Saudi jets in mid-air and repair them on the ground. Every bomb that falls on Yemen has American fingerprints on it, especially the cluster bombs (another war crime) made in America.

Yemen is a nation under siege from the water, where the US Navy enforces a blockade not only of food, medicine, and other humanitarian relief coming in. The US Navy also turns back Yemenis trying to flee, essentially reducing their choices to risking drowning or starvation. And thanks to the effectiveness of the blockades, there is a massive risk of cholera in Yemen as well, as the US and its allies deliberately wage biological warfare.

Yemen is a nation under siege on the ground. The Saudis control Yemen's northern border, which has been under dispute between the two countries for decades. Nothing crosses the border into Yemen without Saudi permission, mostly granted to artillery fire. Little effectual return fire comes from Yemen. Yemen's eastern border is with Oman, which is a friendly state. In between Oman and Yemeni population centers in the west, the territory is mostly controlled by al Qaeda and ISIS, with the Saudi-backed puppet regime tucked in around Aden. All of those forces oppose the Houthis in control of the northwest, which has been their homeland for centuries. Just to be clear: the US is deliberately starving a population that is fighting al Qaeda and Isis.

With its recent governmental purges, Saudi Arabia maybe has become the second most dangerous nation in the world. Not to worry, the USA is still Number One. But the US/Saudi axis can hardly be much better news for the region than it is for Yemen.

On November 8, the United Nations and some twenty international relief agencies issued a statement of alarm at and opposition to the US/Saudi-enforced siege on Yemen. The human cost of two and a half years of US/Saudi aggression is already unforgivably punishing and cruel. Now the US/Saudi siege threatens unprecedented catastrophe:

> There are over 20 million people in need of humanitarian assistance; seven million of them are facing famine-like conditions and rely completely on food aid to survive. In six weeks, the food supplies to feed them will be exhausted. Over 2.2 million children are malnourished, of those, 385,000 children suffer from severe malnutrition and require therapeutic treatment to stay alive. Due to limited funding, humanitarian agencies are only able to target one third of the population (seven million) ... outbreaks of communicable diseases such as polio and measles are to be expected with fatal consequences, particularly for children under five years of age and those already suffering from malnutrition ... the threat of famine and the spread of cholera ... deadly consequences to an entire population suffering from a conflict that it is not of their own making.

Also on November 8, the day of the statement of alarm, UN Emergency Relief Coordinator Mark Lowcock briefed the UN Security Council on the crisis in Yemen. The briefing was secret, on the request of Sweden. After the briefing, Lowcock met with reporters. He warned that, unless there is a significant, massive humanitarian response soon:

> There will be a famine in Yemen. It will not be like the famine that we saw in South Sudan earlier in the year where tens of thousands of people were affected. It will not be like the famine which cost 250,000 people their lives in Somalia in 2011. It will be the largest famine the world has seen for many decades, with millions of victims.

The aggression against Yemen has been a nexus of war crimes from the beginning, when it was sanctioned by the Obama administration to appease Saudi peevishness over international peacemaking with Iran on nuclear development. For almost three years, Yemen has been a holocaust-in-the-making, with this difference: turning most of the country into a death camp, with America's blessing and collusion. Republicans will choose to confirm 300 unqualified judges before they'll choose to intervene in one criminal war, and mostly Democrats will not seriously object to either choice.

If the United States doesn't kill you, it's perfectly happy to let you die (what health care?). The question – with hope embedded – is whether most Americans support the legal reign of terror that is Pax Americana. Given US treatment of Americans from Ferguson to Flint to Standing Rock to Puerto Rico, the prospect is grim.

80.

US Hysteria Blooms in Wake of North Korean Missile Splashdown

Suppose an opportunity for peace arrived – could the US see it?

The most dangerous thing about the North Korean missile launch is the reaction of the unprincipled, under-informed, white identity extremist sitting in the Oval Office. If there's a nuclear war coming out of this manufactured "crisis," the buck will have stopped with him. Not that President Trump doesn't have other fools egging him on to risk global chaos and destruction in response to an imaginary, inflated threat from an impoverished nation of 25 million people. Sadly, this is not a surprising development after more than sixty years of aggressive US behavior toward North Korea.

But first, what about that November 29 missile launch, widely and dishonestly played as showing that that North Korea could hit any point in the US, even Washington or Mar-a-Lago? That meme is a speculative fear-tactic. In the fine print, none of the experts say it's real, not even hawkish defense secretary General Jim Mattis, one of the last supposed grown-ups in Trumplandia. The North Korean missile went higher – roughly 2,800 miles – than any previous North Korean missile, but it didn't go very far, about 600 miles, landing in the ocean short of Japan.

Based on this scant information, mostly provided by the North Korean government, experts like David Wright of the Union of Concerned Scientists extrapolated the missile's potential range from the actual 600 miles to an estimated 8,000 miles. This is not a scientific measurement, but a speculative conjecture based on science as well as the unknown assumptions that the tested missile was carrying an

473

actual warhead. Wright allowed for the possibility that the missile's high performance was because it carried a dummy warhead of almost inconsequential weight. Wright concluded, according the New York Times, that "the distance traveled, while impressive, does not necessarily translate into a working intercontinental ballistic missile that could deliver a thermonuclear warhead." That's something of a non-threat threat lurking in a hypothetical future. For General Mattis, the projected possible threat, free of historical or strategic context, was all too real in his hyperbolic projection:

> The bottom line is, it's a continued effort to build a threat — a ballistic missile threat that endangers world peace, regional peace, and certainly, the United States.

This isn't General Mattis prematurely overreacting to just one unevaluated missile test. General Mattis engages in the standard military operating procedure of threat-inflation on a regular basis, which does not distinguish him from two generations of other official military and executive branch fearmongers scaring us with apparent North Korean intentions, even while driving those intentions with real, constant American threatening. As General Mattis put it in late October:

> North Korea has accelerated the threat that it poses to its neighbors and the world through its illegal and unnecessary missile and nuclear weapons programs.... I cannot imagine a condition under which the United States would accept North Korea as a nuclear power....

He said, "unnecessary." He must know that's absurdly Orwellian. The United States and North Korea have been in a state of war since 1950. The armistice of 1953 suspended the fighting but did not end the war. From then until now, North Korean sovereignty has been irrelevant to American leaders. So here we are, with North Korea already a nuclear power and the US refusing to accept a new reality, never mind US responsibility for creating that new reality through decades of open bellicosity. The Times called the most recent missile launch "a bold act of defiance against President Trump," which is a laughably unaware acceptance of the American assumption that it has any right to any authority over another sovereign state.

American denial of the North Korean perspective is the driving force in this largely artificial confrontation. North Korea has already been overrun by American forces once in living memory, in a war with largely unexamined American atrocities (we've propagandized their atrocities to a fare thee well). Overrun by Americans, only to be counter-overrun by the Chinese, North Koreans might well want to be left alone. The US and its allies, especially South Korea and Japan, have maintained unrelenting hostility to North Korea, whose best friend is an unreliable China. Why wouldn't North Korea want a nuclear deterrent? Deterrence is the American justification for a nuclear arsenal that dwarfs all others but Russia's.

But American leaders insist on calling North Korea a threat. North Korea was a threat in 1950. and that turned out very badly for them. Today, North Korea is a credible threat to no one except perhaps its own people. A North Korean attack on anyone would be met with overwhelming force up to and possibly including nuclear obliteration. North Korea is in check, and any honest observer knows that. Some even say so. Defense Dept. spokesman Colonel Robert Manning, in striking contrast to his shrill boss General Mattis, said:

> We are working with our interagency partners on a more detailed assessment of the launch.... the missile launch from North Korea did not pose a threat to North America, our territories or our allies.... We remain prepared to defend ourselves and our allies from any attack or provocation.

That is so rational and basic that it should hardly need saying. We don't live in a time when basic and rational get much attention. American arrogance and paranoia toward North Korea are longstanding, untreated pathologies that continue to worsen. As our Trump tweeted in early October, with his usual fact-free, threatening bombast:

> Presidents and their administrations have been talking to North Korea for 25 years, agreements made and massive amounts of money paid ... hasn't worked, agreements violated before the ink was dry, makings fools of US negotiators. Sorry, but only one thing will work!

Our Trump coyly avoided saying what he thought that one thing was, but his Secretary of State still says, "Diplomatic options remain viable and open for now." Not that anyone pays much attention to Rex Tillerson these days as he guts the State Dept. of effective, experienced personnel. Much greater play goes to the crazy ranters who are already blaming the victims if it turns out we have to attack them (sounds like domestic violence, doesn't it?). Case in point is Lindsey Graham, who plays a deranged Republican Senator from South Carolina, saying:

> If we have to go to war to stop this, we will. If there's a war with North Korea it will be because North Korea brought it on itself, and we're headed to a war if things don't change.

Or as the battering husband puts it: "She just wouldn't listen to me!" Echoing the blame-the-victim mantra, UN Ambassador Nikki Haley (famous for saying "women don't care about contraception") told the UN Security Council the missile launch was an act of "aggression" with serious potential consequences:

> ... make no mistake the North Korean regime will be utterly destroyed.... The dictator of North Korea made a decision yesterday that brings us closer to war, not farther from it. We have never sought war with North Korea and still today we do not seek it.

But they just won't listen!

In North Korea, after the missile launch, leader Kim Jong Un said that his country has "finally realized the great historic cause of completing the state nuclear force." A nuclear deterrent, in other words. This may or may not be entirely true. But they may or may not be beside the point. As writers in Japan Times note, this missile launch, and its accompanying official statements could be an olive branch:

> [North Korea] then said its pursuit of the "strategic weapon" had been intended to "defend the sovereignty and territorial integrity of the country from the US imperialists' nuclear blackmail policy," and emphasized that it would "not pose any threat to any country and region as long as the interests of the DPRK (the Democratic People's Republic of Korea) are not infringed upon.... The DPRK will make every possible effort to serve the noble purpose of defending peace and stability of the world."

476

Does it matter whether this is true as long as everyone acts like it's true? Our Trump has a random relationship with truth, and his spokeswoman says it doesn't matter whether his racist tweets are real or fake news. So, what we have here is an excellent opportunity for the mocker-in-chief of his Asian allies to seize the opportunity to make white identity extremism great again and— oh, never mind.

81.

Trump Endorses Criminal Conspiracy to Crush Honduras Vote

Once again, the US saves a puppet dictator from his own people

Honduras is bleeding now, and Honduran blood runs from the hands of President Trump and Gen. John Kelly, long a vicar of American violence enforcing the imperial will. In their vicariously murderous way, Trump and Kelly are carrying on with a century-old, bipartisan American tradition of oppression and human disregard in the classic "banana republic" that the US Marines once kept safe for United Fruit. Trump and Kelly now are merely defending the corrupt military coup of 2009, sanctioned by President Obama and Secretary of State Hillary Clinton (who was OK with death squads). Obama and Clinton are the godparents of the present Honduran thugocracy and its unchecked death squads that together provoked the massive emigration of Hondurans seeking safety here, thereby helping to elect Trump in 2016.

Reliable reporting on the current outpouring of protest in Honduras is hard to come by, but it's rooted in the Honduran presidential election in November. The incumbent Honduran president, Juan Orlando Hernandez, 49, of the National Party, is a direct beneficiary of the 2009 coup, which elevated him to the leadership of the National Congress. He is a businessman (coffee, hotels, media) with a master's degree in public administration from the State University of New York. He was first elected president in 2013 (with 34% of the vote) in a corrupt process during which at least 18 opposition-party candidates and supporters were murdered. Additionally, charges of fraudulent voting and corrupt campaign contributions were ignored by authorities, to the benefit of Hernandez. Once he was president, he was barred by the Honduran constitution from running for a second term. This obstacle was removed by the Supreme Electoral Tribunal, which is controlled by the president. Hernandez has a long personal relationship with Gen. John Kelly. Going into the election, Hernandez was considered the favorite.

Opposing Hernandez was democratic socialist Salvador Nasralla, 64, of the Libre-PINU Party (the Opposition Alliance against Dictatorship), the party of the coup-deposed President Manuel Zelaya. Nasralla graduated with honors from the Catholic University of Chile as a civil engineer and later earned an NBA. He was CEO of Pepsi Honduras before starting a television career in 1981. Since then, he has been harshly critical of chronic corruption in Honduras, founding the Anti-Corruption Party in 2013, when he won 13% of the vote for president. He was not expected to win the 2017 election.

As it stands now, the winner may never be known, but more than likely Nasralla won the popular vote. Among election monitors, the Organization of American States (OAS) and the European Union (EU) have rejected the results, while the US Embassy has said everything is hunky-dory. Meanwhile, the US and other anti-democratic forces are on the verge of installing their puppet Hernandez as the re-elected president of Honduras. The timeline of this stolen election illustrates just how secure the dictatorship and its allies in the US feel in their brazen criminality:

November 26. Apparently, something like 57% of Hondurans vote for a field of nine candidates. The Supreme Electoral Council, controlled by Hernandez, closes the polls an hour earlier than in the past, likely suppressing the vote. At first the Electoral Council releases vote totals as they come in, as is customary. Then, with Nasralla surprisingly leading, the Electoral Council suspends the count for seven hours.

November 27. With 57% of the votes counted, the Election Council reports that Nasralla is leading Hernandez by 5 points, roughly 45-40. These totals apparently represent mostly voting machine votes and not paper ballots. The Election Council then suspends the count again, for another 36 hours, telling the public there might be no final results until November 30.

November 28. US Secretary of State Rex Tillerson signs off on State Dept. certification that Honduras has been improving on fighting corruption and supporting human rights, clearing the way for $644 million in US aid.

November 28-29. The Election Council issues sporadic new totals that claim Nasralla's percentage is shrinking and that Hernandez is pulling ahead.

November 29. Nasralla and Hernandez sign "a document vowing to respect the final result after every disputed vote had been scrutinized," a circumstance unlikely ever to be realized. When the Election Council again halts the count, claiming a computer glitch, Nasralla repudiates the agreement and urges his supporters to protest: "They take us for idiots and want to steal our victory." Nasralla supporters in the thousands take to the streets across the country.

November 30. Nasralla accuses the Election Council of election fraud. The Election Council reports 94% of votes are counted, with Hernandez ahead by less than 2 points (42.92 to 41.42%). Nasralla supporters are in the streets. Riot police fired tear gas, pepper spray, and live ammunition at protestors.

December 1. The Election Council announces there will be no further results till all votes are counted. Hernandez declares state of emergency and announces a 6 p.m. to 6 a.m. curfew.

December 2. The Honduran National Roundtable for Human Rights denounces government action as state terrorism against civilians. The group also accuses the government of imposing the curfew as an act of repression to protect the electoral fraud it was perpetrating. By now government forces have killed at least 7 people and injured a score. The second night of curfew sees thousands of people banging pots and pans in protest (cacerolazos).

Substantial numbers of National Police defy the Hernandez government and refuse to enforce the curfew. A member of the elite Cobra riot police reads from a statement: "Our people are sovereign. We cannot confront and repress their rights."

December 5. US State Dept. announces certification of Honduran improvement on human rights so that Honduras can continue to get US military assistance.

December 6. OAS observers cast doubt on the election results so far.

December 9. Hernandez government lifts state of emergency and curfew. Radio Progreso, an independent community station defending democracy, is attacked and taken off the air. Journalists are arrested.

December 10. Thousands of Hondurans march on US Embassy in Tegucigalpa protesting US interference in election.

December 14. The Honduran Election Council, as required by law, begins reviewing some 125 official objections to the November 26 election, including four motions challenging the presidential election.

December 15. The Election Council has finished a recount of ballot boxes with irregularities but has not declared a winner. Protests continue throughout the country. The death toll reaches 16, with 1,675 arrests.

December 17. The Organization of American States (OAS) denounces the Honduran election and calls for a new election in a statement saying: "Facing the impossibility of determining a winner, the only way possible so that the people of Honduras are the victors is a new call for general elections."

Supporting the OAS conclusions is a detailed technical report on the election by Georgetown University professor Dr. Irfan Nooruddin who writes in conclusion: "On the basis of this analysis, I would reject the proposition that the National Party [Hernandez] won the election legitimately."

At the same time, Nasralla has left Honduras to go to Washington to plead his case at the State Dept.

Taking advantage of that opportunity, the Election Council announces that Hernandez has beaten Nasralla by less than two points (42.95 to 41.42%) out of almost 3.5 million votes cast (3,476,419). There are about 6 million voters in the country of 9 million people.

Mexico recognizes Hernandez as winner, an announcement coordinated with the US. Nasralla and his supporters call for the population to keep mobilizing and keep protesting.

December 18. Honduran vice president Ricardo Alvarez rejects OAS (but not US) interference in Honduran affairs:

> This is an autonomous and sovereign country. This is a country that is not going to do what anybody from an international organization tells it to do. I will say it again: The only other election this country will have, the next one, is on the last Sunday of November 2021. There's not another election.

December 20. Three human rights experts (David Kaye, Michel Frost, Edison Lanza) from the United Nations and Inter-American Commission on Human Rights condemn the Hernandez government for the use of lethal force on protestors, and for violating basic human rights to life, free expression, and free assembly. They write:

> We are alarmed by the illegal and excessive use of force to disperse protests, which have resulted in the deaths of at least 12 protesters and left dozens injured. Hundreds of people have also been detained, many of whom have been transferred to military installations where they have been brutally beaten and subjected to torture and other forms of ill-treatment.

December 21. Honduras is one of only eight countries at the UN voting not to denounce the US plan to move its embassy to Jerusalem.

December 22. US Secretary of State Rex Tillerson has the State Dept. issue a statement recognizing Hernandez as winner, adding the absurdly hypocritical caveat that "a significant long-term effort to heal the political divide in the country and enact much-needed electoral reforms should be undertaken."

Congressman Jim McGovern, a Massachusetts Democrat, says the State Dept.'s action left him "angry and disturbed." One of some 50 lawmakers who signed letters urging the US to support the OAS call for a new election in Honduras, McGovern states the obvious: "Very few Hondurans have confidence in the results, and the country remains deeply polarized." McGovern then adds fairy dust: "For the US government to pretend otherwise is the height of blind folly and it will surely harm our influence and undermine our priorities throughout the region." This is real blind folly, unless McGovern or anyone else steps up to do anything about it.

Canada also recognizes Hernandez as the winner.

Nasralla concedes.

Why was the US so concerned about Nasralla? He opposes corruption, violence, law-breaking, dictatorship – are these views now seen as threats to US interests? The US doesn't explain itself. It doesn't have to, it's the US. As reporter Allan Nairn said on Democracy NOW recently:

> And at one point early in December, [acting US ambassador Heide] Fulton and John Creamer, who's a senior State Department official and a former aide to General John Kelly of the White House, met with Nasralla. And he said that the US officials were urging him to stop the protests. The protests were the one popular source of leverage against the electoral fraud, and the US was trying to shut them down—without success—even though Nasralla made a point of saying he wanted to be a friend of the US, he wanted to be an ally of the US He said he wasn't going to touch the military base, he wasn't going to touch the multinationals. He even said he would sign every US extradition order without even reading them....

> So, they decided even Nasralla, who was promising all those things to comply with the US, was not good enough, was not acceptable to them, because he would represent a voting out of the coup regime. The 2009 coup, which had backing from the Pentagon and from Secretary of State Hillary Clinton at the time, put in a series of presidents, of whom Hernández is the latest, who back the oligarchy, give the US a blank check to do whatever they want militarily, and who have very little popular support.

Remember that Honduran constitutional ban on a Honduran president being able to run for a second term? The military coup in 2009 claimed then-president Zelaya was trying to change the constitution. Eight years later, stealing an election in which the Honduran president succeeds himself is justified by changing the constitution. As long as the US puppet wins, principles don't matter any more to Trump and Tillerson than they did to Obama and Clinton.

82.

North Korea and South Korea Are Threatening to Seek Peace

Korean détente puts decades of failed, corrupt US policy at risk

A few gestures of mutual respect between North Korea and South Korea during the first week of January are a long way from a stable, enduring peace on the Korean peninsula, but these gestures are the best signs of sanity there in decades. On January 1, North Korean leader Kim Jong-un called for immediate dialogue with South Korea ahead of next month's Winter Olympics there. On January 2, South Korea's President Moon Jae-in proposed that talks begin next week in Panmunjom (a border village where intermittent talks to end the Korean War have continued since 1953). On January 3, the two Koreas reopened a communications hotline that has been dysfunctional for almost two years (requiring South Korea to use a megaphone across the border in order to repatriate several North Korean fishermen). Talks on January 9 are expected to include North Korean participation in the Winter Olympics that begin February 9 in PyeongChang, South Korea.

Kim Jong-un's call for dialogue may or may not have surprised US officials, but reactions from the White House press secretary, the UN Ambassador, and the State Department were uniformly hostile and negative. The most civil was Heather Nauert at State, who said, with little nuance: "Right now, if the two countries decide that they want to have talks, that would certainly be their choice." She might as well have added "bless their little hearts." Patronize is what the US does when it's being polite. More typical bullying came from UN Ambassador Nikki Haley: "We won't take any of the talks seriously if they don't do something to ban all nuclear weapons in North Korea."

US policy is hopelessly tone-deaf if it believes that bell can be un-rung. But that's the way the US has behaved for decades, tone-deaf and unilaterally demanding, insisting that the US and the US alone has the right to determine what at least some sovereign nations can and cannot do. In December, anticipating a North Korean satellite launch (not a missile test), Secretary of State Rex Tillerson told the United Nations with straight-faced moral arrogance:

> The North Korean regime's continuing unlawful missile launches and testing activities signal its contempt for the United States, its neighbors in Asia, and all members of the United Nations. In the face of such a threat, inaction is unacceptable for any nation.

Well, no, that's only true if you believe you rule the world. It's not true in any context where parties have equal rights. And the US secretary's covert urging of others to take aggressive action tiptoes toward a war crime, as does the implied US threat of aggressive war.

The obtuse inflexibility of US policy revealed itself yet again in the initial groupthink response to a different part of Kim Jong-un's January 1 speech where he indicated that he had a "nuclear button" on his desk and would not hesitate to use it if anyone attacked North Korea. Under constant threat from the US and its allies since 1953, North Korea has made the rational choice to become a nuclear power, to have a nuclear deterrent, to have some semblance of national security. The US, irrationally, has refused to accept this with North Korea even while supporting Israel's nuclear deterrent. Kim Jong-un's button reference elicited a reflexive US reiteration of failed policy in florid Trumpian form when the president tweeted on January 2:

> North Korean Leader Kim Jong Un just stated that the "Nuclear Button is on his desk at all times." Will someone from his depleted and food starved regime please inform him that I too have a Nuclear Button, but it is a much bigger & more powerful one than his, and my Button works!

This twitter feed from the Great Disruptor got the twittering classes much atwitter over nothing more important than sexual innuendo, while fleeing from yet another presidential threat of nuclear destruction. And then came the firestorm of "Fire and Fury," and almost all thought of Korea was driven from public discourse, even though what happens in Korea is orders of magnitude more important than what Michael Wolff says Steve Bannon said about Trumpian treason.

But the facts on the ground in Korea have changed materially in the past year despite US bullying and interference. First, North Korea has become a nuclear power, no matter how puny, and it will continue to become more capable of defending itself unless the US thinks it would be better to do the unthinkable (what are the odds?). The second, more important change in Korea is that South Korea shed itself of a corrupt president beholden to US interests and, in May, inaugurated Moon Jae-in, who has actively sought reconciliation with the North for years before his election.

US policy has failed for more than six decades to achieve any resolution of the conflict, not even a formal end to the Korean War. The conventional wisdom, as posed by The New York Times, is a dead end: "The United States, the South's key ally, views the overture with deep suspicion." In a rational world, the US would have good reason to support its ally, the president of South Korea, in re-thinking a stalemate. Even President Trump seems to think so, in a hilariously narcissistic tweet of January 4:

> With all of the failed "experts" weighing in, does anybody really believe that talks and dialogue would be going on between North and South Korea right now if I wasn't firm, strong and willing to commit our total "might" against the North. Fools, but talks are a good thing!

Talks are a good thing. One of North Korea's chronic complaints, as well as a clearly legitimate grievance, has been the endless US/South Korean military exercises aimed at North Korea several times a year. In his January 1 speech, Kim Jong-un again called for South Korea to end joint military exercises with the US. On January 4, the Pentagon delayed the latest version of that clear provocation – scheduled to overlap with the Olympics. Defense Secretary Jim Mattis denied that the delay was a political gesture, saying its purpose was to provide logistical support to the Olympics (whatever that means). Whatever Mattis says, the gesture is a positive gesture and reinforces the drift toward peace, however slightly. Can it be possible that reality and sanity are getting traction? Who knows what's really going on here? And who are the "fools" Trump refers to?

83.

Why Are We Still in Afghanistan?

Forty years of US terrorism show little sign of success

It must have seemed like a safe, cheap and easy idea back in 1979 when US National Security Advisor Zbigniew Brzezinski, with President Carter's blessing, set about harassing the Russian occupation of Afghanistan by covert means. The US escalated CIA activities, working with Pakistani secret services, including arming, training, and directing Islamic militants (then called the mujahideen) to fight the Russians. The US waged a nine-year-long proxy guerrilla war in Afghanistan (where US allies included Osama bin Laden). When the Russians pulled out in 1989, US proxies remained. Now they were called the Taliban, and they ran the country with the festering Islamic rage that the US had nurtured and supported when it seemed to salve our post-Vietnam, post-Iranian Revolution wounded global pride.

The monster the US had raised from a pup was out of US control and came back to hurt us. Numbed by decades of Cold War denial of American crimes, Americans acted surprised by September 11, 2001.

Remember back in October 2001 when the US government and the US population were almost unanimous in the inchoate idea that we had to rush to do something – almost anything – in response to the downing of the World Trade Center?

The Bush administration had already obstructed justice by protecting nationals from the country that provided 15 of the 19 hijackers. The FBI wanted to interview Saudis in the US to see what connections they might discover to their compatriot suicide bombers. President Bush, fresh from holding hands with Saudi princes, made sure all the Saudis managed to get out of the country without any inconvenient criminal investigation questioning. That was a clear cover-up even if there was nothing to cover up, because it covered up the possibility of finding anything at all. That was the kind of blatant flouting of the law that Nancy Pelosi Democrats refused to think of as an impeachable offense. And the 9/11 Commission's report on the Saudis remains top secret into a third presidency. This is massive, bipartisan political breakdown and abject moral failure that could lead to nothing good. It has in fact metastasized unimpeded into the cancer of the Trump administration.

Remember what it was like in September 2001? Almost no one was sane in those days, or if they were, they laid low. Susan Sontag wrote a sane reflection on the attack in The New Yorker, for which she was roundly castigated, especially by her querulous peers at The New Yorker. On September 14, 2001, Barbara Lee of Oakland was the only member of Congress to vote against giving the president an "Authorization for Use of Military Force" (AUMF) – a carte blanche to wage war almost anywhere for almost any reason, a Congressional license to kill that remains in force today and serves as the legal justification for pretty much every dead Afghan, Iraqi, Syrian, Kurd, Yemeni, and anyone else we're killing for any reason anywhere in the world. Rep. Lee has continued to try to rectify the AUMF of 2001, but presidents and Congress en masse consistently maintain America's right to murder in the name of whatever we happen to think is important at the moment.

On the basis of the Congressional invitation to war, the Bush administration went to war with Afghanistan on October 7, 2001, calling it "Operation Enduring Freedom." The ostensible cause of the war was the refusal of the Taliban to turn over Osama bin Laden, who was in the country if not under their control. The US knew roughly where bin Laden was, but was afraid to surround him militarily for fear of provoking serious resistance. Instead, the US relied on Pakistan to seal the border. Osama bin Laden escaped. Lacking a stated reason to be in Afghanistan, the US stayed. And the US is still there. And the US is complicit in the deaths of a million or more Afghans, and complicit in the forced exodus of more than five million Afghans, and complicit in the devastation of Afghanistan culturally, politically, militarily, and economically. Only US delusions survive more or less intact. In his State of the Union address in 2006, President Bush assured us:

> We remain on the offensive in Afghanistan, where a fine president and a National Assembly are fighting terror while building the institutions of a new democracy.

Actually, that was not what was happening in Afghanistan, but by then Bush's deceitful war on Iraq was getting more attention. Barack Obama, typically too clever for his own good, ran against the war in Iraq while defending the war in Afghanistan as a good war (without ever really explaining why). But the politics of perception don't have to be rooted in reality, and by 2013, in his State of the Union address, President Obama was pitching the perception that the war in Afghanistan was pretty much over (if not necessarily won):

> This spring, our forces will move into a support role, while Afghan security forces take the lead. Tonight I can announce that over the next year another 34,000 American troops will come home from Afghanistan. This drawdown will continue. And by the end of next year, our war in Afghanistan will be over.

Actually, that was not what was happening in Afghanistan, either. In 1979 American pride planned for Afghanistan to become a quagmire, a Russian Vietnam. Now the Russians are long gone, and Afghanistan has become another American quagmire. The mistake is the same as in Vietnam: fighting a native population will take forever, because they have nowhere else to go. Sooner or later, the invader usually goes home. And President Trump seems to be indicating that it will be later, telling a UN Security Council meeting:

> I don't think we're prepared to talk right now. It's a whole different fight over there. They're killing people left and right. Innocent people are being killed left and right, bombing in the middle of children, in the middle of families, bombing, killing all over Afghanistan.... We don't want to talk to the Taliban. We're going to finish what we have to finish. What nobody else has been able to finish, we're going to be able to do it.

Actually, what was happening in Afghanistan in 2017 is that the US was bombing the country more than ever, dropping more bombs during 2017 than in the two previous years combined. The US has used the largest non-nuclear bomb in Afghanistan. The US is using B-52s in Afghanistan, the same plane that carpet-bombed Vietnam with ultimate futility. Now the B-52 has set a new record for dropping smart bombs on Afghanistan. These attacks were in northeastern Afghanistan, near the Tajikistan and Chinese borders, targeting the East Turkestan Islamic Movement accused of attacking China. Until recently, parts of this remote region had gone untouched by war for decades. Chinese and Afghan government officials are currently discussing the establishment of a Chinese military base in this region. China has provided Afghanistan with more than $70 million in military aid in the past three years (compared to some $10 billion from US/NATO countries).

Taliban attacks on Kabul and other cities have also escalated in recent weeks, killing more than 130 people in Kabul alone.

When the Taliban governed Afghanistan before 2001, it came close to eradicating opium growing and the heroin trade (set up by the CIA in 1979 to help finance the mujahideen). Since 2001, under US occupation, opium-growing and the heroin trade have flourished, reaching record levels. During that same period, US heroin-users have increased from about 189,000 to 3.8 million. According to a UN report on drugs and crime in 2017:

> Only a small share of the revenues generated by the cultivation and trafficking of Afghan opiates reaches Afghan drug trafficking groups. Many more billions of dollars are made from trafficking opiates into major consumer markets, mainly in Europe and Asia…. [Drug trafficking constitutes] the third biggest global commodity in cash terms after oil and the arms trade.

According to a 2017 report by the US Government Accountability Office (GAO), during the period 2002-2016, the US provided Afghanistan with $6 billion in security and military aid. An Afghan official estimated that as much as half that money had been stolen through Afghan corruption. The overall cost of the Afghan War to the US is estimated at more than $841 billion to date. Another estimate expects the total cost of the Afghan War to exceed $2 trillion, not including the costs of taking care of veterans. President Trump's escalation of the war is expected to add billions to its eventual cost, which is calculated to have passed $1 trillion by January 2018. In his State of the Union address this year, President Trump reported:

> Our warriors in Afghanistan have new rules of engagement. Along with their heroic Afghan partners, our military is no longer undermined by artificial timelines, and we no longer tell our enemies our plans.

So why are we still in Afghanistan? It's not because Afghanistan poses any threat to US national security – or ever did. It's not because there's any rational military or political reason to stay in Afghanistan. And it's not because the Afghans want us there. There are former Taliban in the Afghan legislature, but the US presence (as in Korea) makes any chance of peaceful resolution that much more difficult.

So why are we still in Afghanistan? Because it seemed like a good idea at the time? Because no one at the time thought it through and decided to leave when the good part was no longer possible? Because presidents have more vanity than integrity? Because the US doesn't admit mistakes because that shows weakness no matter the cost of being self-destructively stupid for 16 years? Because the US government is most comfortable when it's lying to the American people? Because the military-industrial complex makes nothing but profits from remote wars? Because we need killed and wounded veterans to show how much we honor our military? Because a lot of people profit from the drug trade? Because the American people have been systematically numbed emotionally, dumbed-down intellectually, mystified for so many decades, and are angrier with each other than the people who do them real harm? Any or all of the above?

84.

Senate Resolution on Yemen – Better Than Nothing, but Three Years Late

"It is long past time for Congress to exercise its constitutional authority on matters of war, and if the United States is going to participate in the Saudi-led war in Yemen, there must be a debate and a vote. Otherwise, our involvement is unauthorized and unconstitutional, and it must end."

This is the pitch Senator Bernie Sanders uses in a press release to entice people to "sign my petition if you agree." This is also the full text of his Friends of Bernie Sanders petition. The petition seeks support for Senate Joint Resolution 54 "to direct the removal of United States Armed Forces from hostilities in the Republic of Yemen that have not been authorized by Congress." Introduced by the Independent senator from Vermont, the resolution became tri-partisan when it picked up support from a Democrat, Chris Murphy of Connecticut, and a Republican, Mike Lee of Utah.

Ordinarily, an effort to halt an ongoing American war could be shuffled off to committee never to be seen again. In this case, Resolution 54 is offered in the context of the War Powers Resolution, which requires that it be considered "in accordance with the expedited procedures" of the law. We may expect Resolution 54 to be voted on within the next few weeks, barring other developments.

Resolution 54 deserves support not only from people who object to war crimes or undeclared wars of aggression, but from people who believe our government should run in an orderly, transparent, and Constitutional manner. Resolution 54 is getting a big push from organizations on the left (including Demand Progress, Daily Kos, Code Pink, Our Revolution, Win Without War, and 15 others). And it's about time.

494

Almost three years ago, on March 26, 2015, Saudi Arabia and its allies started bombing Yemen, the poorest country in the region, with a population of about 27 million. US military units had operated there with impunity until the Houthis overthrew Yemen's internationally-imposed government. From the start, the Obama administration blessed and enabled the initiation of this aggressive war, itself a war crime. Now it is blessed and enabled by the Trump administration. Besides selling the Saudis their planes and bombs (including cluster bombs, another war crime), the US has provided the Saudi coalition with military intelligence, targeting expertise, and mid-air fueling. The US Navy also supported another war crime, the naval blockade of Yemen that has caused starvation and disease (part of a crime against humanity). From the beginning, the Saudi-led attack on Yemen was a genocidal assault on the Houthis, an ethnic Yemeni minority with whom the Saudis have had territorial squabbles dating back decades, if not centuries. None of this has been a secret. By and large nobody cared any more than the inert US Senate in 2015 (including Sanders, Murphy and Lee). In connection with Resolution 54, Sanders said:

> The United Nations emergency relief coordinator said that Yemen was on the brink of, quote, "the largest famine the world has seen for many decades," end-quote. So far, at least 10,000 civilians have died and over 40,000 have been wounded in the war, and 3 million people have been displaced. Many Americans are also not aware that US forces have been actively involved in support of the Saudis in this war, providing intelligence and aerial refueling of planes, whose bombs have killed thousands of people and made this crisis far worse.

The carnage has been accumulating for three years under daily bombing, constant blockade and the world's silence. That is the profoundly sad thing about Resolution 54 and what it illustrates about the present, diminished state of American democracy: this gesture is the best we've got right now for ending the unauthorized, unconstitutional and criminal war that the US has co-waged for almost three years. It's not just the best we've got, it's all we've got. Resolution 54, important as it is, is way too little and way too late. The senators make a point of noting that the American public is unaware of the devastating

495

war in Yemen. And whose fault is that? All three of them have been in the Senate since well before 2015. That they have now found their conscience while 97 other senators hold their silence in the face of American-sponsored genocide is hardly a sign of political health in a country gone far off the rails since 2001.

The sponsors of Resolution 54 don't mention US complicity in the blockade that starves Yemen. The sponsors of Resolution 54 don't breathe a word about war crimes. The sponsors of Resolution 54 don't come close to calling for the same rules being applied to the unauthorized deployment of US troops in Syria. The authors of Resolution 54 have nothing to say about applying the rules in advance of any attack on Iran. The sponsors of Resolution 54, in their small gesture to the rule of law, are pretty much detached from reality.

Resolution 54 isn't designed to solve anything, but it might lead to a reduction of suffering in Yemen. That's slightly better than just washing your hands clean after the crucifixion.

85.

Pentagon Lies About Yemen, says US Role in Saudi War Is 'Noncombat'

"The US government claims that it's not engaged in hostilities unless US troops are on the ground being shot at by the enemy.... It stretches the imagination, and it stretches the English language beyond its breaking point, to suggest the US military is not engaged in hostilities in Yemen."

SENATOR MIKE LEE, UTAH REPUBLICAN, SENATE FLOOR MARCH 13

The Pentagon, having spent three years creating famine and spreading cholera on an unprecedented scale in one of the poorest countries in the world, Yemen, now lies, baldly but with lawyerly gracelessness, that the American bombs guided by American officers to targets as often as not civilian is somehow "noncombat." Effectively, the Pentagon argues that when US military forces only enable genocide, it's not combat. Strictly speaking, the Pentagon is only following orders to commit ongoing war crimes.

In late March 2015, with US blessing from the Obama administration, Saudi Arabia and its allies started bombing Yemen more or less indiscriminately, making as many as 200 sorties a day. Yemen, with no air force and few air defenses, was helpless. From the start this was an illegal war of aggression, a nexus of war crimes in all its particulars, and so it will be until it ends. Without US approval and participation, it's highly unlikely Yemen would have become the world's most serious humanitarian crisis, regardless of the crimes of others.

The gross criminality of US enabling of and participation in the genocidal war on Yemen is not part of the official discussion of the horror our country perpetuates on a daily basis. From the beginning, US military has engaged in the war by providing tactical advice

497

on bombing, offering intelligence, maintaining warplanes, re-fueling Saudi warplanes in mid-air, providing cluster bombs and smart bombs, and generally offering military support for a bombing campaign as vicious as any since the US dropped more explosives on Vietnam than were used in all of World War II.

This is the official view of the scope of US involvement in the Saudi war on Yemen, along with a perverse insistence on calling it a "civil war," when there is only one outside aggressor: the Saudi coalition and its supporters. Even Senator Elizabeth Warren, a Massachusetts Democrat, accepts this demonstrably false framing, as she did at the Senate Armed Services Committee hearing on March 13. She even accepts as gospel the alleged Iranian involvement in Yemen for which there is scant evidence and less precise definition. That has been a chronic Saudi-American lie about Yemen from the beginning, pretending that a local territorial dispute between the Houthis and the Saudis was some sort of grand geopolitical last stand. It wasn't true when Obama green-lighted the killing, and it's not true now as Trump keeps the slaughter going, but it will continue to be accepted as official truth until people like Warren challenge it. But Warren is also the Senator from Raytheon, the defense contractor that sells billions of dollars worth of precision-guided munitions to the Saudi coalition. Euphemistically, Raytheon says it helps the Saudis "meet their security needs," even though there is no serious threat to anyone from the Houthis in Yemen, and the Saudi war is less about security then aggression.

The Pentagon says what it is doing with the Saudi war is "limited US military support," in the words of Defense Secretary Jim Mattis before the Senate on March 13. Mattis did not acknowledge that the Saudi war could not continue without US support, since the Pentagon position is that the US provides "noncombat assistance." None of the US senators present asked about this big elephant taking a dump in the middle of the room. There was only the slightest objection when the Pentagon Central Command head who runs the American part of the war, General Joseph Votel, told senators with a straight face: "We're not parties to this conflict."

According to General Votel, the US is not party to the conflict even though it chooses targets, programs smart bombs, and re-fuels bombers that have now killed something like 10,000 civilians and an unknown number of combatants. General Votel claims US noncombatant status mainly because once the bombs go up, the US pays no official attention to where they come down.

In late February, three senators introduced Joint Resolution 54, designed to put some Congressional check on US war-making in Yemen and elsewhere. The Pentagon's official response was that Congress has no right to tell the Pentagon what it can and cannot do under presidential authority. This view is spelled out in a February 27 letter from the general counsel of the Department of Defense, opposing Joint Resolution 54 and explaining why all the war-making activities of US forces in Yemen have nothing to do with "hostilities" (even though they do, in any honestly rational world). The letter even refers obliquely to actual "hostilities" that are mostly ignored, "the October 2016 strikes against radar facilities in Houthi-controlled territory in defense of US Navy ships in international waters." That's the whole reference, but even as it confirms the US firing weapons at Houthis, it then defends this engagement as an exception that somehow doesn't count as "hostilities." Navy Times lists the Red Sea/Gulf of Aden region off Yemen as one of the "Navy's 5 most dangerous at-sea deployments." Navy Times frames the issue with a clear statement of the hostilities and a hilarious version of the geopolitical history:

> The fact that sailors have already had full-on missile battles with Yemeni rebels near this global choke-point makes the Bab-el-Mandeb, or the BAM, an obvious pick for the most dangerous place in the world where sailors are deploying.

> The Gate of Tears is the maritime equivalent of the Wild West. Yemen is a failed state in the grip of a bloody civil war that has roped in both Saudi Arabia and to a lesser degree, the United States. But spillover from the conflict, as well as meddling from Iran, has made the waters around Yemen extremely dangerous.

This is all duplicitous kabuki on both sides, Pentagon and Senate. They are arguing within a falsely-framed pseudo reality to perpetuate

deceit they all own. Even if the US role were limited to merely supporting the aerial attacks, everyone lies by omission by failing to
acknowledge (much less object to) the air campaign's role in blockading
Yemen, thereby directly causing famine and disease and toxic drinking
water for more than half the population. This biological warfare is also
a war crime.

As is well established in international law, a blockade is an act
of war. The "non-combatant" US admittedly participates in the aerial
blockade of Yemen. The US does not admit its much greater participation in the naval blockade of Yemen. The US-Saudi naval blockade
depends on the US Navy, which has enforced the blockade since 2015.
Yemen has needed to import food to survive for decades. The US-Saudi
blockade cut off food to Yemen, as well as medical supplies, fuel, and all
the other things needed to support a normal civil society. The US-Saudi
blockade has led directly to starvation and famine. The US-Saudi blockade has led directly to the spread of cholera and other diseases. The
US-Saudi blockade is a war crime of stunning enormity. And no one
talks about it.

When President Bashar al Assad engages in similar tactics in
Syria, as in Ghouta of late, the world hears about it, but doesn't do
much. When the US and its allies in the war on terror terrorize and
destroy places like Raqqa, the world hears much less about it and does
nothing. When the US, Saudi Arabia and its allies spend three years
in Yemen committing war crimes that have yet to end, the world hears
little about it, humanitarian agencies and the United Nations raise
objections, but nothing humane is accomplished. The US in Yemen is
morally indistinguishable from Bashar al Assad in Syria.

86.

First Bomb the Wedding, Then Bomb the Rescue Workers

Textbook terrorist tactic and war crime – who cares?

In an impoverished, remote mountain village in northwest Yemen, the wedding celebration was still going strong when the first airstrike hit around 11 p.m. on April 22. The Saudi attacks killed the bride first in a death toll that came to "at least 33 people." The nearest hospital was miles away in Hajjah. The only two cars in the village were knocked out by the bombing. The first casualties reaching the hospital arrived by donkey after midnight. The hospital, one of 13 in Yemen run by MSF (Médecins Sans Frontières, or Doctors Without Borders), had two ambulances that drove back and forth well into daylight bringing in the wounded sometimes six at a time. MSF reported receiving 63 casualties, none armed, none in uniform:

> The injured had mainly lost limbs and suffered shrapnel wounds. At least three patients required amputation, including two brothers, who each lost a foot. By early morning, many residents of Hajjah had come to the hospital to donate blood. In two hours, 150 bags were collected to treat the wounded.

This was yet another American-sponsored war crime. The US has committed war crimes of this sort all on its own since 2009 in Pakistan (and subsequently in Iraq, Afghanistan, Syria and elsewhere). US complicity in committing war crimes almost daily in Yemen began in March 2015 when the president, without a murmur from a supine Congress, gave the green light to a Saudi-led coalition of mostly Sunni Arab states to wage a genocidal bombing campaign against the Houthi rebels (predominantly Shi'ite Zaidis) who had ruled Yemen for 1,000 years until 1962. (Not that US media often mention US involvement, as the CNN report on this deadly wedding illustrates: "A coalition led by Saudi Arabia has been fighting Iranian Houthi rebels in Yemen for more than two years" — actually three. And the Houthis are Yemeni, *not* Iranian, as the official propaganda would love you to believe.)

As with the desecrated wedding described above, the Saudis, with US blessing and extensive tactical support, like to commit their war crimes especially against weddings and funerals (as the CIA was fond of doing in Pakistan). This is state-sponsored terrorism. The states sponsoring it include the US, Saudi Arabia, the UAE and their allies in Yemen. Weddings and funerals offer large gatherings of innocent people who are defenseless. It doesn't take a smart bomb to see the value of a soft target like that. When the rescue workers and other first responders show up, a second strike kills more innocent, defenseless people. This is a standard terrorist tactic with fiendish efficiency. In terror jargon it's called the double-tap.

That same weekend, US-Saudi strikes also killed a family of five and 20 civilians riding in a bus. The US-Saudi air war on the undefended country (Yemen has no air force and limited air defenses) has displaced millions of people in a country of 25 million that was already the poorest in the region when the Saudis attacked. The relentless bombing of civilians (including the use of cluster bombs) has led to severe hunger, approaching famine conditions; a severe shortage of medical supplies and a massive cholera outbreak; and destruction of infrastructure and the near-elimination of clean water. Describing conditions in Yemen, UN Secretary-General Antonio Guterres said:

> Every 10 minutes, a child under 5 dies of preventable causes. And nearly 3 million children under 5 and pregnant or lactating women are actually malnourished. Nearly half of all children aged between 6 months and 5 years old are chronically malnourished and suffer from stunting, which causes development delays and reduced ability to learn throughout their entire lives.

This is what genocide looks like. But to blur that perception, the Saudis and the UAE have given the UN nearly $1 billion in humanitarian aid, to ameliorate the humanitarian disaster they created, even as they continue bombing without a pause. This picture has prompted Guterres to say that "peace is possible" in Yemen, but "there are still many obstacles to overcome."

One such obstacle would be the Saudi claim on April 21 that the Yemeni rebels had seized 19 oil tankers off the coast and had held them hostage for more than 26 days. That was a lie. It was not a credible lie, coming after 25 days of silence during the alleged hostage crisis. It was a lie based on nonsense, since the Saudi naval blockade had allowed the oil tankers into the port of Hodeidah to deliver fuel to the rebel-held area. A commercial shipping traffic website soon located all the "hostage" ships and learned that they were anchored awaiting off-loading. On April 26, Public Radio International exposed the Saudi lie.

On November 13, 2017, the US House of Representatives passed a lengthy resolution (H.Res.599) "Expressing the sense of the House of Representatives with respect to United States policy towards Yemen, and for other purposes" on a bipartisan vote of 366-30 (with 36 not voting). The resolution expresses basic clichés of US policy, with all their varied levels of inaccuracy, dishonesty and wishful thinking. The general tone of the document is that it's all Iran's fault the US-Saudi offensive is killing Yemenis en masse (no evidence offered). Most to the point, the House acknowledges that the US has no legal authorization for the use of force in Yemen (while omitting specific reference to US participation in the bombing, naval blockade, drone strikes, or other military actions). Having identified the illegality of US involvement in a genocidal war, the House resolution does nothing about it other than to ask all the parties to play nice.

In March 2018, Senate Joint Resolution 54 raised some real issues without actually proposing any solution. The resolution defined itself as a choice: "To direct the removal of United States Armed Forces from hostilities in the Republic of Yemen that have not been authorized by Congress."

In a largely party-line vote on March 20, the Senate voted 55-44 to table the resolution without discussing it or changing the course of carnage and US arms sales.

The Yemen peace process is still a hope more than a reality. The US and the Saudi coalition have shown no willingness to negotiate in good faith, but it's not clear that anyone else has either. The Houthis control most of western Yemen and roughly 80% of the population. Houthi senior leader Saleh al-Sammad, considered a moderate, was open to negotiation. On April 19, a US-Saudi airstrike assassinated him.

The Trump administration is equally useless in any search for peace in Yemen. The president is enthralled by the scale of arms purchases by the Saudis and their allies, with no apparent interest in how the Pentagon helps use those weapons mostly against civilians.

A US citizen named Nageeb al-Omari has attempted to bring his 11-year-old daughter Shaima to the US for medical care. She was born with cerebral palsy, but the US-Saudi bombing has made her care all but impossible there. There is no US embassy in Yemen. Shaima's father took her to Djibouti, where she continued deteriorating rapidly. Despite the US anti-Muslim travel ban, the daughter qualifies for the exemptions that would allow her into the US. Even though her father is a US citizen, US State Department officials would not grant her a visa, a waiver, or, most likely, a chance to live. The family has returned to Idlib in Yemen to await the next random act of cruelty from a rogue state that is the world's greatest purveyor of terrorism.

Why should they expect any better treatment than Iraqi Christians in Michigan who voted for the president and now face deportation?

87.

Israeli Snipers Kill Unarmed, Defenseless People: Isn't That Murder?

Israeli "defense" forces kill coldly, calculatedly, then cheer

Israel's deliberate, methodical, selective assassination of unarmed, peaceful Palestinians in Gaza has gone on for years, punctuated by periods of deliberate but random killing with air strikes and artillery. Gaza is a prison, Gaza is a concentration camp, Gaza has been blockaded for a decade, Gaza's occupation is a perennial crime against humanity, but most of all Gaza is a target. Gaza is a target because it suits the Israelis to have two million captive Palestinian men, women and children (half of them are children) to despise, starve, deny medical supplies, reduce to inescapable and unlivable conditions, kill, and then brand as "terrorists" for not surrendering and disappearing from the face of the earth 70 years ago. From an Israeli perspective, Palestinians committed original sin by merely existing.

From a Palestinian perspective, Israelis committed original sin by merely existing.

They are both right, in a narrow sense that is useless for moving forward. Neither has any moral authority in a wider perspective. But where does one go to find any wider perspective?

After weeks of Israeli snipers killing unarmed, nonviolent civilians, the official view of the United States is as narrow, distorted and misleading as it's been for years. On May 14, the day that Israelis killed some 60 people and wounded thousands more, White House representative Raj Shah recited the US view with robotic repetition (with no supporting evidence) throughout his press briefing:

> *Mr. Shah:* The responsibility for these tragic deaths rests squarely with Hamas. Hamas is intentionally and cynically provoking this response.... we believe that Hamas is responsible for these tragic deaths; that their rather cynical exploitation of the situation is what's leading to these deaths. And we want them to stop.... we think that we shouldn't lose sight of the fact that Hamas is the one that, frankly, bear responsibility for the dire situation right now in Gaza.... We believe that Hamas is responsible for what's going on.
>
> Q: So there's no responsibility beyond that on the Israeli authorities? Kill at will?
>
> *Mr. Shah:* What I'm saying is that we believe that Hamas, as an organization, is engaged in cynical action that's leading to these deaths.... as I said earlier, we believe Hamas bears the responsibility. Look, this is a propaganda attempt. I mean, this is a gruesome and unfortunate propaganda attempt. I think the Israeli government has spent weeks trying to handle this without violence, and we find it very unfortunate.
>
> Q: But people were throwing rocks 50 meters from the wall [perimeter fence] and were faced with sniper attack. I mean, is the White House in denial of the split-screen reality that's occurring?
>
> *Mr. Shah:* Again, we believe that Hamas is responsible for this.

Surely Raj Shah and most of the people in the Trump administration know that this is such a distortion of reality as to constitute a Big Lie in the traditional Nazi propaganda sense. Whatever argument might be made to the contrary, the Palestinians are perennially and incontrovertibly the victims here and have been for 70 years, since the Nakba of 1948. The White House blames the victim. Israel, the enduring monument to a successful terrorist campaign, wages terrorism to fight the terrorism used against it.

The White House also singles out Hamas for blame, which is a form of straw-man demonization of long standing. The White House offers no evidence that Hamas can be, much less is, an all-controlling manipulator of two million Palestinians. But blaming Hamas is a way to ignore the conditions Israel has imposed on these two million prisoners who have no choice but to slowly poison themselves with contaminated water in conditions that are literally "unlivable" (according to a 2017 UN report). Hamas is an easy scapegoat, but it is also the only Palestinian political party that actually won an election (2006) that the US, Israel, Fatah and others prevented from taking effect. Hamas had effective control of Gaza, Fatah of the West Bank. In 2005, in an unusual form of ethnic cleansing, Israel had forcibly removed (with $200,000 individual compensation) all Jewish residents from Gaza creating a Palestinian ghetto: a fenced-in occupied territory controlled by Israel, choked by an Israeli-Egyptian blockade, cut off from humanitarian intervention by the US veto at the UN Security Council. Even so, the US and Israel conspired with Fatah to undo Hamas's election victory by force, setting the stage for Hamas to take control of Gaza by removing Fatah in a week of fighting (estimated 118 dead, 550 wounded) in June 2007. The White House chooses just to ignore the year-old proposal by Hamas to create a Palestinian state based on the 1967 borders with Israel.

Singling out Hamas when a broad spectrum of Gazan civil society is turning out to demonstrate at more than a dozen locations along the roughly 15-mile perimeter fence helps US/Israeli officials (and media) depict a false reality. The unspoken subtext of Shah's comments is that Palestinians have no right to engage in massive, nonviolent civil disobedience. This is so patently false that he really can't say it out loud. And he's helped by the undisciplined fringe of Palestinians who don't seem to get that nonviolent civil disobedience really doesn't include rock-throwing, fire-bomb kites and the like, no matter how ineffectual those tactics are (causing no Israeli casualties or reported damage). More disciplined, sustained, nonviolent protest would frame Israeli conduct far more starkly, and cold-blooded murder would be seen for the terror tactic it truly is, especially now that snipers are targeting doctors and other medical personnel.

Gaza is a continuing crime against humanity in which the US is complicit with the perpetrators (as in Yemen and elsewhere). For decades the US has postured as a peace-maker, sometimes with actual good effect. Those days are long gone, as White House representative Shah made clear at his May 14 briefing:

> **Q: Raj,** on the issue of peace between the Israelis and the Palestinians, when was the last time the White House reached out to Palestinian leadership? And will — given the high numbers of casualties, Palestinians calling what has happened today a "massacre," will the White House be reaching out?

> *Mr. Shah:* Well, I don't honestly have an answer for you on that. I'll get back to you.

What he means is that the White House has no peace plan, there is no coherent policy beyond supporting Israel no matter what, and as far as the US goes, peace is not an option. Senior Advisor to the president and son-in-law Jared Kushner, an Orthodox Jew, has reportedly developed a US peace plan that he's reluctant to present publicly for fear the Palestinians might reject it (even though the president calls it "the deal of the century"). On May 14, when Israeli killing in Gaza peaked, Kushner spoke obliquely of his peace plan at the US embassy ceremony in Jerusalem, claiming that the president:

> ... was very clear that his decision and today's celebration, do not reflect the departure from our strong commitment to lasting peace, a peace that overcomes the conflicts of the past in order to give our children a brighter and more boundless future. *As we have seen from the protests of the last month and even today, those provoking violence are part of the problem and not part of the solution.* The United States is prepared to support a peace agreement in every way we can. We believe that it is possible for both sides to gain more than they give... [emphasis added].

None of this corresponds well to the actual behavior of the Trump administration, which has consisted mostly of provocations and subsidies (that pay for maintaining the unlivable conditions of Gaza and the bullets that kill Palestinians, among other crimes of Israel's illegal occupation). Who can Kushner possibly mean by "our children"? The real message from Kushner, highlighted above, comes down to "blame Hamas" – nonviolent civil disobedience provokes violence, doesn't everyone know that, have we learned nothing from Alabama, South

Africa, India? The White House scrubbed that highlighted passage from its official transcript of Kushner's remarks.

But Ambassador Nikki Haley was even more absurd at the UN. While the US was blocking any Security Council action, such as an "independent and transparent investigation," or even a resolution of "outrage and sorrow," Haley characterized Israel's one-sided killing as "restraint" and lied about Israel's border:

> I ask my colleagues here in the Security Council, who among us would accept this type of activity on your border? No one would. No country in this chamber would act with more restraint than Israel has.

The fence enclosing Gaza is not a border. Both sides of the fence are in Israel. The fence is a demarcation line, with a Palestinian concentration camp on the inside and murderers, maimers and mutilators on the outside. Some Israelis are even proud of this, as an Israeli Defense Force (IDF) spokesman tweeted on March 31:

> Yesterday we saw 30,000 people; we arrived prepared and with precise reinforcements; everything was accurate and measured, and we know where every bullet landed.

When your bullets are landing on civilians, on men, women and children, on doctors and medical personnel, that tweet is a confession. More recently a Knesset member promised that "the IDF has enough bullets for everyone." What can possibly justify hunting unarmed Palestinians in the unspeakable conditions of Gaza, conditions created and enforced by Israel, conditions roughly equivalent to the Warsaw ghetto of 1943? Israel is perpetrating a continuing crime against humanity.

Elsewhere in the world, there is an outcry against state-sanctioned shooting fish in a barrel. The US blames the fish. This is an obscene response to an endless atrocity in which the complicit United States is once again up to its eyeballs in innocent blood.

88.

Democratic Senator Schumer Is a Dishonest Putz on Korea, Peace

Democrats' stupidly rigid, soulless partisanship is worse than Trump

Massive American war crimes, incessant firebombing of North Korean cities full of civilians, helped bring about a formal ceasefire on July 27, 1953. That armistice did not end the Korean War, which is not over yet. American hostility to North Korea has continued unabated, overtly and covertly, for the past 65 years. The American position has never included good faith. The US position has never embraced a rational view of complex realities. The US has demanded surrender, in effect, as the precondition of any normalization. The US has continued to wage relentless economic, diplomatic, psychological and other forms of warfare against North Korea since 1953. And then the US was shocked – shocked! – to find North Korea building a nuclear weapons deterrent.

The collectively delusional American foreign policy establishment has bleated with one long, dishonest bipartisan whine about the sins of North Korea without so much as an honest whimper about American war crimes or later economic crimes that helped starve North Koreans. Well, the US deceitfully said of the dead and dying, that famine was North Korea's fault, they can't feed their own people. Funny how that's very like current US policy in Yemen, where the US enables Saudi Arabia to wage a genocidal war and at the same time ineffectively wrings its hands over the world's most serious humanitarian crisis as if the US were helpless to make a difference.

Now we have the widely-derided President Trump actually contributing to a new peace process nursed into being by the leaders of the two Koreas. Instead of threatening nuclear war, the US is suddenly – at least for the moment – threatening Trump hotels on North Korean beaches. How is this not a better circumstance, no matter how preliminary and tentative? How is this not a peace process that we should want to see reach fruition, if that's possible? Given the uncertain, possibly fragile quality of current US-Korean relations, one might expect any sensible person to take a wait-and-see position on what is clearly a peace process only at the beginning of negotiations that might lead to a settlement of the longest war in US history.

Realistically, nothing has yet happened in Korea. And the cold war robots are doing their best to make sure nothing does happen. But for the moment, Trump has put forward reality-based ambitions. He has, in effect, observed that the Empire has no clothes:

> We have right now 32,000 [officially 28,500] soldiers in South Korea. And I'd like to be able to bring them back home. But that's not part of the equation right now....

> We will be stopping the war games, which will save us a tremendous amount of money, unless and until we see that the future negotiation is not going along like it should. But we'll be saving a tremendous amount of money. Plus, I think it's very provocative.... And we call them war games, and I call them war games, and they're tremendously expensive. The amount of money that we spend on that is incredible.

This is all reasonable. It is all conditional. The surprise is that a US president actually said any of it out loud. After 45 years of open hostility to North Korea, the US has close to zero credibility in North Korea. That's abidingly real. If there's to be any chance of a peaceful Korea emerging from this peace process, the US must make more than a token effort to establish its good faith. This is a start, but it's an easy start, with almost no cost to the US strategically.

Given an opportunity to display statesmanship and patience, Democratic leaders chose to play petty politics and display a foreign policy vision wedded to militarism and bluster (which was one of the factors that cost Hillary Clinton the presidency). Senate Minority Leader Chuck Schumer of New York made the absurd claim that, by meeting with North Korea's Kim Jong Un, Trump had given "a brutal and repressive dictatorship the international legitimacy it has long craved." This is cant. This is the rhetoric of decades of reflexive hostility, barren of insight and absent any recognition that reality has shifted in the year since the South Korean election. Schumer's prim, fake morality notwithstanding, the US does daily business with just about every "brutal and repressive dictatorship" it can find, most notably Saudi Arabia and its allies waging a criminal war on Yemen. The idea that Trump meeting with Kim gives either government any greater "international legitimacy" is a simpleton's fiction long winked at in diplomacy. In the real world, legitimacy derives from behavior, and anyone who looks can legitimately wonder whether North Korea currently treats its citizens any worse than the US treats its Puerto Rican citizens.

Schumer's empty posturing went further than the traditional hypocrisy of American exceptionalism, rooted in denial of American genocide and enslavement. Schumer also felt the need to add nasty little lies to his absurd performance:

> President Trump agreed to freeze joint military exercises with South Korea. And he called them 'provocations' – right out of the North Korean propaganda playbook – without the knowledge of South Korea or our own military. I guarantee you, our military men and women were squirming when President Trump called our joint military exercises 'provocations.'

The president did not "freeze joint military exercises," as the Trump statement above makes clear enough for even Schumer to see. Trump called them "war games" and "provocations" because that's what they have always been. Schumer may be right about US military "squirming" when they heard the truth spoken aloud, but that squirming would most likely be because the military has always known their war games were provocations. That's why the US military wages war games year in and year out, in Europe and the South China Sea and elsewhere, to see what they can provoke. That's the world we've lived in for decades, and to pretend otherwise, as Schumer does, is merely to perpetuate it.

Instead of thoughtless, kneejerk anti-Trumpery, serious leadership in an opposition party would acknowledge the promise inherent in the Korean peace process. It would also acknowledge that the process has just begun, that it will take a long time to complete, and that calling names does nothing to improve the prospect for success. Principled leadership in an opposition party would offer good faith support for a process that moves the world away from a nuclear confrontation. Or do Democrats not think of a denuclearized, secure Korea as a success?

While Democratic Party "leaders" are playing a worn-out cold war script to the cameras, they are also distracting from – and thereby complicit in – a host of US crimes against humanity and crimes against the Constitution. Democrats have long been limp on voting rights, the core of our democratic system. Democrats have long been limp on dark money in politics. Democrats have long been limp on immigration, perhaps never more so than now.

The Democracy NOW edition of June 14 covers the US perpetuation of crime and suffering in agonizing detail which shocks the conscience even now. Human rights attorney Jennifer Harbury sums up decades of US brutalism in this hemisphere:

> Sending any refugee back to a place of danger, it's a violation of international law, which I'm sure President Trump doesn't care about at all. But it's also a violation of US law, and it has been for many years. We're breaking the law. We're ignoring the cartels. And we're punishing the hell out of the victims. How that makes us great, I couldn't tell you.

Why do the Chuck Schumers of the world think it's somehow better to rag on Trump for an uncertain peace process rather than confront him on the deliberate, continuous flouting of international and domestic law? Why do the Chuck Schumers of the world tolerate the cruelty and violence inflicted on poor people fleeing from violence and hopelessness? How do the Chuck Schumers of the world fail to see that they are part of a government that is behaving like a brutal dictatorship and now proposes to build concentration camps for the children the government kidnaps from their parents?

This is more than just political cowardice, this is complicity in criminal atrocities.

89.

Saudi-US Propaganda by PBS NewsHour in Houthi-held Yemen

"One of the poorest countries in the Middle East, Yemen's war has pushed it to the brink of famine. A Saudi blockade has slowed the flow of food and helped push prices up. Markets and businesses are ruined from airstrikes. Millions are destitute. Special correspondent Jane Ferguson smuggled herself across front lines to report on what's happening inside the world's worst humanitarian disaster."

PBS NEWSHOUR SUMMARY, JULY 2, 2018

This is what American tax-supported propaganda looks like when an organization like the PBS NewsHour wants to maintain a semblance of credibility while lying through its intimidated teeth. Yes, Yemen is one of the poorest countries in the world, long dependent on imported food and other life support. But to say "Yemen's war" is major league deceit, and PBS surely knows the truth: that the war on Yemen is American-backed, initiated – illegally – in March 2015 by a Saudi-led coalition that includes the UAE (United Arab Emirates). The US/Saudi war is genocidal, creating famine and a cholera epidemic for military purposes. These are American and Arab war crimes that almost no one wants to acknowledge, much less confront.

The "Saudi blockade" is also a US Navy blockade. The blockade is a war crime. Starving civilians is a war crime.

The most amazing sentence is: "Markets and businesses are ruined from airstrikes." Seems rather bland. But this is a tacit admission of more war crimes – Saudi bombing of civilian businesses, as well as civilian hospitals, weddings and funerals. But PBS makes it sound like the airstrikes sort of come out of nowhere, like the rain. PBS omits

514

the American culpability that makes the airstrikes possible: mid-air refueling, targeting support, intelligence sharing and the rest. Think of Guernica, the fascist bombing of civilians that inspired Picasso's painting. Now think of Guernica lasting three years. That's what the US has supported in Yemen and that's what PBS helps cover up.

Yes, "Millions are destitute," and yes, this is "the world's worst humanitarian disaster." But an honest news organization might go on to note that the destitution and the disaster are deliberate results of the world's most relentless war crime.

From a journalistic perspective, getting the perky blonde reporter Jane Ferguson into northern Yemen, where the Houthis have been in control since 2014, is an accomplishment of note. There has been little firsthand reporting from Houthi Yemen, where the worst war crimes have been committed and the worst suffering continues. Ferguson's presence was certainly an opportunity for serious independent reporting. PBS didn't allow that. Based on no persuasive evidence, PBS NewsHour host Judy Woodruff framed the report as coming from "territory held by the Iranian-backed Houthi rebels." There is no credible evidence of meaningful Iranian support for the Houthis. To believe there is, one has to believe the Iranians are consistently getting through the US-Saudi blockade. PBS ignores such realities, as do most Washington policy-makers. Woodruff does acknowledge in her weaselly way that it's "a brutal war that the United States is supporting through a Saudi-led coalition," which is still a long way from the truth that it's a genocidal bombing campaign made possible by the US.

Reporter Ferguson adds to the distraction by focusing on the poverty and suffering as if they came from nowhere:

> Life is slipping away from Maimona Shaghadar. She suffers the agony of starvation in silence. No longer able to walk or talk, at 11 years old, little Maimona's emaciated body weighs just 24 pounds. Watching over her is older brother Najib, who brought her to this remote hospital in Yemen, desperate to get help. The nurses here fight for the lives of children who are starving....
>
> You were never supposed to see these images of Maimona. A blockade of rebel-held Northern Yemen stops reporters from getting here.

> Journalists are not allowed on flights into the area. No cameras, no
> pictures.

That last bit of self-dramatization of the daring journalist glosses over a harsh reality: in addition to waging a genocidal war on a trapped population, the US-Saudi axis is also enforcing isolation and censorship on the victim population. It is a US-Saudi blockade that keeps reporters out, preventing firsthand reporting of endless war crimes. Who says? Jane Ferguson says: "The Houthis cautiously welcomed me in and, once I was there, watched me closely."

Ferguson's coverage of the hunger and starvation is heart-wrenching, journalism at its most moving but least informative. She frames her narrative falsely:

> In the midst of political chaos in Yemen after the Arab Spring, Houthi
> rebels from the north captured the capital, Sanaa, in 2014, before
> sweeping south and causing the country's then president to flee.
> Neighboring Sunni, Saudi Arabia, views the Houthis, from a Yemeni
> sect close to Shia Islam and backed by rival Iran, as an unacceptable
> threat along their border.

Political chaos in Yemen is decades if not centuries old, often fomented by the Saudis and other outside powers. The Houthis have been there for thousands of years (as Ferguson later acknowledges) and their dispute with the Saudis is ancient and territorial. The Houthis' religion is independent. The influence of Iran is largely a Saudi nightfright made increasingly real by the war the Saudis say is supposed to stop Iran. This is contrary to the official story. Ferguson does not acknowledge it.

Ferguson pitches the second part of her three-part series, deceitfully understating American responsibility for the carnage. She doesn't mention that the war would not have started without a US green light, saying only:

> But there is a role played by the US military, one that is sort of more
> passively behind, not quite as visible. And so we're going to be looking
> at that role.

This is the official position of the Pentagon, which has claimed the US is not involved in combat in Yemen. The US role that is "more passively behind, not quite so visible" is still crucial to killing Yemenis on a daily basis. The war on Yemen began with US blessing and continues only because of US political, logistical and materiel support. Jane Ferguson begins this segment with a reasonably accurate albeit morally numb description:

> Inside rebel territory in Yemen, the war rains down from the sky. On the ground, front lines have not moved much in the past three years of conflict. Instead, an aerial bombing campaign by the Saudi-led and American-backed coalition hammers much of the country's north....

Treating war crimes against defenseless people as a kind of natural disaster that "rains down from the sky" is barren of journalistic integrity and gives the war criminals a pass when they need calling out. Ferguson goes on in her antiseptic, no-one's-responsible manner to illustrate the killing of civilians and the destruction of civilian facilities, including a Doctors Without Borders cholera clinic. She also documents US-made weaponry, including an array of unexploded bombs and a collection of cluster bombs. She doesn't mention that cluster bombs are banned by most of the world and constitute a war crime in themselves. She does note that cluster bombs often wound civilians, then follows this fact with the gratuitously propagandistic comment: "The Houthis have also targeted civilians, throwing anyone suspected of opposing them in jail." She has no follow-up, leaving the audience with a false moral equivalence between blowing off a child's arm and throwing someone in jail. But it gets worse. Ferguson later gets off this political judo move:

> Most people here, whether they support the Houthis or not, know that many of the bombs being dropped are American. It provides a strong propaganda tool for the Houthi rebels, who go by the slogan "Death to America."

What does that even mean, "go by the slogan 'Death to America'?" Again, Ferguson has no follow-up. Later she shows a crowd chanting "Death to America" as if that has relevance. Why wouldn't the defenseless victims wish death on the country that murders them without surcease? The main purpose of introducing "Death to America" (with all its Iran-hostage resonance) seems propagandistic, to inflame American audiences that remain in denial about their own very real war guilt. American-supported bombing of Yemen is a fact. It is, quite literally, "Death to Yemen." For Ferguson to call it a "strong propaganda tool" is a Big Lie in classic propaganda tradition. For PBS to broadcast this lie is to engage in propaganda. PBS and Ferguson not only blame the victim, they characterize their very real victimization as if it weren't true but mere propaganda. At the end of the segment, Ferguson once again engages in false moral equivalence:

> Both the Houthis and the Saudi-led coalition have disregarded innocent civilian life in this war. Every bomb that falls on a hospital, office building or home causes more unease about where they come from.

While it may well be true that "both sides" have killed or wounded civilians, there is absolutely no comparison in scale. The US-Saudi coalition comprises mass murderers; the Houthis don't come close. "Every bomb that falls," Ferguson should have said, is dropped by the US-Saudi side on the Houthi side. There is no doubt where the bombs come from.

In her third and last PBS segment, Ferguson foregoes any effort to explore the reality of hundreds of years of Houthi-Saudi territorial conflict. Instead, she goes to bed with US propaganda, opening with a crowd of Yemenis chanting "Death to America" and then stating:

> These rebels, known as Houthis, seized control of Sanaa City and much of the north of the country in 2014. They are of Yemen's Zaydi sect and closest to Shia Islam. Their growing power caused alarm across the border in Sunni Saudi Arabia, so the Saudis formed a coalition of Arab countries to defeat them, a coalition backed by the United States.

This is so twisted it amounts to intellectual fraud. Yemen has a long, tortured history of foreign interference. In the years before 2014, Yemen served (without much choice) as a base for US drone bases. At the same time, the international community imposed a Saudi puppet as Yemen's president (presently in exile in Saudi Arabia). In 2014, the

Houthi uprising, widely popular among Yemen's 28 million people, drove out both the US drone bases and the Saudi puppet president. The Houthis represented something like Yemeni independence, which the US, Saudis and others opposed with lethal force.

US support for the war in Yemen constitutes an impeachable offense for two American presidents. So do continuing drone strikes, also known as presidential assassinations. The war began because President Obama approved it and the Saudis were willing to bomb a defenseless population. But according to Ferguson:

> The Saudis and the United States say the Houthis are puppets for Tehran, a proxy form of Iranian military power right on Saudi Arabia's doorstep.

This is real propaganda. There is no evidence that the Houthis are anyone's puppets (which is one reason they need to be oppressed). Historically, the Houthis are an oppressed people who keep rising up again and again to re-establish their own freedom and independence. There is no credible evidence of significant Iranian presence in Yemen. PBS and Ferguson certainly present none, and neither have the US or Saudi governments. American demonization of Iran has been a fixed idea since 1979, rooted in two psychopathologies: American unwillingness to accept responsibility for imposing a police state on Iran and American inability to see the hostage-taking of 1979 as a rational response to past American predation. American exceptionalism is a sickness that punishes others, currently millions of innocent Yemenis.

Ferguson concludes her series with a dishonest use of journalistic balance, first with a quote from Senator Bernie Sanders arguing that the US role in the Yemen war is unconstitutional. Rather than assess that straightforward argument, Ferguson turns to an Idaho Republican, Senator James Reich, who offers fairy dust and lies:

> The Iranians are in there and they are causing the difficulty that's there. If the Iranians would back off, I have no doubt that the Saudis will back off. But the Saudis have the absolute right to defend themselves.

Imaginary Iranians aren't there now, and they weren't there when the Saudis attacked in 2015. No one attacked Saudi Arabia. The Saudis are not defending themselves, they are waging aggressive war.

By balancing these quotes, Ferguson creates yet another false moral equivalence. There is no meaningful equivalence between Bernie Sanders challenging the president's right to take the country to war on his own and James Reich using a lie to defend war-making that disregards Congress. PBS should be ashamed. Jane Ferguson offers a fig leaf with another quote from Bernie Sanders:

> I don't know that I have ever participated in a vote which says that the United States must be an ally to Saudi's militaristic ambitions. This is a despotic regime which treats women as third-class citizens. There are no elections there. They have their own goals and their own ambitions.

All this is true, but Ferguson has no follow up. Instead she again offers spurious analysis: "American support for Saudi Arabia is a major propaganda tool for the Houthis." No it's not. American support for the Saudis is not propaganda, it's a lethal reality for the Houthis and a crime against humanity for the world. Ferguson completes her piece with a soppy lament for civilian victims, as if no one is responsible for their suffering. That's one last lie. There are many people responsible for the horror in Yemen today and leading the list is the US-Saudi coalition. It doesn't take much intelligence to see that, but apparently it takes more courage than PBS has to report the obvious.

90.

Yemen Is Not a Wedge Issue, It's an Ongoing Nexus of War Crimes

"Saudi Arabia must face the damage from the past three-plus years of war in Yemen. The conflict has soured the kingdom's relations with the international community, affected regional security dynamics and harmed its reputation in the Islamic world. Saudi Arabia is in a unique position to simultaneously keep Iran out of Yemen and end the war on favorable terms if it change its role from warmaker to peacemaker. Saudi Arabia could use its clout and leverage within Western circles and empower international institutions and mechanisms to resolve the conflict."

JAMAL KHASHOGGI, WASHINGTON POST, SEPTEMBER 11, 2018

On October 2, three weeks after the Post published Khashoggi's column, he entered the Saudi consulate in Istanbul, where unknown Saudis apparently rendered him an un-person. Why? No one knows with certainty, but the conventional wisdom is that he was terminated with prejudice for being too outspoken. He was a journalist in self-imposed exile for fear of losing his freedom if he stayed in Saudi Arabia. Some have referred to him as a "dissident," but the evidence of his writing, especially his last column, reveals him as more of a lap cat whose purring is dissent only in the ears of a frightened listener.

Khashoggi treads very lightly in the piece quoted above. He does not call for anyone to take responsibility for what he fails to call a genocidal war started by the Saudis, unprovoked, but with US blessing and vital tactical support. Khashoggi frets about damage to Saudi reputation, not thousands of dead Yemenis, most of them non-combatants. He affirms the myth of Iranian responsibility for the Yemen civil war. He invites a fantasy of Saudi leadership in peace-making, as if the Saudis were not the aggressors and as if the

Saudis had not sponsored decades of international terrorism (including Saudi involvement in 9/11).

Saudi Arabia is a longstanding, well-oiled, totalitarian monarchy. Khashoggi writes like the classic courtier, trying to nudge his lord and master in the direction of a better way ever so tactfully. Khashoggi is a hat-in-hand near-apologist for the unacceptable. But even that limited suggestion of a better wardrobe for brutality was apparently too much for the naked emperors of the Saudi dictatorship.

Political assassination is a common and useful tool for tyrants. The US assassinates people all the time, most ruthlessly by remote drone killings with little care for collateral damage. US assassination teams have taken out Osama bin Laden and unknown others. That's one reason the US has special forces deployed in more than a hundred countries. For decades US-trained monsters have run puppet tyrannies in places like Guatemala and, still, Honduras. There is a hidden interface between our professional military and the world of non-governmental black ops.

This was most recently illustrated by the BuzzFeed News report of American mercenaries assassinating "undesirables" in southern Yemen, the part of Yemen the Saudis are not bombing. There the UAE (United Arab Emirates), a titular Saudi ally, maintains repressive control on the ground behind a fig leaf of the "legitimate" Yemeni government that exercises no effective authority over anything. In this case, a US company, Spear Operations Group (a Delaware corporation) hires US veterans and contracts with the UAE to execute designated opponents, one of whom was a member of a group that had won the Nobel Peace Prize. Sometimes the contractor is the US itself, as with Blackwater in Iraq. Secret and private, operations like this are likely well-known to the US (on a need-to-know basis in places like the CIA or State Department) but remain unregulated and unacknowledged by Congress.

American assassination activities provide an especially bitter irony to those blathering US senators linking the Yemen war to the Khashoggi disappearance as a human rights violation to which the US must respond to maintain its credibility. Several senators, across the political spectrum (an indication of how narrow and shallow that spectrum is), tried to use the Khashoggi case as a wedge issue for ending the US support for the Saudi-led war on Yemen. That is such a squishy, amoral position (almost prone), but passes in contemporary American politics for something like courage, not because it's brave but because so few will go even that tiny bit of the way toward any truthfully principled stand, when in fact two such stands are needed here.

First, the principled stand on the Yemen war – once Obama's war, now Trump's war: this war is an unspeakable atrocity and has been since the US green-lighted it in 2015. This unjustified, undeclared war on the poorest nation in the region is a nexus of unrelenting war crimes and crimes against humanity. The Saudis and their allies daily bomb a defenseless country without regard for killing civilians in school buses, hospitals, bazaars. The Saudis and their allies, guided by the US and using US munitions, have bombed the country so intensely as to turn the environment itself into a biological weapon, spreading disease and famine to millions of people. There is no innocence here: the US, the Saudis and all their allies have blood on their hands for which global decency demands a full accounting (perhaps in vain). The US should never have participated in this war and should end its participation yesterday.

Second, the principled stand on Khashoggi has nothing to do with Yemen or politics of any sort. The principled stand is simple: the Saudis have no right – none, under any principle of international, local, sharia, or any other law – they have no right to entice any victim into a lethal trap. That is not OK. So why is that so hard to say? Well, some equivocate, we don't know exactly what happened, and our president smears those who see the obvious by claiming we are calling the Saudis guilty until proven innocent. Yes, there's a sense in which that has a whiff of truth, but that whiff comes straight from the Saudi cover-up. The Saudis know what happened in the consulate, the Saudis know who did what to Khashoggi, the Saudis know where Khashoggi is now and what condition he's in, and the Saudis are not telling what they know.

The Saudis could make us all look like fools by simply producing and releasing a healthy, happy Khashoggi, maybe even giving him a wedding present. The president seems to think that might happen. What's the matter with you?

The war in Yemen is criminal and unacceptable. The war in Yemen has been criminal and unacceptable since it began. Now, almost four years later, it's ever more criminal and unacceptable and still few people understand that obvious horror. The war is morally abhorrent and should be rejected for that reason alone.

Luring an inconvenient journalist into your consulate and dismembering him while still alive – if that's what happened – is criminal and unacceptable. Most people seem to get that, even if they don't know what to do about it. State assassination is morally abhorrent and should be rejected for that reason alone.

Linking the assassination of one man to the deliberate slaughter of thousands and the onslaught against millions, as if they have any rational relationship, is an exercise in moral bankruptcy.

* * *

A priest, a rabbi and a Muslim journalist walk into a Saudi Embassy.

The priest and the rabbi come out alive.

And Trump praises the Saudis for religious tolerance.

91.

Afghanistan in 2019: Fewer US Troops, More CIA Torture and Killings

"No other country in the world symbolizes the decline of the American empire as much as Afghanistan. There is virtually no possibility of a military victory over the Taliban and little chance of leaving behind a self-sustaining democracy — facts that Washington's policy community has mostly been unable to accept.... It is a vestigial limb of empire, and it is time to let it go."

OP-ED BY ROBERT D. KAPLAN, THE NEW YORK TIMES, JANUARY 1, 2019

This is the cynical voice of American imperialism speaking through one of its more reliable hand-puppets. Foreign Policy has twice named Robert Kaplan one of the "Top 100 Global Thinkers." In his op-ed, Kaplan blames Afghanistan's current problems on the illegal US war on Iraq in 2003, adding parenthetically and without further explanation: "which I mistakenly supported." The unintended joke here is that he frames the Iraq War as a mistake largely because it diverted the US from nation-building in Afghanistan. Yes, he says exactly that. He has nothing to say about either war's criminality or US atrocities. Those are not serious concerns for the imperial mindset – those are just the necessary inconveniences of maintaining an empire. He even appears unaware that his formulation about Afghanistan and the decline of the American empire perfectly fits the historical reality of US defeat in Vietnam.

On New Year's Eve, the day before Kaplan's op-ed, the lengthy lead story in the Times was headlined: "CIA-Led Afghan Forces Leave Grim Trail of Abuse." This report is based on months of reporting on night raids, torture and summary executions of Afghan civilians carried out by CIA-trained death squads, euphemistically called "strike forces" in the paper. The instances described in the report are horrifying and savage. In one, the death squad puts bags over the heads of two brothers, executing them with their families in the next room. For good measure, the death squad blew up the room where the bodies lay.

Perhaps it's just another sign of American psychic numbing, but the Times story seems to have provoked little response from other media, from politicians of any stripe, or from the public. More American war crimes in some Muslim country? Well, Happy New Year!

The US invaded Afghanistan on October 7, 2001, under Operation Enduring Freedom, accusing the Taliban of harboring some of the 9/11 attackers, most of whom were Saudis. More to the point, the US has been creating havoc in Afghanistan at least since 1979, when we started training the mujahedeen to fight the Russians only to receive "our" Islamist radicals' blowback at the Twin Towers. Afghanistan is a country about the size of Texas with a population of about 35 million (almost 40% literate). Some 63% of the population is under 25 years old and so has little conscious memory of a time when Afghans weren't the targets of the American war machine.

Presently the US has about 14,000 troops in Afghanistan, but nobody now quite knows how long they'll be there. Mostly what US troops do is protect the official government from the apparent majority of the population that prefers the Taliban or some imaginary other option. The Afghan government controls little more than half the country most of the time. All sides have been killing civilians at the rate of about 8,000 a year for several years now, with the US and allies doing most of the killing. At least 18 CIA operatives were killed in Afghanistan from 2001 to 2017. This disproportionately deadly toll has not done much to win the hearts and minds of the people, but in seventeen years, the US hasn't figured out how to do anything else better than create carnage.

The CIA-run death squad campaign isn't new, but it has been seriously expanded during the past two years. Death squad personnel run into the thousands, mostly Afghans, but are recruited, trained, equipped and controlled by CIA agents or CIA contractors. They operate independently of the US military command, typically without the military's knowledge. They are effectively terrorist cells. They carry out night raids, long opposed by the Afghan government and the population at large. The night raids target civilians the CIA thinks it has reason to assassinate or capture and torture. The Times report describes survivors of night raids, all of whom insist on their innocence. There is no official accountability for these terrorist tactics:

> A spokeswoman for the C.I.A. would not comment, nor would Afghans directly involved with the forces. Afghan security officials in Kabul tried to play down the level of the forces' autonomy and the nature of their abuses. When pressed with details of specific cases, they did not respond.

And there is no evidence that these terrorist tactics are doing any good in a country that has despised foreign invaders for centuries. Virtually the same US terror tactics failed spectacularly in Vietnam. There the CIA mounted the infamous Phoenix Program to terrorize South Vietnamese villages with CIA-run death squads who "neutralized more than 80,000 real or suspected Viet Cong."

Once Osama bin Laden escaped capture in 2001, the US war in Afghanistan lacked any clear mission. The Bush administration and the military shifted their attention to making war on Iraq instead. Failing to disengage sensibly from Afghanistan, the US let the war drift on mindlessly. In 2009, President Obama declared Afghanistan the "smart war" and decided to escalate it without really figuring out why. Obama relied particularly on CIA drones to kill massive numbers of people, mostly civilians, ultimately to no useful purpose.

In 2016, President Trump campaigned on getting out of Afghanistan. Once in office, trump appointed Mike Pompeo to run the CIA. Pompeo set out to expand CIA killing, particularly with the death squads discreetly called "strike forces" by the Times. This paramilitary escalation, primarily against the Taliban, was first reported in October 2017, creating little stir. Six months later, the CIA still denied the story was true. In the fall of 2017, Pompeo expressed US policy this way:

We can't perform our mission if we're not aggressive. This is unforgiving, relentless. You pick the word. Every minute, we have to be focused on crushing our enemies.

At the same time, the Institute for Public Policy had a different perspective, offered by former State Department career officer Matthew Hoh, who served in Afghanistan. Hoh had resigned in 2009 in protest against the Obama administration's escalation of the war there. Calling the 2017 CIA's expanded death squads part of "the broader war campaign of the United States in the Muslim world," Hoh accurately predicted:

> This CIA program of using Afghan militias to conduct commando raids, the vast majority of which will be used against civilians despite what the CIA states, falls in line with American plans to escalate the use of air and artillery strikes against the Afghan people in Taliban-held areas, almost all of whom are Pashtuns. Again, the purpose of this campaign is not to achieve a political settlement or reconciliation, but to brutally subjugate and punish the people, mostly rural Pashtuns, who support the Taliban and will not give in to the corrupt American run government in Kabul.

Since 2001, the US has watched passively as three presidents waged war on Afghanistan, each committing war crimes and crimes against humanity that would surely, in a just society, constitute impeachable offenses. For all the public splutter of self-designated serious people over the possible withdrawal of 2,000 US troops from Syria, the absence of real reaction to how badly it's all going in Afghanistan is sort of amazing (or would be for anyone still capable of amazement).

92.

Career War Criminal Elliott Abrams to Lead US on Venezuela

"In 1985, an activist for the relatives of the disappeared [persons in Guatemala], named Rosario Godoy, was abducted by the army. She was raped. Her mutilated body was found alongside that of her baby. The baby's fingernails had been torn out. The Guatemalan army, when asked about this atrocity, said, 'Oh, they died in a traffic accident.'"

"When [US human rights official] Elliott Abrams was asked about this accident, he affirmed also that they died in a traffic accident. This activist raped and mutilated, the baby with his fingernails pulled out, Abrams says it's a traffic accident."

ALLAN NAIRN,
ON DEMOCRACY NOW JANUARY 30, 2019

Some say history repeats itself. Mark Twain said history doesn't repeat, but it rhymes. The January 25 appointment of convicted perjurer Elliott Abrams as the new US Special Envoy on Venezuela is evidence that history just goes on and on and on with ironic cruelty and relentless injustice. That would be especially true if you happen to have the world's largest proven oil reserve, as Venezuela does.

The malign US interference in Venezuela goes back more than a century. For decades the idea of "Venezuelan democracy" was a US-inflected oxymoron. When Venezuela somehow elected Hugo Chávez president in 1999 – legitimately – turnout was 63% and Chávez won 56% of the vote (both better numbers than the 2016 US presidential election). Chávez was a leader of failed coups in 1992 that tried to topple the corrupt kleptocracy of then-president Carlos Andrés Pérez, who had been elected promising to resist US meddling, only to

529

become a corrupt tool of it (and impeached in 1993). The US responded to the democratic process in Venezuela with at least one coup attempt against Chavez in 2002 and chronic economic warfare for two decades. Despite its oil, Venezuela has not prospered and remains a country of about 31 million people, one in five of whom are poor.

Venezuela is now in play once more, with no reasonably decent outcome in sight. Whichever vicious and corrupt side wins, most of the Venezuelan people are likely to lose. In a sense, it was ever thus. Presently, the US has taken sides with self-proclaimed Venezuelan interim president Juan Guaidó. On January 22, Guaidó leveraged his position as President of the Venezuelan National Assembly to make an ingenious but untested argument that the national presidency was "vacant" and he had a constitutional obligation to fill it (or something like that – try to find a coherent explanation of what actually happened). In an alternative reality, Venezuelan President Nicholas Maduro was re-elected president last May and sworn in on January 10. The Venezuelan constitution is invoked on both sides, and there appears to be no institution with sufficient authority to resolve the issue. The constitutional basis of Guaidó's position is specious on its face, since he relies on Article 233 and none of its conditions apply. Guaidó asserts that the National Assembly, controlled by the opposition party, voided the May 2018 election results and that therefore when Maduro's term expired on January 9, the presidency became vacant. On Maduro's side is the Constituent Assembly, a murky institution created in 2017 that runs in parallel with the National Assembly. The CIA acknowledges that the "ruling party" controls the Constituent Assembly, but states: "The US Government [like 40 other countries] does not recognize the Assembly, which has generally used its powers to rule by decree rather than to reform the constitution."

So, of course when Juan Guaidó used the National Assembly's power to rule by decree, the US rushed to recognize his somewhat imaginary government without hesitation, without analysis, without restraint. Even if there is no practical way to sort out the competing constitutional legalities in an orderly, peaceful way, the US might have given the rule of law at least lip service. Instead, the US polarizes the world further, demanding that other nations help make Venezuela worse. On January 26, US Secretary of State Mike Pompeo told the UN Security Council:

> Now, it is time for every other nation to pick a side. No more delays, no more games. Either you stand with the forces of freedom, or you're in league with Maduro and his mayhem.

Whose mayhem? Whose economic sanctions? Whose periodic coup attempts? Pompeo embraces a version of the Big Lie about Venezuela we've been hearing for a long, long time. The day before he spoke at the UN, Pompeo announced the appointment of Attorney Elliott Abrams, a promising sign that the Venezuelan future will be dark and bloody. In his announcement, Pompeo invoked "the Venezuelan people" at least nine times, which should be warning enough. Pompeo said, complete with the contradiction as to which people will be served:

> Elliott Abrams is coming aboard to lead our efforts on Venezuela.... Elliott's passion for the rights and liberties of all peoples makes him a perfect fit and a valuable and timely addition.... Elliott will be a true asset to our mission to help the Venezuelan people fully restore democracy and prosperity to their country.... he is eager to advance President Trump's agenda and promote the ideals and interests of the American people.

President Trump was talking about invading Venezuela in 2017, but was dissuaded by Rex Tillerson, then Secretary of State and National Security Advisor Gen. H.R. McMaster. The idea is still not off the table, as National Security Advisor John Bolton recently confirmed (along with flashing his notepad with "5,000 troops to Colombia," unexplained). Bolton is apparently one of the architects of the current coup effort in Venezuela, along with Pompeo and Vice President Mike Pence. Pence was on the phone assuring US support for Guaidó before he named himself president (on behalf of the Venezuelan people who were not involved).

Adding Elliott Abrams to this team does little to provide hope for the Venezuelan people. Contrary to Pompeo's assertion, Abrams has never demonstrated "passion for the rights and liberties of all peoples," least of all Palestinians. But Abrams's demonstrated capacity for supporting subversion, torture and mass killing does indeed make him "a perfect fit and a valuable and timely addition." After all, Abrams represents the continuity of 40 years of genocidal US global policies. And he participated in many of them, as reported with devastating detail on Democracy NOW as well as the terror timeline in The Intercept, but not so much in mainstream media.

In 1981, at the age of 33, Abrams was unanimously confirmed by the Senate as Ronald Reagan's Assistant Secretary of State for Human Rights and Humanitarian Affairs. Reagan's first choice, Ernest Lefever, had been rejected in part for his view that the US should support vicious regimes if they were our allies.

Abrams managed to carry out that policy very well, starting in El Salvador in the early 1980s, when our Salvadoran government ally could carry out human rights violations and mass killings almost without reproach. The government killed nearly 75,000 people. No atrocity was worthy of Abrams's condemnation. He had no sympathy for those seeking asylum from US-sponsored state violence, telling Congress:

> **Some groups argue that illegal aliens who are sent back to El Salvador meet persecution and often death. Obviously, we do not believe these claims or we would not deport these people.**

Overseeing US involvement in Guatemala, Abrams claimed to be equally oblivious to the human rights depredations of the government of Gen. Ríos Montt, a born-again evangelical Christian. He was a hero to the Reagan administration as his death squads helped kill some 200,000 Guatemalans. Ríos Montt was eventually convicted in a Guatemalan court of waging genocide against his own people. If there's any evidence Abrams regrets his support for crimes against humanity, that evidence is well hidden. In 2017, his status as an unindicted war criminal was enough to keep Trump from naming him Secretary of State.

In 1983, Abrams supported the US invasion of Grenada. He also pushed for a full-scale invasion of Nicaragua, where he was already involved in the support of the terrorist Contras against the Sandinista government. When Congress cut off support to the Contras, Abrams was involved in the criminal activities of the so-called Iran-Contra operation that included selling drugs to support the Contras and shipping arms to Iran to support the Contras. Abrams escaped serious consequences for his crimes, pleading guilty in 1991 to two counts of lying to Congress. Without remorse, Abrams wrote what he thought of his prosecutors: "You miserable filthy bastards, you bloodsuckers." The first President Bush pardoned him and five other Iran-Contra criminals on Christmas Eve 1992. (These pardons were supported by current attorney-general nominee William Barr.)

In 1985, the Reagan administration was aware that Panamanian president Manuel Noriega was a heavy drug dealer. When a former Panama health official was about to release what he said was proof of Noriega's cocaine smuggling, Noriega's agents seized and tortured the man, sawing off his head while he was still alive. When the news became public and caused a stir in the US, Abrams went out of his way to block Congressional hearings, claiming that Noriega was "being really helpful to us" with Nicaragua and that he was "really not that big a problem."

Abrams was reportedly involved in the US-supported coup attempts against Chavez in Venezuela in 2002. In 2003, Abrams played a mysterious role in squelching a peace proposal from Iran that might have ended the US war against Iraq.

In 2006, Abrams was instrumental in suppressing the results of a legitimate democratic election. In support of the corrupt Palestinian Authority, the Bush administration pushed for elections in the West Bank and Gaza. To their surprise, Hamas won. In response, Abrams and others tried to organize a coup. Hamas effected a counter-coup, the Bush administration refused to recognize the election winners, and that US-enforced injustice is at the heart of suffering in Gaza now.

Everywhere Elliott Abrams goes, innocent people are left bleeding or dead. Objections among the predominant political and pundit classes are hard to find. The conventional wisdom, especially among Democrats, is to support the US coup attempt but object to any military intervention, as if that satisfied any standard of national sovereignty. Rep. Tulsi Gabbard seems to be alone in saying that the US "needs to stay out of Venezuela." But now Elliott Abrams is our man for Venezuela. And that suggests that tens of thousands of Venezuelans will soon be having serious "traffic accidents."

93.

Senator Warren Calls for End of US Support of War Crimes in Yemen

"Yemen is the world's largest humanitarian crisis. In 2018, an estimated 22.2 million people – 75 percent of the population were in need of humanitarian assistance. A total of 17.8 million people were food-insecure and 8.4 million people did not know how to obtain their next meal. Conflict, protracted displacement, disease and deprivation continued to inflict suffering on the country's population. Disruption to commercial imports, inflation, lack of salary payments to civil servants and rising prices of basic commodities exacerbated people's vulnerability. Despite a difficult operating environment, throughout the year, 254 international and national partners actively coordinated to assist people with the most acute needs in priority districts across Yemen's 22 governorates. Together they assisted over 7.9 million people monthly with some form of humanitarian assistance."

UN OFFICE FOR THE COORDINATION OF HUMANITARIAN AFFAIRS,
FEBRUARY 7, 2019

That sanitized United Nations assessment above, horrific as it is in its abstract body-counting way, only begins to describe the terrible reality that foreign countries have inflicted on the poorest country in the region.

A starker reality is that the US has aided and abetted a criminal, genocidal war against Yemen, mostly carried out by Saudi Arabia, the United Arab Emirates (UAE) and several allies. From the beginning, this war has been a nexus of war crimes that included using cluster bombs on civilian targets, such as weddings, funerals, hospitals and schools. The US was involved from the start in selecting those and other targets. The US provided intelligence, maintenance, mid-air refueling and support for a naval blockade (an act of war) that helped starve a country that has always needed to import food to survive.

There has never been any justification for the US to unleash this carnage on Yemen. In 2014-2015, the native Houthis won a civil war and regained control of that part of Yemen they had previously controlled for hundreds of years. The internationally-imposed "legitimate" government fled to Saudi Arabia. Further Houthi expansion was limited by a variety of forces that included government loyalists, al Qaeda and ISIS enclaves, independent militias and tribal resistance. Yemen might have been left to sort itself out (the Houthis did eliminate al Qaeda and ISIS from their area of control). In 2015, Yemen posed no serious threat to anyone other than itself.

But the Saudis were sulking, not only because they lost their puppet government in Yemen, but more so because the US was actually treating Iran as a sovereign nation capable of behaving responsibly under the proper circumstances. The US was joining in the multilateral agreement that has so far halted Iran's development of nuclear weapons.

So, when Saudi crown prince Mohammed bin Salman (MBS) floated the idea of low-risk bombing of helpless people, the Obama administration collectively shrugged and said in effect: sure, why not, and we'll even help you commit the international crime of waging aggressive war against a neighboring country in the midst of a civil war. And that's what the US did. And that's what the US is still doing. And the US thinks so little of its criminal bloodletting that the president doesn't even mention it in his state of the union address, and most of Congress and the media and the public have no strong objection to a permanent state of war criminality. Well, 30 former Obama officials last fall said Trump should end all US support for the Saudi war on Yemen, without seriously taking responsibility for their own actions that could put them in a war crimes dock (if such a thing is still imaginable):

> The statement by the former senior officials attempts to acknowledge that America's participation in the war — providing intelligence, refueling, and logistical assistance to the Saudi-led coalition — was now clearly a mistake, given the coalition's failure to limit its myriad violations and end the war. But they justify the Obama administration's

initial decision to support the war as based on "a legitimate threat posed by missiles on the Saudi border and the Houthi overthrow of the Yemeni government, with support from Iran."

Iran's involvement in Yemen has always been largely imaginary, and still is. But the Trump administration sees Iranian ghosties and ghoulies everywhere, without ever managing to demonstrate that they actually exist. Unfortunately for the Houthis, they are Shiite Muslims of their own sect – Zaydi – who have been targeted by Saudi Wahhabism for the past 40 years. Imagining Iran was just an excuse for the Saudis to continue their religious war by other means. In 2015, Iran "supported" the Houthis minimally, mostly diplomatically and politically. There has been no evidence that Iranian involvement has exceeded the scale described by Robert Worth, long-time reporter on Yemen, in the current New York Review:

> Houthis have also benefitted – militarily at least – from their alliance with Iran and Hezbollah, which have provided training on infantry tactics, anti-tank fighting, mine-laying, and anti-ship attacks in the Red Sea. Iran has provided ballistic missiles that the Houthis have fired across the border into Saudi Arabia

That's the whole load of Iranian "support" as iterated by Worth, who is no Houthi apologist. He gives no timeframe nor any measure of the extent of this support. Everything he lists is arguably defensive, including the missiles if they followed the Saudi bombing. But the Iranian strawman is rigidly fixed in the minds of US officials and media reporters, even Worth, who ignores his own later evidence and reflexively writes: "Huge obstacles to peace remain, above all the Houthis' military alliance with Iran, which is what led the Saudis to launch the war in the first place." So at least he acknowledges the Saudis waging aggressive war and even uses an apt Nazi reference to describe the Saudi mindset: "They consider the Houthis an Iranian dagger aimed at their heart."

Southern Yemen is subject to something much more like a real Nazi occupation. Some uncertain amount of southern Yemen, including Aden, is titularly under the control of the "official" Yemeni government. The same area and beyond is more effectively under the control of the UAE military, whose shock troops include thousands of child soldiers from Somalia. The UAE works closely with US advisors on the ground. The UAE is reliably reported to run black sites, a network of secret prisons where they torture and kill prisoners at will. The US military officially testified to the Senate Armed Services Committee on February 5 that the US has not observed such activities. The official US see-no-evil written statement on Yemen and the rest of the region is predictably optimistic and opaque.

Senator Elizabeth Warren questioned the US regional commander, Gen. Joseph L. Votel about UAE prisoner abuses reported by the United Nations, the Associated Press, Human Rights Watch and Amnesty International. The general's response was one of official ignorance or deniability: "I think what I'm saying to you is that we have no observations of our own – our people that have actually seen this…. I have not reached any kind of conclusion that they are conducting these activities…." By omission, the general made clear that the US has made no effort to determine the truth. This is the first rule of any cover-up: "I don't want to know and you don't want to know." (Votel was equally oblivious to reports that Saudi and UAE military were illegally transferring US arms to militias and other third parties in Yemen.)

"Turning a blind eye is not acceptable," was Warren's response. Earlier in the hearing, following up on the US support for Saudi bombing missions, Warren said:

> I'm asking you questions about the details of the help we give the Saudis because they continue to conduct bombing runs. They continue to perpetuate one of the worst man-made humanitarian disasters of the modern era. During this civil war, more than 85,000 children under the age of 5 have starved to death, and tens of thousands of civilians have been killed.
>
> This military engagement is not authorized. We need to end US support for this war now.

If this is the first time you're learning about a US senator and presidential candidate publicly calling for the end of US involvement in the illegal war on Yemen, what does that tell you about American media and politics?

Meanwhile, the December ceasefire brokered by the UN continues to hold shakily, without significant US support, and the civilian death toll from hunger and disease mounts.

94.

Alleged 'Spy' Monica Witt is No Justification for US War on Iran

"Inside the government, some officials called her "Wayward Storm." Her real name was Monica Elfriede Witt, an exemplary Air Force counterintelligence agent who had studied Persian and carried out covert missions in Iraq, Saudi Arabia and Qatar".

NEW YORK TIMES, FEBRUARY 13, 2019

"... American authorities have struggled to conclude exactly why she turned on her country."

NEW YORK TIMES, FEBRUARY 16, 2019

"I served in the Air Force for 10 years and participated in both the Afghanistan and Iraq Wars. After viewing so much corruption and the damage we were doing both to Iraq/Afghanistan and to the perception of the US, I decided I needed to do as much as I could to help rectify the situation."

MONICA WITT'S UNDATED POST ON IRAQ VETERANS
AGAINST THE WAR

With a coordinated offensive of public relations strikes on February 13, the US government did its best to improve the climate for war by demonizing Monica Witt and further demonizing Iran. The Justice Department released a self-congratulatory press release together with a previously sealed indictment of Monica Witt and four Iranian nationals. The Treasury Department issued a dry press release along with sanctions on two Iranian organizations and ten "associated individuals," based on the authority of executive orders declaring national emergencies as far back as 2007. Other US agencies joining in the legal assault included the FBI, the US Attorney for DC and the Air Force.

The government's efforts sparked a few days of news stories generally following the official line as dictated by the Justice Department headline: "Former US Counterintelligence Agent Charged with Espionage on Behalf of Iran." Or as the Justice Department summarized the story:

> Monica Elfriede Witt, 39, a former US service member and counterintelligence agent, has been indicted by a federal grand jury in the District of Columbia for conspiracy to deliver and delivering national defense information to representatives of the Iranian government. Witt, who defected to Iran in 2013, is alleged to have assisted Iranian intelligence services in targeting her former fellow agents in the US Intelligence Community (USIC). Witt is also alleged to have disclosed the code name and classified mission of a US Department of Defense Special Access Program. An arrest warrant has been issued for Witt, who remains at large.

And that's pretty much how it was reported, with no attention to the internal contradiction: If Witt defected in 2013, why are we only hearing about it in 2019? Did anyone ask if the "news" was conveniently related to the US war-drumming coming out of the Trump administration? The US vice president, secretary of state and other high-ranking officials were spending much of Valentine's week trying to tempt its allies to be smitten with America's burgeoning war fever for Iran. This is an obsession shared by Saudi Arabia and Israel. The Europeans were not impressed.

As for Monica Witt, American media soon lost interest, despite the heroic efforts of the Times to drag out a story with no legs. Well, no, that's not right. The legs were there, the story's deeper meaning is rooted in the illegal wars in Afghanistan and Iraq and the myriad American war crimes committed there. But why would American media revisit such old news?

Monica Witt isn't currently available, reportedly in residence in Iran, beyond the reach of American law and all but the most industrious American media (no known example).

But here, chronologically, is what seems to be known or alleged about Monica Witt's life.

She was born in El Paso, Texas, on April 8, 1979. While she was still young, her family moved to Florida. Her father, Harry Witt, currently lives in Longwood.

In 1984, the US secretary of state designated Iran a "state sponsor of terrorism," and has renewed the designation every year since. (The US also designates Syria, Sudan and North Korea state sponsors of terrorism, but does not so designate Saudi Arabia, Turkey, Russia, Israel, or any other country.)

On March 15, 1995, the US president's Executive Order No. 13224 declared a national emergency to deal with the threat from Iran.

Monica Witt's mother died shortly before Witt enlisted in the Air Force "in or around August 1997" (according to the indictment). She served continuously till "in or around March 2008" (indictment). Apparently the Air Force doesn't keep precise records, or the Justice Department doesn't care. Air Force Times says Witt "joined the Air Force on Dec. 17, 1997."

From February 1998, Witt spent 14 months at the US Defense Language Institute in Monterey, California, where she learned to speak Farsi, the Iranian language.

In May 1999, Witt "deployed to several overseas locations in order to conduct classified missions" (indictment). She remained overseas till November 2003. She served at various times in Saudi Arabia, Diego Garcia and Greece.

On March 20, 2003, the US invaded Iraq. Witt's conduct in the war earned her an Air Medal with the citation (omitted from the indictment):

> **Staff Sergeant Monica E. Witt distinguished herself by meritorious achievement while participating in sustained aerial flight from March 29 to April 18. During this period, the airmanship and courage of Sergeant Witt in the successful accomplishment of these important reconnaissance missions in support of Operation IRAQI FREEDOM, under extremely hazardous conditions, demonstrated her outstanding proficiency and steadfast devotion to duty. The professional**

ability and outstanding aerial accomplishments of Sergeant Witt reflect great credit upon herself and the United States Air Force.

In November 2003, Witt was assigned as a Special Agent criminal investigator and counterintelligence officer for the Air Force Office of Special Investigations (AFOSI), which has about 2,000 Special Agents. She conducted classified operations in the Middle East for AFOSI till March 2008. She served a tour in Iraq in 2005 and Qatar in 2006. She separated from the Air Force on June 12, 2008. From then till August 2010 she continued to work for AFOSI, but as a government contractor. According to the indictment, Witt "held a TOP SECRET/SCI security clearance from the time she joined the Air Force in 1997 until she terminated her employment" in 2010. Her career awards and decorations include the Air Medal, three Air Force Commendation medals and three Aerial Achievement medals.

In June 2008, Witt earned her bachelor's degree from the University of Maryland University College. The next few years were somewhat sketchy, according to the Times: In 2011, she lived in low-income housing and at some point was homeless, but she also entered graduate school at George Washington University, from which she graduated in 2012. GW's International Affairs Review published two of her articles sympathetic to Iran. A classmate recalled her having symptoms of PTSD, as well as talking about drone strikes, extrajudicial killings and atrocities against children that her military colleagues would brag about. Later, in August 2012, she wrote a piece for Iranian PressTV about sexual harassment and rape in the US military (which reportedly is worst in the Air Force).

In February 2012, as the Justice Department press release puts it:

> In Feb. 2012, Witt traveled to Iran to attend the Iranian New Horizon Organization's "Hollywoodism" conference, an IRGC [Iranian Revolutionary Guards Corps] sponsored event aimed at, among other things, condemning American moral standards and promoting anti-US propaganda.

As self-described, New Horizon, the International Institute of Independent Thinkers and Artists, openly welcomes people with a wide range of views, including those who are anti-Zionist and anti-Imperialist. New Horizon is routinely demonized in the US as anti-Semitic and anti-American (as in the above quote). But objectively, what's wrong with condemning "American moral standards"? Americans of all stripes do it all the time. And "Hollywoodism," however defined, has long been a staple of moral indignation and cultural criticism. Are we all now vulnerable to federal indictment for such thought-crimes? According to Monica Witt's indictment, this event is at the beginning of the alleged conspiracy to deliver secret information to Iran. The indictment also asserts that Witt's position as a Special Agent during 2003-2008 was also part of the conspiracy beginning in 2012.

The US government also indicts Witt for calling herself a US veteran and making "statements that were critical of the US government, knowing these videos would be broadcast by Iranian media outlets." The US also indicts her for converting to Islam in a ceremony she knew would be broadcast.

On May 25, 2012, the indictment notes, the FBI warned Monica Witt that Iran intelligence services might be trying to recruit her.

In February 2013, Witt attended another New Horizon conference and told Iranian officials that she wanted to emigrate to Iran. The Iranians were suspicious and reluctant. Clearly she was – and is – a possible double agent. The Daily Beast calls her (inaccurately) "Iran's dumbest spy," while inadvertently offering support for the double agent hypothesis: "that Witt's digital fingerprints led to the exposure of a broader spy network." The government's belated indictment could be part of her cover. After several months of back and forth in 2013, Monica Witt allegedly defected to Iran on August 28, and may have been there ever since.

On April 2, 2015, Iran signed a multilateral agreement to limit its nuclear weapons development. On July 14, 2015, Iran and seven other parties signed a joint plan of action. The other signers were the US, France, GB, Russia, China, Germany and the EU. On May 8, 2018, President Trump announced that the US would unilaterally withdraw from the agreement. The rest of the signers, as well as the international inspectors, continue to stand by the agreement that Iran has not violated.

Between 2013 and now, the US government would have you believe that Monica Witt "could have brought serious damage to the United States and we will not stand by and let that happen," according to FBI official Nancy McNamara in 2019. The government alleges a variety of cybercrimes involving Witt in 2014 and 2015. That means that the Air Force was so lax that it took no precautionary measures after Witt left the service in 2008, despite her behavior being so overt that even the FBI noticed by 2012. That level of incompetence really isn't that credible.

No doubt the government is constrained somewhat by security concerns – and embarrassment – but when it gets down to particulars, the most serious actual harm the Justice Department cites in its press release is from 2015:

> The Cyber Conspirators created a Facebook account that purported to belong to a USIC employee and former colleague of Witt, and which utilized legitimate information and photos from the USIC [US Intelligence Community] employee's actual Facebook account. This particular fake account caused several of Witt's former colleagues to accept "friend" requests.

While the government also makes much more serious allegations that Witt revealed the names of US operatives, it does not allege specific damage from such revelations, nor from the naming of particular secret projects already many years old (if they still existed at all). Most of the other six counts in the indictment apply to Iranian nationals and the cyberwarfare that is part of current international reality and very much part of the US arsenal deployed against Iran. It's not news that it's a gritty world out there. For the US government to play the Monica Witt case as if it's something that matters, when the indictment remained sealed for seven months, is dishonest. For mainstream media like the Times to promote threat inflation (especially where there is none) is reckless, especially when it feeds into a government determination to have a war at any cost. The Times helped brings us the illegal war in Iraq in 2003 and it's well on its way to bringing us the war in Iran in 2019.

95.

US Makes Stuff Up to Grease the Skids for War on Iran

"Iran's retention of archives related to its past covert nuclear weapons program (the Amad Plan), as well as its efforts to keep many scientists and technicians from that former weapons program working together under the continued leadership of the former head of that program, raise serious questions regarding whether Iran intended to preserve the option to resume elements of a nuclear weapons program in the future...."

US DEPARTMENT OF STATE REPORT,
"ADHERENCE TO AND COMPLIANCE WITH ARMS CONTROL, NONPROLIFERATION, AND
DISARMAMENT AGREEMENTS AND COMMITMENTS," APRIL 2019

With absolutely zero good reasons for waging war on Iran, the Trump administration goes on making stuff up to lie the country into yet another war. The template looks like the Bush administration's successful effort to lie the US into the Iraq War, the catastrophic effects of which keep unfolding.

The State Department report quoted above garnered some anti-Iran media headlines, but the total fact content is slim. The report states as facts that Iran has an archive and that it has kept some of a scientific team working together. That's it. There are no other alleged facts, damaging or otherwise.

There is a lot of speculation in service to fear-mongering (nothing yet as egregious as then National Security Advisor Condoleezza Rice saying in 2003 – with no basis in fact – "We don't want the smoking gun to be a mushroom cloud.")

The Trump people are working on it, but some are apparently dragging their heels for the sake of some sort of integrity. The State Department first posted its report online on April 15, then pulled it down, then re-posted it April 17 (the quote above is from that version), without yet explaining what was going on.

According to Reuters, the report "provoked a dispute with US intelligence agencies and some State Department officials concerned that the document politicizes and slants assessments about Iran, five sources with knowledge of the matter said." Reuters did not report any details of the supposed dispute. As a factual matter, the politicized and slanted assessments of Iran are confirmed by a straight-forward reading of the text.

The larger issue in the report is international compliance with the 1968 Treaty on the Non-Proliferation of Nuclear Weapons (NPT) to which there are 190 parties. Among the non-parties are nuclear-armed states India and Pakistan, as well as South Sudan. The report does not mention them, but has some sharp words for North Korea, Syria, and Russia.

The State Department also omitted Israel, another nuclear-armed state that is not a party to the treaty. Besides being non-compliant, Israel is allied with the US in obdurate opposition to the NPT's primary purpose of nuclear disarmament.

And in a bookend hypocrisy, the report omitted Saudi Arabia and the US suggestion to give them nuclear technology, which would surely be an NPT violation.

The release of the report follows Secretary of State Mike Pompeo's April 10 appearance before the Senate Foreign Relations Committee in support of State's $40 billion budget request. In his written statement, with no supporting evidence, Pompeo submitted an article of faith that is at least partly false:

> We know that the Islamic Republic of Iran's authoritarian regime will continue to use their nation's resources to proliferate conflict in Iraq, Yemen, Syria, and beyond. It will continue to bankroll terrorist groups like Hamas and Hezbollah. The United States will therefore work together with our allies and partners to counter Tehran's aggressive actions to undermine peace and security in the Middle East and beyond.

Last time anyone checked, it was the US that invaded Iraq in a war of aggression that violated international law. It was Saudi Arabia, with US support, that attacked Yemen in a war of aggression that violates international law. In Syria, the country came apart because of multiple factors including a record drought, popular resistance to a dictator, and broad international interference of which Iran was not a major factor. Or, to put it another way, Pompeo lied, in service to his self-proclaimed Christo-fascist ideology.

Republican Senator Rand Paul of Kentucky challenged Pompeo on the administration's apparent march to war on Iran. After trying to sidestep the questioning, Pompeo asserted that the US could attack Iran based on the Authorization to Use Military Force (AUMF) passed overwhelmingly in 2001 after the 9/11 attacks. The only member of Congress to vote against this blank war-making check was Rep. Barbara Lee of Oakland.

The AUMF requires some connection to the 9/11 attackers to be invoked. There has never been any credible evidence connecting Iran even indirectly to 9/11, which was carried out by mostly Saudi nationals. Nevertheless Pompeo deceitfully asserted: "There is a connection between the Islamic Republic of Iran and al-Qaeda. Period, full stop."

"You do not have our permission to go to war in Iran," Senator Paul rejoined, ignoring Pompeo's assertion that the administration didn't need anyone permission.

Two days earlier, on April 8, the Trump administration had advanced its economic war on Iran by designating a part of Iran's government, the Islamic Revolutionary Guard Corps (IRGC), as a foreign terrorist organization. The deliberate provocation was based on little credible current evidence. Pompeo cited alleged IRGC involvement in an earlier 1996 attack and a foiled plot in 2011, both of which involved Saudi targets. Another State Department official blamed Iran for American deaths in the Iraq War. The official party line demonizing Iran was parroted nicely in President Trump's official announcement:

> Today, I am formally announcing my Administration's plan to designate Iran's Islamic Revolutionary Guard Corps (IRGC), including its

Quds Force, as a Foreign Terrorist Organization (FTO) under Section 219 of the Immigration and Nationality Act. This unprecedented step, led by the Department of State, recognizes the reality that Iran is not only a State Sponsor of Terrorism, but that the IRGC actively participates in, finances, and promotes terrorism as a tool of statecraft. The IRGC is the Iranian government's primary means of directing and implementing its global terrorist campaign.

This designation will be the first time that the United States has ever named a part of another government as a FTO. It underscores the fact that Iran's actions are fundamentally different from those of other governments....

Actually, Iran's actions are not fundamentally different from those of other governments, starting with the US which carries out continuing terrorist attacks in Afghanistan, Pakistan, Somalia, Yemen, Libya, and places we have yet to learn about. On April 16, Iran responded to the US terrorist designation by making one of its own against the region's US Central Command, CENTCOM, whose favored terrorist tactics include death squads and drone strikes.

It gets worse for the US. According to Francis Boyle, professor of international law at the University of Illinois College of Law, the designation of the IRGC is:

... a complete negation and violation of the Third Geneva Convention of 1949 and thus a war crime. It opens us up to reprisals against our own military forces. Under the laws of war, reprisals against military personnel are permissible. This is continuing down the path of Bush Jr. determining that the Taliban and al Qaida are not protected by the Geneva Conventions, which was rejected by the US Supreme Court in the Hamden decision.... Iran could now determine that US Special Forces, Seals, Green Berets, Rangers, etc., are terrorists and thus do not benefit from the Third Geneva Convention. *Apparently, for that reason, the Pentagon was against it.* [emphasis added]

CENTCOM's own official description of Iran is free of Trumpish hysteria, while paying lip service to terrorist activities of more than 20 years ago. The detached CENTCOM summary concludes on a somewhat optimistic note:

The UN Security Council has passed a number of resolutions calling for Iran to suspend its uranium enrichment and reprocessing activities and comply with its IAEA obligations and responsibilities, and in July 2015 Iran and the five permanent members, plus Germany (P5+1) signed the Joint Comprehensive Plan of Action (JCPOA) under which Iran agreed to restrictions on its nuclear program in exchange for sanctions relief.

This possibility of re-establishing regional peace and normalization was one of the first things the Trump administration needed no permission to try to destroy. The Trump administration violated international law with its action, since the Iran agreement is part of a UN Security Council resolution (that the US approved). The other members of the Iran agreement continue to try to hold it together, since Iran has met all its obligations under the agreement. The Trump administration falsely claims otherwise. Judged by its actions to date, the Trump administration will be satisfied with nothing less than Iranian capitulation, and if that requires genocide, so be it, all part of God's plan.

Those persuaded that God is on the side of the US may be getting some perverse satisfaction from the brutal weather visited on Iran (also Afghanistan, Iraq, and Syria) since the last week of March. Record rains have covered the region. Flooding has killed an estimated 80 Iranians while threatening and disrupting the lives of ten million. In an unhumanitarian triumph, US sanctions on Iran have blocked humanitarian aid to the flood victims. US sanctions are blocking cash support to the Iranian Red Crescent, the equivalent of the Red Cross. Iranian President Hasan Rouhani has called on the US to lift sanctions for a year to help Iran cope with its humanitarian crisis.

This natural disaster of climate change dimensions has been little reported in American media, a Swedish report in CounterPunch being an exception. In Iran, serious flooding has hit 28 of the country's 31 provinces. The UN has been responding to the need, and as of April 13 reported that "Armenia, Azerbaijan, France, Germany, Japan, Kuwait, Oman, Pakistan, Russia, Switzerland, Turkey, Vatican have provided relief items to the Government of Iran in support of the response." The US response has been limited to attacks and threats. Most US allies in

NATO or the European Union remain AWOL, perhaps cowed by American threats to enforce US law in their home countries (that's the way sanctions work). Last fall, the International Court of Justice (IJC) at the UN ruled that the US had to remove sanctions that target humanitarian trade, food, medicine and civil aviation. The ruling enforced the terms of the 1955 Treaty of Amity between the US and Iran.

Secretary of State Pompeo promptly responded that the international court couldn't tell the US what to do and, anyway, the US was quitting that treaty, "a decision, frankly, that is 39 years overdue." Pompeo accused Iran of bringing a "meritless case" (that Iran won) and of "attempting to interfere with the sovereign rights of the United States." The Christo-fascist sore loser added that "Iran is abusing the IJC for political and propaganda purposes."

So it's no wonder the North Koreans requested that the US remove Pompeo from further negotiations on denuclearization. They blame Pompeo's "talking nonsense" and being "reckless" and "gangster-like" behavior for the failure of talks in February. The Koreans are looking for someone who is "more careful and mature in communicating with us."

Surely Iranians would agree with that, and so should Americans.

96.

NATO May Have Been a Good Thing Once. It's Not Any More

"I am really truly honoured and grateful for the privilege of addressing you all today. And to represent the 29 members of the NATO Alliance. Seventy years ago, tomorrow, NATO's founding treaty was signed in this great city."

"On that day, President Truman said, "We hope to create a shield against aggression and the fear of aggression; a bulwark which will permit us to get on with the real business of government and society; the business of achieving a fuller and happier life for all our citizens" [emphasis added].

NATO SECRETARY GENERAL JENS STOLTENBERG, IN CONGRESS, APRIL 3, 2019

Like most 70-year-olds, the military alliance of NATO has seen better days. It is an old soldier with dreams of being young and useful again. NATO, the North Atlantic Treaty Organization, hasn't operated in anything like a North Atlantic military theater in decades.

Founded in 1949 with 12 members, NATO spent its first 46 years not fighting anybody. For its first four decades. it held ritual war games aimed at deterring the myth of Soviet aggression while the Warsaw Pact held ritual war games aimed at deterring the myth of Western aggression. Then the Soviet Union collapsed and NATO went on its still-continuing spree of military adventures in Eastern Europe, Central Asia, the Indian Ocean and North Africa, achieving notable successes nowhere.

NATO's 1992 intervention in the former Yugoslavia hasn't ended yet. NATO's 2001 invasion of Afghanistan hasn't ended yet. NATO's 2009 anti-piracy mission in the Indian Ocean hasn't ended yet. NATO's 2011 intervention in Libya has produced a disaster that hasn't ended yet.

NATO receives bipartisan, almost holy reverence from Congress and much of the American public. This mass worship is less reality-based than it is myth-based. Perpetuating a massive military organization with no coherent mission is a nifty way to waste billions of dollars and thousands of lives. That will not change any time soon, what with our Trump demanding that NATO countries double their military spending and our Congress happily pushing American military spending past three-quarters of a trillion dollars a year.

New Cold War thinking appears to be bi-partisan. Congressional leaders Mitch McConnell and Nancy Pelosi invited NATO Secretary General Jens Stoltenberg to celebrate NATO's 70th anniversary with an unprecedented address to a joint session of Congress. That makes a chilling sort of sense. NATO has been a de-stabilizing force in the world for more than two decades. The US has been a de-stabilizing force in the world for much longer. Both are in search of new inflated threats to justify squandering more billions on "defense." If anyone in Congress had any objection to honoring the secretary general of an active war-making alliance, that voice is hard to find.

President Trump has played his NATO cards so cleverly that Congress does his bidding, thinking it's acting in opposition. Once in office after having run an anti-NATO-sounding campaign, in May 2017 Trump signed a NATO expansion bill that Russia opposed. As a result, in July 2017 tiny Montenegro became the 29th member of the NATO alliance. Amidst more NATO-bashing by Trump in 2018, the Senate hurriedly passed a non-binding NATO support measure by 97-2 (the two opposing were Republican Senators Rand Paul of Kentucky and Mike Lee of Utah). In January 2019, Rep. Tulsi Gabbard (and 53 others) chose not to vote on a bill that would prevent Trump from pulling the US out of NATO. But the bill passed the House 357-22, all the nays coming from Republicans. The Senate has not acted on the bill, which would prohibit the use of any funds to withdraw from NATO.

No wonder that the NATO Secretary General got multiple standing ovations after telling worshipful Congress members things like:

The NATO alliance is not only the longest lasting alliance in history, it is the most successful alliance in history.

Ever since the founding of our Alliance in 1949, every Congress, every American president, your men and women in uniform, and the people of the United States of America, have been staunch supporters of NATO.

This is true enough and can also be heard as a subtle swipe at Trump's frequent denigrations of NATO. Stoltenberg made other passing reference to Trump's controversial stands on other issues:

So, we should not be surprised when we see differences between our countries.

Today there are disagreements on issues such as trade, energy, climate change, and the Iran nuclear deal.

These are serious issues and serious disagreements.

And that is absolutely all he has to say about any of them, two of which involve existential threats to the world – nuclear weapons and climate change. Instead, Stoltenberg focused on what he called "a more assertive Russia," pushing a New Cold War agenda less rooted in reality than in the need to create a compelling threat that would justify ever more NATO spending.

Stoltenberg baldly asserted that "In 2014, Russia illegally annexed Crimea." He provided no context, no history, no nuance. Most importantly he ignored the reality of the political aggression by the US and other NATO allies by seeking to make Ukraine a NATO member bordering Russia. How provocative is that by a country still in a snit over decades-old Russian efforts in Cuba? Not only was Ukraine enticed toward NATO, NATO allies destabilized the country and effectively managed to unseat Ukraine's elected president.

The results of NATO's heedless confrontation in Ukraine have not been pretty. Crimea is the least of it compared to the Ukrainian civil war, the Ukrainian kleptocracy, and the rise of Ukrainian fascism. NATO is currently expanding naval operations in the Black Sea to put pressure on shipping around Crimea. Ukraine is now poised to elect a new president, a television comedian who played the president on TV.

Stoltenberg claimed that Russia was engaged in "a massive military build-up from the Arctic to the Mediterranean and from the Black Sea to the Baltic." Russia has no Mediterranean shoreline, not even close. And the reality is that Russia reduced its military spending by 20% in 2017. Russia spends about $66 billion a year on its military, less than a tenth of US military spending, and less than a third of European military spending. NATO countries together spend about $1 trillion a year on the military. Or as Stoltenberg glossily spins it:

> NATO has responded with the biggest reinforcement of our collective defence in decades.
>
> For the first time, we have combat-ready troops deployed in the east of our Alliance.

This is a continuation of years of NATO's political aggression toward Russia. Stoltenberg again teases the possibility of NATO membership for Ukraine. And moving to another, long-active front, Stoltenberg also teases NATO membership for Georgia. He does not explain how pushing the borders of the NATO alliance up against the border of a nuclear superpower is likely to make the world safer for anyone. He does say, with a straight face:

> We do all of this not to provoke a conflict.
>
> But to prevent a conflict.
>
> And to preserve the peace.

To that end, Stoltenberg calls on Russia "to return to compliance with the INF treaty." The INF (Intermediate-range Nuclear Forces) Treaty was signed in 1987 by President Reagan and Chairman Gorbachev. By May 1991, the treaty had removed intermediate-range US nuclear missiles from Europe after years of European public protest. Similar Soviet missiles were removed at the same time. After the break-up of the Soviet Union, six of the newly formed states (including Russia) remained part of the treaty and allowed inspection regimes.

It is generally accepted, as Stoltenberg said, that Russia is at some level in violation of the INF treaty. The nature of the presumed violations are unclear. These "violations" are usually offered as demagoguery without reference to US actions. The Obama administration set out on a trillion-dollar nuclear weapons program that Trump has expanded. Trump has promised to quit the INF treaty. Even if Russia came into full compliance with the INF Treaty (whatever that really means), there is no reason to believe the US will moderate any of its aggressive nuclear war-making policies.

Among other things, it wouldn't be good for business. Stoltenberg boasted of NATO allies increasing their military spending by $100 billion a year, half again as much as the Russian spend annually. Stoltenberg asserted:

> That money allows us to invest in the new capabilities our armed forces need, including advanced fighter aircraft, attack helicopters, missile defence and surveillance drones. This is good for Europe, and it is good for America....
>
> Europe provides the US with a platform to project power around the world. [emphasis added]

This is not good for Europe. This is not good for America. This is not good for almost anyone. Who thinks the world needs any more projection of American power *anywhere*. But our mindless Congress gives the prospect of war and more war one standing ovation after another.

97.

US Constitution Is Now Officially a Joke as Applied to War or Peace

"A joint resolution to direct the removal of United States Armed Forces from hostilities in the Republic of Yemen that have not been authorized by Congress."

CAPTION FOR S.J.RES.7, VETOED BY PRESIDENT TRUMP APRIL 16, 2019

"Congress has the sole power to declare war under article I, section 8, clause 11 of the United States Constitution."

FIRST FINDING OF FACT IN S.J.RES.7

Lawful authority to take the nation to war under the US Constitution has long been an unofficial joke, at least since the US led the "police action" in Korea in 1950. The fighting ended with the armistice in 1953, but not the war. We're still pretending it was constitutionally legitimate even though the Korean War sets a new record every day as America's "longest war." Congress has been ducking its constitutional responsibility ever since, through Vietnam, Afghanistan, Iraq, and all the other, less spectacular military sideshows it's sidestepped around the world for the past sixty-plus years.

US military action in Yemen – boots on the ground – grew out of the War on Terror. From 2007 till 2014, US special forces units carried out drone operations against real or imagined terrorists (including at least one teenaged American citizen), while the Yemeni government claimed responsibility. That government fell to the Arab Spring of 2014, followed by an internationally-imposed government and a civil war that sent it scurrying to Saudi Arabia, and sent US combat forces scurrying out of the combat zone. With the Houthis taking control of

Yemen in early 2015, the Obama administration gave a green light and significant logistical support to Saudi Arabia and its allies to undertake an undeclared, genocidal air war against an opponent with no air force and little air defense (soon eliminated).

The US Congress paid no serious attention to any of this. Republican majorities in both houses were content to allow the Obama-supported carnage in Yemen to continue unimpeded and undiscussed. Minority congressional dissent took years to emerge, as the Trump administration embraced the slaughter in Yemen.

The Joint Resolution to end US involvement in the illegal war on Yemen was introduced on January 30, 2019, by three Senators: Independent Bernie Sanders of Vermont, Republican Mike Lee of Utah, and Democrat Chris Murphy of Connecticut. Another 16 senators signed on as co-sponsors during the next six weeks.

On March 13, the Senate passed S.J.Res.7 on a bi-partisan vote of 54-46 (all the nays were Republicans).

On April 4, the House passed S.J.Res.7 on a bi-partisan vote of 247-175 (all the nays were Republicans).

On April 16, President Trump vetoed S.J.Res.7. His veto message contained a number of falsehoods, including "apart from counterterrorism operations against al-Qa'ida in the Arabian Peninsula and ISIS, the United States is not engaged in hostilities in or affecting Yemen." Translated that means: OK, special forces go in and out of Yemen at will, but I'm going to lie about supporting the air war (which I'll admit later in this statement), and since no one else is talking about the US Navy taking part in the sea blockade of Yemen, neither will I, even though I 've been told that the blockade is a direct act of war against Yemen.

Trump went on to defend the US "non-involvement" in the war on Yemen as a necessary act of patriotism: "it is our duty to protect the safety of the more than 80,000 Americans who reside in certain coalition countries that have been subject to Houthi attacks from Yemen." What countries? What attacks? He doesn't say, other than the airport in Riyadh, which surely qualifies as a defensive act of war against the Saudi aggressor.

Trump asserted the obvious: "Peace in Yemen requires a negotiated settlement." Then he preposterously blamed the Republican-controlled Senate for the failure of peace talks because "inaction by the Senate has left vacant key diplomatic positions, impeding our ability to engage regional partners in support of the United Nations-led peace process." Who sets priorities in this administration? Why is fomenting war against Iran more important than peace in Yemen where half the country, fourteen million people, face famine in the world's worst current humanitarian disaster?

And Trump got off a laugh line near the end: "great nations do not fight endless wars."

He did not mention Korea, but he did pretend that US war-making was almost over in Afghanistan and Syria. And he got off one more joke: "we recently succeeded in eliminating 100 percent of the ISIS caliphate."

On April 16, Rep. Ro Khanna, a California Democrat who has long protested US involvement against Yemen, tweeted:

> With Trump's veto of @BernieSanders' and my War Powers Resolution, which passed with bipartisan support in Congress, he is risking the lives of millions of Yemeni civilians to famine, deadly airstrikes, and the war crimes of the Saudi regime. We must override his veto.

On May 2, the Senate voted on the presidential veto of S.J.Res.7, which required 67 votes to over-ride. The vote failed, 53-45.

In just over three months, the US Congress voted three times to end US involvement in the criminal war on Yemen. The cumulative congressional vote total was 354 against US complicity in a crime against humanity, while 266 Republicans voted to let the famine and disease continue with US help. The majority in Congress, while not going so far as trying to end the war itself, at least made an effort to wash the blood off American hands.

Constitutionally, the country can't even manage a pale imitation of Pontius Pilate. By a vote of 1-0 the president gets to thwart democratic government and to prolong destruction of the poorest country in the region for no decent reason. And it's all constitutional, that's the beauty

559

part, because Congress abdicated its constitutional responsibility over and over and over again since 1950. That's the state of American constitutional democracy today. Congress can't prevent war. Congress can't end war. Congress can't even end American complicity in war crimes.

So, yes, the Senate vote of May 2 officially ratified the US Constitution as a meaningless joke insofar as it applies to the presidential ability to make war whenever and wherever he thinks he can get away with it. Constitutionally, Congress still has the "sole power to declare war." The president has the power to make war without declaring it. Yemen is now Trump's war and he happily blames it on "Iran's malignant activities," unspecified.

Congress has the power, theoretically, to defund any military action it doesn't like. But first it would have to find one. It doesn't have to look far. Now would be the time for a resolution against any military action against Iran without express Congressional approval. That would invite another presidential veto.

According to The Hill on May 10, Rep. Ro Khanna has been discussing with House Speaker Nancy Pelosi whether the House Democrats should appeal Trump's veto to the Supreme Court. Khanna argues that it's unsettled law whether the president has the last word on war and peace.

But after appealing this pro-war veto to the current Supreme Court, where would the country find itself?

The Constitution's not in tatters, it's just irrelevant. That's a bipartisan achievement. And there's little sign that most of the American people care, or even notice.

98.

Tanker Attack Was Imaginary, but US Says Iran Did It

BREAKING OVERNIGHT OIL TANKERS ATTACKED Saudi Arabia Claims Ship Heading To Us Sabotaged

ABC NEWS ON-SCREEN HEADLINE, MAY 13, 2019

BREAKING OVERNIGHT SAUDI OIL TANKERS ATTACKED Energy Minister Says Ships Were Targeted In "Sabotage Attack"

CBS NEWS ON-SCREEN HEADLINE, MAY 13, 2019

These network stories are examples of fake news at its most dangerous, when it plays into the dishonest manipulations of an administration beating the drums for a war against Iran that has no reasonable basis. Not only do the networks and mainstream media generally fail to question the administration's rush to war, they also fail to do basic journalism by independently confirming whether a particular story is true or not.

The story of the "oil tanker attacks" appears to have been mostly or entirely false, as any news organization could have known from the start by exercising basic skepticism. Or the story could have been pimped as terrorism, as Debka.com did, asserting on May 13 that: "A special unit of the Iranian Revolutionary Guards marine force carried out the sabotage on four Saudi oil tankers outside Fujairah port." No evidence, anonymous sources only, and wrong number of Saudi tankers.

The first report of something happening in or near the emirate of Fujairah in the United Arab Emirates (UAE) came from the Lebanon-based

561

Al Mayadeen TV, saying that seven to ten oil tankers were burning in the port of Fujairah on the Gulf of Oman (outside the Strait of Hormuz leading to the Persian Gulf). There is no evidence that any tankers were burning there. Available satellite images show no smoke, explosions, or anything else to support the claim of an accident or an attack.

A few hours later, a new story surfaced. On May 12 at 7:38 pm, the UAE foreign ministry issued a statement carried by the state news agency WAM with the headline: "Four commercial ships subjected to sabotage operations near UAE territorial waters, no fatalities or injuries reported." The report in its entirety offered little detail:

> ABU DHABI, 12th May, 2019 (WAM) -- Four commercial ships were subjected to sabotage operations today, 12th May, near UAE territorial waters in the Gulf of Oman, east of Fujairah, the Ministry of Foreign Affairs and International Cooperation, MOFAIC, has announced.
>
> The Ministry said that the concerned authorities have taken all necessary measures, and are investigating the incident in cooperation with local and international bodies.
>
> It said that there had been no injuries or fatalities on board the vessels and that there had been no spillage of harmful chemicals or fuel.
>
> The MOFAIC statement said that the carrying out acts of sabotage on commercial and civilian vessels and threatening the safety and lives of those on board is a serious development. It called on the international community to assume its responsibilities to prevent such actions by parties attempting to undermine maritime traffic safety and security.
>
> The Ministry also described as 'baseless and unfounded' rumours earlier today, 12th May, of incidents taking place within the Port of Fujairah, saying that operations within the port were under way as normal, without any interruption.

There's not much here. What sort of "sabotage operations" occurred? Who carried them out? What damage was there, if any? Who were the four ships? When was the sabotage discovered? What's really going on here, if anything?

The next day the Saudi Press Agency chimed in with a statement from the Minister of Energy that "confirmed that... two Saudi oil tankers were subjected to a sabotage attack in the exclusive economic zone of the United Arab Emirates, off the coast of the Emirate of Fujairah." The minister claimed structural damage to the two tankers but did not make them available for inspection. Satellite and surface images showed no damage to either tanker.

That's about all that was known on May 13 as ABC News went on the air acting as if the story was factually clear and larger than supported by any evidence. The lead-in to the story was flush with news-hype and propaganda technique: "we begin with that attack overseas on Saudi ships and oil tankers. One about to head to the U.S. This comes in the wake of that warning about threats from Iran." Fundamentally dishonest. There were two Saudi tankers, no Saudi "ships." The other two tankers were from the UAE and Norway. There was no certainty that there was any attack (and there still isn't). Saying that one tanker was about to head to the US was not only irrelevant, but provocative. It was on its way to Saudi Arabia to load oil bound for the US (according to the Saudis). Putting the mis-reported "attack" in the context of "that warning about threats from Iran" is pure propagandistic parroting of US government scare-mongering.

But that was just the lead-in to veteran reporter Martha Raddatz, surely she'd bring some sane perspective to bear, right? Wrong, she made it worse, talking in a tone suitable for a "they-just-attacked-Pearl-Harbor" report. Somberly treating the alleged attack as a matter of fact, Raddatz framed it with a conclusion supported by no evidence whatsoever:

> This comes at an extremely tense time in the region with the U.S. warning just days ago that Iran or its proxies could be targeting maritime traffic in the oil rich Persian Gulf region. Although we do not know who carried out this morning's attack on these ships, we do know four were sabotaged off the coast of the United Arab Emirates in the Persian Gulf and that it caused significant structural damage to two Saudi oil tankers. One of the Saudi ships was on its way to pick up Saudi oil for delivery to the U.S. Last week the U.S. urgently dispatched a carrier strike group, B-52 bombers and a Patriot missile battery to the region after it said there were unspecified threats to American forces in the region. Iran's news agency this morning saying

the dispatch of the warships was to exaggerate the shadow of war and frighten the Iranian people. But this is a very dangerous development.

Could Sarah Huckabee Sanders have said it better?

Posing as a journalist, Martha Raddatz ratchets up the Trump administration's scare campaign based on nothing more than fear tactics. She's so busy trying to scare us, she doesn't even get the geography right. The alleged attack didn't happen in the Persian Gulf. The four ships that were supposedly attacked were in the Gulf of Oman off the coast of the UAE. Almost all the rest of what Raddatz reports as "fact" comes from government press releases.

And that's not the most shameful part for Raddatz and ABC News. Worse than botching facts large and small is the willingness of such mainstream media players to team up with elements of the US government seeking war with Iran at almost any cost.

CBS News coverage was little better, not only putting the action in the Persian Gulf, but upping the number of ships "attacked" to six. CBS did manage a small saving grace, concluding: "Whatever the case, the tensions here have only risen since President Trump withdrew from the 2015 nuclear deal, brokered between Iran and world powers."

Well, yes, THAT is the crux of the mess. The US unilaterally tries to pull out of a multi-lateral international agreement that all other parties say is working and we're supposed to take the US seriously? Seriously? At this point, any reporter who accepts a government press release as authoritative should be summarily fired. At this point, that is inexcusable malpractice. Iran has abided by the nuclear deal, all the inspectors affirm that. The other signatories – China, Russia, GB, France, Germany, and the EU – all affirm that. But they don't stand up to the US effectively. They allow the US to bully them into joining the American economic warfare against Iran.

Over the next several days after it broke, the "oil tankers attacked" story slowly collapsed. Fact-based skepticism started to catch up with the official story. The UAE kept reporters from getting too close to the ships, which showed no serious damage. An anonymous US official blamed Iran, based on no evidence. US military officials in the Persian

Gulf region stopped answering questions about whatever it was, referring questioners to the White House.

At this point, if the oil tanker attacks were either a warmongering hoax or false flag operation, it's not going to have the same success as the sinking of the battleship Maine in Havana Harbor in 1898 or the provocations of US warships in the Tonkin Gulf in 1964. There's even an off-chance that a suspicious Congress and an even more suspicious public will manage to slow the rush to war, or even stop it. There are signs of some increased media wariness, also known as detachment. Perhaps the most hopeful signs are the leaked anonymous stories that the president really, really doesn't want to go to war, which of course he doesn't have to if he doesn't want to, if he knows what he wants.

Another leaked story had it that Secretary of State Mike Pompeo and National Security Advisor John Bolton are confident that they can lead Trump by the nose into the war they want with Iran and that Trump's too stupid to understand what they're up to. If Trump sees that, it might give peace a chance.

PART SIX

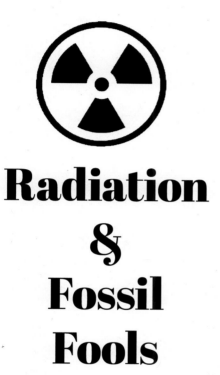

Radiation
&
Fossil
Fools

99.

US Human Radiation Experiments Covered Up by Public Broadcasting

"The bomb will not start a chain reaction in the water, converting it all to gas and letting all the ships on all the oceans drop down to the bottom. It will not blow out the bottom of the sea and let all the water run down the hole. It will not destroy gravity. I am not an atomic playboy."

VICE ADMIRAL WILLIAM P. BLANDY, BIKINI BOMB TEST COMMANDER, JULY 25, 1946

When the military scientists of an advanced technological nation deliberately explode their largest nuclear bomb (and 66 others) over Pacific islands and use the opportunities to study the effects of radiation on nearby native people, which group is best described as "savage"? And what should you call the people who prevent a documentary about these American post-war crimes from reaching a wide audience in the United States?

"Nuclear Savage" is a recent documentary film that explores American nuclear weapons testing in the Marshall Islands, 1946-1958, and particularly the secret Project 4.1: an American experiment in exposing Pacific Islanders to overdoses of radiation – deliberate human radiation poisoning – just to get better data on this method of maiming and killing people. The public broadcasting establishment has spent more that two years keeping this story off the air.

The preview reel of "Nuclear Savage" includes a clip with a stentorian newsreel announcer reporting on the American treatment of Marshall Islanders in April 1957, and explaining to his predominantly American audience:

> The Marshallese caught by fallout got 175 roentgens of radiation. These are fishing people, savages by our standards, so a cross-section

569

was brought to Chicago for testing. The first was John, the mayor of Rongelap Atoll.... John, as we said, is a savage, but a happy, amenable savage.

So how serious is 175 roentgens (assuming the measurement is accurate)? In 1950, the International Commission on Radiological Protection (ICRP) recommended that human radiation contact should not exceed 0.3 roentgen per week for whole-body exposure ["roentgen" as a measure of radiation dose has since been replaced by "rem"]. It's not clear how long the Marshallese were exposed to radiation levels of 175 roentgens – or on how many occasions – but that amount was more than 580 times what was then considered a safe weekly exposure.

Public broadcasting paid for this film – and then suppressed it

In 2005, director Adam Horowitz started work on "Nuclear Savage," his second documentary about the American military use and abuse of the Marshall Islands. Horowitz has a contract with Pacific Islanders in Communications (PIC), which describes itself as "a national non-profit media arts organization" whose mission "is to support, advance and develop programming that enhances public recognition of and appreciation for Pacific Islander history, culture and society. In keeping with the mission, PIC provides funding for new programs primarily for public television. We work with independent producers to create and distribute programs about Pacific Islanders that bring new audiences to public television, advance issues and represent diverse voices and points of view not usually seen on public or commercial television."

Among its efforts to carry out this mission, PIC supported the production of "Nuclear Savage" with $100,000 passed through to Horowitz from the Corporation for Public Broadcasting (CPB). Horowitz delivered a completed, 87-minute version of "Nuclear Savage" in October 2011 – the same month it was nominated for Best Environmental Film at the Amsterdam International Documentary Film Festival. That was also the same month various public broadcasting officials started putting up roadblocks to keep the movie off the air, a delaying tactic that continues into 2014. FAIR (Fairness & Accuracy in Reporting) reported the story in detail as "Nuclear Stalemate" in Extra!

One of the first requests, from Leanne Ferrer at PIC, was for a shorter version at 60 minutes. Rather than have Horowitz cut his film by 27 minutes, PIC hired its own editor and controlled the editing process. Part of Ferrer's concern reportedly was a sort of politically correct reverse racism, her objection that there was too much of Horowitz in the film and he's not a Pacific Islander. The shorter version has less of Horowitz. And the PIC web site pitches "Nuclear Savage: The Islands of Secret Project 4.1" as a "portrait of Pacific Islanders struggling for dignity and survival after decades of intentional radiation poisoning by the US government."

PIC summarizes the film this way: "Some use the term 'savage' to refer to people from primitive cultures, but nuclear experimentation pushed savagery to new levels. In the 1950s, the US conducted 67 atomic and hydrogen bomb tests in the Marshall Islands, vaporizing islands and exposing entire populations to fallout. The islanders on Rongelap received near fatal doses of radiation from one test and were then moved onto a highly contaminated island to serve as human guinea pigs for 30 years. Filmmaker Adam Jonas Horowitz spent 25 years collecting material – including original footage, archival clips and unpublished secret documents – to create this unforgettable and ironic portrait of American cynicism, arrogance and racism. Winner of festival awards in Paris, Chicago and Mexico City."

PBS canceled scheduled broadcasts without public explanation

In 2013, PBS World Channel scheduled "Nuclear Savage" for four showings on May 28 and 29 – and PBS executive Tom Davison emailed Horowitz in advance, saying "Congratulations on this airing." When the airing failed to take place, without explanation from PBS, Horowitz was unable to get a straight answer from Davison, Ferrer, or anyone else in the public broadcasting food chain, although PIC executive Amber McClure wrote with Orwellian deceit: "Your program has not been declined by PBS."

Outright rejection by PBS is required by Horowitz's contract in order for him to regain independent control of his film. In December 2013, in his original letter to the editor of the Santa Fe Reporter, Horowitz summed up his experience to date this way:

PBS "World Channel" executives accepted, scheduled and advertised the show nationally, only to reverse their decision and cancel the show at the last minute. The show was originally accepted and then later rejected by two different branches of PBS, on three different occasions. PBS executives promised to deliver to me, a list of the precise points in the film that they felt represented 'bias,' or questions of 'fact,' and I promised to work with them to fix any problems. But PBS has still never delivered any specifics whatsoever of their complaints about the film, a film by the way that they have already completely reworked with their own editors.

Horowitz has also had support from private foundations, including the Kindle Project, where: "We support whistleblowers and rabble-rousers. We give grants to peacemakers and seed savers. We make awards to artists and activists. We support people and projects working towards solutions and alternatives to systems in transition. We seek out the strange, the bizarre, the unpolished, the less likely to receive funding. We fund individuals and initiatives that may seem risky or radical to mainstream funding sources...."

The unsigned "Notes on Nuclear Savage: The Islands of Secret Project 4.1" on the Kindle Project web site from April 2012 talks about the ways the film was succeeding, despite unofficial quasi-government censorship and beyond "the glamorous festival circuit:"

Heartbreaking is the most poignant word that could be used to describe this film, and in my conversations with Adam this word has been uttered more than once. I've often wondered how he has the stamina for this subject matter; the stamina to expose himself to the worst kinds of atrocities that humans inflict on one another. The people of the Marshall Islands have faced similar catastrophic fates as the victims who underwent Nazi medical tests during WWII. Adam was there to tell the world about it. These days, his perseverance comes from the success of the film – not just from the attention it's getting from the international circuit, but from what's happening in the Islands themselves.

Public information is not always well known by the public

What was happening in the islands was that "Nuclear Savage" was being shown again and again on local and national television channels.

It was shown at the Pacific Island conference of Presidents. People were copying and bootlegging the film across the region, with bootleg copies sometimes turning up on television. And Marshallese activists were using the film to resist US government efforts to re-re-settle some populations back to their home islands that were still dangerously radioactive.

"As of now, no one has moved back," Horowitz told an audience after showing "Nuclear Savage" at the International Uranium Film Festival in Window Rock, Arizona, last December. Despite the American effort to re-re-settle the forced Marshallese refugees on their former home islands, Horowitz said the effort had amounted to "just a bunch of empty houses."

Horowitz has been angry about American treatment of the Marshall Islands for a long time. In late 2013 he told a reporter the US "destroyed an entire country that we were not at war with, that we were at peace with. Not only did they blow up all these islands, but they purposely contaminated all these people as human experiments. It's a very unknown story here."

The story was classified top secret until the 1990s, when the Clinton administration declassified documents related to nuclear testing that including previously unknown information on the Project 4.1 program to use Pacific Islanders as human guinea pigs for assessing the impact of ionizing radiation. Even the official historian of U.C. nuclear testing, Barton Hacker, who tries to minimize the criminality of Project 4.1, ended up writing in 1994 that an "unfortunate choice of terminology may help explain later charges that the AEC [Atomic Energy Commission] had deliberately exposed the Marshallese to observe the effects. Like the American radium dial painters of the 1920s and the Japanese of Hiroshima and Nagasaki in 1945, the Marshallese of 1954 inadvertently were to provide otherwise unobtainable data on the human consequences of high radiation exposures."

The US was an occupying power and effectively still is

Europeans "discovered" these Pacific Islands in the 1520s (they were named the Marshall Islands after the British explorer John Marshall).

In 1874 they became part of the Spanish East Indies. In 1884 Germany bought them as part of German New Guinea. During World War I, the Japanese occupied the islands and later ruled them under a League of Nations mandate. During World War II, the United States took the islands from the Japanese and has effectively occupied them ever since.

In 1946, the US evacuated the entire population of Bikini Atoll (167 people) and logged the first of 23 atomic weapons explosions that have made what's left of the atoll (part of it was vaporized) a largely uninhabitable radioactive tourist destination [one report says 4-6 "caretakers" live there]. Most of the 167 original residents have died, but their descendants number more than 4,000. A 1975 federal lawsuit (seeking roughly $750 million in compensation promised but not paid by the US) was denied review by the US Supreme Court in April 2010, but the effort to make the US provide just compensation continues.

Later in 2010, UNESCO named Bikini a "world heritage site" as a symbol of the "dawn of the nuclear age." The US Environmental Protection Agency has said that Bikini is close to the "safe" radiation level of 15 millirems – but according to the US Department of Energy, the "safe" level is really 100 millirems, and the contradiction remains unreconciled.

In 1947, the United Nations included the Marshall Islands in a Trust Territory controlled by the US, whose obligations included the duty to "protect the inhabitants against the loss of their lands and resources." Later in the year the US evacuated the entire population of Enewetak Atoll, where it would explode another 44 atomic weapons, the last series in 1958.

On March 1, 1954, the US exploded its first deliverable hydrogen bomb that, at 15 megatons, was more than 1,000 times as powerful as the Hiroshima bomb of 1945. The official story, which the US government still defends, is that it was an "accident" that the bomb dumped so much radiation on downwind populations, and that Project 4.1 was initiated after the blast in order to help the victims as well as study them.

The record includes one reference to Project 4.1 prior to March 1 [the government says someone put it there after the fact]. More troubling is the undisputed evidence that the US was aware that the weather had changed, that the wind was blowing toward populated areas, but they went ahead with the test anyway. After the radiation came down like "snow" on Rongelap and other islands, the Navy evacuated American personnel quickly, but left the "happy, amenable savages" to absorb more radiation for another two days.

As early as 1956, the Atomic Energy Commission had characterized the Marshall Islands as "by far the most contaminated place in the world."

For the victor, justice is only optional, not enforceable

In 1979, the US allowed the Marshall Islands to become "self-governing," while the US reserved the sole control of military use and defense of the territory. In 1986 the US granted the Republic of the Marshall Islands "sovereignty" under the Orwellian-named Compact of Free Association, which left the US in military control and free to use Kwajalein Atoll as a missile testing range. Four years later the U.N. ended the "nation's" Trusteeship status. The CIA estimates that the Marshall Islands' GDP is $182 million, of which the US provides $70 million in aid payments, according to the State Department. Both the CIA and State Department omit unpaid compensation from their public summaries of the Marshall Islands.

The movie "Nuclear Savage" includes US Ambassador Greta Morris making a wooden public statement of "deep regrets" for the "hardships" the Marshallese have suffered "as a result of the testing program, as well as the accidental downwind injuries caused by one test, Bravo" – which is the official version of the 1954 H-bomb Castle Bravo. Later Greta Morris is asked at a public event to discuss US "government policy" – the ambassador refuses to talk on camera.

In March 2012, at an event commemorating the anniversary of the H-bomb test, Marshall Islands foreign minister Phillip Muller called on the US to pay more than $2 billion in awards already made by the Nuclear Claims Tribunal, which was created and underwritten by the US. The US moral and financial obligation continues to grow, as the Marshall Islands are reportedly seeing a continually rising cancer

rate more than half a century later. At the same event, according to Overseas Territories Review:

> US Ambassador to the Marshall Islands Martha Campbell told the event in Majuro Thursday evening that 'the United States has provided nearly $600 million in compensation and assistance to the Republic of the Marshall Islands to help the affected communities overcome the effects of nuclear testing,' and noted that the US and Marshall Islands governments had agreed to 'a full and final settlement of all nuclear-related claims' in 1983 [an apparent reference to the Compact of Free Association and its side agreements].

In 1998, staff from the US Centers for Disease Control and Prevention (CDC) made a comparison study to compare the amount of radioactive Iodine-131 at four different radiation-polluted sites, measured in curies (1,000 curies of Cesium-137, as found in a radiation therapy machine, could produce serious health effects in a direct exposure of just a few minutes). The CDC team reported its finding that the atmospheric release of curies of Iodine-137 at the Hanford nuclear processing plant was 739,000 curies; at Chernobyl the release was 40 million curies; at the Nevada bomb test site, 150 million curies; and in the Marshall Islands, 6.3 billion curies (more that 30 times as much radiation as the other three sites combined).

The Republic of the Marshall Islands is ranked #5 in the world among countries with the highest health costs as a percentage of GDP – behind Liberia, Sierra Leone, Tuvalu and the United States.

The history of the treatment of the radiation victims of the Marshall Islands is essentially a paradigm for the treatment of radiation victims everywhere. The perpetrators of radiation-exposure lose patience with the seemingly endless effects of their acts and so they tend to abandon all responsibility for them. So far at least, the Marshall Islands history appears to be foreshadowing Fukushima's future.

Given the unpalatability this story might have for an American television audience, it's little wonder that public broadcasting executives are content to spend public money to keep the public under-informed.

Afternote 2013: "The term 'savage' is used to refer to people from primitive cultures, but this documentary shows how savagery reaches new levels with the advent of advanced technology. In the 1950s, the US conducted 67 nuclear tests in the Marshall Islands, vaporizing islands and exposing entire populations to fallout. The people of Rongelap received near fatal doses of radiation from one of these tests, and were then moved to a highly contaminated island to serve as guinea pigs to test the affects of radiation on humans for almost 30 years, where they suffered from recurring cancers and birth defects that have affected multiple generations. This cynical act by the US government was conducted with such arrogant racism that without incredible archival footage and shocking secret documents, the story would seem unbelievable."

Film Society Lincoln Center, New York City, description of "Nuclear Savage: The Islands of Secret Project 4.1

The Republic of the Marshall Islands covers nearly a million square miles of picturesque islands, thriving coral atolls, and crystal clear blue waters …. undoubtedly one of the most interesting places in the world to visit.

Marshall Islands government promotion for tourism in 2014

Update 2019: The Marshall Islands remain contaminated by radiation from US nuclear testing. For their trouble, the Marshallese are permitted to live and work in the US without a visa (over 22,000 as of 2010 census; about 55,000 remain in the islands).

Director Adam Horowitz wrote in March 2019: "Many of the interview subjects in the film have died, including Foreign Minister Tony DeBrun, Almira Matayoshi and others. Rising sea levels are causing significant troubles across the country, e.g. Erosion, flooding, salinization of fresh water wells, etc." Horowitz owns the rights to the film and will arrange showings on request.

Rising sea levels due to climate change threaten to wipe the country out by as early as 2030. The government has been building sea walls on some of the country's 1,156 islands. In February 2019, the president proposed a massive project to raise the height of selected islands, most of which are now less than six feet above sea level.

In 2014, the Marshall Islands sued the US to enforce the terms of the Nuclear Non-Proliferation Treaty, in particular to force the US (in the words of the treaty) "to pursue negotiations in good faith" to address "the grim legacy of the United States nuclear weapons program." US federal district court dismissed the suit, as did US federal appeals court in July 2017 with a decision that held, in effect, that the US couldn't be forced to do anything since the "claims presented inextricable political questions that were non-justiciable and must be dismissed." – or in layman's language: this is too political, the US is too guilty, and we're not touching it!

100.

Nuke the People?

No radiation is good for you, a little more won't hurt

In something of a stealth maneuver during the 2012 holiday season, the US Department of Energy set about to give every American a little more radiation exposure – and for some, a lot – by allowing manufacturers to use radioactive metals in their consumer products – such as zippers, spoons, jewelry, belt buckles, toys, pots, pans, furnishings, bicycles, jungle gyms, medical implants, or any other metal or partly-metal product.

The Energy Department announced its plan in the Federal Register on December 12th, and invited comment for 30 days, through January 11, 2013. Citing its need to address environmental concerns under the National Environmental Protection Act (NEPA), the agency said, in part, that its plan was:

> ... to delegate authority to manage radiological clearance and release of scrap metal from radiological areas to each Under Secretary for sites under his or her cognizance....

> This Draft PEA for the Recycling of [Radioactive] Scrap Metals Originating from Radiological Areas analyzes the potential environmental impacts associated with resuming the clearance of [radioactive] scrap metal, originating from DOE radiological areas, for recycling pursuant to improved procedures designed to assure that clearance for release is limited to [radioactive] metals meeting stringent criteria.

Translated from the bureaucratese, this is a proposal to lift a ban on recycling radioactive metals left over from American bomb-making and other nuclear activities, and allow them to be used commercially, with "stringent," but largely unenforceable criteria, for their use. The initial ban was ordered in 2000, by then-Secretary of Energy Bill Richardson.

Exactly one Congressman challenges Energy Department

Largely ignored by mainstream media, the plan caught the attention of an alert Congressman, Rep. Edward Markey, D-MA, who wrote a three-page letter to Energy Secretary Steve Chu on January 11th, beginning:

> I write to convey my grave concerns regarding your December 2012 proposal to rescind the agency-wide suspension of the release of radioactively contaminated scrap metal from Department of Energy (DOE) facilities for purposes of recycling it into consumer products that could ultimately by utilized by pregnant women, children or other vulnerable populations. This proposal is unwise, and should be immediately abandoned.

On January 16th, while taking note of Rep. Markey's letter, the *Wall Street Journal* covered the story by starting this way:

> The Department of Energy is proposing to allow the sale of tons of scrap metal from government nuclear sites – an attempt to reduce waste that critics say could lead to radiation-tainted belt buckles, surgical implants and other consumer products....
>
> The approximately 14,000 tons of metal under review for possible initial release is only a fraction of the tens of millions of tons of metal recycled annually, it said. Smaller amounts could be eligible for release in future years.
>
> Selling the metals could bring in $10 million to $40 million a year, the DOE estimates.

Nuclear industry minimizes radiation dangers

As is common in nuclear industry proposals of all sorts, the Energy Department sought to assure readers of its proposal that any radiation exposure resulting from recycling radioactive waste into the commercial mainstream would have minimal impact on any given individual. The article in the *Journal* included a chart from the department that reinforced its claim that "... would at worst expose a person to very low levels of additional radiation."

This approach ignores the current scientific consensus that there is *no* safe level of radiation exposure. Since there is already a measurable level of background radiation worldwide, and since world-wide radiation levels have increased as a result of nuclear weapons testing and nuclear accidents like Chernobyl and Fukushima, the fundamental safety question is whether any additional radiation exposure is safe in any meaningful sense. It's not.

This approach also fails to deal with the reality that once the department has released radioactive materials for commercial use, it loses almost all control over how and where they're used, and in what concentrations. The same material used in a ceiling light fixture will pose less risk than if it is used in a belt buckle, or jewelry worn close to the skin. These uses are less dangerous than material inside a human body, as in a joint replacement or heart valve.

Contaminated products come from everywhere

The issue is of global concern because other countries are recycling their radioactive waste as well, with uncertain control and safety. As Rep. Markey noted in his letter:

> **Just a year ago, Bed, Bath and Beyond recalled tissue holders made in India that were contaminated with low levels of the radio-isotope cobalt-60 that were shipped to 200 of its stores in twenty states.**

> **The Nuclear Regulatory Commission, when discussing the discovery of the contaminated products, said that, "There's no real health threat from these, but we advise people to return them."**

While that may seem contradictory, it's mainly because the choice of the word "real" is not very accurate. It's true that there's no threat of immediate injury from a low level of radiation, whereas a high enough level will be lethal. It's also true that there may be no "realistic" threat from a radioactive tissue box, but that's not the same as "no threat," since harm from radiation exposure is cumulative.

Rep. Markey's letter illustrates this concern, as he notes that the Energy Department is proposing to release contaminated metals into the marketplace, as long as, quoting from the document, it "... can be shown that the release will result in less that 1 millirem (mrem) above background to a member of the public in any calendar year." [One millirem is a tiny amount of radiation.]

Nevertheless, Rep. Markey expresses doubt about even this low standard: "I believe this standard, *even if it were the appropriate standard,* will be impossible to assure or enforce" [emphasis added].

United States has no one in charge of managing risk

There is no federal agency with responsibility for such oversight or enforcement. This regulatory vacuum was illuminated by the discovery in 2009 of thousands of contaminated consumer products from China, Brazil, France, Sweden and other countries, as reported by *Mother Nature Network*:

> The risk of radiation poisoning is the furthest thing from our minds as we shop for everyday items like handbags, furniture, buttons, chain link fences and cheese graters. Unfortunately, it turns out that our trust is misplaced thanks to sketchy government oversight of recycled materials.
>
> The discovery of a radioactive cheese grater led to an investigation that found thousands of additional consumer products to be contaminated. The source is recycled metals tainted with Cobalt-60, a radioactive isotope that can cause cancer with prolonged exposure.

According to a Scripps Howard News Service investigation in 2009, records of the Nuclear Regulatory Commission show:

> ... 18,740 documented cases involving radioactive materials in consumer products, in metal intended for consumer products or other public exposure to radioactive material.
>
> The US Government Accountability Office estimates there are some 500,000 unaccounted for radioactively contaminated metal objects in the US, and the NRC estimates that figure is around 20 million pounds of contaminated waste....
>
> In 2006 in Texas, for example, a recycling facility inadvertently created 500,000 pounds of radioactive steel byproducts after melting metal contaminated with Cesium-137, according to US Nuclear Regulatory Commission records. In Florida in 2001, another recycler unintentionally did the same, and wound up with 1.4 million pounds of radioactive material.

When They Tried This Before, They Failed

Nuclear engineer Arnie Gunderson echoed Markey's warning in his January 13th podcast, pointing out that the nuclear industry has been trying to do something like this for decades. The reason, he explained, was that radioactive materials are now liabilities for those who own them, are responsible for protecting them and, eventually, storing them safely. But, if they can sell the material, the liability instantly becomes an asset.

NIRS, the Nuclear Information and Resource Service, has come out strongly against the Energy Department initiative, noting the long history of the industry to unburden itself of its radioactive waste and any responsibility for it:

> We've fought this battle before. In the late 1980s, NRC adopted a policy it called 'Below Regulatory Concern' (BRC), that would have allowed about 30% of the nation's 'low-level' radioactive waste to be treated as normal garbage and dumped in landfills, be burned in incinerators, and yes, be recycled into consumer products....

> NIRS and our allies responded with one of our largest organizing campaigns ever.... 15 states passed laws banning BRC within their borders. Hearings were held in the House and in 1992, Congress officially overturned the BRC policy.

The grassroots action contributed to Secretary Richardson's ban on selling radioactive metals for commercial use, the ban that the current Energy Department proposal would overturn. The department has offered no new basis for its recycling program beyond streamlining what it proposed before. NIRS counters that:

> Nothing has changed since 2000 that would justify lifting its current ban. Rather, just the opposite: since then the National Academy of Sciences has acknowledged that there is no safe level of radiation exposure, and we've learned that women are even more vulnerable to radiation than men (while children have long been known to be more vulnerable than adults).

NIRS and other advocacy organizations are currently engaged in a campaign to submit comments before the February 11th deadline to ask the Energy Department to withdraw this proposal.

Update 2019: In May 2013, Rep. Markey introduced legislation intended to prevent the Energy Department from implementing its proposal to allow radioactive waste to be used in consumer products. While the legislation was not enacted into law, neither did the Energy Department implement its proposal.

Nuclear waste continues to accumulate in government storage facilities of varying security. According to the General Accounting Office (GAO), the US has roughly 80,000 metric tons of high level nuclear waste generated by nuclear power plants and stored at 80 sites in 35 states, with no final storage plan yet adopted. Military nuclear waste is managed separately at numerous sites, with final storage expected to be at the WIPP site in New Mexico.

On June 5, 2019, the Energy Department issued a proposal to save some $40 billion on the cost of handling high-level radioactive nuclear waste from US weapons production currently stored at sites in South Carolina, Idaho, and Washington where all the waste is classified as highly radioactive. The department would save money by re-classifying some of the waste as low level and treating it under different safety standards.

Among others, the Natural Resources Defense Council has long opposed this proposal, saying it undermines more than 50 years of national consensus, writing in January 2019:

"Under the law, high-level radioactive waste from the U.S. nuclear weapons program must be disposed of in deep, geologic formations, far from human contact. By unlawfully proposing to give itself the authority to 'reinterpret' what is high-level radioactive waste, the Trump administration is trying to walk away from the most toxic, long-lasting waste in the world."

101.

More Radiation Exposure Won't Hurt You, Says US EPA

"Protection Standards for Nuclear Power Operations" means what?

The Environmental Protection Agency (EPA) of the United States is a full-blown oxymoron when it comes to protecting US residents from the danger of increased exposure to ionizing radiation. That's the kind of radiation that comes from natural sources like Uranium and the sun, as well as unnatural sources like uranium mines, nuclear weapons, and nuclear power plants (even when they haven't melted down like Fukushima). The EPA is presently considering allowing everyone in the US to be exposed to higher levels of ionizing radiation.

In 1977, the EPA established levels of radiation exposure "considered safe" for people by federal rule (in bureaucratese, "the regulation at 40 CFR part 190"). In the language of the rule, the 1977 safety standards were: "The standards [that] specify the levels below which normal operations of the uranium fuel cycle are determined to be environmentally acceptable." In common parlance, this became the level "considered safe," even though that's very different from "environmentally acceptable." Acceptable by whom? The environment has no vote.

The phrase "considered safe" is key to the issue, since there is no "actually safe" level of radiation exposure. The planet was once naturally radioactive and lifeless. Life emerged only after Earth's radiation levels decayed to the point where life became possible, despite a continuing level of natural "background radiation." The reality is that there is no "safe" level of radiation exposure.

In January 2014, the EPA issued a very long proposal (in bureau-cratese, an "Advance Notice of Proposed Rulemaking") to consider raising the "safe" radiation levels established in 1977. According to the EPA, the proposal "does not propose revisions to the current regula-tion, but is being issued only to collect information to support EPA's review." The public comment period on the EPA proposal – titled "Environmental Radiation Protection Standards for Nuclear Power Operations" – has been extended to August 4, 2014.

Is the EPA actually immersed in a protection racket?

The studied ambiguity of the proposal's title – "Environmental Radi-ation Protection Standards for Nuclear Power Operations" – goes to the heart of the issue: who or what is really being protected, nuclear power operations?

Quite aware that it is perceived by some as placing the desires of the nuclear power industry above the safety needs of the population, the EPA begins its proposal for changing radiation limits with this defensive and contradictory passage:

> This Advance Notice of Proposed Rulemaking is being published to inform stakeholders, including federal and state entities, the nuclear industry, the public and any interested groups, that the Agency is reviewing the existing standards to determine how the regulation at 40 CFR part 190 should be updated and soliciting input on changes (if any) that should be made.

> This action is not meant to be construed as an advocacy position either for or against nuclear power.

> EPA wants to ensure that environmental protection standards are adequate for the foreseeable future for nuclear fuel cycle facilities.

If the scientific consensus is right, that no level of radiation expo-sure is "safe," how can *any* protection stand that allows any exposure to be "adequate" in any public health sense?

As far as the EPA is concerned, the uranium fuel cycle does not include uranium mining, despite the serious environmental danger that process entails. Only when the environmental and human degradation from uranium mining has been done, does the EPA begin regulating environmental protection from nuclear fuel cycle facilities, beginning with milling and ending with storage or reprocessing facilities for nuclear waste.

According to the agency itself, "EPA's mission is to protect human health and the environment. EPA sets limits on the amount of radiation that can be released into the environment." How does this square with the evidence that NO radiation exposure is healthy?

Radiation exposure is chronic, cumulative and unhealthy

Given the pre-existing radiation load on the environment from natural sources, it's not clear that there is any amount of radiation that can be released into the environment with safety. The EPA pretty much evades that question, since the straightforward answer for human health is: no amount. Besides, the semi-captured protection agency is just as much engaged in protecting economic health for certain industries as it is in protecting human health. This leads it to making formulations that manage to acknowledge human reality without actually supporting it:

> **The Agency establishes certain generally applicable environmental standards to protect human health and the environment from radioactive materials.**

These radioactive materials emit ionizing radiation, which can damage living tissue and cause cancer.

The EPA's 1977 rules were promulgated in an era of optimism about the expansion of nuclear power in the US. Even the EPA was predicting 300 operating reactors within 20 years. In 1973, President Nixon had predicted 1,000 reactors by 2000.

In 1979, the Three Mile Island nuclear power plant accident happened, during which the reactor core partially melted down. The number of operating nuclear power plants has never risen much above 100 since then. The nuclear industry needs a relaxation of limits on radiation releases to stimulate new plant construction.

Lower radiation levels provide more environmental protection

Environmental organizations like the Nuclear Information and Resource Service (NIRS) are urging the EPA to lower radiation release standards, to "protect more, not less." According to NIRS, regulation of nuclear power has a sorry history:

> Nuclear power operations that release radioactivity have been given an enormous "free pass" to expose communities (and the biosphere) to levels of radiation that are too high. When converted to RISK of cancer, the current regulation allows harm 2000 times higher than the EPA's stated goal of allowing only 1 cancer in a million from licensed activities. Even using EPA's more lax allowable risk level of 1 in 10,000 current EPA radiation regulations allow 20 times higher than that.

Nuclear proponents have long argued that there are "safe" levels of radiation, or even that some radiation exposure is good for you. What "safe" means in this context is that there are low levels of radiation that will take a long time to cause harm (cancer, genetic damage) and that in the meantime the odds are close to 100% that you will die from some other cause.

In 2005, the National Academy of Sciences addressed "safe" levels of radiation and concluded that there are none in any scientifically meaningful sense.

Humans are exposed to a basic, damaging level of ionizing radiation from multiple sources from gestation till death. This natural background radiation is at a relatively low level, but the risk from radiation is cumulative. Every additional exposure above background radiation adds to the risk. Some of these risks, like radiation treatment to treat cancer, are widely accepted as reasonable trade-offs. The reasonableness of greater exposure from the nuclear fuel cycle and the uncontrolled growth of nuclear waste is not such an obviously beneficial trade-off.

> **Update 2019:** On February 1, 2019, the Trump administration appointed Brant Ulsh, a health physicist, as chair of the EPA radiation advisory panel. Ulsh has long opposed the EPA's restrictions on radiation exposure. He rejects the scientific consensus that any exposure to ionizing radiation is a cancer risk.

RADIATION & FOSSIL FOOLS

In April 2018, the National Council on Radiation Protection and Measurement, a congressionally chartered non-profit, published a study confirming the consensus that there is no safe level of radiation exposure

In April 2018, the EPA proposed new regulations allowing increased exposure to radiation, on the theory that a little radiation can be good for you, called hormesis. The new regulations – Ionising Radiation Regulations of 2019 (IRR19) – were signed into law on February 5, 2019.

Scientists for Accurate Radiation Information (SARI) was founded in 2013 to counter public concern about radiation after the Fukushima nuclear power plant meltdowns (that have not ended). Mother Jones (February 27, 2019) has a piece about SARI titled: "Thanks to This Advocacy Group, the Trump Administration Believes a Little Radiation is Good for you." Brant Ulsh is a member of SARI and co-authored an article urging the EPA to use hormesis as the standard for regulating ionizing radiation. The paper argued that it was outdated science to consider all radiation dangerous, thereby forcing "unnecessary burdens of costly clean-up" on nuclear power plants, bomb-making factories, or other nuclear facilities.

Hormesis remains controversial in the scientific community.

102.

Kitty Litter Shuts Down Sole US Nuclear Weapons Waste Facility

US nuclear weapons buildup ignores waste dangers

Now it's official: using the wrong kitty litter can cause a severe and expensive nuclear accident at the nation's unique underground radioactive waste containment facility, shutting it down indefinitely.

Last winter, the US Department of Energy (DOE) appointed a Technical Assessment Team of independent experts from other government labs, and the team spent most of a year investigating the 2014 Valentine's Day radiation-release accident at New Mexico's federal Waste Isolation Pilot Project (WIPP). On March 26, 2015, the team produced a 277-page report that concluded that radiation was released from the facility when a single container (Drum 68660) over-heated and failed because the nuclear weapons waste it contained was packed with the wrong kind of kitty litter. That kitty litter was "chemically incompatible" with the other contents of the drum, causing it to overheat, creating gases that forced open the lid in a "thermal runaway" that led to the spill that released radiation to the environment and that still renders a large section of the underground storage area lethal to humans.

The assessment team concluded that the February 14, 2014, drum failure took about 70 days to develop before the drum was breached. The accident released radioactive isotopes of Uranium, Plutonium and Americium in uncertain amounts that are officially thought to be relatively small. As of early April 2015, Drum 68660 is the only drum that has failed. The experts determined that another 677 drums containing radioactive waste were packed with the wrong kitty litter. These drums are scattered among several locations, and could also fail, but the experts "believe" that another failure is unlikely.

In part because the accident site remains largely inaccessible, the assessment team wrote that it "could not determine the cause of the drum breach with absolute certainty."

Los Alamos National Laboratory's multiple radiation risks continue

While most of the drums of nuclear weapons waste laden with organic kitty litter are already underground at WIPP, there are an estimated 113 in temporary storage in Texas and 57 remaining at the Los Alamos National Laboratory (LANL). One of the drums at LANL is a "sibling drum" to the one that burst underground. The two drums were packed with waste from the same "parent drum" and with the same Swheat Scoop kitty litter, but other elements of their contents were slightly different. The drum still at LANL is monitored for heat and remains intact. LANL has shipped more than 1,000 drums of waste to WIPP since it opened in 1999. Remaining LANL waste, stored above ground on-site, was threatened by wildfire in 2011 and remains near an earthquake fault line.

The DOE assessment team did not address the question of why the waste packing process at Los Alamos stopped using non-organic kitty litter as usual and switched to Swheat Scoop. The World Nuclear Association, an industry group in London, explains the kitty litter mix-up by saying: "The DOE did not specify its preferred brand.... However, Swheat Scoop happens to be made from wheat and therefore contains carbohydrates which provided fuel for a chemical reaction with the metal nitrate salts being disposed of." Each 55-gallon drum of nuclear waste typically includes about 50 pounds of kitty litter.

Rumors that the accident at WIPP was caused by the wrong kitty litter used by LANL surfaced soon after it happened. In May 2014, New Mexico's Environment Department (NMED) secretary, Ryan Flynn, issued a formal order to LANL to secure the drums containing the wrong kitty litter, observing that:

Based on the evidence presented to NMED, the current handling, storage, treatment and transportation of the hazardous nitrate salt bearing waste containers at LANL may present an imminent and substantial endangerment to health or the environment.

Was LANL cutting safety corners to cut costs?

In November 2014, after a six-month investigation, the Santa Fe *New Mexican* portrayed LANL as behaving either incompetently, or with reckless disregard for safety, or with something like criminal negligence – perhaps a mixture of all three. Motivating LANL malfeasance, the paper suggests, was the desire of the private contractors running the lab to meet the June 30, 2014, deadline for clearing waste from the site, thereby protecting and extending its $2.2 billion annual operating contract with the US Energy Department as well as another $80 million a year for managing LANL.

Like so much of the US nuclear weapons program, LANL is a cozy, profitable, corporate-welfare monopoly for a private consortium calling itself Los Alamos National Security. The Delaware Limited Liability Company was formed eight years ago by four entities: Babcock & Wilcox Technical Services, URS Energy and Construction, Bechtel, and the University of California. As stated in its by-laws, the company purpose is "to manage and operate the Los Alamos National Laboratory in a manner that furthers the interests of the national security and advances the DOE/NNSA missions, programs and objectives in accordance with the terms of the Prime Contract." In other words, it is a privately held national security profit center that, according to Bloomberg, "engages in the businesses of nuclear defense programs, facilities management, science and technology to homeland security challenges, and safety and security."

Los Alamos National Security LLC is, by its very nature, a limited liability conflict of interest in which at least one conflict is between profit and security.

Santa Fe New Mexican lays out tough case against LANL

As viewed by the *New Mexican*, the parent company, Los Alamos National Security, allowed its employees at LANL to take numerous actions that could protect the company's profits by risking the security of others. The gambit appears to have failed by just one drum. Its elements, perpetrated or allowed by LANL employees or contractors, included, according to the *New Mexican*:

- ... workers packaging the waste came across a batch that was extraordinarily acidic, making it unsafe for shipping. The lab's guidelines called for work to shut down while the batch underwent a rigid set of reviews to determine how to treat it, a time-consuming process that jeopardized the lab's goal of meeting the deadline. Instead, the lab and its various contractors took shortcuts in treating the acidic nuclear waste, adding neutralizer and a wheat-based organic kitty litter to absorb excess liquid.

- Documents accompanying the drum, which were supposed to include a detailed description of its contents ... made no mention of the acidity or the neutralizer, and they mischaracterized the kitty litter as a clay-based material – not the more combustible organic variety that most chemists would have recognized as hazardous if mixed with waste laden with nitrate salts....

- Documents and internal emails show that even after the radiation leak, lab officials downplayed the dangers of the waste – even to the Carlsbad managers whose staff members were endangered by its presence – and withheld critical information from regulators and WIPP officials investigating the leak.

- The waste container that ultimately burst would not have met federal transportation standards to get on the road from Los Alamos to Carlsbad, nor would it have been accepted at WIPP, if its true ingredients had been reported by the lab.

- In documents filed with the New Mexico Environment Department before the accident, LANL reported that the waste in the drum that would later burst "is stable and will not undergo violent chemical change without detonating," and "there is no indication that the waste contains explosive materials, and it is not capable of detonation or explosive reaction. The materials in the waste stream are therefore not reactive wastes.

- LANL has never publicly acknowledged the reason it switched from clay-based litter to the organic variety believed to be the fuel that fed the intense heat.

- Organic kitty litter may have been mixed in up to 5,565 containers of waste at LANL starting in September 2012 that were incorrectly labeled as holding inorganic litter, according to an assessment conducted by WIPP personnel.

LANL did not respond to inquiries by RSN seeking an explanation for the change from inorganic to organic kitty litter during 2012-2014.

Commenting on the story in the *New Mexican*, Greg Mello of the Los Alamos Study Group wrote in part: "The treatment processes [LANL] used were illegal as well as dangerous. Shipping the waste was illegal. Providing the fallacious manifest that accompanied the drums was illegal. Failing to provide accurate information after the fact when NMED asks for it was and is illegal."

In the most recent study group bulletin, Mello notes that not every misdeed in the nuclear world will reach the public and cites an example from December 2014 when eight people at LANL were apparently contaminated with Plutonium but there was no news coverage.

Nuclear safety is an expensive mirage, all for the sake of nuclear war

The cost of failure of the single drum contaminated with organic kitty litter will almost surely run into the hundreds of millions of dollars. WIPP alone estimates its recovery plan will cost at least $500 million, and an additional $200 million or so for an improved, new ventilation system. These estimates do not include the additional costs of holding the nuclear waste stream while WIPP is closed, or the cost of improvement and compliance at LANL or any other facility.

When it opened in 1999, WIPP was supposed to have a 10,000-year leak-proof design life protecting the public from nuclear weapons waste radiation. That design life turned out to be only 15 years of safety, although further releases of radiation since Valentine's Day 2014 have apparently been limited.

The Department of Energy says it is committed to reopening WIPP by March 2016, at least for partial operation, but that's uncertain, since no one has ever before tried to fix an underground nuclear waste facility. Meanwhile, the ceiling of the underground salt cave had a significant collapse in January, when a section of ceiling 8 feet by 8 feet and two feet thick fell in a non-contaminated section of the one square mile storage area. As WIPP management acknowledged at the time: "This event highlights the need to continue prioritizing roof bolting and ground control in both the contaminated and uncontaminated areas of the WIPP underground facility in order to ensure safety and habitability in the underground. This area was originally scheduled to be re-bolted during the annual outage in February 2014."

In March, more than a year after Drum 68660 burst, decontamination of the underground area began, as reported by WIPP: "Employees are using a modified piece of agricultural spraying equipment that allows them to apply a fine water mist to the walls and floor. The water dissolves the salt and washes it down to the floor. When the salt recrystallizes, it encapsulates the contamination and prevents any resuspension of radioactive particles."

And now the federal government has reversed its past practice of paying fines for violating state laws and regulations. In December 2014, New Mexico's Environment Department levied a total of $54 million in fines on the federal (outsourced) operations at WIPP ($17.7 million) and LANL ($36.6 million). The Energy Department is taking the position that it would be illegal to pay New Mexico's fines, even though it has done so in the past.

Underlying this struggle over the safety of nuclear weapons waste is the Obama administration's perpetuation of longstanding reliance on a massive nuclear weapons force comprising more than 7,500 warheads, more than 2,000 of which are presently deployed around the world. The Obama administration has embarked on a program of improving and expanding the American nuclear force. A key element of that program is the fabrication of Plutonium pits (nuclear bomb triggers). Making these essential elements of American weapons of mass destruction has been assigned to the Los Alamos National Laboratory, even though LANL has demonstrated its ability and willingness to gamble on lying about using the wrong kitty litter.

> **Update 2019:** WIPP was closed for about three years, until it started receiving nuclear waste shipments again in April 2017. WIPP took 724 shipments in 2013 before it was closed. It took 133 shipments in 2017, 311 in 2018, and expects another 400 in 2019.
>
> In November 2018, New Mexico settled its $54 million suit against WIPP, agreeing to accept federal funding for roadwork and environmental projects rather than collecting fines.

103.

Law Is to Justice as Treaties Are to Native Americans

"Since the founding of this nation, the United States' relationship with the Indian tribes has been contentious and tragic. America's expansionist impulse in its formative years led to the removal and relocation of many tribes, often by treaty but also by force." Cobell v. Norton, 240 F.3d 1081, 1086 (D.C. Cir. 2001). This case also features what an American Indian tribe believes is an unlawful encroachment on its heritage. More specifically, the Standing Rock Sioux Tribe has sued the United States Army Corps of Engineers to block the operation of Corps permitting for the Dakota Access Pipeline (DAPL).

(OPENING PARAGRAPH OF STANDING ROCK SIOUX TRIBE, ET AL.,
V. US ARMY CORPS OF ENGINEERS, ET AL., CIVIL ACTION #16-1534 (JEB))

After seeming to quote sympathetically another judge's oblique acknowledgement of historic injustice (above), a US District Judge went on to issue an opinion perpetuating that injustice, as required by law. On September 9, 2016, Judge James E. ("Jeb") Boasberg issued his order based on his self-described cursory review of the record ("digging through a substantial record on an expedited basis"). This cursory review is again acknowledged in the judge's conclusion that "the Corps has likely complied with the NHPA [National Historic Preservation Act] and that the Tribe has not shown it will suffer injury that would be prevented by any injunction the Court could issue." The judge took 58 pages to justify his ruling on a likelihood rather than a finding of fact, which was not easily found given the spotty state of the evidence. Judge Boasberg's lengthy exposition of the case is filled with surmises and suggests that few, if any, of the participants have consistently acted in good faith.

Judge Boasberg's decision, to deny an injunction halting construction of the Dakota Access Pipeline (DAPL), appears reasonable enough on its face since the pipeline is already about half built (on private land) and the Standing Rock Sioux made no specific representations of culturally significant sites that would be irreparably damaged in the absence of an injunction, at least according to the judge, who wrote: "These people created stone alignments, burial cairns, and other rock features throughout the area to conduct important spiritual rituals related to the rhythms of their daily life. Along the region's waterways in particular, the prevalence of these artifacts reflects water's sacred role in their deeply held spiritual beliefs." His decision to discount these non-specific monuments ("at least 350") was more of a psychological defeat than a legal one for the tribe. The Standing Rock Sioux had, from the beginning, wanted the Army Corps of Engineers to treat the entire pipeline as a single project. The Corps insisted that its legal jurisdiction applied only to unconnected bits and pieces totaling about 12 miles along the route of the 1,172-mile pipeline. Although Congress has regulated natural gas pipelines, it has passed no law putting oil pipelines under federal jurisdiction, even when a pipeline, like DAPL, passes through several states.

US Justice Dept. plays both sides of pipeline issue

Whatever impact Judge Boasberg's ruling had didn't last long. Apparently the US Justice Dept., having represented the Corps of Engineers in the Standing Rock Sioux case, had anticipated Judge Boasberg's decision. Within minutes of the judge's ruling, the Justice Dept. issued a joint statement that began:

> We appreciate the District Court's opinion on the US Army Corps of Engineers' compliance with the National Historic Preservation Act. However, important issues raised by the Standing Rock Sioux Tribe and other tribal nations and their members regarding the Dakota Access pipeline specifically, and pipeline-related decision-making generally, remain. Therefore, the Department of the Army, the Department of Justice, and the Department of the Interior will take the following steps....

The first step was effectively to impose a non-injunction injunction that halts construction on at least some of the contested areas where the pipeline approaches or encroaches on waterways. For now, the Corps of Engineers will withhold the permits necessary for construction to continue, pending the resolution of cultural site issues along the pipeline as well as the larger issue of how the US relates to the supposedly sovereign tribal governments. This three-agency federal intervention has all the look of a coordinated attempt at political de-escalation of a situation threatening to get out of hand. Starting in April 2016 and increasing at the end of summer, thousands of Native Americans from a number of tribes across the country have gathered near Lake Oahe as "protectors of the waters," using nonviolent direct-action techniques to block pipeline construction. Both the pipeline company and the state of North Dakota have responded with force and violence, as well as unlawful behaviour violating the protesters' rights. As the Justice Dept. statement of September 9 put it:

> ... we fully support the rights of all Americans to assemble and speak freely. We urge everyone involved in protest or pipeline activities to adhere to the principles of nonviolence. Of course, anyone who commits violent or destructive acts may face criminal sanctions from federal, tribal, state, or local authorities. The Departments of Justice and the Interior will continue to deploy resources to North Dakota to help state, local, and tribal authorities, and the communities they serve, better communicate, defuse tensions, support peaceful protest, and maintain public safety.
>
> In recent days, we have seen thousands of demonstrators come together peacefully, with support from scores of sovereign tribal governments, to exercise their First Amendment rights and to voice heartfelt concerns about the environment and historic, sacred sites. It is now incumbent on all of us to develop a path forward that serves the broadest public interest.

Despite the reasonable rhetoric, the only action proposed by the Justice Dept. is to "invite tribes to formal, government-to-government consultations." This is an ancient paradigm that has rarely turned out well for the tribes. The Justice Dept. agenda for the consultations has just two items: (1) "to better insure tribal input" into decisions affecting tribal lands and rights "within the existing statutory framework," and (2) to consider proposing new legislation to Congress. Implicitly, the first point contradicts Judge Boasberg's conclusion that the Corps of Engineers "likely" complied with the law. But what the Justice Dept. proposes will take a long time to reach any satisfactory solution, if it ever does. This is in direct opposition to pressures on the ground, where the white population (roughly 90% of North Dakota) is restive and the owner of the pipeline, Energy Transfer Partners, faces a contractual obligation to start delivering oil in early 2017. There is no middle ground here.

Once again, it's the American empire versus interfering outsiders

Energy Transfer Partners represents the tip of the corporate oligarchy that has no profitable stake in alleviating climate change. The international banks (38 of them according to Bloomberg) that have put up more than $10 billion for DAPL and other oil projects are, in reality, underwriting the burning of more and worse fossil fuels as far as the planet is concerned. Mainstream media coverage, when it exists, typically focuses on protest and confrontation over the local water issue, without meaningful context and without going deeper into underlying issues. Providing detailed coverage of both events on the ground and wider context, Democracy NOW has been reporting the story in depth since early August, as tensions were building.

On July 25, 2016, the Corps of Engineers issued an environmental assessment that found that the pipeline would have "no significant impact" on the tribe's burial grounds or other cultural landmarks. The Corps also instituted a "Tribal Monitoring Plan," under which DAPL was required to notify the tribes when working on sensitive areas so that the tribe could monitor the work. This was roughly seven years since work began on the pipeline, by which time almost half the pipeline had already been built without monitoring.

On August 4, the tribe filed for an injunction to stop work on the pipeline. Judge Boasberg held a hearing on the motion on August 24, promising a decision on September 9. The judge noted that 90% of the clearing and grading, the work most damaging to tribal sites, had been completed in North Dakota. He added: "One of the few exceptions is the crossing leading up to the west side of Lake Oahe, which has not yet been cleared or graded."

On September 2, the tribes filed a supplemental declaration with Judge Boasberg, identifying a number of cultural sites both within and near the pipeline route, areas that had been untouched by construction. The following day, Saturday, September 3, DAPL bulldozers moved in and plowed up the area, without regard for any tribal sites in their way. To get this done, DAPL brought in private security forces from out of state. Local and state law enforcement withdrew and watched or went away. Caught by surprise, tribal protesters belatedly but peacefully swarmed the site to stop the bulldozers. There they were met by aggressive private security forces who used dogs and pepper spray, as well as personal violence, to hold protestors at bay while the bulldozers finished their work. An unknown number of protestors were hit, shoved, pepper sprayed, maced, bitten by dogs and otherwise attacked by DAPL workers and security. And the state of North Dakota responded by issuing a warrant for the arrest of journalist Amy Goodman for criminal trespass.

In his ruling a week later, Judge Boasberg covered this event in a single sentence: "The next day, on Saturday, September 3, Dakota Access graded this area." In the same section, Judge Boasberg went to much greater lengths to minimize the findings of previously unidentified cultural sites. He also conflated them with others that were not in areas that needed permits. His writing sounds like a brief for the pipeline, showing not the slightest displeasure with DAPL's actions. Another judge faced with pre-emptive bulldozing of property in active litigation might have had a word or more to say about actions taken in contempt of court.

Tribal suffering makes a great panopticon for shows of caring

Later in his decision, where he finds that the tribe will suffer no irreparable harm in the absence of an injunction, Judge Boasberg wrote without apparent irony of "the likelihood that DAPL's ongoing construction activities – specifically, grading and clearing of land – might damage or destroy sites of great cultural or historical significance to the Tribe." The judge does not consider whether this is exactly what happened on September 3. Instead, in a growing fog of mock respect, the judge quotes the Standing Rock Sioux Tribal Council chairman, Dave Archambault II:

> History connects the dots of our identity, and our identity was all but obliterated. Our land was taken, our language was forbidden. Our stories, our history, were almost forgotten. What land, language, and identity remains is derived from our cultural and historic sites.... Sites of cultural and historic significance are important to us because they are a spiritual connection to our ancestors. Even if we do not have access to all such sites, their existence perpetuates the connection. When such a site is destroyed, the connection is lost.

With breath-taking sanctimony, the judge then ignores not only the future possibility of irreparable harm from DAPL construction, but also the actual irreparable harm of September 3 as well. Judge Boasberg writes: "The tragic history of the Great Sioux Nation's repeated dispossessions at the hands of a hungry and expanding early America is well known. The threat that new injury will compound old necessarily compels great caution and respect from this Court in considering the Tribe's plea for intervention."

Whereupon the judge exercised no caution whatsoever, denied the request for an injunction and left the tribe at the mercy of the pipeline company (until the Justice Dept. intervened). In his order, the judge then justified his choice with an argument of inevitability as to the destruction of tribal sacred sites: "any such harms are destined to ensue *whether* or not the Court grants the injunction the Tribe desires." [emphasis added] But later the judge admitted that "there may be many sites that ... the Court has missed."

Judge Boasberg, whatever his personal qualities, appears here as an agent of the state, a state that has been hostile for centuries to those who lived here before. Despite his lip service to Native American suffering, Judge Boasberg is little different in cultural representation from Jack Schaaf, 60, the white, angry, North Dakota rancher who is mad at the tribes for legally trying to defend their rights. As reported in the New York Times on September 13, he showed no awareness of self-contradiction:

> Mr. Schaaf said he had no problem with people standing up for a cause, but he was tired of navigating a police checkpoint if he wanted to drive into Mandan for a pizza. He complained that closings at Lake Oahe had prevented him from boating. And he said the protesters had no right to march on a public highway. "I think it's totally wrong," he said. "If they want to protest, they should be in the ditch."

This, like Judge Boasberg, is the voice of the conqueror whose denial of who he is requires him to deny the conquered their rights. This is class war and race war. This is the power to attack the living and disturb the dead without remorse, without hesitation, without even awareness. This is the continuity of American genocide that underlies everything America says it wants to stand for. This is the bedrock of American entitlement, as illustrated by recent events at Standing Rock. This is entitlement that sees no contradiction in denying some of the public access to public roads. This is entitlement that enables law officers to lie about pipe bomb threats when tribal leaders talk about loading up their peace pipes. This is entitlement that shows itself in the actions of a pipeline company that, while waiting for a judge to rule on the protection of a burial ground, sends in its goons and bulldozers to rape the land and then argue that there's no burial ground left to protect.

Entitlement that robs a grave for a skull to use in ritual kissing

This is the deeply pathological American entitlement that has no difficulty sharing blankets laced with smallpox, no difficulty wiping out men, women and children at Sand Creek or Ludlow Colorado, no difficulty slaughtering guards and prisoners at Attica and no difficulty waging war crimes in countries sorely in need of disentitlement, at least in American eyes.

And strangely enough, Judge Boasberg has been beautifully cast by fate as the embodiment of the American pathology as it attacks the tribes once more. Jeb Boasberg is a child of American privilege. From St. Albans School to Yale to Oxford to Yale Law School and on up the federal judicial ladder, there is nothing apparent in his published life story that he will ever understand tribal realities, much less deal fairly or compassionately with them.

Judging by Jeb Boasberg's answers to the US Senate before being confirmed for his next federal judgeship, he is the antithesis of an activist judge. He had no objection to mandatory sentencing. He wrote: "I have not presided over cases in which my desired outcome was contrary to the law." He answered that he does not consider his own personal values (unstated) relevant. With regard to the right to bear arms and to the death penalty, he said he would follow current law as determined by the Supreme Court. He said he does not believe the US Constitution is a living document that can evolve with society. He said a federal judge must do as the Supreme Court says. He said more, much of it repetitive, none of it suggesting any inclination to deviate purposely from current legal doctrine, regardless whatever justice might demand.

These answers create an impression of a legal automaton, insofar as it's possible for a human to be robotic. Asked for his view of "the role of a judge," he answered: "A judge should fairly and impartially uphold the law as it is written and apply it to the cases that appear before him or her." With perfect consistency, he does not address the problem of how to uphold the law fairly when the law itself is unfair (a longstanding, common problem with American law).

The ruling class does as the ruling class does

The ruling class writes the law and the ruling class is not concerned with the law's fairness to others than themselves. Jeb Boasberg, when he was at Yale College, was a member of a secret society of the ruling class, Skull and Bones (familiarly known as "Bones"), founded in 1832 by William H. Russell, heir to an opium-trade fortune. A great many of its members have served the American empire, especially in the CIA. Bonesmen as President include William Howard Taft and both Bushes (and their father/grandfather Prescott Bush). Bones alumni include William F. Buckley, William Sloane Coffin, Averill Harriman, Lewis Lapham, Henry Luce and Secretary of State John Kerry among a long list of other notables.

Judge Boasberg's deference to law, to government agencies, to oil pipeline companies is all consistent with his membership in a ruling class club. What is especially neat about this club is that, by credible legend, it has long been directly involved in Native American grave desecration. As the story goes, Prescott Bush was stationed at Fort Sill, Oklahoma, in 1918. The Apache warrior Geronimo had died at Fort Sill in 1909. Bush and fellow Bonesmen dug him up and brought his skull and other bits back to the Tomb, the New Haven home of Skull and Bones. A lawsuit in 2009, seeking the return of Geronimo's skull to his heirs, ended in dismissal by a federal judge before the truth of the skull could be established. The judge ruled that the Native American Graves Protection and Repatriation Act, under which the suit was filed, did not protect any graves desecrated before 1990, when the law was passed. That let Skull and Bones off the hook. And left Geronimo in limbo, or New Haven.

Assume the legend is literally true: then, as a Yale senior joining Skull and Bones, Jeb Boasberg kissed Geronimo's skull. Metaphorically, that act of atavistic triumphalism shines through in his legal decision against the Standing Rock Sioux.

Kissing the skull of an enemy is just another way of showing who's in control here, whose burial is sacred and whose is not.

104.

Obama Is Pathetic on Human Rights in North Dakota

"We're monitoring this closely. And, you know, I think, as a general rule, my view is that there is a way for us to accommodate sacred lands of Native Americans. And I think that right now the Army Corps is examining whether there are ways to reroute this pipeline in a way.... So—so, we're going to let it play out for several more weeks and determine whether or not this can be resolved in a way that I think is properly attentive to the traditions of the first Americans...."

PRESIDENT OBAMA ON THE NOW THIS NEWS WEBSITE, NOVEMBER 1, 2016

Isn't that sweet? The President gave lip service to "the traditions of the first Americans." He didn't mention treaties between sovereign nations, of course, because he's not about to break with the traditions of the second Americans: that such treaties are only a means to a genocidal end. Such treaties aren't to be taken seriously by the United States of exceptional, manifestly destined Americans whenever such treaties interfere with what the US wants.

That's what "properly attentive" means historically. Freely translated, "properly attentive" means "make a show of peace talk, then roll over them with whatever force necessary after it's too late to affect the election." The legal mind is nothing if not properly attentive to elegant turns of phrase in its unyielding hypocrisy.

If the President had any intention of honoring anything relating to the sacred lands of Native Americans, he would not be planning to "let it play out for several more weeks." Sacred lands have already been destroyed. Sacred lands are being destroyed now, not only by the pipeline construction but also by the massive militarized police response

606

to nonviolent protest. Letting it play out for several more weeks only opens the door to the destruction of more – even all – of the sacred lands in the path of this lethal-to-the-planet pipeline.

What is happening, what has been happening for months in North Dakota, is a travesty – of justice, of common human decency, of the rule of law and standards of international law. And it all feeds the forces hastening climate change. Our president is on the wrong side of all of it, just barely responding with docile, passive, articulate evasiveness.

"We're monitoring this closely," says the President

If the President is monitoring this closely and remains willing to let it play out for several more weeks, that's a pretty clear signal that he has no serious problem with the creation of police state conditions in North Dakota. Besides an unknown number of private security forces working for Energy Transfer Partners (the pipeline sponsor), there are law enforcement officers from at least seven states that have cost about $10 million so far. That seems a ridiculously high price to pay to contain peaceful protest. And it's an even more ridiculous price for taxpayers to shell out to protect private profits.

If the President is monitoring this closely without responding, that is a tacit admission that he has no serious problem with any of the egregious behavior so far by official and quasi-official paramilitaries and their wide-ranging mistreatment (including criminal assault) of American citizens. In particular, he has allowed and continues to allow himself to be seen as approving:

- Unlicensed, apparently untrained private security forces using dogs to bloody peaceful protesters (who call themselves water protectors).

- State officials arresting and over-charging journalists for committing journalism.

- A local sheriff inflaming the public with false reports of "pipe bombs," when what he had actually heard was talk of "peace pipes."

- Law officers shooting nonviolent water protectors in the back and front with rubber bullets.

- State officials housing arrestees in dog cages and conditions that violate international law against torturing prisoners.

- Law officers on the riverbank using mace and pepper spray against nonviolent water protectors standing in the water.

- Official surveillance helicopters flying low to panic horses.

- Official surveillance helicopters mysteriously going off duty just before "persons unknown" start a prairie fire (with such ineptitude that the wind blows it away from the Standing Rock Sioux gathering ground).

- Apparent contempt of court by Energy Transfer Partners, who sent its bulldozers to destroy a burial ground that, once destroyed, could no longer be a reason for a federal court to rule against the pipeline. Desecration is not a criminal act, apparently, when you have a government permit for it, even when that permit is under litigation.

That's a lot of official abuse to tolerate, even for a president, and that's just a sampling of the police state techniques being tested in Middle America these days.

Starting to sound conciliatory, the President said, "And I think that right now the Army Corps is examining whether there are ways to reroute this pipeline in a way ..." The President paused there, leaving the thought unfinished. The pipeline has already been re-routed, away from the state capital city of Bismarck after residents there expressed fear that the pipeline threatened their water supply. Now the pipeline threatens the water supply of the Standing Rock Sioux (and thousands of others), but that is more acceptable to the American power structure. The President has expressed no dismay at the idea that a pipeline rupture along the Missouri River would devastate huge numbers of "the first Americans," who have no other source of water. As one water protector put it: "If it were to be contaminated... it would be a death sentence."

Why does the President think rerouting a climate-hostile pipeline is any kind of an answer to anything other than protecting the speculative bets of Energy Transfer Partners? If he were to consider this pipeline (any new pipeline) in terms of its impact on global climate values, this would be a no-brainer: no more pipelines. This is the Army Corps of Engineers we're talking about – the Army – and the President is the commander in chief who has no difficulty blowing up wedding parties and funerals with drones in some imaginary defense of national security. Why does he have such reluctance to protect planetary security? Why does he not just order the Army Corp of Engineers to go back to square one and re-do this process? Why was it fast-tracked in the first place, with the exclusion of interested parties who had legal standing? President Obama shows no inclination to do any of this well or right. He's apparently much more comfortable with false equivalencies and blaming the victims (also on Now This News):

> Yeah, I mean, it's a challenging situation. I think that my general rule when I talk to governors and state and local officials, whenever they're dealing with protests, including, for example, during the Black Lives Matters protests, is there is an obligation for protesters to be peaceful, and there's an obligation for authorities to show restraint. And, you know, I want to make sure that as everybody is exercising their constitutional rights to be heard, that both sides are refraining from situations that might result in people being hurt.

For someone supposedly monitoring this closely, the President might be expected to know that people have already been hurt and most if not all of those hurt were nonviolent, peaceful protestors set upon by dogs and assaulted by rubber bullets, sound cannons and chemical weapons. What fundamental, callous irrationality prompts this president to bring in Black Lives Matter? That is strange beyond comprehension.

But perhaps it shines a light on that dark place in his soul that allowed him to react with almost no help or pity for the people of Flint, poisoned by their own governments, including the one President Obama is supposed to lead.

105.

Fukushima: Still Getting Worse After Six Years of Meltdowns

Even Fox News reports radiation at "unimaginable levels"

After a week of limited coverage of "unimaginable levels" of radiation inside the remains of collapsed Unit 2 at Fukushima (see below), Nuclear-News.net reported February 11 that radiation levels are actually significantly higher than "unimaginable."

Continuous, intense radiation, at 530 sieverts an hour (4 sieverts is a lethal level), was widely reported in early February 2017 – as if this were a new phenomenon. It's not. Three reactors at Fukushima melted down during the earthquake-tsunami disaster on March 3, 2011, and the meltdowns never stopped. Radiation levels have been out of control ever since. As Fairewinds Energy Education noted in an email February 10:

> **Although this robotic measurement just occurred, this high radiation reading was anticipated and has existed inside the damaged Unit 2 atomic reactor since the disaster began nearly 6 years ago.... As Fairewinds has said for 6 years, there are no easy solutions because groundwater is in direct contact with the nuclear corium (melted fuel) at Fukushima Daiichi.**

What's new (and not very new, at that) is the official acknowledgement of the highest radiation levels yet measured there, by a factor of seven (the previously measured high was 73 sieverts an hour in 2012). The highest radiation level measured at Chernobyl was 300 sieverts an hour. What this all means, as anyone paying attention well knows, is that the triple-meltdown Fukushima disaster is still out of control.

RADIATION & FOSSIL FOOLS

"Sievert" is one of the many mystifying terms of radiation measurement that keep most people from fully understanding the dangers of radiation. A "sievert" is roughly equivalent to a "gray," as each represents a "joule" per kilogram (not to be confused, for example, with "Curie" or Becquerel," or with "rem," "rad," or "roentgen"). In the International System of Units (SI), a "joule" is the "unit of work or energy, equal to the work done by a force of one newton when its point of application moves one meter in the direction of action of the force, equivalent to one 3600th of a watt-hour." Got that? The jargon doesn't much matter as far as public safety is concerned. All ionizing radiation is life-threatening. The more you're exposed, the more you're threatened. As Physics Stack Exchange illustrates the issue:

> The dose [of radiation] that kills a tumor is deliberately aimed at that tumor. If, instead of using a collimated beam, you put a person in a wide beam for radio "therapy", you would be treating their entire body as a tumor and kill them.

Radiation levels at Fukushima are comparable to a nuclear explosion that doesn't end. That's one reason that TEPCO, the Tokyo Electric Power Co. that owns Fukushima, keeps trying to reassure the world that little or no radiation escapes from Fukushima. This is not true, radiation in large, mostly unmeasured or undocumented amounts pours into the Pacific Ocean all the time, without pause. One reason this release is out of control is because no one apparently knows just where the three melted reactor cores have gone. TEPCO says it thinks the melted cores have burned through the reactors' inner containment vessels but are still within the outer containment walls. They keep looking as best they can.

On February 3, 2017, the Guardian reported the high radiation levels discovered by a remote camera sent into the reactor on a telescopic arm. Reader Supported News carried the story from the environmental news site EcoWatch on February 5. Essentially the same story was reported on February 6 by Smithsonian.com, on February 7 by ZeroHedge.com, and on February 8, Fox News reported that "radiation levels at Japan's crippled Fukushima nuclear power plant are now at 'unimaginable' levels."

There have apparently been no such reports on CBS, NBC, CNN, or MSNBC. On February 9, ABC ran an AP story about pulling a robot out of Unit 2 because of "high radiation," without specifying a level and adding: "TEPCO officials reassured that despite the dangerously high figures, radiation is not leaking outside of the reactor."

On February 12, Pakistan Defence ran the AP story of February 9, but included the new level of radiation at 650 sieverts that fried a robot's camera, adding:

> The high levels of radiation may seem alarming, but there's good news: it's contained, and there are no reports of new leaks from the plant. That means that the radiation shouldn't affect nearby townships. Higher levels of radiation could also mean the robot is getting closer to the precise source of radioactivity to properly remove the melted fuel.

All this coverage relates only to Unit 2's melted reactor core. There is no reliable news of the condition of the melted reactor cores in two other units. Last November, in a half-hour talk reviewing the Fukushima crisis, Arnie Gunderson of Fairewinds Energy Education discussed the three missing reactor cores and what he suspected was the likelihood that they had not been contained within the reactor.

The ground water flowing into, through and out of the reactor is contaminated by its passage and is having some impact on the Pacific Ocean. The US, like other governments, is ignoring whatever is happening, treating it as if it doesn't matter and never will. In Carmel, California, residents are finding that tide pools, once vibrant with life, are now dead. They blame Fukushima.

Whatever is going on at Fukushima, it's not good and has horrifying possibilities. It's little comfort to have the perpetrator of the catastrophe, TEPCO, in charge of fixing it, especially when the Japanese government is more an enabler of cover-up and denial than any kind of seeker of truth or protector of its people. It took private researchers five years to figure out that Fukushima's fallout of Cesium-137 on Tokyo had taken a more dangerous, glassy form that wasn't cleaned up effectively.

The US and most of the rest of the world have chosen not to take Fukushima more seriously than a multi-car Interstate pile-up. This policy is one more roll of the dice, saving money now and gambling the future. But now we have Rick Perry heading up the US Department of Energy and Scott Pruitt slated to take over the Environmental Protection Agency – so we can expect big changes, right?

There has been one big change already at the Energy Dept., which uses more contractors than any other US agency. The Government Accountability Office (GAO) found that the Energy Dept. failed to protect whistleblowers who raised legitimate nuclear safety and other concerns. In response, the Energy Dept. prepared a new rule protecting whistleblowers from contractor retaliation.

That rule was blocked from going into effect by President Trump's regulatory freeze on January 20. Metaphorically, the earthquake and tsunami of the American election on November 9, 2016, has produced a political meltdown of unknown and expanding dimensions that will continue unchecked, causing still unmeasured destruction and human suffering far into a dark and dangerous future.

> **Update 2019:** More than eight years after the triple reactor meltdown at Fukushima, the status of the three melted reactor cores remains somewhat contained but uncontrolled, with no end in sight.
>
> Clean groundwater continues to flow into the reactors, then radioactive water flows out into the Pacific. Continuously. A frozen ice wall costing $309 million diverts much of the groundwater around the site to the Pacific. The water flow is not well measured. Some contaminated water is stored on site, but the site's storage capacity of 1.37 million tons of radioactive water may be reached during 2020.
>
> One proposed solution is to dilute the stored radioactive water and then dump it in the Pacific. Fukushima fishermen oppose this. Radioactivity in Fukushima fish has slowly declined, but the local fishing industry is only at 20 per cent of pre-meltdown levels.
>
> Water flowing into the reactors and cooling the cores is vital to preventing the meltdowns from re-initiating.
>
> The summer Olympics are planned for Tokyo in 2020. In 2013, two years after the Fukushima meltdowns, Japan's Prime Minister Shinzo

Abe pitched the Tokyo site by telling the Olympic Committee in reference to Fukushima: "Let me assure you, the situation is under control."

This was a lie. Even now, no one knows where the melted reactors are precisely. One robot has made one contact so far. Radiation levels at the core are lethal. There is, as yet, no way to remove the cores safely. The disaster is not as out of control as it was, but that's about the best that can be honestly said.

Official government statistics show pediatric cancers almost doubling since the Fukushima meltdowns of 2011. Thyroid cancers are reaching epidemic levels. The Japanese government refuses to track leukemia and other cancers. The official Fukushima death toll is more than 18,000, of whom 2,546 have never been recovered. Most of Fukushima prefecture remains uninhabitable due to high radiation levels.

On April 14, 2019, Prime Minister Abe visited the Fukushima meltdown site. He stood on elevated ground wearing no protective clothing about 100 meters from the building holding the melted-down reactors. Radiation where he was standing was in excess of 100 microsieverts per hour, less than safe. Abe's visit lasted six minutes. This was a classic pseudo-event, designed to be reported despite its lack of actual meaning – for all practical purposes it was another nuclear lie.

On March 21, 2019, Dr. Helen Caldicot offered an assessment much closer to the likely truth:

"They will never, and I quote never, decommission those reactors They will never be able to stop the water coming down from the mountains. And so, the truth be known, it's an ongoing global radiological catastrophe which no one really is addressing in full."

106.

With Blood on Its Missiles, US Indicted for Global Nuclear Terror

"The Nuremberg Principles not only prohibit such crimes but oblige those of us aware of the crime to act against it. "Complicity in the commission of a crime against peace, a war crime, or a crime against humanity ... is a crime under International Law....

"The ongoing building and maintenance of Trident submarines and ballistic missile systems constitute war crimes that can and should be investigated and prosecuted by judicial authorities at all levels. As citizens, we are required by International Law to denounce and resist known crimes."

KINGS BAY PLOWSHARES INDICTMENT OF US FOR WAR CRIMES,
APRIL 4, 2018

On April 4, 2018, the Kings Bay Plowshares Seven, three women and four men, all Catholics, carried out their faith-based, nonviolent, symbolic action, pouring blood on the world's largest nuclear submarine base and indicting the US for its perpetual crime of holding the world hostage to the terrorist threat of using nuclear weapons. The US crime that began in 1945 has reached new intensity with Donald Trump's years of casual rhetoric threatening nuclear holocaust on targets from ISIS to North Korea. Every other nuclear-armed state engages in the same criminal threatening every day, but the US has been at it longer and is still the only state to have perpetrated the actual war crimes of not one but two nuclear terror attacks against mostly civilian targets in Japan in 1945.

The target of the Plowshares Seven's radical direct action was the Kings Bay Naval Submarine Base, home to eight Trident nuclear submarines, each capable of launching nuclear missile strikes anywhere in the world. Each 560-foot-long Trident ballistic missile submarine carries sufficient firepower to attack some 600 cities with more destructive force than destroyed Hiroshima. The "small" warheads on Trident missiles have a 100-kiloton payload, roughly seven times more powerful than the Hiroshima bomb. The Kings Bay base covers some 17,000 acres, making it roughly 2,000 acres larger than Manhattan. The base was developed in 1978-79 under President Jimmy Carter, a former nuclear submarine engineer. A prominent Christian protestant all his career, Carter has long made peace with war-making, unlike the radical Catholics in the Plowshares movement since they hammered and poured blood on nuclear nosecones in 1980 (the first of more than 100 Plowshares actions since then).

On April 4, 2018, the fiftieth anniversary of the assassination of the Reverend Dr. Martin Luther King, Liz McAlister, 78, Stephen Kelly S.J., 70, Martha Hennessy, 62, Clare Grady, 58, Patrick O'Neill, 62, Mark Colville, 55 and Carmen Trotta, 55, entered the Kings Bay Naval Submarine Base.

> Carrying hammers and bottles of their own blood, the seven sought to enact and embody the prophet Isaiah's command to: "Beat swords into plowshares." In so doing, they were upholding the US Constitution through its requirement to respect treaties, international law through the UN Charter and Nuremberg principles, and higher moral law regarding the sacredness of all creation. They hoped to draw attention to and begin to dismantle what Dr. King called "the triple evils" of racism, militarism, and extreme materialism.

– Kings Bay Plowshares press release, May 4, 2018

As darkness fell on April 4, the Plowshares Seven were setting out to commit a classic act of civil disobedience, breaking laws that they saw as unjust in light of a higher law. The description of events that follows here is based on the government indictment (signed by five lawyers), the Kings Bay Plowshares account, and a conversation with one of the Plowshares Seven, Martha Hennessy, a retired occupational therapist, at her home in Vermont, where she is confined with an ankle bracelet while awaiting trial.

After penetrating the perimeter fence as a group, the seven split up into three groups, headed for three different destinations on the base, and arrived unchallenged.

The nuclear weapons storage bunkers are in a shoot-to-kill zone. McAlister, Kelly and Trotta managed to unfurl a banner without getting shot but were quickly arrested. The banner read: "Nuclear weapons: illegal/immoral."

The second group, Grady and Hennessy, went to the Strategic Weapons Facility Atlantic Administration, two large, one-story office buildings out of sight and hearing range from the weapons storage bunkers. Here the scene was more surreal: lights were on in the building, people were working inside, but it was very quiet. Grady and Hennessy were alone in the dark outside for almost an hour. That gave them time to post the Plowshares indictment on the door and rope off the area with yellow crime scene tape. They poured blood on the door and the sidewalk. They spray-painted the sidewalk with "Love One Another" and "Repent" and "May Love Disarm Us All."

When they were done, they joined the third group, Colville and O'Neill, at the Trident D5 Monuments, a sculptural, phallic celebration of nuclear weapons delivery systems. There the Plowshares splashed blood on the base logo and the Navy seal. They draped the monument in yellow crime scene tape. They pried back-lit blue letters off the monument. They hung a banner paraphrasing Martin Luther King's admonition that "the ultimate logic of racism is genocide." The banner read: "The Ultimate Logic of Trident is Omnicide." People drove by as they worked, but no one stopped. After about an hour, security officers arrived and very politely, full of Southern good manners, handcuffed the four and took them into custody at a base facility sometime after midnight.

> In days to come, the mountain of the Lord's house shall be established as the highest mountain and raised about the hills. All nations shall stream toward it.... He shall judge between the nations, and impose terms on many peoples. They shall beat their swords into plowshares; and their spears into pruning hooks; One nation shall not raise the sword against another, nor shall they train for war again.

> – Book of Isaiah, 2:2-4

According to Kings Bay Base spokesman Scott Bassett, the Plowshares Seven were quickly transferred to the civilian county jail.

Bassett said there were no injuries and that no military personnel or "assets" were in danger. He said the incident was still under investigation, but "At no time was anybody threatened."

Mainstream media seem to have treated the blooding of the submarine missiles as a one-day story of little import or ignored it entirely. The Navy was treating it as a trivial case of trespass and vandalism. Georgia officials filed charges along the same lines. But by the time the Plowshares Seven had been in county jail for a month, someone had decided to make a federal case of it.

The federal indictment of May 2 is a squalid bit of legalism at its most dishonest. The seven-page charge tries to have it both ways, making out a trespass/vandalism case while suppressing any desecration of US nuclear war-making ability. No wonder it took five lawyers to conjure up a redundantly iterated charge of conspiracy to trespass and "willfully and maliciously destroy and injure real and personal property" of the US Navy. The charge is naked of any hint of a motive, and for good, sordid, corrupt prosecutorial reason. The motive calls into question the legality of the base, the submarines, the nuclear weapons and the right of the US to keep the rest of the world under perpetual threat of annihilation. The feds have a long history of keeping that argument out of court by any means necessary.

Prosecutorial deceit is further illustrated by the indictment's corrupt selection of the alleged overt acts by the defendants. The indictment charges all seven with acts some of them could not possibly have committed. And for all their wordy whining about property being damaged or defaced, the lawyers conspire not to mention any yellow crime tape, or banners, or – most importantly – the defendants' blood. "A True Bill" the document is called on the page where five federal lawyers signed, if not in contempt of court, surely in contempt of truth and justice.

But that's where this case is headed, down the rabbit hole of police state justice, if the government has its way. The Plowshares Seven, all presently proceeding without attorneys of their own, will attempt to argue a necessity defense – that whatever illegal actions they have taken were necessary to prevent a greater harm, in this case nuclear destruction. That case is so patently obvious, the government has never dared to let it be argued (in other countries it has led to some acquittals). Mostly miscarriages of justice like this go on in the shadows, without media attention, without regard to who is president or which party is in power. Anyone who looks carefully soon realizes this is true. In late 2008, Martha Hennessy wrote from England:

> I can't write about my journey coming here to participate in the Catholic Worker Farm community without considering the context of our current world situation. The global financial markets teeter on the brink of chaos, and the US presidential race nears Election Day. It feels as though those who are aware of what is happening are holding their collective breath while others toil on in pain and oblivion. I completed early voting before leaving the States, but I am always left with a feeling of having blood on my hands, trying to be a "responsible" citizen in a so-called democracy. The recent American bailout of the corporate criminals is a theft from the people who need housing, healthcare and education. The horrific war that has been visited on the Iraqi people has turned on its perpetrators. And now people of faith who mount nonviolent protest to these atrocities are being branded as "terrorists" by the domestic security apparatus. How to maintain faith, hope and love with such dark times ahead?

Hennessy and two others are out on bail, but electronically shackled. The other four remain in federal prison in the usually appalling conditions the US justice system deems appropriate, or at least profitable. The prosecutors opposed any bail for any of them. A motions hearing is scheduled for early August, when all seven will seek release to allow them to prepare for trial, representing themselves. No trial date has yet been set. The defendants face potential sentences of 5 to 20 years each. They used their own blood to symbolize redemption and repentance in the shadow of nuclear holocaust. For that, these seven nonviolent Catholics have put themselves at the mercy of a "Christian" nation whose deepest belief is in its own exceptionalism, immersed in a permanent war economy heading toward omnicide, which can't come soon enough for apocalyptic dominionoids who figure their souls are saved so let's get it on. In a sane world, wouldn't that be enough for jury exclusion?

The Kings Bay Plowshares asked the court to dismiss these prosecutions for several reasons. Nuclear weapons are illegal under US law. Nuclear weapons are illegal under US Treaty Law. Nuclear weapons are illegal under international law. And prosecuting peace activists for taking action based on their religious beliefs violates the Religious Freedom Restoration Act.

> **Update 2019:** On November 7 and 19, 2018, the court held evidentiary hearings before a newly-assigned US Magistrate on the Plowshares 7 defense under the Religious Freedom Restoration Act, which is the basis of their motions to dismiss the charges. During the hearings, five of the Plowshares defendants testified, along with two expert witnesses: Fordham Professor of Religion Jeannine Hill Fletcher and Bishop Joseph Kopacz from Jackson, MS. The commander of Naval Station Kings Bay, Capt. Brian Lepine, testified under oath, but refused to acknowledge that nuclear weapons were present on the Trident submarines or stored at the base.
>
> At the end of the November 19 hearing, Magistrate Benjamin Cheesbro denied the Plowshares motion to mitigate their conditions of release (two were still incarcerated at the time). Plowshares asked the court to lessen their bond restrictions and allow them to remove their ankle monitors. Magistrate Cheesbro refused, ruling that the five are a "danger to community safety." He also allowed time for further filings before he would decide the questions raised under the Religious Freedom Restoration Act.
>
> In early April 2019, for the first anniversary of the Plowshares 7 action, supporters launched a global petition calling for the charges against the Plowshares to be dropped and for a revitalization of a worldwide anti-nuclear weapons movement. Three of the early signers were Nobel Peace Prize laureates Rev. Desmond Toto, Mairead Maguire and Jody Williams. Other signers included Noam Chomsky, Daniel Ellsberg, Rev. Dr. William Barber, Medea Benjamin, Phyllis Bennis, Ben Cohen, Chris Hedges, Martin Sheen, Paul Stookey, Alice Slater, Col. Ann Wright and others.
>
> As of mid-April 2019, four of the Plowshares were still out on bail and three were incarcerated. Magistrate Cheesbro had not reported his findings to presiding judge Lisa Godbey Wood to rule on the questions. No trial date had been set.

107.

Climate Crisis Goes Unabated, Nations Most Responsible Still Anti-Future

"Some people say that I should study to become a climate scientist so that I can "solve" the climate crisis. But the climate crisis has already been solved. We already have all the facts and solutions. And why should I be studying for a future that soon may be no more, when no one is doing anything to save that future? And what is the point of learning facts when the most important facts clearly mean nothing to our society?"

"Today we use 100 million barrels of oil every single day. There are no politics to change that. There are no rules to keep that oil in the ground. So we can no longer save the world by playing by the rules, because the rules have to be changed. So we have not come here to beg the world leaders to care for our future. They have ignored us in the past, and they will ignore us again. We have come here to let them know that change is coming, whether they like it or not. The people will rise to the challenge. And since our leaders are behaving like children, we will have to take the responsibility they should have taken long ago."

GRETA THUNBERG OF SWEDEN, AGE 15, ADDRESSING COP24,
THE 24TH CONFERENCE OF PARTIES TO THE UNITED NATIONS FRAMEWORK CONVENTION
ON CLIMATE CHANGE

Happy talk news coverage of COP24 accomplishments tends to prattle on about how 196 nations have agreed on a "rule book" that will help implement the 2015 Paris Agreement to begin cutting back on greenhouse gasses worldwide in an effort to limit the damage of the climate crisis already well underway. This is not bad news. It's not really news at all. The highly technical "rule book" may add clarity to what 195 nations are doing or not doing to mitigate global warming, but it is no more enforceable than the Paris Agreement. The response to the global climate crisis continues to be voluntary, with the world's most useful volunteers refusing to step up. Global greenhouse gas emissions increased in 2017 and are increasing again in 2018. None of this is new, nor is it necessarily an unalterable omen of planetary doom. But to head off the worst of this creeping catastrophe, major nations will need to change their behavior enough to have global impact. That is still a long, long way from happening. The US is in the retrograde vanguard, along with China, Russia, Saudi Arabia, Kuwait and other oil-producing states.

The history of the world's limp response to climate change is an old, consistent story, since long before it reached crisis proportions. Human impact on climate was recognized as early as 1847, in a speech by Whig congressman George Perkins Marsh in a talk before the Agricultural Society of Rutland County, Vermont. His observations were largely cautionary, the kind of environmental concern that was ignored by the industrial revolution for a century, until there were too many toxic waste streams and Superfund sites to ignore, so the costs were passed on to the victims as much as guilty corporations and their quisling political flunkies could manage. It's the same game with the climate crisis; those responsible avoid accountability at whatever cost to anyone but themselves. At COP24, 191 nations were eager to adopt the latest UN climate report that gives the world roughly 12 years to head off the worst effects of the climate crisis. The consensus required to adopt this simple acknowledgement of the best current science available was blocked by the US, Russia, Saudi Arabia and Kuwait. The power politics of denial, led by the US, not only slows any rational response to continued warming, these politics encourage unchecked pursuit of the profitable but globally destructive practices that created the crisis in the first place.

As an example, take the 100 million barrels of oil the world uses every day, referred to by Greta Thornberg (above). Leaving those 100 million barrels in the ground, day after day after day, year after year, would accrue to the health and welfare of billions of people over decades if not centuries. By contrast, a few people, maybe a few thousand people in the oil and gas industry will die before they forego the profit from using every last drop no matter what carnage they cause. In a very real sense, the traditional energy industry is a calculating mafia for whom killing people isn't mass murder, it's just a cost of doing business, and the beauty part is that it's a cost they don't even have to pay.

The UN's Intergovernmental Panel on Climate Change isn't the only credible scientific body warning of the deepening climate crisis. The US government's official 1596-page National Climate Assessment released in November also sounds alarms that increased warming will cost the US billions of dollars and millions of lives. The White House has rejected it and the president said, "I don't believe it." All the same, the evidence is clear, the science is sound, the crisis is real. UN Secretary General António Guterres spoke urgently and lucidly to the COP24 gathering in Katowice, Poland, delivering in his own words essentially the same message as 15-year-old Greta Thornberg – that addressing and ameliorating climate change is not only necessary but entirely possible:

> We have the ways. What we need is the political will to move forward.... Failing here in Katowice would send a disastrous message to those who stand ready to shift to a green economy.
>
> To waste this opportunity would compromise our last best chance to stop runaway climate change. It would not only be immoral, it would be suicidal.

COP24 was neither a failure nor a success. Insofar as the "rule book" was adopted, that's positive, but perhaps a Pyrrhic victory. There's little reason to think that enough of the nations that pose the major threats to the planet are even close to changing their practices sufficiently to make any real difference. There is no reason to expect any reduction in global emissions, which is necessary to mitigate the climate crisis. In the near term, global emissions are going to continue to increase and the only possible good news will be slowing the rate of increase. That is unlikely. The US is hell-bent on burning more oil, coal and gas as well as loosening restrictions on emissions. Canada has long-term plans to decarbonize its economy, but for now it is rushing to capitalize on its tar sands oil. According to the Union of Concerned Scientists, China has become the largest national greenhouse gas producer (once #1, the US is now #2) and that's unlikely to change. Australia is committed to more coal. Brazil is committed to agribusiness at the expense of the Amazon rainforest. Germany is still hooked on coal. And Poland, which hosted COP24, plans to continue to rely on coal. The #3 polluting nation, India, is committed to using coal to bring electricity to hundreds of millions of its people. The #4 polluting nation, Russia, relies heavily on coal and oil. And so it is across the industrialized world where no one wants to get too far from the herd as it ambles toward the cliff.

Precise measurements of particular greenhouse gasses from particular sources are hard to come by and mostly don't exist because the world is a tricky place to measure with precision. But the scale of the problem doesn't seem to be a mystery. More than half the climate-warming emissions come from China, the US and the European Union (add India, Russia and Japan and that's close to 70% of the total). In other words, there's little the rest of the world can do to make much difference. And right now there's no major national leadership anywhere committed to reducing greenhouse gas emissions enough to avert catastrophic warming. The US is deliberately heading for destruction, burning all the fossil fuels it can find. Other nations have a more mixed approach (China burns more coal and has more solar panels than anyone else by wide margins), but collectively it's nowhere near enough to keep the climate crisis from deepening.

Globally, some 70% of greenhouse gasses are created by the energy sector of the economy – primarily electricity generation, transportation, heating/cooling and industrial processes. Of those, electricity and transportation are the worst offenders. That's why solar panels and windmills matter so much (even when discounted for the industrial production emissions). The scale of the problem is huge and hard to grasp. But the laws of physics as applied to greenhouse gasses have brought us to a reality where the control and reduction of a planetary threat is understood and could be implemented, albeit with great difficulty and cultural stress. The main barrier to preserving a livable planet is the intellectual pollution of right-wing and corporatist ideologues who claim reality is a hoax. That's how the official US delegation ends up going to the climate change conference to promote using more coal. Self-preservation is the enemy of the profitable.

In a culture of equal treatment for disinformation, it's little wonder an organization like 350.org has trouble getting heard beyond its committed minority. Founded in 2008, 350.org refers to the presumed reasonable concentration of CO_2 (carbon dioxide) in the atmosphere of 350 parts per million (ppm). In 2008, that reasonable level had long since been passed. In the 1880s, early in the industrial revolution, the CO_2 level in the atmosphere was around 280 ppm. By 2008 the concentration was 386 ppm. Today CO_2 concentration in the atmosphere is over 400 ppm and climbing. In its simplest terms, this is a clear crime against humanity (as well as a suicidal gesture).

Perhaps it's time to start thinking of the climate crisis as a crime and the world as a crime scene. Then we'd need to figure out a way to round up the perpetrators. We know who they are.

PART SEVEN

Impeaching Is Easy,

Removal Is Hard

108.

So This Is What a National Nervous Breakdown Looks Like?

Nobody won the 2016 election

Elections have consequences, as the cliché goes, and those consequences are unpredictable, perhaps never more unpredictable than
when no one wins the election — but *someone* takes office anyway.

When that happens, the country is largely defenseless, as we
learned so disastrously in 2000. That was when we had five unprincipled Supreme Court justices to thank for promoting an actual (but
uncounted) loser to the presidency. George W. Bush proceeded to
reward the country's wary trust by blithely ignoring warnings of a terrorist attack, then using 9/11 to jingo up the fear-laden public mood and
urge us to go shopping while he (and a complicit Democratic Congress)
started wars that have yet to end. For reasons having nothing to do with
decency or justice, Nancy Pelosi led the opposition to impeaching this
war-criminal president who lied us into war. For extra credit, Bush
presided over a bipartisan wave of unchecked criminal capitalism that
brought the economy to its knees and Democrats to the White House.

That didn't help. Barack Obama used his "mandate" for hope
and change to bail out the criminal capitalists and protect them from
prosecution. With Nancy Pelosi's collusion, he squandered whatever
opportunity there was for an effective, single-payer health system, preferring to build a Rube Goldberg health care construct that coddles
insurance companies without even insuring everyone. Obama provided little hope or change to Guantanamo inmates or drone victims,
but he left war criminals and torturers unpunished, while expanding
Bush-era wars to other countries.

Now we have a wartime president-elect who didn't win, and who goes unchallenged by the popular-vote leader who also lost. Roughly half the country is freaking out at the prospect of a future that seems as inherently dangerous and unfair as it is inevitable. Now those freaking out over a Trump presidency have an idea how some #NeverTrump Republicans felt six months ago at the prospect of a Trump nomination. They got over it. The danger is that we will too.

Since November 8, much of the country seems to have spiraled into a slough of despond, feeling helpless, directionless, uncomprehending and hopeless. Even the apparent winners seem joyless in their success, their triumph marked less by celebration than by anger, epithets, Nazi graffiti, shootings and mad tweets. It's as if everyone knows that there's no one prepared or qualified to take power, but they're going to take it anyway, and take it no one knows where.

Whatever we do, we're along for the ride

There is, as yet, no organized resistance, although there seems to be a widespread, disorganized desire to resist. For all that some bewail the triumph of Trump, none of the establishment authorities is actively resisting him on principle except where his or her own sacred cows might be led to the slaughter. The president-elect is a joke (more on that in a moment, but he will still be our president). The Democrats in Congress put multi-millionaire Nancy Pelosi back in power, and in the Senate they elevated the endlessly compromising and compromised Chuck Schumer. Democrats do not choose leaders who would provide bold, principled leadership. Republicans in 2008, faced with Obama, had the courage of their convictions (never mind how ugly those convictions were), circling their wagons in open and constant defiance of the electoral majority.

Democrats, lacking either courage or convictions, are behaving now like a species that doesn't know it's endangered and hunted. The Democratic Party has become an obstacle to achieving the common good. The party seems more than content to enjoy the perks of office while making only occasional token efforts to achieve some minimal public good. Decades of their own failure somehow seem irrelevant to Democrats institutionally.

Hillary Clinton's post-election behavior should be enlightening, even if it's not surprising. How might a real leader have behaved on election night and after? Would she have bailed on her supporters and nursed her personal hurt? Or might she have swallowed hard, publicly acknowledged that this election was more about the country than her identity politics, and gone on to rally her followers to stand for the principles that matter to her, to them and to the nation? She might have done the latter, but that would have required her to have principles, to embrace real change, to have a vision of something better than an elitist police state with fewer and fewer benefits for more and more people.

Another way to put it is that Hillary Clinton might have distinguished herself from the parody of a progressive presidency presented by Obama's eight mostly feckless years in office. She chose, instead, to run on Obama's "legacy."

Whatever Donald Trump's reality, he won the election by appearing to be a candidate who would bring real change to a people longing for it. Enough previous Obama voters and Sanders voters voted for Trump to determine the outcome. Yes, Clinton won the popular vote, an irrelevant fact that allows Democrats to remain in denial about their failures not only to serve the American people well, but to deny their failure to serve even their presumed base constituencies well. Clinton's dissing Black Lives Matter was as much a dog whistle to racists as anything Trump did or said; why was it so hard to take a principled stand against armed law officers killing unarmed black people for no apparent reason? Remember when the Democratic Party was the party of working people? There is no such party any more.

Minority government is what we've had and what we're going to get

Minority government has long existed in the US, because low voter turnout means that no presidency gets votes from much more than a quarter of the country's eligible voters. Minority government has come to mean, at least since Ronald Reagan, a government dedicated to serving a rich and powerful minority of the population who are given more and more opportunities to loot public funds. The Pentagon's unaudited,

631

self-reported waste of $125 *billion* a year is only one of the more recent, grosser examples that can be found pretty much across the government from giveaway oil and mining leases to private prisons to immigration processing to charter schools to privatization in sectors across the board where the enrichment of a few dwarfs the false stereotype of the welfare cheat.

Responding to the Trump triumph with insult and denigration, no matter how valid, is worse than a waste of time. It is an exercise in denial. The Democrats lost this election in just about every substantial and meaningful way, not only by running a corrupt primary process, not only by expecting fealty to a hollow candidate, but by decades of withdrawal from meaningful engagement with too many deserving Americans. Anyone paying attention knew, at least by 2008, that the country was in ferment and that that ferment needed to be addressed honestly and substantively. The scale of Democrats' failure to do that is measured by the rise of the Tea Party in 2010, and now Trump. The country has been hurting for a long, long time, like the tail gunner in *Catch*-22, and Democrats have treated only scratches while the body politic has its guts spilling out.

You can see this in official responses to fracking and oil pipelines with little regard for the future of the planet, or official responses to hunger and homelessness with little regard for the future of fellow citizens, or official responses to drugs and prisons with little regard for science or justice.

Perhaps the most glaring, obvious, cruel official response of this sort was to the governmental poisoning of the population (about 100,000) of Flint, Michigan. Why was this not a national emergency? When a state government accomplishes what amounts to a terrorist attack, why is it not worth the immediate, intense attention of the media, the environmental agencies, or the president? What kind of country settles for half-measures and leaves people still fending for themselves while being charged an exorbitant rate for using a poisoned water supply?

That's pretty much why no one won this election. There was no one to vote for. We've been in the wilderness much longer than we generally acknowledge. Bigots didn't put us there. Misogynists didn't put us there. White nationalists didn't put us there. They all may contribute to keeping us there, but capitalists put us there, and capitalists will keep us there until we develop more effective wilderness survival skills.

109.

Trump Crashes on Take-Off

How long can the country survive in constitutional crisis?

Yes, we're in a constitutional crisis. The crisis has many elements that arose during the first week of the Trump presidency. These include illegal enrichment, complicity in war crimes and most spectacularly, the immigration attack on Muslims.

Our current constitutional crisis began the moment Donald Trump was sworn in as president without resolving his unaddressed conflicts of interest around the globe. This failure put him into immediate, demonstrable violation of the Constitution's Article I, Section 9 "Emoluments Clause," which states in part:

> And no Person holding any Office of Profit or Trust under them, shall, without the Consent of the Congress, accept of any present, Emolument, Office, or Title, of any kind whatever, from any King, Prince or foreign State.

On January 23 at 9 a.m., the organization Citizens for Responsibility and Ethics in Washington (CREW) filed a 37-page complaint in the US federal court for the Southern District of New York, asking the court to issue an injunction to prevent President Trump from further violation of the constitutional ban on receiving payments from foreign entities. This issue is new in constitutional jurisprudence, as no previous president has taken office with such extensive and unaddressed business dealings involving foreign interests. (Jimmy Carter divested and still Republicans investigated him.) Potentially, each of Trump's foreign deals represents an impeachable offense. But the course of this or other litigation on the issue is unlikely to be swift, and the outcome is uncertain.

Our present US constitutional crisis expanded with the administration's continuing to commit the war crimes of the Bush and Obama administrations, in particular the presidential use of drones to assassinate foreign nationals. Over the inaugural weekend of January 21-22, a pair of US drone strikes killed as many as ten people in Yemen, some of them alleged terrorists. Presidential assassination would appear, on its face, to be the kind of high crime the Constitution defines as an impeachable offense. President Trump follows two predecessors who assassinated foreigners without political consequence, so it's unlikely he will face impeachment for assassination any time soon.

The third and so far most volatile element of our constitutional crisis is the president's implementation of his executive order titled *"Protecting the Nation from Foreign Terrorist Entry into the United States,"* an Orwellian title for a presidential fiat that does no such thing and may well make the US less safe. The order is an Islamophobic effort to ban Muslims from selected countries. The order is arguably a violation of the Constitution's "Establishment Clause," the First Amendment's first clause:

> **Congress shall make no law respecting an establishment of religion, or prohibiting the free exercise thereof...**

The rest of the amendment enshrines free speech, a free press, the right peaceably to assemble, and the right to petition the government for a redress of grievances – all together in basic constitutional law that supports vital public response across the country to President Trump's attempt to give religious bigotry the force of law.

On Friday, January 27, at 4:42 p.m., President Trump signed his executive order into law, an act of such utter executive incompetence that it took less than twenty-four hours to create chaos around the globe. The president had not even taken care that his own decree be faithfully executed, having failed to have it competently and objectively vetted, having failed to allow advance review by agencies expected to enforce it, and having failed to implement the order in a rational and orderly fashion. The effects of such incompetence are so easily predictable, in advance, that it's conceivable that the resulting worldwide assault on innocent individuals was a deliberate political disruption.

There is no evidence of good faith in the execution of this law, and less evidence of good faith in designing it to be constitutional. Within 48 hours, federal judges across the country had issued rulings against the president and his Muslim ban. By 9 p.m. Saturday, responding to an emergency petition by the ACLU and others, Federal District Judge Ann M. Donnelly issued a stay that prevents the government from carrying out the order. In remarkable proceedings in court, the government lawyers were unable to offer a rational defense of the order and when the judge offered them a week to do so, they said that would not be enough time.

Reinforcing this legal uncertainty on January 30, Acting US Attorney General Sally Yates ordered Justice Dept. attorneys not to defend Trump's apparently unlawful executive order "unless and until I become convinced that it is appropriate to do so." The oath of office for Acting AG Yates, like the president's oath, commits her to "support and defend the Constitution of the United States." With the US Justice Dept. opposing the US president, presumably one of them is wrong, and we need to know which one to resolve our constitutional crisis. That was made harder hours later, when the president fired Yates and replaced her with US attorney Dana Bent who has promised "to enforce the immigration order" according to the Washington Post.

In Virginia, another federal judge, Leonie M. Brinkema, issued a temporary restraining order against the president, the Dept. of Homeland Security, the Customs and Border Protection agency and others, requiring them to allow detainees to see lawyers and forbidding them to remove detainees. When US senator Cory Booker, D-NJ, showed up Saturday night at Dulles International Airport with a copy of the court order, government officials refused to meet with him and communicated only through written notes. Booker was rare among senators in responding to the immediacy of government thuggishness, which has prompted thousands, perhaps millions of Americans to protest with a moral clarity that their national "leaders" seem not to comprehend.

Mayors across the country, from Boston to Seattle, have had no such timidity standing up for fundamental constitutional values. Some evangelical Christians have also objected to Trump's order, even though one of his stated purposes was to promote their kind of Christianity above other religions. Expressing basic Christian tolerance of all who are made in God's image, these evangelicals pray "that God would continue to grant you wisdom and guidance."

So far, at least seven judges (in New York, Virginia, Boston, Los Angeles and Seattle) have ruled against Trump's executive order, setting off a judicial process that could reach the Supreme Court. The Trump administration has already reversed the order as it applies to travellers with green cards. Whether the Trump administration will fully comply with court orders, and whether defiance of the law rises to the level of impeachable offenses remains to be seen.

For all the legal and political struggles, the grossest offense of Trump's executive order is to reality and honesty. The order cites September 11, 2001, as part of its justification, which is pure demagoguery. Not only was that 15 years ago, but none of the attackers – NONE – came from ANY of the countries covered by the order. The 9/11 attackers came mostly from Saudi Arabia (15), as well as two from the United Arab Emirates and one each from Lebanon and Egypt. None of these countries are covered by the executive order. ALL of these countries are places where Trump has business interests.

Of the seven countries covered by the executive order – Syria, Iraq, Yemen, Iran, Somalia, Sudan and Libya – none are places where Trump has business interests. All but Iran are thought to be places where US combat troops are deployed. The US is engaged in an ongoing criminal war in at least one of the countries, Yemen. The number of terrorist attacks on the US attributed to people from any of the seven sanctioned countries is ZERO – there have been none.

The threat that some "radical Islamic terrorism" attack will kill an American remains minuscule. The Cato Institute point out that you are three times more likely to be killed by a random animal than any terrorist. Statistically over the past 15 years, Islamic terrorists have killed an average of 8 Americans per year while lightning kills 50 a year. Far more dangerous than foreign terrorists are American white nationalist terrorists or anti-abortion terrorists. Who else has assassinated more "enemies" than these people? But the Islamist terror-mongering of government officials has gone on for decades, doing the work of the terrorists by making Americans afraid.

Our Trump has amplified the fear-mongering even above Bush-presidency levels, which smoothed the way into wars that still haven't ended. There is no reason to expect civilized leadership from the Trump administration or either the Republican or Democratic parties, at least until they find the moral and intellectual clarity to escape their own alternate realities.

But what has happened in response to the Muslim ban has been amazing, unexpected and a source of real hope. Across the country, Americans of all sorts – including a host of state officials – have swarmed in public protest against the demonizing of Muslims, against the lies of the alternative fact crowd, against the indecency and cruelty of the decades of political callousness that have been fed by Reagan and Clinton and their successors till they delivered that rough beast slouching in the White House today.

President Trump's approval rating has gone negative in just eight days in the White House, more than 550 days faster than ANY of his recent predecessors.

At last, perhaps, the people are ready to say no. At last, perhaps, the people are ready to reject the worst impulses of a culture designed to impoverish the many without enlightening the few. At last, perhaps, the people are ready to be their own leaders and embrace the possibility of equality even for the most demonized among us. To see so many people determined to protect Muslim travellers, people who are the other, and yet still deserving of the same protections the rest of us deserve – that is truly heartening in the face of a government inclined to achieving order by oppression and violence.

On January 20, Donald Trump took the oath of office as provided by the US Constitution:

I do solemnly swear (or affirm) that I will faithfully execute the Office of President of the United States, and will to the best of my ability, preserve, protect and defend the Constitution of the United States.

Is it a violation of this oath to initiate chaos? Is it a violation of this oath to promulgate executive orders that plainly aim to abrogate current law or that attack basic constitutional rights? Has there been a moment since he took this oath that Donald Trump has not acted in bad faith while failing to preserve and protect the Constitution? Is his performance as president not fairly characterized as a complex of deliberate choices that form a nexus of impeachable acts?

At last, perhaps, the people in growing numbers are taking serious notice. The people are far, far ahead of their "leaders." There is real resistance. There is a real constitutional crisis. And there is a real possibility that Americans can sustain the will to redeem their country.

Update 2019: The Crew lawsuit of January 23, 2017, [Civil Action No. 1:17-cv-00458-GDB] was dismissed in US federal district court for the southern district of New York on December 21, 2017. CREW appealed to the US Court of Appeals for the Second Circuit on February 16, 2018 and filed a 70-page brief on April 24, 2018. Defendant Trump filed a 56-page answer on May 29, 2018. As of June 2019, the case remained undecided.

110.

Trump Betrays the Constitution, Slanders Career Government Attorney

"The acting Attorney General, Sally Yates, has betrayed the Department of Justice by refusing to enforce a legal order designed to protect the citizens of the United States. This order was approved as to form and legality by the Department of Justice Office of Legal Counsel."

WHITE HOUSE STATEMENT, JANUARY 30, 2017

The levels of duplicity in the opening paragraph of this White House statement are impressive. Acting Attorney General Sally Yates was appointed to that position at the request of the Trump administration, for the express purpose of serving only until the confirmation of the Trump appointee for Attorney General. (Later White House characterizations of her as an Obama appointee, while accurate in a sense, are profoundly dishonest, as illustrated by Trump's January 30 tweet calling Yates "an Obama A.G.")

Georgia native Sally Yates, 56, is a career attorney for the Justice Department who was first hired by Reagan-appointed US Attorney Bob Barr (whose decidedly conservative career included leading the effort to impeach Bill Clinton). Her 27-year career in the Justice Department was impressive enough to win Trump's interim appointment despite her two prior Obama appointments (both approved by the US Senate). She was not, in any meaningful sense, anyone's political appointee.

Early on January 30, 2017, reportedly after a weekend of contemplation and consideration of the president's January 27 executive order on immigration, Yates issued a memo to top lawyers at the Justice

Department. That memo, in carefully calibrated language, questioned whether the president's order, already under legal challenge in half a dozen or more federal jurisdictions, was lawful, meaning constitutional. Already Justice Department lawyers in New York had been unable to offer any cogent defense of the order (in part because the Justice Department had almost no part in drafting it). Yates concluded her memo with appropriate caution in response to a murky and chaotic situation created by the order:

> **Consequently, for as long as I am the Acting Attorney General, the Department of Justice will not present arguments in defense of the Executive Order, unless and until I become convinced that it is appropriate to do so.**

This is not a statement of defiance, this is a cautionary note in the midst of a situation spiralling out of control, with the government perpetrating injustice that is being checked by the courts. This is an invitation to be persuaded. The White House made no effort to persuade the acting Attorney General that the order was legally defensible. The White House has not made that argument to anyone publicly. The White House position is that the order is lawful. Because the White House says it is. That is not the way American checks and balances are supposed to work.

In its statement above, the White House asserts baldly that Yates was refusing to "enforce a legal order designed to protect the citizens of the United States." The first problem is that the Justice Department has no enforcement role under the order, which was then being chaotically enforced by the Department of Homeland Security, sometimes in defiance of court orders (Virginia has filed a motion to hold the Trump administration in contempt of court). The Justice Department under Yates was merely declining to defend the erratic, unfair and arbitrary enforcement of an order of dubious legality.

The White House claim that the order was "designed to protect the citizens of the United States" was flat-out false. The chaotic implementation of the order was powerful evidence that it hadn't been "designed" sufficiently, and not at all well. The order, by banning

Muslims from countries whose citizens had never attacked the US, did nothing to protect anyone, while doing much harm to thousands of innocent people including Americans. The terrorism "danger" is so slight that even the order itself had to invoke events of more than fifteen years ago (9/11) to create a simulacrum of credibility.

This is old style demagoguery, using inflated or imaginary threats to make the population afraid, a goal shared by terrorists of all stripes. "Islamic radicalism" is but the latest shibboleth to scare the pants off credulous Americans in the grand tradition of non-existent weapons of mass destruction, fighting "them" (Iraqis, Iranians, Vietnamese, whoever) over there so we don't have to fight them here, or the evergreen vast communist conspiracy (among others). These familiar styles of deceit, even though easy to debunk, remain in use because they still work.

In addition, we face an expanding universe of "alternative facts" (as Kellyanne Conway nicely phrased it), a universe in which demonstrable facts, logic, math, science and the other touchstones of traditional, civilized reality no longer matter. George Orwell described something like this in his novel "1984," where the official language was Newspeak (which had no word for science) and the population learned to believe that "Ignorance is strength."

The White House statement on Sally Yates is closest to pure Newspeak when it says: "This order was approved as to form and legality by the Department of Justice Office of Legal Counsel." This is quintessentially Orwellian in the way it obscures the truth without actually lying. The "approval" alleged here is much less than meets the eye. The Office of Legal Counsel has, in the past, been notoriously solicitous of the president, telling him that almost anything he wants to do is legal. At its nadir, this office in 2002, through the good offices of Assistant Attorney General Jay S. Bybee and his deputy John Yoo, assured President Bush that he could torture almost anyone in almost any manner he chose. Trump's Muslim ban is every bit as "legal" as Bush's torture regime, or as Newspeak has it: $2 + 2 = 5$.

On March 24, 2015, Senator Jeff Sessions, now the Attorney General nominee, questioned Sally Yates about the Office of Legal Counsel during her confirmation hearings (in a clip that has gone viral). Sessions' point was that the Attorney General's office should say "No" to a president "if the views a President wants to execute are unlawful." Yates agreed that was a duty of the Attorney General's office.

The Office of Legal Counsel rubber-stamped unlawful torture, so its imprimatur has no automatic validity. Independent review is called for in any thorough and orderly process. As Sally Yates wrote in her memo:

> **My role is different from that of the Office of Legal Counsel (OLC)....**
> **OLC's review is limited to the narrow question of whether, in OLC's**
> **view, a proposed Executive Order is lawful on its face and properly**
> **drafted. Its review does not take account of statements made by an**
> **administration or its surrogates close in time to the issuance of an**
> **Executive Order that may bear on the order's purpose. And impor-**
> **tantly, it does not address whether any policy choice embodied in an**
> **Executive Order is wise or just.**

Implicitly, the Trump administration may have put the order through such a limited review to avoid precisely the more searching, substantive questions raised by Yates. Whatever the intent, all the available evidence suggests that the administration made a point of avoiding the constitutional issues that are now before the courts. In that behavior, arguably, the president and his aides violated their own constitutional oath to "preserve, protect and defend the Constitution of the United States" (Article II, Section 1). Sally Yates took a similar oath of office to "support and defend the Constitution of the United States."

Recently some legal writers have taken Yates to task for the manner of her legal dissent. Attorney Alan Dershowitz misrepresented her actions, then criticized them, even though he agreed with her assessment of the policy. Law Professor Josh Blackman of the Cato Institute similarly mischaracterized Yates's actions (as well as those of others), then tendentiously used his mischaracterization to justify Trump's firing her. Columnist Edward Morrissey also mischaracterized the actions of Yates and the OLC, calling her carefully worded memo "insubordination" – a falsehood. Insubordination is disobey-ing a direct order, which Trump had not given, and in this instance, had no authority to give. These articles from The Hill, The Week and Politico fail to meet minimal standards of accuracy, using straw man arguments to advance false conclusions.

The substantive issues raised by the executive order on immi-gration remain unresolved. The Trump administration could address them any time it chooses, but intellectual integrity is in short supply at the highest levels of government. The courts will address them in the fullness of time, which may or may not be soon enough. In any fair assessment now, of who was more faithful to their oaths of office, Yates has the clear advantage, so it's no wonder the White House declined her invitation to persuade and instead fired her with a volley of calumny. Yates "betrayed" no one and nothing.

As far as the Constitution goes, the actual traitors here are in the White House.

111.

Constitutional Crisis Deepens as Trump Fights Checks and Balances

"SEE YOU IN COURT, THE SECURITY OF OUR NATION IS AT STAKE!"

TWEET FROM DONALD J. TRUMP, FEBRUARY 9, 2017

Trump's screaming tweet, complete with all caps in the original, captures the essence of this president's bald move to take total power over the United States. When he says, "the security of our nation is at stake," he refers demagogically to the imaginary threat of terrorists from seven countries. He is right to say, "the security of our nation is at stake," but not at all in the way he means – the security of our nation is profoundly at stake in this case because, if he wins, then presidential orders will become dictatorial decrees beyond the reach of the courts. Our constitutional crisis continues.

Executive Order 13769, issued January 27, 2017, established the so-called Muslim ban on immigrants from seven countries (Iran, Iraq, Yemen, Syria, Somalia, Sudan and Libya). The order was prepared with limited vetting and implemented with no advance planning, creating immediate, global chaos that led to numerous court challenges and partial stays of the order. The case brought January 30 by the states of Washington and Minnesota together persuaded a Washington State judge (appointed by President Bush) to issue a nationwide temporary restraining order (TRO), enjoining the US government from enforcing key provisions of the Executive Order (which the government apparently took its time to obey).

The government's motion for an emergency stay of the TRO was heard February 7 by a three-judge federal district Appeals Court (one step below the US Supreme Court). On February 9, the Appeals Court unanimously affirmed the lower court's ruling and left the TRO in place, unmodified, until the lower court holds a duly-scheduled hearing of the government's appeal of the TRO before deciding whether to make the TRO permanent.

Trump's Executive Order has created a watershed crisis in US constitutional government. Trump fired an acting attorney general for questioning his order's constitutionality and legality. Several lower federal courts have found the order, in the words of the Appeals Court, "unconstitutional and violative of federal law." The issue is likely to reach the Supreme Court before long. If the Supreme Court rules for the president, then he will be able to rule by decree. If the Supreme Court upholds the lower courts, that will check the president's power to rule by decree, but only until the next challenge to the US Constitution's traditional balance of powers.

9th Circuit Appeals Court rejects attack on Constitution

What follows is a brief summary of the Appeals Court's 29-page order, including the constitutional issues that court identified. The language of the Appeals Court order is as restrained and dignified as the president's tweets are hysterical and outrageous. The court begins by stating the basis for deciding the issue:

> To rule on the Government's motion, we must consider several factors, including whether the Government has shown that it is likely to succeed on the merits of its appeal, the degree of hardship caused by a stay or its denial, and the public interest in granting or denying a stay.

In sketching the background for the Executive Order, the court notes that the only specific attack or threat cited to justify the danger to national security is 9/11. The court describes elements of the Executive Order and their impact as they were implemented.

In a February 10 tweet, President Trump asserted:

> LAWFARE: "Remarkably, in the entire opinion, the panel did not bother even to cite this (the) statute." A disgraceful decision!

Since the court cites the Immigration and Nationality Act,

codified at 8 U.S.C. (p. 4), it's not clear what statute Trump had in mind. The court writes that in issuing its initial restraining order:

> The district court preliminarily concluded that significant and ongoing harm was being inflicted on substantial numbers of people, to the detriment of the States, by means of an Executive Order that the States were likely to be able to prove was unlawful.

The US government claims that the states have no standing to sue, no right to sue, because the states had not suffered sufficient injury from the Executive Order. The government does not dispute that the state universities "are branches of the States under state law." After reviewing the impact of the Executive Order on members of the state universities, the court holds:

> We therefore conclude that the States have alleged harms to their proprietary interests traceable to the Executive Order. The necessary connection can be drawn in at most two logical steps: (1) the Executive Order prevents nationals of seven countries from entering Washington and Minnesota; (2) as a result, some of these people will not enter state universities, some will not join those universities as faculty, some will be prevented from performing research, and some will not be permitted to return if they leave. And we have no difficulty concluding that the States' injuries would be redressed if they could obtain the relief they ask for: a declaration that the Executive Order violates the Constitution and an injunction barring its enforcement. The Government does not argue otherwise.

According to government lawyers, the federal courts have no legitimate authority to review any presidential orders "to suspend the admission of any class of aliens." The government argues that such orders are even more unreviewable when the president is motivated by national security claims, even if the orders violate constitutional rights and protections. The government claims that court review of unconstitutional orders violates the principle of separation of powers in government. The court rejects these arguments:

> There is no precedent to support this claimed unreviewability, which runs contrary to the fundamental structure of our constitutional democracy.... Within our system, it is the role of the judiciary to interpret the law, a duty that will sometimes require the "[r]esolution of

litigation challenging the constitutional authority of one of the three branches...." We are called upon to perform that duty in this case.

The court notes that the government is so desperate to find support for its claims that it misquotes from a case (Kleindienst v. Mandel) to reach a false conclusion. Even in national security cases, the courts have a legitimate role, contrary to the government argument. The court points out that, while the Supreme Court counsels deference to national security decisions of the White House or Congress, the Supreme Court also made clear that:

> ... the Government's "authority and expertise in [such] matters do not automatically trump the Court's own obligation to secure the protection that the Constitution grants to individuals," even in times of war.... it is beyond question that the federal judiciary retains the authority to adjudicate constitutional challenges to executive action.

Addressing the government's motion to stay the lower court order, the Appeals Court points out that a stay is not a matter of right, but a matter of court discretion based on the particular circumstances of the case. The government, by requesting the stay, bears the burden of showing that those circumstances support the request, as the court explained:

> Our decision is guided by four questions: "(1) whether the stay applicant has made a strong showing that he is likely to succeed on the merits; (2) whether the applicant will be irreparably injured absent a stay; (3) whether issuance of the stay will substantially injure the other parties interested in the proceeding; and (4) where the public interest lies."

The court concludes that the government fails to satisfy ANY of the four criteria. The court cites the Constitution's Fifth Amendment requirement that "No person ... be deprived of life, liberty, or property without due process of law ..." and describes the government position in quietly scathing terms (pp. 19-20):

> The Government has not shown that the Executive Order provides what due process requires, such as notice and a hearing prior to restricting an individual's ability to travel. Indeed, the Government does not contend that the Executive Order provides for such process. Rather, in

addition to the arguments addressed in other parts of this opinion, the Government argues that most or all of the individuals affected by the Executive Order have no rights under the Due Process Clause.

To make this argument, the government lawyers must ignore the plain language of the Constitution referring to "No person" and hope that no one notices that the individuals affected by the Executive Order are, in fact, living, breathing persons. People noticed, and people noticed that this attitude is authoritarian and it is the antithesis of American democratic standards.

The government tries to mitigate the Executive Order by referring to an "Authoritative Guidance" issued by White House Counsel Donald F. McGahn addressing and seeking to remedy certain portions of the order relating to lawful permanent residents. The court rejects this government argument with withering dry scorn:

> The Government has offered no authority establishing that the White House counsel is empowered to issue an amended order superseding the Executive Order signed by the President and now challenged by the States, and that proposition seems unlikely. Nor has the Government established that the White House counsel's interpretation of the Executive Order is binding on all executive branch officials responsible for enforcing the Executive Order. The White House counsel is not the President, and he is not known to be in the chain of command for any of the Executive Departments.

In analyzing this and other poorly thought out, incomplete and incompetent aspects of the government's case, the court points out that "it is not our role to try, in effect, to rewrite the Executive Order." What the court says, with somewhat sly due deference, is that it's up to the White House to do its job correctly.

The court turns to the states' argument that the Executive Order violates both the Constitution's First Amendment's command that "Congress shall make no law respecting an establishment of religion," as well as the Equal Protection Clause of the Constitution. While citing Supreme Court holdings supporting the states' argument, the Appeals Court chooses not to address it in the context of the government's emergency motion.

Neither does the court address the underlying absurdity of an Executive Order based on fear-mongering over imaginary threats. If the "terrorist threats" endlessly uttered by the Chicken Littles of government and media had any basis in reality, then suspending the Executive Order might actually be dangerous and might even lead to "irreparable injury." The court rejects that government argument, too:

> The Government has not shown that a stay is necessary to avoid irreparable injury.... Despite the district court's and our own repeated invitations to explain the urgent need for the Executive Order to be placed immediately into effect, *the Government submitted no evidence to rebut the States' argument that the district court's order merely returned the nation temporarily to the position it has occupied for many previous years.* The Government has pointed to no evidence that any alien from any of the countries named in the Order has perpetrated a terrorist attack in the United States. *Rather than present evidence to explain the need for the Executive Order, the Government has taken the position that we must not review its decision at all.* [emphasis added]

In contrast, the court finds that the states have provided ample evidence that the Executive Order had already caused irreparable damage to some people and that, if reinstated, it would cause irreparable damage to many more.

Assessing the general public interest, the court saw favorable arguments on both sides. The public has a "powerful interest in national security," but the public also has an interest in "free flow of travel, in avoiding separation of families and in freedom from discrimination." At this point, the court denies the government's motion for an emergency stay, in effect because there is no perceptible emergency. Or rather there is no emergency as the government defines it. Taken as a whole, the court's order illustrates a serious constitutional emergency perpetrated by the president against his own government and people. While the court doesn't list other public interests, the public also surely has a substantial interest in a government that follows the constitutional due process of law, that acts in good faith, that supports its arguments with facts based in reality, and that does not claim the right to act dictatorially with no checks and balances.

White House acts as if it is not only ABOVE the law, it IS the law

Late on February 10, Trump administration sources said there would be no appeal of this decision to the Supreme Court. That leaves the future district court decision as a possible vehicle for a Supreme Court ruling. But late on February 10, the president hinted at just issuing a brand new Executive Order (adding "I like to surprise you."). This might be good for the White House, avoiding a possible Supreme Court decision requiring it to act within the constitutional framework of the law. That might also be better than a Supreme Court decision that reinforced the president's power to rule by decree. We don't know how far the Supreme Court will go either for ideology or to protect judicial authority. We can be pretty sure that our constitutional crisis will not be over any time soon and may not turn out well for the Constitution.

112.

Impeachable Offenses Announced Live on TV – by President Trump!

"We were very close [on the health care bill]. It was a very, very tight margin. We had no Democrat support. We had no votes from the Democrats. They weren't going to give us a single vote, so it's a very difficult thing to do. I've been saying for the last year and a half that the best thing we can do, politically speaking, is let Obamacare explode. It is exploding right now.... It's going to have a very bad year.... This year should be much worse for Obamacare.... We'll end up with a truly great healthcare bill in the future, after this mess known as Obamacare explodes.... I know some of the Democrats, and they're good people – I honestly believe the Democrats will come to us and say, look, let's get together and get a great healthcare bill or plan that's really great for the people of our country. And I think that's going to happen."

PRESIDENT TRUMP, PRESS BRIEFING MARCH 24, 2017

Quite a curious piece of Trumpfoolery this exegesis of the failure of the Republicans' American Health Care Act (AHCA) to get enough support even to risk a vote in the House. This wasn't President Trump's healthcare plan – he's *never* proposed a plan – but he's still selling the *possibility* of a plan, bi-partisan at that, even if he has to allow – or cause – millions of people to suffer in the process, which implicitly involves his committing clearly impeachable offenses. Back to that in a moment.

First let's wonder: why would anyone with a grasp on reality be surprised by the absence of Democratic support for eviscerating Obamacare? Obamacare was a rickety compromise trying to satisfy mutually exclusive goals, one of which was NOT universal healthcare coverage. Still it managed to insure some 20 million Americans who were previously without health. And Obamacare passed in the first place with *no Republican votes!* So why would Democrats, even

652

the truly corrupt ones, vote to make a bad situation worse? Trump acknowledged that, stating "Obamacare was rammed down everyone's throats – 100 per cent Democrat." The president suggested that if Obamacare collapses as he predicts, that will pressure Democrats to seek a bi-partisan deal to the Republicans' liking. As a candidate, Trump was selling a healthcare con, and that hasn't changed.

"Obamacare is the law of the land," House Speaker Paul Ryan acknowledged after his bill, the AHCA, was pulled before a vote.

Given that Obamacare is the law of the land, the president has a duty, an affirmative legal duty, to uphold that law unless and until it's constitutionally changed. That's the point of the president's oath of office in Article II, Section 1 of the Constitution:

> I do solemnly swear (or affirm) that I will faithfully execute the Office of President of the United States, and will to the best of my Ability, preserve, protect and defend the Constitution of the United States.

This is reinforced in Section 3, which enumerates many of the president's other Constitutional duties, including: "he shall take Care *that the Laws be faithfully executed.*" [emphasis added]

So when Trump says, "The best thing politically speaking is to let Obamacare explode," he may be cynically correct, but he's Constitutionally wrong. As president, Trump has no right to let Obamacare explode. He has a duty to faithfully execute Obamacare, which may prove easier than he hopes, since Obamacare may not be currently exploding so much as settling into a disappointing, low-level stability.

At this point, no one knows what the Trump administration will or will not be willing to do to undermine the law of the land that it despises. Active measures by the White House could clearly be unconstitutional, but so could passive responses to Obamacare's difficulties. The new Health and Human Services (HHS) secretary, Dr. Tom Price, a former self-dealing Congressman, is a devout Tea Party enemy of Obamacare and was a point man for its repeal. As HHS secretary, Price is responsible for managing Obamacare, obligated to do his best to make sure it doesn't explode. But he is also in a position to make large and small decisions to undermine Obamacare by stealth and connivance. And what Price does or doesn't do is all, ultimately, the president's responsibility.

It's hard to imagine that either the president or his secretary, with their vivid history of bad faith, will act honestly to make Obamacare work as well as possible. Perhaps they will be more or less correct in their prediction of an Obamacare explosion and clever enough to conceal whatever nefarious fingerprints they leave on the wreckage. What will Democrats do then?

The smartest, simplest answer for American health care that benefits the American people has long been in plain sight, and specifically rejected by President Obama in 2009, after campaigning on it in 2008. Senator Bernie Sanders has campaigned for it for decades, but it was specifically rejected by the Democratic leadership in 2016. Now the idea of single payer health care, also known as Medicare for All, is once more being dangled not only before Democrats, but before President Trump as the only way he can fulfill his grandiose campaign promises on health care. Senator Sanders, at a Vermont town hall style meeting with the other two members of the Vermont congressional delegation and an audience of about 1,000 people, said:

> We have got to end the international disgrace of being the only major country on earth not to guarantee healthcare to all people as a right not a privilege. Within a couple of weeks I am going to be introducing legislation calling for a Medicare-for-All, single-payer program.

Over two months earlier, on January 24, 2017, Michigan's Democratic congressman John Conyers introduced exactly such a bill in the House, HR 676 – Expanded & Improved Medicare for All Act, that went unmentioned by Sanders, or even by Vermont's Democratic congressman Peter Welch, who is one of the bill's 72 current co-sponsors. As summarized by Congress.Gov, in part: "This bill establishes the Medicare for All Program to provide all individuals residing in the United States and US territories with free health care that includes all medically necessary care, such as primary care and prevention, dietary and nutritional therapies, prescription drugs, emergency care, long-term care, mental health services, dental services and vision care." The bill is currently before four House committees, none of which have yet voted on it. Media coverage of the Sanders initiative often ignored the Conyers bill, as if Sanders were doing something new. On Democracy Now, Dr. Steffie Woolhandler summed up HR 676 and its long history:

> HR 676, would be, you know, everyone just pays their taxes, and everyone is automatically eligible for a program like Medicare, only it would have no copayments, no deductibles for covered services, no participation by the private health insurance industry, so an expanded and improved Medicare, expanded to everyone, improved so it doesn't have the kind of gaps in uncovered services that do—you know, do exist in the current Medicare program. We've been advocating that plan for decades. Frankly, Congressman Conyers and Senator Sanders have, as well.

Most of Washington's "leadership" class is way behind the Democratic minority, and way behind the country on single payer health care – not least because it requires the constitutionally mandated general welfare of "we, the people" to take priority over the profits of insurance and drug companies. But maybe, out of opposition to Trump if not for better reasons, Democrats can unite around single payer. That would give them the policy high ground by supporting the medical consensus best choice for health care. And it would position them nicely as offering Trump a way, as he put it, to "work out a great healthcare bill for the people of this country,... a truly great healthcare bill in the future,... get a great healthcare bill or plan that's really great for the people of our country. And I think that's going to happen."

The likelihood of that happening is probably increased by the threat of impeachment over failure to enforce Obamacare, assuming that Democrats have the courage to stand behind the Constitution. That should be made easier by the reality that President Trump has been impeachably in violation of the Constitution's emoluments clause (Article I, Section 9) since the moment he took office. Democrats' timidity to date is hardly reassuring, but perhaps they'll be more motivated by the President's weekly trips to promote Trump properties, or the cost of security for Trump family vacationers at Aspen, or the nepotism that puts un-elected millionaires like his daughter Ivanka in one White House office and his son-in-law Jared Kushner in another with apparent czar-like powers derived not from the Constitution nor the Congress, but only from his marriage to the president's daughter. Presumably, at some point, already long overdue, Democrats (and even Republicans with respect for the Constitution) will find the courage and integrity not only to say enough is enough, but this is too much.

113.

CIA Chief Declares War on Truth

"... the American people deserve a clear explanation of what their Central Intelligence Agency does on their behalf.... we are an organization committed to uncovering the truth and getting it right.... And sure—we also admit to making mistakes.... But it is always our intention—and duty—to get it right. And that is one of the many reasons why we at CIA find the celebration of entities like WikiLeaks to be both perplexing and deeply troubling."

CIA DIRECTOR MIKE POMPEO, APRIL 13, 2017

While the snippets above provide a reasonable summary of the substance of Mike Pompeo's first speech as head of the CIA, they don't begin to capture the full demagoguery of the CIA head's rambling 3700-word blather of ad hominem attacks, false claims, hyperbolic rhetoric, irrelevancies, straw man arguments and political deflections. In other words, Pompeo made it clear that he has little regard for truth, for personal decency, or for the Constitutional protections for free speech or for the free exercise of religion. It was an altogether chilling debut for a spy agency head in a country that still imagines itself enjoying some basic freedoms.

Pompeo started with an anecdotal biography of former CIA agent Philip Agee, without mentioning that Agee resigned from the CIA in 1968 and died in 2008. Nor did Pompeo mention that Agee resigned, despite CIA entreaties to stay, because Agee could no longer countenance the Agency's support for brutal dictatorships across Latin America. Instead of confronting the substance of Agee's life and actions, Pompeo reiterated the official CIA demonization of the man who founded the anti-CIA magazine *Counterspy* and revealed many CIA secrets. As the CIA has done for decades, Pompeo blamed Agee for the assassination of CIA agent Richard Welch in Greece in 1975. Barbara

Bush made this same claim in her 1994 memoir. After Agee sued her for libel, the claim was removed from the paperback edition.

As a lawyer who knows he can't libel the dead, Pompeo is unmitigatedly dishonest in his portrait of Agee, concluding it with: "Meanwhile, Agee propped up his dwindling celebrity with an occasional stunt, including a *Playboy* interview. He eventually settled down as the privileged guest of an authoritarian regime." That was a reference to Cuba, where Agee died, but until the very end of his life he also spent time in Germany, his wife's home country. Pompeo utterly fails to meet his duty to get it right. He comes nowhere near the truth, that Agee's life represents the struggle faced by a man of conscience when he realizes the agency he works for also commits horrendous crimes, not just mistakes. An honest historian would put this account of a man's life within the context of the US Senate's 1975 Church Committee, which documented a number of CIA crimes and led, for awhile at least, to significant CIA reform.

Having framed his talk with a false version of Philip Agee, Pompeo spent the rest of it mixing CIA boilerplate promotional material with his main purpose, attacking WikiLeaks based on a big lie:

> WikiLeaks walks like a hostile intelligence service and talks like a hostile intelligence service. It has encouraged its followers to find jobs at CIA in order to obtain intelligence. It directed Chelsea Manning in her theft of specific secret information. And it overwhelmingly focuses on the United States, while seeking support from anti-democratic countries and organizations. It is time to call out WikiLeaks for what it really is – a non-state hostile intelligence service often abetted by state actors like Russia.

Pompeo offers no analysis or evidentiary support for these assertions. There is no public evidence that WikiLeaks is anything like an intelligence service in purpose, structure, or functioning. According to WikiLeaks founder Julian Assange, WikiLeaks has the same mission as the Washington Post or New York Times: "to publish newsworthy content. Consistent with the US Constitution, we publish material that we can confirm to be true irrespective of whether sources came by that truth legally or have the right to release it to the media." The

Times famously did that very thing in 1971 when it released the Pentagon Papers, which affirmed the disastrous dishonesty that produced the Vietnam War.

The record of WikiLeaks is the opposite of most any intelligence service, certainly of the CIA. WikiLeaks is available as a resource for people to publish government secrets. WikiLeaks vets the material it is offered and, so far, has never had to make a retraction. Everything WikiLeaks has offered is true. The CIA lies all the time, although not everything it says is false. What Pompeo says about Chelsea Manning looks like a bald-faced lie. But he needs that lie to undercut the reality that Manning was a soldier with a conscience who objected to US random slaughters of Iraqi civilians, men, women, children, journalists.

Pompeo's reference to "state actors like Russia" is shamelessly hilarious. The best-known WikiLeaks project allegedly involving Russia is the massive release of Democratic National Committee (DNC) emails during the 2016 campaign. These were significantly damaging to Hillary Clinton and Mike Pompeo at the time was saying things like this:

> Well, it's classic Clinton, right? When you find out you got a problem, you deflect, you deny, you create a contretemps where there really is none. Frankly, it's pretty clear who invited the Russians to do damage to America, and it was Hillary Clinton. She put classified information on a private server, inviting the Chinese, the Iranians, the Russians, all to have access to it. I hope they didn't get it, but even the former director of the CIA said he thinks they probably did. So, the person who's put American national security risk isn't Donald Trump, it's Hillary Clinton.

So in July 2016, WikiLeaks was innocent, and Russia was irrelevant? Can you say find the truth and get it right? Can you say serial hypocrite? Or can you say, along with candidate Trump last October, "This just came out. Wikileaks. I love WikiLeaks"?

At the time of Pompeo's speech, mainstream media paid more attention to the so-called "mother of all bombs" dropped on Afghanistan than they did to this much more powerful political bombshell dropped on the US. Recently some mainstream media have been taking another look, as in this headline from Newsweek: "CIA CHIEF POMPEO TAKES AIM AT THE FREE PRESS."

> What can and should CIA, the United States, and our allies do about the unprecedented challenge posed by these hostile non-state intelligence agencies?... First, it is high time we called out those who grant a platform to these leakers and so-called transparency activists.... We know the danger that Assange and his not-so-merry band of brothers pose to democracies around the world. Ignorance or misplaced idealism is no longer an acceptable excuse for lionizing these demons.

Once again, the high hilarity of the deceitful surfaces in Pompeo's calling Assange a threat to democracy. If that is in any sense true, then Mike Pompeo owes his CIA job to the success of Assange's "threat." The real threat is to those who "grant a platform" to WikiLeaks, and those would be all American media for starters. But the scarier part is that Pompeo is not only comfortable demonizing people like Agee or Assange, he literally calls them "demons," and this is not standard political talk, this is fundamentalist Christian visualizing the devil's work. When some of the highest officials in the US government are busy chasing "demons," then US Constitutional government is at serious risk.

Mike Pompeo, 53, the present director of the Central Intelligence Agency, is a West Point trained military veteran, a Harvard trained lawyer, and a self-expressed, profound "Christian" bigot and hypocrite. He has no experience in intelligence. The radical former Tea Party congressman from Kansas was confirmed for his CIA role by a 66-32 Senate vote despite his lengthy, fact-free obsession with the Benghazi attack of 2012, or his avid denial of climate change, or his ardent support for keeping Guantanamo and other torture prisons open (he has called torturers "patriots"). He has advocated covert surveillance to collect "all metadata" on Americans, a program that is currently illegal. Pompeo not only magnifies the threat of terrorists like ISIS, he views that threat through a religious lens and apparently believes in the Manichaean formulation that there is currently "a conflict between the Christian west and the Islamic east."

After his April 13 address, Pompeo took questions, one of which was about President Trump's relationship with the CIA and the other 16 agencies in the intelligence community. The question apparently referred to such things as President Trump's tweets earlier this year, blaming leaks on "the intelligence community (NSA and FBI?). Just like Russia" and later saying "Intelligence agencies should never have allowed this fake news to 'leak' into the public. One last shot at me. Are we living in Nazi Germany?"

Despite this context, Pompeo answered the question about the president's relations with the intelligence community simply: "It's fantastic."

The audience laughed. Pompeo added: "Don't laugh, I mean that."

Good to know that the head of Central Intelligence believes in fantasy. Reassuring to know that the CIA head wants to "make sure that we know that Jesus Christ our savior is truly the only solution for our world."

A nation formed by the ideas of the Enlightenment, the Age of Reason, is now at least partly in the hands of a Christian Taliban.

114.

American Wonderland: Trump World Is Much Stranger Than It Seems

The spring blizzard of the bizarre shows no sign of letting up

When was the last time we had a sitting president and a former FBI director calling each other liars? And something like 100 per cent of the population seems to believe that at least one of the accused liars is a real liar. That's the new American normal.

The James Comey circus produced a holiday atmosphere in DC, with bars open for business before the live hearings came on. And the TV audience for the Comey show was an apparently impressive 19 million-plus viewers. But that's pallid next to the presidential inauguration's 30 million-plus, or the Super Bowl's typical 110 million-plus in the US. Here you may insert the appropriate comment about how these numbers reflect American priorities, with football being five times more engaging than a game where the republic is an underdog.

In this kind of carnival atmosphere, it is little wonder that little attention is paid when the director of National Intelligence stonewalls a Senate Intelligence Committee hearing rather than answer questions about presidential law-breaking. Little wonder that little attention is paid when the director of the Central Intelligence Agency stonewalls rather than answer questions about presidential law-breaking. And little wonder that the Senate Intelligence Committee's Republican majority paid little attention to the stonewalling by their party's top national intelligence community officials. There is some wonder if the Democrats are awake.

Republicans will not entertain pointed questions from uppity black women

The hearing didn't begin to get close to testy until Deputy Attorney General Rod Rosenstein, who was instrumental in getting Comey fired, refused again and again to answer a simple question. The question from Democratic senator Kamala Harris of California (where she was state attorney general) was *whether Rosenstein would assure* the independence of the independent counsel, former FBI director Robert Mueller, who is investigating the relationship between the Trump campaign and Russian power brokers. Rosenstein would not give a direct answer, choosing to stonewall by filibuster. Senator Harris interrupted:

> Sir, if I may, the greater assurance is not that you and I believe in Mueller's integrity ... it is that you would put in writing an indication based on your authority as the acting attorney general that he has full independence.

Again, Rosenstein rambled unresponsively and again Harris intervened. At that point, two Republican senators, chairman Richard Burr of North Carolina and John McCain of Arizona, intervened and curtly lectured the senator from California on the need for "courtesy." It looked for all the world like Republicans playing to their base by trying to put the uppity black woman in her place. As a result, Rosenstein was granted the courtesy of being allowed to stonewall like the others, not even giving lip service to future independence, integrity, or justice.

Senator Burr, by insisting on "the courtesy for questions to get answered," made sure the questions would not get answered. Or rather, Rosenstein's refusal to say he would do what he could to guarantee the independence of the independent counsel was tantamount to warning Robert Mueller that he was on a short leash. Insofar as that warning is the real message, that could also be an obstruction of justice.

Isn't it high time to get the FBI working for Trump interests?

And if that weren't enough to reassure the president that the noose wasn't tightening around his neck any faster than senators who swore an oath to protect and defend the Constitution could obstruct, the

663

president nominated a new FBI director. That's a little like the Gambino Family picking its own prosecutor.

The White House's tweeted choice for James Comey's successor is Christopher Wray, who has been greeted by largely respectful, if muted acceptance, in the words of The New York Times:

> In choosing Mr. Wray, the president is calling on a veteran Washington lawyer who is more low key and deliberative than either Mr. Mueller or Mr. Comey but will remain independent, friends and former colleagues say.... [He] would bring a more subtle management style to the FBI.... [He] is a safe, mainstream pick....

To emphasize that point, the Times ran a picture showing Mueller and Comey, with Wray slightly behind them. The picture was taken in 2004, when Wray was in the Justice Department helping to craft torture policy for President Bush. Wray is overtly political, having given consistently and only to Republican candidates. In 2004, Wray's testimony about the homicide of a CIA detainee was characterized as "less than truthful" by Senate Judiciary Committee chairman Patrick Leahy of Vermont. Wray's most recent high-profile success was helping to keep New Jersey governor Chris Christie from being indicted for the criminal closing of the George Washington Bridge as political payback. A court allowed Wray to withhold potential evidence against his client.

If being a dishonest Republican torture-promoter isn't enough to disqualify, maybe his legal work as a partner in the 900-lawyer King & Spalding international law firm would serve. His clients have reportedly included Trump family members. Another partner is the ethics advisor to the Donald J. Trump Revocable Trust. And then there are Wray's apparent Russian connections reported by USA Today (but not the Times). Wray's firm has a Moscow office. It "represents Rosneft and Gazprom, two of Russia's largest, state-controlled oil companies." Rosneft also has ties to Secretary of State Rex Tillerson who, as Exxon CEO made a $500 billion oil drilling deal with Rosneft, a deal suspended by sanctions imposed by the Obama administration.

Conflicts of interest, dishonesty, torture, corporatocracy, Russian connections – why shouldn't those be the standards of American law enforcement? It's the new American normal.

115.

Trump's In-Your-Face Impeachable Offense

"For seven years I've been hearing about health care, and I've been hearing about repeal and replace and Obamacare is a total disaster, some states had over a two hundred per cent increase, two hundred per cent increase in their premiums, and their deductibles are through the roof, it's an absolute disaster. And I think you'll also agree that I've been saying for a long time, let Obamacare fail and then everybody's going to have to come together and fix it.... Let Obamacare fail, it'll be a lot easier. And I think we're probably in that position, where we'll just let Obamacare fail. We're not going to own it, I'm not going to own it. I can tell you the Republicans, they're not going to own it. We'll let Obamacare fail and the Democrats are going to come to us and we're going to say, "How do we fix it? How do we fix it? Or, how do we come up with a new plan?" ... It would be nice to have Democrat support, but really they're obstructionists, they have no ideas, they have no thought process, all they want to do is obstruct government, and obstruct – period...."

PRESIDENT TRUMP, LUNCHEON COMMENTS, JULY 18, 2017

Responding to a reporter's question, the President's four-minute lunch ramble [excerpted above] is remarkable in many ways, starting with its fundamental incoherence: expecting Democrat obstructionists with no thought process "to come to us" to fix it. The record is clear: when Republicans were in the minority they refused to work on Obamacare, and since the Republicans have been in the majority, they've refused to ask Democrats to work on Obamacare. Republicans are not invested in health care, especially for poor people, Republicans are invested in tax cuts for the rich (to which Democrats are not necessarily opposed).

The President's ramble is even more remarkable for its mischaracterization of reality when he says, "Obamacare is a total disaster." Yes, it has problems, as he points out, without also pointing out that these are problems Democrats embraced rather than enact a single payer health care plan. But for all its problems, Obamacare is far from a total disaster in the real world. The majority of Americans still perceive it as a relative success, and the people who benefit directly from it mostly see it as a godsend.

The President's ramble is remarkable for the oblique way he blames the present mess on Republicans, without naming them. "For seven years" he's been hearing about health care, he says, without adding: and for seven years these ideological idiots haven't been able to craft a single useful alternative. He also doesn't say: believe it or not, some of them actually want to help poor people stay healthy and think it's OK for really rich people to help pay for the common good. "I'm not going to own it," he says frankly. (The same day his White House spokesperson Sarah Huckabee Sanders pushed the same lie about Democrats being responsible for fixing the law even though they have no power to do so.) The reality, however unfair it may be, is always that responsibility lies with those in power. For Trump, health care is all his now, whatever happens.

The President's ramble is even more remarkable for his expressed plan to abandon a duly-enacted law: "we're probably in that position, where we'll just let Obamacare fail." This future course is apparently based on the false and contradictory assessment that Obamacare has already failed ("total disaster"). The President of the United States is blithely embracing a plan that will cause incalculable harm to millions of American citizens, and he seems either uncomprehending or uncaring about the consequential suffering his choice would cause to the country he imagines he's making great again.

But now comes the most remarkable aspect of the President's ramble, his naked embrace of a course of action that clearly comprises multiple violations of the Constitution, multiple impeachable offenses rooted in his oath of office:

> I do solemnly swear (or affirm) that I will faithfully execute the Office of President of the United States, and will to the best of my ability, preserve, protect and defend the Constitution of the United States.
>
> – Oath of office of the President of the United States, US Constitution,

Article II, Section 1

President Trump swore this oath on January 20, 2017, before what he seems to believe was the largest inaugural crowd ever. In case it's not clear enough what it meant to "faithfully execute the Office of President of the United States," the Constitution offers some guidelines, including "he shall take Care that the Laws be faithfully executed" (Article II, Section 3). The Affordable Care Act, aka Obamacare, is a duly-enacted statute that has survived challenge before the Supreme Court. Obamacare is indisputably a law that the President has a constitutional duty to faithfully execute.

The way the Obamacare law is written gives the President considerable authority over the way the law operates, well or badly. Among the techniques of sabotage publicly discussed, the President could cut subsidies that lower the cost of insurance. He could refuse to carry out the law's mandate that most Americans have health insurance or pay a penalty enforced by the IRS. He could undermine enrollment in Obamacare by refusing to promote the open enrollment period in November. He can continue to lie about and exaggerate the flaws of Obamacare until he makes its failure a self-fulfilling prophecy. He could try any or all of these tactics, which would likely have a cascading effect, undermining insurance markets and consumer confidence and turning health care into chaos for millions of people.

Well, guess what? The Trump administration has been attacking the government since day one or thereabouts. Even though the attack is continuous and takes place in plain sight — starting with the appointment of agency heads who hate their agencies, almost all duly approved by collaborators in the Senate — little attention has been paid. Congress members with publicly funded staffs have paid little attention to the daily erosion of the public good across the government. Major media companies with ample staff and budget prefer sitting in video-free White House press-stonewalling sessions to digging into what is actually happening at agencies no longer fulfilling their lawful mandates. One exception to this inattention (no doubt there are some others) is a long piece by Sam Stein (Daily Beast, July 20), detailing some of the ways the Department of Health and Human Services (HHS) under Secretary Tom Price is undermining America's health and human services, Obamacare in particular, immorally and probably illegally. Near the end of his piece we learn that Democratic senators Patty Murray and Ron Wyden flagged this issue in February but have had no response yet from HHS. What's up with that!?

One last remarkable aspect of the President's ramble is that news coverage of it has stressed more concern for protecting insurance markets than acting lawfully in constitutional good faith. (A quick Google search found only one current exception, tarpley.net, other than my piece in Reader Supported News. Constitutionally, Trump has been impeachable since the moment he took office, but only a political process can impeach a President.)

The political will to impeach this deceitful, destructive President and his administration does not exist despite millions of people, even some in Congress and the media, knowing impeachment is abundantly justified. And it's not just Obamacare, or Trumpian self-enrichment in violation of the emoluments clause, or even the Russian hooha (whatever it really is). Every day, with little attention, this administration violates the constitutional duty to faithfully execute the law to protect the environment, to defend the right to vote, to protect civil rights and civil liberties, to support public education, among its other travesties of governing, foreign and domestic.

Faced with the obscenity of Republican "health care," Republican senator Shelley Moore Capito of West Virginia said, "I did not come to Washington to hurt people." That makes her an enemy of her party, for now at least. But it's not as though there's a host of Democrats expressing human decency with such simple, direct eloquence. Not hurting people, defending the Constitution, why is that too much to ask?

116.

Incoherent President Reassures UN That US Policy Is Insane

**"If the righteous many do not confront the wicked few,
then evil will triumph."**

MINORITY PRESIDENT DONALD TRUMP, SEPTEMBER 19, 2017, ADDRESSING THE UNITED
NATIONS

With stunningly unintended precision, about a third of the way into his UN speech, President Trump encapsulated the current brutal reality of the United States in late 2017, where the righteous many do not confront the wicked few and evil oozes its slow and merciless triumph through the body politic. Or perhaps the "righteous many" is another myth and the "wicked few" are the true majority. Wherever one looks, the news is not reassuring, whether it's climate change, civil rights, police state treatment of minorities, rewarding the rich for their wealth, punishing the poor for their poverty, attacking voter rights, or bloating a military that regularly kills civilians. Trump's next sentence drove home the crucifying irony of the American moment: "When decent people and nations become bystanders to history, the forces of destruction only gather power and strength."

Yes, they do. Yes, we do. We live now in a time of literal perpetual war in Afghanistan, Iraq, Syria, Yemen and many of the other 100-plus sovereign states that have US boots on their ground. Before 9/11, the US was at war only most of the time, more spectacularly, but with no better results since 1945. This is not good. Surely most UN members appreciate that, without having the nerve to say so. They did not applaud when Trump boasted:

We will be spending almost $700 billion on our military and defense.

$700,000,000,000 is a lot of money, and it doesn't even include a big chunk for our nuclear arsenal that comes from the Energy Department. $700 billion is more money than anyone else in the world spends on its military. $700 billion is roughly five times what China spends, nine times what Saudi Arabia spends, ten times what Russia spends, eleven times what India, France, Japan, Germany, and the United Kingdom spend. $700 billion is more than what these countries *altogether* spend. For Americans, military spending is an addiction that no longer produces a high, only a craving. Like any addiction, it is deeply destructive. We knew that once. But now we're junkies deeply in denial of our self-destruction. Endless war and out of control military spending have done much to destroy what we once believed was best about the US. Eisenhower belatedly warned us, but he was far from the first. Back in 1795, when the United States was three years old, James Madison wrote:

> Of all the enemies of true liberty, war is, perhaps, the most to be dreaded, because it comprises and develops the germ of every other. War is the parent of armies; from these proceed debt and taxes; and armies, and debts, and taxes are the known instruments for bringing the many under the domination of the few.... No nation could preserve its freedom in the midst of continual warfare.

That's pretty much the way it's turning out, except there's a possibility that the many are actually in favor of being dominated by the few. Or they're intimidated. Or they're mystified. Whatever is happening with the American people, Donald Trump represented them at the UN with a 41-minute pastiche of clichés, political pablum, incomprehensible nonsense and meaningless feel-good rhetoric. (All the quotes that follow are from the official White House posting of the speech, reportedly written by 32-year-old hardliner Stephen Miller, a senior advisor for policy.) The speech begins in a curious campaign mode as Trump assures the representatives of 192 other countries that, much to their presumed relief:

> The American people are strong and resilient, and they will emerge from these hardships more determined than ever before.

670

This referred to the US suffering from hurricanes. Trump said nothing of the suffering of Caribbean islands from hurricanes, or Bangladesh from flooding, or Mexico from earthquakes, or any other pain and anguish in the world. America first.

Then came a sloppy, unpersuasive best-of-times/worst-of-times passage in which Trump threat-mongered "terrorists and extremists" and then, with presumed unawareness, described the United States roguishness of recent decades:

> Rogue regimes represented in this body not only support terrorists but threaten other nations and their own people with the most destructive weapons known to humanity.

The next sentence was perhaps the best of several instances of impenetrable nonsense:

> Authority and authoritarian powers seek to collapse the values, the systems, and alliances that prevented conflict and tilted the world toward freedom since World War II.

The record includes dozens of wars since 1945, wars that the US promoted or participated in, with millions of casualties. The US has been at war 93% of the time since 1792. The US has been in covert or overt war, or both, or several, pretty much continuously since 1945. Soon after that, Trump launched into hyperbolic fantasy:

> We have it in our power, should we so choose, to lift millions from poverty, to help our citizens realize their dreams, and to ensure that new generations of children are raised free from violence, hatred, and fear.

These are fine sentiments, to be sure, but not what most members of the UN are committed to achieving, and surely not what the Trump administration is about. The passage was preamble to what struggled to be the thematic thread of the speech, the purported pillars of the Marshall Plan, "three beautiful pillars ... peace, sovereignty, security and prosperity." Four "beautiful" pillars. Trump offered no plan to achieve these "pillars," nor did he make a coherent argument beyond the platitudinous:

> Our success depends on a coalition of strong and independent nations that embrace their sovereignty to promote security, prosperity, and peace for themselves and for the world.

Trump ran through several descriptions of what sovereign nations do without addressing the apparent contradiction inherent in the US defining how other nations should be sovereign. In this context, God made a first of several odd appearances before this most multicultural of assemblies:

> And strong, sovereign nations allow individuals to flourish in the fullness of the life intended by God.

In concluding his litany of fuzzballs, Trump arrived at his first applause line (there were four), although why this line drew applause is somewhat mysterious:

> As President of the United States, I will always put America first, just like you, as the leaders of your countries will always, and should always, put your countries first. (Applause.)

The sentiment must surely appeal to Saudi Arabia, Burma (Myanmar), Israel, or Egypt as much as to Cuba, Yemen, Venezuela, or North Korea, but Trump has a double standard for which leaders he will allow to "put your countries first." Trump took a cheap shot at both Russia and China, but did it in a single sentence without any indication that he actually meant anything by it:

> We must reject threats to sovereignty, from the Ukraine to the South China Sea.

As widely reported, Trump gave major attention to North Korea "for the starvation deaths of millions of North Koreans, and for the imprisonment, torture, killing and oppression of countless more." That sounds like a familiar sovereign pattern, especially if you substitute "Native Americans" for "North Koreans." Trump did not go *there*, of course, preferring to suggest vaguely that it was up to the UN to deal with North Korea:

> That's what the United Nations is all about; that's what the United Nations is for. Let's see how they do.

"Let's see how *they* do?" The US is no longer in the UN? Trump's Freudian slip is showing. Trump's next big thing was Iran, about which he pretty much lied shamelessly, even blaming Iran for "Yemen's civil war," which doesn't really exist. Yemen is a humanitarian catastrophe made obscenely worse by constant Saudi bombing with US collusion and support since it began in 2015. In this, Trump is as much a war criminal as Obama.

Once again casting the US as saintly, Trump disingenuously talked about all the US had done to help refugees, especially refugees from Syria and Iraq. You know, the ones he tried to ban. In this context he offered a priceless rationalization for American inhumanity:

> For the cost of resettling one refugee in the United States, we can assist more than 10 in their home region. Out of the goodness of our hearts, we offer financial assistance to hosting countries in the region, and we support recent agreements of the G20 nations that will seek to host refugees as close to their home countries as possible. This is the safe, responsible, and humanitarian approach.

That's a fairly clever, if transparent way of saying keep those raghead terrorists in their own countries, or at least the ones next door. In the context of trashing Cuba and Venezuela, Trump uttered a bald-faced lie:

> America stands with every person living under a brutal regime.

That's never been true, as Palestinians in Gaza know, as Yemenis know, as Rohingya in Burma know, as black Americans in Missouri know, as native Americans know, as any sentient human should know. In this context, the ruthless hypocrisy of Trump's closing stands in bold relief:

> So let this be our mission, and let this be our message to the world: We will fight together, sacrifice together, and stand together for peace, for freedom, for justice, for family, for humanity, and for the almighty God who made us all.

Really? Is that why Trump was whining earlier in this speech about how much the US paid to keep the UN going?

Trump's appearance at the UN was another confirmation of just how awful he and his administration are, and probably no one has a clear understanding of the full extent of the Trump awfulness. And it just keeps coming. Turkish President Erdogan says Trump apologized to him for US indictments of Turkish security guards attacking peaceful protestors. The White House says Trump didn't apologize for that. Does it matter either way? Trump's America does not stand with Turks living under Erdogan's brutal regime.

117.

Who's a Laughingstock?
And Why Aren't You Laughing?

Remember, in Trump's wonderland shooting up a church is not a guns issue

In his latest impersonation of the Red Queen from *Alice in Wonderland*, the president of the United States stopped just short of shouting "Off with his head!" at the latest New York terror suspect. But pretty much everyone knows that's *exactly* what he meant. Lewis Carroll intended the Red Queen to be an entertaining caricature by virtue of her absurdity. That's a luxury we don't have when considering our Trump's affinity with the Red Queen's jurisprudence: "Sentence first – verdict afterwards." That's just what our Trump demands again and again from legal proceedings, with appalling disregard for the Constitution and any other law that happens to displease him.

On its face, that disregard for law, that open hostility to anything like a fair process that might produce a result displeasing to Trump – all that would seem to be an obvious and constant violation of his oath office ("preserve, protect and defend the Constitution"), as well as an obvious and constant violation of the constitutional mandate (Article II, section 3) that the president "shall take Care that the Laws be faithfully executed."

As recently as 1970, presidential messing with the judicial process was generally taken seriously, as when Richard Nixon at a press conference said of Charles Manson, *"Here is a man who was guilty*, directly or indirectly, of eight murders without reason." Manson's defense attorneys promptly called for a mistrial, the presiding judge took it under advisement, and amidst public outcry Nixon backed off on his prejudicial

675

public comments, claiming that he didn't mean to imply that Manson was guilty. Nixon's attorney general (and later convicted felon) John Mitchell, who was present at the press conference, said later: "I don't believe the President made the charge or implied one." [At the time, with killings in Vietnam, Cambodia, Kent State and Fred Hampton's bedroom, among other places of extra-judicial execution, it would have been more to the point to note that Nixon was a man who was guilty, directly or indirectly, of thousands of murders without good or just reason.]

On October 31, the FBI charged Sayfullo Saipov with the truck-murder of eight people in lower Manhattan. Saipov waived his Miranda rights and said he had planned the attack for Halloween and asked to display an Islamic State flag in his hospital room. Referring to Saipov's attack the next day, in the midst of a long statement that first blamed immigration policy with no coherent argument, Trump said to reporters at a cabinet meeting:

> Terrorists are constantly seeking to strike our nation, and it will require the unflinching devotion to our law enforcement, homeland security, and intelligence professionals to keep America safe....
>
> We have to get much tougher. We have to get much smarter. And we have to get much less politically correct. We're so politically correct that we're afraid to do anything.... We also have to come up with punishment that's far quicker and far greater than the punishment these animals are getting right now. They'll go through court for years....
>
> We need quick justice and we need strong justice — much quicker and much stronger than we have right now. Because what we have right now is a joke and it's a laughingstock.

In other words, Trump is arguing for an American police state that is somehow omniscient enough to keep out immigrants who will commit crimes seven years after being admitted to the country. Saipov was an accountant came here in 2010 under a Diversity Immigrant Visa and became a permanent resident with a green card. And for anyone who doubted the police state drift of the commander in chief, there was this exchange near the end of the press event, referring to the Guantanamo prison that is an ongoing crime against humanity:

Q: Mr. President, do you want the assailant from New York sent to Gitmo?

The President: I would certainly consider that, yes.

Q: Are you considering that now, sir?

The President: I would certainly consider that. Send him to Gitmo — I would certainly consider that, yes.

If it weren't such an abomination of torture and legal horror, Guantanamo would be a laughingstock to the world. Instead it's a shock to civilized countries and a great recruiting tool for Islamic extremists. Guantanamo, whether Americans like it or not, is America's face to the world. Established in panic and fear by the Bush administration, perpetuated mostly by Congressional panic and fear by an Obama administration that didn't care all that much, now it is a dark joke that is a fact of American life, where we keep people charged with no crime without a chance of release and let them starve themselves in protest until they're too weak to resist force-feeding, by which we keep them alive to prolong the endless torture of hopeless, painful lives. Trump has long missed the brutal joke of Guantanamo reality while tweeting lies about how many Guantanamo detainees have returned to the field (relatively few), feeding a fake news story of long standing.

That's not the joke and laughingstock our Trump was referring to, although it should be. But Guantanamo is a fine example of "Sentence first – verdict afterwards" jurisprudence, so Trump is willing to overlook Obama's fingerprints all over this particular legacy. Trump's laughingstock is the constitutionally-based American judicial system. Except that in the White House wonderland of 2017, they say Trump never said what the White House transcript says he said. He didn't call the American judicial system a joke and a laughingstock. That's what White House press secretary Sarah Huckabee Sanders lied on November 2:

> **That's not what he said. He said that process has people calling us a joke and a laughingstock.**

677

EXCEPTIONAL

To be fair, only her first statement is a demonstrable lie. The second statement, that people are calling us a joke and a laughingstock is actually true, just not at all in the way Sanders wants us to believe it. And the Justice Department had already charged Saipov in federal court in New York amidst widespread reports of how well the federal court system has dealt with terrorism cases, especially as compared to the dismal record of the military tribunals at Guantanamo. Even Trump seemed to acknowledge that reality when he tweeted, once again interfering in the judicial process:

> Would love to send the NYC terrorist to Guantanamo but statistically that process takes much longer than going through the Federal system...

Not to leave bad enough alone, Trump tweeted four minutes later with a sentiment that out-Nixoned Nixon:

> ...There is also something appropriate about keeping him in the home of the horrible crime he committed. Should move fast. DEATH PENALTY!

Our Trump knows no bounds. Every time he tweets like this it's another impeachable offense that the cowardly majority in Congress will ignore, or even follow. We know what kind of government our Trump would like us to have. He made that clear to the Washington Post:

> The saddest thing is, because I am the President of the United States, I am not supposed to be involved with the Justice Department. I'm not supposed to be involved with the FBI. I'm not supposed to be doing the kind of things I would love to be doing. And I am very frustrated by that. I look at what's happening with the Justice Department, why aren't they going after Hillary Clinton with her emails and with her dossier, and the kind of money — I don't know, is it possible that they paid $12.4 million for the dossier, which is total phony, fake, fraud and how is it used?

Our Trump wants to be emperor, perhaps not in name, but in fact. He wants no checks and balances, he wants no rational consideration, he just wants obedience. He wants to punish his enemies:

678

"Sentence first – verdict afterwards." He wants the kind of judiciary they already have in Guantanamo, where the presiding judge (a colonel) feels justified in convicting defense counsel (a higher ranking general) of contempt of court, not just for standing up for his client, but for standing up for his client's civilian attorneys. This was the first military tribunal conviction since 2008, not of a terrorist but an American general, John Baker, sentenced to 21 days in confinement. The convicted general is the chief defense counsel for military commissions and the second highest ranking general in the Marines. The general's underlying offense was his objection to the government wiretapping defense attorney conversations with their clients. He was freed after three days' confinement. The case is continuing, with Pentagon lawyers uncertain whether any of the developments so far are within the officials' legal authority, and a federal civilian judge reluctant to hear any appeal. This would all be breathtakingly funny if it were fiction. But it's a real-world laughingstock.

There are laughingstocks everywhere. We have a government of laughingstocks. Our president is a laughingstock, as are his cabinet and his veep. The Congress is a laughingstock – that's the one truly bipartisan thing about Congress. For the moment, only the judiciary is not a complete laughingstock, although the Supreme Court is teetering toward the bad joke category. The federal judiciary continues to maintain centers of rationality, coherence and constitutional principle. But time is against the judiciary. As our Trump appointees fill more and more vacancies, we can expect to be governed by a full laughingstock. And the joke will be on us. Unless we can somehow regain our full civic size and become another Alice who tells them all: "Who cares for you? You're nothing but a pack of cards!"

Update: On June 18, 2018, Brig. Gen. Baker's contempt conviction was overturned by a DC Circuit federal judge. Judge Royce Lamberth ruled that the prosecutor, Col. Vance Spath lacked the judicial authority to rule unilaterally on a contempt charge. In his 27-page opinion: Judge Lamberth wrote in part:

Judge Spath acted unlawfully when he unilaterally convicted General Baker of criminal contempt and sentenced him for that contempt. He usurped a power that belongs solely to the members of the commission, voting as a body. [The statute does not] authorize unilateral findings of guilt and sentencing by the military judge without the input of members. Such an interpretation would undermine the entire military commission system and essentially authorize bench trials for all the crimes [under the statute].

118.

House Democrats Vote to Block Consideration of Impeachment

Led by Pelosi and other usual suspects, Dems duck critical issue

On December 6, a *majority* of Democrats in the House joined *all* House Republicans in voting to prevent the House of Representatives from even debating articles of impeachment against President Trump. The House voted 364-58 (with 10 non-votes) to table impeachment articles (H RES 646) sponsored by Texas Democrat Al Green. Over the strong objections of Democratic leaders (an oxymoron), Green had brought his impeachment resolution to a vote by invoking his personal privilege as a House member. Green's resolution began:

ARTICLE I

In his capacity as President of the United States, unmindful of the high duties of his high office and the dignity and proprieties thereof, and of the harmony and courtesies necessary for stability within the society of the United States, Donald John Trump has with his statements done more than insult individuals and groups of Americans, he has harmed the society of the United States, brought shame and dishonor to the office of President of the United States, sowing discord among the people of the United States by associating the majesty and dignity of the presidency with causes rooted in white supremacy, bigotry, racism, anti-Semitism, white nationalism, or neo-Nazism on one or more of the following occasions...

There is nothing surprising or false in this observation. The remainder of Article I lists well-reported occasions when Trump acted as described. There is no doubt that the events occurred. Article I concludes that: "Donald John Trump by causing such harm to the society of

681

the United States is unfit to be President and warrants impeachment, trial and removal from office."

There is no question about what Trump's behavior has been. The argument would be whether his behavior constitutes an impeachable offense under the Constitution's Article II, section 4, which provides only that:

> **The President, Vice President and all civil Officers of the United States, shall be removed from Office on Impeachment for, and Conviction of, Treason, Bribery, or other high Crimes and Misdemeanors.**

So what are "other High Crimes and Misdemeanors"? The Constitution does not say, and no one knows with certainty what the Constitution's framers thought they were. What it comes down to in any case of impeachment is whether the president's behavior is serious enough or damaging enough to the good of the country as a whole that he should be removed from office. Is it enough that he openly violates his oath of office? Is it enough that he issues orders illegal on their face? Is it enough that he continues to commit the war crimes of his predecessors? Is it enough that he trumpets impeachable offenses on TV? Is it enough that he has flouted the Constitution since Inauguration Day? Is it enough that he publicly corrupts the legal process? In any healthy society, the behavior of Donald John Trump would be enough to provoke serious debate as to whether the country should suffer it any further.

A majority of Democrats have now gone on record in opposition even to debating Trump's behavior on its merits. Those Democrats, 128 of them, mostly white-privileged, have voted in tacit support of the racism, bigotry and prejudice streaming from the Trump administration. Led by Nancy Pelosi, these 128 Democrats (including all the party leadership except James Clyburn) have taken a public pass on discussing real issues of conscience with national importance. Only 58 Democrats voted with conscience. The corruption of our system is expressed by Washington's surprise that there were so many, not so few.

Surprise that there were "only" 128 cowards among Democrats in the House is well founded. Nancy Pelosi is the same leader who lacked the stomach to try to impeach George Bush for lying us into a war that the country continues to pay for in money and blood, albeit mostly other people's blood. In Pelosi-World, if lying the country into war isn't an impeachable offense, what is?

And let's be clear here, it's not as if the votes of any of those 128 Democrats were going to make *any* material difference in the outcome. The Republican majority in the House was going to table the impeachment resolution no matter how any of the Democrats voted. The Democrats voting not to consider articles of impeachment had no practical grounds for doing so. Each of them put personal politics ahead of any moral reckoning, much less the desperate need of the country for principled leadership. Each of them cast a squalid vote not to confront the profoundly destructive behavior outlined in the impeachment articles, the second (and last) of which began:

ARTICLE II

In his capacity as President of the United States, unmindful of the high duties of his high office, of the dignity and proprieties thereof, and of the harmony, and respect necessary for stability within the society of the United States, Donald John Trump has with his statements done more than simply insult individuals and groups of Americans, he has harmed the American society by publicly casting contempt on individuals and groups, inciting hate and hostility, sowing discord among the people of the United States, on the basis of race, national origin, religion, gender, and sexual orientation, on one or more of the following occasions ...

Again, the resolution lists illustrative instances of the offending behavior, all of which happened without any doubt.

But 128 Democrats don't want to object, or even to be seen as being willing to object to Trump behavior. These 128 Democrats prefer to be seen voting not to discuss outrages even when there is no chance whatsoever that these outrages will be subject to public debate. They all knew before they voted that Republicans wouldn't allow it. Yet given an absolutely no-risk opportunity to object to Trump behavior, 128 Democrats chose instead to vote as if they have no serious objection to racism-based policy dominating American government. How can we know that's not exactly true?

Democrats have been fleeing from the impeachment process for months now, ever since Green first brought out his articles in May. At least six other House Democrats have filed articles of impeachment against Trump, none of which have been voted on yet. Five new articles of impeachment were introduced in mid-November, charging Trump with obstruction of justice, illegally taking money from foreign entities, illegally taking money from American entities, undermining the courts in violation of his oath of office, and undermining public media in violation of the First Amendment – all producing demonstrable damage to the United States as a constitutional democracy.

This is all denied by the Democratic leaders, including Pelosi and her minority whip Steny Hoyer of Maryland, who said without apparent irony:

> **Do we disagree with the policies? We do. But disagreeing with the policies is not enough to overturn an election, a free and fair election.... There are a large number of Democrats that believe this president ought to be impeached, we have just a made a judgment that the facts aren't there to pursue that....**

According to Hoyer, 2016 was – unquestionably – a "free and fair election," despite evidence that it was anything but, especially the Democratic primaries. He and Pelosi might well have reason to keep anyone from looking too closely at any of that. Their personal culpability in a corrupt primary process involves, at the very least, doing nothing about it. And the troubles of the Democratic party leadership run much deeper than that, as lucidly articulated by Nomiki Konst, member of the Democratic National Committee Unity Reform Commission, who wonders why the DNC spent $700 million on five "consultants" but didn't have money for yard signs in Michigan and Wisconsin.

And there's no sense or decency coming from old line Doug Jones, who was just elected Senator from Alabama. He says the sexual aggression allegations against Trump don't much matter now. He dismisses the women who have come forward recently, he dismisses the movie *16 Women and Donald Trump*, recently released by Brave New Films, and he dismisses calls for Trump's resignation or impeachment.

Senator-elect Jones, a lawyer who probably knows better, told CNN's Jake Tapper in his pseudo-folksy Alabama manner:

> You know, Jake, where I am on that right now is that those allegations were made before the election. And so people had an opportunity to judge before that election. I think we need to move on and not get distracted by those issues. Let's get on with the real issues that are facing the people of this country right now.

That expresses the specious heart of the Democratic Party these days, a party of dishonesty and denial. Jones must know that the allegations raised during the election were not fully vetted. Jones must know that the allegations have expanded and taken on more weight and credibility as strong, articulate women have come forward to support them. Jones dismisses issues that matter significantly to more than half the population. And what does Jones mean by "real issues"? Does he really think a corrupt, bigoted president threatening nuclear war is not a real issue?

The reality of the Trump presidency is that the president has not spent a single minute in office when he wasn't committing at least one impeachable offense. Advised after the election to divest himself of conflicts of interest, Trump complied in part but continues to profit from foreign and domestic businesses in clear violation of the Constitution's emoluments clauses. In a lawsuit pending since June, almost 200 House and Senate Democrats have sued Trump to enforce the emoluments clauses. On Inauguration Day 2017, attorney John Bonifaz of Free Speech for People started an impeachment campaign based on the emoluments clauses. In his view, impeachment can and should proceed as a civil action parallel to the criminal action headed by special counsel Robert Mueller. On Democracy NOW December 15, Bonifaz spoke of the difference between criminal and civil procedures:

> The question here are crimes against the state. That is what impeachment is about – abuse of power, abuse of public trust, and not only through the violations of the anti-corruption provisions. There is now, of course, evidence of obstruction of justice. There's evidence of potential conspiracy with the Russian government to interfere with the 2016 elections and violate federal campaign finance laws, among

others. There is now evidence of abuse of the pardon power in the pardoning of former Maricopa County Arizona Sheriff Joe Arpaio. There's recklessly threatening nuclear war against a foreign nation. There's misuse of the Justice Department to try to prosecute political adversaries. And there's the giving aid and comfort to neo-Nazis and white supremacists. All of this—all of this deserves an impeachment investigation in the US House of Representatives.

Realistically, no impeachment proceeding can go forward without some Republicans, an unlikely development before the 2018 elections. The Democrats in charge seem to have the same blind assumption of winning that they had in 2016, which is hardly reassuring. Waiting for that "certain" victory, those Democrats are content to subject the country to another year of unchecked Trump behavior, with no Plan B should Democrats fail to take the House. Meanwhile, Democratic shucking and jiving does nothing to bring Republicans face to face with their own monstrosities. Democratic dishonesty at the top seems to know no shame, as Pelosi said with counter-factual fatuity:

> If you're going to go down the impeachment path, you have to know you can do it not in a partisan way..... We have an investigation in the Justice Department that is seeking facts. We don't want it to look political.... [My goal is] for our country is to come together to win the next election.

Impeachment is inherently partisan, with the possibility of being bipartisan in part. In reality, "not partisan" is a lie or a delusion. The Mueller investigation is a criminal investigation that may or may not lead directly to indicting a sitting president. It cannot lead directly to impeachment and removal from office. It might lead there indirectly, but that's a long process that took three years with Nixon. The goal of the country coming together is a fantasy, and winning the next election is purely partisan – what Pelosi says is obscurantist garbage, but that seems to be the best Democratic leaders can give us these days.

Update 2019: Some 200 Democrats in Congress filed a lawsuit [No. 17-cv-01154] in US District Court in the District of Columbia on June 14, 2017 (just a few days before the 45th anniversary of the Watergate break-in on June 17, 1972). This suit asked the court to enforce the emoluments clause of the Constitution by "enjoining [President

Trump] from accepting emoluments from foreign states without first obtaining the consent of Congress...."

On June 7, 2018, the court held its first hearing a motion hearing. On September 28, 2018, the court partly denied and partly deferred a motion to dismiss the case. As of March 2019, the case had not gone to trial and remained pending.

On June 12, 2017, the Attorneys General of Maryland and Washington, DC, filed their own emoluments lawsuit against Trump in federal district court in Maryland (#8:17-cv-01596-PJM). After the court ruled that plaintiffs had standing and could begin discovery, plaintiffs issued multiple subpoenas on December 3, 2018. On December 20, the US 4th Circuit Court of Appeals issued a stay, ordering plaintiffs to defend their right to seek relief from the president.

On March 19, 2019, a three-judge panel of the 4th Circuit held a hearing on the question. According to the NY Times: "A panel of federal appeals court judges on Tuesday sharply challenged the legal basis for a lawsuit alleging that President Trump's profits from his luxury Washington hotel violate the Constitution's anti-corruption clauses." The Justice Department argued that the president was immune to the constitutional claims. The question of what constitutes an illegal emolument is unsettled law. As of June 2019, the appeals court had not issued a decision.

119.

War on Iran Is US Policy Now, According to Secretary of State

Former CIA head offers a policy of prevarication and tortured truth

On May 21, in his first formal public address as US Secretary of State, Mike Pompeo (sworn in May 2) effectively declared war on the sovereign nation of Iran.

Pompeo has no constitutional authority to declare war on anyone, as he well knows, so his declaration of war is just short of overt, though it included a not-so-veiled threat of a nuclear attack. Pompeo's declaration of war is a reactionary move that revitalizes the malignant Iranophobia of the Bush presidency, when predictions were rife that Iran would have nuclear weapons by next year, next month, next week, predictions that never came true over 20 years of fearmongering. In effect (as we'll see), Pompeo wants us to believe that everything bad that happened in the Middle East after Saudi terrorists attacked us on 9/11 in 2001 has been Iran's fault, starting with Afghanistan. Almost everything Pompeo had to say to the Heritage Foundation on May 21 was a lie or, more typically, an argument built on lies.

Heritage Foundation host Kay Coles James called Pompeo's 3,700-word speech "Bold, concise, unambiguous" and "a bold vision – clear, concise, unambiguous." It was none of those, except perhaps bold in its willingness to go to war with an imaginary monster. Even without open warfare, warmongering has its uses both for intimidating other states and creating turmoil among the populace at home. Buckle your seatbelts.

The 2012 Iran nuclear deal (officially the Joint Comprehensive Plan of Action or JCPOA) was, by all reliable accounts, working effectively in its own terms up until May 8: inspectors confirmed that Iran had eliminated the nuclear programs it had promised to eliminate, that its uranium enrichment program for nuclear power plants was nowhere close to making weapons-grade material, and so on. Whatever perceived flaws the deal may have had, and whatever other problems it didn't cover, the deal was working to the satisfaction of most of its signatories: Iran, France, Great Britain, Germany, Russia and China. As a measure of international cooperation, the deal not only worked, it was an available precedent for further negotiations among equal parties acting in good faith. The US was not such a party. On May 8, the US president, unilaterally and over the clear objections of all the other parties to the agreement, pulled the US out of the deal for no more clearly articulated reason than that he didn't like it. Or as Pompeo tried to re-frame it in his May 21 declaration of war:

> President Trump withdrew from the [Iran nuclear] deal for a simple reason: it failed to guarantee the safety of the American people from the risk created by the leaders of the Islamic Republic of Iran.

This is a Big Lie worthy of Nazi Minister of Propaganda Joseph Goebbels. What "risk created by the leaders of the Islamic Republic of Iran" is there? Iran poses NO imminent threat to the US and wouldn't even if it had nuclear weapons (as North Korea and eight other countries have). Iran has no overseas bases; the US has more than 600, including a couple of dozen that surround Iran. A classified number of US bases and aircraft carriers around Iran are armed with nuclear weapons. Iran lives every day at risk from the US military while posing almost no counter-risk (and none that wouldn't be suicidal). There is no credible threat to the American people other than fevered speculation about what might happen in a world that does not exist.

To clarify Pompeo's lie, the president withdrew from the deal for a simple reason: to protect the American people from a non-existent threat. In reality, peremptorily dumping the deal without any effort to improve it first may well have made Americans less safe in the long term. There's no way to know. And given the current US ability to manage complicated, multifaceted problems, there's little reason for hope. Since no one else seems as reckless as the US, we may muddle through despite massive inept stupidity and deceit.

The frame for Pompeo's deceitful arguments is the familiar one of American goodness, American exceptionalism, American purity of motive. He deploys it with the apparent self-assurance that enough of the American people still fall for it (or profit from it) that it gives the government near carte blanche to make the rest of the world suffer our wilfulness. Pompeo complains about "wealth creation for Iranian kleptocrats," without a word about American kleptocrats, of whom his president is one and he is too, presumably. And then there's the unmentioned collusion with Russian kleptocrats. Better to divert attention and inflate the imaginary threat:

> The deal did nothing to address Iran's continuing development of ballistic and cruise missiles, which could deliver nuclear warheads.

Missiles were not part of the nuclear agreement, so of course it didn't address missiles. And even if Iran, which has a space program, develops missiles under the agreement, it still wouldn't have nuclear warheads to deliver. There is no threat, but the US could move the projected threat closer by scrapping the agreement rather than seeking to negotiate it into other areas. That move both inflames the fear and conceals the lie. In effect, Pompeo argues metaphorically that we had to cut down the cherry orchard because it failed to produce beef.

Pompeo goes on at length, arguing that all the problems in the Middle East are Iran's fault. He never mentions the US invasions of Afghanistan or Iraq, or US intervention in other countries creating fertile ground for ISIS in Libya and genocide in Yemen. Pompeo falsely claims that "Iran perpetuates a conflict" in Syria that has made "that country 71,000 square miles of kill zone." Pompeo falsely claims that Iran alone jeopardizes Iraq's sovereignty. Pompeo falsely blames Iran for the terror and starvation in Yemen caused by US-supported Saudi terror bombing. Pompeo falsely blames Iran for US failure in Afghanistan. Pompeo uses these and other lies to support the longstanding

Big Lie that "Iran continues to be ... the world's largest sponsor of terror."

This is another Bush administration lie that lived on under Obama and now gets fresh life from Pompeo, but without evidence or analysis. US sponsorship of Saudi bombing of defenseless civilians in Yemen probably accounts for more terrorist acts than Iran accomplishes worldwide. Israeli murder of unarmed protestors in Gaza has killed more people than Iran's supposed terror. The demonization of Iran persists because of the perverse US public psychology that has neither gotten over the 1979 hostage-taking nor accepted any responsibility for destroying Iranian democracy and subjecting Iran to a brutal US-puppet police state for a quarter-century. The Big Lie about Iran is so ingrained in American self-delusion, Pompeo may not be fully aware of the extent to which he is lying to his core (he surely knows the particulars of specific smaller lies).

Only someone who is delusional or dishonest, or both, could claim with apparent sincerity that one goal of the US is "to deter Iranian aggression." Pompeo offers no particulars of this Iranian "aggression." So far as one can tell, in the real world, Iran has not invaded any other country in the region, or elsewhere. The US has invaded several countries, including Afghanistan, Iraq, Syria, Somalia and by proxy Yemen. American aggression has been real and deadly and constant for decades, but because the US is the one keeping score, the US doesn't award itself the prize it so richly deserves year after year as the world's number one state sponsor of terror. This is how it's been since long before 1967, when Martin Luther King tried speaking "clearly to the greatest purveyor of violence in the world today — my own government." That's the way it was, that's the way it still is, that's the future Pompeo points us toward with a not so veiled threat of nuclear war:

> And I'd remind the leadership in Iran what President Trump said: If they restart their nuclear program, it will mean bigger problems – bigger problems than they'd ever had before.

And then Pompeo launched on a lengthy description of Iran as he sees it, a self-serving interpretation of Iranian events that may or may not mean what Pompeo says they mean. What is most remarkable about the passage is that it could as well apply to the US today. Just change the Iran references to American references, as I have done in the text below, leaving everything else Pompeo said intact, and the likely unintentional effect is eerily like looking in a black mirror reality:

> Look, these problems are compounded by enormous corruption inside of [the U.S.], and the [American] people can smell it. The protests last winter showed that many are angry at the regime that keeps for itself what the regime steals from its people.

> And [Americans] too are angry at a regime elite that commits hundreds of millions of dollars to military operations and terrorist groups abroad while the [American] people cry out for a simple life with jobs and opportunity and with liberty.

> The [American] regime's response to the protests has only exposed the country's leadership is running scared. Thousands have been jailed arbitrarily, and at least dozens have been killed.

> As seen from the [#MeToo] protests, the brutal men of the regime seem to be particularly terrified by [American] women who are demanding their rights. As human beings with inherent dignity and inalienable rights, the women of [America] deserve the same freedoms that the men of [America] possess.

> But this is all on top of a well-documented terror and torture that the regime has inflicted for decades on those who dissent from the regime's ideology.

> The [American] regime is going to ultimately have to look itself in the mirror. The [American] people, especially its youth, are increasingly eager for economic, political, and social change.

As an analysis of the US by a US official, that might suggest we were headed toward enlightened and progressive policy changes. Even for what it is, Pompeo's self-deceiving pitch to "the Iranian people," it could have led in a positive direction. It didn't. Pompeo followed this assessment with a dishonest offer for new talks. It was dishonest because it came with non-negotiable US preconditions, "only if Iran is willing to make major changes." Then came a full page of preconditions, "what it is that *we demand from Iran*," as Pompeo put it [emphasis added]. Meeting those US demands would be tantamount to a surrender of national sovereignty in exchange for nothing. Pompeo surely understood that he was making an offer Iran couldn't do anything but refuse.

The secretary of state's bullying chest-puffery continued for another two pages of falsehoods and repetitions. He called for a global alliance of democracies and dictatorships "to join this effort against the Islamic Republic of Iran." Linking Egypt and Australia, Saudi Arabia and South Korea, Pompeo spun into a fully delusional statement about nations with little in common:

> They understand the challenge the same way that America does. Indeed, we welcome any nation which is sick and tired of the nuclear threats, the terrorism, the missile proliferation, and the brutality of a regime which is at odds with world peace, a country that continues to inflict chaos on innocent people.

Wait a minute! Nuclear threats! Missile proliferation! Brutality at odds with world peace! A country that continues to inflict chaos on innocent people! That's us! That's the US since 1945. And that's absolutely not what Pompeo meant, insofar as anyone can be absolutely sure of anything. He made that clear with yet another lie: "we're not asking anything other than that Iranian behavior be consistent with global norms."

Pompeo came to the predictable conclusion familiar to other countries: Iran will "prosper and flourish ... as never before," if they just do what we tell them to do. And to illustrate US *bona fides* and good faith in all its dealings, Pompeo showed himself, however unintentionally, capable of true high hilarity:

> If anyone, especially the leaders of Iran, doubts the President's sincerity or his vision, let them look at our diplomacy with North Korea.

That is funny. It's just not a joke.

120.

Trump Isn't Just a Problem, He's a Manifestation of America's Id

"The speed of America's moral descent under Donald Trump is breathtaking. In a matter of months, we've gone from a nation that stood for life, liberty and the pursuit of happiness to a nation that tears children from their parents and puts them in cages."

PAUL KRUGMAN, NEW YORK TIMES COLUMN, JUNE 21, 2018

Economist Paul Krugman is a smart Princeton professor who won a Nobel Prize, and most of what he says in this column is heartfelt, decent and humane. His argument is relatively simple: since there is no present immigration crisis, there is no basis – practical, moral – no decent basis whatsoever for the current government's inhumane, illegal, brutal treatment of immigrants and their children. Therefore, in an apparently deliberate exercise of hatred and bigotry, the Trump administration is committing crimes against humanity.

That's all quite true, quite obvious, and millions of people already recognize the government's mindless cruelty for what it is – mindless cruelty that stimulates the mindlessly cruel base of Trump supporters from the cabinet on down.

But the way Krugman opens his column is mind-bogglingly delusional at best, dishonestly partisan at worst. Yes, "America's moral descent under Donald Trump is breathtaking," but *not* because of its speed. America's moral descent has been with us from the beginning. America's beginning was a struggle to *ascend* from the accepted moral order rooted in slave-holding authoritarianism, where inequality was God-given, and women and children were property. The big difference between now and then is that then the angry white men making

694

a revolution had enlightened ideals that conflicted with the darker angels of their nature. The core dynamic of American history has always been the struggle between those who want to realize American ideals and those who don't. The record is decidedly mixed, but the big victories mostly belong to the exploiters and killers. Trump is clearly in that line of descent.

Krugman asks us to believe that, in January 2017, America was "a nation that stood for life, liberty and the pursuit of happiness." This is just a fantasy. These are words from the Declaration of Independence and have no weight in law that defines the nation. The preamble to the Constitution sets our national goals as a more perfect Union, Justice, domestic Tranquility, the common defence, general Welfare, and the Blessings of Liberty. In January 2017, our common defence was secure, except in the paranoid rantings of demagogues. Every other aspiration of the Constitution was in a shambles of long duration.

As he rose to the Presidency, Donald Trump was not so much a unique persona in triumph as he was the cobbled-together excrescence of more than 40 years of collective struggle by right-wing operatives trying to build their own fantasy of America, which Trump now embodies, perhaps imperfectly in the eyes of the idealist right. But he's their Frankenstein creation and the rabble loves him, contradictory sewn-together bits and all.

Trumpenstein was a long time in the making, but one could see the early bits taking shape at least as early as Ronald Reagan's 1980 presidential campaign. The racist veins were pulsing clearly in his "states' rights" speech at his kick-off in Philadelphia, Mississippi. That event was a racist Republican dog whistle quietly celebrating the 1964 lynching of the three civil rights workers, Goodman, Chaney and Schwerner, who went unmentioned. The racism of the right has only grown with race-based drug laws, race-populated prisons, race-based poverty, police executions and on and on. The Clintons were shameful accomplices. No president since Reagan has dialed back American racism. Obama spoke eloquently about race, but that didn't keep Republicans from racializing politics, much to the glee of the Tea

Party, and Obama never pushed back effectively, instead becoming the deporter-in-chief after blessing the military coup in Honduras that later fed the immigration wave fleeing oppression and murder.

Yes, we are now officially "a nation that tears children from their parents and puts them in cages." We are also a nation that took years to notice our official brutality to immigrants, especially asylum seekers, and most especially those seeking asylum from brutal dictatorships that we nurture and support. American brutality on the border is hardly a serious departure from American brutality in Iraq or Vietnam or Korea or in nations of Native Americans where we took children and put them in cages we called Christian schools.

Krugman surely knows all this and more, so why won't he see it or say it? It's as if he's drunk the Kool-Aid of American exceptionalism and must deny anything not pre-blessed by our cultural cult. Republicans were rabid to impeach Clinton for lying about a blow-job, Democrats couldn't even impeach Bush for lying us into war (a war we've yet to escape). Obama couldn't even close Guantanamo, but he refused to prosecute the torturers, and now one of them runs the CIA. It's taken America years of bipartisan betrayal to get where we are now, but how can we change if we can't even say clearly and directly who we are and how we got this way?

Krugman is wholly justified in any moral outrage he may feel about the Trump administration, but he is not justified, morally or intellectually, in making Trump a scapegoat embodying longstanding American evils long promoted by the right with little opposition. Trump is a mirror for the country, and if the country doesn't like what it sees, the country needs to change.

121.

Beyond Any Treasonable Doubt – Isn't the President There Yet?

Author's note: The following collage of more and less hysterical reactions to President Trump's embrace of President Putin includes cries of "Treason!" without any call to action. What can we do if this is as true as it seems? The answer, such as it is, follows at the end of this piece.

Today's press conference in Helsinki was one of the most disgraceful performances by an American president in memory. The damage inflicted by President Trump's naiveté, egotism, false equivalence, and sympathy for autocrats is difficult to calculate.... No prior president has ever abased himself more abjectly before a tyrant.

U.S. SENATOR JOHN MCCAIN, REPUBLICAN OF ARIZONA, OFFICIAL STATEMENT, JULY 16

Donald Trump's press conference performance in Helsinki rises to & exceeds the threshold of "high crimes & misdemeanors." It was nothing short of treasonous. Not only were Trump's comments imbecilic, he is wholly in the pocket of Putin. Republican Patriots: Where are you???

JOHN O. BRENNAN, FORMER DIRECTOR, U.S. CENTRAL INTELLIGENCE AGENCY

[Trump] gives every impression of betraying his oath of office.... Trump's own national security adviser said the Russian election attack constituted an "act of war." So what does that make his boss? Some – including former CIA director John Brennan – now dare call it treason. That conclusion was once unthinkable. No longer.

MAX BOOT, WASHINGTON POST COLUMNIST

Everyone in this body [US Senate] should be disgusted by what happened in Helsinki today.

SENATOR BEN SASSE, REPUBLICAN OF NEBRASKA

697

I am a tea party conservative, that will never change. But Trump was a traitor to this country today. That must not be accepted. Speak out.

JULY 16 TRUMP/PUTIN TWEET FROM REPUBLICAN FORMER CONGRESSMAN JOE WALSH,
NOW A SYNDICATED RADIO HOST

The Trump team were colluding with the Russians in 2016 – and they are still colluding.

CARL CAMERON, FORMER CHIEF POLITICAL CORRESPONDENT FOR FOX NEWS

Persistent and disruptive cyber operations will continue against the United States and our European allies, using elections as opportunities to undermine democracy, sow discord and undermine our values.... Frankly, the United States is under attack.

DIRECTOR OF NATIONAL INTELLIGENCE DAN COATS TOLD THE SENATE INTELLIGENCE
COMMITTEE IN FEBRUARY 2018

Some [Republican officials] now reportedly seek to impeach [US Deputy Attorney General] Rosenstein on trumped up charges. To attack one of our national defense leaders as we are being attacked, and to do so to benefit our foreign adversary, is *textbook treason*. [emphasis in original]

DAVID ROTHKOPF, CEO AND EDITOR, FOREIGN POLICY MAGAZINE

This is an incredible, unprecedented moment. America is being betrayed by its own president. America is under attack and its president absolutely refuses to defend it. Simply put, Trump is a traitor and may well be treasonous."

CHARLES M. BLOW, NEW YORK TIMES COLUMNIST

Treason against the United States, shall consist only in levying war against them, or in adhering to their enemies, giving them aid and comfort. No person shall be convicted of treason unless on the testimony of two witnesses to the same overt act, or on confession in open court.

UNITED STATES CONSTITUTION, ARTICLE III, SECTION 3

Since his first moment in office, President Trump has been guilty of impeachable offenses, most obviously by violating the emoluments clause of the Constitution: using the office of the presidency for

698

personal profit for himself, his family and his friends. At least some of the corruption of the Trump administration has been widely reported and even resulted in a few official resignations. But the impeachable corruption continues uninterrupted.

Now it appears more than likely that, since his first moment in office, President Trump has also been a traitor. And the apparent treason continues uninterrupted.

Among Republicans the response to Trumpian high crimes and misdemeanors has been largely limited to the wringing of hands, backed by mock-pious tut-tutting, and expressions of shock – shock! – to see sycophantic Putin-worship practiced so openly. Senator McCain's exceptional response should shame the others, but smart money says it won't. We live in a country where the expression "Republican patriot" is usually an oxymoron.

After hours of silence, Senator Mitch McConnell of Kentucky, the Senate majority leader, refused to answer any questions after making a brief statement lacking any noticeable principle:

> The Russians are not our friends. I've said that repeatedly, I say it again today. And I have complete confidence in our intelligence community and the findings that they have announced.

Equally inert and unprincipled, Speaker of the House Paul D. Ryan of Wisconsin issued a statement that had slightly better rhetoric but to no better point, given his own lack of effort to lead the House to seek the whole truth of the 2016 election:

> There is no question that Russia interfered in our election and continues attempts to undermine democracy here and around the world.... The president must appreciate that Russia is not our ally.... The United States must be focused on holding Russia accountable and putting an end to its vile attacks on democracy.

Republican corruption is neatly crystallized in that last sentence, which harbors two viciously false ideas essential to Republicans' hanging on to power. The first deceit is the notion that only the Russians are at fault, which is part of the cover-up of Trump allies engaging with Russians in a manner that has resulted in several of them pleading guilty to felonies. The recent arrest of Russian national Maria Butina for conspiring against the US as a secret agent involves a nexus of Americans that includes Republican operative Paul Erickson, Donald Trump Jr., two National Prayer Breakfasts and the National Rifle Association, among others.

The second, even more important deceit is that there's no need to put an end to Republicans' own vile attacks on democracy over the past two decades. Republicans have used voter caging, voter purges, vote-counting manipulations, disenfranchisement of voters, gerrymandering and other techniques, legal and illegal, to shape a false electorate that will vote Republican. They have done this with little opposition from Democrats and a big assist from the Supreme Court's denial of reality in weakening the Voting Rights Act. This Republican elephant has been in the room for a long time as officials avert their attention in what is metaphorically treason by default – and makes Russian manipulations that much easier.

OPEN TREASON

NEW YORK DAILY NEWS FRONT PAGE HEADLINE,
JULY 17, FEATURING A DRAWING OF DONALD TRUMP HOLDING HANDS
WITH A TOPLESS PUTIN WHILE SHOOTING UNCLE SAM IN THE HEAD,
SPATTERING BRAINS ON FIFTH AVENUE.

This is an extraordinary moment. It is without equal, not only in American history but in modern history. A hostile foreign power intervened in our election to help elect a man president who has since actively served their interests and has defended them at every turn.

DAVID ROTHKOPF, FOREIGN POLICY MAGAZINE

BETTER OFF NOW

NEW REPUBLICAN SLOGAN, JULY 11, 2018

Trust no one.

VLADIMIR PUTIN AT HELSINKI

The argument that Trump is a traitor who has committed treason as defined by the Constitution is pretty straight-forward but depends on applying modern reality to the 18th century document.

At this point, there is no reason to believe Trump has levied war against the United States. There is good reason to believe that cyber-war is war within the intended meaning of the Constitution, and that Russia (among others) has waged cyberwar against the US, and that the president has failed in his sworn constitutional duty to defend the United States. That would qualify Russia as an enemy of the United States (a longstanding pillar of US foreign policy).

Is there any serious doubt, then, that Trump has met the Constitutional requirement for treason, by adhering to enemies of the United States, giving them aid and comfort (most recently and spectacularly at Helsinki)? But what can be done with that obvious reality? No matter how much more evidence piles up, the Constitution has a booby trap: Article III, section 3, provides that "The Congress shall have power to declare the punishment of Treason...." That's it. For now at least, the country is at the mercy of a Republican Congress that has been committing the moral equivalent of treason for decades. There's no constitutional alternative.

122.

Climate Change Response Pits Trump Against US Government

"I don't believe it."

DONALD TRUMP, NOVEMBER 26TH,
REFERRING TO THE 1596-PAGE FOURTH NATIONAL CLIMATE ASSESSMENT, RELEASED BY
THE WHITE HOUSE AT 2 P.M. ON BLACK FRIDAY,
NOVEMBER 23RD, THE DAY AFTER THANKSGIVING.

"I don't believe it" is not, by definition, a rational argument supported by evidence. It's a statement of faith, not susceptible of proof or rebuttal, and as such is useless to effective governance.

"I don't believe it" is the empty opposite of the Fourth National Climate Assessment that is part of a continuing, multi-disciplinary, real-world examination of climate change that began in 1990 (more on this under-publicized report later). Produced by the 13 government agencies that comprise the US Global Change Research Program, the Assessment is the latest report in a thirty-year climate watch that has seen steady, unchanging trends toward catastrophic global impact. Climate change is a dynamic process, driven by human activity that humans have done little to mitigate for a generation. Climate change is happening, it is irreversible, but there is still time to mitigate its worst effects, to save lives, to preserve habitat, to adjust economies, to sustain a somewhat civilized world.

"I don't believe it" is Donald Trump's response to all of this. Researchers in the Trump administration are forbidden – forbidden! – from even mentioning climate change, never mind developing strategies to cope with its varied impacts. Sorry about that, Puerto Rico. Sorry about that, Houston and North Carolina. Sorry about that, California. Sorry about that, everyone.

702

"I don't believe it" has a corollary in White House practice: "I don't want *you* to believe it." The White House considered suppressing the report, but that would require overt law-breaking, since the National Climate Assessment is mandated by Congress. The White House reportedly considered editing or censoring the report, but feared that would make things worse (as it had when a Bush administration oil executive falsified an earlier climate report). So the White House went with a traditional subterfuge, releasing the Assessment when it would be least likely to get significant news coverage – at 2 p.m. on a Friday, not only a traditional black hole for bad news but super-shopper Black Friday after Thanksgiving as well. For a report that signaled the inevitably of an uninhabitable planet within decades, unless the US and others make major changes of public policy, the story has received rather muted attention.

As one Trump advisor summed up the dishonest White House approach, adding a touch of conspiratorial paranoia:

> We don't care. In our view, this is made-up hysteria anyway.... Trying to stop the deep state from doing this in the first place, or trying to alter the document, and then creating a whole new narrative — it's better to just have it come out and get it over with. But do it on a day when nobody cares, and hope it gets swept away by the next day's news.

To reinforce distraction from news that affects every American for generations, the White House also chose to lie about it. The White House issued a statement on November 23rd that falsely claimed that "the report is largely based on the most extreme scenario." The report included a range of scenarios. White House spokesperson Sarah Huckabee Sanders repeated this lie on November 27th, falsely claiming the official US government position on climate was "not based on facts." Sanders also lied when she claimed that the National Climate Assessment process was not transparent. Sanders also made false environmental claims that are irrelevant to and a distraction from climate questions.

In a sense, it's not news when Donald Trump and his followers double down on climate denial. These are veteran birthers, after all.

But the scale of climate change is vast and daunting. The stakes in dealing with climate change are intimidatingly high: millions of lives, billions of acres, trillions of dollars. It's enough to give the most careful, rational leader pause.

"I don't believe it" is not an answer. It's not a policy. It's cowardice or worse.

At this point, the world is past the point of preventing climate change from doing serious damage. That damage is already happening. Bigger and more powerful storms, coastal and inland flooding, larger and more intense forest fires, water scarcity, lethal heat waves and more, all exacerbated by climate change, take more lives and property every year. The problem is global. Political dithering is pandemic, reinforced by political corruption. We've known – or should have known – for at least thirty years that we have a problem we need to face. Exxon and other oil companies have known for fifty years or more that their profitability came at the cost of putting the planet at risk. Coal companies have *always* known that coal was unhealthy for people, if not the globe.

"I don't believe it" is an abdication of leadership. "I don't believe it" is what you say, whether you believe it or not, when your goal is to put a prohibitive tariff on solar panels, to slow the rush away from fossil fuels.

We didn't have to get to this place, where our choices are all stark. In 1989, President George H.W. Bush initiated the US Global Change Research Program. In 1990, Congress passed the Global Change Research Act, designed to develop and coordinate "a comprehensive and integrated United States research program which will assist the Nation and the world to understand, assess, predict, and respond to human-induced and natural processes of global change." From that rational beginning of intellectual integrity, we have drifted through one feckless presidency and Congress after another, squandering thirty years of opportunity to save ourselves from ourselves.

"I don't believe it" seems to have become the national motto, sometimes expressed as "In God We Trust," long since replacing *e*

704

pluribus unum or any other aspirational goal. The reigning cultural stupidity of the United States, its *suicidal* cultural stupidity, was neatly encapsulated by Utah Republican senator Mike Lee on November 25th, when he expressed the widely shared mindlessness that passes for conventional wisdom on addressing climate change:

> All the proposals I've seen so far that would address any of these issues would devastate the US economy and have little or no benefit that is demonstrable from our standpoint. And so I have yet to see a proposal that would bring this about. I think if we're going to move away from fossil fuels, it's got to be done through innovation. And innovation can be choked out through excessive government regulation.

He doesn't mention regulation like a tariff on solar panels. He has no proposal of his own. He's not even sure fossil fuels are bad (*"if* we're going to move away from fossil fuels"). For the foreseeable future the Mike Lees of the world, who hold positions of power everywhere, are content to let the planet creep toward further catastrophe rather than disturb the profit centers of their patrons. He may as well as have said, "I don't believe it."

While it is true that climate change is a global problem that needs a global solution, it is also true that the US is the single largest contributor of greenhouse gases driving the problem. And the US is led by people committed to creating ever more greenhouse gases until some uncertain future date when something unspecified will change their course. In February, the US Energy Department reported that there was likely to be *no decrease* in US carbon emissions for more than 30 years. That would mean *the rest of the world* would have to achieve zero carbon emissions, immediately, just to maintain the already damaging status quo.

Thirty years ago, Bill McKibben published "The End of Nature," an early warning about what was then called "the greenhouse effect." McKibben's recent piece in the New Yorker of November 26th is a long, angry, despairing piece about our collective path to self-destruction:

> The extra heat that we trap near the planet every day is equivalent to the heat from four hundred thousand [400,000] bombs the size of the one that was dropped on Hiroshima.

As a result, in the past thirty years we've seen all twenty of the hottest years ever recorded. The melting of ice caps and glaciers and the rising levels of our oceans and seas, initially predicted for the end of the century, have occurred decades early. "I've never been at ... a climate conference where people say, 'that happened slower than I thought it would,'" Christina Hulbe, a New Zealand climatologist, told a reporter for Grist last year....

All this has played out more or less as scientists warned, albeit faster. What has defied expectations is the slowness of the response. The climatologist James Hansen testified before Congress about the dangers of human-caused climate change thirty years ago.

The cultural vacuity of American leadership is as stunning as is it self-willed. Confronted with an official US government report, American leadership chooses to ignore three decades of conscientious, consistent, accumulating research that a real problem is getting steadily worse, choosing instead to ignore, deny, lie and maintain the policy that feeds the crisis. This is beyond rearranging deck chairs on the Titanic. This is maintaining full speed ahead while betting that there are no icebergs.

No matter what happens next, the failed American leadership of the past thirty years has assured that we, and the rest of the world, will go on suffering unnecessary losses for a long time into the future. Perhaps the new Democrats in Congress will force the failed party leadership to adopt a "Green New Deal" and perhaps that can make some difference, though it's too late to make much difference in time. But that's one of the two grim choices we face: do something to reduce carbon emissions as quickly as possible and risk the possibly severe economic consequences – or perhaps remarkably positive economic outcomes. Or a mix. Nobody really knows.

"I don't believe it" is the alternative, the choice to follow current policy and risk almost certain, severe economic consequence – as well as even more certain, severe ecological consequences – as well as severe consequences to human well being, health and life. This is the path of our Trump's climate leadership. It is fraudulent, irresponsible and criminal.

Criminal? We have seen the carnage caused by climate change already. We know there will be more and worse to come unless we take efforts to mitigate the consequences. Our Trump shows no evidence that he knows the risk or cares about it, so how is that not criminal negligence on a global scale?

Lock him up.

123.

US Adopts Christian Ideology to Guide Foreign Policy

"This trip is especially meaningful for me as an evangelical Christian, coming so soon after the Coptic Church's Christmas celebrations. This is an important time."

"We're all children of Abraham: Christians, Muslims, Jews. In my office, I keep a Bible open on my desk to remind me of God and His Word, and The Truth."

"And it's the truth, lower-case "t," that I'm here to talk about today. It is a truth that isn't often spoken in this part of the world, but because I'm a military man by training, I'll be very blunt and direct today: *America is a force for good in the Middle East."*

"We need to acknowledge that truth, because if we don't, we make bad choices – now and in the future."

U.S. SECRETARY OF STATE MIKE POMPEO, JANUARY 10, 2019

Secretary of State Mike Pompeo went to the American University in Cairo early this year to deliver what may be the clearest statement of foreign policy principles that will come from this administration. Pompeo's speech began (see above) with his acknowledgement that he views the world through a pair of self-reinforcing ideologies: Christian evangelism and American Salvationism. The 3,600-word speech has little overall coherence as Pompeo meanderingly applies his muscular Christian Americanism (he never suggests his view is shared by the president or anyone else) to a self-serving selection of issues. What follows are highlights from the speech in the order they appear, with whatever commentary seems helpful. Pompeo has this to say about the Arab Spring that started in early 2011 and spread across the Middle East:

708

These lands witnessed convulsions from Tunis to Tehran as old systems crumbled and new ones struggled to emerge. That's happened here [in Egypt], too.

And at this critical moment, America, your long-time friend, was absent too much. Why? Because our leaders gravely misread our history, and your historical moment.

The preposterous dishonesty of this telegraphic summary of a complex nexus of only semi-related events tells you all you need to know about the sophistication and nuance of analysis at work at the top of the US government. Pompeo conflates developments in countries as varied and far apart as Morocco, Tunisia, Egypt, Syria, Bahrain and Iran (even though Iran isn't Arab). The US absence from Tunisia and Morocco was more or less beneficial to both countries. The US was hardly absent from Bahrain, where the US naval base benefited from the monarchy's heavy-handed crushing of protest. The US was excessively involved in Libya, which hasn't recovered yet from our support.

Pompeo's soft-pedaling of Egypt ("That's happened here, too") is particularly revelatory, not only because he's being polite to his host country, but even more so because he's shoving a whole lot of ugly history down the Orwellian memory hole. Egypt, remember, went from one of the uglier, US-supported military dictatorships (happy to do our torture for us) to a constitutional democracy that chose Mohamed Morsi for President. When Morsi turned out to be too Islamist for the Egyptian military (and the US), he was overthrown in a military coup and replaced with a proper military-imposed democracy that elected a general to re-establish the current police state that isn't quite as bad as the one before. See? America brings progress! But Egypt raises issues – democracy, freedom of speech, rule of law – whose absence in Egypt's police state are of no great concern to Pompeo. That's probably why he offers no explanation of what he means by "our leaders gravely misread our history, and your historical moment."

That's because he raised the whole Arab Spring nuisance (without naming it, of course) for quite another purpose: to attack President Obama, who also gave a foreign policy speech (5800 words) at the

American University back in June 2009, one that was far more thoughtful and actually coherent, regardless of what Pompeo said in his sleazy
way without naming his boss's predecessor:

> **He told you that radical Islamist terrorism does not stem from an
> ideology.**

> **He told you that 9/11 led my country to abandon its ideals, particularly
> in the Middle East.**

These are demonstrably false statements.

Obama did not use the word "ideology" or the right-wing buzz
phrase "radical Islamist terrorism," which only the credulous and
uninformed would believe. Nor did Obama say 9/11 led the US "to abandon its ideals," though that would be more true than not, what with
torturing innocents, bombing civilians and invading two countries
that had not attacked us. What Obama actually said of 9/11 was that "in
some cases, it led us to act contrary to our ideals" – which is precisely
true. But Pompeo's attack on Obama garnered him headlines, with few
in the media making the effort to point out that Pompeo was lying by
attacking words that were never said. Maybe that's because Pompeo
does that a lot. Even so, it's not honorable journalism.

Pompeo fulminates at length about ISIS, Iran, "Hizballah," and
Bashar Assad without actually making any cogent or fully accurate
point. He asserts that "... our desire for peace at any cost led us to strike
a deal with Iran ..." even though we were already at peace with Iran. He
ignores the reality that the nuclear agreement with Iran has stopped
Iran's development of nuclear weapons and that this is confirmed by
Iran's cooperation with international inspectors. He also ignores the
other parties to the deal – Russia, China, France, UK, Germany and the
European Union – all of whom continue to support the deal despite the
US pulling out (which has not yet taken effect). Pompeo and his cronies
are the only ones claiming the deal is a failure, but those claims are
false, disingenuous, dishonest and supported by no evidence whatsoever. For all his name-calling on Iran, Pompeo offers no specifics,
only loose allegations with no factual support. Pompeo reaches this
conclusion about his quartet of bad actors:

> So today, what did we learn from all of this? We learned that when America retreats, chaos often follows. When we neglect our friends, resentment builds. And when we partner with enemies, they advance.

This must be mere demagoguery. If Pompeo believes it, he's delusional. Where has America retreated? Not from Iraq, not from Syria (yet), not from any of our myriad bases surrounding Iran and elsewhere across the Middle East, and certainly not from Afghanistan (Pompeo never mentions Afghanistan). There was chaos in Libya because we intervened, there's chaos in Syria and Gaza, there's chaos in Iraq and Afghanistan, there's chaos in Yemen. Most of that chaos is at least partly due to US involvement (except Gaza, where the US supports Israel's crimes against humanity).

When Pompeo says, "when we partner with enemies, they advance," he might be onto something. He probably means Iran, but Iran hasn't "advanced" and hasn't invaded anyone in centuries (even though the US prompted Iraq to invade Iran in 1980). No, what Pompeo unwittingly reveals most obviously is that when the US partners with Saudi Arabia, the Saudis advance by propagating their own radical Islamist extremism – Wahhabism – across the globe, by making war on Yemen with our blessing and in violation of international law, and by threatening various of their neighbors including Iran and Qatar. Saudi Arabia is an autocratic, repressive state in which human rights and freedoms exist at the fringes when they exist at all. The other Arab states (as well as Turkey) are similarly autocratic, violent, and anti-democratic. Or as Pompeo calls them, our friends.

Pompeo's speech has a long passage designed to show how brilliantly the US has changed in the past two years, virtually bringing a new Eden to the Middle East. None of it is credible or reality-based, but it does have its share of hilariously absurd assertions:

> America has always been, and always will be, a liberating force, not an occupying power....

> And when the mission is over, when the job is complete, America leaves....

> Life is returning to normal for millions of Iraqis and Syrians ...

Whatever Pompeo may think "normal" means, life is not likely to return to normal for Iraqis or Syrians any time soon, even if "normal" doesn't mean living under a stable dictatorship. When the mission, as Pompeo argues, is fighting terrorism, then the mission is never over. And America does not have a pattern of leaving anywhere. America has combat forces in 165 countries these days, give or take a few. America hasn't left Syria, Iraq, or Afghanistan, never mind South Korea, Japan, Germany, Britain, Italy and lord knows where else. The reality is that the United States, for its entire existence, has been an occupying power on the American continent.

All this may seem just too obvious for words but remember this is a rebuttal of what the American Secretary of State – third in line for succession to the presidency – is telling the world what he claims to be the truth. And it's not even close. And it gets worse.

Pompeo spends the last third of his speech rambling through all the reasons the United States will remain at war for the foreseeable future. His argument goes something like this, and I paraphrase: Iran, Iran, Iran in Yemen, Hizballah, Iran, Iran, Libya, Iran, rockets in Lebanon, Iran, Iran. He never mentions human rights. Anywhere.

Pompeo's hypocrisy shines most brightly when he talks about Yemen. He doesn't mention Saudi killing of civilians or other war crimes, or Yemeni cholera epidemics, or Yemeni starvation, or any of the other horrors perpetrated on the poorest nation in the region. Instead, he claims the US has provided "robust humanitarian aid" and supported peace talks (albeit almost invisibly). Despite decades of American efforts to de-stabilize Yemen, Pompeo boasts: "And in Yemen, we will continue to work for a lasting peace." This is a criminal war of endless atrocity that Pompeo fully embraces because: Iran (no evidence needed). But he's too petty to give credit for the war where it's deserved, since that would mean praising Obama. Pompeo is happy to take the credit for continuing the work no matter who gets slaughtered, hopefully Iran:

> America will not retreat until the terror fight is over....

> For our part, airstrikes in the region will continue as targets arise....

The United States fully supports Israel's right to defend itself against the Iranian regime's aggressive adventurism....

First, it's never easy to recognize truth. But when we see it, we must speak it... one thing we've never been is an empire-builder or an oppressor.

That pretty much sums up the ideology of a self-defined, exceptional ideologue. America has never been an oppressor. America has never been an empire builder. America always was, is, and will be a force for good – no matter who has to suffer for it.

Epilogue/Epitaph

124.

US Policy: Mass Murder of Migratory Birds Not Our Problem

"Birds are, quite literally, the proverbial "canary in the coal mine." How birds fare in the world indicates how all wildlife and habitat, and by extension human populations, will fare. It is not just poetry that led Rachel Carson to title her seminal work, Silent Spring. All the past administrations for which we have worked have struck a balance and worked diligently and in good faith with industries that had significant impacts on birds, such as oil and gas, coal, electric utilities, commercial fishing, communications, transportation, national defense, and others to reasonably address unintended take. It can be done. In fact, it has been done. Successes in applying this law to minimize the incidental killing of birds are numerous."

LETTER OF JANUARY 10, 2018, FROM 17 FORMER GOVERNMENT
CONSERVATION PROFESSIONALS OBJECTING
TO DEPARTMENT OF INTERIOR MEMORANDUM UNILATERALLY
VOIDING CENTURY-OLD LAW

One of the ways American fascism works these days is to ignore the rule of law while putting on a great fake show of legal probity. The example here is the Trump Administration's secret reversal of migratory bird protection law, later imposed on the nation by its own authoritarian fiat, making law without the participation of Congress or any other government agency. The Trump administration's procedure effectively reduces due process of law to the arbitrary ruling of one person. This seems patently unconstitutional on its face, since the Constitution (Article II, section 3) requires that the president "shall take Care that the Laws be faithfully executed."

The bilateral 1916 Migratory Bird Treaty was signed by the United States and Canada, then still part of Great Britain. The Bird Treaty was one of the earliest environmental protection laws, incorporated by Congress into US law in 1918 as the Migratory Bird Treaty Act (16 USC 703ff). For a hundred years administrations of both US parties have faithfully executed the act to protect migratory birds from a host of evolving threats from industries to whom the life or death of birds was inconsequential. These industries became increasingly resentful toward government intrusion on their profits for the sake of wild birds, of all things.

The US Fish and Wildlife Service (FWS) enforced migratory bird law on behalf of the Interior Department in bipartisan fashion across all administrations since the 1970s, from Nixon through Obama.

In 1989, the *Exxon Valdez* oil tanker wreck in Alaska killed some 300,000 birds. The Exxon oil company settled criminal misdemeanor charges brought by the US under the migratory bird act, paying $125 million in fines and restitution (part of Exxon's overall liability of about $1 billion in other legal actions). At the time, Exxon's fine was the largest ever imposed for an environmental crime. As of July 2013, Exxon still had not paid $92 million of the settlement. In October 2015, the US abandoned its claim against Exxon. The Alaskan coast remains polluted by Exxon oil.

In 2010, the *Deepwater Horizon* oil rig explosion and 87-day oil gusher killed 11 people and hundreds of thousands of birds in the Gulf of Mexico. BP (British Petroleum) settled criminal misdemeanor charges brought by the US under the migratory bird act, paying $100 million in fines (part of BP's overall liability of more than $20 billion in other legal actions). In 2012, BP pled guilty to manslaughter (among 14 felony counts) and paid $4 billion in criminal fines and penalties. The BP oil spill (over 200 million gallons) was 20 times larger than Exxon's.

The penalties generated by these two events, Exxon and BP, represent 97 percent of the total revenue generated by the migratory bird law for the Fish and Wildlife Service, according to the Washington Post. As of March 2017, the US Fish and Wildlife Service website stated misleadingly:

> **The Migratory Bird Treaty Act makes it illegal for anyone to take, possess, import, export, transport, sell, purchase, barter, or offer for sale, purchase, or barter, any migratory bird, or the parts, nests, or eggs of such a bird except under the terms of a valid permit issued pursuant to Federal regulations.**

The FSW misstated the law, which includes the word "kill" among its illegalities. The law (16 US Code 703) is titled: "Taking, killing, or possessing migratory birds unlawful." The law states in relevant, unambiguous part:

> Unless and except as permitted by regulations made as hereinafter provided in this subchapter, it shall be unlawful at any time, by any means or in any manner, to... kill... any migratory bird....

Until 2017, administrations of both parties understood the law to apply equally to any migratory bird killing without a permit, regardless of whether the killing was intentional or unintentional. The Exxon and BP mass bird kills were presumably unintentional. Neither Exxon nor BP challenged that long-established understanding of the law under which they were charged and accepted guilt.

Before 2017, efforts to weaken or repeal the migratory bird law had been ineffective. Congress made changes in migratory bird law on numerous occasions including 1960, 1986, 1998, 2002, and 2003 without once changing the law's clear prohibition against killing migratory birds, intentionally or not.

In 1986, in response to a Sixth Circuit federal court ruling, Congress required that any felony charged under the law required an element of intent by the wrongdoer. Congress, as it had before, left misdemeanors to be prosecuted without intent, under strict liability. In other words, if you kill migratory birds then you're liable, whether you intended to or not.

In 2002, Congress explicitly carved out an exception to migratory bird law, allowing the US military to kill birds unintentionally, but only during military readiness activities." Other military activities that killed migratory birds, intentionally or not, were still prohibited. The legislation directed Fish and Wildlife to issue regulations under the authority of the Migratory Bird Treaty Act, which FWS did in 2007. In 2015, Republicans in the House introduced bills to reduce the scope and the financial penalties of the Migratory Bird Treaty Act. Neither bill became law.

In December 2011, the American Bird Conservancy petitioned Fish and Wildlife to undertake the rulemaking process to create

719

regulations under the authority of the migratory bird act that would regulate the impacts of industrial wind power projects on migratory birds. In March 2012, FWS responded, agreeing with the conservancy's analysis of its authority under the law to regulate unintentional bird kills by windmills. But FWS denied the conservancy's request for regulation on the basis that FWS was still working with the wind industry on voluntary guidelines.

The American Bird Conservancy renewed its call for regulation in 2015. On May 26, FWS issued a notice of intent to undertake an Environmental Impact Statement (consistent with the National Environmental Policy Act) in support of regulating unintentional bird kills by windmills, and invited public input in the process.

On January 10, 2017, in the waning days of the Obama administration, the Interior Department's solicitor (agency lawyer) issued a memorandum now deleted from the department's website. The memorandum, Opinion M-37041, was titled "Incidental Take Prohibited Under the Migratory Bird Treaty Act," referring to unintentional bird kills by industrial and commercial operations, specifically including windmills. This memorandum of 30 pages confirmed the department's policy over preceding decades. Solicitor Hilary Pompkins pointed out that, regarding some disputed words in the law:

> ... even if the traditional common-law meaning of "take" introduces some ambiguity as to whether that term applies to incidental take, "kill " is unambiguous.

In other words, the government's consistent reading of the law is that killing migratory birds, regardless of intent, is nevertheless illegal. It is incumbent on industrial and commercial actors to anticipate obvious dangers and take actions to mitigate them, otherwise they risk prosecution by the government.

The incoming Trump administration didn't see it that way. Trump and many of his supporters were generally anti-regulation, almost any regulation. One billionaire Trump supporter, Harold Hamm, founder and CEO of the oil company Continental Resources had characterized regulation as "death by a thousand cuts." In 2015, Hamm leaned on the University of Oklahoma to dismiss scientists studying the connection between oil fracking and more frequent earthquakes.

In 2011, Hamm had his own unpleasant encounter with the Migratory Bird Treaty Act. Continental and several other oil companies operating in North Dakota were charged with killing birds by failing to put protective netting over oil waste pools. That allowed birds to fly in, get oil-soaked, and die. Continental was charged with killing one phoebe. Hamm was outraged and challenged the charges in US District Court in North Dakota. In January 2012, Judge Daniel Hovland granted the oil companies' motion and dismissed the charges, ruling that the migratory bird law of 1918 was too vague to justify the indictments, even though the law had been enforced this way for decades. The judge wrote, in part, ultimately relying on mind-reading the intent of the 1918 Congress:

> All parties involved in this dispute have acted in good faith, and there is case law which supports the legal arguments both sides have presented. Nevertheless, the criminalization of lawful, commercial activity which may indirectly injure or kill migratory birds is not warranted under the Migratory Bird Treat Act as it is currently written.

> This Court believes that it is highly unlikely that Congress ever intended to impose criminal liability on the acts or omissions of persons involved in lawful commercial activity which may indirectly cause the death of birds protected under the Migratory Bird Treaty Act.

This is an apt expression of the mindset of many members of the incoming Trump administration, especially the political appointees at the Interior Department. It's not as though there's no reasonable argument to be had here. Indicting a company on the basis of a single dead phoebe seems ludicrous, but the danger of unprotected waste oil pits is real. The rule of law provides numerous avenues for addressing such competing interests. The Trump administration demonstrated no interest in following anything like the rule of law in any substantive way.

On February 6, 2017, shortly after taking office, the Trump administration suspended the Interior Department's January memorandum supporting decades of precedent in enforcing the Migratory Bird Treaty Act. What happened next was ugly, as described in a lawsuit filed by the National Audubon Society in May 2018:

> Representatives of the oil and gas industry, among others, then lobbied DOI [Interior Dept.] to issue a new directive that would eviscerate any obligation to take migratory bird impacts into consideration when engaging in various industrial activities. For example, on August 31, 2017, the Western Energy Alliance, which represents oil and natural gas companies, sent Secretary of the Interior Ryan Zinke a letter complaining that the "implementation and enforcement of incidental take of migratory birds (including nests and their habitat) . . . is inhibiting oil and natural gas development." The letter urged Secretary Zinke to issue "guidance that [the] MBTA [Migratory Bird Treaty Act] does not give FWS the authority to regulate incidental take for [sic] migratory birds."

> On November 3, 2017, the Director of Government Relations for the Independent Petroleum Association of America wrote to the Deputy Director of DOI's Office of External Affairs with the subject line "MBTA," asking "Any word on the solicitor's opinion yet?"

Within the Interior Department, the review of the migratory bird law was proceeding in private.

The Administrative Procedure Act of 1946 relating to rule making (5 USC 553) requires the rule making agency to make public announcement of and provide for public comment on any rule before adopting it: "the agency shall give interested persons an opportunity to participate in the rule making through submission of written data, views, or arguments...." Without explaining why, the Trump administration ignored this federal law. The only interested persons known to be involved in the process were lobbyists for oil, gas, and other industries.

The National Environmental Policy Act (NEPA) of 1969 contemplates public knowledge of and participation in environmental policy decisions. A November 2017 federal court decision in Montana addressed the failure of the Obama administration to conduct a proper environmental impact statement before approving the TransCanada pipeline:

> No agency possesses discretion whether to comply with procedural requirements such as NEPA. The relevant information provided by a NEPA analysis needs to be available to the public and the people who play a role in the decision-making process. This process includes the President.

The environmental policy act requires that for all "major federal actions significantly affecting the quality of the human environment," the federal agency taking the action must prepare an environmental impact statement that analyzes the "impact of the proposed action," and "alternatives to the proposed action." (42 U.S.C. 4332(C)) The Trump Interior Department did not undertake an environmental impact statement relating to migratory bird law and it did not explain its inaction.

The environmental policy act also allows an agency to prepare an environmental assessment to determine the need for an environmental impact statement. The Trump Interior Department did not undertake an environmental assessment relating to migratory bird law and it did not explain its inaction.

On December 22, 2017, without prior notice, the Interior Department's solicitor Daniel Jorjani issued a memorandum, M-37050, holding that "the Migrant Bird Treaty Act does not prohibit incidental take," meaning that oil companies and others can kill migratory birds without limit as long as they didn't intend to do so. Jorjani's memo took effect immediately, with force of law, permanently replacing the January memo that had restated settled law regarding migratory birds. Smithsonian.com had a December 27 story with a ho-hum attitude although it did include oil industry lies about lax enforcement against windmills that kill birds.

Effectively Jorjani determined that black is white. He did it in secret with industry and bureaucratic co-conspirators. There is no evidence that he acted in good faith and there is no further review possible of his memo within the executive branch. He reversed a hundred years of evolving environmental policy protecting migratory birds. He did it with one fell fascist swipe of his pen.

This blatantly undemocratic manner of law-making was largely ignored at the time and has been ignored ever since, with occasional quiet and polite demurrers. There were limited, minor media reports, but no objection from Congress over its usurped authority.

On January 10, 2018, less than three weeks after the decision was made public, 17 former government conservation professionals wrote the letter quoted at the top of this piece. They are "very concerned" by Jorjani's memo and beseech Interior Secretary Ryan Zinke to modify the memo. They wrote:

> This is a new, contrived legal standard that creates a huge loophole in the MBTA [Migratory Bird Treaty Act], allowing companies to engage in activities that routinely kill migratory birds so long as they were not intending that their operations would "render an animal subject to human control." Indeed, as your solicitor's opinion necessarily acknowledged, several district and circuit courts have soundly rejected the narrow reading of the law that your Department is now embracing....

> The MBTA can and has been successfully used to reduce gross negligence by companies that simply do not recognize the value of birds to society or the practical means to minimize harm. Your new interpretation needlessly undermines a history of great progress, undermines the effectiveness of the migratory bird treaties, and diminishes U.S. leadership.

There is no record that the ethically-challenged Zinke responded before he left office under a cloud. But there is no record of anyone else at the Interior Department responding either. After a few months of stonewalling silence, the department issued a memo on April 11, 2018, offering "Guidance on the recent M-Opinion [37050] affecting the Migratory Bird Treaty Act," addressing "what changes to prior practice should be made" to conform to the 180-degree reversal of department policy. The Washington Post covered this superficially, as if it was both recent and unimportant. The Interior Department memo asserts, without apparent irony, that:

> The mission of the Service is to work with others to conserve, protect, and enhance fish, wildlife, plants, and their habitats for the continuing benefit of the American people. Migratory bird conservation remains an integral part of our mission.

This dishonest assertion seems designed to blur reality. It states that the National Environmental Policy Act should be followed, even though it was ignored in creating the memo it purports to explain. In the real world, the changes that the Interior Department has made amount to an abdication of any significant responsibility for migratory birds. The Fish and Wildlife Service is no longer enforcing any law against industrial bird kills. The Fish and Wildlife Service is no longer investigating or even keeping records on industrial bird kills. Elizabeth Shogren reports that FWS "saved about $2.5 million by not filling ten positions primarily related to investigating violations of the Migratory Bird Treaty Act." After a century of some protection by the US government, migratory birds are on their own.

Canada has indicated that it will continue to enforce the Migratory Bird Treaty as best it can. It's not clear what Mexico, Japan, and Russia are doing about American treaty violations. It's not clear whether the Trump administration has bothered to inform any other governments of its reversal of the treaties' lawful requirements.

On May 24, 2018, four plaintiffs – the National Audubon Society, the American Bird Conservancy, the Center for Biological Diversity, and the Defenders of Wildlife – filed suit against the Interior Department, the Fish and Wildlife Service, and solicitor Jorjani. The plaintiffs' 35-page filing in US District Court for the Southern District of New York challenges Jorjani's 2017 memo as "unlawful and arbitrary and capricious." The complaint argues that:

> For decades Defendants [US government agencies] have construed the MBTA [Migratory Bird Treaty Act], consistent with its plain language, as protecting migratory bird populations from foreseeable "incidental" killing or "take" caused by major industrial activities that are not specifically directed at migratory birds but nevertheless kill them in large numbers. This interpretation has helped to conserve migratory birds for decades in keeping with the purpose of the MBTA and the international treaties the Act implements.

The plaintiffs ask the court to reinstate the January 2017 solicitor's opinion that restated the settled law of the past century. They also ask the court to vacate Jorjani's December 2017 memo as well as the

April 2018 memo issuing "guidelines." The government has moved to dismiss the case. Federal judge Valerie Caproni has not yet ruled on the government's motion. The judge was appointed by President Obama in 2013, before which she was General Counsel of the FBI under Robert Mueller. There have been no hearings on the merits of the case.

On September 5, 2018, the attorneys general for eight states filed suit against the same Defendants – Interior Department, Fish and Wildlife Service, and Jorjani. Led by Barbara Underwood of New York, the other states were California, Illinois, Maryland, Massachusetts, New Jersey, New Mexico, and Oregon. The states' 26-page complaint asks the court to declare "that the Jorjani opinion is arbitrary, capricious, or not in accordance with law" and to vacate the opinion, which would restore the Solicitor's memo of January 2017 restating a century of settled law. The states argue in part that:

> The Jorjani opinion is inconsistent with the Act's text and purposes, is contrary to defendants' previous longstanding interpretation of the Act and decades of consistent application of that interpretation, drastically limits the scope of the Act, subjects migratory birds to increased likelihood of death or injury from industrial and other human activities that immediately take or kill or are foreseeably likely to take or kill migratory birds, and harms the States' sovereign, ecological, and economic interests in robust federal protections of migratory birds.

This case is also before Judge Valerie Caproni. There have been no hearings and none are scheduled. The only pending motion is for Dianna Shin of New Jersey to appear pro hac vice.

On April 11, the Senate voted 56-41 to confirm David Bernhardt as Secretary of the Interior, a career lawyer/lobbyist for the oil industry and their ilk. While he served as deputy secretary, Bernhardt was deeply involved in gutting the Migratory Bird Treaty Act as reported by Elizabeth Shogren of Reveal (and not much of anyone else). Solicitor Jorjani's email October 27, 2017, confirms that Bernhardt "has been plugged in since Day 1" in gutting the migratory bird law. Bernhardt was unanimously confirmed by Republican Senators with their longstanding antipathy to environmental laws. They were joined by three other corrupt senators, Democrats-in-name-only Joe Manchin of West Virginia, Martin Heinrich of New Mexico, and Kyrsten Sinema of Arizona.

On April 15, the inspector general of the Interior Department opened an investigation into ethics complaints against Interior Secretary David Bernhardt. The investigation was requested by eight Senate Democrats and four government watchdog groups.

This is about more than just corrupt Democratic Senators, this is about more than notoriously corrupt Republican Senators, this is about more than just a US cabinet agency engaging in a secret process that reverses a hundred years of legal precedent, this is about more than the failure of mainstream media to cover blatantly unlawful government, this is about more than the failure of the court system to respond in timely fashion to contempt for law, this is about more than the failure of Democrats generally and Democratic presidential candidates in particular to notice the raw success of the Trump administration carrying off the impeachable offense of failing to take care that the law be faithfully executed.

This is about the institutional triumph of American fascism.

125.

The American Gulag Thrives as Trump's Immigration Police State Persistently Violates the Law

When you physically abuse immigrants, sexually abuse immigrants, or refuse to provide them the medical care that they need, you break the law of the United States of America....

In a Warren administration, I'll launch a task force in the Department of Justice to investigate the Trump administration's criminal abuses at the border, and we'll hold perpetrators accountable....

When people come here who are desperate — people who come here whose lives have been turned upside down, people who come here to try to build a better future — then we need to treat them with humanity, and we need to follow the law.

SENATOR ELIZABETH WARREN, MASSACHUSETTS DEMOCRAT

The US government's treatment of immigrant children not only shocks the conscience, it is also a chronic, blatant violation of US law. The US government's deliberate, unlawful cruelty to its child hostages was vividly illustrated by government attorney Sarah Fabian, a self-described mother, as she tried to explain to the disbelieving three judges of the US Ninth Circuit Court of Appeals how the US government could say it held children in "safe and sanitary" conditions as required by law. Fabian's stunning performance went viral, showing her defending conditions in which the government deprives its child-prisoners of soap, toothpaste, toothbrushes, or beds. A lower federal district court had already ruled that these conditions were not "safe and sanitary." Fabian's coldly deceptive responses to the judges' incredulous questions is a stunning illustration of an attorney zealously representing her client, the US, with little regard for truth, humanity, decency, fundamental honesty, or the plain language of the governing law. Given the manifest bad faith of the US government in immigration matters over decades, one wonders: at what point does "just following orders" become a form of co-conspiracy in violating human rights?

The governing law for this case is the 1997 Flores Settlement Agreement of a 1985 class action lawsuit against the US for its treatment of immigrant minors held in detention. Subsequent Congressional action has codified parts of the settlement, but Congress has done nothing to disturb the settlement, as courts have previously ruled. The settlement itself is 28 pages long (including 14 pages of exhibits). It sets out nationwide policy that covers "the detention, release, and treatment" of all immigrant minors detained by US immigration authorities. The intent of the settlement is to assure that US immigration authorities treat, "and shall continue to treat, all minors in its custody with dignity, respect and special concern for their particular vulnerability as minors."

This is the current law of the land and will remain the law of the land until Congress enacts any change that is signed by the president. For the Ninth Circuit Appeals Court, the critical question of "safe and sanitary" conditions is addressed in Section V of the settlement, "PROCEDURES AND TEMPORARY PLACEMENT FOLLOWING ARREST." It is hard to find any legal or moral ambiguity in this section, which establishes a clear expectation that US Immigration authorities will treat the children in their custody with care and respect:

> Whenever the [US] takes a minor into custody, it shall expeditiously process the minor and shall provide the minor with a notice of rights, including the right to a bond redetermination hearing if applicable. Following arrest, the INS shall hold minors in *facilities that are safe and sanitary* and that are consistent with the [US's] *concern for the particular vulnerability of minors.*
>
> Facilities will provide access to toilets and sinks, drinking water and food as appropriate, medical assistance if the minor is in need of emergency services, adequate temperature control and ventilation,

adequate supervision to protect minors from others, and contact with family members who were arrested with the minor.

The [US] will segregate unaccompanied minors from unrelated adults. Where such segregation is not immediately possible, an unaccompanied minor will not be detained with an unrelated adult for more than 24 hours.

If there is no one to whom the [US] may release the minor pursuant to Paragraph 14, and no appropriate licensed program is immediately available for placement pursuant to Paragraph 19, the minor may be placed in a [US] detention facility, or other [US]-contracted facility, having separate accommodations for minors, or a State or county juvenile detention facility. However, minors shall be separated from delinquent offenders.

Every effort must be taken to ensure that the safety and well-being of the minors detained in these facilities are satisfactorily provided for by the staff [emphasis added].

Every minute you spend reading this, like every minute before and after, is another minute of trauma inflicted on children and infants by the US government, trauma deliberately and callously inflicted on children held in concentration camps for children, concentration camps run by US agencies with the moral standards of a Gestapo. These are all the unforced choices of the American government, choices that have been getting worse and worse for decades, choices that are now tantamount to crimes against humanity committed by an American government rendered monstrous by the overwhelming psychic numbness of its leaders and too much of its population.

Concentration camps? Of course they are, they're part of an American gulag across the South and West designed to punish and intimidate immigrants regardless of their age or health. These are concentration camps, many of them for profit. They are not yet death camps, but they are killing people – deliberately or carelessly hardly matters. These concentration camps are torturing people by design with harsh conditions and harsh treatment and callous neglect. They inflict sleep deprivation on children, which is a form of torture.

The atrocity of American treatment of immigrants has been documented for years. Immigrants flee their countries that have become unlivable, in great part thanks to American support for brutal dictatorships. So they seek asylum here. The US, having punished them in their home countries, turns around and punishes them for coming here. The inspector general at Homeland Security documents the agency's criminal treatment of children and adults in report after report. This is an old story getting worse, and media report it in brutal detail. Attorney Holly Cooper, who represents immigrant children and co-directs the Immigration Law Clinic at the University of California, Davis, told AP:

> **In my 22 years of doing visits with children in detention, I have never heard of this level of inhumanity.**

Another attorney, Warren Binford, was part of a monitoring team sent by the plaintiffs in the case before the Ninth Circuit Appeals Court. On Democracy NOW, she gave harrowing, eyewitness detail of her observations of the disgraceful treatment of children by US authorities at the Clint, Texas, Border Patrol station. That's the one that got so much bad publicity of late that the US moved its child prisoners elsewhere. Then it moved them back.

In addition to the pornography of child brutalization, which is good at upsetting people but not so much at motivating them, attorney Binford noted that roughly half the children in custody have parents in the US. Statistically, of all the children in US custody, only about 12 per cent have no parent or other relative to go to (as defined in the 1997 *Flores* Settlement). Despite cries of helplessness by the Trump administration, Binford said, "We are nowhere near the highest level of apprehensions that have been taken by the Border Patrol over the last several decades.... And when they say that, it's simply not true." She noted that taxpayers are paying $775 per day per child to keep them in squalid conditions, when most of them have family to go to, only because the Trump administration prefers to break the law:

... they are absolutely breaking the law.

They're breaking law as to the conditions of detention.

They're breaking the law as to the number of hours that they can keep the children in Border Patrol facilities.

They're breaking the law as far as how long these children are being kept in ORR facilities.

They're breaking the law by taking the children away from their families.

And they're also breaking the law by transporting them on Texas state highways without the appropriate child seats and infant carriers and, you know, these booster seats that are required by law.

Everywhere I look, this administration is breaking the law.

This is an ongoing, intentional atrocity. Committing human rights crimes is the Trump policy for controlling immigration. Not only is it illegal, it's failing. There is outrage over the inhumanity, there are many hands wringing, but where is the outrage at the Perpetrator in Chief?

The torture and killing of immigrant children are not only crimes but impeachable offenses. The failure to faithfully execute and enforce the law is an impeachable offense. You might think there's been enough suffering and criminality to make even Nancy Pelosi and her fellow dodo Democrats come out of their politically motivated passivity and moral blindness on this US crime against humanity. We shall see.

126.

Failure to Impeach Trump Is
a Way to Reaffirm Him

And if we don't impeach, here's what the president will say. He will say that the Democrats had the House by overwhelming numbers. He will say that they did not impeach me. He will say, "By their inaction, I have been vindicated, I have been exonerated." Mr. Mueller did not exonerate him. Why would the House of Representatives exonerate him? And he will say, "By virtue of this, you ought to elect me meaning him, President Trump — president again." And let me share this with you. He will make a powerful argument that we were complicit, in a sense, in his actions by not having our action in the House of Representatives.

REP. AL GREEN, D-TEXAS, ON DEMOCRACYNOW, MAY 22, 2019

Would the American people re-elect a president caught in the midst of a multi-faceted impeachment inquiry? One never knows.

Or would the American people be more likely to re-elect a president free from any impeachment inquiry?

With no commanding presidential candidate likely to emerge till well after the Iowa caucus on February 3, 2020, the center of Democratic Party power is now in the House of Representatives, largely in the hands of Speaker Nancy Pelosi. Pelosi is so determined to give Trump a pass on impeachment that Trump's lawyers cite her position in their court briefs. That seems like a pretty bad place for a supposed opposition party to find itself.

Pelosi and other Democratic Party leaders have indicated a willingness to pursue impeachment if "the people want it." Then the same leaders do little or nothing to encourage the people to want it. That is the opposite of leadership. That is also a failure to understand how the impeachment of Richard Nixon became supportable through

733

the conscientious evidence-gathering that persuaded the public that Nixon had committed impeachable offenses.

Pelosi is slippery to the point of dishonesty on the question of impeachment. New York Times columnist Maureen Dowd wrote a long wet-kiss article titled "It's Nancy's Parade" in the Sunday Times of July 7. Dowd asked Pelosi if she had said about Trump, as reported, "I don't want to see him impeached, I want to see him in prison." That's a classic false-choice deflection to begin with, but Pelosi danced it disingenuously further:

> I didn't exactly say that.... You can't impeach everybody. People wanted Reagan impeached but that didn't happen. O.K., they impeached Clinton for something so ridiculous — getting impeached for doing a dumb thing as a guy. Then they wanted to impeach Obama.... [Trump] has given real cause for impeachment.

This is scattershot distraction Trump-style, seeming to make some point while avoiding the underlying question. If Trump, as Pelosi says, "has given real cause for impeachment," then why has the House not begun to impeach him?

There is a glaring omission in Pelosi's list of recent presidents – Reagan, Clinton, Obama, but neither Bush. The second Bush lied the country into war, the Iraq war that continues to cost us dearly. Even that was not enough for Pelosi. She opposed impeaching Bush for the war crimes he so plainly committed. Does she lack principle? Does she lack courage? Does she always make her decisions on the narrowest partisan political calculation? What is really going on?

Democrats have the power to initiate impeachment proceedings. Democrats have the power to control the pace of those proceedings. There are numerous impeachable offenses, in almost every area – immigration, environment, climate, census, war-making, emoluments, regulating contrary to statute across the government – the list of failures to faithfully execute the laws or the office of the President is long and easily demonstrated. Even Pelosi says, "he every day practically self-impeaches by obstructing justice and ignoring the subpoenas" – which she allows him to do with impunity.

There are about 80 Democratic House members on record in favor of moving ahead on impeachment. That leaves another 155 Democratic House members either uncommitted or opposed to impeachment. These Democrats are not outspoken on the question. Many of them oppose impeaching a flagrantly dishonest, probably criminal president mainly because it might put their own re-election at risk. No profiles in courage there. We saw them flex their muscles recently when they forced Pelosi to capitulate on protecting immigrant children and accept the Senate bill that would do little to assure that the Department of Homeland Security follows the law.

Impeachment is a process that requires careful management

Pelosi misleadingly talks about impeachment, characterizing it as if it's a compact, unitary event. It's not. "Impeachment" itself is only a formal accusation, a Congressional indictment that requires an investigation of uncertain length by the House Judiciary Committee, including having hearings, drawing of articles of impeachment, publicly debating and voting on them, and delivering those approved to the full House for a final vote. Only then do the articles of impeachment go to the Senate for a trial of indeterminate length and a final vote.

The impeachment process for Bill Clinton began in January 1994 with the appointment of a special prosecutor (Ken Starr took over in August 1994). The process ended more than five years later when the Senate acquitted Clinton on February 12, 1999.

The impeachment process for Richard Nixon began formally with the creation of the Senate Watergate Committee in February 1973, less than eight months after the Watergate burglary. The House Judiciary Committee started its investigation in October, voting for articles of impeachment at the end of July 1974. Nixon resigned on August 9, before the full House considered the impeachment articles. That abbreviated impeachment process took about 550 days.

As of July 9, the November 3, 2020, presidential election was 483 days away. That is plenty of time for the House Judiciary Committee to accomplish something meaningful without having to risk defeat in the Senate.

735

So it's a calculated question for 2020: Would a prolonged, careful, substantive impeachment inquiry make Trump stronger or weaker by election day? Would a prolonged period of sniping at Trump's faults, without daring to impeach him, make Trump stronger or weaker on election day? Regardless of who the Democratic candidate turns out to be, it seems more likely that he or she will be strengthened by a House impeachment inquiry carried on with integrity before the election. Yes, it will be partisan, but that is offset if it is also principled. But first, Pelosi has to help it happen. According to Dowd:

> **Now Pelosi is in her element, ready for the fight of her life with Trump.... Pelosi keeps moving forward, a shark with a permagrin.... If combating an inhumane Trump requires a superhuman effort, Pelosi may be just the woman to do it.**

But Dowd does not say how this will be done. Dowd supports her hope with nothing more than an anecdote about Pelosi carrying on bravely at an Irish political event just after having her right hand smashed in a car door. This shows grit, to be sure. But it was only for one night, and the struggle with Trump has more than a year to go.

Reflecting the traditional political timidity of mainline Democrats, Pelosi has taken potshots at fellow Democrats in the House like Alexandria Ocasio-Cortez, mocking the Green New Deal, or Ilhan Omar, reinforcing the right wing's anti-Semitic canard. Pelosi has demonstrated that, in a pinch, she does not have their backs or Rashida Tlaib's or Ayanna Pressley's. Pelosi again denigrated all four women of color to Dowd. This is ugly, gratuitous infighting, not principled leadership. Little wonder, perhaps, that Corbin Trent, an aide to Ocasio-Cortez, told reporter Ryan Grim that the Democratic leadership is "driven by fear. They seem to be unable to lead."

"The greatest threat to mankind," according to Trent, a co-founder of Justice Democrats, "is the cowardice of the Democratic Party."

The Democrats Pelosi denigrates are all agents of change. Pelosi talks about defeating Trump, but she doesn't embrace much change of any other sort. She cavils at the more ambitious proposals of Democratic presidential candidates. Why has the House pushed so little legislation that challenges the status quo? Is there anything Pelosi truly believes in besides herself? Dowd characterizes her as the most powerful woman in the country (with Trump the most powerful man). Pelosi seems to have made the calculation that she'd rather preserve her speakership than take any serious risk. Are the ambitions of a 79-year-old multimillionaire really more important than the good of the country?

If this is really "Nancy's Parade," where is it headed?

The crisis that is the Trump administration has no easy solution. No one has control of a future full of "what-ifs." That's what makes the need for courageous leadership so dire. An impeachment inquiry has no time limit. The areas in which Trump has committed impeachable offenses are almost unlimited. That's not the hard part. An impeachment inquiry that has multiple subjects that are heading toward multiple articles of impeachment should take a long time and can be credibly managed to conclude before or after the election, or never. In that sense, impeachment can't fail.

A continuing, multi-faceted, public inquiry into even just a handful of Trump's most egregious constitutional violations has the potential for educating that part of the American public still capable of being educated (a majority, one hopes). It is a constitutional vehicle to create change quite different from Pelosi's apparent choice of waiting for change to happen spontaneously. An extended impeachment inquiry is a positive, powerful way to focus with the full force of the Constitution on issues that matter

For example, an article of impeachment for carrying out a bigoted immigration policy of deliberate, illegal cruelty that includes family separation and other crimes against humanity, violations of domestic and international law – that's easy to imagine – and the public hearings leading up to such an article would have the advantage of addressing an issue many Americans care about and all Americans should care about. And it would do so in a formal, lawful context where evidence matters.

Perhaps Pelosi really is in a no-win situation, along with the US. And perhaps not. Either way, no one knows, no one can know, so why not choose an aggressive and principled public course of action that takes the fight to Trump instead of forever reacting ineffectively? If Trump's success teaches us nothing else, it reaffirms the hugely obvious lesson that boldness impresses the American people – and that the bold are more likely to win against high odds.

Thanksgiving For a Grateful Empire   MURRAY NGOIMA

Who Thought All This Was a Good Idea?

William Boardman is also the author of *Woodstock Country School – A History of Institutional Denial* (Yorkland Publishing, Revised Edition, 2018). He was a lay judge in Vermont for 20 years. For five years in the 1970s, he taught English, US History and Drama at the Woodstock Country School. For 12 years he produced, directed, wrote for and performed on the award win-

ning Panther Program (comedy and comment in songs and sketches) on Vermont Public Radio, with national distribution supported by the National Endowment for the Arts. His television credits include *The News Is The News* and *That Was The Week That Was* (both on NBC) and *Captain Kangaroo* (CBS). He is currently an online and print reporter and columnist. Since 2012, he has been publishing on Reader Supported News. His work has also appeared elsewhere, including Dissident Voice, CounterPunch, OP-ED News, Consortium News, Polizeros, Smirking Chimp, Agonist, Transcend Media Service, Global Research, Truthout, Second Vermont Republic, AlterNet, Hawaii Daily News, Rise Up Times, Exploded View, Middleboro Review, Montpelier Bridge, Liberals Unite, Firedoglake, Vermont Commons, Liberty Underground Virginia (LUV), Dandelion Salad, The Free Press, Vermont Digger, Rebel Mouse, Newsvine, Vermont Standard, Independent Voter Network and Z Magazine.

William Boardman was born and raised in Manhattan. He graduated from Yale College and the Yale School of Drama. He has lived in the same old farm house in Woodstock, Vermont, for 48 years. He shares it with two female pets, a black cat named Nuit and a black dog named Roger. He hopes for the best, regardless of rational expectations.